P9-CDK-361

THE REPORT
OF THE
COMMISSION ON
OBSCENITY
AND
PORNOGRAPHY

NOTE

This edition of
*The Report of the Commission on
Obscenity and Pornography*
was set in type from the materials
released by the Commission to the press
on September 30, 1970.

A NEW YORK TIMES BOOK

THE REPORT OF THE COMMISSION ON OBSCENITY AND PORNOGRAPHY

Special Introduction by Clive Barnes of
The New York Times

RANDOM HOUSE
NEW YORK

All rights reserved under International and Pan-American
Copyright Conventions. Published in the United States by
Random House, Inc., New York, and simultaneously in Canada
by Random House of Canada Limited, Toronto. By Arrangement with
Bantam Books, Inc.
ISBN: 0-394-46994-1
Library of Congress Catalog Card Number: 70-144227
Manufactured in the United States of America
First Edition

This book is available in a paperback edition
from Bantam Books, Inc., 666 Fifth Avenue,
New York, New York 10019

Contents

SPECIAL INTRODUCTION
by Clive Barnes

There are two remarkable things about the *Report of the Commission on Obscenity and Pornography*. The first is its findings. The second, and even more remarkable, is that the President of the United States should have found such a commission necessary. Surely we know where we stand on the issue of pornography or obscenity. We do know, don't we? It seems that we do not.

We are living in a permissive society, and yet few of us can decide how permissive we want our society to be, or, alternatively, how nonpermissive we think our society should become. How divided is the nation on the subject of obscenity and pornography? The majority report of the Commission suggests not very much. It says: "Public opinion in America does not support the imposition of legal prohibitions upon the rights of adults to read or see explicit sexual materials."

On the other hand, Charles H. Keating, Jr., founder of Citizens for Decent Literature, Cincinnati, one of the dissenting commissioners, and the only commissioner appointed by President Nixon, takes the opposing view. "Credit the American public with enough common sense," he writes, "to know that one who wallows in filth is going to get dirty. This is intuitive knowledge. Those who spend millions of dollars to tell us otherwise must be malicious or misguided, or both."

Strong words. More strong words came in another dissenting viewpoint put by the Rev. Morton A. Hill, S.J., president of Morality in Media, New York, and the Rev. Winfrey C. Link, administrator of the McKendree Manor Methodist Retirement Home, Hermitage, Tennessee. These two commissioners started their minority opinion with the striking words: "The Commission's majority report is a Magna Carta for the pornographer." They clearly feel that the pornographer should not have a Magna Carta. Yet other people could well feel that there may be grave dangers, even grave political dangers, in giving the pornographer anything less.

Most of Washington's commissions happily come at least close to unanimity. Yet here out of eighteen members, only twelve voted for the basic recommendation that: "Federal, state and local legislation prohibiting the sale, exhibition and distribution of sexual materials to consenting adults should be repealed." Five other commissioners dissented and one abstained.

The nature of the dissent varied. Father Hill and Reverend Link have already been mentioned. Mr. Keating, while filing his own dissenting report and concurring with the findings of the Hill-Link dissent, actually abstained from voting on the Commission's findings. Thomas C. Lynch, the attorney general of California, voted against the majority report, as did Rabbi Irving Lehrman, of Temple Emanu-El in Miami Beach, and Mrs. Cathryn Spelts of the South Dakota School of Mines and Technology, one of the two women commissoners. Rabbi Lehrman and Mrs. Spelts, however, subscribed to the bulk of the majority report, but said that the evidence was insufficient to warrant repeal of all restrictions on adults.

There were even minor disagreements over emphasis from the commissioners signing the majority report, and four commissioners felt it necessary to issue separate opinions. Morris A. Lipton, professor of psychiatry and director of research development at the University of North Carolina, and Edward D. Greenwood, psychiatrist at the Menninger Foundation, Topeka, Kansas, merely wanted to stress their opinion that the studies contracted for by the Commission, while possibly having flaws, were uniform in the direction in which they were pointing. "This direction," Mr. Greenwood and Professor Lipton considered, "fails to establish a meaningful causal relationship or even significant correlation between exposure to erotica and immediate or delayed antisocial behavior among adults." On the subject of pornography generally they said: "We find it to be a nuisance rather than an evil. The American public apparently agrees."

These two psychiatrists were only, in effect, underlining the majority viewpoint of the Commission. But the two sociologists on the Commission, Otto N. Larsen, professor of sociology at the University of Washington, and Professor Marvin E. Wolfgang, director of the Center of Criminological Research at the University of Pennsylvania, wished to push the Commission's findings rather further than the majority.

Professors Larsen and Wolfgang recommended "no specific

statutory restrictions on obscenity or pornography." They believe that "the First Amendment to the Constitution is abrogated by restrictions on textual and visual material that may be deemed by some as 'obscene' or 'pornographic.'" They would have repealed all existing federal, state and local statutes regarding obscenity, and would not preclude the distribution of pornographic materials to juveniles.

Recommending the repeal of such statutes, these two sociologists said: "Advocating repeal is not advocating anarchy, for we believe that informal social controls will work better without the confusion of ambiguous and arbitrarily administered laws. With improvements in sex education and better understanding of human sexual behavior, society can more effectively handle, without legislation, the distribution of material deemed by some to be offensive to juveniles or adults."

It was Congress that found the traffic in obscenity and pornography to be "a matter of national concern," and, having regard to the federal government's responsibilities in the matter, established an advisory commission whose purpose was: "After a thorough study which shall include a study of the causal relationship of such materials to antisocial behavior, to recommend advisable, appropriate, effective, and constitutional means to deal effectively with such traffic in obscenity and pornography."

The commission was requested by Congress to address itself to "a matter of national concern." But one of the Commission's most significant, and in some quarters most disputed, findings is that obscenity and pornography are not matters of public concern at all. Indeed, this evidence might suggest that Congress might save its money, and that the American people, contrary to such individualized evidence as collected by Mr. Keating and others, have very little interest in the subject. The Commission suggests that we are permissive about permissiveness. Few congressional commissions can have sought so eagerly to saw away at the branch they were sitting on. But evidence is evidence—or, in this instance, is it?

At the request of Congress the Commission not only utilized such sociological and psychological evidence as had already been garnered on pornography, but also instituted a considerable amount of basic research.

Who cares about pornography, apart, of course, from Congress? Obviously Congress, with its eye admirably fixed upon the flexible vote of the electorate, fondly imagined that everyone cared. On September 30, 1970 the Commission urbanely contradicted Congress's most grass-rooted hopes.

In what must become one of the most controversial surveys ever initiated by a congressional commission, it discovered that only 2 percent of our populace placed concern over erotic materials among "the two or three most serious problems facing the country today."

One can accept this finding. Yet the question that supports its statistics was perhaps a trifle naively put. A man who is asked what are the two or three most serious problems facing the country today might well say (and 54 percent did) that the Vietnam war is what worries him the most. And should we be surprised to find 36 percent primarily interested in racial conflict, 32 percent looking askance at inflation, taxation, unemployment and other middle-class nightmares? Nineteen percent it appears are concerned with pollution and 4 percent show a more than passing interest in what is described as the failure of the educational system.

There are facts, lies and statistics, and it would be a bold man who would contend that statistics bear more resemblance to facts than they do to lies. Statistics are as pliable as toffee, even if they do, once in a while, stick in your teeth.

The present statistics—so basic to the Commission's undertaking—were responsive to the following question: "Would you please tell me what you think are the two or three most serious problems facing the country today?" So only 2 percent expressed concern over erotic materials. But look once more at the question. In our present sand-slip society a man has the duty to be worried about many things. We look to our nation, to ourselves and to our children. In the desperate hierarchy of troubles probably only 2 percent of us can enjoy the luxury of nominating obscenity as one of the two or three major contemporary issues.

The rest of us are looking toward such primary needs as peace and prosperity. But our primary concern with such basic issues does not mean that we are not worried—and not only engaged for ourselves but for our children—about the ever-increasing availability of erotica.

It needs no statistics to tell us that our children are far more bombarded with sexual material than we were ourselves when we made our own nervous transitions to maturity. This is important. It is, surely, as Congress originally said, "a matter of national concern," and to refuse acceptance of that concern, or to underrate it, is unrealistic. The findings—and the dispute over those findings—of this congressional commission are vitally important to us.

It is easy, perhaps dangerously easy, to mock the nature of statistics and findings offered by this Commission, and unquestionably some of the evidence suggested in its report is of the kind in which science is painfully following in the wake of common sense. It will surprise few people, for example, to discover that men are more stimulated by nude photographs of women than they are by photographs of other men—unless of course, they are homosexuals to whom different valuations apply. Such data savor of the simplistic.

Yet the research of the Commission has delivered its quota of surprises. Perhaps the greatest—perfectly evident from the findings—is that women are virtually as interested in erotica as are men. This, probably, will be a surprise to many people—although the cause of it may originate in areas not everyone will be prepared to discuss.

Normally, or even abnormally, it seems that there is not a single sexual interest that is not catered to by the diligent pornographer. Yet it is evident to the most casual of investigators that most pornography is aimed at the male heterosexual. If the female heterosexual is virtually as interested in such material as the male—and, give or take a certain feminine modesty, the findings here suggest that she is—she is painfully underrepresented in available erotic material.

There are obvious reasons for this, among which social custom can probably not be placed too high. Yet the suspicion remains that women are the underprivileged sex when it comes to erotica and that this underprivilege derives from male supremacy. Women's Lib could well make a plank in their platform out of the missing opportunity to either reject or embrace smut. At present comparatively little pornography— very little indeed—is aimed at women. And yet it seems that they respond to it as warmly as men.

Another surprising, or at least possibly surprising, attitude revealed by the report, is the purely educational aspects of pornography. It seems from the evidence presented that one significant function of pornographic material is the dissemination of information about sex, and the encouragement of less inhibited attitudes toward sex.

The dissidents to the Commission's majority stress, in various ways, their anxiety that the prevailing currents of opinion place an undue value upon sexual gratification. Whether this is true or not is a matter upon which everyone should formulate his own opinion. Community standards and individual attitudes have quite clearly changed enormously, even over the past couple of decades. However, if you accept, as immediately previous generations probably did not, that sexual desire is an appetite that should be satisfied rather than curbed, the possible educational function of pornography is a factor worthy of consideration.

The majority view of the Commission implies that obscenity, like beauty, is in the eye of the beholder. This is obviously true. Whatever value we choose to place upon the Commission's findings—and the evidence of the dissidents, while naturally less scientifically garnered, must nevertheless be most seriously regarded—it really does seem that for the majority of Americans questions of obscenity and pornography are much more questions of taste than questions of morality. If this is true, and if this is established, the Commission will have fulfilled a very valuable function. For as a society we lack guidance in this matter. Our courts talk about community standards, while having only the vaguest ideas of what, currently, those standards are. And as a nation we are very uncertain of our own attitude.

This report clarifies the situation. If nothing else, it does this simply by stating that such a situation exists. On her deathbed Gertrude Stein murmured: "What is the answer?" There was no reply from the friends gathered around her. Just a silence. So Miss Stein said, falteringly: "Then, what is the question?"

The great virtue of this report is not that it offers answers, but simply that it asks questions. At the moment, on the entire subject of obscenity, including what and why it is, we desperately need questions.

Our difficulty is simply expressed. We have as a community decisions to make that affect sexual mores. Traditionally we have had Judeo-Christian precepts to guide us. Those precepts are today more honored in the breach than in the observance, and as a community we lack the universally accepted certainty of religious dogma which was able to provide a clear demarcation between right and wrong, good and evil. We have, perhaps, to build a new society, and our attitudes toward sex, pornography, obscenity and censorship are possibly—indeed, almost certainly—of vital interest.

Censorship is a dirty word—perhaps the dirtiest. The easiest thing to censor—or if you prefer it, to suppress—is something of a sexual nature. You merely have to say that it offends you morally, and in breathless, bible-tapping guilt, a considerable part of the community is likely to support you.

The correlation between censorship of sexual material and a rejection of the First Amendment to the Constitution has been spotted more than once, even before this report. Even if one believes in the desirability of censorship of matters pertaining to sex, it is obviously difficult to legislate in a manner that will not ill-advisedly embrace politics. An example might be offered here. During the past two or three years a state of total permissiveness has been established upon the New York stage. Total nudity and simulated sexual acts have been accepted by the police and, therefore by implication, by the community. The only drama that has been prosecuted on moral grounds in the past few years has been *Che,* written by Lennox Raphael.

It was a monstrously bad play—but many plays are monstrously bad. But it did show scenes of male and female nudity, together with simulated sexual acts of unequivocal significance.

The problem is that *Che* also presented an ill-considered, political attack upon the United States—an attack that could not but be offensive to many Americans in the audience.

Yet the play—the feeblest of things, but totally sincere in its political beliefs—was prosecuted and, in effect, damned. It did nothing that two or three other off-Broadway shows —including the notorious *Oh! Calcutta!*—had not also done. But *Che,* the only play to be busted in recent years, was not only obscene, it was also political. It attacked American policy in Cuba—it attacked it in a very confused way but the political purpose of the play was always evident.

It would be most dangerous if political opinions were to be assailed on grounds of obscenity. The so-called underground press contains papers that mix lightweight obscenity with heavyweight political opinion. It would be a bad day for America if these papers were banned. We need dissent—it is part of the pattern of democracy. And if this dissent comes in packages that we do not always find acceptable to our taste, we must remember that it is more honorable, and democratically more useful, to honor dissent rather than ban it.

There is one point concerning obscenity that does not appear in the report as forcibly as might have been expected. We all know what pornography is, and what pornographic materials are. But in art there is an enormous difference, in intention if in nothing else measurable, between the erotic and the pornographic.

Eroticism is to the artist the expression of a very precious part of life. The artist's intention is not pornography but truth. Eroticism is woven into the web of his words and offered as part of life.

It is clear that the artist wishing to employ eroticism in his work should in no way be hindered. However, if the erotic artist can be allowed his privileges, then he must also recognize his duties. Art is not pornography, and while simple pornography can be easily categorized as such, so that no one buying would be under any illusion regarding his purchase, art, be it a novel, a motion picture, a play, or a painting, is more difficult to label.

Here and now in the English-speaking world, almost everything we hear and see in the form of art is controlled by a comparatively small group of highly sophisticated men in New York, Los Angeles, and London. These people live in a particular society that may well have community standards that diverge from those of the nation as a whole.

All media should be vigilant of such divergence. It is fatally easy for media executives to imagine that their standards of taste represent the entire nation. This may not be so. There surely comes a point when obscenity, however urbanely presented, becomes an invasion of privacy. One person in a theater, outraged by a four-letter word, has been indecently offended. Artists should not be censored—but neither should they imagine that their own standards of taste are universal. To impose such standards unilaterally, without concern or regard for the audience, savors rather nastily of fascism. Our arts must be free, but they also must be careful.

Perhaps the most important thing about pornography is to prevent it from coming up on one unexpectedly. Pornography should always be very clearly labeled, so that people buying it know what they are purchasing and no one could be exposed to it through inadvertence or innocence.

What effect is this report likely to have? It is unusual in that it tells Congress something that Congress did not expect to hear. Legislation along the lines recommended by the Commission seems, at present, a trifle unlikely. But this report is bound to affect the decisions of our courts, and its majority view, while much disputed, is very likely to become the yardstick of contemporary community standards in such matters.

The Report of the Commission on Obscenity and Pornography provides all of us for the first time with data and evidence on this terribly complex subject. It seriously requires the attention of every citizen concerned with the quality of our lives. As much as any other public document it represents the United States of America, 1970. Read it. You may love it or hate it, accept it or challenge it, but you shouldn't ignore it.

THE REPORT
OF THE
COMMISSION ON
OBSCENITY
AND
PORNOGRAPHY

COMMISSION ON OBSCENITY AND PORNOGRAPHY

1016 — 16th STREET, N.W.
WASHINGTON, D.C. 20036

September 30, 1970

To the President and Congress of the United States:

Pursuant to Section 5(b), Public Law 90-100, I have the
honor to transmit the final report of the Commission on
Obscenity and Pornography containing its findings,
conclusions and recommendations.

By direction of the Commission

William B. Lockhart, Chairman

The President
The President of the Senate
The Speaker of the House of Representatives

Preface

Congress, in Public Law 90-100, found the traffic in obscenity and pornography to be "a matter of national concern." The Federal Government was deemed to have a "responsibility to investigate the gravity of this situation and to determine whether such materials are harmful to the public, and particularly to minors, and whether more effective methods should be devised to control the transmission of such materials." To this end, the Congress established an advisory commission whose purpose was "after a thorough study which shall include a study of the causal relationship of such materials to antisocial behavior, to recommend advisable, appropriate, effective, and constitutional means to deal effectively with such traffic in obscenity and pornography."

Congress assigned four specific tasks:

"(1) with the aid of leading constitutional law authorities, to analyze the laws pertaining to the control of obscenity and pornography; and to evaluate and recommend definitions of obscenity and pornography;

"(2) to ascertain the methods employed in the distribution of obscene and pornographic materials and to explore the nature and volume of traffic in such materials;

"(3) to study the effect of obscenity and pornography upon the public, and particularly minors, and its relationship to crime and other antisocial behavior; and

"(4) to recommend such legislative, administrative, or other advisable and appropriate action as the Commission deems necessary to regulate effectively the flow of such traffic, without in any way interfering with constitutional rights."

Public Law 90-100 became law in October, 1967, and the President appointed members to the Commission in January, 1968.[1] Funds were appropriated for the Commission's operation in July, 1968; at the same time the tenure of the Commission was extended to provide it the originally intended two years for its studies.

1

The Commission held its first meeting in July, 1968. It gave exploratory consideration to the various areas of its responsibilities, making use of experts who presented preliminary analyses of the available information about law, traffic and effects.

The Commission elected William B. Lockhart as chairman and Frederick H. Wagman as vice-chairman. The Commission then organized itself into four working panels: 1) Legal; 2) Traffic and Distribution; 3) Effects; and 4) Positive Approaches. It appointed a committee to recommend a director and a general counsel for the Commission's staff.[2] Upon the recommendation of this committee, the Executive Director and General Counsel were appointed by the Commission effective the last week in August, 1968. The remainder of the staff was appointed by the Executive Director; the nucleus of the staff was assembled in September, 1968.

The Commission fully subscribed from the beginning to the Congressional directive to make recommendations only after thorough study. To implement this approach, it was determined that confidentiality by Commission members should be maintained. This was felt to be necessary to encourage maximum exploration and free discussion of opinions, data and new ideas at meetings of the Commissioners, to enhance open and unbiased investigations in sensitive areas, to avoid public misinterpretations of research data and to prevent premature conclusions. Moreover, the Commissioners felt it was important, in order to avoid confusion as to the activities of the Commission, to have but one spokesman prior to the completion of its Report. Commissioner Charles H. Keating, Jr., a replacement for one of the original Commissioners,[3] did not subscribe to this decision after his appointment.

Because its initial survey of available information relating to the various tasks assigned by Congress amply demonstrated the insufficiency of existing factual evidence as a basis for recommendations, the Commission initiated a program of research designed to provide empirical information relevant to its tasks. The responsibility for the details of the research program was delegated to the four working panels which reported to the Commission on their progress and direction from time to time. The Commission's energies were devoted at the beginning principally to the design and implementation of the research program, at a later point to the assimilation and integration of the results of the research, and finally

2

to the discussion of alternatives and the making of decisions regarding recommendations.

Some members of the Commission suggested that public hearings be held at the beginning of the Commission's life. The Commission concluded, however, that in the first stage of its work public hearings would not be a likely source of accurate data or a wise expenditure of its limited resources. Approximately 100 national organizations were invited to express their views on the problems of obscenity and pornography by submitting written statements, and views were also solicited from those involved in law enforcement, from the legal profession generally, and from constitutional law experts. The Commission left open the possibility of holding public hearings at a later date when it would be possible to invite witnesses to focus on particular issues and proposals as those evolved from the Commission's studies and discussions. Public hearings were held in Los Angeles, California, on May 4 and 5, 1970, and in Washington, D. C. on May 12 and 13, 1970. Fifty-five persons, representing law enforcement agencies, courts, government at many levels, civic organizations, writers, publishers, distributors, film producers, exhibitors, actors, librarians, teachers, youth organizations, parents and other interested groups, were invited to appear before the Commission. Thirty-one of these persons accepted the Commission's invitation. In addition, the Commission heard statements from numerous private citizens who attended the hearings. A broad spectrum of views was presented to the Commission through these hearings. Because of financial limitations, the transcript of the Commission's hearings will not be printed but may be found in the Archives of the United States.

Material may be deemed "obscene"[4] because of a variety of contents: religious, political, sexual, scatological, violent, etc. The Commission has limited its concern to sexual obscenity, including sadomasochistic material, because the legislative history indicated this as the focus of congressional concern as reflected by the linking of obscenity with pornography in the Act creating the Commission. The application of obscenity laws has been directed in recent times almost exclusively to sexual obscenity; indeed, court decisions regarding permissible legal definitions of the term "obscene" have appeared in recent years to delimit its application to such sexual obscenity. Thus, the Commission's inquiry was

3

directed toward a wide range of explicit sexual depictions in pictorial and textual media.[5]

Just as obscenity may involve a variety of contents and judgments, so also may "antisocial" behavior and moral character. A declining concern with established religions, new questions as to the wisdom and morality of war, changes in attitudes toward races and minorities, and conflicts regarding the responsibility of the state to the individual and the individual to the state may all be considered to represent changes in the moral fiber of the nation. To some, these phenomena are considered to be signs of corroding moral decay; to others, signs of change and progress. It was impossible during the brief life of the Commission to obtain significant data on the effects of the exposure to pornography on nonsexual moral attitudes. Consequently, the Commission has focused on that type of antisocial behavior which tends to be more directly related to sex. This includes premarital intercourse, sex crimes, illegitimacy, and similar items.

Discussions of obscenity and pornography in the past have often been devoid of fact. Popular rhetoric has often contained a variety of estimates of the size of the "smut" industry and assertions regarding the consequences of the existence of these materials and exposure to them. Many of these statements, however, have had little anchoring in objective evidence. Within the limits of its time and resources, the Commission has sought, through staff and contract research, to broaden the factual basis for future continued discussion. The Commission is aware that not all issues of concern have been completely researched nor all questions answered. It also recognizes that the interpretations of a set of "facts" in arriving at policy implications may differ even among men of good will. Nevertheless, the Commission is convinced that on most issues regarding obscenity and pornography the discussion can be informed by important and often new facts. It presents its Report, hopeful that it will contribute to this discussion at a new level. Since it may be anticipated that in any controversial area some of the research will be questioned as to method and the validity and reliability of the results, the Commission hopes that responsible scientific organizations will carefully scrutinize these studies and that new and continuing research will result.

The Commission's Report consists of this preface, an overview of the findings of the Commission, a set of nonlegislative and legislative recommendations, and the full reports of the four Panels.

The Commission will also publish a series of Technical Reports which will make available the details of the data developed by the Commission, its staff, and those individuals and groups who contributed to its research program.

NOTES

1. Upon the resignation from the Commission of Kenneth B. Keating to accept appointment as Ambassador to India, the President appointed Charles H. Keating, Jr., as his replacement in June, 1969. Commissioner Charles H. Keating, Jr., chose not to participate in the discussions and deliberations which led to the formulation of this Report and its recommendations. His views appear in his separate statement.

2. The Committee consisted of the Chairman and Vice-Chairman and Commissioners Edward D. Greenwood, Joseph T. Klapper, Otto N. Larsen and Irving Lehrman.

3. Kenneth B. Keating.

4. The area of the Commission's study has been marked by enormous confusions over terminology. Some people equate "obscenity" with "pornography" and apply both terms to any type of explicit sexual materials. Other persons intend differences of various degrees in their use of these terms. In the Commission's Report, the terms "obscene" or "obscenity" are used solely to refer to the legal concept of prohibited sexual materials. The term "pornography" is not used at all in a descriptive context because it appears to have no legal significance and because it most often denotes subjective disapproval of certain materials, rather than their content or effect. The Report uses the phrases "explicit sexual materials," "sexually oriented materials," "erotic," or some variant thereof to refer to the subject matter of the Commission's investigations; the word "materials" in this context is meant to refer to the entire range of depictions or descriptions in both textual and pictorial form—primarily books, magazines, photographs, films, sound recordings, statuary, and sex "devices."

5. The Commission did not investigate directly the phenomenon of "live" sex shows, such as simulated or actual sexual activity on the stage, or before an audience. These activities are governed most often by local laws regulating actual sexual conduct, such as prohibitions upon indecent exposure, disorderly conduct, fornication, or sodomy. The terms of such prohibitions vary widely from locality to locality and the reasons for them may diverge substantially from the concerns underlying obscenity prohibitions. The Commission, therefore, did not deem recommendations in these various areas of sexual conduct to be within its primary assignment.

5

Part One

OVERVIEW
OF FINDINGS

I. The Volume of Traffic and Patterns of Distribution of Sexually Oriented Materials*

A. The Industries

When the Commission undertook its work, it could find no satisfactory estimates of the volume of traffic in obscene and pornographic materials. Documented estimates describing the content of materials included therein were not available. The first task was to determine the scope of the subject matter of investigation. The very ambiguity of the terms "obscene" and "pornographic" makes a meaningful single overall estimate of the volume of traffic an impossibility. It is clear that public concern applies to a broad range of materials. Therefore, the Commission determined to report on the commercial traffic and distribution of sexually oriented materials in motion picture films, books, and periodicals. The Commission's examination included these materials, whether publicly or privately exhibited or sold in retail outlets, by individual sales, or through the United States mails.

Two overall findings may appropriately be stated at the outset. Articles appearing in newspapers, magazines, and in other reports have variously estimated the traffic in the "pornography" or "smut" industry to be between $500 million and $2.5 billion per year, almost always without supporting data or definitions which would make such estimates meaningful.

The Commission can state with complete confidence that an estimate of $2.5 billion sales grossly exaggerates the size of the "smut" industry in the United States under any rea-

*The Report of the Traffic and Distribution Panel of the Commission provides a more thorough discussion and documentation of this overview.

sonable definition of the term. In addition, a monolithic "smut" industry does not exist; rather, there are several distinct markets and submarkets which distribute a variety of erotic materials. Some of these industries are fairly well organized, while others are extremely chaotic. These industries vary in terms of media, content, and manner of distribution. Some of the industries are susceptible to fairly precise estimates of the volume of materials, others are not.

We will describe briefly, and provide estimates of dollar and unit volume for most of the industries involved in the production and distribution of broadly defined sexually oriented material.

MOTION PICTURES

Movies have long been one of the primary recreational outlets for Americans. Box office receipts from nearly 14,000 theaters were estimated at $1.065 billion for 1969, and approximately 20 million persons attended motion pictures weekly.

Until the past year or two, motion pictures distributed in the United States fell rather neatly into three categories: general release, art, and exploitation films. By far the most important and familiar are general release films produced and distributed by well-known companies, starring well-known actors, and exhibited in 90% or more of the theaters across the country. These account for the vast majority of theater attendance in the United States. Art films are an undefined, amorphous group of films which appeal to a limited audience. Exploitation films, usually known in the industry as "skin flicks," are low-budget sex-oriented movies which have a rather limited exhibition market.

In addition to these well-defined types of films recognized by the industry for many years, in the past year or two quite a number of highly sexually oriented hybrid films (which combine elements of all three traditional types) and films of a totally new genre have appeared. Another group of films, known in the trade as "16mm" films, which are generally among the most sexually explicit available, have also come onto the market.

The Rating System. The recent acceleration in sexual content of films has been approximately coincident in time with the initiation of a movie-rating system for the guidance of viewers. The rating system represents an industry judgment

8

of the appropriateness of the content for children, and reflects to some degree the explicitness of the sexual content of a rated movie. The rating system contains four classifications, two that are not age restricted and two that are age restricted: "G," all ages admitted; "GP," all ages admitted, parental guidance suggested; "R," restricted because of theme, content, or treatment to persons under 17 unless accompanied by a parent or adult guardian; and "X," no one under 17 admitted.

The rating system provides rough guidelines for judging the sexual content of rated films. "G" rated films contain little in the way of sexual matter or vulgar language. Although the "G" rating of a few films has been criticized in the past, the application of this rating has probably become more strict in the past year or so. Little beyond conventional embracing and kissing is allowed. Films with an "antisocial" theme are not rated "G."

"GP" rated films are rated with the "maturing adolescent" in mind. Some degree of sexual implication is allowed, flashes of nudity from a distance are sometimes shown, and some vulgar language is permitted. If discussion of sexual topics becomes "too candid" or if approval is expressed for such activities as premarital sex or adultery, the film will be rated "R" or "X."

"R" rated films can contain virtually any theme. Considerable partial nudity is allowed as is a good deal of sexual foreplay. Several "R" films have contained scenes of full female nudity (genitalia). The chief difference between "R" and "X" rated films is the quantity and quality of the erotic theme, conduct or nudity contained in the film rather than a set of absolutes which automatically classify a film as "R" or "X."

"X" rated films are those which, in the judgment of the industry organization charged with rating, cannot be given any other classification. Films which concentrate almost exclusively on eroticism are placed in this category. An "X" rating may be self-applied by producers who do not submit their product to the Code and Rating Administration (the only classification which can be so applied).

General Release Films. Since the beginning of the motion picture industry, the sexual content and themes of movies have been the target of criticism. In recent years, general release films have become more sexually explicit. They are the target of the most public criticism because of their nation-

9

wide distribution to large diversified audiences. This criticism is magnified because of the large volume of newspaper advertising, gossip columns, and stories, articles, and pictures appearing in periodicals.

The trend towards increased sexual content of general release films has accelerated in the past two years. The candid treatment of sexual subjects has affected all aspects of films, i.e., theme, activity depicted, and degree of nudity. At present, there are few areas of sexual conduct which have not been the central subject of widely distributed general release films, including adultery, promiscuity, abortion, perversion, spouse-swapping, orgies, male and female homosexuality, etc. These themes, which were sometimes dealt with discretely in an earlier era, are now presented quite explicitly. Further, the requirement of an earlier day for "just retribution" for sexual misdeeds is no longer a requirement.

Sexual activity depicted on the screen has also become much more graphic. Scenes of simulated intercourse are increasing. Other sexual acts, including masturbation, fellatio, and cunnilingus, are sometimes suggested and occasionally simulated.

Partial nudity (female breasts and buttocks and male buttocks) may be seen in many general release films. The depiction of full female nudity (pubic area) has been increasing, and a few general release films have shown both sexes totally nude (genitalia).

Art Films. During the 1950s, "art films" treated sexual matters with a degree of explicitness not found in general release films of the same era. Today only the "foreignness" or limited audience appeal sets such films apart from many general release movies.

Exploitation Motion Pictures. Exploitation films (usually known as "skin flicks"), are low-budget films which concentrate on the erotic. Ordinarily, these films are shown only in a limited circuit of theaters and the film titles, though advertised, are not familiar to most people for lack of publicity. Until one or two years ago, the lines of demarcation between these films and general release movies were quite clear. However, the increase of sexually related themes and the incidence of nudity in the latter have blurred many of the former distinctions to a point where there is a considerable overlap. Today, perhaps the chief distinction between some sexually oriented general release films and exploitation films is that the latter (a) are much less expensive to produce (an

10

average cost of $20,000 to $40,000); and (b) are ordinarily exhibited in far fewer theaters (about 6% of all theaters exhibit such films at least on a part-time basis).

The vast majority of exploitation films are directed at the male heterosexual market. Relatively few films are produced for a male homosexual audience, but the number of these films has apparently increased in the past year or two. Full female nudity has become common in the last year or two, although full male nudity is virtually unknown except in those films directed at the male homosexual market. Sexual activity covering the entire range of heterosexual conduct leaves very little to the imagination. Acts of sexual intercourse and oral-genital contact are not shown, only strongly implied or simulated; sexual foreplay is graphically depicted.

The majority of theaters exhibiting exploitation films are old, run-down, and located in decaying downtown areas. However, there has been a trend toward building new theaters and opening such theaters in suburban areas.

"Hybrid" and "New Genre" Motion Pictures. Within the past two years, there has been a radical increase in sexually oriented motion pictures which receive relatively wide distribution. These "hybrid" films combine the sexual explicitness of exploitation films with the distribution patterns of general release films. In addition, an entirely new genre of highly sex-oriented films has been created. Some of these films graphically depict actual sexual intercourse on the screen, an activity which had previously been shown only in private or semi-private exhibitions.

Exploitation films normally achieve relatively limited exhibitions in an established circuit of theaters (perhaps 500-600 theaters on the average). Popular general release films can expect to be exhibited in 5,000 or more theaters. The market for popular hybrid sexually oriented films falls somewhere in between; many have been exhibited in 1,000 to 2,000 theaters and extended runs are common. In addition, such films are not limited to exhibitions in run-down theaters in decaying downtown areas; many play in first-class theaters in downtown and suburban areas. The most sexually explicit of all motion pictures (herein labeled "new genre" films) as yet have received only limited distribution in major cities.

Sixteen Millimeter Motion Pictures. Recently, an additional form of sexually oriented motion pictures shown in

11

theaters has emerged—known in the industry as "16mm films." As of August, 1970, a majority of the 16mm theaters in the country exhibit silent color films of young females displaying their genitals, but in a few cities 16mm films graphically depict sexual intercourse and oral-genital contact. Usually, 16mm films are the most sexually graphic films shown in the locality.

It is very difficult to estimate the number of 16mm theaters currently in operation, but a figure of 200 seems reasonably accurate.

As yet there are no recognizable film titles moving from city to city, and there is almost no nationwide distribution of such films. However, although 16mm films are in their infancy and as yet are a minor factor in the traffic of sexually oriented materials, the market definitely seems to be expanding.

Box Office Receipts of Motion Pictures. An analysis of reported box office receipts for films since the rating system has been in effect reveals no dramatic differences in reported grosses among "G," "GP," and "R" rated films, although as a group "G" films tended to have consistently higher grosses.

Total box office receipts are not available for either individual films or for classes of films. Each year, however, a trade journal reports on the movies which returned the greatest film rental fees to their distributors. In 1969, 25 "G" movies returned $119 million; 28 "GP" films returned $92 million; 18 "R" rated films accounted for $57 million; 3 "X" films returned $14 million; and 16 unrated films (most of which were released before the rating system went into effect) returned $56 million; of these, four were clearly sex-oriented and returned over $11 million in rentals. Box office receipts for these films were probably between 2 and 2.5 times the rental fees.

Final figures for 1970 are not available, but an analysis of the reported 50 top box office films each week in 20-24 cities for the first six months of 1970 (a total of 222 films) can be summarized as follows:

TABLE 1

Breakdown of ''Top Fifty'' Films, January-July, 1970

Rating	Number Of Films	Percentage Of Films	1970 Gross Receipts [1] (in millions)	Percentage of Gross Receipts
G	44	19.7 %	$44.4	25.9 %
GP	69	30.9 %	57.3	33.5 %
R	46	20.6 %	44.9	26.2 %
X	15	6.8 %	12.4	7.2 %
Non-Sex Unrated	15	6.8 %	2.7	1.6 %
Sex-Oriented Unrated [2]	33	15.2 %	9.5	5.6 %
TOTAL	222	100.0 %	$171.1	100.0 %

---

[1] Many of the films listed in the ''Top Fifty'' during the first six months of 1970 were originally released in 1969. Only 1970 gross receipts for these films were included.

[2] These films are characterized as hybrid or new genre films in this Report. Judgments on the classification were made by the Commission Staff.

TABLE 2

Box-Office Receipts, by Classification

Rating	1970 Projected Receipts (in millions) [1]	Percentage of Receipts
G	$ 259	23.5 %
GP	335	30.5 %
R	262	23.8 %
X	72	6.6 %
Non-Sex Unrated	16	1.5 %
Sex-Oriented Unrated [2]	56	5.0 %
Art Films [3]	35	3.2 %
Exploitation Films [4]	65	5.9 %
TOTAL	$1,100	100.0 % [5]

---

[1] The first six figures in this column are projected from the ''Percentage of Gross Receipts'' column in Table 1 against an estimated gross of $1 billion for all but art and exploitation films.

[2] These films are characterized as hybrid or new genre films in this Report. Judgments on the classification were made by the Commission Staff.

[3] ''Art films'' play in between 500 and 600 theaters in an established ''art circuit.'' Few if any of these films reach the Top 50, but the total box-office receipts can be estimated at $30-$40 million simply on the basis of the number of theaters exhibiting such films.

[4] Estimated at $60-$70 million; see succeeding section of this Report.

[5] SOURCE: U.S. Industrial Outlook, 1970.

for sexually oriented films because theaters in many smaller cities and towns do not exhibit such films at all. Thus, the actual nationwide percentage accounted for by "G" and "GP" films is probably significantly greater than the projection, and "R," "X," and unrated sexually oriented hybrid films prob- ably account for less of the national market than indicated. However, the projection is useful in that it marks the maxi- mum traffic in sexually oriented films.

Exploitation Films. Estimates by the exploitation film in- dustry indicate a $60 million box office business in 1969. Additional studies indicate gross receipts for all exploitation theaters may have been as high as $70 million in 1969. Indus- try sources have indicated that 1970 receipts are likely to be considerably lower because of increased competition from sexually oriented motion pictures playing outside the exploi- tation market.

BOOKS AND MAGAZINES

The distribution and sale of sexually oriented publications in the United States can be roughly divided into two cate- gories: (a) those which are a part of the mass market, i.e., books and periodicals available to a general audience; and (b) so-called "adults only" publications, a sub-market of sexually oriented printed matter which receives relatively limited distribution.

The Mass Market. There are several channels by which mass market publications are distributed from the publisher to the consumer: national distributors, national jobbers, book clubs, local wholesale distributors, and retailers. In many cases, publications skip over some of the intermediate steps, and flow directly from publisher to retailer and from publisher to consumer.

The book publishing industry in 1968 (latest figures avail- able) estimated its receipts at almost $2.6 billion. Of that total, materials which could conceivably be within the areas of study by the Commission would be found only in "Adult Trade Books" ($179 million), "Paperback Books" ($167 mil- lion) and "Book Club" ($204 million)—a total of $550 mil- lion, or some 21% of the entire book industry.

The periodical industry in the latest official consensus of business (1967) reported total receipts of approximately $2.6 billion. Of this, only general periodicals such as comics, wom- en and home service magazines, news, business, and entertainment magazines could possibly be of interest to the Commission. These produced receipts of $1.445 billion, of which $560 million came from single copy and subscription sales (25% of total receipts) and $885 million from advertising.

The Commerce Department estimates that during 1970 publishers' receipts will reach approximately $5.6 billion (both books and periodicals) but the proportion of the market of interest to the Commission will probably remain about the same as before.

The book and periodical publishing industry in the United States is the largest and most diversified in the world. For example, over 10,000 periodicals are published per year and their sales per issue range from a few thousand copies to over 17.5 million. The total average sales, per issue, for all mass market magazines is almost 250 million copies and the total number of magazines sold in 1969 has been estimated at more than 2.5 billion. Approximately 30,000 new book titles have been published each year for the past several years.

Although there are no official estimates of the total number of copies of mass market paperbacks distributed yearly, industry sources estimate that over 700 million paperback books are distributed each year and that over 330 million of these are sold. The retail sales volume of mass market paperback books exceeded $340 million in 1968.

Mass market paperback and hard-cover books and periodicals which might be classified as sexually oriented are distributed in basically the same manner as other mass publications. Such materials are usually not the most sexually explicit available in most localities and certainly not in any of the larger population centers. These publications are the most widely available sexually oriented printed material, however. There are approximately 110,000 retail outlets for general magazines, 80,000 of which display and sell paperback books; 10,000 sell mass market hard-cover books. Even more copies of both books and periodicals are sold through the mails by subscription and book clubs.

Sexually Oriented Mass Market Periodicals. Although the wide range of periodicals makes it difficult to distinguish which publications should be classified as sexually oriented, the mass market industry recognizes certain types of magazines as such.

"Confession" or "romance" magazines emphasize fictional accounts of the sexual problems of young women. These magazines do not explicitly describe sex organs or sexual activ-

15

ity and always resolve sexual problems in a moral context. In 1969, 38 confession magazines had total sales of 104.4 million copies and total retail sales of nearly $40 million. These magazines accounted for the vast bulk of the market.

"Barber shop" magazines, aimed at a male readership, primarily feature "action" stories, some of which are sex-oriented. Pictorial content primarily consists of "glamour" or "pin-up" photographs, but recently there has been an increase in photos of partially nude females. During 1969, sales of 20 such magazines (which make up almost the entire market) were approximately 30 million copies and retail sales totaled approximately $12 million.

The mass market magazines with the highest degree of sexual orientation are known in the industry as "men's sophisticates." These magazines generally have a standardized formula which devotes a substantial portion to photographs of partially nude females (with breast and buttock exposure) in modeling poses. Total 1969 sales figures for 62 "sophisticate" magazines were approximately 41 million copies, and the total retail sales were at least $31 million. Almost all the market was included. Publishers and distributors agree that during 1969 and into 1970, the market for men's sophisticates has declined.

There is a special group of sex-oriented mass market magazines which do not adequately fit any of the above classifications. Preeminent among these is Playboy, unique in the periodical industry. Each issue of Playboy contains no less than three, and sometimes four or five, pictorial layouts which feature partially nude females. In most cases, there is only breast and buttock exposure, although on occasion very discrete photographs of feminine pubic hair have been printed. Some of the articles and fiction contain a significant degree of sexual orientation, but many articles on other topics are written by well-known authors and distinguished persons. During 1969, just under 64 million copies were sold, and retail dollar sales were over $65 million.

There are a few other mass market magazines which contain a substantial amount of sexual orientation, but are not easily categorized. Total combined copy sales of these magazines are less than 20 million copies, and retail dollar sales are less than $15 million.

Sexually Oriented Mass Market Books.   Most major paperback publishers produce titles which might be classified as sexually oriented. For example, Bestsellers, a trade journal for magazine and paperback wholesalers and retailers, lists the 20 best-selling paperback books each month. Between January, 1969, and July, 1970, eighteen paperbacks which could easily be considered to be sexually oriented appeared on the Bestsellers list for more than one month. Three of these reached the number one position, and five ranked as high as second. Almost all of the major book lines were represented.

Although it is impossible to arrive at total sales figures, tens of millions of paperback books with some degree of sexual orientation are sold each year.

An indication of the interest in sexually oriented hard-cover books can be projected from the fact that two of the top ten best-selling fiction titles of 1968 were regarded as "sexy books." In 1969, six of the top ten hard-cover fiction "best sellers" and eight of the top 20 were regarded as sexually oriented. During 1968 and 1969, none of the top ten non-fiction best sellers were related to sex. As of June 1970, three of the top four non-fiction best sellers relate to sex.

Newspapers.   The sexual content of daily newspapers was not investigated. Most newspapers, however, reflect a somewhat increased candor in articles and news stories relating to sexual matters.

The sexual content of one genre of newspaper, the so-called "underground press," has been the subject of considerable comment, although these are primarily political in nature. It has been estimated that there are 200 such newspapers in the United States with a readership of 6,000,000. The accuracy of such claims, however, is open to question. Sales figures for five of the best known newspapers indicated average weekly sales of over 200,000 and yearly sales of 10,500,000 in 1969.

The Secondary or "Adults Only" Market   Self-labeled "adults only" printed materials are of far less economic importance than are mass market publications. Separate or "secondary" channels of national and local wholesale distribution and of local retail sales have been created for this "adult" market. However, there is an overlap of sexually oriented materials between the mass and the "adult" markets; some publishers produce materials for both, and many other publishers constantly seek to expand distribution of their "secondary" product into the mass market.

Twenty or 30 of approximately 100 publishers producing primarily for the secondary market are important market-

17

place factors. Most are located either in California or the New York City area.

Sexual Content of "Adults Only" Paperback Books. The sexual content of paperback books published for the "adults only" market has become progressively "stronger" in the past decade. Today, the content of "adults only" paperback books runs the gamut from traditional "sex pulp" books (stories consisting of a series of sexual adventures tied together by minimal plot, in which the mechanics of the sex act are not described, euphemistic language is substituted for common or clinical terms, and much of the sexual content is left to the reader), through modern "sex pulp" (common terms for sexual activity and detailed descriptions of the mechanics of sex act are used), "classic" erotic literature, "pseudo-medical" (alleged case-study analysis of sexual activity), illustrated marriage manuals, and illustrated novels (with photographs in which young females pose with the focus of the camera directly on their genitalia), to "documentary" studies of censorship and pornography containing illustrations depicting genital intercourse and oral sex. Insofar as the textual portions of many of these books are concerned, it is probably not possible to exceed the candor, graphic descriptions of sexual activity, and use of vulgar language in some currently distributed "adults only" paperback books. The pictorial content of some illustrated paperback books similarly cannot be exceeded in explicit depictions of sexual activity.

The vast majority of "adults only" books are written for heterosexual males, although about 10% are aimed at the male homosexual market and a small percentage (less than 5%) at fetishists. Virtually none of these books is intended for a female audience.

Sexual Content of "Adults Only" Magazines. "Adults only" magazines of today contain little textual material and are devoted principally to photographic depictions of female and male nudity with emphasis on the genitalia. Some of these depictions contain two or three models together and some pose both males and females in the same photograph. The posing of more than one model in a single photograph has resulted in a considerable amount of implied sexual activity, either intercourse or oral-genital contact, but neither actual sexual activity nor physical arousal of males is depicted at the present time. Nearly 90% are intended for a male heterosexual audience. About 10% are directed to male homosexuals and feature male nudes. Fetish and sadomasochistic magazines featuring bondage, chains, whips, spanking,

18

rubber or leather wearing apparel, high-heeled boots, etc., are a rather insignificant part of the total production (less than 5%).

Production Costs. The cost of producing "adults only" paperback books and magazines is usually greater than the cost of these items for a mass general audience. Press runs for mass market paperback books seldom are below 100,000; only a very few "adults only" publishers had press runs as high as 40,000 in 1969 and 1970, and the typical press run of these publishers did not exceed 15,000 or 20,000. Since the fixed costs are apportioned to a much smaller number of copies, the unit cost is significantly higher for the "adults only" publications. "Adults only" paperback books usually cost between $.10 and $.20 to produce although some are considerably higher; "adults only" magazines are considerably more expensive to produce, in the $.45 to $.60 range, because of higher printing and preparation costs.

Distribution Channels. Many publishers of "adults only" materials act as their own distributors directly to retail outlets. However, there are now approximately 60 local wholesale distributors of "adults only" materials almost all of whom are located in large metropolitan areas.

There are approximately 850 self-labeled retail "adult" bookstores and 1,400 retail outlets which provide a restricted access section for "adult" material in addition to selling other products in a non-restricted access area. Most of these are located in metropolitan areas of 500,000 or more population. Many of these stores have estimated average gross sales of $200 to $300 a day and gross yearly sales of nearly $100,000. Average yearly retail sales are probably closer to $60,000 to $70,000. Net profits sometimes are in excess of $20,000 per store per year.

Retail outlets displaying and selling "adults only" material tend to be located in downtown or central city areas; a few are found in suburban shopping centers or in local neighborhoods. The stores range in appearance from seedy to respectable with the majority in the former category. The primary product of these retail "adult" bookstores are paperback books and magazines, although some sell sexual devices and some operate arcade type movie machines. A store may display as few as 200 or as many as 1,000 or more titles of paperback books and from 100 to 500 or more separate titles of magazines.

Total Sales of "Adults Only" Publications. The total volume of "adults only" materials sold at retail in the U.S.

was estimated by several different means. The most useful of these was an industry-wide analysis conducted by the Internal Revenue Service which disclosed that 20 of the largest "adult" publishers had gross receipts of approximately $21 million and an aggregate profit of $450,000 in tax year 1968. Combining all sources of information, the Commission estimates that 25 to 30 million "adults only" paperback books were sold in 1969 for a total retail value of $45 to $55 million; "adults only" magazine sales were approximately $25 to $35 million for 14 to 18 million copies. The best estimate is that "adults only" materials in the U.S. accounted for between $70 and $90 million in retail sales in 1969.

MAIL ORDER

Method of Doing Business. The American public is inundated annually by over 21 billion pieces of mail which advertise products and solicit purchases. A small percentage of this volume (less than 0.25%), attempts to sell sexually oriented materials. The number of businesses advertising sexually oriented materials through the mails varies greatly over time because the market offers easy and inexpensive entry and is in a constant state of flux. There are probably several hundred individuals or firms dealing in mail-order erotica at present, most of whom are located in the New York City and Los Angeles metropolitan areas. Of these, fewer than 20 are major factors and only about five generate a substantial volume of complaints from the public.

Mail-order operators offer a wide variety of sexually oriented materials for sale and cater to almost every conceivable taste. The most popular items are heterosexually oriented magazines, books, 8mm movies, sexual devices, and advertisements for "swingers" clubs. There are also materials designed for male homosexuals (10%) and a small amount for fetishists.

There are three types of advertising in this industry: solicited, semi-unsolicited, and unsolicited. Solicited advertising is that received by an individual who has made a request to be put on a specific mailing list. Semi-unsolicited advertising is usually received after a purchase or inquiry, or from a mailer who has obtained the individual's name and address from another mailer in the same business. Unsolicited advertising is received by an individual who has never made a purchase from, or inquiry of any dealer in sexually oriented materials. Most mail-order dealers in sexually oriented ma-

20

terials mail only to solicited or semi-unsolicited names. However, a few mail a large volume of advertising to unsolicited names. These are responsible for the majority of public complaints about erotica in the mails.

The business of advertising and selling sexually oriented materials through mail order is subject to the same rules of economics as any mail order operation. Mail-order selling can be profitable, but it is an expensive way of doing business. The cost to reach the potential customers with an advertising message is high and responses to sexually oriented mail advertising do not greatly differ from responses to mail advertising of any other products. The mail-order erotica business is very tenuous and stories that vast fortunes have been made overnight are apocryphal for the most part. Even the giants of the industry (fewer than ten) are relatively small-time operators and the profit of the largest probably does not exceed $200,000 before taxes per year.

Public Complaints. In April, 1968, the federal Anti-Pandering Act went into effect and allowed recipients of unsolicited sexually provocative advertisements to request the Postmaster General to issue an order to the mailer to refrain from further mailings to the addressee. During the first two years of operation, the Post Office received over 450,000 requests for prohibitory orders and issued over 370,000. Prohibitory orders have been issued against hundreds of separate business firm names. However, two mailers accounted for nearly 40% of the total prohibitory orders and three others accounted for another 20%. Approximately 5% of prohibitory orders were issued on behalf of minors under the age of 19. Although the number of prohibitory orders issued since the law went into effect is substantial, less than ½ of 1% of all sexually oriented advertising results in a complaint to the Post Office. Post Office figures show a decline of approximately 50% in requests for prohibitory orders during the first six months of fiscal 1970 as compared with the same period in fiscal 1969.

Volume of Mail and Sales. Twenty-eight major mailers and three mailing services specializing in processing sexually oriented advertising spent over $2 million on postage during fiscal 1969. This was enough to mail approximately 36 million letters. It is estimated that these dealers accounted for approximately 75% to 80% of the total mail volume. Therefore, the total volume of sexually oriented mail was approximately 45 to 48 million letters during fiscal year 1969. Retail sales value of the sexually oriented materials bought

21

through mail order probably did not exceed $12 to $14 million in fiscal 1969. (The Internal Revenue Service analyzed the receipts and income of most of the volume mailers for the tax year of 1968. These mailers had gross sales of $5.5 million and reported an aggregate loss of $3,000 for that year. However, the majority of the mailers did make a profit for the year).

"Under-The-Counter" or "Hard-Core" Materials. In 1970, a very limited amount of sexual material is being sold "under the counter." Such materials, which the market defines as "hard-core pornography," generally are limited to photographic reproductions of sexual intercourse depicting vaginal, anal, or oral penetration. These photographic materials are generally available in three forms: motion pictures (popularly called "stag films"), photo sets, and picture magazines. It has been estimated that between 3,000 and 7,000 stag films have been produced in the last 55 years, but an accurate estimate of the number on the market is virtually impossible to make. The stag film production is primarily a localized business with no national distribution and is extremely disorganized. There are no great fortunes to be made in stag film production. It is estimated that there are fewer than half a dozen individuals who net more than $10,000 per year in the business.

The traffic in picture magazines of sexual intercourse is apparently increasing. Today, the source of these materials appears to be principally Scandinavia or domestic copies of foreign publications. Photos or photo sets depicting sexual activity are a very minor part of the market at present.

Traffic and distribution of under-the-counter materials appears to be a very minor part of the total traffic in erotic materials. Imports of such materials from Scandinavia, however, appear to be increasing. Although the retail sales of these imports is almost certainly less than $5 million per year, this market appears to be growing. The total market in under-the-counter materials is estimated to be between $5 and $10 million.

Organized Crime Law enforcement officers differ among themselves on the question of whether "organized crime" is involved in the pornography business. Some believe very strongly that it is; others believe just as strongly that it is not.

There is some evidence that the retail "adult bookstore"

business, which purveys materials that are not only at the periphery of legitimacy but also at the margin of legality, tends to involve individuals who have had considerable experience with being arrested. The business does involve some risk of arrest and, therefore, would be avoided by persons with more concern for legitimacy and general reputation. There is a greater likelihood that persons with some background of conflict with the legal system will be found among "adult" bookstore proprietors. This is not the same, however, as being an adjunct or subsidiary of "organized crime." At present, there is insufficient data to warrant any conclusion in this regard.

B. The Consumers

ADULT EXPERIENCE WITH SEXUALLY EXPLICIT MATERIALS

Approximately 85% of adult men and 70% of adult women in the U.S. have been exposed at sometime during their lives to depictions of explicit sexual material in either visual or textual form. Most of this exposure has apparently been voluntary, and pictorial and textual depictions are seen about equally often. Recent experience with erotic materials is not as extensive as total experience, e.g., only about 40% of adult males and 26% of adult females report having seen pictorial depictions of sexual intercourse during the past two years.

Experience with explicit sexual materials varies according to the content of the depictions; depictions of nudity with sex organs exposed and of heterosexual intercourse are most common; depictions of homosexual activities and oral sex are less common; and depictions of sadomasochistic sexual activity are least common in Americans' experience. Thus portrayals of sex that conform to general cultural norms are more likely to be seen than are portrayals of sexual activity that deviate from these norms.

Experience with explicit sexual materials also varies according to the characteristics of the potential viewer. Men are more likely to be exposed to erotic materials than are women. Younger adults are more likely to be exposed than are older adults. People with more education are more likely to have experience with erotic materials. People who read general books, magazines, and newspapers more, and see general movies more also see more erotic materials. People who are more socially and politically active are more exposed

23

to erotic materials. People who attend religious services more often are less likely to be exposed to erotica.

Although most males in our society have been exposed to explicit sexual materials at some time in their lives, a smaller proportion has had relatively extensive experience with erotica. From one-fifth to one-quarter of the male population in the U.S. has somewhat regular experience with sexual materials as explicit as depictions of heterosexual intercourse.

Few people report that they buy erotic materials. Between one-quarter and one-half of people who have ever seen explicit sexual materials have ever purchased such materials. A major proportion of the acquisition of erotic materials occurs by obtaining it from a friend or acquaintance at no cost. Unsolicited mail accounts for a very small proportion of the exposure to erotic materials. Thus, most exposure to erotica occurs outside the commercial context and is a social or quasi-social activity. Erotica is a durable commodity for which there are several consumers for each purchase.

The informal distribution of erotica among friends and acquaintances is asymmetrical. Many more people have had sexual materials shown or given to them than report showing or giving these materials to others. Sharing is predominantly with friends of the same sex or with spouses. Only 31% of men and 18% of women report knowing of a shop which specializes in sexual materials.

Although the percentage of the population purchasing erotic materials is relatively small, the total number constitutes a sizeable market.

The patterns of experience of adults in Denmark and Sweden with erotic materials are similar to that described for American adults.

YOUNG PEOPLE'S EXPERIENCE WITH SEXUALLY EXPLICIT MATERIALS

First experience with explicit sexual materials usually occurs in adolescence for Americans. Roughly three quarters of adult American males report having been exposed to such materials before age 21. Retrospective reporting on adolescent experience by adult males indicates that the experience with erotica during adolescence was not isolated but rather both extensive and intensive.

Several recent studies of high school and college age youth are quite consistent in finding that there is also considerable exposure to explicit sexual materials on the part of minors

24

today. Roughly 80% of boys and 70% of girls have seen visual depictions or read textual descriptions of sexual intercourse by the time they reach age 18. Substantial proportions of adolescents have had more than an isolated exposure or two, although the rates of exposure do not indicate an obsession with erotic materials. A great deal of this exposure occurs in pre-adolescent and early adolescent years. More than half of boys have had some exposure to explicit sexual materials by age 15. Exposure on the part of girls lags behind that of boys by a year or two. Exposure of adolescents to depictions of genitals and heterosexual intercourse occurs earlier and more often than does exposure to oral-genital and homosexual materials. Experience with depictions of sadomasochistic material is much rarer, although it does occur.

Young people below the age of 21 rarely purchase sexually explicit books, magazines, and pictures; the mails and underground newspapers are negligible sources of exposure to erotica. By far the most common source of exposure to sexually explicit books, magazines, and pictures is a friend about the same age, and this exposure occurs in a social situation where materials are freely passed around. There is some suggestion that young people who are less active socially are less likely to be acquainted with sexual materials.

Thus, exposure to explicit sexual materials in adolescence is widespread and occurs primarily in a group of peers of the same sex or in a group involving several members of each sex. The experience seems to be more a social than a sexual one.

PATRONS OF ADULT BOOKSTORES AND ADULT MOVIE THEATERS

Patrons of adult bookstores and adult movie theaters may be characterized as predominantly white, middle class, middle aged, married males, dressed in business suit or neat casual attire, shopping or attending the movie alone. Almost no one under 21 was observed in these places, even where it was legal for them to enter.

The average patron of adult bookstores and movie houses appears to have had fewer sexually related experiences in adolescence than the average male in our society, but to be more sexually oriented as an adult. The buyers of erotica report frequencies of intercourse fairly similar to those of nonconsumers, and report a similar degree of enjoyment of

25

intercourse. Their high degree of sexual orientation in adult-hood encompasses, in addition to pictorial and textual erotica, a variety of sexual partners and of sexual activities within a consensual framework. Activities most frowned upon by our society, such as sadomasochism, pedophilia, bestiality, and nonconsensual sex, are also outside the scope of the interests of the average patron of adult bookstores and movie houses.

II. The Effects of Explicit Sexual Materials[1]

The Effects Panel of the Commission undertook to develop a program of research designed to provide information on the kinds of effects which result from exposure to sexually explicit materials, and the conditions under which these effects occur. The research program embraced both inquiries into public and professional belief regarding the effects of such materials, and empirical research bearing on the actual occurrence and condition of the effects. The areas of potential effect to which the research was addressed included sexual arousal, emotions, attitudes, overt sexual behavior, moral character, and criminal and other antisocial behavior related to sex.

Research procedures included (1) surveys employing national probability samples of adults and young persons; (2) quasi-experimental studies of selected populations; (3) controlled experimental studies; and (4) studies of rates and incidence of sex offenses and illegitimacy at the national level. A major study, which is cited frequently in these pages, was a national survey of American adults and youth which involved face-to-face interviews with a random probability sample of 2,486 adults and 769 young persons between the ages of 15 and 20 in the continental United States.[2]

The strengths and weaknesses of the various research methods utilized are discussed in Section A of the Report of the Effects Panel of the Commission.[3] That Report is based upon the many technical studies which generated the data from which the Panel's conclusions were derived.

26

A. OPINION CONCERNING EFFECTS OF SEXUAL MATERIALS

There is no consensus among Americans regarding what they consider to be the effects of viewing or reading explicit sexual materials. A diverse and perhaps inconsistent set of beliefs concerning the effects of sexual materials is held by large and necessarily overlapping portions of American men and women. Between 40% and 60% believe that sexual materials provide information about sex, provide entertainment, lead to moral breakdown, improve sexual relationships of married couples, lead people to commit rape, produce boredom with sexual materials, encourage innovation in marital sexual technique and lead people to lose respect for women. Some of these presumed effects are obviously socially undesirable while others may be regarded as socially neutral or desirable. When questioned about effects, persons were more likely to report having personally experienced desirable than undesirable ones. Among those who believed undesirable effects had occurred, there was a greater likelihood of attributing their occurrences to others than to self. But mostly, the undesirable effects were just believed to have happened without reference to self or personal acquaintances.

Surveys of psychiatrists, psychologists, sex educators, social workers, counselors and similar professional workers reveal that large majorities of such groups believe that sexual materials do not have harmful effects on either adults or adolescents. On the other hand, a survey of police chiefs found that 58% believed that "obscene" books played a significant role in causing juvenile delinquency.

B. EMPIRICAL EVIDENCE CONCERNING EFFECTS

A number of empirical studies conducted recently by psychiatrists, psychologists, and sociologists attempted to assess the effects of exposure to explicit sexual materials. This body of research includes several study designs, a wide range of subjects and respondents, and a variety of effect indicators. Some questions in this area are not answered by the existing research, some are answered more fully than others, and many questions have yet to be asked. Continued research efforts which embrace both replicative studies and inquiries into areas not yet investigated are needed to extend and clarify existing findings and to specify more concretely the conditions under which specific effects occur. The findings of available research are summarized below.

Experimental and survey studies show that exposure to erotic stimuli produces sexual arousal in substantial portions of both males and females. Arousal is dependent on both characteristics of the stimulus and characteristics of the viewer or user.

Recent research casts doubt on the common belief that women are vastly less aroused by erotic stimuli than are men. The supposed lack of female response may well be due to social and cultural inhibitions against reporting such arousal and to the fact that erotic material is generally oriented to a male audience. When viewing erotic stimuli, more women report the physiological sensations that are associated with sexual arousal than directly report being sexually aroused.

Research also shows that young persons are more likely to be aroused by erotica than are older persons. Persons who are college educated, religiously inactive, and sexually experienced are more likely to report arousal than persons who are less educated, religiously active and sexually inexperienced.

Several studies show that depictions of conventional sexual behavior are generally regarded as more stimulating than depictions of less conventional activity. Heterosexual themes elicit more frequent and stronger arousal responses than depictions of homosexual activity; petting and coitus themes elicit greater arousal than oral sexuality, which in turn elicits more than sadomasochistic themes.

SATIATION

The only experimental study on the subject to date found that continued or repeated exposure to erotic stimuli over 15 days resulted in satiation (marked diminution) of sexual arousal and interest in such material. In this experiment, the introduction of novel sex stimuli partially rejuvenated satiated interest, but only briefly. There was also partial recovery of interest after two months of nonexposure.

EFFECTS UPON SEXUAL BEHAVIOR

When people are exposed to erotic materials, some persons increase masturbatory or coital behavior, a smaller proportion decrease it, but the majority of persons report

28

no change in these behaviors. Increases in either of these behaviors are short lived and generally disappear within 48 hours. When masturbation follows exposure, it tends to occur among individuals with established masturbatory patterns or among persons with established but unavailable sexual partners. When coital frequencies increase following exposure to sex stimuli, such activation generally occurs among sexually experienced persons with established and available sexual partners. In one study, middle-aged married couples reported increases in both the frequency and variety of coital performance during the 24 hours after the couples viewed erotic films.

In general, established patterns of sexual behavior were found to be very stable and not altered substantially by exposure to erotica. When sexual activity occurred following the viewing or reading of these materials, it constituted a temporary activation of individuals' preexisting patterns of sexual behavior.

Other common consequences of exposure to erotic stimuli are increased frequencies of erotic dreams, sexual fantasy, and conversation about sexual matters. These responses occur among both males and females. Sexual dreaming and fantasy occur as a result of exposure more often among unmarried than married persons, but conversation about sex occurs among both married and unmarried persons. Two studies found that a substantial number of married couples reported more agreeable and enhanced marital communication and an increased willingness to discuss sexual matters with each other after exposure to erotic stimuli.

ATTITUDINAL RESPONSES

Exposure to erotic stimuli appears to have little or no effect on already established attitudinal commitments regarding either sexuality or sexual morality. A series of four studies employing a large array of indicators found practically no significant differences in such attitudes before and after single or repeated exposures to erotica. One study did find that after exposure persons became more tolerant in reference to other persons' sexual activities although their own sexual standards did not change. One study reported that some persons' attitudes toward premarital intercourse became more liberal after exposure, while other persons' attitudes became more conservative, but another study found

29

no changes in this regard. The overall picture is almost completely a tableau of no significant change.

Several surveys suggest that there is a correlation between experience with erotic materials and general attitudes about sex: Those who have more tolerant or liberal sexual attitudes tend also to have greater experience with sexual materials. Taken together, experimental and survey studies suggest that persons who are more sexually tolerant are also less rejecting of sexual material. Several studies show that after experience with erotic material, persons become less fearful of possible detrimental effects of exposure.

EMOTIONAL AND JUDGMENTAL RESPONSES

Several studies show that persons who are unfamiliar with erotic materials may experience strong and conflicting emotional reactions when first exposed to sexual stimuli. Multiple responses, such as attraction and repulsion to an unfamiliar object, are commonly observed in the research literature on psychosensory stimulation from a variety of nonsexual as well as sexual stimuli. These emotional responses are short-lived and, as with psychosexual stimulation, do not persist long after removal of the stimulus.

Extremely varied responses to erotic stimuli occur in the judgmental realm, as, for example, in the labeling of material as obscene or pornographic. Characteristics of both the viewer and the stimulus influence the response: For any given stimulus, some persons are more likely to judge it "obscene" than are others; and for persons of a given psychological or social type, some erotic themes are more likely to be judged "obscene" than are others. In general, persons who are older, less educated, religiously active, less experienced with erotic materials, or feel sexually guilty are most likely to judge a given erotic stimulus "obscene." There is some indication that stimuli may have to evoke both positive responses (interesting or stimulating), and negative responses (offensive or unpleasant) before they are judged obscene or pornographic.

CRIMINAL AND DELINQUENT BEHAVIOR

Delinquent and nondelinquent youth report generally similar experiences with explicit sexual materials. Exposure to sexual materials is widespread among both groups. The age of first exposure, the kinds of materials to which they are exposed, the amount of their exposure, the circumstances of exposure, and their reactions to erotic stimuli are essentially the same, particularly when family and neighborhood backgrounds are held constant. There is some evidence that peer group pressure accounts for both sexual experience and exposure to erotic materials among youth. A study of a heterogeneous group of young people found that exposure to erotica had no impact upon moral character over and above that of a generally deviant background.

Statistical studies of the relationship between availability of erotic materials and the rates of sex crimes in Denmark indicate that the increased availability of explicit sexual materials has been accompanied by a decrease in the incidence of sexual crime. Analysis of police records of the same types of sex crimes in Copenhagen during the past 12 years revealed that a dramatic decrease in reported sex crimes occurred during this period and that the decrease coincided with changes in Danish law which permitted wider availability of explicit sexual materials. Other research showed that the decrease in reported sexual offenses cannot be attributed to concurrent changes in the social and legal definitions of sex crimes or in public attitudes toward reporting such crimes to the police, or in police reporting procedures.

Statistical studies of the relationship between the availability of erotic material and the rates of sex crimes in the United States presents a more complex picture. During the period in which there has been a marked increase in the availability of erotic materials, some specific rates of arrest for sex crimes have increased (e.g., forcible rape) and others have declined (e.g., overall juvenile rates). For juveniles, the overall rate of arrests for sex crimes decreased even though arrests for nonsexual crimes increased by more than 100%. For adults, arrests for sex offenses increased slightly more than did arrests for nonsex offenses. The conclusion is that, for America, the relationship between the availability of erotica and changes in sex crime rates neither proves nor disproves the possibility that availability of erotica leads to crime, but the massive overall increases in sex crimes that have been alleged do not seem to have occurred.

Available research indicates that sex offenders have had less adolescent experience with erotica than other adults. They do not differ significantly from other adults in relation to adult experience with erotica, in relation to reported arousal or in relation to the likelihood of engaging in sexual behavior during or following exposure. Available evidence suggests that sex offenders' early inexperience with erotic material is a reflection of their more generally deprived sexual environment. The relative absence of experience appears to constitute another indicator of atypical and inadequate sexual socialization.

In sum, empirical research designed to clarify the question has found no evidence to date that exposure to explicit sexual materials plays a significant role in the causation of delinquent or criminal behavior among youth or adults.[4] The Commission cannot conclude that exposure to erotic materials is a factor in the causation of sex crime or sex delinquency.

NOTES

1. The Report of the Effects Panel of the Commission provides a more thorough discussion and documentation of this overview.
2. The study was conducted by Response Analysis Corporation of Princeton, New Jersey, and the Institute of Survey Research of Temple University, Philadelphia, Pennsylvania.
3. See also the Preface of the Commission's Report.
4. Commissioners G. William Jones, Joseph T. Klapper, and Morris A. Lipton believe "that in the interest of precision a distinction should be made between two types of statements which occur in this Report. One type, to which we subscribe, is that research to date does not indicate that a causal relationship exists between exposure to erotica and the various social ills to which the research has been addressed. There are, however, also statements to the effect that 'no evidence' exists, and we believe these should more accurately read 'no reliable evidence.' Occasional aberrant findings, some of very doubtful validity, are noted and discussed in the Report of the Effects Panel. In our opinion, none of these, either individually or in sum, are of sufficient merit to constitute reliable evidence or to alter the summary conclusion that the research to date does not indicate a causal relationship."

III. Positive Approaches: Sex Education, Industry Self-Regulation, and Citizens Action Groups*

Regardless of the effects of exposure, there is still a considerable amount of uneasiness about explicit sexual materials and their pervasiveness in our society. In discussions about obscenity and pornography, the fact is often overlooked that legal control on the availability of explicit sexual materials is not the only, or necessarily the most effective, method of dealing with these materials.

*The Report of the Positive Approaches Panel of the Commission provides a more thorough discussion and documentation of this overview.

Apart from legal controls, a great deal of support exists in our society for several other methods of dealing with obscenity and pornography. According to a national survey, nearly everyone approves, for example, of parents teaching children "what is good for them and what is not." A very large proportion, approximately three-quarters, of the adults in our survey also approve of dealing with sexual materials by providing instruction in school that teaches children "what is good for them," by industry regulating itself in terms of the kinds of materials it makes available, by librarians keeping "objectionable materials" off the shelves, and by groups of citizens organizing themselves to keep "objectionable things" out of the community.

The Commission has explored the effectiveness of sex education, industry self-regulation, and organized citizen action as methods of dealing with the availability of sexually explicit materials.

A. SEX EDUCATION

A large majority of sex educators and counselors are of the opinion that most adolescents are interested in explicit sexual materials, and that this interest is a product of natural curiosity about sex. They also feel that if adolescents had access to adequate information regarding sex, through appropriate sex education, their interest in pornography would be reduced.

There is mounting evidence of dissatisfaction with existing sources of sex information. Although adults indicate that parents are the most preferred source of sex information for children and that other children are the least preferred source, these same adults indicate that child peers had been a principal actual source of *their* sex information. Other sources of information indicated by adults as preferred sources, such as church, school, and physician, were also minor actual sources for them. Studies of today's adolescents reveal that their peers are still the principal source of sex information and that parents, church, and physician are minor sources. Schools, however, are a more important source of sex information today than they were a generation ago.

This trend toward delegating some responsibility for sex education to the schools is approved by a substantial majority of adults in our country. The amount of support for sex education in the schools varies among different segments of our society, however: People who are older, who have less

33

formal education, and who have conservative attitudes toward sex are less likely to support sex education.

Young people report dissatisfaction with the sex information they get both at home and at school. They report that at home parents are frequently embarrassed or uninformed and most do not talk openly and honestly about sex, while at school, the information they are given tends to be irrelevant, insufficient, or is made available too late. In the absence of satisfactory information from preferred sources, young people tend to turn to their friends, and to books and periodicals, although they recognize that these may not always be reliable sources. Young people would prefer to receive information from more appropriate and more reliable sources and in a more timely fashion, and think that more responsibility should be delegated to the schools.

More desired sources of sex information are not necessarily more reliable. Parents, a preferred source of sex information, are often neither well informed about sex nor expert in communicating with children. Formal courses in sex education are relatively new in universities and colleges and there are few teachers who are well prepared for imparting sexual information to young people. Studies indicate that physicians are often no better informed about some significant aspects of human sexuality than the generally educated citizen and may be no more at ease in discussing some sexual matters. This is also true for professional religious workers.

Training of professional workers in the area of sex education is beginning to receive some attention, but opportunities for formal training are still not widely available. Less than 15% of our colleges and universities offer any training in this area and such training is frequently only in summer workshops. Even so, the amount of professional training currently available represents a considerable increase in opportunity over what was available as recently as two years ago. The American Association of Sex Educators and Counselors devotes a great part of its annual national meeting to practical seminars and workshops in order to supplement the sparse existing training opportunities.

Medical schools are now beginning to include courses in normal human sexuality in their curricula. At the present time, about half of the medical schools in the United States devote any portion of their curricula specifically to human sexuality and for the most part the courses offered are elective. This represents a tremendous increase in training opportunity as compared with two years ago. Within theological schools discussion of sex education is only beginning.

Commercially prepared teaching materials for sex education courses at all levels are now becoming available; however, materials for use in the training of professionals are still severely limited. In fact, at least two medical schools and one religiously affiliated private training institute for professional workers have used what is generally termed "hard-core pornography" in their sex education courses because no other materials are available explicitly depicting the wide range of sexual behavior with which professionals in human sexuality must be familiar.

Training of professionals in sex education must overcome not only the absence of adequate information about sex, but also existing attitudes which inhibit the open discussion of sex without embarrassment or titillation. The experience of the two medical schools and the private training institute suggests that the use of pictorial depictions of explicit sexual activity with discussion provides not only information but also a reduction of inhibition and embarrassment in talking about sex. It should be noted that a similar finding was obtained in some of the experimental studies of the effects of explicit sexual materials.

Many schools have implemented sex education programs in the past few years and these represent a wide variety of approaches in terms of content and context. Some courses start in elementary school and continue through high school, while others are initiated only in junior high or even senior high school. Some sex education courses are integrated with other courses, and some are separate courses under a variety of different titles. The content of different courses varies from principal focus on comparative structure of reproductive systems, to focus on the social content of sexual activity, to emphasis on moral sanctions constraining sexual expression. Thus, there is little professional consensus regarding the appropriate scope of sex education.

The recency of the introduction of sex education into the curriculum and the pluralism that exists regarding the definition of goals, content and context, have resulted in the almost total absence of empirical research aimed at evaluating programs of sex education. The Commission has been able to discover only two formal studies. One is still in the process of data analysis and no results are as yet available. The other indicates that girls who had a particular sex education course were less likely to have illegitimate children

35

than girls who had not taken the course and that boys who took the course were less likely to be divorced later, at the time the study was conducted, than were boys who had not had the course in sex education.

Sex education in the schools has been advocated because the existing alternatives for communicating about sex with young people are felt by so many people, both adults and young people themselves, to be inadequate or undesirable.

Although sex education has been endorsed by a variety of national organizations, such as the National Congress of Parents and Teachers, the National Council of Churches, the National Education Association, the American Medical Association, and the American Psychiatric Association, and although a majority of adults in our society favor sex education in the schools organized opposition to sex education has emerged in the past two years at both national and local levels. This opposition has resulted in a decelerating rate of introduction of new sex education programs in the schools. It has also engendered sensitivities which have made it very difficult to conduct empirical research to evaluate the consequences of sex education. Such opposition has also, however, forced the advocates of sex education in the schools to assess their programs more critically and to recognize the need for more empirical research data about the consequences of these programs as well as the need for education of parents and the general public.

It is increasingly apparent that parents, as well as children, are in need of adequate information about sexuality. Education of parents may help to bridge the communication gap between them and their children and thereby reduce some of the burden of sex education on other institutions.

Institutions other than the school are now recognizing the need for more adequate sex education and are beginning to assume responsibilities in this area. This is particularly true of religious institutions. A number of national religious organizations have begun to discuss sexuality seriously and several are active in producing and disseminating sex education materials.

At the present time, the amount, and frequently the quality, of sex education available to young people is limited. However, to the extent that interest in erotica on the part of young people is motivated by natural curiosity and the desire to know more about sex, sex education would appear to be potentially powerful in reducing this interest and thereby decreasing the possibility of exposure to misinformation or information outside of its proper context. Sex education programs also offer the opportunity for parents, school, and church to cooperate in helping to form within the individual a set of positive values and attitudes toward sexuality.

B.   ORGANIZED CITIZEN ACTION

Organized citizen action groups can be a positive force in dealing with obscenity and pornography, though limited empirical information now exists regarding the structure and methods of operation of groups organized around such issues. The studies which do exist of such groups point up both their strengths and weaknesses.

The hypothesis has been offered that citizen action groups tend to arise when the formal and informal sanction systems that have previously inhibited traffic in explicit sexual materials no longer effectively operate. A further hypothesis has been offered which suggests that the actions of these groups and the motives of their members may be interpreted as an attempt to reinforce and reinstate value systems and behavioral standards which are perceived to be disintegrating. Because a number of people will no longer voluntarily subscribe to these systems and conform to these standards under the pressure of informal sanctions, an attempt is made to arouse the community to a reaffirmation of values and standards in this area and to formalize them with new external sanction systems, usually in the form of new laws or prosecutions under existing laws. An intensive analysis of two citizen action groups supports these hypotheses.

A national survey of prosecuting attorneys revealed that citizen action groups organized to deal with obscenity and pornography were much more often reported to exist in large cities and in communities where the traffic in pornography was generally perceived to be a serious problem rather than in smaller cities or in communities where pornography was not at that time so perceived.

Prosecuting attorneys are quite divided in their opinions of the helpfulness to law enforcement of citizen action groups. A slight majority feels that these groups are helpful, but a very large minority feels that they are not of much help. The important factor determining whether they are helpful or not appears to be whether the group is representative of the total community and not whether pornography is perceived as a problem in the community. The more representative of the total community the group is, the more likely it

37

is to be considered helpful. About one quarter of the prosecuting attorneys report that the citizen action group in their community is very representative of their community's opinions, somewhat more than half of the prosecutors report that it is fairly representative, and about 20% report that it is not very representative.

These law enforcement officials report that citizen action groups can be helpful to them by locating and reporting obscenity law violators, communicating to merchants about the nonacceptability of certain kinds of materials in the local community, and alerting the community to the problem. However, they also report that these groups tend to hinder law enforcement by not knowing what the law is, by pressing for action that is unwarranted, and by overzealousness in attempting to impose their own standards on the total community.

Members of citizen action groups tend to feel that there is widespread community support for their position, whether this is true or not. Those individuals who want the most restrictions on the availability of these materials, even when they are a minority, tend to think that most others in the community want the same degree of restriction.

Evaluating the effectiveness of citizen action groups organized against pornography is relatively difficult because their goals tend to be amorphous and ill-defined. An intensive study of two such groups that were evaluated as successful by their members indicated that their practical effect on the availability of erotica in their respective communities had been quite minimal. This research suggests that citizen action groups may be more successful as symbols than as effective tools. It is important to the participants to demonstrate belief in and support for an enduring set of basic values in the face of threatened change.

In summary, citizen action groups more frequently arise in communities where informal sanction systems and voluntary compliance are no longer effective in controlling the flow of explicit sexual materials. They can seriously interfere with the availability of legitimate materials in a community by generating an overly repressive atmosphere and by using harrassment in seeking to implement their goals. However, they can be effective if they genuinely reflect the opinion of the community and if they pursue specific, positive, well-defined, constructive goals.

C.   Industry Self-regulation

Most of the mass communication media attempt some sort of self-regulation. This is usually voluntary and overtly aimed at protecting consumers; often, it is designed to ward off external threats of control or censorship. The usual vehicle for self-regulation in the mass communication media is a voluntary code such as the Comic Magazine Code or the National Broadcasting Code. These usually specify the kinds of content that should not be included in that medium's operation. Particular concern is focused on the potential offensiveness of certain kinds of content and on protecting children and adolescents from possible harmful effects of exposure to themes and treatments of themes considered suitable only for adult consumption.

COMIC BOOK INDUSTRY

The comic book industry has maintained a code since 1954 specifying standards that must be met by each issue of each member publication. All material produced by each member must be submitted for review prior to publication. Any material that treats of obscenity, nudity, horror, and excessive violence is not acceptable for publication. One hundred seventy-nine comic publishers (90% of the industry) are members of the Comic Magazine Association and adhere to the industry code. Very few complaints have come to public notice during the past decade concerning the sexual content of children's comic books. The CMA has been commended for its vigilance in effective self-regulation by several national organizations concerned with the protection of children. During the past year or so several publications have appeared which treat explicit sexual themes in a comic book format. These are somewhat reminiscent of the "eight pagers" of the 1920s and 1930s. They are circulated clandestinely and, are not available in the same racks as children's comic magazines. This situation illustrates one of the weaknesses of voluntary industry self-regulation; it is powerless to control noncompliance by nonmembers.

RADIO AND TELEVISION

The National Association of Broadcasters has long maintained radio and television codes as guidelines and standards against which all member stations are advised to review their programming and broadcasting practices. Circumspection is advised in dealing with adult themes. Profanity, obscenity, sexual material, and vulgarity are forbidden. Both codes stress that the broadcaster should develop programs which foster and promote the commonly accepted moral, social and ethical standards and ideals characteristic of American life. Both radio and television operate in a commercial system which causes them to be extremely responsive to what they interpret to be community sentiment regarding program content. The size of the audience is a crucial factor in determining advertising revenue and often determines whether a program remains on the air. The resulting quality of many programs illustrates the weaknesses inherent in such an approach.

MOTION PICTURES

The motion picture industry instituted a new attempt at self-regulation in November, 1968, when the motion picture rating system went into operation. This rating system was designed to inform potential consumers of the content of films and to inform parents as to the suitability of rated films for viewing by children and adolescents. It also incorporates some voluntary restrictions by theaters regarding admittance of children and adolescents to certain films. The rating system is comprised of four categories of films, two without age restrictions and two with age restrictions on admissions. The explicitness of sexual content in a film and the amount and kinds of violence shown determine the rating that any particular film receives.

The movie rating system appears to be well known to the public, especially to that part of the public most frequently attending the movies. It also appears to be used a great deal by the public. A substantial majority of parents with children at home report using the ratings to select movies for their children. Formal observations of patrons at restricted movies reveal that very few underage persons attempt to enter these theaters. During the first 10 months of the rating system's existence, roughly 80% of the film features released were rated. Most of those that were not rated were minor films having limited distribution. Approximately 93% of the exhibitions of feature films advertised in newspapers in 40 cities throughout the United States in the summer of 1969 were accounted for by rated films. The movie rating system does not function with maximum efficiency, however. A study of newspaper advertising for movies revealed that the display of rating information was defective in almost half of the advertisements.

Comparisons of the industry's ratings of its movies with ratings given the same movies by other groups indicate that the industry ratings are not completely agreeable to everyone. This is not surprising, however, for not all of the nonindustry ratings are consistent with each other. Newspaper movie critics agreed with 70% of the industry's ratings and when they disagreed tended to think that the industry's ratings were too restrictive rather than too permissive. A comparison of industry ratings with the ratings of several other agencies revealed agreement in three-quarters of the cases, with the industry more permissive in approximately one-quarter of the cases. The greatest discrepancy in ratings was between the industry and the National Catholic Office for Motion Pictures. The greatest degree of agreement with industry ratings was found with two municipal rating agencies, which by nature should be more representative of the wide range of viewpoints in society.

The weakest element in the rating procedure is probably the local enforcement of age restrictions for admission. Enforcement varies from theater to theater and tends to be least strict at drive-in theaters. Enforcement tends to be firm at "X" rated movies and at theaters which regularly show "adult" films.

The Commission has not been able to ascertain what impact, if any, this preventive form of self-regulation has had on creativity and innovation in the several forms of mass media considered here. It is very possible that self-regulation, often reinforced by pressures from a vigilant minority, not only sets up rules and internal procedures for deleting or blunting material deemed offensive, but also inhibits experimentation with new ideas, dampens response to social change, and limits the sources of cultural variety. Any final assessment of self-regulation must include a consideration of such possible consequences as a cost to be weighed against any advantages to be gained from the regulation of sensitive materials.

41

IV. Law and Law Enforcement[1]

A. Existing Obscenity Legislation and Cost of Enforcement[2]

FEDERAL STATUTES

There are presently five federal laws which prohibit distributions of "obscene" materials in the United States. One prohibits any mailing of such material (18 U.S.C. section 1461); another prohibits the importation of obscene materials into the United States (19 U.S.C. section 1305); another prohibits the broadcast of obscenity (18 U.S.C. section 1464); and two laws prohibit the interstate transportation of obscene materials or the use of common carriers to transport such materials (18 U.S.C. sections 1462 and 1465).[3] In addition, the 1968 federal Anti-Pandering Act (39 U.S.C. section 3008[4]) authorizes postal patrons to request no further mailings of unsolicited advertisements from mailers who have previously sent them advertisements which they deem sexually offensive in their sole judgment, and it further prohibits mailers from ignoring such requests. There is no present federal statute specifically regulating the distribution of sexual materials to young persons.

Five federal agencies are responsible for the enforcement of the foregoing statutes. The Post Office Department, the Customs Bureau, and the Federal Communications Commission investigate violations within their jurisdictions. The F.B.I. investigates violations of the statutes dealing with transportation and common carriers. The Department of Justice is responsible for prosecution or other judicial enforcement.

The cost to the federal government of enforcing the five federal statutes generally prohibiting the distribution of obscene materials appears to be at least $3 to $5 million per year. Enforcement of the Anti-Pandering Act has cost the Post Office about an additional $1 million per year.[5]

STATE STATUTES

Forty-eight of the States have statutes which generally prohibit the distributions[6] of "obscene" materials. In addition, the statutes of 41 states contain some type of special prohibition regarding the distribution of sexual materials to minors. The cost of enforcing these statutes cannot be determined with any precision. The total of all state and local enforcement activity, however, far exceeds federal enforcement in terms of number of arrests and prosecutions, so that the aggregate cost of state law enforcement for all jurisdictions is, conservatively, $5 to $10 million per year. More than 90% of all state and local prosecutions recently have involved distribution to adults rather than enforcement of juvenile statutes.

FEDERAL AND STATE STATUTORY DEFINITIONS OF "OBSCENITY"

None of the federal statutes generally prohibiting the distribution of "obscene" material defines that term. State statutes generally prohibiting the distribution of "obscene" material either do not define the term or verbally incorporate the constitutional standard established by the Supreme Court and discussed below. State juvenile statutes frequently incorporate relatively specific descriptive definitions of material prohibited for minors, qualified by subjective standards adapted from the constitutional standard for adults.

B. The Constitutional Basis for Prohibitions upon the Dissemination of Explicit Sexual Materials

For many years the Supreme Court assumed, without deciding, that laws generally prohibiting dissemination of obscenity were consistent with the free speech guarantees of the Constitution. In 1957, in the case of Roth v. United States, the Court held that such laws were constitutional, but it required that they utilize a narrowly restrictive standard of what is "obscene."

In upholding the constitutionality of obscenity prohibitions, the Roth decision did not rely upon findings or conclusions regarding the effect of sexual materials upon persons who are exposed to them. Rather, the fundamental premise of Roth was that "obscene" materials are not entitled to the protections accorded to "speech" by the First and Fourteenth Amendments to the Constitution. The Court based this conclusion upon its findings (1) that the Framers of the Bill of Rights did not intend the free speech guarantee of the First

43

Amendment to apply to all utterances and writings, (2) that "obscene" speech—like libel, profanity and blasphemy—was not intended to be protected by the Amendment, and (3) that a universal consensus had existed for many years that the distribution of obscenity should be legally prohibited.

In 1969, in Stanley v. Georgia, the Supreme Court modified the premise of the Roth decision to some extent by holding that the constitutional guarantee of free speech protects the right of the individual to read or view concededly "obscene" material in his own home. Some lower federal courts have held that the Stanley decision gives constitutional protection to some distributions of obscenity, as well as to its private possession. Specifically, courts have held unconstitutional the federal importation prohibition as applied to the importation of obscene material for private use, the federal mail prohibition as applied to the mailing of obscene material to persons who request it, and a state prohibition applied to films exhibited to adults at theaters to which minors were not admitted. These courts have held that the constitutional right to possess obscene materials established in Stanley implies a correlative right for adults to acquire such materials for their own use or to view them without forcing them upon others. Other lower federal courts have not applied the Stanley decision to these situations. The Supreme Court has not yet explicitly passed upon these questions, but has set for argument in the 1970 term three cases raising these issues.

C. Constitutional Limitations upon the Definition of "Obscene"

Adult Obscenity Statutes

Although upholding the constitutionality of broad prohibitions upon the dissemination of obscene materials, the Roth decision imposed a narrow standard for defining what is "obscene" under such prohibitions. Subsequent decisions have narrowed the permissible test even further.

The prevailing view today in the Supreme Court of the United States, the lower federal courts and the courts of the States is that three criteria must all be met before the distribution of material may be generally prohibited for all persons, including adults, on the ground that it is "obscene." These criteria are: (1) the dominant theme of the material, taken as a whole, must appeal to a "prurient" interest in

44

sex; (2) the material must be "patently offensive" because it affronts "contemporary community standards" regarding the depiction of sexual matters; and (3) the material must lack "redeeming social value." All three criteria must coalesce before material may be deemed "obscene" for adults.

The requirement that the material appeal to a "prurient" interest in sex is not clear in meaning but appears to refer primarily to material which is sexually arousing in dominant part. Material must appeal to the prurient interest of the "average" person, unless it is designed for and distributed to a particular group, in which case it is the interests of the members of that group which are relevant. The Supreme Court has never settled the question whether the "community" by whose standards "offensiveness" is to be determined is a "national" community or whether it is the State or locality where the distribution occurs. Whatever the relevant community, a substantial consensus that particular material is offensive is apparently required to violate the community's "standard." There is some disagreement in the Supreme Court over the precise role played by the "social value" criterion. All the Justices have agreed that social value is relevant to obscenity determinations. A plurality (not a majority) has held that unless material is "utterly" without redeeming social value it may not be held to be obscene; a minority of Justices would permit a small degree of social value to be outweighed by prurience and offensiveness. Nor has the Court authoritatively defined what values are redeeming "social" values, although it has suggested that these may include entertainment values as well as the more firmly established scientific, literary, artistic and educational values. Finally, the Court permits the manner of distribution of material to be taken into account in determining the application of the three criteria, at least where the material itself is close to the line of legality.

The application of these three Roth criteria to specific materials requires a great deal of subjective judgment because the criteria refer to emotional, aesthetic and intellectual responses to the material rather than to descriptions of its content. As noted above, the precise meaning of the criteria is also unclear. This subjectivity and vagueness produces enormous uncertainty about what is "obscene" among law enforcement officials, courts, juries and the general public. It is impossible for a publisher, distributor, retailer or exhibitor to know in advance whether he will be charged with a criminal offense for distributing a particular work, since his un-

45

derstanding of the three tests and their application to his work may differ from that of the police, prosecutor, court or jury. This uncertainty and consequent fear of prosecution may strongly influence persons not to distribute new works which are entitled to constitutional protection and thus have a damaging effect upon free speech. These definitional problems are also cited by law enforcement officials at all levels as their chief difficulty in enforcing existing obscenity laws. There is, therefore, almost universal dissatisfaction with present law.

A series of decisions of the Supreme Court, generally rendered without opinion, has given an exceedingly narrow scope of actual application to the constitutionally required three-part standard for adult legislation. These decisions leave it questionable whether any verbal or textual materials whatever may presently be deemed "obscene" for adults under the constitutional standard and suggest that only the most graphic pictorial depictions of actual sexual activity may fall within it. Present law for adults is therefore largely inef-· fective.

The results of empirical research regarding the application of the three constitutional criteria confirm the difficulties of application as well as their exceedingly narrow scope. Several studies have found that "arousingness" and "offensiveness" are independent dimensions when applied to sexual materials; that is, material that is offensive may or may not be arousing, and material that is arousing may or may not be offensive. Only a very restricted range of material seems to be capable of meeting both of these criteria for most people. Further, there is very little consensus among people regarding either the "arousingness" or the "offensiveness" of a given sexual depiction. A wide distribution of judgments in these two areas occurs, for example, for depictions of female nudity with genitals exposed, for explicit depictions of heterosexual sexual intercourse, and for graphic depictions of oral-genital intercourse. In addition, judgments differ among different groups: Males as a group differ from females as a group in their judgments of both "offensiveness" and "arousingness"; the young differ from the old; the college-educated differ from those with only a high school education; frequent church attenders differ from less frequent church attenders.

An additional and very significant limiting factor is introduced by the criterion of social value. In the national survey of American public opinion sponsored by the Com-

46

mission, substantial portions of the population reported effects which might be deemed socially valuable from even the most explicit sexual materials. For example, about 60% of a representative sample of adult American men felt that looking or reading such materials would provide information about sex and about 40% of the sample reported that such an effect had occurred for himself or someone he personally knew. About 60% of these men felt that looking at or reading explicit sexual materials provided entertainment and almost 50% reported this effect upon himself or someone he personally knew. Half of these men felt that looking at or reading explicit sexual materials can improve sex relations of some married couples, and about a quarter of the sample reported such an effect on themselves or on someone they knew personally. Fewer women reported such effects, but 35%, 24% and 21% reported, respectively, information, entertainment, and improved sexual relations in themselves or someone they personally knew as a result of looking at or reading very explicit sexual materials. As previously indicated, two experimental studies found that a substantial number of married couples reported more agreeable and enhanced marital communication and an increased willingness to discuss sexual matters with each other after exposure to erotic stimuli.

In pursuit of its mandate from Congress to recommend definitions of obscenity which are consistent with constitutional rights, the Commission considered drafting a more satisfactory definition of "obscene" for inclusion in adult obscenity prohibitions, should such prohibitions appear socially warranted. To be satisfactory from the point of view of its enforcement and application, such a definition would have to describe the material to be proscribed with a high degree of objectivity and specificity, so that those subject to the law could know in advance what materials were prohibited and so that judicial decisions would not be based upon the subjective reactions of particular judges or jurors. In light of the empirical data, described above, showing both the lack of consensus among adults as to what is both arousing and offensive and the values attributed by substantial numbers of adults to even the most explicit sexual materials, the construction of such a definition for adults within constitutional limits would be extremely difficult. In any event, the Commission, as developed in its legislative recommendations set forth later in this Report, does not believe that a sufficient social justification exists for the retention or en-

47

actment of broad legislation prohibiting the consensual distribution of sexual materials to adults. We, therefore, do not recommend any definition of what is "obscene" for adults.[7]

SPECIFIC OBSCENITY STATUTES

The extreme definitional problems which occur for adult obscenity under the Roth case do not apply to statutes which do not seek to interfere with the right of adults to read or see material of their own choice. In 1967, in Redrup v. New York the Supreme Court noted that, in contrast with general obscenity laws prohibiting sale to adults, legislatures have much wider latitude when formulating prohibitions which restrict themselves to impeding only certain types of distributional conduct—such as distribution of explicit sexual materials to minors and the thrusting of explicit sexual materials upon unwilling recipients through unsolicited mail and public display. Definitions in these areas need only be rationally related to the problem which the legislation seeks to address and no particular definitional formulation is constitutionally required.

Specific prohibitions incorporating broader definitions than are permissible in adult legislation must be restricted in their application to the specific area of their concern. Thus, statutes designed to protect minors from exposure to material which may not be deemed obscene for adults may only prohibit distributions to minors; prohibitions may not be placed upon all adults in order to protect minors. Public display and unsolicited mail prohibitions which restrict material which may not constitutionally be deemed obscene for adults must also be carefully drafted to avoid interference with consensual adult distribution or exhibition.

The areas of latitude for greater control overlap the areas of greatest public concern. Prosecuting attorneys who reported a serious community concern about obscenity to the Commission attributed this concern primarily to the thrusting of offensive materials upon unwilling recipients and to fear that materials would be distributed to minors. It is in these areas that effective legislative prohibitions may be formulated and enforced.

Although greater latitude is allowed constitutionally in restricting explicit sexual materials in the areas of public display, unsolicited mailings and direct disseminations to minors, satisfactory definitions again require the use of explicit objective provisions specifically describing the material to be

48

restricted. Concern about rigidly codifying in law definitions which may soon be outmoded by changing social custom can be alleviated by building into laws a periodic review
of their content.

D. Public Opinion Concerning Restrictions on the Availability of Explicit Sexual Materials

A national survey of American public opinion sponsored
by the Commission shows that a majority of American adults
believe that adults should be allowed to read or see any
sexual materials they wish. On the other hand, a substantial
consensus of American adults favors prohibiting young persons access to some sexual materials. Almost half the population believes that laws against sexual materials are impossible to enforce. Americans also seem to have an inaccurate
view of the opinions of others in their communities; the
tendency is to believe that others in the community are more
restrictive in outlook than they actually are.

Public opinion regarding restrictions on the availability of
explicit sexual materials is, however, quite divided in several
ways. Principally this split of opinion is related to the characteristics of the person expressing the attitude and the issue
of potential harmfulness of the material.

CHARACTERISTICS OF PERSONS EXPRESSING THE ATTITUDE

Advocacy of restrictions on the availability of explicit
sexual materials is more likely to be found accompanying an
orientation against freedom of expression generally. In addition, females tend to be more restrictive than males, older
people more restrictive than younger people, those with a
grade school education more restrictive than the high school-
educated, who in turn tend to be more restrictive than the
college educated, and people who attend church regularly
tend to be more restrictive than those who attend less
often.

THE POTENTIALITY OF HARMFUL EFFECTS

When questioned as to whether they favored access of
adults or young persons to sexually explicit materials, about
40% of all the respondents on the national survey made
their responses contingent on the issue of whether or not
such materials cause harm. About two thirds of the persons

49

who favor no legal restrictions said their views would be changed if it were clearly demonstrated that certain materials have harmful effects. On the other hand, about one-third of the persons who favor some restrictions or extensive restrictions would change their views if it were clearly demonstrated that sexual materials have no harmful effects.

E. OBSCENITY LAWS IN OTHER COUNTRIES

Countries other than the United States differ widely in the terms of and extent of their legal restrictions regarding the distribution of explicit sexual materials. A summary of existing legal provisions in fifteen other countries is contained in the Report of the Legal Panel of the Commission.

A trend has appeared in recent years toward substantial re-evaluation and revision of obscenity laws, often through the use of commissions similar to this Commission. Such an official commission report in Denmark has resulted in the repeal of that country's adult obscenity legislation (with juvenile and nonconsensual exposure restrictions being retained). A similar recommendation has been made in Sweden and final enactment of the repeal of adult legislation in that country will apparently take place in the fall of 1970. Advisory commissions in Israel and the United Kingdom have also recently recommended elimination of prohibitions upon distribution of sexual materials to consenting adults. The constitutional court of West Germany presently has under consideration the question of the constitutionality of that country's adult legislation in view of free speech guarantees. Advisory commissions in countries other than the United States have, like this Commission, all concluded that consensual exposure of adults to explicit sexual materials causes no demonstrable damaging individual or social effects.

NOTES

1. The Report of the Legal Panel of the Commission provides a more thorough discussion and documentation of this overview.
2. A description of the history of obscenity prohibitions is set forth in the Legal Panel Report.
3. Two other statutes impose supplementary regulations. 39 U.S.C. section 3006 (Numbered 39 U.S.C. section 4006 prior to the 1970 Postal Reorganization Act.) authorizes the Postmaster General to block incoming mail to persons using the mails to solicit remittances for obscene matter. 47 U.S.C. section 503(b)(E) imposes civil penalties upon prohibited broadcasts of obscene matter.
4. This Act was numbered 39 U.S.C. section 4009 prior to the 1970 Postal Reorganization Act.
5. The cost to the Post Office Department in fiscal 1968 is estimated by

that department as approximately $1 million—$.75 million allocated to the Postal Inspection Service, which attempts to detect violations, and $.25 million allocated to the General Counsel's Office. The cost to the Customs Bureau in fiscal 1968 is estimated by that Bureau at approximately $1 million. Neither the F.B.I. nor the Justice Department supplied cost figures to the Commission. Other data supplied by the Justice Department indicate significant enforcement activity on the part of the F.B.I., Justice and several United States Attorneys' offices throughout the country of the statutes within their jurisdictions. The Commission believes that these costs would aggregate at least $1 million per year.

To the foregoing total of about $3 million must be added the costs to federal courts and the cost to the Federal Communications Commission. In addition, obscenity enforcement activities on the part of at least two of the Departments—Post Office and Justice—have increased substantially since fiscal 1968.

6. Several of these statutes contain narrowly drawn exemption provisions such as exemptions for persons distributing materials in the course of scientific or artistic pursuits.

Part Two

RECOMMENDATIONS
OF THE COMMISSION

I. Non-Legislative Recommendations

The Commission believes that much of the "problem" regarding materials which depict explicit sexual activity stems
from the inability or reluctance of people in our society to be
open and direct in dealing with sexual matters. This most
often manifests itself in the inhibition of talking openly and
directly about sex. Professionals use highly technical language when they discuss sex; others of us escape by using
euphemisms—or by not talking about sex at all. Direct and
open conversation about sex between parent and child is too
rare in our society.

Failure to talk openly and directly about sex has several
consequences. It overemphasizes sex, gives it a magical, non-
natural quality, making it more attractive and fascinating. It
diverts the expression of sexual interest out of more legitimate channels, into less legitimate channels. Such failure
makes teaching children and adolescents to become fully and
adequately functioning sexual adults a more difficult task.
And it clogs legitimate channels for transmitting sexual information and forces people to use clandestine and unreliable
sources.

The Commission believes that interest in sex is normal,
healthy, good. Interest in sex begins very early in life and
continues throughout the life cycle although the strength of
this interest varies from stage to stage. With the onset of
puberty, physiological and hormonal changes occur which
both quicken interest and make the individual more responsive to sexual interest. The individual needs information
about sex in order to understand himself, place his new

53

experiences in a proper context, and cope with his new feelings.

The basic institutions of marriage and the family are built in our society primarily on sexual attraction, love, and sexual expression. These institutions can function successfully only to the extent that they have a healthy base. Thus the very foundation of our society rests upon healthy sexual attitudes grounded in appropriate and accurate sexual information.

Sexual information is so important and so necessary that if people cannot obtain it openly and directly from legitimate sources and through accurate and legitimate channels, they will seek it through whatever channels and sources are available. Clandestine sources may not only be inaccurate but may also be distorted and provide a warped context.

The Commission believes that accurate, appropriate sex information provided openly and directly through legitimate channels and from reliable sources in healthy contexts can compete successfully with potentially distorted, warped, inaccurate, and unreliable information from clandestine, illegitimate sources; and it believes that the attitudes and orientations toward sex produced by the open communication of appropriate sex information from reliable sources through legitimate channels will be normal and healthy, providing a solid foundation for the basic institutions of our society.

The Commission, therefore, presents the following positive approaches to deal with the problem of obscenity and pornography.

1. The Commission recommends that a massive sex education effort be launched. This sex education effort should be characterized by the following:

a) its purpose should be to contribute to healthy attitudes and orientations to sexual relationships so as to provide a sound foundation for our society's basic institutions of marriage and family;

b) it should be aimed at achieving an acceptance of sex as a normal and natural part of life and of oneself as a sexual being;

c) it should not aim for orthodoxy; rather it should be designed to allow for a pluralism of values;

d) it should be based on facts and encompass not only biological and physiological information but also social, psychological, and religious information;

e) it should be differentiated so that content can be shaped appropriately for the individual's age, sex, and circumstances;

54

f) it should be aimed, as appropriate, to all segments of our society, adults as well as children and adolescents;

g) it should be a joint function of several institutions of our society: family, school, church, etc.;

h) special attention should be given to the training of those who will have central places in the legitimate communication channels—parents, teachers, physicians, clergy, social service workers, etc.;

i) it will require cooperation of private and public organizations at local, regional, and national levels with appropriate funding;

j) it will be aided by the imaginative utilization of new educational technologies for example, educational television could be used to reach several members of a family in a family context.

The Commission feels that such a sex education program would provide a powerful positive approach to the problems of obscenity and pornography. By providing accurate and reliable sex information through legitimate sources, it would reduce interest in and dependence upon clandestine and less legitimate sources. By providing healthy attitudes and orientations toward sexual relationships, it would provide better protection for the individual against distorted or warped ideas he may encounter regarding sex. By providing greater ease in talking about sexual matters in appropriate contexts, the shock and offensiveness of encounters with sex would be reduced.

2. The Commission recommends continued open discussion, based on factual information, on the issues regarding obscenity and pornography.

Discussion has in the past been carried on with few facts available and the debate has necessarily reflected, to a large extent, prejudices and fears. Congress asked the Commission to secure more factual information before making recommendations. Some of the facts developed by the Commission are contrary to widely held assumptions. These findings provide new perspectives on the issues.

The information developed by the Commission should be given wide distribution, so that it may sharpen the issues and focus the discussion.

3. The Commission recommends that additional factual information be developed.

The Commission's effort to develop information has been limited by time, financial resources, and the paucity of previously existing research. Many of its findings are tentative and many questions remain to be answered. We trust that our modest pioneering work in empirical research into several problem areas will help to open the way for more extensive and long-term research based on more refined methods directed to answering more refined questions. We urge both private and public sources to provide the financial resources necessary for the continued development of factual information so that the continuing discussion may be further enriched.

The Federal Government has special responsibilities for continuing research in these areas and has existing structures which can facilitate further inquiry. Many of the questions raised about obscenity and pornography have direct relevance to already existing programs in the National Institute of Mental Health, the National Institute of Child Health and Human Development, and the United States Office of Education. The Commission urges these agencies to broaden their concerns to include a wider range of topics relating to human sexuality, specifically including encounters with explicit sexual materials.

4. The Commission recommends that citizens organize themselves at local, regional, and national levels to aid in the implementation of the foregoing recommendations.

The sex education effort recommended by the Commission can be achieved only with broad and active citizen participation. Widespread discussion of the issues regarding the availability of explicit sexual materials implies broad and active citizen participation. A continuing research program aimed at clarifying factual issues regarding the impact of explicit sexual materials on those who encounter them will occur only with the support and cooperation of citizens.

Organized citizen groups can be more constructive and effective if they truly represent a broad spectrum of the public's thinking and feeling. People tend to assume, in the absence of other information, that most peoples' opinions are similar to their own. However, we know that opinions in the sexual realm vary greatly—that there is no unanimity of values in this area. Therefore, every group should attempt to include as wide a variety of opinion as is possible.

The aim of citizen groups should be to provide a forum whereby all views may be presented for thoughtful consideration. We live in a free, pluralistic society which places its trust in the competition of ideas in a free market place. Persuasion is a preferred technique. Coercion, repression and censorship in order to promote a given set of views are not tolerable in our society.

II. Legislative Recommendations

On the basis of its findings, the Commission makes the following legislative recommendations. The disagreements of particular Commissioners with aspects of the Commission's legislative recommendations are noted below, where the recommendations are discussed in detail. Commissioners Link, Hill, and Keating have filed a joint dissenting statement. In addition, Commissioners Keating and Link have submitted separate remarks. Commissioners Larsen and Wolfgang have filed statements explaining their dissent from certain Commission recommendations. A number of other Commissioners have filed short separate statements.[1]

In general outline, the Commission recommends that federal, state, and local legislation should not seek to interfere with the right of adults who wish to do so to read, obtain, or view explicit sexual materials.[2] On the other hand, we recommend legislative regulations upon the sale of sexual materials to young persons who do not have the consent of their parents, and we also recommend legislation to protect persons from having sexual materials thrust upon them without their consent through the mails or through open public display.

The Commission's specific legislative recommendations and the reasons underlying these recommendations are as follows:

A. STATUTES RELATING TO ADULTS

The Commission recommends that federal, state, and local legislation prohibiting the sale, exhibition, or distribution of sexual materials to consenting adults should be repealed. Twelve of the 17 participating members[3] of the Commission join in this recommendation.[4] Two additional Commissioners[5] subscribe to the bulk of the Commission's Report, but do not believe that the evidence presented at this time is sufficient to warrant the repeal of all prohibitions upon what adults may obtain. Three Commissioners dissent from the recom-

mendation to repeal adult legislation and would retain existing laws prohibiting the dissemination of obscene materials
to adults.[6]

The Commission believes that there is no warrant for
continued governmental interference with the full freedom of
adults to read, obtain or view whatever such material they
wish. Our conclusion is based upon the following considerations:

1. Extensive empirical investigation, both by the Commission and by others, provides no evidence that exposure to or
use of explicit sexual materials play a significant role in the
causation of social or individual harms such as crime, delinquency, sexual or nonsexual deviancy or severe emotional
disturbances.[7] This research and its results are described in
detail in the Report of the Effects Panel of the Commission
and are summarized above in the Overview of Commission
findings. Empirical investigation thus supports the opinion of
a substantial majority of persons professionally engaged in
the treatment of deviancy, delinquency and antisocial behavior, that exposure to sexually explicit materials has no
harmful causal role in these areas.

Studies show that a number of factors, such as disorganized family relationships and unfavorable peer influences,
are intimately related to harmful sexual behavior or adverse
character development. Exposure to sexually explicit materials, however, cannot be counted as among these determinative factors. Despite the existence of widespread legal
prohibitions upon the dissemination of such materials, exposure to them appears to be a usual and harmless part of
the process of growing up in our society and a frequent and
nondamaging occurrence among adults. Indeed, a few Commission studies indicate that a possible distinction between
sexual offenders and other people, with regard to experience
with explicit sexual materials, is that sex offenders have seen
markedly *less* of such materials while maturing.

This is not to say that exposure to explicit sexual materials
has no effect upon human behavior. A prominent effect of
exposure to sexual materials is that persons tend to talk more
about sex as a result of seeing such materials. In addition,
many persons become temporarily sexually aroused upon
viewing explicit sexual materials and the frequency of their
sexual activity may, in consequence, increase for short periods. Such behavior, however, is the type of sexual activity
already established as usual activity for the particular individual.

58

In sum, empirical research designed to clarify the question has found no evidence to date that exposure to explicit sexual materials plays a significant role in the causation of delinquent or criminal behavior among youth or adults.[8]

2. On the positive side, explicit sexual materials are sought as a source of entertainment and information by substantial numbers of American adults. At times, these materials also appear to serve to increase and facilitate constructive communication about sexual matters within marriage. The most frequent purchaser of explicit sexual materials is a college-educated, married male, in his thirties or forties, who is of above average socio-economic status. Even where materials are legally available to them, young adults and older adolescents do not constitute an important portion of the purchases of such materials.

3. Society's attempts to legislate for adults in the area of obscenity have not been successful. Present laws prohibiting the consensual sale or distribution of explicit sexual materials to adults are extremely unsatisfactory in their practical application. The Constitution permits material to be deemed "obscene" for adults only if, as a whole, it appeals to the "prurient" interest of the average person, is "patently offensive" in light of "community standards," and lacks "redeeming social value." These vague and highly subjective aesthetic, psychological and moral tests do not provide meaningful guidance for law enforcement officials, juries or courts. As a result, law is inconsistently and sometimes erroneously applied and the distinctions made by courts between prohibited and permissible materials often appear indefensible. Errors in the application of the law and uncertainty about its scope also cause interference with the communication of constitutionally protected materials.

4. Public opinion in America does not support the imposition of legal prohibitions upon the right of adults to read or see explicit sexual materials. While a minority of Americans favors such prohibitions, a majority of the American people presently are of the view that adults should be legally able to read or see explicit sexual materials if they wish to do so.

5. The lack of consensus among Americans concerning whether explicit sexual materials should be available to adults in our society, and the significant number of adults who wish to have access to such materials, pose serious problems regarding the enforcement of legal prohibitions upon adults, even aside from the vagueness and subjectivity

59

of present law. Consistent enforcement of even the clearest prohibitions upon consensual adult exposure to explicit sexual materials would require the expenditure of considerable law enforcement resources. In the absence of a persuasive demonstration of damage flowing from consensual exposure to such materials, there seems no justification for thus adding to the overwhelming tasks already placed upon the law enforcement system. Inconsistent enforcement of prohibitions, on the other hand, invites discriminatory action based upon considerations not directly relevant to the policy of the law. The latter alternative also breeds public disrespect for the legal process.

6. The foregoing considerations take on added significance because of the fact that adult obscenity laws deal in the realm of speech and communication. Americans deeply value the right of each individual to determine for himself what books he wishes to read and what pictures or films he wishes to see. Our traditions of free speech and press also value and protect the right of writers, publishers, and booksellers to serve the diverse interests of the public. The spirit and letter of our Constitution tell us that government should not seek to interfere with these rights unless a clear threat of harm makes that course imperative. Moreover, the possibility of the misuse of general obscenity statutes prohibiting distributions of books and films to adults constitutes a continuing threat to the free communication of ideas among Americans—one of the most important foundations of our liberties.

7. In reaching its recommendation that government should not seek to prohibit consensual distributions of sexual materials to adults, the Commission discussed several arguments which are often advanced in support of such legislation. The Commission carefully considered the view that adult legislation should be retained in order to aid in the protection of young persons from exposure to explicit sexual materials. We do not believe that the objective of protecting youth may justifiably be achieved at the expense of denying adults materials of their choice. It seems to us wholly inappropriate to adjust the level of adult communication to that considered suitable for children. Indeed, the Supreme Court has unanimously held that adult legislation premised on this basis is a clearly unconstitutional interference with liberty.

8. There is no reason to suppose that elimination of governmental prohibitions upon the sexual materials which may

be made available to adults would adversely affect the availability to the public of other books, magazines, and films. At the present time, a large range of very explicit textual and pictorial materials are available to adults without legal restrictions in many areas of the country. The size of this industry is small when compared with the overall industry in books, magazines, and motion pictures, and the business in explicit sexual materials is insignificant in comparison with other national economic enterprises. Nor is the business an especially profitable one; profit levels are, on the average, either normal as compared with other businesses or distinctly below average. The typical business entity is a relatively small entrepreneurial enterprise. The long-term consumer interest in such materials has remained relatively stable in the context of the economic growth of the nation generally, and of the media industries in particular.

9. The Commission has also taken cognizance of the concern of many people that the lawful distribution of explicit sexual materials to adults may have a deleterious effect upon the individual morality of American citizens and upon the moral climate in America as a whole. This concern appears to flow from a belief that exposure to explicit materials may cause moral confusion which, in turn, may induce antisocial or criminal behavior. As noted above, the Commission has found no evidence to support such a contention. Nor is there evidence that exposure to explicit sexual materials adversely affects character or moral attitudes regarding sex and sexual conduct.[9]

The concern about the effect of obscenity upon morality is also expressed as a concern about the impact of sexual materials upon American values and standards. Such values and standards are currently in a process of complex change, in both sexual and nonsexual areas. The open availability of increasingly explicit sexual materials is only one of these changes. The current flux in sexual values is related to a number of powerful influences, among which are the ready availability of effective methods of contraception, changes of the role of women in our society, and the increased education and mobility of our citizens. The availability of explicit sexual materials is, the Commission believes, not one of the important influences on sexual morality.

The Commission is of the view that it is exceedingly unwise for government to attempt to legislate individual moral values and standards independent of behavior, especially by restrictions upon consensual communication. This is certainly true in the absence of a clear public mandate to do so, and our studies have revealed no such mandate in the area of obscenity.

The Commission recognizes and believes that the existence of sound moral standards is of vital importance to individuals and to society. To be effective and meaningful, however, these standards must be based upon deep personal commitment flowing from values instilled in the home, in educational and religious training, and through individual resolutions of personal confrontations with human experience. Governmental regulation of moral choice can deprive the individual of the responsibility for personal decision which is essential to the formation of genuine moral standards. Such regulation would also tend to establish an official moral orthodoxy, contrary to our most fundamental constitutional traditions.[10]

Therefore, the Commission recommends the repeal of existing federal legislation which prohibits or interferes with consensual distribution of "obscene" materials to adults. These statutes are: 18 U.S.C. Section 1461, 1462, 1464, and 1465; 19 U.S.C. Section 1305; and 39 U.S.C. Section 3006.[11] The Commission also recommends the repeal of existing state and local legislation which may similarly prohibit the consensual sale, exhibition, or the distribution of sexual materials to adults.

B. Statutes Relating to Young Persons

The Commission recommends the adoption by the States of legislation set forth in the Drafts of Proposed Statutes in Section III of this Part of the Commission's Report prohibiting the commercial distribution or display for sale of certain sexual materials to young persons. Similar legislation might also be adopted, where appropriate, by local governments and by the federal government for application in areas, such as the District of Columbia, where it has primary jurisdiction over distributional conduct.

The Commission's recommendation of juvenile legislation is joined in by 14 members of the Commission. Two of these,[12] feel the legislation should be drawn so as to include appropriate descriptions identifying the material as being unlawful for sale to children. Three members disagree.[13] Other members of the Commission, who generally join in its recommendation for juvenile legislation, disagree with various detailed aspects of the Commission's legislative proposal.

These disagreements are noted in the following discussion.

The Commission's recommendation of juvenile legislation flows from these findings and considerations:

A primary basis for the Commission's recommendation for repeal of adult legislation is the fact that extensive empirical investigations do not indicate any causal relationship between exposure to or use of explicit sexual materials and such social or individual harms such as crime, delinquency, sexual or nonsexual deviancy, or severe emotional disturbances. The absence of empirical evidence supporting such a causal relationship also applies to the exposure of children to erotic materials. However, insufficient research is presently available on the effect of the exposure of children to sexually explicit materials to enable us to reach conclusions with the same degree of confidence as for adult exposure. Strong ethical feelings against experimentally exposing children to sexually explicit materials considerably reduced the possibility of gathering the necessary data and information regarding young persons.

In view of the limited amount of information concerning the effects of sexually explicit materials on children, other considerations have assumed primary importance in the Commission's deliberations. The Commission has been influenced, to a considerable degree, by its finding that a large majority of Americans believe that children should not be exposed to certain sexual materials. In addition, the Commission takes the view that parents should be free to make their own conclusions regarding the suitability of explicit sexual materials for their children and that it is appropriate for legislation to aid parents in controlling the access of their children to such materials during their formative years. The Commission recognizes that legislation cannot possibly isolate children from such materials entirely; it also recognizes that exposure of children to sexual materials may not only do no harm but may, in certain instances, actually facilitate much needed communication between parent and child over sexual matters. The Commission is aware, as well, of the considerable danger of creating an unnatural attraction or an enhanced interest in certain materials by making them "forbidden fruit" for young persons. The Commission believes, however, that these considerations can and should be weighed by individual parents in determining their attitudes toward the exposure of their children to sexual materials, and that legislation should aid, rather than undermine, such parental choice.

63

Taking account of the above considerations, the model juvenile legislation recommended by the Commission applies only to distributions to children made without parental consent. The recommended legislation applies only to commercial distributions and exhibitions; in the very few instances where noncommercial conduct in this area creates a problem, it can be dealt with under existing legal principles for the protection of young persons, such as prohibitions upon contributing to the delinquency of minors. The model legislation also prohibits displaying certain sexual materials for sale in a manner which permits children to view materials which cannot be sold to them. Two members of the Commission,[14] who recommend legislation prohibiting sales to juveniles, do not join in recommending this regulation upon display; one member of the Commission[15] recommends only this display provision, and does not recommend a special statute prohibiting sales to young persons.

The Commission, pursuant to Congressional direction, has given close attention to the definitions of prohibited material included in its recommended model legislation for young persons. A paramount consideration in the Commission's deliberations has been that definitions of prohibited materials be as specific and explicit as possible. Such specificity aids law enforcement and facilitates and encourages voluntary adherence to law on the part of retail dealers and exhibitors, while causing as little interference as possible with the proper distribution of materials to children and adults. The Commission's recommended legislation seeks to eliminate subjective definitional criteria insofar as that is possible and goes further in that regard than existing state legislation.

The Commission believes that only pictorial material should fall within prohibitions upon sale or commercial display to young persons. An attempt to define prohibited textual materials for young persons with the same degree of specificity as pictorial materials would, the Commission believes, not be advisable. Many worthwhile textual works, containing considerable value for young persons, treat sex in an explicit manner and are presently available to young persons. There appears to be no satisfactory way to distinguish, through a workable legal definition, between these works and those which may be deemed inappropriate by some persons for commercial distribution to young persons. As a result, the inclusion of textual material within juvenile legislative prohibitions would pose considerable risks for dealers and distributors in determining what books might legally be

64

sold or displayed to young persons and would thus inhibit the entire distribution of verbal materials by those dealers who do not wish to expose themselves to such risks. The speculative risk of harm to juveniles from some textual material does not justify these dangers. The Commission believes, in addition, that parental concern over the material commercially available to children most often applies to pictorial matter.

The definition recommended by the Commission for inclusion in juvenile legislation covers a range of explicit pictorial and three-dimensional depictions of sexual activity. It does not, however, apply to depictions of nudity alone, unless genital areas are exposed and emphasized. The definition is applicable only if the explicit pictorial material constitutes a dominant part of a work. An exception is provided for works of artistic or anthropological significance.

Seven Commissioners would include verbal materials within the definition of materials prohibited for sale to young persons.[16] They would, however, also include a broad exception for such textual materials when they bear literary, historical, scientific, educational, or other similar social value for young persons.

Because of changing standards as to what material, if any, is inappropriate for sale or display to children, the Commission's model statute contains a provision requiring legislative reconsideration of the need for, and scope of, such legislation at six-year intervals.

The model statute also exempts broadcast or telecast activity from its scope. Industry self-regulation in the past has resulted in little need for governmental intervention. If a need for governmental regulation should arise, the Commission believes that such regulations would be most appropriately prepared in this specialized area through the regulating power of the Federal Communications Commission, rather than through diverse state laws.

The Commission has not fixed upon a precise age limit for inclusion in its recommended juvenile legislation, believing that such a determination is most appropriately made by the States and localities which enact such provisions in light of local standards. All States now fix the age in juvenile obscenity statutes at under 17 or under 18 years. The recommended model statute also excludes married persons, whatever their age, from the category of juveniles protected by the legislation.

The Commission considered the possibility of recommending the enactment of uniform federal legislation requiring a notice or label to be affixed to materials by their publishers, importers or manufacturers, when such materials fall within a definitional provision identical to that included within the recommended state or local model juvenile statute. Under such legislation, the required notice might be used by retail dealers and exhibitors, in jurisdictions which adopt the recommended juvenile legislation, as a guide to what material could not be sold or displayed to young persons. The Commission concluded, however, that such a federal notice or labelling provision would be unwise.[17] So long as definitional provisions are drafted to be as specific as possible, and especially if they include only pictorial material, the Commission believes that the establishment of a federal regulatory notice system is probably unnecessary; specific definitions of pictorial material, such as the Commission recommends, should themselves enable retail dealers and exhibitors to make accurate judgments regarding the status of particular magazines and films. The Commission is also extremely reluctant to recommend imposing any federal system for labelling reading or viewing matter on the basis of its quality or content. The precedent of such required labelling would pose a serious potential threat to First Amendment liberties in other areas of communication. Labels indicating sexual content might also be used artificially to enhance the appeal of certain materials. Two Commissioners[18] favor federally imposed labelling in order to advise dealers as clearly and accurately as possible about what material is forbidden for sale to young persons, placing the responsibility for judging whether material falls within the statute on the publisher or producer who is completely aware of its contents and who is in a position to examine each item individually.

Finally, the Commission considered, but does not affirmatively recommend, the enactment by the federal government of juvenile legislation which would prohibit the sale of certain explicit materials to juveniles through the mails. Such federal legislation would, the Commission believes, be virtually unenforceable since the constitutional requirement of proving the defendant's guilty knowledge means that a prosecution could be successful only if proof were available that the vendor knew that the purchaser was a minor. Except in circumstances which have not been found to be prevalent, as where a sale might be solicited through a mailing list composed of young persons, mail order purchases are made without any knowledge by the vendor of the purchaser's age.

Certificates of age by the purchaser would be futile as an enforcement device and to require notarized affidavits to make a purchase through the mails would unduly interfere with purchase by adults. The Commission has found, moreover, that at present juveniles rarely purchase sexually explicit materials through the mail, making federal legislative machinery in this area apparently unnecessary.

C. PUBLIC DISPLAY AND UNSOLICITED MAILING

The Commission recommends enactment of state and local legislation prohibiting public displays of sexually explicit pictorial materials, and approves in principle of the federal legislation, enacted as part of the 1970 Postal Reorganization Act, regarding the mailing of unsolicited advertisements of a sexually explicit nature. The Commission's recommendations in this area are based upon its finding, through its research, that certain explicit sexual materials are capable of causing considerable offense to numerous Americans when thrust upon them without their consent. The Commission believes that these unwanted intrusions upon individual sensibilities warrant legislative regulation and it further believes that such intrusions can be regulated effectively without any significant interference with consensual communication of sexual material among adults.

PUBLIC DISPLAY

The Commission's recommendations in the public display area have been formulated into a model state public display statute which is reproduced in the Drafts of Proposed Statutes in Section III of this Part of the Commission Report. Three Commissioners dissent from this recommendation.[19]

The model statute recommended by the Commission (which would also be suitable for enactment in appropriate instances by local government units and by the federal government for areas where it has general legislative jurisdiction) prohibits the display of certain potentially offensive sexually explicit pictorial materials in places easily visible from public thoroughfares or the property of others.[20] Verbal materials are not included within the recommended prohibition. There appears to be no satisfactory way to define "offensive" words in legislation in order to make the parameters of prohibition upon their display both clear and sufficiently limited so as not to endanger the communication of messages of serious social

67

concern. In addition, the fact that there are few, if any, "dirty" words which do not already appear fairly often in conversation among many Americans and in some very widely distributed books and films indicates that such words are no longer capable of causing the very high degree of offense to a large number of persons which would justify legislative interference. Five Commissioners disagree[21] and would include verbal materials in the display prohibition because they believe certain words cause sufficient offense to warrant their inclusion in display prohibitions.

Telecasts are exempted from the coverage of the statute for the same reasons set forth above in connection with discussion of the Commission's recommendation of juvenile legislation.

The recommended model legislation defines in specific terms the explicit sexual pictorial materials which the Commission believes are capable of causing offense to a substantial number of persons. The definition covers a range of explicit pictorial and three-dimensional depictions of sexual activity. It does not apply to depictions of nudity alone, unless genital areas are exposed and emphasized. An exception is provided for works of artistic or anthropological significance. The Commission emphasizes that this legislation does not prohibit the sale or advertisement of any materials, but does prohibit the public display of potentially offensive pictorial matter. While such displays have not been found by the Commission to be a serious problem at the present time, increasing commercial distribution of explicit materials to adults may cause considerable offense to others in the future unless specific regulations governing public displays are adopted.

UNSOLICITED MAILING

The Commission, with three dissents,[22] also approves of federal legislation to prevent unsolicited advertisements containing potentially offensive sexual material from being communicated through the mails to persons who do not wish to receive such advertisements. The Federal Anti-Pandering Act, which went into effect in 1968, imposes some regulation in this area, but it permits a mail recipient to protect himself against such mail only after he has received at least one such advertisement and it protects him only against mail emanating from that particular source. The Commission believes it more appropriate to permit mail recipients to protect themselves against all such unwanted mail advertisements from any source. Federal legislation in this area was enacted just prior to the date of this report as part of the 1970 Postal Reorganization Act. Public Law 91-375, 91st Cong., 2nd Sess., 39 U.S.C. Sections 3010-3011; 18 U.S.C. Sections 1735-1737.

The Commission considered two possible methods by which persons might be broadly insulated from unsolicited sexual advertisements which they do not wish to receive. One approach, contained in the 1970 Postal Reorganization Act, authorizes the Post Office to compile and maintain current lists of persons who have stated that they do not wish to receive certain defined materials, makes these lists available at cost to mailers of unsolicted advertisements, and prohibits sending the defined material to persons whose names appear on the Post Office lists. A second approach, described in detail in the Commission's Progress Report of July, 1969, would require all mailers of unsolicited advertisements falling within the statutory definition to place a label or code on the envelope. Mail patrons would then be authorized to direct local postal authorities not to deliver coded mail to their homes or offices.

In principle, the Commission favors the first of these approaches employed by Congress in the 1970 Postal Reorganization Act. The Commission takes this view because it believes that the primary burden of regulating the flow of potentially offensive unsolicited mail should appropriately fall upon the mailers of such materials and because of its reluctance to initiate required federal labelling of reading or viewing matter because of its sexual content. The Commission believes, however, that under current mail-order practices it may prove financially unfeasible for many smaller mailers to conform their mailing lists to those compiled by the Post Office. Use of computers to organize and search mailing lists will apparently be required by the new law; few, if any, small mailers utilize computers in this way today. If the current lists maintained by the Post Office came to contain a very large number of names—perhaps one million or more—even a computer search of these names, to discover any that were also present on a mailing list sought to be used by a mailer, might be prohibitively expensive. If such were the case, the Commission would believe the second possible approach to regulation to be more consistent with constitutional rights. This approach, however, might place serious burdens upon Post Office personnel. The Commission was not able to evaluate the practical significance of these burdens.

In considering the definition appropriate to legislation regulating unsolicited sexual advertisements, the Commission examined a large range of unsolicited material which has given rise to complaints to the Post Office Department in recent years. A definition was then formulated which quite specifically describes material which has been deemed offensive by substantial numbers of postal patrons. This definition is set forth in the footnote. The Commission prefers this definitional provision to the less precise definitional provision in the 1970 Postal Reorganization Act.

D. DECLARATORY JUDGMENT LEGISLATION

The Commission recommends the enactment, in all jurisdictions which enact or retain provisions prohibiting the dissemination of sexual materials to adults or young persons, of legislation authorizing prosecutors to obtain declaratory judgments as to whether particular materials fall within existing legal prohibitions and appropriate injunctive relief.[23] A model statute embodying this recommendation is presented in the Drafts of Proposed Statutes in Section III of this Part of the Commission Report. All but two[24] of the Commissioners concur in the substance of this recommendation. The Commission recognizes that the particular details governing the institution and appeal of declaratory judgment actions will necessarily vary from State to State depending upon local jurisdictional and procedural provisions. The Commission is about evenly divided with regard to whether local prosecutors should have authority to institute such actions directly, or whether the approval of an official with state-wide jurisdiction, such as the State Attorney General, should be required before an action for declaratory judgment is instituted.

A declaratory judgment procedure such as the Commission recommends would permit prosecutors to proceed civilly, rather than through the criminal process, against suspected violations of obscenity prohibition. If such civil procedures are utilized, penalties would be imposed for violation of the law only with respect to conduct occurring after a civil declaration is obtained. The Commission believes this course of action to be appropriate whenever there is any existing doubt regarding the legal status of materials; where other alternatives are available, the criminal process should

70

not ordinarily be invoked against persons who might have reasonably believed, in good faith, that the books or films they distributed were entitled to constitutional protection, for the threat of criminal sanctions might otherwise deter the free distribution of constitutionally protected material. The Commission's recommended legislation would not only make a declaratory judgment procedure available, but would require prosecutors to utilize this process instead of immediate criminal prosecution in all cases except those where the materials in issue are unquestionably within the applicable statutory definitional provisions.

WITHDRAWAL OF APPELLATE JURISDICTION

The Commission recommends against the adoption of any legislation which would limit or abolish the jurisdiction of the Supreme Court of the United States or of other federal judges and courts in obscenity cases. Two Commissioners[25] favor such legislation; one[26] deems it inappropriate for the Commission to take a position on this issue.

Proposals to limit federal judicial jurisdiction over obscenity cases arise from disagreement over resolution by federal judges of the question of obscenity in litigation. The Commission believes that these disagreements flow in largest measure from the vague and subjective character of the legal tests for obscenity utilized in the past; under existing legal definitions, courts are required to engage in subjective decision making and their results may well be contrary to the subjective analyses of many citizens. Adoption of specific and explicit definitional provisions in prohibitory and regulatory legislation, as the Commission recommends, should eliminate most or all serious disagreements over the application of these definitions and thus eliminate the major source of concern which has motivated proposals to limit federal judicial jurisdiction.

More fundamentally, the Commission believes that it would be exceedingly unwise to adopt the suggested proposal from the point of view of protection of constitutional rights. The Commission believes that disagreements with court results in particular obscenity cases, even if these disagreements are soundly based in some instances, are not sufficiently important to justify tampering with existing judicial institutions which are often required to protect constitutional rights. Experience shows that while courts may sometimes reverse convictions on a questionable basis, juries and lower

71

courts also on occasion find guilt in cases involving books and films which are entitled to constitutional protection, and state appeals courts often uphold such findings. These violations of First Amendment rights would go uncorrected if such decisions could not be reversed at a higher court level.

The Commission also recommends against the creation of a precedent in the obscenity area for the elimination by Congress of federal judicial jurisdiction in other areas whenever a vocal majority or minority of citizens disagrees strongly with the results of the exercise of that jurisdiction. Freedom in many vital areas frequently depends upon the ability of the judiciary to follow the Constitution rather than strong popular sentiment. The problem of obscenity, in the absence of any indication that sexual materials cause societal harm, is not an appropriate social phenomenon upon which to base a precedent for removing federal judicial jurisdiction to protect fundamental rights guaranteed by the Bill of Rights.

NOTES

1. Commissioners Joseph T. Klapper, Morris A. Lipton, G. William Jones, and Edward D. Greenwood, and Irving Lehrman.
2. The term explicit sexual materials is used here and elsewhere in these recommendations to refer to the entire range of explicit sexual depictions or descriptions in books, magazines, photographs, films, statuary, and other media. It includes the most explicit depictions, or what is often referred to as "hard-core pornography." The term, however, refers only to sexual materials, and not to "live" sex shows, such as strip tease or on-stage sexual activity or simulated sexual activity. The Commission did not study this phenomenon in detail and makes no recommendations in this area. See Preface to this Report.
3. Commissioner Charles H. Keating, Jr., chose not to participate in the deliberation and formulation of any of the Commission's recommendations.
4. Commissioner Edward E. Elson joins in this recommendation only on the understanding that there will be prior enactment of legislation prohibiting the public display of offensive sexual materials both pictorial and verbal, that there will be prior enactment of legislation restricting the sales of explicit sexual materials to juveniles, and that there be prior public and governmental support for the Commission's nonlegislative recommendations before such repeal is enacted.
5. Commissioners Irving Lehrman and Cathryn A. Spelts.
6. Commissioners Morton A. Hill, S.J., Winfrey C. Link, and Thomas C. Lynch.
7. See footnote 4 in the Overview of Effects.
8. See footnote 4 in the Overview of Effects.
9. See footnote 4 in the Overview of Effects.
10. Commissioner Thomas D. Gill has amplified his position with reference to this finding as follows: Legislation primarily motivated by an intent to establish or defend standards of public morality has not always been, as the Report of the Commission would have it, inappropriate, unsound, and contrary to "our most fundamental constitutional traditions."
In fact for at least 140 years after its adoption, the Constitution never appears to have been considered a barrier to the perpetuation of the belief held in the 13 original colonies that there was not only a right but a duty to codify in law the community's moral and social convictions. Granted

homogeneous communities and granted the ensuing moral and social cohesiveness implied in such uniformity of interest the right of these solid and massive majorities to protect their own values by legislation they deemed appropriate went unchallenged so long as it did not impinge upon the individual's right to worship and speak as he pleased.

Only in the 20th century has an increasingly pluralistic society begun to question both the wisdom and the validity of encasing its moral and social convictions in legal armour, and properly so, for if all laws to be effective must carry into their implementation the approval of a majority, this is peculiarly and all importantly the case with laws addressed to standards of morality, which speedily become exercises in community hypocrisy if they do not embody the wishes and convictions of a truly dominant majority of the people.

The Commission's studies have established that on a national level no more than 35% of our people favor adult controls in the field of obscenity in the absence of some demonstrable social evil related to its presence and use.

The extensive survey of the prosecutorial offices of this country gives added affirmation of the principle that acceptable enforcement of obscenity legislation depends upon a solid undergirding of community support such as may be and is found in the smaller, more homogeneous communities, but is increasingly difficult to command in the largest urban areas where the divisiveness of life leads to splintered moral and social concepts. In effect this report tells us that where you have substantial community concern you don't require the law, but lacking such concern, the law is a substitute of uncertain effectiveness.

If, then, legal rules controlling human conduct are designed to emphasize and reinforce society's moral convictions only in those areas where the pressures for transgression are the greatest and the resulting social consequences the most serious, there is a notable lack of justification for such intervention in the Commission's findings as to the magnitude of the public's concern and the efficacy of the enforcement of current obscenity laws. As has so often occurred, an approach which was both defendable and workable in one era has become vulnerable and suspect in another.

Fairness, however, requires that despite these formidable considerations something more be said and therein is to be found the primary reason for this individual statement. It is by no means certain that the Commission's national study, accurate as it has every reason to be in presenting a national consensus, has an equal validity in depicting the group thinking of a given geographical area, state, or community. It is believable, therefore, that notwithstanding the findings in the national reports, and quite consistent with them, there well may be found geographical pockets of homogeneous conviction, various regional, state, and local units where the requisite massive majority support essential for the legal codification of community standards does exist. My concurrence in the recommendation for the abolition of obscenity controls for consenting adults is not intended to express my disapproval of the right of any such group, so constituted, to challenge and attempt to override the substantial findings of law and fact which the Commission has determined to be persuasive in order to sustain their own deeply and widely held beliefs: a very considerable body of legislation in this country rests on just such a base of moral and social traditions. It is a base, however, which is being undercut and eroded by the currents of the time and because this is so it may not now upon fair and objective examination be found to be of sufficient dimensions to sustain its burden.

11. The broadcasting or telecasting of explicit sexual material has not constituted a serious problem in the past. There is, however, a potential in this area for thrusting sexually explicit materials upon unwilling persons. Existing federal statutes imposing criminal and civil penalties upon any broadcast of "obscene" material do not adequately address this problem because they do not describe with sufficient specificity what material would be prohibited, or under what conditions. Hence, the repeal of these statutes is recommended, upon the understanding that the Federal Communications Commission either already has, or can acquire through legislation, adequate power to promulgate and enforce specific rules in this area should the need arise.

12. Commissioners Edward E. Elson and Winfrey C. Link.

13. Commissioners Otto N. Larsen and Marvin E. Wolfgang disagree for reasons stated in their separate statement. Commissioner Morton A. Hill, S.J. disagrees for reasons stated in his separate statement.

14. Commissioners Edward E. Elson and Freeman Lewis believe that segregating that material prohibited for sale to juveniles from that which is available to all would only enhance its appeal. Further, Commissioner Elson believes that juveniles would be protected from viewing sexually explicit materials if the Model Public Display Statute were extended to apply to those places technically private but public in the sense that they offer free and open access to all. Moreover, such an extension would significantly insulate the general public from such materials being thrust upon them without their consent.

15. Commissioner Morton A. Hill, S.J. See his separate statement for his reasons.

16. Commissioners Edward E. Elson, Thomas D. Gill, Joseph T. Klapper, Irving Lehrman, Winfrey C. Link, Thomas C. Lynch, and Cathryn A. Spelts.

17. Commissioners Thomas D. Gill finds this conclusion acceptable at the present time, but if experience demonstrates that the effective enforcement of juvenile statutes which proscribe written as well as pictorial material is hampered by the problem of scienters, he believes the labelling statute promises to be an appropriate method of correction and should be tried. Commissioners Irving Lehrman and Cathryn A. Spelts join in this footnote.

18. Commissioners Edward E. Elson and Winfrey C. Link.

19. Commissioners Otto N. Larsen, Freeman Lewis, and Marvin E. Wolfgang believe that a public display statute specifically aimed at erotic material is unnecessary. Very few jurisdictions have such a statute now. The execution of existing statutes and ordinances concerned with the projection of generally offensive objects, erotic or not, before the public provides all the spatial boundaries on public display of offensive erotica that is needed. Moreover, these three Commissioners believe that the offensiveness which may be caused by undesired exposure to sexual depictions is not so serious in scope or degree to warrant legislative response.

20. Commissioners Edward E. Elson and Winfrey C. Link believe that the model display statute should be so extended as to apply to those places technically private but public in the sense that they offer free and open access to all. The statute would then cover, for example, retail stores, transportation terminals, and building lobbies. It would then prevent potentially offensive sexually explicit materials from being thrust upon the public unexpectedly at any time.

21. Commissioners Edward E. Elson, Morton A. Hill, S.J., Winfrey C. Link, Thomas C. Lynch, and Cathryn A. Spelts.

22. Commissioners Otto N. Larsen and Marvin E. Wolfgang. See their separate statement. Commissioner Freeman Lewis dissents for two reasons: (1) that legislation restricting only the mailing of sexually oriented materials when so many other kinds of unsolicited mail also produce offense is bad public policy because it is too particular and too arbitrary; and (2) that the frequency of offense caused by unsolicited sexually oriented mail is demonstrably so minute that it does not warrant either the costs of the requisite machinery for operation and enforcement or the exorbitant expenses which would be forced upon this particular small category of mailers in order to comply. In his opinion, the most effective resolution of this problem is to employ the same technique commonly used for any other kinds of unwanted, unsolicited mail: throw it in the garbage pail.

23. Potentially offensive sexual advertisement means:

"(A) Any advertisement containing a pictorial representation or a detailed verbal description of uncovered human genitals or pubic areas, human sexual intercourse, masturbation, sodomy (i.e., bestiality or oral or anal intercourse), direct physical stimulation of unclothed genitals or flagellation or torture in the context of a sexual relationship; or

"(B) Any advertisement containing a pictorial representation or detailed verbal description of an artificial human penis or vagina or device primarily designed physically to stimulate genitals;

"Provided that, material otherwise within the definition of this subsection shall not be deemed to be a potentially offensive sexual advertisement if it constitutes only a small and insignificant part of the whole of a single catalogue, book, or other work, the remainder of which does not primarily treat sexual matters and, provided further, that the Postmaster General shall, from time to time, issue regulations of general applicability exempting certain types of material, or material addressed to certain categories of addressees, such as advertisements for works of fine art or solicitations of a medical, scientific, or other similar nature addressed to a specialized audience, from the definition of potentially offensive sexual advertisement contained in this subsection, where the purpose of this section does not call for application of the requirements of this section."

24. Commissioners Morton A. Hill, S.J. and Winfrey C. Link.
25. Commissioners Morton A. Hill, S.J. and Winfrey C. Link.
26. Commissioner Cathryn A. Spelts.

III. Drafts of Proposed Legislation

A. RECOMMENDED FEDERAL LEGISLATION

REPEAL OF EXISTING LAWS

The following federal statutes prohibiting the consensual distribution of "obscene" material to adults are hereby repealed: 18 United States Code, Sections 1461, 1462, 1464, 1465; 19 United States Code, Section 1305; 39 United States Code, Section 3006.

B. RECOMMENDED STATE LEGISLATION

SECTION 1. REPEAL OF EXISTING LAWS

The state statutes which appear to the Commission presently to impose prohibitions upon the consensual distribution of sexual material to adults are the following: Ala. Code tit. 14, Section 374(4) (1958); Alaska Stat. Section 11.40.160 (1962); Ariz. Reg. Stat. Ann. Section 13-532 (1956); Ark. Stat. Ann. Section 41-2701, 2703, (1947); Cal. Penal Code Section 311.2 (West 1969); Colo. Rev. Stat. Ann. Section 40-9-16 (1963); Conn. Gen. Stat. Ann. Section 53-244 (1958); Del. Code Ann. tit. 11, Section 711 (1953); Fla. Stat. Ann. Section 847.011 (1965); Ga. Code Ann. Section 26-2101 (1969); Hawaii Rev. Stat. Section 727-8 (1968); Idaho Code Ann. Section 18-4101 (3, 4, 5), 4102 (1947); Ill. Ann. Stat. Ch. 38, Section 11-20 (Smith-Hurd 1954); Ind. Ann. Stat. Section 9-601(Fifth); Section 9-604(b); Section 10-2803 (1956); Iowa Code Ann. Section 725.3-6 (1950); Kan. Stat. Ann. Sections 21-1102, 1115, 1118 (1964); Ky. Rev. Stat. Section 436.101 (1962); La. Rev. Stat. Section 14.106 (1950); Me. Rev. Stat. Ann. tit. 17, Sections 2901, 2904, 2905 (1964); Md. Ann. Code Art. 27, Section 418 (1957); Mass. Ann. Laws Ch. 272, Section 28A,

B, Section 31, 32 (1932); Mich. Comt. Laws Section
750.343a-b (1968); Minn. Stat. Ann. Section 617.241; Section 617.26 (1964); Miss. Code Ann. Sections 2280, 2286,
2288, 2674.03 (1942); Mo. Ann. Stat. Sections 563.270,
.280, .290 (1953); Mont. Rev. Codes Ann. Sections 94.3601,
.3602 (1969); Neb. Rev. Stat. Sections 28.921, .922 (1964);
Nev. Rev. Stat. Section 201.250 (1969); N.H. Rev. Stat.
Ann. Section 571A (1955); N.J. Rev. Stat. Section 2A:
115-2 (1951); N.Y. Penal Law Sections 235.00, .05, .10, .15
(McKinney's 1967); N.C. Gen. Stat. Section 14-189. 189.1,
.2, 14-190 (1969); N.D. Cent. Code Section 12-21-09
(1960); Ohio Rev. Code Ann. Sections 2905.34, .342(A),
.36, .40, .41 (Page 1953); Okla. Stat. Ann. tit. 21, Sections
1021(3)(4), 1040.8, .13 (1958); Ore. Rev. Stat. Section
167.151 (1969); Pa. Stat. Ann. tit. 18 Sections 4524, 4528
(1963); R.I. Gen. Laws Ann. Sections 11-31-1, 3, 4 (1956);
S.C. Code Ann. Section 16-414.1 (1962); S.D. Compiled
Laws Ann. Sections 22-24-11, 12 (1967); Tenn. Code Ann.
Section 39-3003 (1955); Tex. Penal Code Art. 527(1)
(1948); Utah Code Ann. Section 76-39-5(1-5) (1953); Va.
Code Ann. Sections 18.1-228, 229, 230 (1950); Wash. Rev.
Code Sections 9.68.010, .020 (1961); W. Va. Code Ann.
Sec. 61-8-11 (1966); Wis. Stat. Sections 944.21, .22, .23
(1958); Wyo. Stat. Ann. Sections 6-103, 104 (1957); D.C.
Code Ann. Section 22-2001 (Supp. III, 1970).

SECTION 2. SALE AND DISPLAY OF EXPLICIT SEXUAL
MATERIAL TO YOUNG PERSONS

(a) Purpose. It is the purpose of this section to regulate the direct commercial distribution of certain explicit
sexual materials to young persons in order to aid parents in
supervising and controlling the access of children to such
material. The legislature finds that whatever social value such
material may have for young persons can adequately be
served by its availability to young persons through their
parents.

(b) Offenses Defined. A person is guilty of a misdemeanor if he
     (i) knowingly disseminates explicit sexual material,
as hereinafter defined, to young persons or
     (ii) if he knowingly displays explicit sexual material
for sale in an area to which young persons have access,
unless such material has artistic, literary, historical, scien-

76

tific, medical, educational or other similar social value for adults.

(c) Penalty.   Whoever violates the provisions of this section shall be liable to [left to state option].

(d) Definitions.   For the purposes of this section:
(i) "Young person" means any person less than ___ years of age;
(ii) "Explicit sexual material" means any pictorial or three dimensional material including, but not limited to, books, magazines, films, photographs and statuary, which is made up in whole or in dominant part of depictions of human sexual intercourse, masturbation, sodomy (i.e., bestiality or oral or anal intercourse), direct physical stimulation of unclothed genitals, or flagellation or torture in the context of a sexual relationship, or which emphasizes the depiction of uncovered adult human genitals; provided however, that works of art or of anthropological significance shall not be deemed to be within the foregoing definition.
(iv) "Disseminate" means to sell, lease or exhibit commercially and, in the case of an exhibition, to sell an admission ticket or pass, or to admit persons who have bought such a ticket or pass to the premises whereon an exhibition is presented.
(v) "Display for sale" in an area to which young persons have access means display of material for sale so that young persons may see portions of the material constituting explicit sexual pictorial material.
(vi) An offense is committed "knowingly" only if (A) the defendant knew that the recipient of material was a young person, as herein defined, or had grounds to believe it probable that the recipient was a young person as herein defined and failed to make reasonable inquiries to determine the age of the recipient; and if (B) (1) the defendant was aware of contents of the material clearly within the definition of explicit sexual material contained in part (ii) of this subsection, or (2) had reason to know that the contents of the material were likely to fall within the definition of explicit sexual material and failed to examine the material to ascertain its contents.

(e) Defenses.   It shall be an affirmative defense to a prosecution under this section for the defendant to show:
(i) That the dissemination was made with the con-

77

sent of a parent or guardian of the recipient, that the defendant was misled as to the existence of parental consent by a misrepresentation of parental status, or that the dissemination was made to the recipient by his teacher or clergyman in the discharge of official responsibilities;

(ii) That the recipient was married, or that the defendant was misled in this regard by a misrepresentation of marital status.

(f) Exemption for Broadcasts. The prohibition of this section shall not apply to broadcasts or telecasts through facilities licensed under the Federal Communications Act, 47 U.S.C. Section 301 et seq.

(g) Limitation Upon Effective Period of Legislation. This Act shall be effective for six years from the date of enactment and shall become null and void thereafter unless reenacted.

SECTION 3. PUBLIC DISPLAYS OF EXPLICIT
SEXUAL MATERIALS

(a) Purpose. It is the purpose of this section to prohibit the open public display of certain explicit sexual materials, in order to protect persons from potential offense through involuntary exposure to such materials.

(b) Offense Defined. A person is guilty of a misdemeanor if he knowingly places explicit sexual material upon public display, or if he knowingly fails to take prompt action to remove such a display from property in his possession after learning of its existence.

(c) Penalty. Whoever violates the provisions of this section shall be liable to [left to state option].

(d) Definitions. For the purposes of this section:
(i) "Explicit sexual material" means any pictorial or three-dimensional material depicting human sexual intercourse, masturbation, sodomy (i.e., bestiality or oral or anal intercourse), direct physical stimulation of unclothed genitals, flagellation or torture in the context of a sexual relationship, or emphasizing the depiction of adult human genitals; provided, however, that works of art or of anthropological significance shall not be deemed to be within the foregoing

78

definition. In determining whether material is prohibited for public display by this section such material shall be judged without regard to any covering which may be affixed or printed over the material in order to obscure genital areas in a depiction otherwise falling within the definition of this subsection.

(ii) Material is placed upon "public display" if it is placed by the defendant on or in a billboard, viewing screen, theater marquee, newsstand, display rack, window, showcase, display case or similar place so that matter bringing it within the definition of subparagraph (i) of this subsection is easily visible from a public thoroughfare or from the property of others.

(e) Exception for Broadcasts. The prohibition of this section shall not apply to broadcasts or telecasts through facilities licensed under the Federal Communications Act, 47 U.S.C. Section 301 et seq.

(f) Limitation Upon Effective Period of Legislation. This Act shall be effective for six years from its date of enactment and shall become null and void thereafter unless re-enacted.

C. MODEL DECLARATORY JUDGMENT AND INJUNCTION STATUTE

(a) Creation of Remedy. Whenever material is being or is about to be disseminated in violation of [insert citation to applicable legal prohibition or prohibitions], a civil action may be instituted by the State against any disseminator or disseminators of the material in order to obtain a declaration that the dissemination of such material is prohibited. Such an action may also seek an injunction appropriately restraining dissemination. Such action may be initiated by any county prosecutor [or other prosecuting official authorized to represent the State in criminal proceedings].[2]

(b) Venue. Such an action may be brought only in the _____ Court of the county in which any disseminator resides, or where the dissemination is taking place or is about to take place.

(c) Parties. Any disseminator of or person who is about to be a disseminator of the material involved may intervene as of right as a party defendant in the proceedings. In addition to the named defendant, the Attorney General shall undertake to give notice to the producer, manufacturer or importer of the material, and the wholesale distributor (if any), that they may exercise this right.

(d) Procedure. [The court of initial jurisdiction] shall give expedited consideration to actions brought pursuant to this section. A hearing shall be held within _____ days of the filing of the complaints and final judgment rendered within _____ days of the termination of the hearing. Appeal from the decision of the [court of initial jurisdiction] lies only to the [highest court of the jurisdiction].[3] A notice of appeal shall be filed within _____ days of the final judgment of the [court of initial jurisdiction] and the [highest court] shall hear and consider the appeal within _____ days of the filing of a notice of appeal and shall render final decision within _____ days after hearing the appeal. A declaration in an action brought pursuant to this section shall not be deemed final for any purpose until the final decision of the [highest court] is rendered or until the time to file a notice of appeal from the decision of the [court of initial jurisdiction] has expired. No restraining order or injunction of any kind shall be issued restraining the dissemination of any work on the ground of its obscenity prior to the completion of the adversary hearing required by this subsection.

Any defendant may assert a right to the trial of the issue of obscenity by jury in actions brought pursuant to this section.

(e) Use of Declaration. A final declaration obtained pursuant to this section may be used to establish scienters, or to form the basis for an injunction and for no other purposes. The Attorney General may undertake to notify any person of final judgment pursuant to this section as a means of affording such person actual notice of that judgment, but such notice shall not have effect in establishing scienters, if the person to whom it is communicated was known to the Attorney General as a producer, manufacturer, importer or wholesale distributor of the material involved and was not given notice of his right to intervene pursuant to subsection (c) of this section.

(f) Definitions. For purposes of this section:

(i) "Disseminate" means to sell, lease, or exhibit commercially

(ii) "Disseminator" means any person who imports, produces, manufactures or engages in wholesale distribution of any material intended to be disseminated, or any person who disseminates any material.

(g) Inconsistent Laws Superseded.　All laws regulating the procedure for obtaining declaratory judgments or injunctions which are inconsistent with the provisions of this section shall be inapplicable to proceedings brought pursuant to this section.

(h) Prosecution Policy.　From and after the enactment of this Act criminal prosecutions shall be brought prior to the obtaining of a declaration under this Act only in cases of material which is unquestionably within the applicable definitional provision. In all other cases, the provisions of this Act shall be used prior to prosecution, which shall not be based upon conduct engaged in before notice of a declaration obtained pursuant to this Act. Prosecutions brought contrary to this subsection shall be dismissed by the trial court; the trial court's decision in this regard shall not be reviewable in appeal.

NOTES

1. This statute could also be adapted to use in connection with federal legislation.
2. About half the members of the Commission favor requiring local prosecutors to obtain the approval of a law enforcement official with state-wide jurisdiction, such as the Attorney General, before instituting an action.
3. A different appeal route or procedure may be deemed appropriate in States with three levels of courts.

Part Three

REPORTS
OF THE PANELS

I. TRAFFIC AND DISTRIBUTION OF SEXUALLY ORIENTED MATERIALS IN THE UNITED STATES

Report of the Traffic and Distribution Panel to the Commission on Obscenity and Pornography.

Commission Panel Members
Thomas C. Lynch—Chairman
Edward E. Elson
Freeman Lewis
Winfrey C. Link
William B. Lockhart— ex officio

Staff Members
John J. Sampson
Bernard Horowitz
Anthony F. Abell
W. Cody Wilson—Executive Director and Director of Research

Introduction—Scope of the Report

Congress, in Public Law 90-100, established a Commission on Obscenity and Pornography to which it assigned various tasks. One of these was: "To ascertain the methods employed in the distribution of obscene and pornographic materials and to explore the nature and volume of traffic in such materials."

The Commission appointed a Traffic and Distribution Panel to concentrate on the study of this particular subject and to report its findings to the full Commission. Because public concern applies to such a broad range of materials in this area, the Panel decided to limit its investigations to those areas of greatest concern. These it determined to be: books;

83

periodicals; certain additional materials such as sexual devices, 8mm films, and photo sets sold in retail outlets, by individuals, or through the mails; and motion picture films, whether exhibited publicly or privately. The Panel did not investigate live performances, such as burlesque shows, night club acts, or stage plays. Nor did it make a concentrated effort to measure erotic stimuli in broadcast or telecast media or in newspapers, except for that limited area represented by the sensational and/or "underground" press.

This Report is divided into sections dealing with various categories of materials. In Part I, the Panel describes the nature of the materials, the methods by which they are distributed, exhibited, and sold, and where possible, the volume of traffic in units and in dollars. In Part II, the Panel describes the patterns of exposure to these materials and the characteristics of the eventual customers or users.

There have been many estimates made concerning the size of the "pornography" or "smut" industry, without providing definitions which would make such estimates meaningful and without supporting data. These have ranged from $500 million to $2.5 billion. To eliminate the confusion which has resulted, it should be helpful to note the following figures:

The book publishing industry in 1968 (latest figures available) estimated its receipts at $2.57 billion (American Book Publishers Council plus American Educational Publishers Institute). Of that total, materials which could conceivably fall within the areas of study by the Commission (because such books could contain sexually oriented materials) could be found only in "Adult Trade Books" ($179 million), "Paperback Books" ($167 million), and "Book Clubs" ($204 million)—total publishers' receipts of $550 million or about 21% of the receipts of the book publishing industry. The balance of publishers' receipts was accounted for by textbooks and special interest books such as religious, juvenile, technical, scientific, professional, and reference books. Assuming publishers recover an average 55% of the retail sales price of hard-cover and paperback books (book club sales are at retail), total retail sales of these books were approximately $833 million in 1968.

The periodical publishing industry, in the last official census of business (1967), reported total receipts of approximately $2.6 billion (Department of Commerce, 1970a, p. 3). Of this, only periodicals such as comics, women and home service, general interest, news, business, and enter-

84

tainment magazines were of interest to the Commission. These produced publishers' receipts of $1.445 billion, of which $560 million came from single copy and subscription sales and $885 million from advertising.

The Department of Commerce (1970b, p. 437) estimates that in 1969 total box office receipts from all motion pictures were $1.065 billion. All motion pictures were within the interest of the Commission.

The materials represented by these figures are: $833 million for books (1968 at retail); $560 million for periodicals (1967 publishers receipts—retail receipts not practical for estimating, particularly because of the subscription.factor); and $1.065 billion for motion pictures (1969 estimated box office receipts), for a total of $2.458 billion.

The market for unquestionably explicit sexually oriented materials must be determined largely by areas not covered by the official statistics above, and this Report will isolate and pinpoint the volume of such traffic. A summary here may, however, be useful.

The Panel estimate of the volume of traffic in relatively explicit sexual materials of the kinds which it was intended by Congress to investigate is contained in Table 1.

TABLE 1

Total Volume in Sexually Oriented Materials

Books ("adult only" at retail): $45-55 million
Periodicals ("adult only" at retail): $25-35 million
Motion Pictures (Box Office): $450-460 million[1]
Mail Order (all materials): $12-14 million
Under-the-Counter (all materials): $5-10 million

TOTAL $537-574 million

[1]Includes "R", "X," sex-oriented unrated, and exploitation films.

The range of investigation which follows is much broader than the materials covered in Table 1. Extensive citations and supporting documentation will be limited in the interest of readability, but these will be found in the Technical Reports upon which this Panel Report largely is based and which will be separately published by the Commission (see particularly Volume 4, John J. Sampson, "Commercial Traffic in Sexually Oriented Materials in the United States, 1969-1970").

Section A. Sexually Oriented Motion Pictures

THE MOTION PICTURE
INDUSTRY—IN GENERAL

Movies have long been one of the primary recreational outlets for Americans, although motion pictures are no longer as significant a part of the entertainment industry as they were 25 years ago. The industry hit its high-water mark in 1946, with box office receipts estimated at $1.7 billion from approximately 80 million admissions per week. The percentage of the recreational dollar spent on motion pictures fell from 19.8% in 1946 to 3.1% in 1968 (Motion Picture Almanac, 1969, p. 58A). In recent years, box office receipts have increased from a post-War low of $900 million in 1962 to an estimated $1.065 billion in 1970 (Department of Commerce, 1970b, p. 437). The increased receipts are due to higher admission prices rather than an increase in attendance. Between 1960 and 1969, total receipts rose by less than 10% while the admission price index rose by over 90%. Less than 20 million attended motion pictures weekly in 1969. The number of theaters has also declined in the past 25 years from over 19,000 in 1946 to an estimated 13,750 in 1970 (Department of Commerce, 1970b, p. 438). The industry continues to be a major economic force, however, with nearly 14,000 theaters and a $1 billion plus box office business.

Until the past year or two, motion pictures distributed in the United States fell rather neatly into three categories: general release, art, and exploitation films. Recent innovations in the market have altered these traditional classifications and blurred former distinctions—the vast majority of the motion pictures exhibited in 1969-1970 can easily be classified as falling within one of these three types.

By far, the most important and familiar are general release films, which account for most of the theater attendance in the U.S. General release films are those produced and distributed by well-known companies, starring well-known actors, and exhibited in 90% or more of the theaters across the country (Randall, 1970a). A popular film of this type may be exhibited in 5,000 or more theaters.

Art films are an amorphous group of films which are exhibited on a rather limited scale (ordinarily between 500 to 800 bookings per film). The exact characteristics of "art" films are almost impossible to define with specificity, except to note that the majority are foreign films, which, are aesthetic, intellectual, artistic, or other reasons, appeal to a limited audience. American-made pictures falling into this category are generally low-budget films designed to appeal to the "art film" audience.

Exploitation films, usually known in the industry as "skin flicks," are low-budget sex-oriented movies which are not acceptable to the majority of exhibitors and, therefore, have a rather limited exhibition market (the potential is usually about 500 theaters). This marketing pattern is one measure which serves to distinguish exploitation films from general release films in 1970.

In the past year or two quite a number of highly sexually oriented hybrid films which combine elements of all three traditional types of films of a totally new genre have appeared. Still another group of films has come onto the market. These are presently known in the trade as "16mm" films, and are among the most sexually explicit available. This Report will deal with these after the traffic in sexually oriented films falling into the traditional classifications has been discussed.

SEXUALLY ORIENTED GENERAL RELEASE FILMS

Since its very beginning, the motion picture industry has been the target of criticism directed at the sexual content and themes in movies. Today, there are general release films which are sexually quite explicit. They are the target of the most public criticism because of their nationwide distribution to large, diversified audiences. This criticism is magnified because of the large volume of newspaper advertising, gossip columns and stories, pictures, and articles appearing in periodicals.

From 1920 to 1950, the motion picture industry was dominated by a few large companies (the "majors") which produced the vast majority of movies and also controlled a large number of theaters. As a result of public criticism of the sexual content of many motion pictures, a trade association of the major studios (now the Motion Picture Association of America or MPAA) was founded in the 1920s to provide a system of self-regulation. Criticism continued, however; in 1934, this led to the formation of the Production

Code Administration (PCA), which granted a "code seal of approval" to those motion pictures deemed suitable for exhibition. The code seal was required in order for a movie to be shown at theaters controlled by one of the "majors." In effect, in order for a motion picture to receive wide distribution, approval by the PCA was a necessity.

The PCA and the majors thus rigorously controlled the sexual content of general release motion pictures for over 20 years. However, the end of World War II signalled the beginning of a new era of turmoil and change in the motion picture industry which has continued to the present day. Economic and social changes in the past 25 years have contributed to the relative decline of the industry. During this same period, the sexual content of general release films has increased markedly. Whether the two are related can only be speculated upon; it is by no means certain that the relative decline of the industry has a direct causal relationship to the increased sexual content in the motion pictures of 1970. The MPAA denies there is any relationship, and takes the position that movies reflect society rather than lead in changing it (Valenti, 1970).

Factors which have contributed to the changes in both the economic structure of the industry and in the sexual content of general release movies are as follows:

1. An antitrust decision in 1948 (United States v. Paramount Pictures) forced the "majors" to divest themselves of control of theaters. This greatly reduced the ability of the major studios to control the sexual content of all widely distributed movies.

2. During the 1950s, foreign "art" films, which did not carry the PCA seal, began to attract American audiences in such large numbers that an "art film" circuit became established. Many of these films treated sexual topics in a manner not acceptable to the PCA.

3. Much of the power of local censor boards was eliminated by judicial decisions such as Freedman v. Maryland (see Report of the Legal Panel). Only one state has a state censorship board today.

4. In the post-World War II period, social and sexual mores changed significantly in the United States.

5. Television displaced the motion picture industry as the most popular and least expensive form of family entertainment. Between 1950 and 1960, the number of television sets increased by 400% while theater admissions fell by 50% (Randall, 1968, p. 3).

6. There are also indications that the composition of the movie-going audience has changed with a shift towards audiences of young adults.

Whatever impact these various factors individually may have had upon general release films, it is clear that the sexual content of popular motion pictures has changed radically since World War II. Changes in content, of course, have gone beyond the sexual realm and have resulted in increased candor in films dealing with many previously taboo subjects as well, such as drug addiction, political dissent, racism, and a wide range of anti-establishment themes. It is also clear that the trend towards dramatically increased sexual content in movies has accelerated in the past year or two. Major themes of recent general release films have included perversion, abortion, orgies, wife-swapping, prostitution, promiscuity, homosexuality, nymphomania, lesbianism, etc. These themes, which sometimes were dealt with in a very discreet manner in motion pictures of another era, are now presented quite explicitly. At present, there are few areas of human sexual behavior which have not been explored. Further, the "formula" treatment of earlier times is often ignored. For example, "just retribution" for sexual behavior outside the standards of conventional morality, once a standard for movies, is no longer viewed as a necessity by today's film makers.

Graphic sexual activity is often depicted in general release films. Simulated intercourse is relatively common, although the degree of explicitness varies from film to film (a number are quite candid). Other sexual activities, such as masturbation, fellatio, and cunnilingus have been implicit in many films and shown in rather explicit detail in some (stopping short of actually depicting the act).

The rapidity of the change in the sexual content of general release movies is perhaps best exemplified by the treatment of the female body on the screen. Although legs, sweater-girls, and some decolletage have been featured in the movies for decades, a woman's navel was not shown in a major motion picture until the early 1960s. By 1967, flashes of female genitalia had appeared in a general release movie. Today, partial nudity (female breasts and buttocks and male buttocks) is quite common in general release films. Full female nudity (pubic areas shown) is increasingly common, and a few general release films have shown both sexes totally nude (genitalia).

The trend toward highly sex-oriented motion pictures is

being followed by most industry members. Only one well-known producer-distributor has not distributed movies directed toward the "adult" or "mature" audience.

Since November, 1968, certain guidelines for general release films have been provided by the industry through use of a rating system.[1] Almost all general release films are rated by the Code and Rating Administration (CRA), the successor of the PCA, according to the following system:

G—All ages admitted. General audiences.

GP—All ages admitted. Parental guidance suggested.

R—Restricted. Under 17 requires accompanying parent or adult guardian.

X—No one under 17 admitted. (Age limit may vary in certain areas).

In addition, an "X" may be self-applied by a producer or a distributor who chooses not to submit his picture to the CRA. No other rating may be self-applied.

Since the initiation of the rating system on November 1, 1968, through May 12, 1970, the CRA has rated a total of 655 films. A summary of these by rating appears in Table 2.

TABLE 2

Rated Movies, November 1968-May 1970

Rating	Number	Percentage
G	188	28.7%
GP	259	39.5%
R	171	26.1%
X	37	5.7%
TOTAL	655	100.0%

A survey of the trade press for the first ten months of the rating system's existence disclosed that 20% of all films released during that period were unrated (Randall, 1970a). Many of these were minor films with limited exhibition.

The MPAA states that the ratings are intended only as a guide to parents and express only the industry's opinion of the suitability of rated films for young people (Valenti, 1970). Supposedly the rating of a film provides a rough guideline as to the degree of sexual content in the film. Neither the MPAA nor the CRA have ever published rating standards; however, a study of the rating system by the Positive Approaches Panel included a study of the criteria used for various ratings as of summer 1969 (Randall, 1970a). Apparently, it is the intent of the CRA to remain flexible in

90

order to adapt the system to changing times, the changing content of movies, and public criticism of previous ratings. The following is a summary of interviews with Code and Rating Administration officials in January, 1970:

G-Rated Movies. Films rated "G" must be sexually pure. Little beyond conventional embracing and kissing is allowed. No "G" film may contain anti-social themes. The standards for "G"-rated films have certainly not been liberalized, and, in fact, probably will become stricter in the future. The CRA recognizes that a few "mistakes" may have been made in rating certain films. In the view of the CRA, a "mistake" in a rating is one which generates an appreciable amount of criticism (either from the public or from critics) because a rating has been too permissive or too strict. Criticism is almost invariably directed at ratings which are thought to be not sufficiently restrictive. The CRA claims to be responsive to letters of protest from the public and can adjust its criteria to apply more restrictive ratings in the future. Incidentally, not all objections to "G" rated films are sexual in nature; some "G" rated films have been criticized for excessive violence or "vulgar" language.

GP-Rated Movies. Motion pictures are rated "GP" with the maturing adolescent in mind. Moderately explicit indication of sex is permitted. Originally, no nudity (female breast or buttock or male buttock) was allowed, but, as of January, 1970, brief "flashes" of partial nudity in a "long shot" did not automatically disqualify a movie from a "GP" rating. While sex may be discussed, if the discussion becomes "candid," the film is classified "R." A minimum amount of vulgarity is permitted, but no "extreme vulgarity" is allowed. Detailed discussions or dramatizations of perversion are not allowed in "GP" rated films. For example, a "GP" picture may intimate or present the fact of homosexuality, but dramatization of a homosexual relationship is not permissible. Similarly, films involving premarital sex or adultery without open approval may be rated "GP." Under the former Production Code standards, such activities were required to be either denounced or punished by "moral compensation" in order to receive a code seal. However, the rating system does not require compensatory moral values. If approval is expressed for such conduct, however, the film will be rated "R" or "X."

R-Rated Movies. The "R" rating allows for virtually any theme. As of January, 1970, quite a bit of breast and buttock nudity was permitted in this category. Officials of CRA, however, did not believe that this line would be held, a prediction which was fulfilled later in 1970. The CRA has been criticized for rating certain motion pictures as "X" rather than "R" but such complaints have come only from the industry and critics, not from the public. A wide range of sexual behavior is allowed in "R" rated films. Brief breast touching and caressing and simulated intercourse are permissible, but not for a lengthy period, as of January, 1970. In addition, the quantity of sexual content has an effect on the rating. While a few limited scenes of sexual activity or nudity are allowed in "R" pictures, an "excessive quantity" may result in an "X" rating. There are almost no language restrictions in "R" rated films, so long as vulgarity or "four-letter words" are not used "excessively." Any legitimate discussion of sex is permissible if, in the opinion of the CRA, it does not exceed the bounds of good taste. The chief difference between "R" and "X" films is a subject appraisal of the quantity and quality of erotic themes, conduct, or nudity, rather than a set of absolutes which automatically classify a film as "X."

X-Rated Movies. The final classification, "X", serves as a catch-all for motion pictures which cannot be rated "G," "GP," or "R." In addition, films rated "X" do not receive the code seal of approval (carry-over from the earlier system). The CRA allegedly does not make judgments regarding the sexual content of "X" pictures; if the motion picture is judged too strong for an "R" rating, it is rated "X." As of January, 1970, genital exposure, graphic simulated intercourse, strong specific indications of oral-genital contact, and films which concentrate almost exclusively on eroticism were placed in the "X" classification.

The above description of the rating criteria as of January, 1970, has been modified as of August, 1970. The restrictive ratings of "R" and "X" have undergone constant revision. For example, some current "R" rated films contain sexual content which, according to the CRA officials, when interviewed in January, 1970, would have necessarily resulted in an "X" rating. Included are large amounts of total female nudity and graphic sexual activity, including masturbation, coitus, group sex, and strong implications of fellatio and cunnilingus.

Because of the flexibility of the CRA ratings and the changing criteria, categorical statements about rating criteria cannot be relied upon in the future. In this rapidly changing area, predictions about the sexual themes and content in motion pictures in the future are impossible to make.

SEXUALLY ORIENTED ART FILMS

During the 1950s, when art films were very popular in the United States, many treated sexual matters with a degree of explicitness not permissible under the Production Code then in effect. Many were charged as being obscene, but in virtually every instance the courts ruled otherwise.

Art films of today, at least those cast in the traditional mold, contain less sexual content than many general release films, and cannot be distinguished by their relative sexual candor, as once was the case. Today only the "foreignness" or limited audience appeal set such films apart from many general release movies.

Because of their relatively low sexual content and limited appeal, no special effort was made to measure the box office success of these films. Parenthetically it should be noted that some very highly sexually oriented films which have achieved great success resemble art films in some respects. Because of other distinguishing characteristics, however, these films are classified separately and discussed below (see "Sexually Oriented 'Hybrid' and 'New Genre' Motion Pictures").

EXPLOITATION MOTION PICTURES

Exploitation films (often known as "skin flicks," "adults only," or "sexploitation films") are low-budget films which concentrate on the erotic. Until one or two years ago, the lines of demaraction between these films and general release movies were quite clear. However, the increase of sexually related themes and the incidence of nudity and sex play in the latter have blurred many of the former distinctions to a point where there is a considerable overlap. Today, perhaps the chief distinction between at least some sexually oriented general release films and exploitation films is that the latter (a) are much less expensive to produce (which is usually obvious to the viewer) and (b) are ordinarily exhibited in far fewer theaters.

History Exploitation films are not a recent phenomenon; they have existed for almost 50 years. During most of this time, the films were usually exhibited as "special events," rather than under a continuing policy of exhibition. Initially,

93

exploitation films of the 1920s featured total nudity and little plot or erotic conduct (demonstrations of affection were usually confined to a passionless embrace). The 1930s and 40s saw the virtual elimination of total nudity and the development of more refined story lines. The most typical theme was the wayward girl in the city; "jungle" pictures and "nudist camp" movies were also popular.

The first exploitation film to be a significant economic success was produced in 1959, reportedly for $24,000 (Knight and Alpert, 1967, p. 124). The film, which told the story of a man who was unable to see clothing on females, eventually grossed more than $1,000,000. In the early 1960s, many producers imitated this formula (an abundance of partial nudity, breasts and buttocks, with no erotic conduct, known in the trade as "nudie-cuties"). Others produced an abundance of nudist camp films, which featured totally nude females almost exclusively.

Between 1964 and 1968, exploitation films moved in a variety of directions. Some producers dropped all pretense of a plot and substituted nudity for a story line. Others produced "roughies," a mixture of sex and violence. Some films depicted women as aggressors (nymphomaniacs, lesbians, and prostitutes); others portrayed them as victims. A few films were self-styled "documentaries" dealing with sexual mores and aberrations. Still others were known as "kinkies" (dealing with fetishes) and "ghoulies" (minimizing nudity and maximizing violence).

In 1969, and continuing into 1970, exploitation films dealt with the same themes often found in general release motion pictures: perversion, abortion, drug addiction, wayward girls, orgies, wife-swapping, vice dens, prostitution, promiscuity, homosexuality, transvestism, frigidity, nymphomania, lesbianism, etc. Almost all of the popular movie-making formulas have been utilized as settings for presenting these themes, including westerns and historical epics, although contemporary settings are still the most widely used.

The vast majority of exploitation films are directed at the male heterosexual market. Relatively few films are produced for a male homosexual audience, but the number of these films has increased in the past year or two. A small number of theaters exclusively exhibit male homosexual films and a few exhibit such films on occasion. This market is quite small at present, and is included in the estimate for the entire exploitation film market, although "male" films are developing their own producers and theaters.

Full female nudity in exploitation films has become common in the last year or two, although male genital exposure is almost unknown except in those films directed at the male homosexual market. Sexual activity covering the entire range of heterosexual conduct leaves almost nothing to the imagination. Actual sex acts, however, are not shown, only strongly implied or simulated. Self-imposed restrictions on the use of "vulgar" language have also disappeared in many films.

Current distinctions in sexual content between exploitation and some general release films are rather subtle; the difference is primarily one of emphasis and degree. For instance, a sexually oriented general release film may show total femal nudity on the screen for 1% to 5% of the total running time, while exploitation films may show the same degree of nudity for 10% or even 50% of the running time.

Thus, in 1970, factors which classify a movie as "exploitation" are (a) the manner in which the film is marketed and (b) the cost of production. The position of unquestioned leadership in explicitness of sexual content in motion pictures formerly held by exploitation movies has disappeared in today's market. Quite a number of general release movies produced and distributed by major companies have approached or exceeded the sexual content of the typical "skin flick." In addition, as discussed in a succeeding section, a new genre of motion pictures has replaced the exploitation feature as the most sexually explicit available for exhibition in conventional theaters. However, in mid-1970, exploitation films continue to be shown in the limited market which they created. Whether traditional exploitation films will be able to withstand the assaults of more expensively produced films in the future is problematical.

Production In the past two years, more than 50 and perhaps as many as 100 business firms have produced exploitation films. Production budgets range from $3,000 to $100,000 with an average cost of between $20,000 and $40,000. Producers who grind out films for less than $5,000 are a very minor factor in the market place. Some producers spend at least $40,000 to make a feature film and upwards of $60,000 to release it. Two or three claim to have spent $75,000 to $100,000 on recent films, but costs at this level are unusual. Budgets are controlled carefully by most producers; script costs are kept at a minimum; unknown actors are invariably used and there is a constant turnover of players; film production crews are kept to a minimum,

95

usually non-union; and the movies are hurriedly made, usually in less than one week.

Industry sources estimated that at least 135, and perhaps as many as 200, full-length feature exploitation films were produced in 1969. The exact number is very difficult to ascertain, because many extremely low-budget films have very limited distribution. In addition, exploitation films have an extended release time and sometimes remain in circulation for several years because only a small number of prints are made (usually 10 to 25). Thus, it takes some time for a film to be exhibited on the exploitation circuit.

Most large exploitation producers act as their own distributors and also distribute films for smaller companies; some purchase films and market them under their own label as well. Producers agree that the normal maximum return for an exploitation film is between $150,000 and $200,000, and that a more typical return of $75,000 will show a profit for most films. Gross profits in relation to costs have historically been relatively high (returns on investment of from 100% to 400%). However, the market ordinarily limits the gross dollar receipts to levels far below those of the general release market. The lowest budget general release films generally cost more to produce than the gross box office receipts of all but a very few of the most successful exploitation films.

Films come and go in this market with great rapidity; the typical movie is exhibited for only one week in the average "skin house." Few films achieve recognition beyond the exploitation market, and only a small number are promoted extensively. The oversupply of films is such that very few have an opportunity to develop into "hits." Of course, the relatively low quality of most such films (from a technical standpoint) precludes much chance of wide success in any event.

Exploitation Theaters. There is a definite trend for exploitation theaters to be held by chain operators, some of whom are also producer-distributors (even though this practice is forbidden to majors by U.S. v. Paramount Pictures), and the trend toward centralized management has brought new capital into the market. This has resulted in the remodeling of old theaters or construction of new theaters which exclusively exhibit exploitation films, especially in the western part of the country. The majority of such theaters, however, are shabby and run down, and are usually located in decaying downtown areas. There has been a recent trend toward establishing exploitation theaters in suburban areas, especially drive-ins.

Most exploitation theaters are medium sized (500-700 seats), and are in operation an average of 14 hours a day. Admission prices vary considerably (i.e., from 89 cents along 42nd Street in New York to $5.00 in some cities). Nationwide, the average admission price is between $2.00 and $2.50 (considerably higher than the national average for general release theaters). Exploitation theater owners appear to be very strict about enforcement of minimum age entrance requirements, which are usually set at either 18 or 21 (Winick, 1970b). The typical exploitation theater exhibits multiple features, and in most theaters feature films are changed weekly; extended runs are very rare.

Most exploitation theater owners are said to retain 75% of the box-office receipts (general release theater owners supposedly retain 50% on the average), and more often than not, they are able to rent films on a flat-rate basis. Because of the oversupply of exploitation films, film rental fees are often less than 25% of the weekly gross, with a concomitant increase in profit for exhibitors. Weekly box-office receipts vary considerably, but the average theater probably takes in about $2,000, although some theater owners have reported record weekly grosses of over $15,000, and averages of over $6,000 per week.

As of early 1970, approximately 880 theaters exhibited exploitation films at least on a part-time basis (one-fourth of which are drive-ins); these represented over 6% of all theaters in the United States. Of this number, over 500 had a full-time exploitation film policy.

Two surveys of exploitation theaters were made on behalf of the Panel. The first, conducted by the Bureau of the Census (Sampson, 1970), matched a list of over 500 full-time exploitation theaters (as of 1970) against the 1967 official census of business. Approximately 50% of the reports made by these theaters in 1967 were located, and the following economic data for that year were disclosed.[2] Gross receipts for 256 theaters were $32.7 million (including taxes and concession receipts); and reported receipts from admissions for 100 theaters were $23 million. Slightly less than 6% of the reporting theaters had receipts of more than $300,000; 42% reported receipts of $100,000 to $300,000; 30% reported receipts of $50,000 to $99,000; 16% had receipts of between $20,000 and $49,000; and 6% had receipts of less than $20,000.

The Bureau of Census does not average data because a varying number of theaters report for each question asked. Because the purpose of this report is to provide a general picture of the market, such distinctions can be disregarded. The typical or average exploitation house in 1967 had total receipts from all sources of $128,000; (receipts from admission were $115,395) the average indoor exploitation theater had 83,553 annual individual admissions, and the average drive-in had approximately 65,121. The average seating capacity in conventional exploitation theaters was 627, and the average drive-in theater could accommodate 458 vehicles. In 1967, most exploitation theaters showed multiple features more than 50% of the time.

At the behest of the Panel, a very fragmentary survey was made by the Adult Film Association of America (AFAA), the trade association of exploitation film producers, distributors, and exhibitors (only 20 theaters reported). These theaters claimed an average of over 73,000 individual admissions and average receipts of nearly $175,000 in 1969 (average admission price was $2.30). The theaters reporting had an average of 467 seats, most had been in business for 15 years or more, and all were at least two or three years old. All booked multiple features more than 75% of the time.

SEXUALLY ORIENTED "HYBRID" AND "NEW GENRE" MOTION PICTURES

Within the past two years, the increase in sexual content of widely distributed motion pictures has made labeling and categorization of many sexually oriented films almost impossible. Certain pioneering films and their imitators have, in effect, smashed the neat classifications of general release, art, and exploitation films which formerly existed as yardsticks for analyzing the sexual content of movies. The industry recognizes that something unique is happening, but the creation of any commonly recognized labels for these new "sex" films has not yet occurred.

In the last two years, there has been both a hybridization of the recognized categories of films and, in addition, a creation of an entirely new genre of highly sex-oriented films.

In general, this Report discusses the traffic in sexually oriented materials in general terms and avoids specific references, but this new market can only be described by examples.

One version of hybrid sexually oriented films is a combination of general release and exploitation films. Some of these apparently were originally intended for the exploitation film market, but, because of skillful promotion or other reasons not immediately apparent, "broke out" of the limited confines of that market into a much broader exhibition. A good example is Vixen which was produced for under $100,000 by the leading exponent of exploitation films and had nearly 1,500 playdates in 1969, with a reported box office gross of several million dollars—over $2 million in only 20-24 cities (Variety, 1970b, p. 9). Hybrid films of this type also are produced by major companies, but on much higher budgets; Beyond the Valley of the Dolls is the most current example, a film directed by the producer of Vixen for a major studio.

A few films seem to be a marriage of exploitation and art films, appealing to a limited audience and combining elements of those two types. Coming Apart is an example.

By far, the most important of the hybrid films combine elements of all three recognized categories. That is, these films resemble exploitation films in the high degree of explicit sexual activity depicted. Indeed, many of these films go well beyond the sexual content of the typical exploitation film, i.e., more explicit simulated sexual foreplay, coitus, or oral-genital contact and full nudity of both sexes, etc., features not found in typical exploitation films made at the same time. These films also resemble art films in that many are low-budget foreign films exhibited in the original language with subtitles or dubbed into English. Finally, these hybrid films are exhibited widely in respectable theaters for extended periods of time, a characteristic formerly limited to general release films. A comprehensive list of such films would be rather lengthy; good examples are I am Curious (Yellow); Without a Stitch; Fanny Hill; Inga; The Libertine; Fuego; Monique; Female Animal; Camile 2000; I a Woman (I & II); Tropic of Cancer; and De Sade.

In addition to the hybrid films described above, an entirely new genre of sexually oriented motion picture has been exhibited in 1969 and 1970, almost exclusively in major metropolitan areas. These films graphically depict actual sexual intercourse on the screen, activity which was previously unknown in public theaters and had been confined to private or semi-private exhibitions at "smokers" or "stag nights." The

99

first of these films, Man and Wife, and a number of imitators, were cast in a "sex education for married couples" mold; in other words, they purported to be cinematic marriage manuals.

Later films have been presented as sexual documentaries, and not only depicted coitus, but also examined sexual mores, taboos, erotic art, etc., e.g., Sexual Freedom in Denmark and Freedom to Love. Other films of this revolutionary type are documentaries of pornography in Scandinavia, especially Denmark; e.g., Pornography in Denmark and Pornography: Copenhagen 1970 (also known as Wide Open Copenhagen). These films are the most explicit of all, and depict fellatio and cunnilingus as well as coitus on the screen.

Not only is the sexual content of this "new wave" of films much greater than in films of only two or three years ago, but the marketing patterns do not follow the traditional lines heretofore readily identifiable. As noted above, both sex-oriented exploitation films and art films normally achieve relatively limited exhibitions in an established circuit of theaters (perhaps 500-600 theaters on the average). Popular general release films can expect to be exhibited in as many as 5,000 or more theaters. The market for popular hybrid sexually oriented films falls somewhere between these two extremes; many have been exhibited in 1,000 to 2,000 theaters. In addition (contrary to the experience of a typical exploitation film), extended runs are common; some of these films have played in a theater for six months to a year, in much the same manner as "hit" general release films. In addition, such films are not limited to exhibition in run-down theaters in decaying downtown areas; such films play in first-class general release theaters in downtown and suburban areas and receive considerable exhibition in local neighborhood theaters. The most sexually explicit of all motion pictures, the "new genre" films, have not yet received wide exhibition and, in fact, have thus far been exhibited in fewer theaters than successful exploitation films (under 50 theaters). However, these films have received extended runs in the cities in which they have been shown.

SIXTEEN MILLIMETER MOTION PICTURES

Within the past two or three years, an additional form of sexually oriented motion picture shown in theaters has emerged—known in the industry as "16mm films."[3]

As of August 1970, a majority of the 16mm theaters in the country exhibit silent color films of young females displaying their genitals, usually accompanied by music from phonograph records (although some exhibitors present movies with sound tracks). Usually, 16mm films are the most sexually explicit films shown in the locality, although the wave of "movie marriage manuals" and sex documentaries in 1970 are even more sexually explicit than most 16mm films. In a few cities, (at present primarily Los Angeles and San Francisco) 16mm films are the equivalent of old-style "stag movies," and depict sexual intercourse and oral-genital contact with penetration shown in detail. These films cannot be exceeded in candor and in graphic depictions.

Many 16mm theaters are located in decaying downtown areas and are converted store fronts, although some are conventional theaters. Most are quite small and have from 50 to 200 seats; the average seating capacity is probably about 150. It is very difficult to estimate the number of 16mm houses currently in operation, but a figure of 200 is probably reasonably accurate. At present, these theaters are located only in major metropolitan centers such as Los Angeles, San Diego, San Francisco, Seattle, Dallas, Detroit, and New York City.

Sixteen millimeter films are both simple and inexpensive to produce. The equipment is portable, and films can be made in lofts, apartments, and wooded areas without difficulty. As a result, many 16mm theater owners produce their own films, while others purchase prints. Film rental is virtually unknown. As yet there are no recognizable film titles moving from city to city, and there is almost no nationwide distribution of such films.

The operation of a 16mm theater can be quite profitable, primarily because of the typical $4-$5 admission charge, and because the theaters are usually open for at least 12 to 14 hours per day.

Local sources in San Francisco estimated that the gross box-office receipts for an average 16mm theater in that city are approximately $3,000–$4,000 per week, and a few very successful theaters gross as much as $8,000 weekly. As yet, 16mm theaters have remained primarily a local phenomenon. However, although 16mm films are in their infancy and as yet are a minor factor in the traffic of sexually oriented materials, the market definitely seems to be expanding.

General Release, Art, "Hybrid," and "New Genre" Films
Reported box office receipts in trade journals for the period
since the rating system has been in effect have been analyzed.
Although there was no dramatic differences in reported
grosses among "G," "GP," and "R" rated films, as a group
"G" films tended to have consistently higher grosses. This, of
course, does not mean that "G" films are the most profitable;
the cost of production must be taken into account. However,
it is clear that "G" films (which contain relatively little in the
way of sexual content) do not "die" at the box office, as
has often been claimed in some quarters of the industry
(Randall, 1970b).

Data regarding the success of films rated "X" by the CRA
is mixed. Some "X" films do very well at the box office and
most have initial success during the early weeks of exhibition.
In addition, some films not rated by the CRA but reported
on by the trade journals do well at the box office.

Total box office receipts are not available for either individual films or for classes of films. However, it is possible
to make reasonable estimates of receipts from data supplied
by the trade journals (primarily Variety). Each year, Variety
reports on the movies which allegedly returned the greatest
film rental fees to their distributors.

For 1969, of the top 20 films returning $5 million or more
in fees, eight were rated "G," four were rated "GP," three
were rated "R," one was rated "X," one was unrated, and
the other three were released before the rating system went
into effect.

It should be noted, however, that a few of the "G" movies
in this list have been reported in the trade press to have lost
money for their producers, while all of the "R," "X," and
unrated films reputedly returned a profit, and some are alleged
to have been exceptionally profitable (Variety, 1970a, p. 15).
Ninety films reportedly returned over $1 million to the distrib-
utor in 1969 for a total of $338.5 million; of these, 25 "G"
movies returned $119 million; 28 "GP" films returned $92
million; 18 "R" films accounted for $57 million; 3 "X" films
returned $14 million; and 16 unrated films returned $56 million (of these, four were clearly sex-oriented and returned
over $11 million).

Final figures for 1970 are not available, but an analysis
of the reported 50 top box office films each week for the
first six months indicates that many "R," "X," and several

102

unrated sexually oriented films are doing very well at the box office (Randall, 1970b). Each week Variety reports box office receipts of the "50 Top Grossing Films" in 20-24 cities (at the date of last listing). Table 3 summarizes an analysis of the box office experience of those films which appeared in the "Top Fifty" list at least once.

TABLE 3

Breakdown of "Top Fifty" Films, January-July, 1970

Rating	Number of Films	Percentage of Films	1970 Gross Receipts (in millions)[1]	Percentage of Gross Receipts
G	44	19.7%	$44.4	25.9%
GP	69	30.9%	57.3	33.5%
R	46	20.6%	44.9	26.2%
X	15	6.8%	12.4	7.2%
Non-Sex Unrated	15	6.8%	2.7	1.6%
Sex-Oriented Unrated[2]	33	15.2%	9.5	5.6%
TOTAL	222	100.0%	$171.1	100.0%

[1] Many of the films listed in the "Top Fifty" during the first six months of 1970 were originally released in 1969. Only 1970 gross receipts for these films were included.
[2] These films are characterized as hybrid or new genre films in this Report. Judgments on the classification were made by the Panel.

Although only 650–800 theaters in 20–24 cities are included in the survey summarized by Table 3 (5% of total theaters), their receipts in the first six months of 1970 represent approximately 31% of the Department of Commerce projected total of box-office receipts of all motion pictures this year. Therefore, while the "Top Fifty" chart is not definitive it is a good barometer of films in current exhibition and their relative position in regard to each other.

Table 3 does not include two categories studied by the Panel—art and exploitation films. To provide an estimate of box office receipts of all films for 1970, the Panel constructed Table 4. Figures in the six categories in Table 3 were projected to total $1 billion. To this was added $35 million for art films and $65 million for exploitation films (the Panel estimates $30–$40 million and $60–$70, respectively, for these categories). New percentages were then calculated for the eight categories in Table 4 using the total figure of $1.1 billion projected by the Department of Commerce (1970b).

TABLE 4

Box-Office Receipts, by Classification

Rating	1970 Projected Receipts (in millions)	Percentage of Receipts
G	$259	23.5%
GP	335	30.5%
R	262	23.8%
X	72	6.6%
Non-Sex Unrated	16	1.5%
Sex-Oriented Unrated[1]	56	5.0%
Art Films[2]	35	3.2%
Exploitation Films[3]	65	5.9%
TOTAL	$1,100	100.0%

[1] These films are characterized as hybrid or new genre films in this Report. Judgments on the classification were made by the Panel.

[2] "Art films" play in between 500 and 600 theaters in an established "art circuit." Few if any of these films reach the Top 50, but the total box-office receipts can be estimated at $30-$40 million simply on the basis of the number of theaters exhibiting such films.

[3] Estimated at $60-$70 million; see succeeding section of this Report.

The weekly list of the top 50 box-office grossers used in Table 3 undoubtedly distorts the importance of "R," "X," and unrated sexually oriented films to some degree because it is limited to 20–24 major metropolitan cities. Theaters in many smaller cities do not exhibit such films. When these figures are projected nationally, as was done in Table 4, this distortion is increased. The Panel estimates that a 75% reduction in the 100% projection for "R," "X," and unrated sexually oriented films in Table 4 would produce a more accurate estimate of nation-wide box office receipts in 1970. Such a reduction would produce an increase in the figures shown for "G" and "GP" films. Despite this probable inaccuracy, Table 4 is useful in that it marks the maximum 1970 box-office receipts for sexually oriented films.

Estimated Total Box-office Receipts for Exploitation Films —1969 Exploitation industry sources estimate that the average theater grosses $2,000 weekly, or $100,000 per year, and that approximately 600 theaters exhibited exploitation films each week during 1969. Thus, estimates of the industry indicate a $60 million box office business in 1969 for such films. The Panel, projecting incomplete data supplied by the Census Bureau, estimates that the 1969 volume may have been as high as $70 million.

Industry sources claim that 1970 receipts are running 10%–20% behind 1969 because of increased competition from sexually oriented motion pictures playing outside the exploitation market.

Section B. Sexually Oriented Books and Magazines

The distribution and sale of sexually oriented publications in the United States can be roughly divided into two categories; (a) those which are a part of the "mass market," i.e., books and periodicals distributed to a general audience; and (b) so-called "adults only" publications, a submarket of sexually oriented printed matter which receive relatively limited distribution.

THE MASS MARKET

The book and periodical publishing industry in the United States is the largest and most diversified in the world. Every year hundreds of separate publishing companies, some very large and many quite small, produce tens of thousands of new titles and reissues of hard cover books, paperbound books, and periodicals. The majority of all publications are directed to special interests, but thousands are published for general consumption.

BOOK PUBLISHING

Approximately 30,000 new book titles and new editions have been published during each of the past three years. The Department of Commerce (1970b) estimates that receipts by publishers in 1970 will total over $2.5 billion, and the last official census of business in 1967 disclosed receipts by publishers of $2.1 billion. The latest estimates available from the industry are for 1968; the American Book Publishers Council and the American Educational Publishers Institute estimated receipts of the industry at $2.57 billion. Of that total, materials which could conceivably be within the areas of study by the Panel would be found only in "Adult Trade Books" ($179 million), "Paperback Books" ($167 million) and "Book Clubs"

105

($204 million)—a total of $550 million or some 21% of the whole book industry. The balance of publishers' receipts was accounted for by textbooks and special interest books such as religious, juvenile, technical, scientific, professional, and reference books. Assuming publishers recover an average of 55% of the retail sale price of books (book club sales are at retail prices), total retail sales of these books in 1968 were approximately $833 million.

There are 80,000 paperback book titles currently in print (Paperbound Books in Print, 1970); between 20,000 and 25,000 of these sell in the general market, and the balance are school books, technical texts, special interest books, etc. Although there are no official estimates of the total number of copies of mass market paperbacks distributed and sold at retail yearly, industry sources estimate that over 700 million paperback books are distributed and over 330 million of these are sold. The retail sales volume of mass market paperback books exceeded $340 million in 1968. (Publishers' Weekly, 1970b, p. 79.)

PERIODICAL PUBLISHING

The Department of Commerce (1970b, p. 64) estimates that receipts by periodical publishers will be in excess of $3 billion in 1970, an increase of over $1 billion from 1960. The last official census of business, in 1967, disclosed receipts by publishers of approximately $2.6 billion. Of this, only periodicals such as comics, women and home service, general interest, news, business, and entertainment magazines could possibly be of interest to the Panel. These produced receipts of $1,445 billion, of which $560 million came from single copy and subscription sales and $885 million from advertising revenue. An analysis of the leading 200 periodicals for the first six months of 1969 disclosed that a total of almost 157 million copies per issue were sold by subscription and 64.5 million single copy sales were made for each issue of these periodicals. Unfortunately, because of the varying price structures of subscription sales of magazines, it is not possible to estimate total retail sales of periodicals.

Over 10,000 periodicals are published per year, many of which are special interest magazines. Sales per issue range from a few thousand copies per issue to over 17.5 million for the largest periodical. The total sales for all mass market periodicals distributed in 1969 has been estimated at more than 2.5 billion copies.

Publishers use a wide variety of marketing channels to distribute their products to the mass market. Each type of publication (hard-cover and paperback books and periodicals) is distributed in different ways. In addition to the publishers themselves who sell directly to retailers, especially hard-cover books and paperback books, or directly to customers, especially periodical subscriptions, there are a number of business organizations which assist in distributing publications:

1. National Distributors. Most paperback and periodical publishers employ one of 15 major national distributors to supply local wholesalers. National distributors set the quantity to be distributed, handle all returns (unsold merchandise), make billings and collections, and perform selling and some promotion functions. Some publishers act as their own national distributors while others use one of several smaller organizations (other than the 15 largest).

2. National Jobbers. These organizations purchase paperback books and periodicals from the publisher and sell directly to retailers (on a returnable basis).

3. Book Clubs. These organizations lease or purchase publications from the publisher (almost always hard-cover books) and sell these directly to the customer by mail order.

4. Local Wholesale Distributors. Over 600 local wholesale distributors (known as I.D.'s in the trade) in the United States are franchised on a geographical basis to distribute mass market periodicals and paperbacks in a given territory to retailers.

5. Retail Outlets. It has been estimated there are approximately 110,000 regular outlets for general magazines, including independent and chain drugstores, supermarkets, variety stores, stationery stores, cigar stores, and newsstands. Of these it has been estimated 80,000 display and sell paperback books. Some 10,000 outlets sell mass market hard-cover books; the vast majority of these also sell paperback books. (Publishers' Weekly, 1970a, p. 28).

In brief, the typical patterns of distribution for the various type of publications directed to the mass market can be described as follows. Periodicals are ordinarily sold through the following distribution channels: (a) single copy sales: publisher to national distributor, local wholesale distributor to retailer; or publisher to national jobber, to retailer; and (b) subscription sales: publisher to subscriber. The distribution of paperback books is more complex: publisher to national distributor to local wholesale distributor, to retailer; or publisher to national jobber, to retailers; or publisher to retailer. Hard-cover books usually are distributed as follows: publisher to national jobber to retailer or institution (library, school, etc.); or publisher to book club to reader; or publisher to retailer; or publisher to reader.

MASS MARKET SEXUALLY ORIENTED PUBLICATIONS

Mass market paperback and hard-cover books and periodicals which might be classified as sexually oriented are distributed in basically the same manner as other mass publications. Such materials are usually not the most explicit printed materials available in most localities, and certainly not in any of the larger population centers. However, these publications are the most widely available sexually oriented materials available in the U.S.

The succeeding sections describe the traffic of certain publications which generally can be categorized as containing a higher degree of sexual content than is generally found in the average mass market publication. These have been broken down into magazines, paperback and hard-cover books, and newspapers.

It should be noted that as far as can be discovered, mass market sexually oriented materials are distributed and sold only on a voluntary basis. Because almost all periodicals and books are distributed on a fully returnable basis, pressure from publishers or wholesalers to distribute unwanted merchandise would be self-defeating. In today's fiercely competitive mass market, very few (if any) sellers can demand that a buyer handle a certain item.

Sexually Oriented Mass Market Periodicals The wide range of sexually oriented periodicals makes it particularly difficult to distinguish which publications should be classified as sexually oriented; for example, some persons might argue that one or more pictures of a nude or scantily clad female makes a particular issue of that magazine "sexually oriented." Others might argue that articles dealing with human sexuality should cause a periodical to be so classified. By that standard, most of today's popular magazines could be classified as sexually oriented, at least for some issues. Instead of examining the sexual content of individual issues of mass market magazines, the Commission Staff concentrated on those magazines which regularly contained a significant degree of sexual orien-

108

tation. These magazines are classified by the industry as "confession," "barber shop," "men's sophisticates," "sensational," and "special" (a catch-all for periodicals not falling into any of the other categories.)

Confession Magazines. Stories in confession magazines primarily emphasize the sexual problems of young women and are aimed at an audience of adolescent girls and young women. These magazines do not explicitly describe sex organs or sexual activity and the problems are always resolved in a moral context (Sonenschein, et al., 1970).

Almost every confession magazine is published monthly. From October 1, 1968, to September 30, 1969, average sale per issue of 38 selected confession magazines was approximately 10.4 million, and total sales for the period were 104.4 million copies. Slightly more than two million sales per issue were through subscriptions.

Assuming total yearly sales of approximately 110 million copies (to account for magazines not included in the survey), and an average retail price of $.35, total retail sales for this particular genre of sexually oriented publications in 1969 amounted to at least $38.5 million.

Barber Shop Magazines. "Barber shop" magazines, aimed at a male readership, primarily feature "action" stories, some of which are sex-oriented. Pictorial content primarily consists of "glamour," or "pin-up" photographs, a secondary feature of these magazines. Recently, however, there has been an increase in photos of partially nude females (breast and buttock exposure). During 1969, the average paid sale per issue (usually monthly or bi-monthly) for 20 selected barber shop magazines was 3.5 million copies (only 6,000 of which are subscriptions), and the yearly total was almost 30 million copies. Minimum retail sales for the barber shop magazines surveyed totaled approximately $12 million in 1969.

Sensational Newspapers and Magazines. "Sensational" newspapers (sometimes called "tabloids") such as the National Enquirer specialize in "expose" stories. Formerly these papers contained a substantial percentage of "sexual adventure" stories. However, in recent years, the sexual content has been so reduced as to make them generally acceptable to the most conservative retail outlets, such as supermarkets and variety stores, which cater to female audiences.

Men's Sophisticates. The mass market magazines with the highest degree of sexual orientation (especially nudity) are known as "men's sophisticates" (also as "girlie" or "East Coast girlie"). These magazines generally have a standardized

109

formula which devotes a substantial portion to photographs of partially nude females, (with breast and buttock exposure) in modeling poses. A self-imposed taboo against the depiction of female genitalia is rigidly observed. Little if any sexual activity is presented, and males rarely, if ever, appear in the photographs. In addition to the pictorial features, men's "sophisticate" magazines contain numerous articles, most of which are sexually oriented.

Sixty-two selected men's sophisticate magazines sold approximately 41 million copies in 1969, and total retail sales were at least $31 million.

Publishers and distributors interviewed by the Panel agree that during 1969 the market for men's sophisticates fell substantially from the 1968 level. While no overall figures were available for this decline in sales, circulation figures for five well-known men's sophisticates magazines were obtained for the first six months of 1969 and compared to sales for the first six months of 1968; sales had declined 37% for these five magazines. Comparison of newsstand sales figures for an additional 29 men's sophisticates from another source showed a 5% decrease.

Special Magazines.   There is a special group of sex-oriented mass market magazines which do not adequately fit any of the above classifications. Preeminent among these is Playboy, unique in the periodical industry and more of an institution than just another magazine. Each issue of Playboy contains no less than three, and sometimes four or five, pictorial layouts which feature partially nude females. In most cases, there is only breast and buttock exposure, although on occasion very discreet photographs of feminine pubic hair have been printed. In addition, Playboy always contains a number of drawings, both cartoon and "pin-ups," depicting nude females. It is not unusual for some of these drawings to depict couples in positions of sexual intercourse without showing genitalia. Some of the articles and fiction contain a significant degree of sexual orientation, but many articles on other topics written by well-known authors and distinguished persons are also included. Playboy sells for $1.00 monthly (except for two holiday issues priced at $1.50) and during 1969, had average paid sales of 5,324,000 copies per issue (1,417,000 subscriptions and 3,907,000 single copy sales). During 1969, just under 64 million copies were sold, and retail dollar sales were approximately $64 million. Playboy ranks twelfth in average total paid sales of all magazines, and first in profits to retail dealers. In addition, the magazine's yearbook sells

110

more than 500,000 copies (at $2.50 each), and more than two million calendars are sold annually. Thus, retail sales of Playboy publications are over $66 million. It should be noted that dollar sales of Playboy are more than twice those of all the men's sophisticate magazines combined.

A few other mass market magazines, such as Penthouse, English-American version of Playboy, Cosmopolitan, which in recent years has been known in the trade as "the woman's Playboy," and Sexology, Evergreen Review, and Avant Garde contain a substantial amount of sexual orientation, but are not easily categorized. Total combined copy sales of these magazines are less than one-third of Playboy's sales, and retail dollar sales are less than one-quarter those of Playboy.

Sexually Oriented Mass Market Paperback Books There is no universal agreement on paperbacks which should be classified as sexually oriented. In addition, even if a list were produced, obtaining sales figures would be virtually impossible.

Most major paperback publishers produce titles which might be classified as sexually oriented. For example, Bestsellers, a trade journal for magazine and paperback wholesalers and retailers, lists the 20 best selling paperback books each month. This list provides an indication of the popularity of particular mass market paperbacks, although sales figures are not given. During the period January, 1969–July, 1970, eighteen paperbacks which could easily be considered to be sexually oriented appeared on the Bestsellers list for more than one month. Three of these reached the number one position, and five ranked as high as second. Almost all of the major book lines were represented.

Sexually Oriented Hard-Cover Books An indication of the interest in sexually oriented hard-cover books can be projected from the fact that two of the top ten best selling fiction titles of 1968 were regarded in the trade as "sexy books." In 1969, six of the top ten fiction best selling hard-cover books and eight of the top twenty were regarded by the industry as sexually oriented. During 1968 and 1969, none of the top ten nonfiction best sellers were related to sex.

As of June, 1970, the market has yet to produce a sexually oriented best seller in hard-cover fiction, but three of the top four nonfiction best sellers relate to sex.

Newspapers The Panel made no attempt to investigate the sexual content of daily newspapers. Most newspapers,

111

however, reflect a somewhat increased candor in articles and news stories relating to sexual matters.

The sexual content of one genre of newspaper, the so-called "underground press," has been the subject of considerable comment. Although underground newspapers are primarily political in nature, quite a few devote considerable space to sexual topics as well—especially in classified advertisements. It has been estimated that there are 200 such newspapers in the United States with a readership of 6,000,000 persons per week. The accuracy of such claims, however, is open to question. Sales figures were available for only five selected newspapers and indicated average weekly sales of over 200,000 and yearly sales of 10.5 million in 1969. These five newspapers are the best known in the field.

THE SECONDARY OR "ADULTS ONLY" MARKET

Self-labeled "adults only" printed materials are of far less economic importance than are mass market publications. For example, the combined copy sales of all "adult only" magazines in a year are less than one month's sales of Reader's Digest. Separate "secondary" channels of national and local wholesale distribution, and local retail sales, have been created for this "adults only" market. However, there is an overlap of sexually oriented materials between the mass and the "adult" markets; some publishers produce materials for both, and many other publishers constantly seek to expand distribution of their "secondary" product into the mass market.

There are 80 to 100 publishers producing primarily for the secondary market, of whom approximately 20 to 30 are important factors. Most are located either in California or the New York City area, although three or four important publishers are located in other states.

SEXUAL CONTENT OF "ADULTS ONLY" PAPERBACK BOOKS

"Sex Pulp" Books Until the Late 1960s   The sexual content of paperback books published for the "adults only" market has become progressively "stronger" in the past decade, primarily because of court decisions involving books such as Tropic of Cancer and Fanny Hill (See Legal Panel Report).

Until the mid-1960s, most paperback books published for the secondary market were known as "sex pulps." These followed a rather rigid set of ground rules: vulgar terms describ-

112

ing sexual acts, genitalia, excretion, etc., were not used, but rather euphemistic or symbolic language was substituted; the books consisted of a series of sexual adventures tied together by a minimal plot; sexual foreplay was described in great detail, but the mechanics of the sex act was not; and much of the sexual content was left to the imagination of the reader.

By the late 1960s, however, the "sex pulp" formula had become relatively passe. A new breed of sexually oriented secondary books came onto the market, in which all restraints upon both language and descriptions of sexual activity were eliminated. In many there was little pretense of a story line; many books were little more than a compilation of non-stop sexual activity.

Some paperback novels of the "sex pulp" type of the early 1960s are still published, probably because a portion of the market prefers less explicit material. However, the industry's criteria for "sex pulp" books has been broadened; this classification now includes any paperback which is badly written, edited, and typeset, and is apparently aimed at relatively poorly educated readers, irrespective of the degree of explicitness of its language or descriptions of sexual activity.

Wholly Textual Sex Oriented Paperback Books in the Secondary Market, 1969-1970 Virtually every English language book thought to be obscene when published, and many similar books translated into English, have been reissued by secondary publishers. The entire stockpile of "classic erotic literature" (e.g., The Kama Sutra, Frank Harris, De Sade, etc.) published over centuries has thus come onto the market. Another type of sexually oriented book has become popular in the last few years—pseudo-medical, alleged case-study analysis of sexual activity. Although such books purport to be written by medical doctors or Ph.D.s, they primarily consist of graphic descriptions of sexual activity.

As of 1970, publishers of sex-oriented, wholly textual paperback books are convinced that there are no legal restrictions on the content of any wholly textual publication. As a result, "adults only" paperback books published and sold in the United States cannot possibly be exceeded in candor, graphic description of sexual activity or use of explicit language. The overwhelming majority of these books are intended for a heterosexual male readership. Almost no such books are written for a female audience. Perhaps 10% or more are directed at the male homosexual market, and less

113

than 5% are specifically written for any of the various fetishes.

Illustrated Paperback Books, 1969-1970 In the past two or three years, some secondary publishers have included photographs in their books. Initially, such paperbacks included photographs in which young females posed with the focus of the camera directly upon their genitalia. In 1968 and 1969, however, two additional types came onto the market which revolutionized the sexual content of illustrated paperback books. One was the illustrated "marriage manual" containing photographs of couples engaging in sexual intercourse "for an educational purpose." The most recent marriage manual of this type depicts fellatio and cunnilingus in addition to vaginal intercourse (penetration shown in detail). The second "breakthrough" occurred in 1969 with the publication of books purporting to be serious studies of censorship and pornography. These books contain illustrations ranging from Oriental and European erotic art to reproductions of "hard-core" photographs taken from Danish magazines, which graphically depict sex activities such as vaginal and anal penetration, fellatio, and cunnilingus. Following this lead, a number of publications containing "hard-core" photographs with textual commentary have been published and are in circulation in many major metropolitan areas.

To some extent, therefore, the pictorial content of a number of paperbacks published and sold in the United States has reached the level of sexual explicitness found in Danish materials. However, Danish-type "pornographic" magazines (consisting entirely of photographs of sexual activity) have yet to be published and sold openly in this country; domestic publishers apparently believe that the inclusion of text is required to provide a legal defense in the event of an obscenity prosecution.

Production Costs of "Adults Only" Paperback Books Printing secondary paperbacks is relatively expensive because press runs are normally rather small. Press runs for mass market paperback books were seldom below 100,000 during 1969 and 1970, but very few secondary publishers had initial press runs as high as 40,000, and most did not exceed 15,000 or 20,000. Thus, initial costs (type-setting, art work for the cover, press make-ready, etc.) are apportioned over many fewer copies, and unit costs are significantly higher. Costs vary considerably, depending on the length of the book,

114

the size of the press run, the cost of the manuscript (free for "classics"), etc. Most secondary paperbacks cost between $.10 and $.20 per copy to produce (not including company overhead), but per unit costs may run as high as $.30 to $.40 for small press runs of large books with considerable art work and a high manuscript cost.

Secondary publishers usually recover only 40% to 50% of the cover price for every copy of a new title sold. To compensate for increasing unit costs and declining sales, the average cover price of secondary paperback books rose steadily during 1969-1970; typical prices now range from $1.50 to $2.25 and even $3.00. Some prices are considerably higher; at least one secondary paperback had a cover price of $20.00.

For the most part, 1969 and 1970 have been poor years for secondary book publishers. A serious oversupply of materials reduced profits for all but the most successful. Quite a number of large publishers experienced serious financial difficulty, and a few went bankrupt. Some survived only by "dumping" unsold copies on the "remainder" market.

SEXUAL CONTENT OF "ADULTS ONLY" MAGAZINES

"Adult" Magazines Until the Late 1960s Court decisions overruling obscenity convictions of sexually oriented magazines have affected the market almost as profoundly as similar court decisions dealing with textual material. In 1958, the Supreme Court reversed an obscenity conviction involving two nudist magazines containing pictures clearly revealing the genitalia of men, women, and children. During the early 1960s, nudist magazines slowly broke down the practice of segregating the sexes in photographs which had been observed earlier. Publishers remained very restrained about the situations portrayed in the photos. Any scene implying sexual activity was scrupulously avoided, and body contact was allowed only in situations of a wholly non-sexual nature. Nudist magazines of the early 1960s contained numerous articles extolling nudism and portrayed nudists only at work and play.

By the mid-1960s, secondary publishers had become much bolder in pictorial nudity. Implied erotic activity became an integral part of pseudo-nudist magazines. The so-called "legitimate" nudist magazines, which attempted to reproduce candid shots of nudist camp activities, passed into oblivion because they could not compete in the marketplace with magazines which copied the nudist format, but contained more erotic pictures and more attractive models. By 1967 or 1968, a whole new group of magazines featured nude females posed in a manner which emphasized their genitalia in complete detail (known in the industry as "spreader" or "split beaver" magazines). Most contained little, if any, text.

At the same time, male homosexual magazines developed along the same lines, also assisted by favorable Supreme Court decisions which overturned previous obscenity convictions. Homosexual magazines through the late 1960s consisted primarily of posed pictures of nude males. The genitals of the models, the focal points of the photographs, were flaccid. Photographs were usually of a single model, although group scenes were not unusual. There was little or no physical contact between models, and sexual activity was generally not even implied.

Relatively small quantities of fetish books and magazines were produced featuring uses of items such as rubber and leather wearing apparel, lingerie, high heeled boots, etc. Sadomasochistic depictions or descriptions of bondage, spanking, and "domination" by clubs, whips, etc. were also available in limited quantities. Sexual explicitness in these materials was usually far less than in typical "girlie" magazines. Although quite a number of titles were produced, these magazines were not a major factor in the marketplace.

Sexual Content of "Adult" Magazines—1969-1970 Through June, 1970, there have been few dramatic innovations in the sexual content of "adults only" magazines. Additional female models have been added to the photographs, and many magazines have integrated male and female models. This has led to considerable implied sexual activity in the photographs. Actual sexual activity, or arousal of the male models is seldom depicted.

Magazines aimed at male homosexuals have changed somewhat in the last year or two, and self-imposed restrictions on implied sexual activity are eroding slowly. Most homosexual magazines, however, are considerably less graphic than magazines featuring females.

Fetish magazines continue to be a rather insignificant part of the total production, and have changed relatively little from the mid-1960s.

Production Costs of "Adults Only" Magazines Magazines are considerably more expensive to produce than paperback books. A much higher quality paper is required to reproduce

116

photographs, and color reproduction is mandatory to some degree. The "package" cost of a magazine, which includes model and photography fees, type setting, etc., usually ranges from $1,000 to $4,000 per issue. Some "adult" magazines contain only 24 pages, although 32 pages is usually the minimum, and some are as long as 96 pages. Press runs tend to be very small, even when compared to secondary paperbacks. Few publishers had press runs as high as 25,000 in 1969, and most limited production to 10,000 or 15,000. A few reduced their production to as low as 6,000 to 8,000 per title.

Secondary magazines may cost as little as $.30 per copy to produce, but often unit costs are as high as $.60-$.65 because of low press runs, expensive production costs and a liberal use of color photographs.

DISTRIBUTION OF "ADULTS ONLY" PUBLICATIONS

Publishers Almost all secondary publishers act as their own national distributors. As a result, the distribution pattern of "adults only" magazines and paperback books is chaotic. Many secondary publishers deal directly with retailers if a wholesaler is not available in a territory or will not handle the publications. Another method of distributing the product is through mail-order (either directly by the publisher or by supplying other mailers). Finally, merchandise which does not sell on its initial introduction to the market is often sold on the "remainder" market, where buyers purchase materials at large discounts and are not given return privileges.

I.D. Wholesale Distribution An undetermined number of I.D. wholesalers distribute some "adults only" materials to selected customers. Those who do normally limit themselves to paperbacks and, on occasion, some of the "milder" secondary magazines. Rarely do they distribute the most graphic materials. This refusal to deal in "strong" material is undoubtedly a combination of personal taste, fear of adverse publicity, or fear of prosecution, depending on the individual.

Secondary Wholesale Distributors Because most I.D. wholesalers refuse to distribute "adults only" material, several individuals have seized the opportunity to distribute this material to retail outlets. These wholesalers are known as "secondaries" because they distribute few, if any, mass market publications. Sex-oriented material comprises 80% or more of their stock, and a majority handle sex-oriented publications almost exclusively. The inability of secondary distributors to obtain mass market publications means that such wholesalers are relatively small-time operators.

The chief distinction in the manner of doing business between secondary wholesalers and I.D. wholesalers is that the former deal directly with publishers. Orders are placed with, and returns are made directly to the publishers. Publications are normally shipped on a fully returnable (consignment) basis, although outright purchase of previously unsold publications are increasingly important. Ordinarily, new titles are automatically shipped in a fixed quantity to secondary distributors, who then apportion the new titles to retail accounts and, after a certain time (usually between one and four weeks), pick up unsold merchandise. These "returns" are then shipped back to the publisher for credit to the distributor's account.

Because of the extensive overproduction of new titles in 1969, shelf life for most publications was extremely short. If a paperback book or magazine failed to sell almost immediately after its introduction, it would be withdrawn from display within a week or two. Publishers and secondary distributors interviewed stated that the average exposure of a new title (either paperbacks or magazines) seldom exceeded three or four weeks during 1969.

New titles are usually billed to secondary distributors for 50% or less of the cover price. One popular distributor's rate used extensively during 1969 was 50% off the cover price plus 10% off for cash payment within 30, 60, or 90 days (55% discount). The secondary wholesaler distributes his materials to retailers for approximately 60% of the cover price (a 33% mark-up). In comparison, discounts for mass market publications are approximately 30% to 40% on periodicals and 40% to 46% on paperbacks to the wholesaler. Discounts to retailers on periodicals are 20% to 30% and on paperbacks are 20% to 36%.

The Panel, through a variety of sources, gathered a list of the important secondary distributors in the United States as of Fall, 1969. The 60 secondaries on the list service from 12 to over 300 accounts each. In addition, information sources report that there are probably an equal number of book store owners who act as secondary distributors in their localities. In both New York and California, there are four or more relatively large secondary wholesalers and a number of smaller ones. Twelve states have two, 13 have one, and

25 states do not have any secondary distributors. This is in stark contrast to the mass market distribution system where virtually every locality in the United States is served by an I.D. wholesaler.

Most of the secondary distributors interviewed stated that their profits provide only "a living," and that most of the money in the "adults only" market goes to publishers and retailers. Secondary distributors interviewed were very reluctant to discuss either gross sales or profits in detail. A 1967 survey in California (Lynch and O'Brien, 1967) stated that a large secondary distributor made gross sales of more than $150,000 a year, with profits ranging from $7,500 to $22,500 per year.

One of the Commission's contractors obtained an estimate from a wholesaler that he made a 20% gross profit before expenses on all materials he sold to retailers, and that his annual gross sales were approximately $700,000 (Nawy, 1970). This is consistent with the reports received from other wholesalers (Finkelstein, 1970a; Massey, 1970), and with the estimates made for California distributors in 1967. The average wholesaler's mark-up to retailers ranges between 20% and 40%, and only those few who do a volume business are likely to make substantial profits.

"Junk" Dealers and Discount Houses Secondary whole-sale distributors are facing increasing competition from two sources: "junk dealers" and the discount houses. Both deal in "remainders" which are almost never dated, and thus are often indistinguishable from new titles. A "junk dealer" operates from a car or pick-up truck and visits individual retail outlets. He carries a variety of remainder publications which he offers for sale at greatly reduced prices (50% or 60% discount) on a "no-return" basis. Junk dealers are not an important factor in the business since their operations are sporadic and unsystematized. Discount houses, also known as "remainder houses," operate on a volume basis, selling paperback books and magazines on a no-return basis after purchasing them from the original publisher. Some publishers "remainder" their own publications. Because of high volume, a discount house offers discounts as high as 75% to 90%. Indeed, many publications have recently been offered on the market at prices below the original printing cost.

Retail Outlets The final step in the distribution of secondary books and magazines is the retail outlet. Self-labeled "adults only" bookstores are the keystone in the distribution of secondary materials at the present time. Several methods of selling secondary books and magazines are used today.

"Adult" Bookstores. These retail outlets handling the materials under discussion are devoted exclusively to sexually oriented material, are usually self-labeled as "for adults only," and access to the store is actually restricted to adults. Nationwide, the most common age minimum for entrance into such stores seems to be 21, although in numerous communities those 18 and over are permitted to enter.

Stores with a Special "Adult" Section. An even larger number of stores carry a wide range of reading matter, including mass market periodicals and paperback books, and provide a segregated area for secondary materials. This type of retail outlet usually restricts access to the special secondary publications section to "adults only."

Unsegregated "Adult" Materials. Some stores do not segregate secondary materials from mass market publications and usually do not restrict access to the materials to adults, although some limit sales of secondary materials to adults.

Retail outlets displaying and selling "adults only" materials tend to be located in downtown or central city areas. Areas of a city which contain bars featuring live entertainment tend to attract retail outlets selling secondary materials. However, not all "adults only" stores are limited to the central city in decaying downtown areas; a few are found in suburban shopping centers, near colleges, etc.

Most self-labeled "adults only" bookstores are open for 12 to 14 hours per day, at least six days a week. The interiors vary considerably, but the majority are rather seedy. However, a substantial number are as well-kept as the average bookstore, and a few might even be described as "fancy."

The primary products of "adults only" bookstores are secondary paperback books and magazines. Some stores may display as few as 200 or 300 paperback book titles, others as many as 1,000 titles. With few exceptions, paperback books are displayed on racks in the same fashion as in drug stores or conventional bookstores, and browsing is permitted. Most paperbacks have a cover price printed on the book, and are rarely sold above this price. However, the "hottest" paperbacks, especially the illustrated books containing graphic photographs of sexual activity, are sometimes marked up over the cover price (as much as twice the normal price). In addition, there is often a special rack for "sale" items. An adult bookstore may display anywhere from 100 or 200 to as many as 500 or more separate magazine titles. Prices are often increased over the publishers intended cover price by use of stickers, even on magazines which have a price printed on the cover. Many, and perhaps a majority of the "adults only" stores prohibit browsing in magazines by enclosing them in sealed plastic bags.

"Adults only" retail outlets also occasionally display a limited number of hard-cover books which are priced considerably higher than most (e.g., $15) and constitute a very small percentage of the total sales of retail outlets. Many bookstores also sell a wide range of other sexually oriented materials, including 8mm home movie films (usually priced at $15 and $25), sexual devices (such as artificial vaginas and dildoes), a variety of lotions and potions, allegedly designed to improve sexual prowess, and miscellaneous items such as whips and chains, plastic life-size female dolls, etc.

The most important sideline, economically, for many self-labeled adult bookstores is arcade movie machines, also known as "peepshows."[5] Customers pay $.25 to view three or four minutes of an erotic 8mm movie. To view the entire reel, a customer is required to spend between $1 and $2. These "peepshows" usually depict fully nude females exposing their genitals, and many depict sexual foreplay between couples (sometimes male-female, sometimes female-female). This business apparently is an extremely lucrative one. Receipts from such operations are alleged to exceed the return from sales of books and magazines in many stores. A further advantage of a "peepshow" operation is that the cash receipts are not recorded in a systematic manner.

Number of "Adults only" Retail Outlets in the United States According to a survey conducted for the Panel,[6] the following approximate figures can be projected for the total secondary outlets in the United States as of Spring, 1970.

1. There are 850 self-labeled "adults only" bookstores selling secondary books and magazines, over half of which sell only those materials, and a quarter of which sell other sex-related products;

2. An additional 1,425 retail outlets provide a special restricted access section for "adult" material in addition to selling other products, primarily mass market publications, but also liquor and cigars, in a nonrestricted access area;

3. Approximately 175 self-labeled adult bookstores, or

stores with a special adult section, operate arcade-type movie machines; and

4. The majority of both self-labeled bookstores and stores with an "adults only" section are located in metropolitan areas of 500,000 or more.

If these projections are accurate, less than 2% of all retail outlets for books and magazines in the United States sell "adults only" materials.

A separate study (Sampson, 1970) was initiated to determine the number of such outlets in the 30 major cities of the United States (central cities in metropolitan areas of over one million population). This survey revealed that, as of Spring, 1970, approximately 420 self-labeled "adults only" bookstores were operating in the central cities of the 30 major metropolitan centers. Information relating to retail outlets containing a special "adult" section was fragmentary, but about 400 such outlets were reported in 20 of the 30 cities (the majority of which were located in the Los Angeles area). An additional 130 outlets sold secondary materials on an unsegregated basis.

SALES AND PROFITABILITY

Most publishers, distributors, and retailers engaged in the "adults only" or secondary market interviewed by the Commission Staff stated that the average retail store had daily gross sales of approximately $300, although estimates ranged from $200 to $500. Some allegedly had gross retail sales of $100,000 or more in 1969. A conservative estimate of yearly gross sales for the average "adults only" store of $60,000 to $75,000 per store seems warranted. Although sales in retail outlets which do not deal solely in sexually oriented adult material are difficult to estimate, industry sources estimate that most outlets selling both mass market and secondary publications expect to average at least $200 per day from sales of adult materials.

TOTAL RETAIL SALES OF SECONDARY MATERIALS

Total sales of secondary materials can be estimated by projecting average gross sales of "adults only" bookstores and other outlets for secondary material. There are perhaps 850 exclusively "adults only" bookstores in the United States. If average retail sales during 1969 in each store were $60,000 to $75,000, the minimum suggested by three studies of such

122

outlets, sales in all such stores totaled between $51 and $64 million. It must be noted that although the bulk of the sales in such stores are books and magazines, "they also sell home movies, sex devices, etc., and a number have arcade movie machines. Sales of these items accounted for a substantial percentage of the total store revenue. The proportion of total sales of secondary materials sold by "adults only" bookstores as opposed to sales in the approximately 1,425 stores with "adult" sections, and in stores displaying secondary materials which are segregated, can only be estimated. The best estimate, based on available information, is that sales in these other outlets are between 50% and 100% of sales made in "adults only" stores.

One further important study on the gross sales of the secondary industry is still being completed. The Internal Revenue Service has studied the income tax returns of 20 of the largest secondary publishers for the tax year 1968, the last available year. Almost all of the largest publishers in the industry were included. Their gross receipts reported for 1968 were slightly less than $21 million; net profits were less than $500,000.

The Panel attempted to estimate the sales volume in secondary materials in various other ways.

One source estimated that retail sales of "genital-oriented magazines" totaled $30 to $35 million in 1969, and that retail sales of secondary paperback books totaled $25 to $30 million; retail sales of the secondary industry are thus placed at between $55 and $65 million (Magazine Industry Newsletter, 1969).

Twenty of the top 30 publishers of secondary materials were interviewed. They disclosed that they published at least 200 new titles of paperbacks per month during most of 1969. Press runs at the time of the interviews (Summer-Fall, 1969) ranged from 10,000 to 50,000 copies per title, averaging 15,000 to 20,000. Subsequent discussions with many of these publishers indicated that press runs fell steadily during 1969. Based on these interviews, between 30 and 35 million paperbacks were produced by these publishers during 1969. Most publishers stated that paperback sales per title ran between 40% and 50% of production, with 45% a "reasonable average sale" per title. The average cover price was probably $1.75 to $2.00. Publishers interviewed thus claimed about 13.5 to 15.75 million copies sold, using the 45% rate; retail sales would then range from $28 to $32 million. Assuming a 40% rate, 12 to 14 million copies were sold with receipts in the vicinity of $21 to $28 million. These figures should be increased to account for the entire industry. Thus, the Panel estimates that the industry, at a maximum, sold 25 to 30 million paperbacks in 1969; retail sales volume would then be approximately $45 to $55 million.

Most of the major magazine publishers interviewed stated that they were producing almost 100 new magazine titles per month in 1969. The average press runs for these magazines probably did not exceed 12,000 copies, and ranged from 8,000 to 25,000 copies per issue. Subsequent discussions with publishers revealed that an oversupplied market caused press runs to decline during 1969. Sales of magazines were estimated by most publishers to range between 50% and 70% of the 1969 total of 12 million copies. If sales averaged 50% to 60%, a total of six to eight million copies were sold. Cover prices for magazines averaged at least $3.00, and possibly $4.00 per copy. These publications generated total retail sales of $18 to $32 million in 1969.

In order to particularize further the total volume of production of secondary materials, assistance was sought from the American Publishers and Distributors Association (APDA), the embryonic trade association of secondary publishers. In a survey conducted by an attorney from Los Angeles (Laven, 1970), 40 of approximately 80 publisher-distributors replied to a questionnaire sent under the auspices of the APDA. Summarized totals of these responses were supplied to the Panel as follows:

TABLE 5

Secondary Material (in units)

	Magazines	Paperback Books
Titles per year	1,000	2,750
Average press run	12,000	14,000
Total press run	12,000,000	38,500,000
Average sales per title	8,200	7,800
Total sales	8,400,000	21,450,000
Total remainder sales	2,000,000	12,000,000

The attorney estimated that responses to the questionnaire accounted for approximately 50% of the total production of the industry. He suggested the above figures be doubled to achieve an accurate account of the total production of the industry. It seems likely, however, that the magazine publishers reporting do well over 50% of the total. It is conceiv-

124

able that sales figures were somewhat exaggerated by the responding publishers. If the results of this survey are projected as suggested, industry gross annual retail sales ranged between $125 and $150 million in 1969.

An overall appraisal of the total retail volume of secondary materials can be made by combining all these estimates. The Panel believes the most reasonable estimate which can be made is that 60 to 70 million copies of secondary paperback books were published in 1969, 25 to 30 million were sold, and total retail sales were between $45 and $55 million. Magazine sales accounted for perhaps $25 to $35 million. The entire secondary publication market thus had retail sales of between $70 and $90 million in 1969. It is probable that actual gross retail sales of the secondary market were closer to the lower figure.

Section C. Mail-Order Erotica

According to the President's Commission on Postal Organization (1968), the American public annually receives over 21 billion pieces of mail which advertise products and solicit purchases. While the vast majority of direct mail advertisers are involved in conventional business operations a small percentage of these operators use the mails to advertise sexually oriented materials. In contrast to the other media examined by this Report, the advertising and sale of sexually oriented material through the mails is, for the most part, not distributed along a continuum from "mild" to more explicit material, and does not involve producers in both a mass market selling and a group of smaller, secondary producers. Instead a well-defined dividing line exists between those who advertise and sell such merchandise and those who do not.

MATERIALS FOR SALE

Mail-order operators offer a wide variety of sexually oriented materials for sale and cater to almost every conceivable taste. The most widely advertised items are heterosexually oriented magazines, books (both paperback and hardcover), 8mm movies, and sexual devices. There is also a substantial amount of material available for male homosexual

125

customers, and a relatively small amount designed for a wide range of fetishists and sadomasochists.

Magazines, which have a publication cost of between $.30 and $.70 (for full color), are usually sold in the $2.00–$5.00 price range, although prices range as high as $10.00. Paperback books are produced for between $.10 and $.40 per copy on an average, and are usually sold for $2.00 to $5.00, although prices of $7.50 to $10.00 are not unusual, and have been noted as high as $20.00. Hard-cover books, which are rather widely advertised through the mails, cost $.75 to $2.00 to produce, and usually sell for $5.00 to $15.00. The sexual content of these publications is either identical with or very similar to those produced for and sold in the secondary or "adults only" market at retail.

"Home movie" films are substantial items in mail-order erotica, although they generate considerably fewer sales than do books. Production costs average between $1.00 and $2.00 for black and white films and $2.00–$4.00 for color, and typically sell for $15.00 to $25.00 (b/w) and $20 to $40 (color). Mail-order film advertisers almost always advertise photographs as well, usually in the $5–$10 range. The vast majority of 8mm films are heterosexually oriented, and depict nude females (one or more) and often men and women (two or more) in a wide variety of erotic settings. In addition, a small number of films are produced for male homosexuals depicting one or more nude males; few films are produced which are intended to appeal to fetishists and sadomasochists.

Sexual devices are also advertised extensively, primarily artificial male and female genitals. These are usually advertised together with a variety of pseudo-medical elixirs and lotions which claim to improve sexual prowess or delay sexual climax. The devices are very inexpensive to produce (the usual cost is less than $1.00 or $2.00) and ordinarily command prices from $10.00 to $25.00 or higher. The patent medicines cost very little to produce, and command prices of $3.00 to $10.00 on the average.

In addition, "swingers" clubs (advertising for sexual partners) and fetish materials, such as chains, belts and leather wearing apparel, are also advertised through the mails. These account for a very small percentage of mail-order advertising and are not an important factor in the market.

While the mark-up on all sexually oriented materials sold through mail-order advertising is relatively high—probably higher than for related non-sex items sold by mail order—the cost of goods sold is usually a relatively minor factor in the cost of doing business. The cost of direct mail advertising is many times the cost of the item sold.

Some individuals advertising mail-order erotica operate fraudulently, promising the purchaser much more than he will actually receive. These are known as "scam operators" in the trade. The advertisements are designed to entice, but the materials themselves are hardly what the purchaser expects. This type of operation has markedly declined in the past two years.

THE ADVERTISING PROCESS

Sellers of sexually oriented materials use both space advertising and direct mail to promote their wares. Space advertising often uses coupons to solicit orders and/or inquiries, but its major purpose is not so much to sell goods, always a welcome result, as to collect names of interested potential buyers who can be solicited for further sales by direct mail advertising.

Direct mail efforts can be put into three classifications:

1. Solicited—that is, mailings to names of people who have made a specific request.

2. Semi-unsolicited—that is, mailings to names of people who have previously responded to space or direct mail advertising, either from the mailer or from some other mailer whose list has been rented or traded.

3. Unsolicited—that is, mailings to names of people with no known record of having made previous responses to space or direct mail advertising in the hope of culling out new customer names.

The basic ingredient of direct mail advertising is the mailing list. Mailers constantly strive to enlarge and update lists to increase the possibility of future sales. Advertising in magazines or newspapers which are likely to appeal to the potential customer are a popular (and expensive) source of new names. The cost of advertising in nationally distributed magazines of the type preferred for such ads is such that the advertising is not usually an immediate money-maker. However, the list of potential customers obtained can prove to be extremely valuable for future sales.

After a mailing list is established, it is used not only to advertise the mailer's products, but is also rented to other mailers for a fee. Before a complete list is rented, a test mailing is usually made to determine whether the use of the entire list will prove profitable. Similarly, lists are often traded by

127

mailers. These procedures are a popular method of expanding sales. The name of any individual making a purchase from a mailer who has traded or rented a list becomes his "property" and is added to his customer list for future solicitations.

Ordinarily, neither rental nor a trade of mailing lists results in an actual exchange of lists. Arrangements are made to have brochures sent to those on a list without the list-owner losing control. The security of mailing lists is very important. Many mailers do not allow lists out of their custody: often when a list is rented or traded, the owner insists that a reputable mailing service process the advertising to insure the list is not "stolen" (i.e., copied).

List brokers collate a number of small lists onto master sheets (15,000 is usually the minimum number of names on such a list), and rent them. A few such brokers are primarily in the business of list rental, and often have dozens of lists available. The lists often are segregated by type of interest, i.e., heterosexual books, home movies, sexual devices, homosexual and fetish materials, etc.

In the conventional mail-order industry, list rental fees sometimes are as low as $5 or $6 per 1,000 names, although fees for many lists are considerably higher. Fees for rental of a sexually oriented list ordinarily begin at $20 or $25 per 1,000 names, and fees for a "golden list" (proven purchasers) may be as high as $100 per 1,000 names.

The total number of names on sexually oriented lists is impossible to estimate because of substantial duplication (a regular purchaser of erotica may be on any number of lists). Most industry sources claim that present mailing lists contain two to three million names of those who have either purchased or inquired about sexually oriented material in the past two or three years, and some of those in the industry claim much higher figures (i.e., eight to ten million). It is probable that even the most conservative estimate from the industry (two million names) is an exaggeration.

MAILING COSTS

The cost of direct mail advertising varies greatly, depending on a number of factors. Out-of-pocket costs include brochures, outer envelopes, return envelopes, addressing, brochure insertion, postage, and list rental. The amount expended for each, except for postage (which is almost invariably first class), varies considerably depending on the quantity and the quality of the advertising.

128

If a mailer spends the least amount possible for each variable cost factor, and uses his own mailing list, the minimum direct cost is about $100 per 1,000 letters, or $.10 per piece. The average cost of mailing is about $.12 or $.13 per letter. Two of the largest direct mailers in the United States (not in the sexual product industry) made a cost analysis of several typical sexually oriented advertisements for the Panel. Advertisements which had generated a large volume of complaints to the Post Office were included. The most expensive mailing analyzed was estimated to cost $184 per 1,000 for a volume of 10,000 letters ($.184 each); the least expensive would have cost $116 per 1,000 on distribution of 1,000,000 letters ($.116 each).

PERCENTAGE OF RESPONSE

Mail-order operators do not measure their success by the percentage of response to their advertisements; instead, they divide incoming receipts by the total number of letters mailed, arriving at a figure known as a "per letter return." For example, a 2½% sales response on an advertisement for a $10.00 item and a 1% sales response on a $25.00 item both yield $250.00 for each 1,000 letters mailed, or $.25 per letter.

Books and magazines are generally the lowest-priced sexually oriented materials sold in any quantity through the mail. If the average purchase is only $2 or $3, the percentage of response must be exceptionally high (on the order of 5%—10%, which is virtually unattainable) to realize a profit. Therefore, many major mailers of advertisements for books do not advertise books selling for less than $10. This allows the mailer to make a profit on a response rate of 2% or less ($.20 per letter or $200 per 1,000).

There is considerable variation in the response rate to advertisements for 8mm movies, depending on factors such as the time of year, the "appeal" of the items for sale and the competition at the time of the mailing. Home movies are priced considerably higher than books (the minimum purchase is usually $15 to $25), and a lower rate of response can be profitable. For example, a 1% response will return $.15 to $.20 per letter, considered to be the minimum break-even point. Responses vary between $.10 and $1.75 per letter: as of mid-1969, most mailers claimed a $.50 per letter average return on mailings to known film buyers.

Although the response rate for sexual devices, potions, etc. is probably as low as for home movies, prices for these products can produce a profit with as low as a 1% response with a return of $.15 to $.25 per letter.

HYPOTHETICAL MAIL-ORDER OPERATION

Table 6 presents a hypothetical example of a mail-order dealer selling sexually oriented materials (in this instance, books).

The mailer advertises a "high-quality" illustrated marriage manual for sale through the mails at $10 per copy. The cost of the book to the mailer may be as low as $.25 to $.40, or as high as $.60 to $.70, depending on the quantity printed, the cost of the manuscript, royalty payments (if any), and the overall technical quality. Assume, for ease of computation, that the book delivered to the customer costs the mailer $1.00. Each month 500,000 advertisements are mailed at a cost of $.12 per letter (including postage, brochures, envelopes, list rental, etc.). A 2% ($.20 per letter) response leads to the following results:

TABLE 6

Hypothetical Mail-Order Operator I

Mailing Cost (500,000 letters @ 12¢)	$60,000
Cost of Goods Sold (10,000 books @ $1)	10,000
Overhead	10,000
Total Expenses	80,000
Gross Receipts (100,000 books @ $10)	100,000
Profit	+$20,000

HYPOTHETICAL MAIL-ORDER OPERATION I

If this level of response is maintained, a substantial income can be generated. If the response rate drops to 1.5% ($.15 per letter), however, the business becomes unprofitable:

TABLE 7

Hypothetical Mail-Order Operator II

Mailing Cost (500,000 letters @ 12¢)	$60,000
Cost of Goods Sold (7,500 books @ $1)	7,500
Overhead	10,000
Total Expenses	77,500
Gross Receipts (7,500 books @ $10)	75,000
Loss	−$ 2,500

Advertising and selling sexually oriented materials by mail order is subject to the same economic rules as any mail-order operation. Mail-order selling can be profitable, but it is an expensive way to reach potential customers. As a matter of fact, the projected 1.5% to 2% response above does not differ greatly from responses to mail-order advertising of more conventional books and magazines. Although there is a profit to be made, mail-order erotica is certainly a tenuous business. Stories to the effect that vast fortunes have been made almost overnight are apocryphal for the most part. Even the "giants" of the industry are relatively small-time operators. Of course, sales of $1 and $2 million yearly and gross yearly incomes of $200,000 are substantial when viewed from the standpoint of the average citizen. However, businesses with such levels of sales and income can hardly be viewed as major economic forces. Most mailers content themselves with a better-than-average "living," rather than with vast riches.

Number and Location of Mailers

It is difficult to estimate the number of such businesses; the market offers easy and inexpensive entry and therefore is in a constant state of flux. Compounding the difficulty in making an exact count of the mailers is the business practice of many to change the business name of the operation (known as "d/b/a," or doing/business/as) very frequently. There are, however, at least several hundred individuals or firms dealing in mail-order erotica at present, most of whom are located in the New York City and Los Angeles area (including all of the largest mailers). Approximately 85% of all sexually oriented advertising originates from these two locations, and nearly 99% of the advertising causing public complaints has had a California or New York return adddress.

Public Complaints about Sexually Oriented Advertising

Prior to April, 1968, the only recourse for the recipient of "objectionable" mail was to complain to the Post Office, which, in turn, investigated with the object of initiating prosecution if the material was legally obscene. On April 14, 1968, the Anti-Pandering Act (39 U.S.C. 4009) went into effect, which provides offended recipients of advertising a legal recourse. Requests can be made to the Postmaster General to "issue an order ... directing the sender and his agents to refrain from further mailings to the addressee." A parent or guardian may also request a prohibitory order on behalf of a child or ward under the age of 19 who resides with him. Under the act, the mailer must delete the name(s) of the addressee(s) from all his mailing lists, and he is forbidden to rent or trade the list unless the appropriate deletions have been made. Failure to comply results in a federal court order to do so and failure to obey the court order can result in a contempt of court citation.[7]

If the intent of the Anti-Pandering Act was to reduce the volume of sexually oriented mail, to date the law has been a failure. All those interviewed agree the volume of such advertising increased in 1968-1969, although it was not possible to measure the reported increase. It is certain that the volume of sex-oriented advertising has not visibly decreased. More complaints were made to the Post Office in 1969 than during any year before the enactment of the law. This may be accounted for, at least in part, by the fact that for the first time the law provided a postive means of redress for offended citizens. Incidental effects of the law have been to increase the costs of doing business in sexually oriented advertising and the costs incurred by the Post Office.

The Post Office supplied the following data for its experience under the Anti-Pandering Act, April 14, 1968 to June 30, 1970:

TABLE 8

Prohibitory Order Data

Requests for Prohibitory Order	467,516
Prohibitory Orders Issued	381,559
Violation Cases Sent to Justice Department	3,806
Court Orders Directing Compliance with Prohibitory Orders	295

PROHIBITORY ORDER SURVEY

In fiscal 1969, a record of 235,000 complaints were received by the Post Office (182,000 of which resulted in prohibitory orders). The previous record was set in 1966 when slightly less than 200,000 complaints were made. For the time period April, 1968 through December, 1969, an

132

examination of several thousand prohibitory orders was made by the Commission Staff in order to establish the mailers being complained against, and a random sample of orders was taken at 12 of the 64 Postal Service Centers in the country (Charlotte, N.C.; Chicago; Dallas; Houston; Indianapolis; Kansas City; Los Angeles; Nashville; New York; Phoenix; San Francisco; and Washington, D.C.). This sampling disclosed that:

1. Prohibitory orders had been issued against nearly 400 separate business firm names mailing sexually oriented materials; orders were also issued against dozens of business firms advertising nonsexual products.

2. Seventeen mailers, using one or more business firm names, were each responsible for 75%-80% of all prohibitory orders issued (ranging from 1% to over 27% of the total sampled). Of this number, five mailers were responsible for 62% of all orders issued and two of these mailers accounted for over 40% of the total.

3. The major offending mailers sent their advertising on a "nationwide basis," and generated complaints in every Postal Service Center sampled.

4. Measured by the population served, there was a discernible relationship between geographic regions and the number of orders issued by the Postal Centers. Citizens residing in the Western United States caused nearly twice as many prohibitory orders to be issued on their behalf as did residents of the South. Probably mailers have much greater advertising coverage in the West because a higher percentage of persons residing in that region are on mailing lists.

5. Mailers of sexually oriented advertising inevitably offend some recipients even if the mailer prints a warning on the envelope as to the content of the letter, or if the advertising brochure is not illustrated and vulgar language is not used.

6. Mailers who attempt to control their mailings generate few complaints. A majority of mailers appear to follow this practice. Those who mail indiscriminately to general mailing lists account for a disproportionate share of the prohibitory orders. The number of orders issued against a particular mailer is primarily a result of the mailing lists used, rather than the sexual content of the advertising, and is also not an accurate indicator of the size of the business. Based on the practices of those mailers generating most of the complaints, it is obvious that the vast majority of orders issued are on behalf of those who have received unsolicited advertising.

133

7. Some mailers take certain steps to avoid having mail opened by minors, such as printing a "warning" on the envelope forbidding minors to open the letter. Obviously age requirements cannot be enforced in the mail-order business. Approximately 5% of the total orders were issued on behalf of minors (under age 19).

8. Although a substantial number of prohibitory orders have been issued, only about 0.5% of all sexually oriented advertising mailed result in a complaint to the Post Office, and even less resulted in a prohibitory order. Requests for prohibitory orders in the first half of 1970 were less than half of the number of such requests in the first half of 1969.

VOLUME OF SEXUALLY ORIENTED MAIL—FISCAL 1969

In conjunction with the Postal Inspection Services[8] the Commission undertook a survey of postal expenditures of the most important mailers. Because important mailers use postage meters or bulk mailing permits instead of stamps to make their mailings, this study of the actual purchases of postage is an accurate measure of the volume.

Data on the traceable postage expenditure during fiscal 1969 were obtained for 28 mailers and three mailing services specializing in sexually oriented advertising in New York City and the Los Angeles area. According to the Postal Inspection Service, all the major mailers in the country were included in this survey. The mailers studied spent a total of $2,170,000 on postage in fiscal 1969, an amount sufficient to mail approximately 36 million letters.

There is no certain way to determine the percentage of the total sexually oriented advertising mailed during fiscal year 1969 which was sent by the 28 dealers and three mailing services studied. However, the percentage of prohibitory orders issued against these mailers during the same time period is available. Between 75% and 80% of all prohibitory orders issued for the comparable time period were issued against the mailers in the postal expenditure survey.

A possible method of determining the total volume of sexually oriented advertising is to project the known volume of advertising in fiscal 1969 of the mailers studied for postage purchases (36 million letters) and the percentage of prohibitory orders issued against those same mailers (75% to 80%). This procedure has one substantial defect: mailing methods vary considerably, and there is no direct relationship between mail volume and prohibitory orders issued against the mailers studied (although perhaps in the overall this relationship exists). In any event, any error is not likely to be large, probably no more than plus or minus 10%. It can, therefore, be estimated that the total volume of sexually oriented mail in fiscal 1969 was approximately 45 to 48 million letters. This represents almost exactly 0.1% of all first class mail mailed in the United States and slightly more than 0.05% of all mailing in fiscal 1969. (Postmaster General's Report, 1969).

The average return to mailers is certainly no more than $.50 per letter, and the more probable average return is $.25 or $.30 per letter. Therefore, the maximum possible retail sales volume of sexually oriented materials through mail order during fiscal 1969 would have been approximately $24 million and it is more likely actual sales were in the $12-$14 million range.

The Internal Revenue Service analyzed tax returns for 1968 for 15 of the 20 largest mailers studied for postal purchases during 1969.[9] Total reported gross receipts of the mailers studied were slightly in excess of $5½ million, and reported combined net profits showed a loss of just under $3,000. Most mailers claimed 1968 was a "banner year" for mail order sales. While this claim is hardly borne out by the IRS report, this is at least an indication of the insignificant size and relative unprofitability of the industry.

The IRS report lends credibility to the estimated figure of $.25 or $.30 as an average per letter return for most mailers. Thus, the estimate of $12-$14 million in sales for fiscal 1969 should be regarded as a maximum. An estimate of under $10 million in sales could be justified on the basis of the IRS study.

HARD-CORE PORNOGRAPHY IN THE MAILS

As of 1970, mailers dealing in sexually oriented materials define "hard-core pornography" as "photographic depictions of actual sexual intercourse with camera focus on the genitals and no accompanying text to provide a legal defense." This, of course, is not a legal definition; it only reflects the industry's belief or understanding of the meaning of the term. This "market" definition may be proven incorrect by judicial decisions, but until that event, mailers will conduct their operations under the supposition that they are correct in their understanding. Under this restrictive definition, almost

135

none of the material advertised and sold by domestic mailers is classified as "hard-core." Promises in advertisements to the contrary are generally spurious. However, some domestic mailers have apparently agreed with foreign (primarily Scandinavian) mailers to supply the advertising while the foreign mailer ships the "hard-core" product to the United States.

In addition, foreign mailers increasingly advertise "hard-core" products in the United States. These mailers are often able to deliver materials ordered, even though outgoing orders for and incoming shipments of foreign pornography are prohibited by law. There seem to be several dozen mailers in Scandinavia doing a volume of business in hard-core exports.

The amount of hard-core materials seized in 1969 (100,000 packages per year in New York) can be ascertained, but the total volume is more difficult to estimate. The Director of the Bureau of Customs Division in New York City charged with enforcing prohibitions against hard-core materials estimates that 30%-35% of the hard-core pornography imported into the port of New York is intercepted. Based on his estimate that the average seizure had an approximate retail value of $20 in 1969, about $2 million worth (retail value) of hard-core material was intercepted of a total volume of $6 million. He states that the majority of foreign mail of this type enters through the port of New York, but that perhaps an additional 25% enters through other ports (almost none of which is seized). If he is correct, approximately $5.5 million worth (retail) of hard-core material was successfully imported in 1969. In light of the projected size of the domestic mail-order business ($12 to $14 million), which all experts agree is much larger than the import business, it is likely that either the Customs Bureau is more efficient than it believes or that the estimated value of the seizures has been overstated. The former seems much more likely.

Section D. The "Under-The-Counter" or "Hard-Core" Pornography Market[10]

In addition to the traffic in sexually oriented materials described in Sections A, B, and C, in most localities some material is sold in an under-the-counter manner—that is, covertly, with an apparent belief by the seller that the material sold is illegal. Ordinarily, materials sold under-the-counter are the most explicit material available in the place of sale. Under-the-counter materials are sold both at established retail outlets for books or other products and in a nonretail setting, such as in bars, barbershops, factories, etc. The shorthand reference to such material used in the marketplace is "hard-core pornography."

Over the past 25 years, the specific characteristics of sexual content in materials sold under-the-counter have changed considerably. At one time, wholly textual "erotic classics" were sold in that manner. Similarly, photographs of human genitalia were also thought by sellers to be hard-core (i.e., obviously illegal). Today, in most localities, materials which were once sold under-the-counter are now freely available, i.e., photographic depictions of human nudity and books by famous authors of erotica—Henry Miller, DeSade, Frank Harris, etc. Nonetheless, there is no nationwide standard regarding materials which are sold openly. Books or magazines which circulate without restriction in one city may be sold covertly in another locality.

There is one genre of sexually oriented material which is almost universally sold under-the-counter in the United States: wholly photographic reproductions of actual sexual intercourse graphically depicting vaginal and/or oral penetration. These materials have been available virtually since the invention of the camera and have always been the most explicit sexual stimuli available in general circulation. Generally, they are available in three forms: motion pictures, photo sets, and picture magazines or brochures.

At present, distinctions between materials sold openly and those sold covertly have become extremely unclear. Prior to about mid-1969, producers of erotic materials were of the opinion that graphic photographic depictions of human sexual intercourse were illegal irrespective of the context in which such photographs were presented. However, in the past year there has been the revolution in both motion pictures and illustrated paperback books (Sections A and B) which has altered this concept. In many metropolitan areas, motion pictures are openly exhibited and illustrated books are openly sold which contain graphic photographic depictions of coitus, fellatio, and cunnilingus. At least to some extent, these materials have made any discussion of the "under-the-counter" concept passe.

Sales of under-the-counter materials have not been eliminated by the more explicit materials available in the past year, however. Wholly pictorial materials unaccompanied by some textual or narrative "justification" of the graphic photography in books and magazines still are sold covertly. The traffic in those materials sold openly has been reported upon in Sections A and B; the under-the-counter market is, in large part, a separate market.

In all other aspects of its research, the Panel was able to receive apparently honest and straightforward answers in interviews with producers of sexually oriented materials. Those connected with "borderline" or "questionable" sexually oriented materials operate openly; their die has been cast and their cause is contested in the courts. They have taken the position that they are protected under the First Amendment. Those who traffic in under-the-counter materials, however, are conscious of the fact that they are operating in an illegal fashion. Therefore, they attempt to keep themselves and their operations out of the public eye. This considerably altered the Staff's investigatory methodology and limited interviews to law enforcement officials, prosecutors, and academicians. As a result, this section of the Report is composed entirely of a compilation of expert opinion. It should be noted that the experts consulted expressed a remarkable unanimity on all substantive points.

Stag Films

Although there are federal, state, and local laws which make the production, sale, distribution, and exhibition of hard-core pornography a criminal offense, stag films are a familiar and firmly established part of the American scene. Stag films, while publicly condemned, are shown privately not only by individual citizens, but also by civic, social, fraternal and veterans' organizations. The National Survey conducted by the Commission (Abelson, 1970) revealed that 44% of the male adults acknowledged having seen one or more stag films in their lifetimes.

The first stag films reached the market in the early 1900s, and the format has been in circulation ever since. In the 70-year history of stag films, production has changed only in form, not in sexual content.

Stag films feature a full range of sexual activities, including fellatio, cunnilingus, and mutual masturbation. Because pornography historically has been thought to be primarily a

138

masculine interest, the emphasis in stag films seems to represent the preferences of the middle-class American male. Thus, male homosexuality and bestiality are relatively rare, while lesbianism is rather common. In recent years, there has been an increased emphasis on group sex, usually three or four individuals, but as many as seven have been noted in a single film. Many stag films attack certain forbidden social and sexual themes; for example, taboos against miscegenation, cunnilingus, and fellatio are constantly assaulted in American stag films, while foreign countries with a strong religious base have a significant anti-clerical strain in their stag films. The taboo against pedophilia, however, has remained almost inviolate. The use of pre-pubescent children in stag films is almost nonexistent.

Relatively few individuals produced stag films prior to World War II. The expertise of these producers contributed to relatively professional movies in comparison to many modern stag films. Pre-World War II stag films can often be recognized by experts because they contain (a) more humor; (b) more emphasis on plot; (c) more attention to nonsexual activities; and (d) greater technical adequacy.

Pre-war films were restricted to 16mm camera equipment, which was relatively costly to own, and severely limited the market for stag films. Ownership of home movie equipment became relatively common in the post-war period with the introduction of inexpensive 8mm cameras and projectors, and many amateurs began to produce stag films. The market changed rapidly from a few operators producing a large number of films to large numbers of operators each producing a small number of films. The "amateur" film maker introduced a commensurate decline in the technical quality of the films, but at the same time, the physical attractiveness of the models and locations was improved.

The changeover from 16mm to 8mm home movie equipment also had a profound effect on the market for stag films. In the early days of the stag film industry (until 1950), most of the traffic was in rental fees rather than sales. Certain individuals traveled a designated route with their own projector and films and displayed their wares on a one- or two-hour show. The rental fee was usually between $25 and $100, and the audiences for these "smokers" or "stag nights" varied from 50 to 200 persons.

Since the early 1950s, after the popularization of 8mm movie equipment, customers have preferred to rent or purchase films for private screenings. The operators of the

139

"road shows" found their services required less and less, so they became the first distributors, wholesalers, and retailers for this market. As the market expanded and more outlets for the films came into existence, the so-called "traveling road shows" began to die out, and, as of 1970, are relatively infrequent in most parts of the country.

It is impossible to determine the number of stag films currently on the market. Some films are shown for decades and are apparently indestructible "classics;" other old films are retitled and redistributed; conversely, many different films have the same title. The Institute for Sex Research at the University of Indiana has estimated that between 3,000 and 7,000 stag films have been produced in the last 55 years, but an accurate estimate of the number on the market at any one time is virtually impossible.

It will cost the producer between $900 and $1,500 to produce 100 copies each of four stag films (a typical number of new titles produced from one filming session); the "performers" are paid $100 to $300; if a photographer is hired, the fee ranges between $100 and $500; if the producer does his own filming and owns his own equipment, this cost will be negligible; the producer will probably spend $800 for raw film and 400 prints. For this expenditure, the producer can expect to recover between $1,200—$2,000 (at $3.00 to $5.00 per reel) if he sells to a distributor, and $4,000 (at $10.00 per reel) if he sells directly to retailers. If the producer is his own distributor, he can sell his films directly to a wholesaler for approximately $6.00 per reel (or $2,400).

A wholesaler, who is usually otherwise employed in a business which calls for a great deal of travel (such as a salesman or a truck driver), ordinarily purchases 100-200 reels of film from a distributor and sells to retailers located along his regular business route. Today, probably most retail outlets are "adults only" bookstores, although clandestine retailers are also found in bars, gas stations, barber shops, factories, etc.

The selling price of stag films varies considerably across the country. Prices for 200 feet, black and white films varied from a low of $12 in one East Coast city to a high of $40 on the West Coast. It is probable that established customers pay approximately $15-$16 per reel. In addition, in many areas, customers can trade a used film back to the retailer and pay a discounted price for a new film.

The availability of stag films today varies considerably from city to city, depending on the mores of the community

140

and the activity of the police. The market has traditionally been localized, and films usually find their way into different regional areas through copying by other sellers rather than through an organized distribution system. In recent years, these markets have overlapped thus allowing films to travel slowly across the country, local market by local market. Nationwide distribution is also facilitated because some wholesalers serve more than one market. At present, law enforcement authorities indicate that the restriction to local markets is breaking down, but, as of Fall, 1970, there is no evidence of a national distribution system for stag films produced at a central location.

There are no great fortunes to be made in stag film production. Local distribution is too disorganized to support the multi-million dollar business which has sometimes been alleged to exist. The experts consulted by the Panel were in agreement that the stag film market at present is rather small. Although hundreds, and perhaps thousands, of individuals have produced hard-core films over the years, most of these productions have been "one-shot" efforts. A comprehensive list of stag films and producers identified only 51 individuals or groups who have produced more than five films. One expert stated that there are fewer than a half-dozen individuals who net more than $10,000 per year in the business.

HARD-CORE PHOTOGRAPHS OR PHOTO SETS

Historically, the widest circulation of hard-core pornography has been accomplished through photographs or photo sets. The proliferation of these materials precludes an accurate estimate of the numbers, although there are certainly millions of such photographs in existence.

The commercial traffic in these materials has declined steadily in the past ten years, however, because of the ease and inexpensiveness with which photographs can be duplicated or produced by self-developing cameras. The content and distribution of hard-core photographs and photo sets are roughly identical to stag films. Prices vary considerably, depending on the availability of the materials. The average price for a packet of six or eight 3 inch by 5 inch black and white photographs is usually between $5 and $10, although prices may be as low as $2.50 or as high as $20.00. Hard-core photographs and photo sets are not regarded by experts as a significant factor in the marketplace.

Hard-core magazines and brochures are generally composed of nothing more than a series of photographs which have been bound together to form an eight to 32 page book. Historically, magazines of this type have often been produced in their entirety in the United States. Today, however, major sources for this type of material are original Scandinavian imports (usually printed in full color) and domestic copies of such magazines (usually printed in black and white. See Section C). The domestic copying process leaves much to be desired; the resulting magazines are technically inferior to the foreign originals.

The primary outlet for this type of erotic material appears to be some "adult" bookstores. Many "adult" bookstores carry a small stock of these magazines which are sold in an under-the-counter fashion. While these materials are usually sold only to regular customers, in some cities they are proffered almost as soon as a customer enters the establishment.

SUMMARY

The traffic and distribution of under-the-counter materials is a very minor part of the total traffic in erotic materials. The legal restrictions on mass distribution curtail any large-scale operations, making this segment of the market economically unattractive to any sizable producer. Many dealers in hard-core are individual entrepreneurs, otherwise gainfully employed, who "moonlight" to supplement their incomes. All experts consulted refused even to attempt an estimate of the size of the under-the-counter market, but most said it was certainly less than 10% of the "adult" materials market. If this is so, total under-the-counter sales are probably well under $10 million yearly.

Section E. Erotica and Organized Crime

Although many persons have alleged that organized crime works hand-in-glove with the distributors of adult materials, there is at present no concrete evidence to support these statements.

One author reported that crime syndicate members stated in interviews that it was not worthwhile for the syndicate to enter the business, primarily because there was no real economic inducement (Sonenschein, 1969, p. 13). The authors of Commission-sponsored research consisting of interviews with police and prosecutors in 17 cities, stated that "police and prosecutors reported strong suspicions that there was a relationship between the distributors of adult books and magazines and organized crime . . . but they had no concrete evidence." Answers in this survey ranged from "it's too big not to be" to "there is no local connection" (Smith and Locke, 1970).

Another contractor who made specific case studies in New York, Chicago, Boston, Los Angeles, and San Francisco was told by officials in every city but San Francisco that organized crime was involved. In some of the studies, well-known members of syndicated crime were involved with the transportation of illegal sex-oriented materials. The cases were too widespread to indicate any genuine organized involvement, but rather, suggested individual activities. This seeming consensus of opinion was apparently based on assumptions of "guilt by association" or because quite a few dealers in adult materials have criminal records (Finkelstein, 1970b).

There is some evidence that the retail adult bookstore business which purveys materials that are not only at the periphery of legitimacy but also at the margin of legality, tends to involve individuals who have had considerable arrest records (Finkelstein, 1970b). The business does involve some risk of arrest and, therefore, would be avoided by persons with more concern for legitimacy and general reputation. Therefore, there is a greater likelihood that persons with some background of conflict with the legal system will be found among "adult store" proprietors. This is not the same, however, as being an adjunct or subsidiary of "organized crime."

The hypothesis that organized criminal elements either control or are "moving in" on the distribution of sexually oriented materials will doubtless continue to be speculated upon. The Panel finds that there is insufficient evidence at present to warrant any conclusion in this regard.

Section F. Patterns of Exposure to Erotic Material

The following pages contain an attempt to spell out in some detail patterns of experience with sexually explicit materials among adults and young people.

Not many scientific investigations have collected data on experience with erotic materials. Those few studies that have been reported asked a variety of questions that are often not strictly comparable. Nevertheless, there is a growing body of knowledge regarding this experience, and a consistent picture is beginning to emerge.

ADULTS

Abelson and his associates (1970) carried out a large national survey to provide information regarding the nature of the experience that adults in the United States have had with erotic materials. This survey involved face to face interviews with a sample of 2,486 adults, age 21 and older, who were selected into the sample by a technique that provided an approximately equal probability for each adult in the United States to be included. The results of this survey should accurately reflect the experience of adults in the United States. The survey asked questions about both seeing and reading depictions of the following five types: emphasizing the sex organs of a man or woman; mouth-sex organ contact between a man and woman; a man and woman having sexual intercourse; sexual activities between people of the same sex; and sex activities which include whips, belts or spankings. Eighty-four percent of the men and 69% of the women in the representative national sample reported having been exposed to at least one of these kinds of depictions.

Athanasiou (1970) analyzed the responses of over 20,000 readers of the magazine, Psychology Today, to a questionnaire on sex attitudes and practices that was contained in the July 1970 issue of the magazine. The respondents were obviously not representative of the general population: 77% were less than 35 years old and 89% had some college experience. In

144

response to the question, "Have you voluntarily obtained or seen erotic or pornographic books, movies, magazines, etc.?", 92% of the males and 72% of the females said, "Yes."

The same question was asked of over 450 members of professional and community service groups in metropolitan Detroit (Wallace & Wehmer, 1970). About 63% were men and 37% women. Eighty percent of these people indicated that they had voluntarily obtained erotic materials.

Goldstein and his associates (1970) conducted intensive clinical interviews regarding experience with a variety of sexual materials with a sample of normal males in metropolitan Los Angeles. These subjects were predominantly lower-middle class in the age range of 20-40 years. The sample included 53 whites and 39 blacks. At least 85% of the whites and 76% of the blacks reported having been exposed to photographic depictions of sexual intercourse and at least 92% of the whites and 90% of the blacks had seen photos of fully nude females.

Massey (1970), in a questionnaire study of several hundred predominantly middle-class men and women members of social, professional, service, and church groups in Denver, found that 83% had seen at sometime in their life depictions of people engaged in a sex act, and a similar percentage had seen depictions of people with all private sex organs fully exposed.

These several studies of selected samples are quite consistent in their results and provide estimates of exposure very similar to that provided by the national survey reported by Abelson and his associates (1970). Approximately 85% of men and 70% of women report specific instances of having been exposed to explicit sexual materials depicting at a minimum nudity with genitals exposed.

The proportion of people in the United States who have been exposed to erotic materials is very similar to the proportion of adults in Copenhagen, Denmark, who report having seen pornographic books and magazines. Kutschinsky (1970) surveyed a representative sample of 398 men and women regarding their attitudes toward sex crimes and toward pornography. The responses to a series of questions regarding exposure to pornography indicated that 87% of men and 73% of women had consumed at least one book and a similar percentage had consumed at least one pornographic magazine (Kutschinsky, 1970).

Fewer adults report recent experience with erotic materials than report ever having been exposed. The national survey

145

(Abelson, et al., 1970) reveals that whereas 84% of males report having been exposed at some time in the past to at least one of the ten depictions that were included in the study, only 40% report having experience with visual depictions of intercourse during the past two years. The comparable figures for women are 69% and 26%. Goldstein and his associates (1970) report a similar phenomenon among normal male adults. Whereas at least 85% of the white males report having been exposed to photos of heterosexual intercourse at sometime in their life, only 71% report exposure to such photos in the past year; the corresponding figures for blacks are 76% and 54%.

Three studies reveal no consistent differences between textual and visual media as being the more likely medium of exposure (Abelson, et al., 1970; Goldstein, et al., 1970; Massey, 1970). The more common medium changes from group to group and from depiction to depiction and does not form a coherent pattern.

Experience does vary, however, according to the content of the material. The national survey indicates that depictions of sex organs and heterosexual intercourse are most common, homosexual activities and oral sex are in between, and sadomasochistic materials are the least common (Abelson, et al., 1970). The data of Goldstein and his associates (1970) on normal adult males are in general agreement with the national survey, but they found more differentiation between full nudity and intercourse, and between homosexual and oral sex content. The rank ordering of likelihood of having been seen was: fully nude women, heterosexual intercourse, oral sex, homosexual, and sadomasochistic. Thus, portrayals of sex that conform to general cultural norms are more likely to be seen, and portrayals of sexual activity that deviate from these norms are less likely to be seen. Portrayals of combinations of sex and violence are relatively rare in the experience of normal adults in our society. Massey (1970) found that reported exposure decreased as material became more explicit within the range from partial nudity to sexual activity with full exposure of sex organs.

Experience with sexual materials also varies according to the characteristics of the viewer. Our chief source of information on this topic is the national survey referred to above (Abelson, et al., 1970). We have already seen that men are more likely to be exposed to erotic materials than are women, and that this gender difference holds in Copenhagen, Denmark, as well as in the United States. Younger adults are more likely to have experience with sexual materials than are older adults, and this holds for both men and women. People with some college attendance are more likely to have experience with erotic materials than people with only high school attendance who are, in turn, more likely to have been exposed to erotica than people who attended school eight years or less. These educational differences hold for both men and women. Males living in relatively large metropolitan areas are likely to have more experience with sexual materials than males living in small metropolitan areas of nonmetropolitan areas, but this does not hold for females. There are differences in amount of exposure among different geographical areas of the country for males but not for females. The most exposure for males occurs in the Northeast section and the least in the North Central section. People who read general books, magazines, and newspapers more and who see general movies more also see more erotic stimuli. People who are socially and politically active are exposed to more erotic materials. Both of these latter two findings hold for both men and women. People who attend religious services more often are somewhat less likely to be exposed to erotica.

Several of these differences in exposure to erotica were also found by Wallace and Wehmer (1970) in their more circumscribed study. They report that college students were most likely among their subjects to have voluntarily obtained or seen erotic or pornographic stimuli, followed by members of professional groups, community service groups, and church groups in that order.

Prosecuting attorneys from large urban areas are more likely to report that the volume of traffic and patterns of distribution are a matter of serious concern in their community than are prosecuting attorneys from smaller communities (Wilson, Horowitz, and Friedman, 1970).

These differences in experience with sexual materials may be summarized by the following profiles. Persons who have the greater amount of experience with erotic materials tend to be male, younger, better educated, urban, to consume more mass communication media, to be more socially active, more politically active, and less active in religious affairs. Those who have less experience with erotic materials tend to be female, older, less educated, to live in small cities or rural areas, to be less exposed to general communication media, less socially active, less politically active, and more active in religious affairs. Similar profiles are reported for Sweden by Zetterberg (1970).

147

Although most males in our society have been exposed to erotic stimuli at sometime in their lives, a small proportion have had relatively extensive experience with erotica. Eighty percent of the male adults in the national sample reported having ever seen in a visual medium at least one of the five kinds of depictions asked about, but only 49% reported having seen three or more of these types of stimuli. Yet, approximately a third (34%) report having seen four or five of these different types. Only 17% of the females have seen three or more of these different kinds of stimuli.

The national survey data on more recent experience with erotica also demonstrates that extensive experience with sexual materials is not the usual case. Whereas 61% of the men report having been exposed to at least one of the above depictions in either visual or textual form during the past two years, only 26% have been exposed to five or more of the ten possible depictions. The figures for women are 50% and 11%.

The national survey also asked how many different times an individual had seen a given visual depiction during the past two years. Fourteen percent of the men and 5% of the women report having seen the given depiction more than five times in the two-year interval (Abelson, et al., 1970). These figures are low estimates because the depiction queried varied from individual to individual in such a way as to more often ask about the types of depictions that are least often seen.

Goldstein and his colleagues (1970) also report data on frequency of recent exposure. Thirty-two percent of the normal white males report seeing photos of heterosexual intercourse more than ten times during the past year, 27% report seeing photos of oral-genital activity that frequently, and only 14% report seeing sadomasochistic materials that frequently. The figures for the black sample are 36%, and 19%, and 9%. The frequency of exposure to textual and movie stimuli is less than that for still photographic depictions. It should be noted that the people in this sample were relatively young and lived in a large urban community and would, therefore, be expected to have had greater exposure than average for males.

Thus, somewhere around one-fifth or one-quarter of the male population in the United States has somewhat regular experience with sexual materials as explicit as intercourse.

There are no exactly comparable figures for frequency of exposure for countries other than the United States. Kutschinsky (1970) found that 18% of the representative adult male sample from Copenhagen, Denmark, report having consumed 50 or more pornographic magazines in their lifetime, and 39% reported having seen a pornographic magazine within the past month at the time of the interview.

Americans have their first exposure to erotic materials at a relatively young age. Three-quarters (74%) of the national sample (Abelson, et al., 1970) of male adults report having seen sexual materials at least as explicit as nudity with genitals before they were 21 years old, over half (54%) before age 18, and nearly one-third (30%) before age 15. Women report a later age of first exposure: about one-half (51%) before 21, one-third (33%) before 18, and one-sixth (17%) before 15. This early age of exposure will be explored further when we look at the experience of adolescents.

Few people report that they buy erotic materials. Only 5% of the men who have seen nonmovie visual depictions in the past two years report having bought the most recent depiction that they have seen; an additional 8% report having seen it at a newsstand or bookstore; but 53% report having been shown the depiction or given it by someone else. A larger proportion of men report having bought the most recent textual depiction they have read, 26%; only 4% read it at a bookstore or newsstand; 64% report having obtained it from someone else at no cost. The figures for women are roughly comparable (Abelson, et al., 1970). These figures may be low estimates because the depiction asked about varied in explicitness from person to person and the more explicit materials are less often purchased.

Massey (1970) asked his subjects if they had ever seen and if they had ever purchased sexual materials of several degress of explicitness. Fifty-nine percent of those who had ever seen depictions of private sex organs but no sex activity had also bought such materials; 47% of those who had ever seen depictions of sexual activity but no sex organs exposed had bought; 35% of those who had ever seen depictions of sex play with sex organs exposed but not in contact had bought; and only 26% of those who had seen depictions of sex acts with full exposure of sex organs had also bought these materials at some time. These figures are perhaps higher than one would obtain in general since the subjects of the study were relatively well educated, young middle aged, urban and socially active. The figures are also not comparable to the ones reported in the national survey since Massey's figures reporting having *ever* bought, and the national survey figures report having bought the most recent exposure.

Several generalizations may be derived from these data. First, most exposure to erotica occurs outside the commercial context. Two, erotica is a durable material for which there are several consumers for each purchase. Three, although the proportion of the population purchasing erotic materials is relatively small, the absolute number of purchasers may constitute a sizable market.

The responses to the national survey (Abelson et al., 1970) indicate that approximately 3% of the most recent exposures to erotic material occurred as a result of unsolicited mail.

Within the general adult public, exposure to erotica is a social or quasi-social activity. The principal source of both visual and textual erotica is a friend or acquaintance. Most people go to see skinflicks or "stag" movies with someone else, although a sizable minority of men (14%) go alone. The sexes differ in terms of with whom they attend erotic movies: men most often go in the company of other men, while women most often go in the company of men or a mixed group of both sexes (Abelson, et al., 1970).

The informal distribution of erotica among friends is an asymmetrical communication network. Many more people have had sexual materials shown or given to them than have shown or given these materials to others. A relatively few people seem to be the central points of the communication network and initially obtain sexual materials and then share them with several others. Only 31% of men and 18% of women report knowing of a shop which specializes in sexual materials. Sharing is predominantly with a friend of the same sex or with a spouse (Abelson, et al., 1970).

MINORS

Although much concern has been expressed regarding young people's potential exposure to explicit sexual materials, there have been until recently almost no formal reports of information about how often this occurs. Two adults may in a conversation about pornography recall certain experiences that occurred in their own childhood, but the sharing of these recollections seldom occurs. Kinsey included questions about age of exposure to erotic materials in his interviews, but these data have never been formally reported.

The national survey funded by the Commission and reported by Abelson and his associates (1970) did ask adults

150

to try to recall the age at which they had first been exposed to explicit sexual materials. We mentioned earlier that of this representative sample of American adult males roughly three-quarters reported having been exposed before age 21, one-half before age 18, and one-third before age 15; and that females report being exposed about two years later than males. These figures may report later exposure than actually occurred, however, because it may be difficult for older people to make differentiations of a few years when recalling teenage experience. For example, although 19% of all male adults report first exposure at 12 years of age or younger, 34% of men age 21-29 report first exposure at age 12 or younger. This difference in reporting may reflect errors in recall among the older respondents or it may reflect actual changes in experience in more recent decades. In either case, we may expect higher rates of earlier exposure to be reported by today's youth.

Goldstein and his associates (1970) asked their subjects (normal, lower middle class, young and middle-aged males) to report on their exposure in adolescence. More than 90% of both whites and blacks reported exposure to photos of fully nude women and about 70% of both groups reported having seen these depictions more than ten times during adolescence. Eighty percent of the whites and 75% of the blacks reported seeing photos of heterosexual intercourse in adolescence, with approximately half of both groups reporting more than ten different exposures to these depictions. Over half of both groups reported seeing photos of homosexual activity, 75% of the whites and 58% of the blacks had seen photos of mouth-genital activity, and 43% of the whites and 30% of the blacks had seen photos of sadomasochistic activity in adolescence.

Both of these studies suggest that there has been considerable exposure to explicit sexual materials by adolescents in the past.

A recent national survey of sex educators and counselors (Wilson and Jacobs, 1970) asked the respondents to estimate the age at which roughly half of boys had been exposed to explicit sexual materials. A similar question was asked about girls. There was virtual consensus (91%) that half of the boys had been exposed to explicit sexual materials by the time they were 16 years old. About two-thirds (64%) of the sex educators and counselors felt that half of the boys are exposed to these materials by the time they are 14 years old. Generally, these experts estimated that girls were one to

151

two years later than boys in their exposure to erotica.

White (1970) asked a total of 300 college students, male and female, from five different universities in New York, Providence, and Boston, at what age they were first exposed to pornography in any form. (Pornography was not defined, but each respondent had been asked to define the term earlier. Their responses indicate that they were thinking of explicit portrayals of genitals and sexual activity.) Nearly three-quarters (71%) said they had been exposed by age 13 and 97% had been exposed by age 17. Only 12% reported that they had never voluntarily exposed themselves to pornography, and 20% reported that they often voluntarily exposed themselves to pornography.

Roach and Kreisberg (1970) asked similar questions in a self-administered questionnaire to a total of 625 students of both sexes from eight colleges in Westchester County, New York. Nearly half of the males (49%) reported having been exposed to pornography before age 13 and 50% of the females had been exposed by age 15. Seven percent of the males and 12% of the females reported never having been exposed voluntarily to pornography, while 32% and 15%, respectively, reported voluntary exposure often.

Berger and his associates (1970a) report on a survey of a national random sample of college students conducted in 1967. The survey asked if the person had seen pornographic photographs depicting sexual activity, pornographic or stag movies depicting sexual intercourse, or pornographic writing. Ninety-eight percent of the males and 82% of the females reported exposure to at least one of these. There was no relationship between having been exposed and year in college, and the authors concluded that first exposure is primarily a precollege phenomenon. Thirty-nine percent of the males and 10% of the females reported frequent exposure to at least one of these types of pornography.

The reports of the college students indicate a greater degree of exposure to explicit sexual materials during adolescence than do the retrospective reports of older adults. This difference may be due to differential recall of the teenage experience, different experiences across generations, different experiences across social class groupings, or all three. Fortunately, we are not limited to inferences based on retrospective reporting for information about contemporary experience of minors with erotic materials. Several recent investigations have directly questioned minors themselves about their experiences in this realm.

The national survey conducted for the Commission also included a sample of 769 adolescents age 15-20 who were living at home; the sample leaves out household members age 15-20 who were away at school, in the armed services, etc. The adolescent sample was asked many of the same questions that were asked the adults, including whether they had seen the various kinds of depictions of explicit sexual material in both pictorial and textual form and the circumstances of a recent exposure experience.

Ninety-one percent of the males and 88% of the females in this national sample age 15-20 reported having seen at least one of the ten depictions queried. Forty-nine percent of the males and 45% of the females reported having seen five or more of the depictions. Thirty-two percent of the males and 29% of the females report that they have seen a given visual depiction more than five times during the past two years. This is probably a low frequency estimate because different depictions were asked about for different respondents, and some of the depictions are likely to have lower frequencies of exposure than others. Minors report considerably more exposure to erotica than do adults in general. However, the experience of the minors with sexual materials is similar to that of adults who are nearest them in age, the 21-29 year olds (Abelson, et al., 1970).

Other studies of more circumscribed groups of minors are consistent with these findings.

Fersch (1970) asked several mixed male and female groups, including public high school students, private high school students, street corner gangs, and college students, about their exposure to books with stories of sadism, masochism, orgies, or wild parties in them, to "girlie" picture magazines, and to "more-censored" pictures and magazines. The subjects ranged from 14 to 22 years old, cut across several socio-economic status classifications, and represented a variety of religious groups. Ninety-seven percent reported that they had read books with sexual stories, 95% had looked at "girlie" picture magazines, and 80% had seen "more-censored" magazines. Half of these minors reported seeing "currently-censored" materials at age 13 or younger and two-thirds at age 14 or younger.

Berger, Gagnon and Simon (1970b) used a self-administered questionnaire to gather information from 473 working-class, white, predominantly Catholic, adolescents age 13-18. Ninety-five percent of the males and 65% of the females had seen pictures of nudes with genitals exposed; 53% of the

153

males and 16% of the females reported having seen such pictures more than ten times. Seventy-seven percent of the males and 35% of the females had seen pictures of sexual intercourse; 32% of males and 4% of females had seen such pictures more than ten times. Sixty percent of the males and 38% of the females had seen movies of sexual intercourse; 27% of the males and 9% of the females had seen such movies five or more times. Seventy-nine percent of the males and 78% of the females had been exposed to books describing sexual activities in slang terms; 20% of the males and 10% of the females had read more than ten such books.

Elias (1970) administered a questionnaire to over 300 11th and 12th grade students in a public school in a working-class suburb of Chicago. The respondents were nearly all white and Christian with slightly over half belonging to the Catholic Church. Ninety-four percent of the males and 66% of the females reported that they had seen photographs of nude females showing genitalia. Eighty-one percent of the males and 43% of the females report having seen photographs of nude males and females engaging in sex behavior. Ninety-five percent of males and 72% of females report having been exposed to printed material describing sexual intercourse. Among the males 40% report seeing photographs of nude females "often," 16% report seeing pictures of intercourse often, and 24% report seeing textual descriptions of intercourse often.

Propper (1970) studied inmates in a youth reformatory in a Northeastern city. The subjects were mostly ages 17-20 (97%), and predominantly from minority ethnic groups (67% black and 21% Puerto Rican). Eighty-five percent reported having seen visual depictions of sex organs, 82% had seen depictions of mouth-sex organ contact, 84% had seen pictures of heterosexual intercourse, 62% had seen homosexual pictures, and 46% had seen visual depictions of sex activities involving whips, belts, and spankings. With regard to frequency, the following percentages had been exposed more than ten times to visual depictions of sex organs, oral sex, intercourse, homosexual activities, and sadomasochistic activity, respectively: 49%, 36%, 44%, 23%, and 13%.

These various studies are quite consistent among themselves in finding that there is considerable exposure to explicit sexual materials on the part of minors. We may conservatively estimate from all these figures that 80% of boys and 70% of girls have seen visual depictions or read tex-

154

tual descriptions of sexual intercourse by the time they reach age 18. Substantial proportions of adolescents have had more than an isolated exposure or two, although the rates of exposure do not indicate an obsession with erotic materials. A great deal of exposure to explicit sexual materials occurs in the preadolescent and early adolescent years. More than half of the boys would appear to have some exposure to explicit sexual materials by age 15. Exposure on the part of girls lags behind that of boys by a year or two. Exposure to genitals and to heterosexual intercourse occurs earlier and more often. Exposure to oral-genital and homosexual materials occurs later and less frequently. Experience with depictions of sadomasochistic materials is much rarer, although it does occur.

Sex educators and counselors are overwhelmingly of the opinion that the principal source of sexual materials on the part of adolescents is from friends about the same age (Wilson & Jacobs, 1970). Eighty-seven percent mention this source. Twenty percent mention a newsstand or bookstore, 15% mention an older relative or find it at home, while 3% mention the mails, buying from an adult, and from an older person who is trying to seduce the adolescent.

The data from the national survey (Abelson, et al., 1970) are not adequate for a definitive statement on this topic, but they do seem to confirm, in general, the sex educators' opinions. About 5% of the adolescents who reported being exposed to a visual sexual depiction in the past two years said that they had bought it at a bookstore or newsstand, and another 5% said that they had seen it at a bookstore or newsstand. The mails, both solicited and unsolicited, are reported as negligible sources of exposure to erotica; and no one reported underground newspapers as a source. The most common source of exposure to sexual materials is a friend and this exposure appears to be a part of the normal social activity centered around house and school.

These findings of the national survey are consistent with the findings of the other more intensive studies carried out with more circumscribed groups.

Berger, Gagnon and Simon (1970b) found that friends were reported to be the most common source of exposure to pictures of sexual intercourse by 70% of the male adolescents and 59% of the female adolescents; other members of family were named by 5% of the males and 11% of the females; stores were named by 6% of the males and none of the females; and mails (about half solicited and half unsolicited) were named by 4% of both males and females. Similar kinds of findings were obtained regarding nudes with genitals exposed and books describing sexual activity in slang terms, except that stores were a more common source for the latter. Exposure to erotic materials appears to be primarily defined as a social activity rather than a sexual activity. Only 11% of these adolescents reported that the usual setting for viewing pictures of sexual intercourse was to be alone, and only 6% indicated that the usual setting was with the other sex. Forty-eight percent usually viewed these pictures with friends of the same sex only and 35% in a mixed sex group. There were sex differences in these reports, with females being more likely to view in mixed company and less likely to view only with their sex. Similar results were found for males regarding viewing movies of sexual intercourse, but females were more likely to view these movies with the opposite sex. Reading books describing sexual activity is more of a solitary activity than viewing pictures with about half the adolescents reporting that the usual setting for reading was to be alone. Still, a social setting with either friends of the same sex only or with mixed company is reported about 12 times more often than reading in the company of the other sex only.

Elias (1970) reports on the basis of interviews with over a hundred high school students that friends approximately the same age are the predominant sources of erotic material, although 45% have found erotic materials hidden at home.

In Propper's (1970) sample only 7% indicate that they bought a picture of sexual intercourse while 72% indicate that they either borrowed it, were given it or saw it some place. Mail is mentioned by 7% as a source of such pictures and stores are mentioned by 4%, while friends are mentioned as a source by over half.

Fersch (1970) reports that his subjects ranked friends, then stores, then adults, and finally mails as a source of "censored" materials, with friends named as source by approximately 60%.

These data suggest very strongly that exposure to explicit sexual materials in adolescence is widespread and occurs primarily in a group of peers of the same sex or a group involving several members of each sex, at school or at home or in the neighborhood. There are some suggestions in the data (Berger, et al., 1970a; Propper, 1970) that young people who are less active socially are less likely to be acquainted with sexual materials. Young people rarely pur-

156

chase explicit sexual materials; most of their exposure comes in a social situation where materials are freely passed around among friends.

Section G. Patrons of Adult Bookstores and Movies

The "consumer of pornography" has been a vague and shadowy concept in American folk myth, not well defined but nevertheless obviously an undesirable type. Yet, in spite of the debate regarding the legal control of obscenity that has been growing the past 15 years, not one empirical study had been reported of the characteristics of people who bought erotic materials when the Commission came on the scene. The Commission has funded a few pilot studies of the patrons of adult bookstores and movie theaters, and these together begin to sketch in a more definite image of the "consumer of pornography."

ADULT BOOKSTORE PATRONS

Massey (1970) observed 2,477 people who entered two bookstores carrying sex-oriented materials in Denver, Colorado. The observations were made over a six-day period in August 1969. One of the stores carried exclusively sex-oriented materials, while the other was a segregated section of a larger bookstore-newsstand. The sex-oriented sections were clearly marked "for adults only." Trained observers attempted to classify each patron in terms of sex, age, ethnic group membership, type of dress and the presence or not of a wedding band.

The patrons were almost exclusively male. Almost three-quarters (74%) were estimated to be in the age range of 26-55, while 22% were 21-25, and 4% were over 55; less than 1% were possibly under 21. Eighty-nine percent of the patrons were white, 4% black, and 5% Spanish-American. Over half the sample were casually dressed, 26% wore suits and ties, 13% were blue-collar workers; the remainder were soldiers, students, tourists, hippies and clergymen. One-third of the patrons whose left hands were observable had on

157

wedding bands. Jewelers estimate that roughly half of married males wear wedding bands, so well over half of these patrons were probably married.

Massey also inserted postcards in the purchases of 500 customers asking for demographic information. Only 52 of these postcards were returned, but the results were very similar to the observations. The purchaser who returned the postcard was male, age 26-35, had some education beyond high school, was married, a resident of the city, had an annual income of $10,000-$15,000, and had a professional or white collar occupation.

Massey reports that approximately one-third of the patrons in the 26-55 age group made purchases, but only about one-quarter of the younger and older groups purchased anything.

Massey attempted to interview some of the patrons, but soon gave up. The customers were quite skittish and generally silent while in the store; they appeared poised for flight. If someone spoke to them, they tended to respond in a monosyllable and move away. Customers did not interact with each other and interacted with the cashier-clerks as little as possible.

Finkelstein (1970a) reports the results of a total of 14 hours of observation of 10 adult bookstores in Boston. The observations were made on three week days between 10:00 a.m. and 3:30 p.m. in May 1970. A total of 493 people were observed entering the stores, all but one of whom were male. Sixty-one percent were estimated to be 40 years of age or older and 39% to be in their 20's and 30's. Only one or two cases that might have been under 21 were observed. Fifty-one percent were dressed in jacket and tie, 38% were neat and casually dressed, 7% had on work clothes, and less than 1% had on a military uniform. Only 3% were disheveled in appearance. Ninety-five percent were white with the remaining equally divided between black and oriental. Ninety-five percent of the patrons entered the stores alone; younger shoppers were more likely to enter the stores in the company of others. Slightly more than one-third of the shoppers (36%) made purchases, and this figure was essentially the same across age groups and dress groups.

Booksellers' descriptions of their customer populations were quite consistent with the objective observations. Most of the stores claim a steady clientele who buy materials regularly, as well as transients who rarely come in more than once, but no estimates of the proportions of these two types could be made.

Nawy (1970) observed 950 customers in 11 adult bookstores in San Francisco. Only three percent of these were females and they were mostly accompanied by a male escort. About 8 out of 10 of the customers were over 25 years old and less than 1% were possibly under 18. The ethnic composition of the customers approximated the ethnic composition of San Francisco as given in the United States Census; predominantly white with a small proportion of blacks and orientals. Middle-class customers, as indicated by dress style, predominated. It is estimated, based on the number of wedding bands observed, that most customers were married. Nine out of ten shopped alone. Approximately one customer in every five made a purchase.

Winick (1970a) reports observations of 1800 patrons of bookstores, 300 in each of six cities: Mid-town Manhattan, Los Angeles, Chicago, Detroit, Atlanta, and Kansas City. Ninety-nine percent of the patrons were male. Approximately 80% were white, 15% black, and smaller percentages were Spanish-American and oriental. The variations across cities in ethnic composition of customers seemed to reflect the differing ethnic composition of the cities. A little over one-third (36%) were in the age range 19-27, 39% were 28-40, and 24% were 41-60. Borderline youth cases were extremely rarely observed (far less than 1%) and few elderly men entered the stores. The age distribution was roughly the same across the cities. Twenty-six percent of the patrons wore business clothes, 41% casual, and 33% work clothes; few military uniforms were observed. There were considerable variations from city to city regarding costume: Atlanta, New York, and Kansas City had lower proportions of business attire and higher proportions of work clothes; Chicago and Los Angeles had higher proportions of business attire. The observers estimated the social class of the patrons as 44% lower class, 47% middle class, and 8% upper middle class. The downtown Manhattan figures inflated the lower class proportions considerably. Almost all (96%) shopped alone.

The profile of the patron of adult bookstores that emerges from these observations in different parts of the United States is: white, middle aged, middle class, married, male, dressed in business suit or neat casual attire, shopping alone.

Kutschinsky (1970) made systematic observations in about half of the pornography shops in Copenhagen in the winter

159

of 1970. His characterization of the people in these shops was: middle aged, middle class, white males. This characterization is very similar to that of the American adult bookstore patron. At least one-fourth of the patrons of the Danish shops were estimated to be from another country on the basis of their language or accent. Approximately one out of four people who entered the shops made purchases. Although selling pornography to 16-19 year olds is legal in Denmark, no persons under age 20 were observed in the shops.

Adult Movie Theater Patrons

Winick (1970a) observed 5,000 customers of adult movie theaters in nine different communities that provided a considerable spread of size, geographic, cultural, ethnic, and socioeconomic characteristics. The observations in eight of these locations were relatively consistent, but one was quite different from the others. We will describe the results of the observations on the eight and then discuss the ninth location.

Seventeen percent of the attendees were estimated to be in the age category 19-27, 32% in the 28-40 category, 41% in the 41-60 age group, and 10% were estimated to be over 60 years old. These figures did not vary significantly from city to city. Eighty percent were white, 14% black, 5% Spanish-American and 2% oriental. These figures did vary from city to city, but the variation appears to reflect the ethnic makeup of the community. Ninety-eight percent of the patrons were male; more females were observed in suburban locations than in downtown locations. All the females were with a male escort or in a mixed-gender group. Ninety percent of the men attended alone. Attending alone was even more characteristic for the downtown theaters; roughly 15% of the patrons of neighborhood theaters attended in groups of two or more males. Twenty-nine percent of the patrons were estimated to be lower class, 55% middle class, and 16% upper middle class. These proportions differed widely from situation to situation reflecting the character of the area in which the theater was located. For example, 62% of the patrons of New York neighborhood theaters were lower class, 69% of those in Kansas City were middle class, and 48% of patrons of New York suburban adult theaters were upper middle class. Forty-one percent wore suits and ties, 50% wore neat casual clothes, and 10% wore work clothes. This also varied by community. Downtown and suburban theaters had more suits and ties and neighborhood

160

theaters had more work clothes; Los Angeles had more casually dressed patrons. Approximately 15% of the customers scrutinized the outside display and a similar proportion exhibited a conflicted demeanor in entering the theater. Very few juveniles were observed looking at the displays outside the theater.

The one theater whose patrons did not fit this general description was a theater in a relatively small city that contained several colleges. The patrons of this theater were more likely to be younger, white, and casually dressed; there was also more attendance of male-female couples.

Winick (1970b) also conducted interviews with 100 patrons of an adult movie theater which provided validation for the classifications based on external observation. He classified each of the patrons in terms of age, ethnicity, and social class on the basis of external observations before the interview and then again after the interview on the basis of the interview data. The two sets of classifications correspond very closely; the main difference was reclassification of a few cases from upper middle class to middle class. These data confirm the possibility of making such judgments accurately from external observation and heightened our confidence in the descriptions provided by such observations.

A small pilot study of theater patrons in Denver (Massey, 1970) produced observations that fit well within the range of the observations reported by Winick (1970a).

Nawy (1970) observed a total of 2,791 customers at three adult theaters in San Francisco. Ninety-seven percent of these customers were male. Eleven percent were age 18-25, 28% were age 26-35, 32% were age 36-45, 20% were age 46-55, and 9% were over age 55. Very few customers appeared to possibly be under 18 years old. Seventy percent of the patrons were white, 5% were black, 14% were Chinese, and 8% were Japanese. Blacks are underrepresented and Chinese overrepresented in comparison to their population in the city. Thirty-nine percent wore suit and tie, 49% wore neat casual clothes, 6% were dressed in sloppy casual clothes, 4% were in "hip" costumes, and 2% in blue collar work clothes. Thirty-one percent wore a wedding band, 58% did not, and 11% could not be observed; this provides an estimate that about 60% are married based on the assumption that half of married men wear wedding bands. Eighty-five percent of the customers entered the theater alone, 6% were with the opposite sex, and 8% were in a group of the same sex.

161

Twenty-three percent of the patrons appeared to be regular customers.

Nawy (1970) also collected questionnaire data from 251 of these adult movie theater patrons. The demographic data on this questionnaire sample is very similar to the description of the total sample of patrons based on external observation. Thirteen percent were under age 26, 78% were age 26-55, and 9% were over 55 years old. Fifty-eight percent of the questionnaire sample were married. Fifty-two percent of this sample were college graduates. Forty-three percent report professional, managerial, or semi-professional occupations, and another 24% report other white collar occupations; 11% did not report on occupation. Forty-one percent of these patrons reported annual incomes over $15,000 and 26% reported incomes between $9,000 and $15,000 a year; 12% did not report their income. Thus, the external observations are validated and amplified by the self reports.

Patrons of adult movie theaters may be characterized on the basis of these observations to be predominantly white, middle class, middle aged, married, males, who attend alone. This contrasts very much with the characteristics of patrons of general movie theaters who tend to be young heterosexual couples (Yankelovich, 1968).

Nawy (1970) reports that his observations revealed that over half of the adult movie theater business is conducted during the 9:00 a.m. to 5:00 p.m. working day. This may be less true for neighborhood and suburban theaters than for downtown theaters. This busines pattern contrasts sharply with that of the general motion picture theaters which often do not open until 6:00 p.m.

Nawy (1970) and Winick (1970a) both noted that black and Spanish-American customers tend to be younger than the white customers in both bookstores and movie houses.

ARCADE PATRONS

Two pilot studies of adult film arcade patrons have been made (Massey, 1970; Nawy, 1970). Both of these indicate that females are not allowed in these arcades.

Massey (1970) observed 236 persons entering an adult film arcade in a single day's complete coverage. He concludes that, "the general type and characteristics of consumers observed in the bookstores continued to be seen in the arcade."

Nawy (1970) observed a total of 367 patrons in all six of the known adult film arcades in San Francisco. The

162

characteristics of these customers were similar to those of the patrons of the bookstores and the movie houses: white, middle aged, middle class, married males. Chinese were less often found in the arcades than in the movies. During business week lunch hours and around 5:00 p.m., three out of four patrons of the arcade were dressed in suit and tie.

INTERVIEW AND QUESTIONNAIRE STUDIES OF CONSUMERS OF EROTIC MATERIALS

Several investigators (Goldstein, et al., 1970; Massey, 1970; Nawy, 1970; Winick, 1970b) have attempted to study patrons of adult bookstores and adult movie theaters. All have reported a great deal of difficulty in securing the cooperation of members of these potential subject populations. Customers in adult bookstores appear more reluctant to participate in a study than patrons of adult movie houses. The response rates in the successful studies were all less than 50%. This low response rate may introduce an undetermined bias into the results because those who agree to filling out the questionnaire or to the interview may be different in some other way from those who do not agree to participate. The distribution of demographic data on the people who participated in the more intensive studies is very similar to that found for the larger samples of observed customers, however; this would suggest that the other data may be fairly representative, too. The fact that data from three independent investigations are consistent with each other lends additional support to the possibility that the findings are representative.

Winick (1970b) conducted informal "discussion interviews" with 100 patrons of adult movie theaters. These interview subjects were selected so as to have a distribution on a variety of externally observable demographic characteristics similar to the distribution of these characteristics among a larger sample of adult movie patrons (Winick, 1970a). Fifteen percent of the sample reported attending such movies once a week or more; 37% attended less than once a week but more often than once every two months; 23% reported attending occasionally; 18% did not see such movies on a systematic basis; and no information was obtained from 7%. Regular customers of adult movies usually have been attending such films for several years and have well developed consumer patterns. Many of the theater patrons also referred in the interviews to other types of erotic materials, with the

163

suggestion that they are familiar with several forms of erotica.

The most common response to the movies made in the interviews was a critical and comparative evaluation of adult movies from the viewpoint of the connoisseur. Sixty-five percent of the patrons commented along these lines; these people tended to be older and fairly frequent movie goers. Fifty-six percent of these viewers identified aspects of information as significant elements in adult films. Fantasy reactions to the movies, usually sexual and often humorous, were commented upon by 56% of the interviewees. Thirty-nine percent of the subjects mentioned the social context of viewing the film. The majority of these expressed positive sentiments regarding the sharing of an experience with others even though the sharing was very impersonal—indeed the impersonal aspect appeared to be essential. The minority of negative and ambivalent aspects of the social context specifically referred to the need to remain alone and separate from the others. Approximately one-quarter (27%) referred to the sexual stimulus value of the movies. The kind of content which acts as a stimulus to these people is the literally and explicitly sexual, with novel or forbidden fruit providing a further increment.

Nawy (1970) administered questionnaires to two samples of patrons of adult movie theaters, using two different methods. In one case, questionnaires were left at an accessible place in the theater to be filled out and returned; of 800 questionnaires, 190 or 24% were returned. In another case every third person leaving the theater was approached and requested to complete the questionnaire; 44% of those approached complied with the request, and this resulted in 61 completed questionnaires. The distribution of demographic variables was very similar and the two samples were combined for analysis. The distribution on demographic variables for this combined sample was not statistically significantly different from the total sample of over 3,000 patrons observed.

Nawy (1970) found that the patrons of adult movies generally lead active and varied sex lives. Ninety-three percent have a regular partner; most have intercourse twice a week or more often; and most report having had intercourse with more than one person during the past year. Most of these viewers of adult movies say that their sex partners are aware of their interest in sex films. Fifty-four percent report that sex is more enjoyable since they have been viewing sex films and less than one percent report that attendance at such films has had a negative effect on their sexual relations.

Seventy-nine percent report that the films have motivated them to introduce new variety into their sex lives. This variety was within fairly circumscribed limits, however, for these people were overwhelming heterosexual; only one of the respondents indicated an interest in experimenting with sadomasochism, and none indicated a desire to engage in bestiality or pedophilia.

Thirty-six percent of these patrons report attending adult movies once a week or oftener. They do not feel guilty about such attendance. Their reported reasons for attending these movies are: for entertainment only, 45%; to get new ideas, 36%; viewing is satisfying in itself, 35%; to pass time, 24%. Seventy-one percent of the movie patrons have purchased material at adult bookstores. Forty percent of these people report having spent more than $100 in the past year on erotic materials.

These customers of adult movie theaters manifest a good deal of upward socioeconomic mobility. Consistent with this upward mobility is that they report larger percentages delaying first intercourse experience until after high school years than does a national sample of men generally (Kinsey, 1948) or a national sample of college students (Berger, et al., 1970a).

Goldstein and his colleagues (1970) interviewed 52 volunteer customers of adult bookstores and adult movie theaters using standardized clinical interviews of approximately two and one-half hours length that inquired intensively into history of experience with erotic materials, attitudes toward sex, and sexual history. The responses from this sample are compared with responses from 53 control subjects to the same interview. The two groups are fairly similar in terms of a variety of demographic variations except that the consumers of erotic materials are better educated and have higher level current occupations.

The buyers of erotic material tend to report more parental permissiveness when they were growing up regarding nudity around the home and exposure to erotic materials than do the controls, but there were no differences in the amount of either erotica around the house or conversation about sex. The two groups report essentially the same source of sex information, but the buyers of erotica tend to have been less likely to have had a sex education course in school.

The buyers are more likely to have had their first sexual intercourse after age 18 than are the controls, and they report less experience with erotica during adolescence.

As adults, the buyers of erotica report frequencies of intercourse fairly similar to that of the controls and a similar degree of enjoyment of intercourse. They are more permissive toward a variety of sexual practices, feeling that every individual should be free to decide for himself what to do in the sexual realm. In practice they also are more likely to have extramarital sexual experience and more often to achieve orgasm through nonintercourse means. The buyers of erotica differ from the controls most in the amount of experience that they have had with pictorial and textual erotic materials; they do not differ, however, in exposure to live erotic shows.

Most patrons of adult bookstores and movies houses appear to have had less sexually related experiences in adolescence than the average male, but to be more sexually oriented as an adult. This high degree of sexual orientation in adulthood encompasses, in addition to pictorial and textual erotica, a variety of partners and a variety of activities within a consensual framework. Activities most frowned upon by our society, such as sadomasochism, pedophilia, bestiality and nonconsensual sex, are also outside the scope of their interest.

NOTES

1. Reference should be made to the Report of the Positive Approaches Panel of the Commission which conducted an in-depth analysis of the movie rating system.

2. No individual reports were disclosed, of course; only aggregate statistics were furnished by the Census Bureau.

3. Of course, 16mm can refer merely to the size of film used, not to the content of the film. All of the films discussed previously are exhibited in 35mm, although a few may originally have been filmed in 16mm and "blown up" for presentation in theaters. In the industry, however, the term "16mm films" has come to denote the type of sexually oriented films described in this section, primarily because such films are almost always exhibited in 16mm (sometimes in 8mm, but never in 35mm).

4. Sixteen millimeter films are not included in this estimate.

5. At one time, many arcades were not operated in conjunction with retail book and magazine sales, but in 1970 most arcades are part of "adult bookstores."

6. Based on a response of 220 of the 550 members of the Council for Periodical Distributors Association, who were asked by the Commission to provide such data because they were familiar with the areas they serve, although they do not handle secondary materials.

7. For a more complete discussion of the legal aspects of mail-order advertising, see the Report of the Legal Panel.

8. The Postal Inspection Service was extremely cooperative throughout the survey. Indeed, all divisions of the Post Office were extremely helpful.

9. Disclosures of individual or corporate tax returns are prohibited; the Internal Revenue Service supplied only industry-wide sales and income statistics.

10. Some judges have employed the term "hard-core pornography" as a synonym for "material which can be legally suppressed." In this Report, the term is used as a synonym for "under-the-counter" or covertly sold materials. This is, in effect, the definition of hard-core applied in the marketplace. It can be argued that because of the confusion about the meaning of the term,

which stems primarily from an undefined legal concept, it would be well to avoid the use of the term altogether.

REFERENCES

Abelson, H., Cohen, R., Heaton, E., and Suder, C. Public attitudes toward and experience with erotic materials. *Technical reports of the Commission on Obscenity and Pornography,* Vol 6. Washington, D. C.: U. S. Government Printing Office, 1970.

Annual report of the postmaster general, 1969. Washington, D. C.: U. S. Government Printing Office, 1970.

Athanasiou, R., Shaver, P., and Tavris, C. Sex, *Psychology today,* July, 1970, pp. 39-52.

Berger, A., Gagnon, J., and Simon, W. Pornography: High school and college years. *Technical reports of the Commission on Obscenity and Pornography,* Vol. 9. Washington, D. C.: U. S. Government Printing Office, 1970. (a)

Berger, A., Gagnon, J., and Simon, W. Urban working-class adolescents and sexually explicit media. *Technical reports of the Commission on Obscenity and Pornography,* Vol. 9. Washington, D. C.: U. S. Government Printing Office, 1970. (b)

Bestsellers. January, 1969-July, 1970.

Department of Commerce, Bureau of the Census. *1967 census of business.* (Preliminary Report) Washington, D. C.: U. S. Government Printing Office, 1970. (a)

Department of Commerce, Business and Defense Services Administration. *U. S. Industrial Outlook, 1970.* Washington, D. C.: U. S. Government Printing Office, 1970. (b)

Elias, J. Exposure to erotic materials in adolescence. Unpublished manuscript, Commission files, 1970.

Fersch, E. The relationship between students' experience with restricted-access erotic materials and their behaviors and attitudes. Unpublished manuscript, Commission files, 1970.

Finkelstein, M. M. Traffic in sex-oriented materials, Part I: Adult bookstores in Boston, Massachusetts. *Technical reports of the Commission on Obscenity and Pornography,* Vol. 4. Washington, D. C.: U. S. Government Printing Office, 1970. (a)

Finkelstein, M. M. Traffic in sex-oriented materials, Part II: Criminality and organized crime. *Technical reports of the Commission on Obscenity and Pornography,* Vol. 2. Washington, D. C.: U. S. Government Printing Office, 1970. (b)

Goldstein, M. J., and Kant, H. Exposure to pornography and sexual behavior in deviant and normal groups. *Technical reports of the Commission on Obscenity and Pornography,* Vol. 7. Washington, D. C.: U. S. Government Printing Office, 1970.

International motion picture almanac, 1969. New York: Quigley Publications, 1969.

Knight, A., and Alpert, H. The history of sex in the cinema, Part XVI: The nudies. *Playboy,* June, 1967, p. 124 ff.

Kutschinsky, B. Pornography in Denmark: Studies on producers, sellers, and users. *Technical reports of the Commission on Obscenity and Pornography,* Vol. 4. Washington, D. C.: U. S. Government Printing Office, 1970.

Laven, F. D. APDA survey of secondary publishers. Unpublished manuscript, Commission files, 1970.

Lynch, T., and O'Brien, C. A report to the California legislature on obscenity: The law and the nature of the business. Unpublished manuscript, Commission files, 1967

Magazine industry newsetter. December 9, 1969.

Massey, M. E. A market analysis of sex-oriented materials in Denver, Colorado, August, 1969—A pilot study. *Technical reports of the Commission on Obscenity and Pornography,* Vol. 4. Washington, D. C.: U. S. Government Printing Office, 1970.

Nawy, H. The San Francisco erotic marketplace. *Technical reports of the Commission on Obscenity and Pornography,* Vol. 4. Washington, D. C.: U. S. Government Printing Office, 1970.

Paperback books in print. New York: R. R. Bowker, 1970.

President's Commission on Postal Organization. *Towards postal excellence.* Washington, D. C.: U. S. Government Printing Office, 1968.

Propper, M. Exposure to sexually oriented materials among young male prison offenders. *Technical reports of the Commission on Obscenity and Pornography,* Vol. 9. Washington, D. C.: U. S. Government Printing Office, 1970.

Publisher's weekly. May 25, 1970. (a)

Publisher's weekly. June 29, 1970. (a)

Randall, R. S. *Censorship of the movies.* Madison: University of Wisconsin Press, 1968.

Randall, R. S. Classification by the motion picture industry. *Technical reports of the Commission on Obscenity and Pornography,* Vol. 10. Washington, D. C.: U. S. Government Printing Office, 1970. (a)

Randall, R. S. Gross receipts for MPAA—rated and unrated films. Unpublished manuscript, Commission files, 1970. (b)

Roach, W. J., and Kreisberg, L. Westchester college students' views on pornography. *Technical reports of the Commission on Obscenity and Pornography,* Vol. 1. Washington, D. C.: U. S. Government Printing Office, 1970.

Sampson, J. J. Commercial traffic in sexually oriented materials in the United States, 1969-70. *Technical reports of the Commission on Obscenity and Pornography,* Vol. 3. Washington, D. C.: U. S. Government Printing Office, 1970.

Smith, A., and Locke, B. Response of police and prosecutors to problems in arrests and prosecutions for obscenity and pornography. *Technical reports of the Commission on Obscenity and Pornography,* Vol. 2. Washington, D. C.: U. S. Government Printing Office, 1970.

Sonnenschein, D. Pornography: A false issue. *Psychiatric opinion.* February, 1969.

Sonnenschein, D., Ross, M., Bauman, R., Swartz, L., and Maclachlan, M. A study of mass media erotica: The romance or confession magazine. *Technical reports of the Commission on Obscenity and Pornography,* Vol. 9. Washington, D. C.: U. S. Government Printing Office, 1970.

Valenti, J. Testimony before the Commission on Obscenity and Pornography, May 12, 1970. *Technical reports of the Commission on Obscenity and Pornography,* Vol. 11. Washington, D. C.: U. S. Government Printing Office, 1970.

Variety, January 7, 1970. (a)

Variety. June 17, 1970. (b)

Wallace, D., and Wehmer, G. Contemporary standards of visual erotica. *Technical reports of the Commission on Obscenity and Pornography,* Vol. 9. Washington, D. C.: U. S. Government Printing Office, 1970.

White, D. M. College students' experience with erotica. *Technical reports of the Commission on Obscenity and Pornography,* Vol. 1. Washington, D. C.: U. S. Government Printing Office, 1970.

Wilson, W. C., Horowitz, B., and Friedman, J. The gravity of the pornography situation and the problems of control: A survey of prosecuting attorneys. *Technical reports of the Commission on Obscenity and Pornography,* Vol. 2. Washington, D. C.: U. S. Government Printing Office, 1970.

Wilson, W. C., and Jacobs, S. Sex educators' opinions regarding adolescents' experience with erotica: A national survey. *Technical reports of the Commission on Obscenity and Pornography,* Vol. 10. Washington, D. C.: U. S. Government Printing Office, 1970.

Winick, C. A study of consumers of explicitly sexual materials: Some functions served by adult movies. *Technical reports of the Commission on Obscenity and Pornography,* Vol. 4. Washington, D. C.: U. S. Government Printing Office, 1970. (a)

Winick, C. Some observations of patrons of adult theaters and bookstores. *Technical reports of the Commission on Obscenity and Pornography,* Vol. 4. Washington, D. C.: U. S. Government Printing Office, 1970.

Yankelovich, Inc. Public survey of movie-goers—1967. In *A year in review,* New York: Motion Picture Association of America, 1968, pp. 11-12.

Zetterberg, H. L. The consumers of pornography where it is easily available: The Swedish experience. *Technical reports of the Commission on Obscenity and Pornography,* Vol. 9. Washington, D. C.: U. S. Government Printing Office, 1970.

II. THE IMPACT OF EROTICA

Report of the Effects Panel to the Commission on Obscenity and Pornography.

Weldon T. Johnson
Lenore R. Kupperstein
and
W. Cody Wilson, Executive Director and
Director of Research
and
THE EFFECTS PANEL
Otto N. Larsen—Chairman
G. William Jones
Joseph T. Klapper
Morris A. Lipton
Marvin E. Wolfgang
William B. Lockhart—ex officio

Preface

If a case is to be made against "pornography" in 1970, it will have to be made on grounds other than demonstrated effects of a damaging personal or social nature. Empirical research designed to clarify the question has found no reliable evidence to date that exposure to explicit sexual materials plays a significant role in the causation of delinquent or criminal sexual behavior among youth or adults.

Existing legislation and judicial decisions are based upon considerations other than demonstrable effects of this nature, although the possibility of such effects seems to underlie this body of law. Legal judgments and social policy established without consideration of effects would seem to be inherently limited. The Effects Panel has examined existing popular and scientific literature and has initiated new empirical research. In drawing conclusions, we have been sensitive to both the quantity and quality of the research. The conclusion to be drawn from the totality of these research findings is that no dangerous effects have been demonstrated on any of the populations which were studied.

The adequacy of research related to policy decisions certainly requires careful evaluation. Questions will be raised about the studies reported here. Were the most relevant criteria of effects employed? How valid were the measures of impact? How much reliance can be placed on self report of responses to erotica? How representative were the populations studied; Do statistical correlations provide a strong basis for inference? We welcome the discussion of these questions by the scientific community. The basic source material will be published in a series of ten volumes of Technical Reports to facilitate this discussion.

The Commission's research program had two important general limitations. First, a narrow time scope was employed. The life of the Commission was approximately two years and the time available for conducting research was considerably less than that. One consequence of this lack of time is that long-term effects could not be adequately investigated. A second consequence of the time limitation is that this report is of necessity not a completely finished product. The preparation and polishing of so detailed a report on the findings of dozens of studies realistically require a period of at least half a year. The brief time actually available to the Panel between the receipt of the reports of the Commission initiated research and the terminal date of the Commission has made it impossible to apply the editorial rigor customary in scientific reports. Thus, for example, tables and references to them will be found, on occasion, to fall somewhat short of easy cross reference. Although every effort within the limits of time available has been made to insure the accuracy of this report, it has been impossible to double check each and every one of the thousands of discrete statistics cited in this report against the dozens of different manuscripts from which they are drawn. In brief this report should and, were the time available, could be rendered more fully consonant with the canons of scientific editing than it now is. Such polishing, however, would not affect the major conclusions which are presented.

Second, access to populations of younger age groups was restricted. Although the research involved several surveys of adolescents and experimental studies with young adults, children generally were deemed inaccessible for direct inquiry.

170

Despite these limitations, the Effects Panel believes that the studies undertaken for the Commission from a wide variety of settings and employing a wide array of effect indicators does add significantly to our understanding of the conditions under which specified types of erotica are, or are not, apt to evoke various physiological, attitudinal, judgmental, and behavioral responses. Because of the Panel's awareness of the pioneering nature of the research, the report includes not only research findings but also specific references to major problems remaining for the study of effects and some suggestions as to how these may be approached.

The Panel has attempted to present a straightforward account of problems, procedures, and findings without explicit reference to policy implications. Policy was the responsibility of the entire Commission and recommendations are presented by the full Commission. Nevertheless, the Effects Panel regards it as appropriate to assert that any recommendations proposing blanket restrictions on all forms of sex-oriented material cannot be based on a reasonable interpretation of the effects here presented even when the limitations of the data are considered. Available research on the impact of erotica clearly suggests that greater latitude can safely be given to adults in deciding for themselves what they will or will not read and view.

One of the contributions of the work of the Panel has been to place the dimension of human sexual behavior on the agenda for continuing inquiry. By providing resources in terms of funds and technical guidelines, the Panel has helped to legitimate systematic inquiry into an area that heretofore has either been ignored or feared. We strongly recommend that such research be further funded and encouraged.

In submitting this report to our colleagues on the Commission, to the President of the United States, to the Congress of the United States, and to the American people we wish to acknowledge a debt to the industrious investigators who have produced the findings, herein summarized. To our Executive Director and Director of Research, Dr. W. Cody Wilson, we are grateful for the creative manner in which he implemented the research program. Finally, to the principal writers of this account, Dr. Weldon T. Johnson and Lenore Kupperstein, we offer special thanks for their dedicated and talented labors in organizing and preparing this report on the impact of erotica.

The members of the Effects Panel, who have participated actively in all phases of the work from research planning

171

to reviewing results and presenting these results in this report, endorse the report and accept responsibility for its contents.

The Effects Panel
Otto N. Larsen, Chairman
G. William Jones
Joseph T. Klapper
Morris A. Lipton
Marvin E. Wolfgang

Section A. Orientation to the Study of Effects

In July of 1968, the Commission established an Effects Panel, as one of four working Panels, and charged it with principal responsibility for three activities: (a) to review and evaluate existing research bearing on the effects of exposure to sexual stimuli; (b) to design a program of new research in the area; (c) to summarize, evaluate, and report the findings of these studies to the full Commission.

CONCEPTUALIZING EFFECTS

The first task facing the Panel was to identify presumed effects of erotic materials and refine these for purposes of research. Two sources were consulted for guidance: (a) previous research in this area, and (b) the claims which had been made about the consequences of reading and viewing erotic material. Reviews of this literature generated several basic questions. If exposure to erotic materials does, in fact, have harmful effects, what kinds of effects are these and who experiences them? Distinctions can be made, for example, between "short-term" effects and "long-term" effects; between "direct" and "indirect" effects; and between effects upon conduct, and effects upon emotions, attitudes, opinions, and moral character. Are these effects experienced by adequately socialized "normal" individuals or only by persons who have already experienced some form of psychopathic or sociopathic condition? Are adults affected, or only children, or both? Various other questions can be asked, but these will perhaps suffice as examples.

172

A review of empirical studies published prior to 1968 revealed little research directly relevant to the total assessment
of effects (Cairns, Paul, and Wishner, 1962).

The Panel learned that existing empirical knowledge pertained generally to sexual arousals, responses, and it could
be summarized briefly: (a) Pictures and words depicting
various aspects of human sexuality produce sexual arousal in
a considerable proportion of the adult population; (b) materials which elicit arousal differ according to the sex of the
viewer; (c) persons differ in their preference for, and response to, sexual stimuli; and (d) the context in which the
viewing occurs is a significant determinant of the extent to
which persons will be aroused by the materials. The reviewers
found no research indicating the duration of arousal or how
this stimulation might affect overt behavior, attitudes governing behavior, or mental health. A later Commission-sponsored
review of the literature concluded that "we still have precious
little information from studies of humans on the questions
of primary import to the law . . . the data 'stop short at the
critical point.' Definitive answers on the determinants and
effects of pornography are not yet available" (Cairns, 1970).

FORMULATIONS FROM POPULAR LITERATURE

In the popular literature about sexually oriented material,
the Panel found that statements about effects typically employed general terms such as "crime" and "anti-social behavior." Socially disapproved consequences and, occasionally,
some socially approved consequences were suggested.

Of all the assertions about erotic material, four are especially prominent: (a) erotica is an offense against community
standards of good taste; (b) exposure to erotica is harmful
for individuals; (c) the existence of erotica has harmful
consequences for society; and (d) exposure to erotica is
harmless or beneficial for individuals.

Offensiveness. Many public statements about erotica reveal that some persons are disgusted or offended by exposure,
or that they simply disapprove of its existence. Pornography
is alleged to be a stench in the public nostril "quite analagous
to keeping a goat in a residential area, or urinating in public"
(Gagnon and Simon, 1967), and there is a tendency to move

from this argument to the "harmful effects" assertion without recognizing the shift in concern. The "offensiveness" effect has been articulated forcefully. For example,

> . . . I am convinced that this traffic in hard-core pornography is indeed an evil of considerable magnitude. This stuff is pollution, as surely as sewage, and it ought to be equally subject to Federal control through the commerce clause. I cannot prove that it is harmful even to young people, but I doubt that the contrary can be proved either—that it is not harmful. There are times when reasonable men have to rely upon their instincts and upon their common sense (Kilpatrick, 1967:24).

> . . . whether the smut incites to crime or not, there can be no doubt that it does degenerate taste and debauch truth (Banning, 1952:135).

Erotic materials have sometimes been regarded as offensive because of their literary deficiencies:

> Pornography, as I have indicated, is harmless so long as we do not corrupt our taste by mistaking it for literature . . . (Burgess, 1970:6).

> After fifty pages of hardening nipples, softly opening thighs, and hot rivers flowing in and out of the ecstatic anatomy, the spirit cries out, not in hypocritical outrage, not because I am a poor Square throttling by libido, but in pure, nauseous boredom. Even fornication can't be as dull, as hopelessly predictable, as all that (Steiner, 1970:103).

The increasing availability of erotic materials typically has been described as a "flood," "avalanche," "growing weeds," "creeping obscenity," or "the pernicious flow of filth which daily gluts our postal system."

Such claims in the current literature indicate that erotic materials do offend and disgust some persons. The Panel concluded that it would be important to regard reactions of disgust and offensiveness, or their opposites, as potential effects. This required differentiating such judgments from other behavioral effects.

Exposure Is Harmful For Individuals. This class of assertions, the Panel found, has generated more attention and discussion than any other. Two characteristics are noteworthy: First, assertions differ according to whether an adult or a child is the affected agent, and the alleged effects upon children generally are different from those which adults are thought to experience. Second, a wide range of behaviors, sexual and nonsexual, criminal and noncriminal, are thought to be effects of exposure. Figure 1 shows an inventory of the presumed effects of exposure which have appeared in the popular literature.

FIGURE 1

Presumed Consequences of Exposure to Erotica

	Sexual	Nonsexual
Criminal or Generally Regarded as Harmful	1. sexually aggressive acts of a criminal nature 2. unlawful sexual practices 3. nonconsensual sex acts 4. incest 5. sexually perverse behavior 6. adultery 7. illegal sexual activities 8. socially disapproved sexual behavior 9. sexual practices harmful to self 10. deadly serious pursuit of sexual satisfaction 11. dehumanized sexual acts 12. preoccupation (obsession) with sex 13. change direction of sexual development from natural pathway 14. block psychosexual maturation 15. misinformation about sex 16. moral breakdown	17. homicide 18. suicide 19. delinquency 20. criminal acts 21. indecent personal habits 22. unhealthy habits 23. unhealthy thoughts 24. reject reality 25. ennui 26. submission to authoritarianism
Neutral	27. sex attitudes 28. sex values 29. sex information 30. sex habits	
Beneficial/ Helpful	31. drains off illegitimate sexual desires 32. provides outlet for otherwise frustrated sexual drives 33. releases strong sexual urges without harming others 34. pleasure 35. provides discharge of "antisocial" sexual appetites 36. assists consummation of legitimate sexual responsibilities	

Assertions vary from predicting general consequences such as:

> . . . if pornography were allowed to proliferate unchecked, it might influence both public and private attitudes and sensibilities, and, therefore, ultimately actions (van den Haag, 1970:125).

and:

> . . . eroticism frees the imaginations not only of children but of the child that is in the hearts of all men, leading them to go much further than they would go on their own. Inflamed fantasy leads to inflamed action (Kubie, 1967:69).

to specific predictions about concrete behavior:

> . . . A notable increase in homosexual offenses can be

175

traced to the availability of magazines devoted to these perversities . . . (Frignito, 1967:86).

Critics often use very general concepts when they attempt to describe the social psychological mechanisms which produce the alleged effects. For example,

Guilt and fear and love serve our needs for mutual security by holding tight rein on the wild horses within every man. Only in exceptional instances do fantasies go over into action, whether of murder, suicide, robbery, or rape. But their unbridled representation removes these restraints (Kubie, 1967:69).

. . . pornography deindividualises and dehumanises sexual acts; by eliminating all the context it reduces people simply to bearers of impersonal sensations of pleasure and pain. This de-humanisation eliminates the empathy that restrains us ultimately from sadism and nonconsensual acts (van den Haag, 1967:53).

Much of the concern about the effect of sexual materials has been addressed specifically to the presumed impact upon children. These assertions are based on the principle that where no strong attitudinal and behavioral commitments exist a priori, the impact of exposure to erotic material is especially pronounced. The following statements are representative of the claims that exposure to erotic materials among children and adolescents is associated with nonsexual crime and delinquency:

Pornography is designed for instant self-gratification and that is a dangerous, decadent character-deforming way of life to teach children. It blunts sensibility, leads to a society of selfish, disengaged, uninvolved individuals, results in sex without love and violence solely for the pleasure it begets and leads ultimately—not to utopia— but, as settled history demonstrates, to delinquency (Carroll, 1967:37).

The publication and distribution of salacious materials is a peculiarly vicious evil; the destruction of moral character caused by it among young people cannot be overestimated. The circulation of periodicals containing such materials plays an important part in the development of crime among youth of our country (Hoover, 1956:2).

Statements about socially disapproved sexual behaviors, are equally prominent.

These pornographic materials are bound to produce in the lives of the teenagers acts of masturbation, acts of

176

self-abuse, acts of unnatural things between fellows and girls, and this is shown up, then, in the sense of guilt, and that reveals itself in emotional problems in the classrooms (Egan, 1955:72).

During psychiatric treatment of institutionalized adolescent delinquent girls, a significant number of incidents of incestuous assaults are reported. The sexually aggressive fathers, brothers or other relatives, are devotees of smut (Frignito, 1967:86).

A number of assertions refer to inappropriate, incomplete, or inaccurate sexual information:

. . . The gravest charge is the damage it does to the youngster's "image" of sex. Pornography degrades sex. It blinds the youngster to the higher values of sexuality. It reduces this noble function to a mere self-indulgence, a plaything with dirty overtones, connected with smutty words on the walls of the public toilet (Levin, 1967:51).

. . . The prepubertal child and the already disturbed adolescent are the most vulnerable to the injurious effects of sexual information which is inaccurate, frightening and obscene. However, it is just these minors who would be apt to be interested in and to seek out pornography (Slap, 1967:54).

The Panel attempted to organize its research priorities around many of these assertions, including the effects upon behavior, attitudes, character, and emotions.

Erotic Materials Are Harmful For Society. Two distinct claims appear in this class of assertions. First, it is argued that the existence and use of erotic materials have an adverse effect upon the sexual and nonsexual morality of society. For example:

. . . it [pornography] has become a threat to the moral fiber of our society, particularly because of the effect upon young people, whose minds, are yet malleable, but whose responsibility it will become to safeguard this society and to pass it on to future generations (Miller, 1967:15).

No one can accurately estimate the incalculable harm that is being done to American society by the deliberate publication, widespread distribution, and open sale in food markets, drug stores, newstands, and many other retail outlets of literature that appeals to the lowest instincts of man (Fitzgerald, 1952:47).

A second type of claim implying harmful consequences for

society is that erotic materials result in social disorganization. For example, it has been stated that:

> If we indulge pornography, and do not allow censorship to restrict it, our society at best will become ever more coarse, brutal, anxious, indifferent, deindividualised, hedonistic; at worst its ethos will disintegrate altogether (van den Haag, 1967:55).

> It [pornography] blunts sensibility, leads to a society of selfish, disengaged, uninvolved individuals . . . (Carroll, 1967:37).

These assertions led the Panel to examine and attempt to employ recent methodological developments designed to assess moral development and moral character.

Exposure To Erotica Is Harmless Or Beneficial. The Panel also encountered statements which suggested that use of erotic materials is either (a) harmless or (b) potentially beneficial to the user under certain circumstances of use.

Those who assert that exposure to erotic materials is harmless argue that the capacity of graphic or literary material to affect behavior is negligible. For example:

> Among all the various sexual stimulations which a human being undergoes, what can be the relative weight of obscene literature as a factor affecting conduct? Particularly in our society, a steady stream of such influences impinges upon the individual from all quarters. It is argued that the impact of sex literature must be quite trivial compared to all these (Clor, 1969:151).

> . . . I am convinced that were all so-called objectional books and like material to disappear from the face of the earth tomorrow this would in no way affect the statistics of crime, delinquency, amoral and anti-social behavior, or personal illness and distress. The same frustrating and denying society would still exist, and both children and adults would express themselves mutinously against it. These problems will be solved only when we have the courage to face the fundamental social issues and personal perplexities that cause such behavior (Linder, 1959:273).

> . . . Conversations with sexual neurotics will almost invariably reveal that in their childhood any mention of sexual subjects was tabooed in their homes. One gets the impression that they have been told too little about sex life and that they have read too little rather than too much erotic literature . . . (Hughes, 1970:xv).

178

Some arguments conclude that erotic materials are not only harmless, but at times also produce beneficial or desirable effects. It has been suggested that sexual materials perform a useful function for individuals by extending opportunities for sexual expression. For example:

... it is in periods of sexual deprivation—to which the young and the old are far more subject than those in their prime—that males, at any rate, are likely to reap psychological benefit from pornography (Mercier, 1970: 21).

For men on long journeys, geographically cut off from wives and mistresses, pornography can act as a portable memory, a welcome shortcut to remembered bliss, relieving tension without involving disloyalty (Tynan, 1970:112).

Others argued that erotic material serves a cathartic function, i.e., it serves as a sexual "release," "safety valve" or neutralizer. It has been asserted that:

... these "unholy" instruments may be more often than not a safety valve for the sexual deviate and potential sex offender (Kronhausen and Kronhausen, 1959:273-274).

... people who read salacious literature are less likely to become sexual offenders than those who do not, for the reason that such reading often neutralizes what aberrant sexual interests they may have (Karpman, 1959:274).

... it is possible that obscene materials provide a way of releasing strong sexual urges without doing harm to others (Cairns, Paul and Wishner, 1962:1,036).

Finally, some have suggested that erotic materials may have instructional value and may discourage sexual inadequacy. For example:

The open distribution of pornography and obscenity would thus encourage heterosexuality, and discourage impotence and frigidity. As such, it is life-giving, a stimulus to joy and a source of socially harmless pleasure. Despite the forces of censorship, sexual intercourse is not a depraved shameful vice. It is a normal body function, habitual to the judge's parents, George Washington, and many leaders of the Girl Scouts. It will become habitual to our innocent daughters, or we should hope that it will (Hyman, 1970:40).

The foregoing questions indicate, at the very least, that men of good will in various professions differ in their views regarding the effects of erotica. The Panel concluded that em-

179

pirical research testing the validity of these varied assertions was urgently needed, and that such research should investigate both allegedly harmful and allegedly neutral or beneficial effects.

The Research Framework

In order to move from an inventory of asserted effects to a program of empirical research, the Panel next undertook to: (a) formulate a set of general goals; (b) outline appropriate research designs; and (c) examine feasible methods of inquiry.

RESEARCH GOALS

After discussing the contributions of previous research and the variety of unanswered questions in this area, the Panel set several goals for its program of studies. These were:

To investigate the relationship between use or availability of erotic material and sexual and nonsexual behavior, both antisocial and socially acceptable.

To investigate the relationship between availability and use of erotic materials and attitudes toward sex, moral outlook regarding sex, and standards of conduct in sex.

To investigate the relationship between exposure to erotic materials and sexual arousal in order to ascertain whether there is a cumulative effect or a satiation effect.

To investigate the relationship between exposure to erotic materials and general social and political attitudes in nonsexual areas.

To investigate the relationship between exposure to erotic materials and mental health or psychopathology.

To ascertain the attitudes of the population of the United States toward erotic materials and the effects of such materials.

RESEARCH DESIGNS

Two decisions were important in designing a program of studies: (a) establishing a satisfactory conception of the relevant stimuli; and (b) specifying the effects to be studied.

Specification Of The Stimulus. Substantial difficulties exist with regard to the terms "obscenity" and "pornography." There is no adequate definition of either in legal parlance or in ordinary language. Justice Stewart's remark ". . . I know

180

it when I see it . . ." is an example of the subjectivity associated with these terms. In general, various attempts to define either "obscenity" or "pornography" included the capacity of certain stimuli to elicit both sexual arousal and judgments of offensiveness. The Panel, however, did not limit its attention to the specific materials which the Courts have judged "obscene,"[1] but rather attempted to explore the effects of a wide range of erotic stimuli.

In the absence of well-defined and generally acceptable definitions of both obscenity and pornography, the Commission conceptualized the relevant stimuli as erotic materials, sexual materials, or sexually explicit stimuli over a range of media (photographs, snapshots, cartoons, films, and written materials in books, magazines and typewritten stories) which are capable of being described in terms of the sexual theme portrayed: e.g., "a man and a woman having sexual intercourse" or "mouth-sex organ contact between man and woman." Thus, judgmental terms such as "pornography" were eliminated from the research vocabulary and "erotic" and "sexual" used in their place.

This decision did not solve all or many of the problems associated with adequate description. In an effort to alleviate some of these problems, all researchers who used visual erotic stimuli in their studies were asked to standardize their stimuli by utilizing a set of erotic films (Schmidt, et al., 1969) and photographic slides (Levitt and Brady, 1965) produced specifically for psychological research. Other researchers who used questionnaires or interview schedules were asked to standardize their questions which described types of erotic materials. The visual stimuli (films and slides) selected for use in these studies included a range of depictions from the display of genitalia to various modes of sexual action, including fellatio, cunnillingus, coitus, and displays of "discipline" (e.g., flagellation and sexual bondage). When written materials were used as stimuli, an effort was made to select depictions from this range of themes.

Identification Of Effects. The act creating the Commission mentions specifically two broad areas of possible effects—crime and antisocial behavior. Just as the conceptualization of the relevant stimuli involved problems, so also did the refinement of "anti-social behavior." The term "antisocial behavior," while obviously including heinous crimes, does not carry consensual limits. Various attitudes and behaviors regarded by some persons as antisocial are not to regarded by

181

others. The Panel clearly could not, within its limited time and budget, investigate the relationships between erotica and every behavior or condition which might be regarded as antisocial. Specifically, the Commission's funded research addressed itself with varying degrees of depth and success to: (a) relationships between availability of erotica and the incidence of juvenile and adult sex offenses, with particular emphasis on forcible rape; (b) similarities and differences in experiences with erotica between delinquents and nondelinquents, and between nonoffender adults and adult sex offenders (particularly rapists and pedophiles), adult nonsex offenders (incarcerated for burglary, homicide, forgery, robbery, etc.) and sex deviants (homosexuals, transsexuals); (c) experimental analyses of the effects of exposure to erotica on psychosexual stimulation, on sexual behavior (masturbation, premarital, marital, and extramarital coitus, and other specified sexual practices), on attitudes (about sex and sexual materials), and on emotions (sexual and nonsexual).

Other behaviors and conditions, which might be regarded as antisocial, have not as yet been investigated. No data have been developed by the Commission, for example, in reference to the relationships between experience with erotica and venereal disease, or divorce.

RESEARCH METHODS

A variety of research methods was judged to be potentially responsive to the Panel's goals, and the members of the Panel agreed not to recommend one or two to the exclusion of others. Rather, effects studies followed a "multiple method approach" so that alternative strategies might be used to complement and supplement one another. The following methods were employed: surveys employing various types of sampling procedures (as described immediately below) quasi-experimental studies of selected populations, studies of rates and incidence at the community level, and controlled experimental studies.

Each of these methods was utilized to approach the general question: under what conditions do certain effects take place? The special suitability and limitations of each method should be noted.

SURVEY METHODS

A number of survey studies were undertaken in which samples of adults and youth were interviewed about their experiences with erotic materials and about attitudes and behavior, sexual and nonsexual. In general, persons having relatively more experience with erotic material were then compared with less experienced persons on a number of other relevant variables such as social and sexual attitudes, social and sexual behavior, and standards of sexual conduct. In some surveys (e.g., Berger, et al., 1970b), it was possible to ask respondents specifically about histories of delinquent and criminal conduct.

The Commission-funded surveys included probability samples of American adults and youth (Abelson, et al., 1970), residents of Copenhagen, Denmark (Kutschinsky, 1970c), high school students in a large midwestern school district (Elias, 1970), American sex educators and counselors (Wilson and Jacobs, 1970), and prosecuting attorneys within the United States (Wilson, et al., 1970). In addition, the Commission contracted for secondary analyses[2] of probability surveys of American college students (Berger, et al., 1970a) and adults and youth in Sweden (Zetterberg, 1970). The Commission also contracted for nonprobability sample surveys of Philadelphia sex offenders (Johnson, et al., 1970): young male inmates of a northeastern reformatory (Propper, 1970) and high school age working class youth (Elias, 1970; Berger, et al., 1970b).

One of the Commission's major research efforts was the national survey of American adults and youth.[3] The survey involved face-to-face interviews with a random sample[4] of 2,486 adults and over 700 young persons[5] age 15 to 20 in the 48 contiguous states. The survey had three general purposes: (a) to identify the amount, frequency, and circumstances of the public's exposure to erotic materials; (b) to describe community standards and norms pertaining to distribution, consumption, and control of erotica; and (c) to collect other relevant data concerning the correlates of exposure to erotic materials. Results of various aspects of the survey are summarized in the appropriate Panel Reports.

Surveys such as Abelson, et al., (1970) which employ "probability samples" may be "generalized to the population as a whole" within known limits which depend on certain technical characteristics of the procedure. Tables of "sampling tolerances" for this survey (adult and adolescent) appear in the Appendix to this Report. The "sampling tolerances" range up to 7% on a .95 confidence level for any subgroup of 400 or more, and as low as 4% for adult groups of 1,500 or more. This is to say that if the survey cites a given percentage in reference to 400 or more respondents (e.g., x%), it may be assumed that if the entire population of similar age and characteristics, were surveyed the chances are 95 out of 100 that the percentage obtained would be within the range X plus or minus 7%. The "tolerance" is at its maximum in reference to percentages close to 50%, and becomes progressively smaller as percentages depart from 50% in either direction. Percentages cited for groups of substantially less than 400 in number have a larger sampling tolerance. Example: 61% of 400 or more respondents say they believe "ABC." If *all* adults in the United States were asked the question, the chances are 95 out of 100 that the percentage saying "ABC" would be between 54% and 68%. Put another way, if *all* questions were asked of *all* adults, the replies would fall within indicated limits roughly 19 out of 20 times.

The limitations of survey design generally, and the survey findings presented in this Report should be noted. Data collection procedures, either face-to-face interview or self-administered questionnaires, may be affected by inaccurate recall or by dissimulation, i.e., respondents may not remember past experiences, or they may inaccurately report them, particularly in the area of private behavior. Although various methods may be employed to detect either, findings based on data provided by the respondent should be qualified in terms of these problems. Another limitation of survey design is the difficulty of casually interpreting statistical correlations. Although such relationships between variables may be strong and reliable, correlation in itself is not an adequate basis for inferring causality. Since the survey researcher typically has little knowledge about antecedent or intervening variables, extreme caution must be exercised in drawing causal inferences from such data. A third limitation of survey design is the problem of generalizing findings to other populations. Systematic sampling procedures (e.g., Abelson, et al., 1970; Kutschinsky, 1970c; Zetterberg, 1970) are employed to produce generalizable findings, but the population to which findings are generalizable must always be specified. For example, the findings of a probability survey of American college students (Berger, et al., 1970a), reported below may be generalized to the bulk of American college students, but not to students over the age of 24, part-time undergraduates, students attending schools with direct religious affiliations, or black students.

Quasi-Experimental Methods.   Although true experimental

designs were not always possible, the Commission contracted for a number of studies which approximated experimental design through retrospective comparisons of matched groups. In these studies groups of individuals that manifested a supposed consequence of exposure to erotica (e.g., juvenile delinquents, sex offenders, etc.) were compared with groups, similar in most characteristics except the misbehavior, in terms of past experiences with erotic materials. Such studies attempted to determine the extent to which the past experiences of the groups were similar or different by comparing: sex offenders and sex deviants with matched nonsex offenders or nonoffender adult groups (Cook and Fosen, 1970; Goldstein, et al., 1970; Walker, 1970), and young male prisoners with matched nonoffender males (Davis and Braucht, 1970b).

The principal limitations of these studies are problems associated with adequate matching and reliance upon respondent reports, both of which complicate the inference of causality.

The logic of quasi-experimental analysis was extended to statistical comparisons of the incidence of delinquency and crime with estimates of the availability of erotic materials in both Denmark (Ben-Veniste, 1970; Kutschinsky, 1970c) and the United States (Kupperstein and Wilson, 1970). The limitations of these studies are those associated with analysis of social indicator statistics: the adequacy of available statistical records and the problematic success of including other relevant variables. These problems also impose severe limitations upon attempts to assert or refute causal relationships.

Controlled Experiments. Situations in which two or more groups of individuals are given a controlled differential exposure to sexual materials and the consequences of exposure observed at later points provide the most rigorous test of causality. The Commission supported 14 such studies, which included a range of erotic stimuli and subjects. Erotic stimuli included textual material (Byrne and Lamberth, 1970; Howard, et al., 1970; Kutschinsky, 1970a), photographic slides (Amoroso, et al., 1970; Byrne and Lamberth, 1970; Cook and Fosen, 1970; Katzman, 1970a, 1970b; Wallace, et al., 1970) and erotic film (Mann, et al., 1970; Mosher, 1970a, 1970b; Howard, et al., 1970; Davis and Braucht, 1970a; Tannenbaum, 1970). Subjects in these experiments[6] included married adults (Byrne and Lamberth, 1970; Mann, et al., 1970; Kutschinsky, 1970a; Wallace, et al., 1970) young, unmarried males and females (Amoroso, et al., 1970; Mosher,

185

1970a, 1970b; Tannenbaum, 1970) and incarcerated sex and nonsex offenders (Cook and Fosen, 1970). Exposure to erotic stimuli occurred either in one 60 to 90 minute session (Amoroso, et al., 1970; Byrne and Lamberth, 1970; Cook and Fosen, 1970; Mosher, 1970a, 1970b; Davis and Braucht, 1970a; Kutschinsky, 1970a) or in several sessions spanning several weeks (Howard, et al., 1970; Mann, et al., 1970). In one study, subjects had an opportunity to view and read erotic materials 90 minutes a day for three weeks (Howard, et al., 1970). Behavioral consequences were assessed 24 hours after exposure (Amoroso, et al., 1970; Cook and Fosen, 1970; Davis and Braucht, 1970a; Howard, et al., 1970; Mann, et al., 1970), several weeks after the experiment (Howard, et al., 1970; Kutschinsky, 1970a; Mann, et al., 1970) and two months after exposure (Howard, et al., 1970).

The most important limitations of these experiments are the potential nongeneralizability of findings from self-selected (volunteer) subjects to other populations, and the extent to which study designs accounted for, or controlled, the influence of nonexperimental variables. In addition, reliance upon self reported responses may create problems of interpretation, especially introspective reports. The use of a range of subjects, no-exposure control groups, and multiple measurements reduce the problems of causal analysis in these studies.

In sum, the research program[7] on effects to be reviewed in this report is one that may be characterized as a multidisciplined pioneering approach to questions about the impact of erotica. As such, certain limitations must be emphasized. The pressure of time did not afford a fully comprehensive effort. Difficult choices had to be made about resources to be allocated for carrying out studies. Some areas of concern, as for example, the linkage of violence and sex, did not receive thorough inspection, and some modes and methods of inquiry were emphasized at the expense of others—statistical versus clinical case material, for example. Moreover, every study cited in this report has limitations. Some studies are more adequate than others. Many questions about effects remain unanswered. And even those findings that are rooted in careful research are tentative in the sense that they need to be checked again by further studies.

Despite these qualifications, the research reviewed in the following chapters provides specific findings and a pattern of evidence that begins to answer pertinent questions about effects. The Technical Reports on which this review is based also record experience that can help formulate more penetrating and productive inquiry in the future.

Section B. Public Opinion About Sexual Materials

The relative absence of research on the effects of erotica has not deterred the formation of strong opinions about (a) the extent to which available pornography constitutes a social problem and (b) the possible effects of exposure to sexually explicit depictions. Prior to 1970, however, opinion surveys had not attempted to assess in any depth the state of general public opinion in this sensitive area.

Systematic assessment of opinion is especially important in policy-related areas where community judgments may provide a basis for government action. In areas which lend themselves to empirical investigation, but where research is absent or available research is inadequate, the role of public opinion in the formulation of policy and legal statutes can be of critical importance. Although the issues of obscenity and pornography have been pronounced upon by the courts and the Congress, as well as by innumerable experts from various fields, these judgments could not have been illuminated by knowledge of public opinion until very recently.

Results of a Commission-sponsored survey are reported in the following pages. The findings show that in 1970, American public opinion on the effects of erotica is more varied than critics may have anticipated.

CURRENT PUBLIC OPINION

In 1970, a survey involving face-to-face interviews with a random sample of 2,486 adults and 769 young persons (ages 15 to 20) was conducted at the Commission's request (Abelson, et al., 1970). One of the purposes of the survey was to determine whether Americans regard and define the area of erotic materials as a significant or important social problem. Adult respondents in the survey were asked: "Would you please tell me what you think are the two or three most serious problems facing the country today?" Only 2% of the

187

population referred to erotic materials, and many of these comments alluded to erotica through criticism of mass media or contemporary sexual standards. The most frequently mentioned problems were: war (54%), race (36%), the national economy (32%), youth rebellion (23%), breakdown of law and order (20%), drugs (20%), pollution and misuse of resources (19%), poverty and poverty programs (12%), moral breakdown (9%), and dissatisfaction with government (9%). About 4% of the population mentioned education, overpopulation, and foreign policy as serious problems, and only 2% mentioned erotic materials.

FIGURE 2

Spontaneously Mentioned National Problems

(Question: "Would you please tell me what you think are the two or three most serious problems facing the country today?")

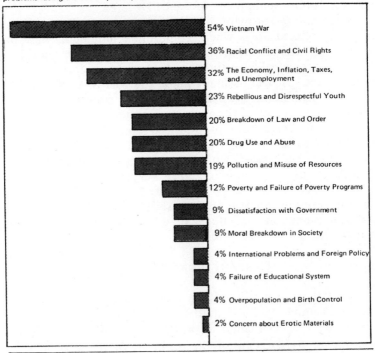

Note — Adapted from Abelson, H., Cohen, R., Heaton, E., & Slider, C. Public attitudes toward and experience with erotic materials. *Technical reports of the Commission on Obscenity and Pornography.* Vol. 6.

The study also showed that persons who did mention sexual materials as a serious social problem often implied a more basic concern with the general area of sexuality and sexual morality than with erotica. Abelson and his colleagues (1970) reported the following responses as illustrative of statements about erotic materials:

Sex—going around everywhere. In the movie—bad shows —too many nude people. Ugly movie—bad morals on the screen. People doing bad things, nasty things. Nude people.

Sex—I don't think views concerning sex and moralities have really changed drastically. It's coming only within a person's mental makeup, which has just been heading for many years. In other words, just going back to the animal structure of man. They're going back (for example) to wearing less clothes—exhibitionism.

I imagine the literature being put out—there seems to be a lot of emphasis on sex. Always using sex in advertisement in movies, T.V. Take a car—a beautiful girl somewhere. Sex—no moral standards at all.

Sex exploitation. The only place I come in contact with this is in the movie theaters. Many movies include unnecessary sex and abusive language. Seemingly for its shock emphasis rather than as an integral part of the scene. I don't think sex in movies is a bad thing if it is a part of the theme and makes a profound statement.

T.V.—they are showing the young generation too much. Stealing, killing, sexy mess—too much for the young generation.

I don't go to the movies. I hear talk about them. Nude movies. Nudity in the movies. It shouldn't be in it.

Sex—I think it's ruining our younger generation. I think it's a bad thing bringing it into the schools. Dress is too immodest. T.V. is rotten.

Morals—the general low moral standards displayed in T.V., movie theaters, fashions. People don't seem to give a darn.

Moral decay—I feel that books nowadays—the popular books—there isn't very much that is private in either books or movies. They talk about things that are private.

It is the stamp of approval of society to accept any sexual behavior in public that I am against. I think that a story can be told without people going naked. Pornography is shown in magazines in even the neighborhood drug stores.

Neither the substance of these statements nor the frequency with which they were mentioned constitutes a strong indict-

189

ment of sexual materials or establishes erotica as a major concern.

Opinion surveys sometimes appear to report contradictory findings, and the findings of the Commission study (Abelson, et al., 1970) may appear to be inconsistent with reports that 85% of the American adults "favor stricter laws on pornography (Gallup, 1969)" and that "76 percent want pornographic literature outlawed and 72 percent believe smut is taking the beauty out of sex (Harris, 1969)." Certain complexities of the issues appear to be responsible for these inconsistencies.[8] Actually, Abelson's first, and extremely generic question on the topic revealed that 68% of the sample felt that "some people should not be allowed to read or see some" sexual materials (32% felt that "people should be allowed to read or see anything they want to"). Further questioning revealed, however, that many opinion on both sides of the issue are actually conditional or qualified. Careful analysis showed that, although substantial proportions of the population endorse some form of restriction on the availability of erotic materials, nearly half (44%) qualify their response in terms of knowledge about the effects of such materials. For example, it was found that 51% of the population would be inclined to sanction availability of erotic materials if it were clearly demonstrated that such materials had no harmful effects on the user. About eight persons in ten (79%) would oppose the availability of such materials if they were convinced that such materials were harmful. At the polar positions, about a third (35%) of the population would oppose availability even if it were shown that such materials were not harmful and 7% would favor availability even if it were shown that there were harmful effects (Abelson, et al., 1970)

These findings underline the degree to which public opinion regarding the availability of erotica is contingent upon whether such material is shown to have, or not to have, harmful effects.

PUBLIC OPINION ABOUT THE EFFECTS OF EROTICA

Most Americans express opinions about how erotic materials affect the user, but there is substantial diversity in the specific effects mentioned. There is no presumed effect upon which more than two-thirds of the adult population agree.

Substantial proportions of men and women believe that sexual arousal and the provision of sex information are effects of visual or textural erotic materials.[9]

190

Table 1 shows that 67% of all adults[10] believe that "sexual materials excite people sexually" (17% disagree), and 61% believe that "sexual materials provide information about sex," although 27% disagree. About half the population (48%) believe that "sexual materials provide entertainment." Less than half believes that boredom, novel marital sexual activity, or becoming "sex crazy" are results of exposure. Somewhat more than half (56%) believe that "sexual materials lead to a breakdown of morals" (30% disagree), and about half (48%) believe that they lead to rape.

TABLE 1

Presumed Effects of Erotica: All Adults

[Question: "On this card are some opinions about the effects of looking at or reading sexual materials. As I read the letter of each one please tell me if you think sexual materials do or do not have these effects." (Q. 55; multiple responses]

Presumed Effects	Has that effect: (N = 2486)		
	Yes	No	Not Sure, No answer
Sexual materials excite people sexually	67%	17%	16%
Sexual materials provide information about sex	61%	27%	12%
Sexual materials lead to a breakdown of morals	56%	30%	14%
Sexual materials lead people to commit rape	49%	29%	22%
Sexual materials provide entertainment	48%	46%	6%
Sexual materials improve sex relations of some married couples	47%	32%	22%
Sexual materials make people bored with sexual materials	44%	35%	21%
Sexual materials lead people to lose respect for women	43%	41%	16%
Sexual materials make men want to do new things with their wives	41%	28%	32%
Sexual materials make people sex crazy	37%	45%	18%
Sexual materials provide an outlet for bottled up impulses	34%	46%	20%
Sexual materials give relief to people who have sex problems	27%	46%	26%

Note — Adapted from Abelson, H., Cohen, R., Heaton, E., & Slider, C. Public attitudes toward and experience with erotic materials. *Technical reports of the Commission on Obscenity and Pornography.* Vol. 6.

Respondents were also asked about their personal experience with these effects cf exposure. Specifically, they were asked, "Have sexual materials had this effect on you, on someone you know personally, or neither?"

The responses as reported by Abelson et al., 1970, are shown in Table 2. It will be noted that Abelson grouped

191

presumed effects under three headings: "socially desirable," "not clearly socially approved or disapproved," and "socially undesirable." While some persons may disagree with the classification of one or another of the effects as "desirable" or "neutral," there will probably be no disagreement regarding the social undesirability of the effects so listed.

TABLE 2
Presumed Effects: Respondents' Own Experience and
Their Perceptions of the Experiences of Others

| | (N=2486) | | |
Presumed socially desirable effects:	% who say "yes, has effect"	Effect on respondent	On someone known personally	On no one known
Provide information about sex	61%	24%	15%	22%
Provide entertainment	48%	18%	16%	17%
Improve sex relations of some married couples	47%	10%	14%	23%
Provide an outlet for bottled up impulses	34%	3%	5%	21%
Give relief to people who have sex problems	27%	2%	7%	17%
Presumed effects not clearly socially approved nor disapproved:				
Excite people sexually	67%	15%	22%	32%
Make people bored with sexual materials	44%	20%	7%	18%
Make men want to do new things with their wives	41%	7%	13%	20%
Presumed socially undesirable effects:				
Lead to a breakdown of morals	56%	1%	13%	38%
Lead people to commit rape	49%	*	9%	37%
Lead people to loose respect for women	43%	5%	11%	26%
Make people sex crazy	37%	*	9%	27%

(Partial Table)

* Less than .5%

Note — Adapted from Abelson, H., Cohen, R., Heaton, E., & Slider, C. Public attitudes toward and experience with erotic materials. *Technical reports of the Commission on Obscenity and Pornography.* Vol. 6.

The table indicates, to begin with, that people are generally far more likely to say they have personally experienced "socially desirable" or "neutral effects" than they are to say they have personally experienced socially undesirable effects. In reference to undesirable effects, they are far more likely to say that the effects occurred to someone other than themselves rather than that they personally experienced such effects. Finally, and for the most part, those who believe undesirable effects occur, simply believe that they occur, without reference either to themselves or to anyone known to them personally. In reference to undesirable effects, the

"on no one known" entries systematically account for 60%
to 76% of those who believe the effects occur. The only other
presumed effects of which this is true are providing "an outlet for bottled up impulses" (62%) and providing "relief to
people who have sex problems" (63%). In all other cases
the percentage is under 50.

The survey also found that in general persons who had
considerable recent experience[11] with sexual materials were
more likely than those with less (or no) experience recently
to see socially neutral or desirable effects, and less likely than
those with less (or no) recent experience to see socially
undesirable effects. Thus, persons reporting more experience
recently were much more likely than persons with less experience recently to believe that sexual materials are arousing
and provide information. Highly experienced[12] adult males
also believe that erotic materials are entertaining and highly
experienced adult women are more likely to believe this than
are women with less experience recently. Those persons with
the most exposure to erotic materials are less likely than those
with no or some experience recently to believe that exposure
leads to moral breakdown. Persons with higher levels of
education were significantly more likely to believe that sexual
materials produce sexual arousal, and provide information
and entertainment. Among men, but not women, those with
less than a high school education were more likely to believe
that sexual materials resulted in moral breakdown. Persons
with comparatively liberal[13] sex attitudes were more likely to
regard arousal, information, and entertainment as effects of
erotica, and much less likely to believe that moral breakdown
was an effect (Abelson, et al., 1970).

To summarize, contemporary public opinion about the
effects of exposure to erotic materials is diverse and varied.
Although most Americans have some opinion about the effects
of erotica, there is no consensus as to what those effects are.
Substantial proportions of the population identify socially
approved effects; and substantial though generally lesser proportions see socially disapproved effects. Interestingly, persons
who envision undesirable effects rarely or never report having
personally experienced them, are more likely to say they
occurred to someone else, are most likely simply to believe in
the effect occurring without reference either to themselves or
to anyone they personally know. Persons who have seen and
read less erotic material recently, who are less educated, who
are older, and who generally hold more conservative attitudes
about sex are more likely than their counterparts to identify

socially undesirable effects of exposure to erotic stimuli.

Persons who believe that the effects of exposure to sexual materials generally are not harmful are more likely to have personally experienced harmless or beneficial effects and to have seen and read more sexual material recently. They also tend to be younger, more highly educated, and more liberal in their sexual attitudes.

PROFESSIONAL AND EXPERT OPINIONS

Certain persons, or groups of persons, are sometimes asked for guidance in areas where available knowledge does not answer important questions. A wide range of opinions about the impact of erotic materials has been accepted as "expert testimony." Recently, several professional and occupational groups have been surveyed systematically in an effort to establish representatives, professional opinion, and the results of these studies are briefly summarized.

EXPERTS ON JUVENILES

Several years ago, the University of Minnesota Library School conducted a survey of two groups experienced with the conduct and problems of juveniles (Berninghausen and Faunce, unpublished, 1965). The survey asked both police chiefs and professionals in child guidance, psychiatry, psychology, sociology, and social work to assess the extent to which sexual materials should be regarded as a cause of juvenile delinquency.[14] Table 3 shows that over three-quarters (77%) of the professional workers believed that "obscene"

TABLE 3

Juvenile Workers' Opinions About Erotic Books

[Question: "Do you think that reading obscene books plays a significant role in causing juvenile delinquency? "]

Respondents	N=1,188	% Yes	% No	Don't know; no response
Police Chiefs	389	57.6	31.4	11.0
Professionals[1]	799	12.4	77.1	10.5

[1]This group consisted of professional workers in child guidance, psychiatry, psychology, sociology, and social work.

Note — Adapted from Berninghausen, D. K., & Faunce, R. W. Some opinions on the relationship between obscene books and juvenile delinquency. 1965, unpublished.

194

books did not "play a significant role in causing juvenile delinquency" (12% disagreed). Fifty-eight percent of the police chiefs believed that such books did play a significant role in delinquency causation, while 31% disagreed. These groups were also asked to assess the relative importance of obscene books in relation to other alleged causes of delinquency. The data indicated substantial differences. Police chiefs ranked such books fourth and the professionals ranked them eleventh out of fifteen possible factors (Berninghausen and Faunce, 1965).

PSYCHIATRISTS AND PSYCHOLOGISTS

Another study of other professional workers in the area of human conduct generally regard erotic materials as unrelated to delinquent or criminal behavior. Researchers affiliated with the University of Chicago recently surveyed 3,423 American psychiatrists and clinical psychologists (Lipkin and Carns, 1970).[15] Table 4 shows that 80% of these clinicians reported that they had never encountered a case in which "pornography" appeared to be a factor in producing antisocial sexual behavior, while 9% said they had suspected such cases and 7% reported being convinced of such a case. The study

TABLE 4

Psychologists' and Psychiatrists' Opinions
About the Effects of Pornography

[Question: "In your professional experience have you encountered any cases where it appeared that pornography was a causal factor in other antisocial behavior as defined above? "]

	N = 3,423
Yes, convinced:	7.4%
Yes, suspected:	9.4%
No such cases:	80.0%
Not ascertained:	3.2%

[Question: "Persons exposed to pornography are more likely to engage in antisocial sexual acts than persons not exposed? "]

Strongly agree:	1.1%
Agree:	12.9%
Disagree:	56.4%
Strongly disagree:	27.3%

Note — Adapted from Lipkin, M., & Carns, D. E. Poll of mental health professions. Cited in the University of Chicago Division of the Biological Sciences and the Pritzker School of Medicine *Reports*, Winter 1970, *20*, (1).

also found that 84% of the psychiatrists and psychologists disagreed (14% agreed) with the statement "persons exposed to pornography are more likely to engage in antisocial sexual acts than persons not exposed."

SEX EDUCATORS AND COUNSELORS

A national survey of American sex educators and counselors (Wilson and Jacobs, 1970)[16] found that adolescents are viewed by these professional workers as being interested in sexual materials, and that this interest is regarded (77% agreed) as "natural curiosity." Table 5 shows that a majority of the sex educators agreed that exposure to sexual materials is not likely to cause harmful or undesirable effects. When asked to speculate about the probable consequence of such exposure, 62% mentioned sexual excitement, 53% suggested that it provided social status for the user, 42% stated that it was a "harmless outlet," and 39% thought erotic materials provided information about sex. In contrast, deleterious effects were thought to be "likely consequences" by minorities ranging from 4 to 19%.

TABLE 5

Opinions of Sex Educators
About Erotic Materials

[Question: "What, in your experience, are the likely consequences of adolescents' exposure to explicit sexual material?" (multiple response)]

Possible Effects	%	N
Sexual excitement	62	208
Provides status	53	176
Harmless outlet	42	140
Provides information	39	130
Little influence	21	69
Preoccupation	19	63
Undesirable sexual behavior	10	33
Lose respect for women	5	18
Moral breakdown	5	16
Boredom	4	13
Other		20

Note — Adapted from Wilson, W. C., & Jacobs, S, Survey of sex educators and counselors. *Technical reports of the Commission on Obscenity and Pornography.* Vol. 10.

A majority of sex educators believed that adolescents who are most experienced with erotic materials are no different

196

from less experienced youth in terms of academic performance (60%) or socioeconomic background (65%).

SUMMARY AND DISCUSSION

Studies of general public opinion and surveys of professional workers in the area of human conduct show that there is substantial variety in opinions about the probable effects of sexual material. The research shows that those who have personally experienced more sexual material recently were significantly less likely to identify harmful effects. Studies of the opinions of persons in the "helping" professions show that a large majority believe that sexual materials do not have harmful effects.

Collectively, these studies suggest that the topic of erotica is generally defined and discussed in ways very different from those commonly supposed by articulate critics. Public opinion in America as of 1970 has not congealed with reference to many important questions about erotic materials. Clearly, a number of contingencies qualify the views that people are willing to endorse or express in this area. Prime among them are the presumptions about effects. However, it is also clear that even if adequate evidence could be developed concerning effects, public opinion would not be structured along the lines of a total consensus regarding the desirability of unrestricted availability of erotic materials. The present data do suggest that the demonstration of harmful effects would create greater agreement among the public about control issues than would the demonstration of harmless effects.

Section C. Behavioral Responses to Erotica

There are two elementary, but fundamental, questions about erotic materials upon which nearly all concerns with the subject are based. First, does exposure to erotic stimuli sexually excite and arouse the viewer? Second, does such exposure affect the subsequent sexual behavior of the user? An adequate answer to the first requires carefully designed experimental studies. The second question can best be answered by research which extends beyond the laboratory, longitudinally, into the natural environment, where sexuality is expressed in a context of established attitudes, individual interests, needs and social relationships.

Studies in this area were not undertaken until recently and there is not yet a large research literature. Substantial beginning have been made, however, in both the measurement of sexual arousal and sexual behavior and in identifying the important variables which affect sexuality.

What follows is a review and discussion of contemporary knowledge about the relationship between exposure to erotic stimuli and (a) psychosexual stimulation (sexual arousal), and (b) sexual behavior.

Psychosexual Stimulation

Of all the presumed consequences of exposure to erotic stimuli, the effect of sexual excitement is probably the most widely held and commonly mentioned. In the national survey conducted for the Commission (Abelson, et al., 1970) 72% of adult males and 63% of adult females indicated that they believed that "sexual materials excite people sexually," although considerably fewer reported experiencing this effect themselves. The growing body of research which bears on this question shows, in general, that photographs, stories, and films which depict various aspects of human sexuality produce excitement in a large proportion of the population.

Available knowledge in this area, however, continues to be complicated by certain technical problems in the measurement and interpretation of physiological and psychological responses to sexual stimulation.[17]

MEASUREMENT OF HUMAN SEXUAL AROUSAL

Human sexual arousal is apparently manifested by a wide range of somatic, psychological, and behavioral responses. Hence, sexual arousal may be associated with physiological changes, in, for example, blood volume, temperature, muscle tension, respiration, and pupil dilation. Changes in these parameters may also occur, however, with the arousal associated with other emotions, such as fear, anger, disgust, etc., and hence are not specific to sexual arousal. The nonspecificity of physiological responses to sexual stimulation is thus a methodological problem in this area (Mann, 1970; Zuckerman, 1970). The most direct methods of assessing physiological arousal involve measurement of changes in the sexual organs. But such methods are subject to two major limitations:

198

(a) such direct measurements entail problems pertinent to the invasion of privacy; and (b) there is a danger that the instrumentation involved in such measurements may itself have an excitatory or inhibitory influence on the object which is measured.

Masters and Johnson (1966) have utilized such direct measurements and have demonstrated that the limitations are not as great as might have been supposed. Their procedures were administered, however, to a select population of volunteers and may or may not be feasible in reference to the population at large.[18] Consequently, these direct measurements are yet to be employed in studies which attempt to survey "normal" populations for the purpose of measuring the degree of sexual arousal generated by erotic stimuli. In the male, a simple penile plethysmograph which can be self-administered may offer such a solution. Alternatively, the measurement of urinary acid phosphatase (derived from the prostate gland) requires only that the subject submit urine samples. However, it remains to be demonstrated whether this indicator is wholly specific and whether it is sufficiently sensitive to discriminate various levels of arousal. In the female, the problem appears to be still more difficult. Devices have been created to measure vaginal blood flow or temperature but these have not yet been used widely. Devices for measurement of vaginal lubrication have yet to be refined. Urine analysis for females appears useless because there are no accessory sexual glands in the female which secrete into the urinary tract.

It has been suggested that each sexually aroused individual shows a pattern of autonomic responses characteristic for him in this specific state. Multiple measures of such functions may permit indirect measurements in a reliable fashion, but the instrumentation and the data processing is formidable.

Sexual arousal in man also involves complex affective and cognitive responses. Arousal appears to be usually accompanied by affective responses which may range from feelings of love, affection, and tenderness, to shame, anger, and quiet, depending upon the past history of the individual, and the context in which arousal is generated. So complex a state renders subjective (self) reports (retrospective or introspective) unreliable unless the subject is carefully questioned. Thus, sexual arousal accompanied by feelings of disgust may be reported by an individual as disgust even though physiological evidence of arousal is present. As is true in many areas of phychological research, self-report verbal scales have been frequently used as a measure of sexual response. In several experimental studies, for example, subjects viewed erotic slides or film and then judged or rated each stimulus on the extent to which they regard it as "sexually arousing" or "stimulating." Such rating scales have been of varying lengths and design (Mann, 1970). A recent variation on this method is to ask specific questions about physiological responses (penile erection, vaginal lubrication, etc.).

Survey studies which have attempted to assess sexual arousal generally employ retrospective reports in which the respondent is asked to recall specific responses to erotic stimuli at some previous point in time. Even in these studies, there are measurement problems in addition to dissimulation or inaccurate recall. Surveys often differ in question wording: some ask about "sexual arousal," while others ask about particular physiological manifestations of arousal, such as genital sensations, etc. Some surveys employ the terms "obscene books" or "pornography," and others refer to "sexual materials."

In the 17 years since the last Kinsey survey, a number of advances have been made in both the conceptualization and measurement of sexual arousal as a response to erotic stimuli. One of the more important findings is that exposure to sex stimuli typically produces multiple and often ambivalent emotional reactions. It has been found that many persons experience, in addition to arousal, feelings of guilt and disgust when viewing or reading sex stimuli. Guilt and disgust responses interact with sexual arousal and affect the way in which arousal is experienced and defined, and more importantly, reported.[19]

This brief assessment of the problems associated with the measurement of human sexual arousal suggests the need for continuing scientific efforts in this area. Future studies might focus upon the refinement of existing techniques for abstracting sexual arousal from global autonomic changes, and identifying the relationships of these to changes in subjective emotional states. Many important questions in this area seem to be awaiting the refinement of current scientific methodology (Mann, 1970; Zuckerman, 1970).

INCIDENCE OF PSYCHOSEXUAL STIMULATION

What proportion of the general population is aroused sexually by erotic materials is difficult to assess. Pertinent research findings derive from widely different research procedures, which are themselves extremely varied. Thus, Kinsey, (et al., 1948, 1953) employing an intensive "clinical" interview with repetitive questioning and self-selected (volunteer) respondents, found that 77% of males and 32% of females reported having been at some time sexually aroused by "photographs, drawings, motion pictures, and other portrayals of sexual action." In considerable contrast Abelson, et al. (1970), asked a national probability sample whether they believed various alleged effects of sexual materials actually occurred and whether they had experienced such effects personally. Twenty-three percent of the males and 8% of the females reported that they had at some time been sexually excited by sexual materials. Still another set of figures is provided by Berger, et al., (1970), who asked a probability sample of American university students "does this type of material (pornographic photographs, drawings, comic books, movies, writing) greatly arouse you, somewhat arouse you, are you indifferent, or does it disgust you?" Forty-six percent of the males and 14% of the females reported arousal. A number of experimental studies to be reviewed here, and which involved volunteer subjects almost exclusively, suggest that between 60% and 85% of both sexes experience sexual arousal when reading or viewing certain erotic stimuli.[20]

Medium of Presentation. Kinsey, et al. (1953), found not only sex-specific differences in reported arousal from erotic stimuli, but also differences across various media (e.g., film, photographs, literature, etc.). The data summarized in Table 6 show that males more often reported arousal from visual depictions of sexual action (77%) than from general literature (59%), reading or hearing erotic stories (47%), or commercial film (36%). Females more often reported arousal from general literature (60%) than from commercial film (48%), visual depictions of sexual action (32%), or erotic stories (14%). It was found that only in regard to motion picture film and romantic literature did as many females as males, or more females than males, report arousal. Females, more often than males, reported "disgust" and "offense" as a response to visual depictions of sexual action. Kinsey suggested that among females, erotic stimulation may depend on the emotional (romantic) atmosphere created by continuous stimuli such as motion pictures and literature.

Several recent studies bear on these points. Abelson and his colleagues (1970) recently asked for retrospective reports of arousal as well as other kinds of reactions to respondents'

201

TABLE 6

Summary of Kinsey's Findings on Arousal to Sex Stimuli

Erotic Material	"Definite," "frequent," and "some" response	Never aroused	N
Visual depictions (photographs, drawings, film) of sexual action			
Male	77	23	3,868
Female	32	68	2,242
General literature			
Male	59%	41%	3,952
Female	60%	40%	5,699
Erotic stories (heard or read)			
Male	47	53	4,202
Female	14	86	5,523
Commercial film			
Male	36	64	3,231
Female	48	52	5,411
Portrayals (photographs, drawings, paintings) of nude figures			
Male	54	46	4,191
Female	12	88	5,698

Note — Adapted from Kinsey, A. C., Pomeroy, W. B., Martin, C. E., & Gebhard, P. H. *Sexual Behavior in the Human Female.* Philadelphia: W. B. Saunders, 1953.

most recent experience with erotic materials. Respondents who had seen or read erotic materials in the past two years were asked: "Think back to your reaction when you last saw this. Were you mostly aroused sexually, disgusted, pleased or what?" The data in Table 7 shows that this form of questioning produced considerably fewer "arousal" responses than reported by Kinsey.[21] The commonly mentioned response by both sexes was "disgust" (24% to 54%). "No effect" was reported by 10% to 24%, and "pleased" by 3% to 17%. Among males, "arousal" was more frequently mentioned as a response to textual material (15%) and "stag films" or "skin flicks" (12%) than to other visual[22] material (8%). Female resondents less often than males reported "arousal" from either textual (6%), film (4%) or other visual media (3%). In general, however, textual stimuli more often "pleased" and "aroused" both sexes than either visual or film media.

In contrast with these findings, results of several experimental studies suggest that erotic film stimulates greater sexual arousal than textual or photographic stimuli. Studies utilizing blood pressure as a measure of sexual arousal in males and females (Davis and Buchwald, 1957) and males (Corman, 1968; Wenger, et al., 1968) found that sexual response to pictures of female nudes or printed erotic passages were not pronounced, but larger changes were produced by

202

TABLE 7

American Adults' Reported Reactions
to Sexual Materials

[Question: Think back to your reaction when you last saw this. Were you mostly aroused sexually, disgusted, pleased or what? (Q22, Q30, Q51: partial table)]

Reactions	Visual		Medium Textual		Movies[1]	
	Men	Women	Men	Women	Men	Women
Number of people who have experienced a depiction recently[2]	534	583	444	528	509	216
Disgusted	36%	54%	27%	41%	24%	40%
No effect	24	16	22	18	12	10
Pleased	9	3	17	10	17	5
Aroused sexually	8	3	15	6	12	4
Amusement	8	6	7	2	8	7
Shock, surprise	4	5	3	5	1	5
Informative, interesting, learned from it	3	4	8	6	2	2
General dissatisfaction or disapproval	4	5	2	5	2	5
Other	3	5	3	4	5	7
DK, N. A.	5	5	5	7	25	22

[1] "Stag films" or "skin flicks"
[2] Each respondent reported about one visual depiction, one text depiction, and stag movies or "skinflicks."

Note — Adapted from Abelson, H., Cohen, R., Heaton, E., & Slider, C. Public attitudes toward and experience with erotic materials. *Technical reports of the Commission on Obscenity and Pornography.* Vol. 6.

erotic film. A recent review of physiological measures (Zuckerman, 1970) concludes that "blood pressure seems to be one of the few variables that shows a graded reaction, with some response to still pictures of nudes, greater response to erotic film, and even greater response during coitus and orgasm." An experimental study with male university students found that sexual arousal assessed by urinary acid phosphatase, was generally greater in response to erotic film than to other erotic media (Howard, et al., 1970).

Recent research (Schmidt and Sigusch, in press) at the University of Hamburg Institute of Sex Research suggests that films and pictures explicitly depicting heterosexual activity (e.g., petting, coitus, oral sexuality) generate sexual arousal in substantial proportions of both males (86%) and females (65%). These findings have been generally confirmed by two subsequent American studies of erotic film. In one study

(Mosher, 1970), 194 single males and 183 single female undergraduate students, 18-21, viewed erotic films.[23] Subjects rated degree of sexual arousal on a seven-point scale. Both males and females reported a moderate level of sexual arousal, with modal ratings of 5 (males) and 4 (females). There was little gender difference in reported arousal to the film depicting coitus, but males significantly more often than females reported arousal to the film depicting oral sexuality. Subjects were also asked to report physiological responses experienced during film viewing. The data in Table 8 shows that physiological responses in the genital region were reported by both males and females while viewing the films. Almost 80% of the males reported partial tumescence and about 20% reported full tumescence, lasting at least 3 minutes. Eighty-five percent of the females reported "mild genital sensations." Females reported more and stronger genital responses to the film depicting coitus than to the film depicting oral sexuality. Among females, more sexually experienced persons reported significantly more physiological indication of sexual arousal.

TABLE 8

Frequencies[1] of Physiological
Responses to Two Erotic Films

Male Physiological Reactions (N=194)	Yes	Uncertain	No
Partial Erection	152	1	40
Full Erection/Less than 3 minutes	44	6	142
Full Erection/3-6 minutes	37	6	149
Full Erection/More than 6 minutes	8	5	179
Female Physiological Reactions (N=183)			
No Genital Sensations	24	0	157
Mild Genital Sensations	153	1	27
Moderate Genital Sensations	84	3	94
Strong Genital Sensations	26	2	153
Breast Sensations	17	4	160
Vaginal Lubrication	35	18	128
Orgasm	1	6	174

[1]Two females did not report. One male did not report for two items, and two other males did not report for two items.

Note — Adapted from Mosher, D. L. Psychological reactions to pornographic films. *Technical reports of the Commission on Obscenity and Pornography.* Vol. 8.

In another experiment (Mann, et al., 1970b), married couples, aged 40 to 50, viewed erotic films[24] once a week for four weeks. Subjects rated on a five-point scale the degree to which they were aroused or repelled by each of the films and the sexual activities portrayed. It was found that both males and females tended to rate most of the films relatively low in sexual arousal. More subjects reported aversive than arousing features; males, compared to females, reported a higher mean number of arousing features, and females, relative to males, reported a higher mean number of aversive features. In general, reports of physiological responses paralleled subjective ratings of the films as "arousing" or "disgusting," "aversive," "favorable—unfavorable."

The data in Table 9 indicate that as many as 57% of the males reported tumescence and 59% of the females reported genital responses during film-viewing. The smallest proportion of females reporting genital responses (31%) and male reports of tumescence (16%) was in response to filmed depictions of male homosexuality. For some films, the sexual arousal scale ratings did not correlate highly with subjects' reports of physiological-sexual responses to the films. Males, for example, judged the "group sex" film as less arousing than three other films, but reported themselves to be more physiologically responsive to this film than to any other.

The studies reviewed do not demonstrate that medium of presentation, e.g., textual, film, etc., is independent of the sexual depiction in producing sexual arousal. The studies do suggest, however, that erotic film generates sexual arousal in substantial proportions of both young and middle age adult males and females, and that the incidence of such arousal may not be apparent in rating scale methods which call for an overall arousal judgment to a particular medium or stimulus.

One other finding regarding medium of presentation is pertinent. Two studies (Byrne and Lamberth, 1970; Tannenbaum, 1970) suggest that less sexually explicit media may generate more sexual arousal than more explicit media. Byrne and Lamberth (1970) compared the arousal valence of similar sexual themes across different media. The data in Table 10 show that arousal ratings of identical sexual themes varied according to the medium of presentation. Males judged photographic slides and written materials about equally arousing, but females judged literary material to be more arousing than photographic. When subjects were asked to imagine or think about these sexual themes without visual cues,[25] the levels of arousal were nearly twice as high as those reported by both sexes for literary stimuli. The greater arousal valence of imagination was also observed in a study of films with erotic

205

TABLE 9

Percentage of Male (N=49) and Female (N=32) Ss Reporting
Physiological Responses During Film-Viewing

Physiological Response	1 Female Masturb. M	F	2 Inter-course M	F	3 Female Homo. M	F	Film 4 Group Sex M	F	5 Male Homo. M	F	6 Sado-Masoch. M	F	7 Oral-Genital M	F
Increased heart rate	32.65	15.63	36.74	25.00	40.82	18.75	46.94	18.75	18.37	21.88	18.37	21.88	22.45	18.75
Increased breathing rate	16.33	12.50	20.41	12.50	14.29	12.50	26.53	15.63	8.16	21.88	12.24	15.63	8.16	18.75
Dry mouth	6.12	3.13	14.29	9.38	10.20	0	12.24	5.88	12.24	3.13	12.24	6.25	6.12	9.38
Erection	42.86	—	57.15	—	44.90	—	55.11	—	16.33	—	24.49	—	42.86	—
Genital sensations	44.90	37.50	46.94	53.13	44.90	37.50	57.15	59.38	22.45	31.25	32.65	37.50	40.82	43.75
Muscle tension	14.29	15.63	16.33	12.50	18.37	18.75	18.37	15.63	18.37	9.38	18.37	15.63	4.08	21.88
Muscle relaxation	2.04	3.13	0	6.25	0	3.13	0	3.13	2.04	6.25	0	3.13	2.04	9.38
Flushing	18.37	18.75	16.33	18.75	18.37	6.25	24.49	12.50	10.20	15.63	10.20	9.38	4.08	6.25
Sweating	2.04	3.13	4.08	6.25	4.08	0	2.04	0	2.04	0	4.08	3.13	2.04	3.13
Other	0	6.25	2.04	6.25	2.04	9.38	2.04	3.13	2.04	9.38	2.04	9.38	2.04	3.13
Mean Percentage	17.96	12.81	21.43	20.00	19.80	11.88	24.49	15.32	11.22	13.12	13.46	13.42	13.46	15.00

Note — Adapted from Mann, J., Sidman, J., & Starr, S. Effects of erotic films on sexual behaviors of married couples. *Technical reports of the Commission on Obscenity and Pornography.* Vol. 8.

sequences deleted or edited. It was found, for example, that persons reported higher levels of arousals, to films which deleted a rape scene, but implied its occurrence, than an identical film which retained the sequence (Tannenbaum, 1970).[26]

TABLE 10

Average Sexual Arousal to Same
Erotic Themes Over Three Media

Media	Males (N=42)	Females (N=42)	Total (N=84)
Photographic stimuli	22.71[1]	19.53[1]	21.12[1]
Literary stimuli	23.07	25.60	24.33
Imaginary stimuli[2]	41.20	45.10	43.15
Total	28.99	30.00	

[1]Each of 19 sexual themes was rated as arousing or not arousing on a six point scale. Table values are average (mean) ratings for each medium.
[2]Subjects were asked to read 19 erotic descriptive phrases such as "oral-genital contact, two males" and to imagine "what they would be like" in movies, books, etc.

Note — Adapted from Byrne, D., & Lamberth, J. The effect of erotic stimuli on sex arousal, evaluative responses, and subsequent behavior. *Technical reports of the Commission on Obscenity and Pornography.* Vol. 8.

Sexual Themes. Several studies have attempted to specify the extent to which different sexual themes generate arousal. In a study of erotic literature (Jakobovits, 1965), 20 males and 20 females, age 21 to 31, were provided with 700-word stories prepared for the study. Subjects read both erotically "realistic" stories as well as "hard core" stories, and rated them on a seven-point "sexually stimulating" scale. It was found that males and females did not differ significantly in the extent to which they judged erotically "realistic" stories as sexually stimulating. It was also found, however, that females judged "hard core" stories as significantly more stimulating than did males. Males rated "realistic" stories more stimulating than "hard core" stories, while females judged "hard core" stories more stimulating than "realistic" stories.

In a study (Byrne and Lamberth, 1970) of 19 specified sexual themes presented in three media (i.e., photographic, literary, "imaginary"), 42 young married males and females did not differ significantly in "overall arousal" ratings,[27] although they did differ in arousal response to certain themes (See Table 11). Regardless of the subject's sex or the medium of presentation of themes of cunnilingus, ventral-ventral intercourse, fellatio, female masturbation, nude heterosexual petting, and dorsal-ventral intercourse were rated as sexually arousing. Similarly, the least arousing themes were judged to be male nudity, "female torturing a male," and homosexual anal intercourse. It was also found that specific themes yielded a number of gender differences. Males rated depictions of group oral sex as significantly more arousing than did females, while depictions of homosexual fellatio and male masturbation were judged significantly more arousing by females than by males.

TABLE 11

Rank Order of Mean Sexual Arousal of Specific
Sexual Themes for Males and Females and for
Three Experimental Conditions

Theme	Subjects		Photographic	Stimuli Literary	Imaginary
	Males (N=42)	Females (N=42)			
Nude females petting	10	13	14	5.5	9.5
Male torturing female	13	15	12.5	13	12.5
Clothed female	12	19	11	17	15
Homosexual fellatio	16	12	18.5	7	17
Ventral-ventral intercourse	3	2	2	3	1
Group oral sex	2	8	3	5.5	6.5
Cunnilingus	1	1	1	1	2
Fellatio	4	6	5.5	10	5
Female masturbating	5	7	5.5	2	8
Male in undershorts	19	16	17	19	18
Nude heterosexual petting	6	3	7.5	4	3
Nude female	8	1	9	8	14
Homosexual cunnilingus	11	9.5	10	9	11
Homosexual anal intercourse	17	18	18.5	15	19
Female torturing male	14	17	16	16	16
Male masturbating	15	9.5	12.5	14	9.5
Dorsal-ventral intercourse	7	5	7.5	11	4
Nude male	18	11	15	18	12.5
Partially clad homosexual petting	9	4	4	12	6.5

Note — Adapted from Byrne, D., & Lamberth, J. The effect of erotic stimuli on sex arousal, evaluative response and subsequent behavior. *Technical reports of the Commission on Obscenity and Pornography.* Vol. 8.

Other studies of sexual themes presented on photographic slides indicate that depictions of heterosexual petting and coital activity are judged to be the most arousing by both males (Amoroso, et al., 1970; Levitt and Brady, 1965; Schmidt, et al., 1969; Sigusch, et al., 1970; Wallace, et al., 1970) and females (Sigusch, et al., 1970; Wallace, et al., 1970). Studies using erotic film suggest that depictions of heterosexual intercourse, especially variations in coital position and oral sexuality, are more often judged to be arousing by males than females (Mann, et al., 1970; Mosher, 1970a; Schmidt and Sigusch, in press).

It may be noted that studies of sadomasochistic themes in visual media (Brady and Levitt, 1965; Byrne and Lamberth, 1970; Mann, et al., 1970; Wallace, et al., 1970) and in written stories (Byrne and Lamberth, 1970) indicate that such themes are generally regarded as not very arousing, or as simultaneously arousing and repelling. (See Table 12 and Fig. 3).

TABLE 12

Male and Female Ss' Mean Ratings[1] of
Sexual Arousal by Filmed Activity

Filmed Activity	Males (mean rating) (N=48)	Females (mean rating) (N=32)
Intercourse	1.77	2.60
Lesbian Acts	2.96	3.85
Oral-Genital Contact	2.24	2.78
Male Homosexual Acts	3.82	3.97
Group Sex	2.55	3.91
Sado-Masochistic Acts	4.14	4.50
Female Masturbation	2.36	3.56

[1] Five point scale: 1 = greatly aroused; 2 = slightly aroused; 3 = no reaction; 4 = mixed arousal and repulsion; 5 = repelled.

Note — Adapted from Mann, J.; Sidman, J., & Starr. S. Effects of erotic films on sexual behaviors of married couples. *Technical reports of the Commission on Obscenity and Pornography.* Vol. 8.

FIGURE 3

Arousal Valence By Sexual Theme In Photographic Slides

High Arousal
1. Heterosexual coitus in the ventral-ventral position
2. Heterosexual coitus in the ventral-dorsal position
3. Heterosexual petting, participants nude
4. Heterosexual petting, participants partly clad
5. Heterosexual fellatio
6. Nude female
7. Heterosexual cunnilingus
8. Masturbation by a female
9. A triad of two couples and one male in conjunctive behavior involving coitus and oral-genital activity
10. Partly clad female
11. Homosexual cunnilingus
12. Homosexual petting by females
13. Sado-masochistic behavior, male on female
14. Homosexual fellatio
15. Sado-masochistic behavior, female on male
16. Masturbation by a male
17. Homosexual anal coitus
18. Nude male
Low Arousal   19. Partly clad male

Note — Adapted from Levitt, E. E. Pornography: some new perspectives on an old problem. *The Journal of Sex Research,* November 1969, *5*(4), 247—259.

Differences in sexual orientation, personality characteristics, and sexual experience are associated with arousal among both males and females. A recent development in research on individual differences pertains to the question of gender differences. A number of recent studies suggest that although males generally judge erotic stimuli as more arousing than do females, the sexes do not differ greatly in the proportion who report physiological-sexual responses to these stimuli (Kutschinsky, 1970a; Mann, et al., 1970; Mosher, 1970a; Schmidt and Sigusch, in press; Sigusch, et al., 1970).

In one experiment (Schmidt and Sigusch, in press) over 200 young adult males and females viewed erotic films and slides. Subjects rated sexual arousal on a nine-point scale and reported physiological-sexual responses experienced. Results indicated that male and female ratings did not differ significantly for two themes (heterosexual petting and coitus), but males judged oral sex themes to be more arousing than did females. Analysis of physiological-sexual responses, however, revealed that substantial proportions of both males (87%) and females (72%) reported genital responses. This finding has been substantially replicated with identical or similar film stimuli in studies of married college students (Kutschinsky, 1970a), unmarried college students (Mosher, 1970a), and middle-age married couples (Mann, et al., 1970).

Sexual Orientation and Arousal. Research does show that an individual's predominant sexual orientation determines phychosexual stimulation. Males, for example, report being more highly aroused by depictions of nude females (Byrne and Lamberth, 1970; Kinsey, et al., 1953; Sigusch, et al., 1970), show more interest in depictions of nude females (Buchwald, 1962; Bullock, 1959) and exhibit higher GSR reading when viewing female nudes (Davis and Buchwald, 1957); Koegler and Kline, 1965) than females. It has also been found that males show pupil dilation in response to nude women but show little change in response to pictures of nude men, and female subjects respond with dilation to pictures of males (Bernick, et al., 1968; Hess and Polt, 1960; Nunnally, et al., 1967). This body of literature suggests that gender differences in sexual arousal are principally a function of stimulus content, and as many have observed a large proportion of commercially available erotic materials is designed for a conventional male sexual orientation.

210

Several other studies have investigated the arousal responses of individuals with unconventional and deviant sexual orientations. It has been found that homosexual males are more likely than heterosexual males to prefer portrayals of nude males (Brown, 1964; Hess, et al., 1965; Zamansky, 1956), record higher phalloplethysmographic levels than heterosexual males to portrayals of nude males (Freund, 1962, 1963; Freund, et al., 1958; McConaghy, 1967), and record higher GSR levels (Solyom and Beck, 1967). These studies suggest that heterosexual and homosexual subjects respond differently to the gender of the model displayed in the stimulus. Several other studies show that, unlike heterosexual or homosexual subjects, pedophiles tend to respond to age of the model displayed in the stimulus, rather than to its gender (Freund, 1965, 1967a, 1967b). A recent study of persons with deviant sexual orientation (Goldstein, et al., 1970) found that homosexuals and pedophiles reported more frequent exposure to erotic depictions of nude males and homosexual activity than did heterosexually oriented persons. Transsexual males reported the least experience and interest in erotic materials, and they identified clothing and other items as more arousing than erotic books, magazines, or films.

In an experimental study (Cook and Fosen, 1970), 63 incarcerated adult sex offenders and 66 adult nonsexual offenders viewed erotic slides and rated each in terms of sexual stimulation. Results indicated that the offender groups did not differ in their ratings. The data in Table 13 show that both groups regarded the most arousing themes to be heterosexual intercourse (ventral-ventral and ventral-dorsal), and heterosexual nude petting. It should be noted that these themes are also typically identified as the most arousing by other heterosexual males and females in the natural environment.

Sex offenders appear to be no different from other groups in what sexual themes are preferred or regarded as arousing (Cook and Fosen, 1970; Gebhard, et al., 1965; Goldstein, et al., 1970; Johnson, et al., 1970).

Certain personality characteristics appear to correlate with sexual arousal. Sexual guilt, for example, has been found to inhibit sexual fantasy after exposure to stimuli (Clark, 1952; Leiman and Epstein, 1961; Mussen and Scodel, 1955) and inhibits, but does not preclude, sexual arousal (Mosher, 1970a). Certain dimensions of attitudinal and behavioral liberalism are also associated with arousal responses to sex stimuli. Persons who hold sexually liberal attitudes are more likely to judge erotic portrayals as arousing (Giese and

TABLE 13

63 Sex Offenders' Ratings of Sexual
Arousal From Erotic Slides

Content of Erotic Slide	Mean Rating[1]
1. Intercourse, ventral-ventral. F over M	3.26
2. Intercourse, ventral-dorsal, F over M	3.23
3. Nude petting, M hand on F genitals	3.14
4. Nude petting, M hand on F genitals, kissing breast	3.04
5. Intercourse, ventral-dorsal, F over M	3.02
6. F masturbating	3.01
7. M approaching cunnilingus	2.90
8. Cunnilingus	2.89
9. M and F in underclothes, hands on genitals	2.86
10. Fellatio, M over F	2.85
11. Fellatio, F over M	2.84
12. Intercourse, ventral-dorsal, each on side	2.83
13. M over F, genitals on breasts	2.75
14. Intercourse, M over F, ventral-ventral	2.73
15. Fellatio, M over F	2.65
16. Nude F reclined on back	2.61
17. Petting, partially clothed, F hand on M genitals	2.60
18. F partially clothed, undressing M	2.37

[1]Six point scale: 1 = Neutral, not exciting; 2 = slightly exciting; 3 = moderately exciting; 4 = very exciting; 5 = extremely exciting.

Note — Adapted from Cook, R. F., & Fosen, R. H. Pornography and the sex offender: patterns of exposure and immediate arousal effects of pornographic stimuli. *Technical reports of the Commission on Obscenity and Pornography*. Vol. 7.

Schmidt, 1968; Schmidt, et al., 1969) and more often report physiological-sexual responses during exposure (Davis and Braucht, 1970a) and retrospectively report sexual arousal (Abelson, et al., 1970; Berger, et al., 1970a). Sexually in-experienced individuals report less arousal to erotic film than those with more sexual experience (Abelson, et al., 1970; Brady and Levitt, 1965; Mosher, 1970a)[28] and prior experience with erotic materials is associated with higher levels of reported arousal (Abelson, et al., 1970; Davis and Braucht, 1970a; Kutschinsky, 1970a; Mann, et al., 1970) although it was also found that prolonged and intensive exposure to a variety of sexually explicit stimuli substantially reduces reported and observed sexual arousal (Howard, et al., 1970).

Age and Arousal to Erotica. Several studies show that arousal to sex stimuli is determined to some extent by the age of the viewer or reader. National survey data (Abelson, et al., 1970) suggest that arousal to sex stimuli becomes less probable with age. For textual sex stimuli, males and females aged 21 to 49 report proportionately more arousal than older males and females (Abelson, et al., 1970), although a recent study in which married couples aged 40 to 50 viewed erotic films showed that about 60% of both males and females reported genital responses to a filmed depiction of group sexual behavior (Mann, et al., 1970). In this experiment between 45% and 55% of persons 40 to 50 reported physiological responses to a filmed depiction of heterosexual intercourse (Mann, et al., 1970) compared with 70% to 85% of males and females aged 20 to 25 for comparable films (Mosher, 1970a; Schmidt and Sigusch, in press).

CIRCUMSTANCES OF EXPOSURE

Recent experimental studies suggest that psychosexual stimulation as an effect of exposure to sex stimuli depends not only on stimulus content and sexual orientation but also on the context of exposure. Specifically, it has been found that the presence or absence of an audience during exposure and the use of certain measurement instrumentation may affect responses to sex stimuli. Research indicates that a permissive or informal setting, in comparison to a formal setting, results in freer expression of sexual thoughts and fantasy as assessed by projective testing (Clark, 1952; Mussen and Scodel, 1955) and in more time spent in viewing erotic stimuli (Amoroso, et al., 1970; Martin, 1964; Walters, Bowen and Park, 1964). Amoroso and his colleagues (1970) conducted an experiment in which 56 male university students viewed erotic slides either alone or in the presence of three observers (identified as graduate students interested in the experiment). All subjects were instructed to judge the slides on certain criteria, and each subject controlled advancement of the slide projector. The data in Table 14 show that the average "viewing time" was significantly longer when subjects viewed the slides alone. Subjects accompanied by observers spent an average of about 11 seconds less in viewing each erotic slide.

These findings were interpreted to indicate that the presence of an audience is threatening and inhibitory. The more limited variability in viewing time in the audience condition suggested to the investigators that the subjects accompanied by observers spent only as much time viewing the slides as was necessary to permit the required judgments (Amoroso, et al., 1970). The presence of an audience did not, however, inhibit psychosexual stimulation (Amoroso, et al., 1970).

TABLE 14

Effect of Audience Upon Sexual Arousal

Sexual Theme	Looking Time (seconds)	
	Alone	Audience
Couple in bed, under blanket	16.54	10.45
Couple undressing each other	19.41	9.92
Girl with breasts exposed	19.95	10.10
Couple in underwear	21.99	11.83
Girl wearing panties, sitting and legs separated	20.92	11.21
Nude male, standing, front	15.41	7.13
Manual-genital/oral-breast contact	26.28	11.48
Male masturbating, lying on bed	18.90	8.69
Fellatio: man on back; female above	23.85	10.88
Coitus: ventral-dorsal, couple on side	27.57	11.07
Cunnilingus	29.20	11.14
Girl on bed, posterior elevated, genitals and anus exposed	24.89	10.21

Note — Adapted from Amoroso, D. M., Brown, M., Pruesse, M., Ware, E. E., & Pilkey, D. W. An investigation of behavioral, psychological, and physiological reactions to pornographic stimuli. *Technical reports of the Commission on Obscenity and Pornography*. Vol. 8.

One other finding of technical interest was observed in three studies of psychosexual stimulation. It appears that the self-administration of sexological inventories in and of itself produces sexual arousal (Kutschinsky, 1970a; Mann, et al., 1970) as does the attachment of electrodes designed to measure physiological correlates of sexual arousal (Amoroso, et al., 1970).

EROTIC STIMULI AND SATIATION

It has been hypothesized (a) that repeated exposure to sex stimuli "results not in continued excitement, but in boredom" (Sonenschein, 1969); and (b) that the capacity of erotic stimuli to excite the viewer or user diminishes after a few hours of exposure, that "the half-life of pornography is approximately two-to-three hours in one's total life time" (Money, 1970). A systematic study of the sexual behaviors and habits of nearly 3,000 American males, including sex offenders, concluded that: "We have often found that men with large collection [of erotic materials] of longstanding lose much of their sexual response to the materials, and while their interest in collecting may continue unabated, their motivation is no longer primarily sexual" (Gebhard, et al., 1965).

A recent experimental study (Howard, et al., 1970) appears

to confirm the hypothesized satiation effect. Subjects consisted of 23 volunteers, all of them male university students, aged 21 to 23. Each weekday for three weeks, each subject spent 90 minutes a day alone in a room containing a large collection of erotic material (films and textual) as well as generally nonerotic materials such as Readers' Digest. Subjects were free to view or read whatever interested them, or, if they chose, to ignore these materials. Psychosexual stimulation was assessed by introspective self reports and by monitoring selected cardiovascular and physiological functions: penile volume, urinary acid phosphatase, and heart rate. Interest in these materials was assessed by recording the proportion of time subjects spent in each session reading or viewing erotic materials. A variety of psychological tests and inventories were employed in addition to three psychiatric interviews with each subject.

The data presented in Fig. 4 show that during the first few

FIGURE 4

Satiation of Interest in Sexual Material

(Percent time spent looking at, or reading in each category and total)

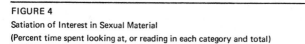

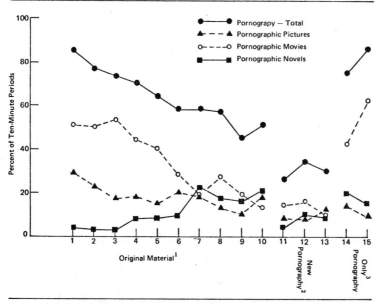

Note — Adapted from Howard, J. L., Reifler, C. B., & Liptzin, M. B. Effects of exposure to pornography. *Technical reports of the Commission on Obscenity and Pornography.* Vol. 8.

[1] "Original material" consisted of both erotic photographs, books, and films and nonerotic books.
[2] "New pornography" indicates that additional erotic material was made available.
[3] "Pornography only" indicates nonerotic material not available.

sessions of the experiment, subjects spent most of the experimental time reading or looking at erotic material. During those days, subjects reported substantially more time thinking about sexual matters and reported increased levels of general sexual arousal. All subjects reported being initially stimulated by the erotic materials, and physiological measurements confirmed high levels of reported psychosexual stimulation.

During the second week of experimental sessions, sexual feelings and both physiologically measured and reported arousal continued, generally, to decline. Fig. 5 shows that after the first 90-minute session, subjects' sexual arousal (average levels of urinary acid phosphatase) dropped significantly.

Concomitant with increasingly attenuated levels of sexual

FIGURE 5

Satiation of Sexual Arousal

(Daily mean levels of urinary acid phosphatase activity)

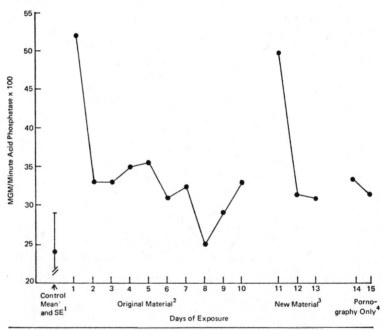

Note — Adapted from Howard, J. L., Reifler, C. B., & Liptzin, M. B. Effects of exposure to pornography. *Technical reports of the Commission on Obscenity and Pornography*. Vol. 8.

[1] Baseline values were obtained from specimens obtained during four successive days prior to the 90-minute sessions.
[2] "Original material" consisted of both erotic photographs, books, and films and nonerotic books.
[3] "New pornography" indicates that additional material was made available.
[4] "Pornography only" indicates nonerotic material was not available.

216

arousal, all subjects reported and showed a marked decline of interest in viewing or reading the materials. Subjects' interest in continued participation in the experiment showed a steady and significant decrease over the three weeks. The proportion of time actually spent with erotic stimuli during each exposure session dropped to approximately 30% by the eleventh session. At this point, novel sexual materials were introduced and both reported and observed sexual arousal increased to the initially high level obtained during the first session, but returned to a declining level immediately. It is also of interest to note that at the beginning of the experiment, all subjects reported interest in viewing erotic material, including a willingness to pay for the opportunity to participate. Nine weeks after the daily exposure sessions ended, however, all subjects reported boredom and a number reported refused private opportunities to view erotica.

The experiment was designed in such a way that prior to, and twice after, the series of 90-minute exposure sessions, the subjects and a group of control subjects, who did not participate in the exposure sessions, viewed an erotic film. Comparison showed that before the 90-minute exposure sessions, both experimental and control subjects reported equally high levels of sexual arousal. Physiological measurement confirmed these reports. In reference to the second film, viewed after the end of three week 90-minute exposure sessions, the observed and reported arousal levels of the two groups differed substantially: Fig. 6 indicates that subjects who had participated in the daily exposure sessions showed about 60%

FIGURE 6

Long-Term Satiation Effects

(Mean acid phosphatase value as a measure of sexual arousal for experimental and control groups before, one week after, and eight weeks after daily sessions)

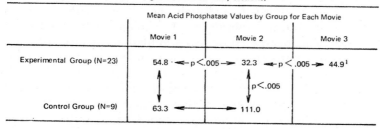

	Mean Acid Phosphatase Values by Group for Each Movie		
	Movie 1	Movie 2	Movie 3
Experimental Group (N=23)	54.8 ◄─ p < .005 ─► 32.3 ◄─ p < .005 ─► 44.9 [1]		
	↕	↕ p < .005	
Control Group (N=9)	63.3 ◄────────► 111.0		

Note — Adapted from Howard, J. L., Reifler, C. B., & Liptzin, M. B. Effects of exposure to pornography. *Technical reports of the Commission on Obscenity and Pornography.* Vol. 8.

[1] Was not different than the value for Movie 1.

as much phychosexual stimulation as they did for the first film and were significantly less aroused than the controls. Two months after the daily exposure sessions, subjects who participated in the daily sessions viewed a third erotic film. Level of arousal for these subjects increased slightly from that observed during the second film, and was no longer significantly below the level observed during the first film.

The results obtained from both physiological measures and reported levels of phychosexual stimulation support the hypothesis that repeated exposure to sexual stimuli results in decreased responsiveness. In addition, degree of interest in both the study and the stimulus materials declined predictably among the subjects. Although complete satiation in the sense of total inhibition of response did not occur, the physiological data and reported levels of arousal and interest point toward satiation in terms of diminished response. At no time during the course of the experiment did the subjects report detrimental effects of the experiment upon sleep, mood, study or work habits or any other aspect of their personal or social behavior. Satiation was specific to erotic material and did not extend to their personal sexual activities.

This particular experiment marks the first attempt to study the effects of repeated and prolonged exposure to sexual stimuli. Additional studies with a broader range of subjects and different intervals of exposure under different social conditions will be necessary before these results can be generalized, although the observation of short-term phychosexual stimulation is certainly consistent with several other studies.[29]

SEXUAL RESPONSES TO EROTIC STIMULI

Even brief exposure to erotic stimuli produces psychosexual stimulation in most males and females. This finding appears to be well established, although there are variations in the amount of arousal experienced. It remains to be determined, however, whether psychosexual stimulation, in turn, produces additional heterosexual, autosexual or homosexual activity. Recent national surveys show that persons who are sexually active are likely to have seen or read erotic materials. A study of American adults shows that persons most experienced recently with erotic stimuli are more likely to have begun heterosexual intercourse at an earlier age than persons with less (or no) recent experience. The survey also found that men and women 21-29 with the most experience recently reported higher frequencies of current sexual intercourse, although this relationship did not hold for other age categories (Abelson, et al., 1970). Among American college students, frequency of exposure to erotic materials is associated with relatively high rates of sociosexual experimentation (hugging, kissing, light and heavy petting, coitus) during both high school and college years, especially among males (Berger, et al., 1970a).

A comparable survey of adults in Sweden shows similar results. Persons with more experience recently with erotic materials were also more likely to have begun heterosexual intercourse at an earlier age, to have higher rates of current intercourse, to have had more sexual experience, and to report more sexual satisfaction (Zetterberg, 1970).

The American survey also shows that both men and women having the most experience recently with sexual stimuli were more likely than others to report an earlier age of first masturbation (Abelson, et al., 1970), although frequency of exposure was unrelated to the frequency of masturbation during high school and college years (Berger, et al., 1970a).

One additional survey of men between 18 and 30 included persons with a range of life styles, from imprisoned offenders to college and theology students. The study shows that persons reporting earlier and more frequent heterosexual petting, coitus, and masturbation were also more likely to report having more exposure to a range of erotic materials. In addition, it was found that both exposure and sexual activity were strongly associated with reported peer group approval and encouragement to engage in a variety of sexual activities (Davis and Braucht, 1970b).

Collectively, these studies show that frequency and amount of exposure to erotic stimuli are associated with frequency and amount of sexual activity (i.e., there is a statistical relationship between the two). These findings suggest several alternative explanations or hypotheses:

First, that relatively frequent exposure to sexual stimuli, or to large amounts of sexual stimuli, predisposes the viewer or user to relatively early and frequent sexual activity. In this case, exposure may either generate new sexual behaviors or activate (increase the probability of occurrence of) already established behaviors.

Second, that high frequencies of established sexual activity predispose the individual to earlier or more frequent experience with erotic materials. Here, sexually active individuals may, as a consequence of their sexuality, become more interested in erotic materials, or may find that the socio-sexual

219

environment in which they participate also includes greater availability of erotic materials, and hence increases the probability of early and frequent exposure.

Third, both sexual activity and exposure to erotica may be a function of some other condition or circumstance which makes both events highly probable. In this case, the third variable may be a friendship (peer) group in a variety of socioeconomic contexts, such as working-class neighborhoods, industrial work groups, or fraternal organizations which encourage, value, and reward certain modes of sexual expression.

Any one, or all, of these explanations is compatible with the survey findings reported earlier; experimental investigations, however, may clarify the direction of the relationships and suggest which, if any, of these hypotheses is appropriate. Pertinent discussion follows the presentation of experimental findings at the end of this section.

Until three years ago, there were no experimental studies of sexual behavioral consequences of exposure to erotic stimuli. At present there are eleven such experiments, variously involving married and unmarried persons[30] (Amoroso, et al., 1970; Byrne and Lamberth, 1970; Davis and Braucht, 1970a; Howard, et al., 1970; Kutschinsky, 1970a; Mann, et al., 1970; Mosher, 1970a; Schmidt, et al., 1969; Schmidt and Sigusch, in press; Sigusch, et al., 1970), and, in one case, sex offenders (Cook and Fosen, 1970). In addition, there is now a growing research literature on both male and female behavioral responses (Byrne and Lamberth, 1970; Kutschinsky, 1970a; Mann, et al., 1970; Mosher, 1970a; Schmidt and Sigusch, in press; Sigusch, et al., 1970) and in reference to persons 18 to 50 years of age. In general, and as discussed below, these studies show that established patterns of premarital, marital and extramarital coitus, petting, homosexual activity, and sexual fantasy are very stable and are not substantially altered by exposure to sexually explicit stimuli. Relatively high rates of sexual activity prior to exposure to sex stimuli are associated with similarly high rates after exposure (Byrne and Lamberth, 1970; Davis and Braucht, 1970a; Schmidt and Sigusch, in press; Sigusch, et al., 1970) and relatively infrequent sexual activity prior to exposure is associated with similarly infrequent activity after exposure, particularly among coitally inexperienced individuals (Amoroso, et al., 1970; Mosher, 1970a). In some circumstances, exposure to erotic stimuli temporarily activates sexual behavior. Such activation, when it occurs, follows established patterns and tends to be short-lived, diminishing markedly within 48 hours (Kutschinsky, 1970a; Mann, et al., 1970). The presence or availability of an established sexual partner appears to determine whether the activated behavior is masturbatory or coital (Kutschinsky, 1970a).

MASTURBATION

The role of erotic stimuli as an adjunct to masturbation has been cited frequently in both sociological analyses (Gagnon and Simon, 1967a; Polsky, 1967) and other statements concerning the effects of exposure to erotic stimuli. The relationship between exposure to erotic stimuli and the frequency of masturbatory activity is clarified by several recent experimental studies. Table 15 summarizes the findings of eight of

TABLE 15
Masturbatory Frequency 24 Hours Before and After Exposure to Sex Stimuli

Population	N	No change	Decreased	Increased	
Married Danish males, 22-34[1] (Kutschinsky, 1970a)	42	79%	7%	14%	No
Married Danish females, 18-28[1] (Kutschinsky, 1970a)	28	89%	0	11%	test
Single German males, 19-27[2] (Sigusch, et al., 1970)	50	66%	6%	28%	No
Single German females, 19-27[2] (Sigusch, et al., 1970)	50	82%	4%	14%	test
Single German males, 19-27[2] (Schmidt and Sigusch, in press)	128	59%	11%	30%	(.001)
Single German females, 19-27[2] (Schmidt and Sigusch, in press)	128	82%	4%	14%	(.01)
Single German males, 19-29[2] (Schmidt, et. al., 1969)	99	68%	5%	26%	(.001)
Single Canadian males, 18-25[2] (Amoroso, et al., 1970)	60	65.5%	8.6%	25.8%	(.05)
Single American males, 18-20[2] (Mosher, 1970a)	194	81%	7%	7%	(NS)
Single American females, 18-20[2] (Mosher, 1970a)	183	90%	1%	2%	(NS)
Single American males, 18-30[2] (Davis and Braucht, 1970a)	121	72%	--	28%	(.001)
Married American males, 30-59 (Mann, et. al., 1970)	48	--	--	4%	(NS)
Married American females, 30-64 (Mann, et. al., 1970)	32	--	--	2%	(NS)

[1] Subjects included some unmarried but coitally experienced persons.
[2] Subjects included both coitally experienced and inexperienced persons.

221

these studies. In the 24 hours following exposure to erotic stimuli, frequencies of masturbation increased among a minority of unmarried males (Amoroso, et al., 1970; Davis and Braucht, 1970a; Schmidt, et al., 1969; Schmidt and Sigusch, in press; Sigusch, et al., 1970) and unmarried females (Schmidt and Sigusch, in press) but did not increase among young, married couples (Byrne and Lamberth, 1970),[31] middle aged married couples (Mann, et al., 1970), males and females whose permanent sexual partner was available (Kutschinsky, 1970a), or coitally inexperienced college freshmen and sophomores (Mosher, 1970a).

Thus, studies of unmarried, but coitally experienced individuals found that between 14% and 30% of the males and between 10% and 14% of the females reported increased frequencies of masturbation after exposure (Amoroso, et al., 1970; Kutschinsky, 1970a; Schmidt and Sigusch, in press; Sigusch, et al., 1970). Studies of both married persons and unmarried, and coitally inexperienced young persons found that, in both cases, about 4% to 7% of the males and about 2% of the females reported increased frequencies of masturbation after exposure (Mann, et al., 1970; Mosher, 1970a).

Davis and Braucht (1970a) found that increased masturbatory activity in the 24 hours after exposure was associated with a history of frequent masturbation ($r=+.22$), relatively high frequencies of recent masturbation ($r=+.60$), a relatively late onset of heterosexual petting ($r=-.35$) and coital behavior ($r=-.28$), infrequent recent heterosexual coitus ($r=-.18$), and higher reported levels of sexual arousal and tension during exposure. Masturbation was associated with more frequent sexual fantasy after exposure (Davis and Braucht, 1970a; Schmidt and Sigusch, in press).

These studies indicate that exposure to sex stimuli increases the frequency of masturbation among minorities of various populations, and principally among individuals with either established masturbatory patterns or established but unavailable sexual partners. In either case, increased frequencies of masturbation apparently disappear within 48 hours after exposure (Kutschinsky, 1970a; Mosher, 1970a).

HETEROSEXUAL COITUS

Recent survey data indicate that American adults who have had the most experience recently with erotic stimuli also report heterosexual intercourse at an earlier age than persons with "some" or no such experience. (Abelson, et al., 1970). This

222

survey also found that young adults, 21 to 29, with the most experience recently with erotica report a higher frequency of current sexual intercourse than do persons with no recent experience. Among American college students, frequency of exposure to erotic materials is associated with relatively high rates of sociosexual experimentation (hugging, kissing, light and heavy petting, coitus) during both high school and college years, especially males[32] (Berger, et al., 1970a).

TABLE 16

Coital Frequency 24 Hours Before
and After Exposure to Sex Stimuli

Population	N	No change	Decreased	Increased	
Married Danish males, 22-34[1] (Kutschinsky, 1970a)	42	71%	2%	26%	No
Married Danish females, 22-34[1] (Kutschinsky, 1970a)	28	68%	0	32%	test
Single German males, 19-27[2] (Sigusch, et al., 1970)	50	80%	4%	16%	(NS)
Single German females, 19-27[2] (Sigusch, et al., 1970)	50	82%	6%	12%	(NS)
Single German males, 19-27[2] (Schmidt and Sigusch, in press)	128	76%	9%	15%	(NS)
Single German females, 19-27[2] (Schmidt and Sigusch, in press)	128	81%	5%	14%	(.001)
Single German Males, 19-29[2] (Schmidt, et. al., 1969)	99	71%	11%	17%	(NS)
Single Canadian males, 18-25[2] (Amoroso, et al., 1970)	60	77.6%	10.3%	12.1%	(NS)
Single American males, 18-20[2] (Mosher, 1970a)	194	91%	4%	2%	(NS)
Single American females, 18-20[2] (Mosher, 1970a)	183	95%	2%	3%	(NS)
Single American males, 18-30[2] (Davis and Braucht, 1970a)	121	82%	11%	7%	(NS)
Married American males, 30-59 (Mann, et al., 1970)	48	---	---	36%	(.01)
Married American females, 30-64 (Mann, et al., 1970)	32	---	---	28%[3]	(.01)

[1]Subjects included some unmarried but coitally experienced persons.
[2]Subjects included both coitally experienced and inexperienced persons.
[3]Percent increase of experimental over control Ss. Additional tests found that mean sexual activity levels on film viewing nights exceeded those for the rest of the four-week period at high levels of significance for males (T=5.31,=48, p<.001) and females (T=4.19,=48,p<.001).

Several experiments found that, in the 24 hours following exposure to erotic stimuli, coital frequencies did not change among coitally inexperienced young persons (Amoroso, et al., 1970; Mosher, 1970a), but did increase among married (Kutschinsky, 1970a; Mann, et al., 1970) and single but coitally experienced persons (Schmidt and Sigusch, in press; Sigusch, et al., 1970).[33] Table 16 summarizes the results of eight pertinent studies. Of the experiments which assessed coital responses to sex stimuli, the proportion of subjects reporting increased activity was statistically significant in only two,[34] among unmarried but coitally experienced females

223

(Schmidt and Sigusch, in press) and among 40 to 50 year-old married couples (Mann, et al., 1970).

It is of interest to note that in four studies in which coital increase was reported, small but about equal proportions of males and females reported such increases (Kutschinsky, 1970a; Mosher, 1970a; Schmidt and Sigusch, in press; Sigusch, et al., 1970). Two studies of married couples suggest that availability of preferred sexual partner and exposure to sex stimuli by both spouses increased the probability of activated coital rates. Men whose permanent coital partners also viewed sex stimuli reported increases in coital frequency but not in masturbation (Kutschinsky, 1970a; Mann, et al., 1970).

Among coitally experienced young persons, increased frequencies of coitus after exposure were associated statistically with greater arousal during exposure, more favorable dispositions toward the erotic stimuli, and generally higher levels of sexual satisfaction prior to exposure (Kutschinsky, 1970a). In another study (Davis and Braucht, 1970a) of young males, 7% reported increased coital frequencies after exposure (11% reported decreases). The increases were associated with greater sexual desire during exposure, less recent coital experience, and more restrictive attitudes about the availability of erotic materials. Coital responses were also associated with an increase in heterosexual petting after exposure ($r=+.84$), and postexposure conversations about sexual matters with both males and females were related both to increased frequencies of petting and coital activity (Davis and Braucht, 1970a).

In general, these experiments indicate that when masturbatory and coital responses to exposure do occur, they tend to be mutually exclusive, and the occurrence of one rather than the other appears to be determined principally by the availability of an established sexual partner.

LOW-FREQUENCY BEHAVIOR

Several sexual practices, for example, oral sexuality, anal intercourse, sadomasochistic activity, group sex, homosexuality, extramarital sexuality, and sexual relations with prostitutes, etc., are presumed to occur relatively infrequently within American society. Two recent experimental studies, in particular, bear on the question of whether exposure to erotic stimuli generates, or increases the probability of occurrence of such "low frequency" behaviors.

In one experiment (Mosher, 1970a), 194 single males and 183 single females, undergraduate students, average 19 years of age, viewed two erotic films.[35] All students' histories of sexual experiences were assessed prior to film viewing. Analysis of the data pertaining to the sexual histories of these subjects revealed that about half of the males and a third of the females had coital experience. A minority of the males and females reported experience with fellatio (40% males; 30% females) and cunnilingus (36% males: 36% females). Homosexual experience was reported by 13 males and 3 females.

All subjects answered specific questions, on a self-administered questionnaire, about twelve specific sexual behaviors engaged in during the 24 hours before and after film-viewing. In addition, two weeks later, all subjects were asked to report "any new sexual behavior in which they had engaged and beneficial or detrimental changes attributable to viewing the films."

TABLE 17

Frequencies[1] of Unmarried Males (N=193) and Females (N=181) Engaging in Sexual Behavior 24 Hours Before and 24 Hours After Viewing Film

Behaviors	Neither Before Nor After		Both Before and After		Before But Not After		After But Not Before	
	Females	Males	Females	Males	Females	Males	Females	Males
Manual Breast Play	146	156	6	14	11	9	13	7
Oral Breast Play	154	166	4	8	7	8	11	4
Manipulated Another's Genitals	154	169	7	7	7	6	8	4
Another Manipulated My Genitals	150	174	5	5	11	5	10	2
Fellatio	166	179	4	2	3	3	3	2
Cunnilingus	167	178	4	4	2	3	3	1
Coitus	163	173	4	4	3	7	6	3
Homosexual Relations	176	185	0	1	0	0	0	0

[1] Seven females and eight males did not report.

Note — Adapted from Mosher, D. L. Psychological reactions to pornographic films. *Technical reports of the Commission on Obscenity and Pornography.* Vol. 8. .

Results of the 24 hour before-after questionnaire are shown in Table 17. The data indicate that overwhelming majorities of the subjects (over 85% of each sex group) did not engage in coitus, fellatio, cunnilingus, or homosexual behavior in either the 24 hours before or the 24 hours after viewing the films. The small number of subjects who engaged in one or more of these activities after viewing (from zero for homosexual behavior to 5% of females for coitus) are virtually the same as the number who engaged in such activity before viewing, with only trivial differences occurring in both directions.

Another study (Mann, et al., 1970) examined the effects

225

of viewing erotic films on middle-aged married couples.[36] The study involved a 12-week period, during which all subjects recorded daily sexual activities in unidentifiable diaries. Subjects viewed erotic films (a control group viewed nonerotic film) once a week for 4 weeks. The sexual behavior of subjects was analyzed for a 4 week base period before exposure to erotic film (phase 1), for the 4 weeks of exposure (phase 2), and for 4 weeks following exposure (phase 3). As reported earlier, transitory increases in coital frequency and variation in technique on film-viewing nights were attributed to the sex stimuli. Subjects were also asked to indicate on the daily diaries each sexual activity that had occurred for the first time in his life or for the first time in six months.

Table 18 describes the "low frequency" behaviors which occurred for the first time or for the first time in six months during the entire course of the study (i.e., prior to, during, and after film-viewing).

The incidence of reported "innovative" acts (first time in life) is noted in parenthetical figures; reactivated (first time in six months) incidence is noted in nonparenthetical figures. As the footnotes to Table 18 indicate, Groups 1 and 2 were composed of couples who saw erotic films together, Group 3 was composed of males who saw erotic films without their wives, and Group 4 was a control group consisting of couples who saw only nonerotic films.

The Table is chiefly remarkable in that most of the entries are "1" and the remainder "2." The total incidence figures indicate that no difference in innovation or reactivation rates for the cited behaviors approaches statistical significance. Such differences as exist are trivial and conform to no meaningful pattern. Thus, total incidence figures show that during phase 2 (viewing) compared with phase 1 (previewing) innovative behavior increased by 1 in one experimental group and remained constant or decreased in the others, but increased from 0 to 3 in Group 4 which saw only nonerotic films. Comparison of totals of both innovative and reactivated acts for phase 2 and 3 combined, as compared with the previewing phase, reveals increases for all groups; but when the combined phase 2 and phase 3 totals are corrected to refer to the same time period as phase 1, the only remaining increase is in the control group. In reference to specific behaviors, extramarital activity was initiated (first time in life) during the experiment by three people, but two of the three were members of the control group. Some form of oral-genital activity was initiated by five males, but one did so in the previewing

226

TABLE 18

Incidence of Activities Performed by Married Male and Female
Ss for First Time in Six Months or First Time in Life[1]

Males

Activity	Group1[2]			Group 2[3]			Group 4[3]			Group 4[5] (Nonerotic film)		
	Phase[6]			Phase			Phase			Phase		
	1	2	3	1	2	3	1	2	3	1	2	3
Performed oral-genital activity				1	1			1				(1)
Received oral-genital activity										1		
Performed oral-genital activity to climax		(1)										
Received oral-genital activity to climax	(1)	1					(1)					(2)
Masturbated spouse to climax							(1)	2	1		1	
Spouse masturbated S to climax	1									1		
Anal intercourse								2				
Achieved climax	1						1					
Extra-marital activity		1		1							(1)	
Activity with prostitute					1							
Performed sado-masochistic behavior									(1)			

Females

Activity	1	2	3	1	2	3	1	2	3	1	2	3
Performed oral-genital activity	1(1)											
Received oral-genital activity	(2)		(2)									
Performed oral-genital activity to climax								(2)	1(1)		(1)	
Received oral-genital stimulation to climax											(1)	
Masturbated self to climax				1			1			1	1	
Masturbated spouse to climax	(1)											
Spouse masturbated S to climax	1						2(1)	1	(1)			
Anal intercourse	(1)						(1)					
Achieved climax								1				
Extra-marital activity	(1)				1			1				(1)
Performed sado-masochistic behavior								(1)				
Group sexual activity								(1)				1
Total incidence by phase												
First time in 6 mos.	3	1	2	2	4	0	4	8	2	3	2	1
First time in life	3	4	3	0	0	0	6	3	2	0	3	4

[1] Figures in parantheses indicate first time in life; other figures indicate first time in six months.
[2] Couples in Group I viewed erotic films.
[3] Couples in Group II viewed erotic films and were advised that "viewing the films might facilitate their marital sexual relationships."
[4] In Group III, husbands viewed erotic films and wives, in separate sessions, viewed nonerotic films.
[5] Couples in Group IV viewed nonerotic films.
[6] Phase 1 = 4 weeks prior to film viewing; phase 2 = 4 weeks of film viewing; phase 3 = 4 weeks after film-viewing (total = 12).

Note — Adapted from Mann, J., Sidman, J., & Starr. S. Effects of erotic films on sexual behaviors of married couples. *Technical reports of the Commission on Obscenity and Pornography.* Vol. 8.

period and another was a member of the control group. Further examples appear superfluous. In sum, and as earlier stated, changes in incidence of innovative or reactivated behaviors of the types cited are nonsignificant, trivial and conform to no meaningful pattern.

It has been argued that a strong response to erotic stimuli requires imagination, the ability to project, and sensitivity, and that such characteristics are found disproportionately among young and well-educated persons (Gebhard, et al., 1965; Kinsey, et al., 1953). More recent studies appear to confirm this argument. National survey data show that men and women in their early twenties report a higher frequency of erotic dreams and sexual fantasy after exposure than do older people. Thirty-five percent of men in their twenties and 30% of women in their twenties report having erotic dreams frequently or occasionally, as against smaller proportions for later ages (Abelson, et al., 1970). These data also show that more highly educated persons, particularly males, are somewhat more likely than those with less education to report higher frequencies of erotic dreams and sexual fantasy. Experimental studies suggest that exposure to sexual stimuli activates the frequency of sexual dreaming or sexual fantasy among young males (Amoroso, et al., 1970; Davis and Braucht, 1970a; Howard, et al., 1970; Schmidt and Sigusch, in press) and young females (Mosher, 1970a; Schmidt and Sigusch, in press), but not among young or middle-aged married couples (Byrne and Lamberth, 1970; Mann, et al., 1970). Again, however, the increased frequency and fantasy and dreaming declined shortly after exposure (Howard, et al., 1970).

CONVERSATION ABOUT SEX

The impact of sex stimuli upon subsequent verbal behavior was first observed by Schmidt and Sigusch in experiments conducted in Germany. It was found that in the 24 hours after viewing erotic film, "talk about sex" increased among a significant proportion of both young males (34%) and females (46%) (Schmidt and Sigusch, in press). Generally similar results were obtained in studies of American youth (Davis and Braucht, 1970a; Mosher, 1970a) and middle-aged married couples (Mann, et al., 1970).

Mosher (1970a) reports that increased frequencies of conversation about sex and sex fantasy were the *only* significant behavioral changes among 194 single males and 183 single females following exposure to erotic film (See Table 19). Although these undergraduates had established high frequencies of sexual conversation, 20% of the males and 25% of the females increased these rates in the 24 hours after exposure.

TABLE 19

Frequency[1] of Conversation About Sex 24 Hours
Before and After Exposure to Erotic Film

	Males (N=187)	Females (N=176)	Total
Increased frequency	20%[2]	25%[2]	23%[2]
Decreased frequency	7%	6%	6%
Unchanged	73%	69%	71%

[1]Seven males and seven females did not report.
[2]Significant (p<.001) by sign test comparing number increasing with number decreasing.

Note — Adapted from Mosher, D. L. Psychological reactions to pornographic films. *Technical reports of the Commission on Obscenity and Pornography.* Vol. 8.

In another study (Mann, et al., 1970), couples married for 15 to 19 years viewed erotic films once a week for four weeks. After the study, the subjects were asked if participation in the study had changed their own or their spouse's sexual patterns. Those who reported changes were asked to evaluate the importance of those changes. The data in Table 20 show that "increased openness in discussing sex" was the change most frequently reported and most frequently cited as "most important" by both husbands and wives in reference to both themselves and their spouses. Forty-three percent of the males reported this change for themselves and 44% report it for their spouses (18% ranked it as most important for themselves and 21% as most important for their spouses). Forty percent of the females reported this change for themselves and 30% for their spouses. Also ranked high was "lowered inhibitions toward spouse" (24% of the males and 21% of the females); an almost equal proportion of males (6%) and females (7%) ranked it as the most important change in themselves, although 11% of the males ranked this as the most important change in their spouses. In general, it was found that "subjects rated the study as exercising a helpful rather than harmful influence upon their own and their spouses' marital and sexual functioning" (Mann, et al., 1970).

It was also found, however, that when couples who viewed erotic films were compared with those who did not, not all of the reported changes could be attributed to erotic film-viewing. Among males, persons who viewed nonerotic films as well as

229

those who viewed no films did not differ greatly in the proportions who reported, for example, "lowered inhibitions." In regard to "increased openness in discussing sex," more of the males who viewed nonerotic films (59%) reported this effect than those who viewed erotic films (42%). Among females, however, those who viewed erotic films were generally more likely than those who did not to report these changes. The researchers suggested that males and females may have been differentially influenced by viewing erotic films, and that completing daily questionnaires concerning sexual activity, may have had a more pronounced effect than film-viewing (Mann, et al., 1970).

TABLE 20

Changes in Own and Spouse's Sexual Patterns
Attributed to Participation in Study

(Figures Represent Percentage of Sample Responding)

Change	Self		Spouse	
	Males (N=80)	Females (N=81)	Males (N=80)	Females (N=81)
Lowered inhibitions toward spouse	23.7	21.0	27.5	7.4
Increased inhibitions toward spouse	3.7	6.2	3.7	0
Increased satisfaction with marital sex life	16.2	12.3	11.2	3.7
Decreased satisfaction with marital sex life	5.0	6.2	3.7	4.9
Increased urge to try new techniques	23.7	21.0	20.0	30.9
Increased desire for extra-marital sex	11.2	3.7	2.5	3.7
Increased frequency of extra-marital sexual activity	0	1.2	1.2	0
Increased frequency of masturbation	0	3.7	1.2	1.2
Increased frequency of awareness of sexual arousal	26.2	18.7	16.2	16.0
Increased openness in discussing sex	42.5	39.5	43.8	29.6
Disruption of sex life	5.0	6.2	5.0	2.5
Disruption of general marital relationship	0	3.7	1.2	1.2
Desire for marital counseling or therapy	1.2	11.1	1.2	2.5

Note — Adapted from Mann, J., Sidman, J., & Starr, S. Effects of erotic films on sexual behaviors of married couples. *Technical reports of the Commission on Obscenity and Pornography.* Vol. 8.

NOTE ON CAUSATION

Earlier in this chapter it was noted that considerable experience with erotic materials was associated with certain sexual attitudes and behavior. It was noted that this relationship in and of itself indicated nothing about cause and effect, i.e., it did not explain whether the attitudes and behavior led to exposure to erotica, or whether erotica led to the behavior and attitudes, or whether both were the result of a third factor, such as a particular life style.

The findings of the experiments here reviewed indicate that neither single nor repeated exposure produced any qualitative or even any long-lasting quantitative effects on the populations studied. Fantasies increased, and masturbation and coital frequencies temporarily increased in the 24 hours after exposure, primarily among groups who habitually engaged in one or the other of these particular behaviors. Qualitative changes in behavior virtually did not occur.

In sum, these findings cast considerable doubt on the thesis that erotica is a determinant of habitual extent or nature of sexual behavior among youth of college age or older adults. The data remain susceptible to either of the other two explanations, that persons who are more sexually active are, therefore, likely to see more erotica, or that the relationship is a product of a third variable such as differences in overall life style.

SUMMARY AND DISCUSSION

PSYCHOSEXUAL STIMULATION

Accumulated research on psychosexual stimulation shows that exposure to erotic photographs, narratives, and film produces sexual arousal in substantial proportions of both males and females. Studies in this area also demonstrate that differences among individuals in psychosexual response are largely a function of sexual orientation and preferences. Regardless of the medium of presentation, however, depictions of heterosexual coitus and petting elicit more frequent and stronger arousal responses than depictions of homosexuality, sadistic and masochistic sexuality. One study found that erotic fantasies or imagined sexual depictions were reported to be considerably more sexually stimulating than explicit textual or visual presentations.

Several recent studies suggest that traditional hypotheses of gender differences in psychosexual responses may require revision. These studies indicate that while males tend to judge erotic stimuli as more arousing than females, the sexes do not differ substantially in physiological-sexual response to these stimuli. Not surprisingly, research indicates that females are

231

less responsive to male-oriented erotica, but about equally responsive to heterosexual action themes. Differences in psychosexual response between the sexes appear to be essentially qualitative, rather than quantitative.

A systematic analysis of the consequences of repeated exposure of young males to erotic stimuli found that continued exposure results in satiation of both sexual arousal and interest in erotic material. After 15 viewing sessions, these males showed substantial reductions in stimulation and reported increased boredom and indifference to sex stimuli; diminished responsiveness was observed as long as eight weeks after the study.

SEXUAL BEHAVIOR

Studies of human sexual behavior show that established patterns of premarital, marital and extramarital coitus, petting, homosexual activity, and sexual fantasy are very stable and are not altered substantially by exposure to erotic stimuli. In some circumstances, exposure to sex stimuli temporarily activates frequencies of masturbation and coitus. Increased frequencies of masturbation occurred principally among individuals with established masturbatory patterns or established but unavailable coital partners, and in both cases apparently disappeared within 48 hours after exposure. Increased coital frequencies tended to occur among sexually experienced persons with established and available sexual partners and tended to disappear within 48 hours. Studies of married couples suggest that viewing erotic films may result in temporary, but substantial, increases in both the frequency and variety of coital performance.

Studies show that exposure to erotic stimuli may also temporarily increase the frequencies of erotic dreams and sexual fantasy, particularly among unmarried persons, and may increase conversation about sexual matters among both married and unmarried persons. Studies of married couples' responses to erotic stimuli found that after exposure, husbands and wives reported more agreeable and "increased openness" in marital communication.

Finally, it should be noted that in none of the studies of effects of exposure to sex stimuli were any significant differences found in relation to any behavioral consequences other than temporary activation of masturbation, coitus, sexual dreams, fantasies, and conversations.

The findings of available research cast considerable doubt

232

on the thesis that erotica is a determinant of either the extent or nature of individuals' habitual sexual behavior. Such behavioral effects as were observed were short-lived, and consisted virtually exclusively of transitory increases in masturbation or coitus among persons who habitually engage in these activities.

Section D. Attitudinal, Emotional, and Judgmental Responses to Erotica

Inappropriate or undesirable attitudes, values, moral standards, thoughts, feelings, and emotions are often mentioned as consequences of exposure to sexual stimuli. Some have argued that studies which look for effects in crime and antisocial behavior will not uncover the real effects of erotica— i.e., the effects upon moral character and sexual orientation. These alleged effects are particularly difficult to investigate empirically because they do not lend themselves to precise formulation and because their occurrence would not necessarily be manifested in overt, physical behavior. In the past two years, however, several studies have been undertaken to investigate attitudinal, emotional, and judgmental responses of users and viewers of erotica. The findings are summarized and discussed in the following pages.

ATTITUDINAL RESPONSES TO EROTICA

The argument that exposure to sexual stimuli results in unconventional sexual attitudes and orientations may be investigated by (a) determining whether persons with differing amounts and frequencies of exposure differ attitudinally, and (b) measuring attitudes and orientations before and after exposure.

SEX ATTITUDES AND EXPOSURE TO EROTICA

A recent national survey (Abelson, et al., 1970) shows that there is still a considerable heterogeneity within American society in the attitudes people hold about sex. There are great differences between people according to age, gender, religious orientations, and level of education. Persons who have sexually liberal attitudes tend to be younger, less religiously active, and

233

more highly educated, while sexually conservative attitudes are associated with those who are older, more religiously active, and who have less formal education. In general, men tend to be more liberal than women.

The survey also shows that people who have more experience recently [37] with sexual materials tend to hold more liberal sex attitudes than those with less exposure. Analysis of a sex attitude scale, composed of seven items, showed that persons who are more experienced recently with erotica are more likely than less experienced persons to agree that:

When it comes to sex, there is a great difference between what most people do and what they would like to do;

Young people today have healthier attitudes toward sex than do their parents;

There is an element of homosexuality in all of us.

In addition, persons with more experience recently tend, more than those with less experience to disagree with the following statements:

Homosexuals should be excluded from regular society;

A girl who goes to bed with a boy before marriage will lose his respect;

It is important that the government strongly enforce existing sex laws.

Americans who have had more experience recently with erotic materials tend to tolerate homosexuality, premarital intercourse, and the nonreproductive functions of intercourse more often that persons inexperienced with erotica. The data in Table 21 show that recent experience with erotica is more strongly associated with liberal sex attitudes that either age or religiosity.

The study (Abelson, et al., 1970) shows that persons with more recent erotica experience tend to hold liberal sexual attitudes, are more tolerant of the sexual activities and preferences of others, and are less likely to respond punitively with either social ostracism or the demand for activation of legal sanctions than the less experienced segment of the population. Another finding of the survey shows more concretely how sexual tolerance among this group manifests itself. Respondents were asked what they thought a parent should do if he were to observe his child masturbating. The results, shown in Table 22, indicate that Americans generally are tolerant of child masturbation, that they would "discuss" or "discourage," rather than "punish" or "forbid" it. Those most experienced recently with erotica were even more likely

TABLE 21

Sex Attitudes and Exposure to Erotica,
Age and Church Attendance

		No. of people	Very liberal	Somewhat liberal	Somewhat consevative	Very conservative
Men		911	21%	27	36	16
Women		1370	12%	25	39	23
Recent exposure to erotica:						
Men:	Most	256	42%	29	26	4
	Some	342	18%	26	40	17
	None	313	11%	26	40	23
Women:	Most	189	31%	32	31	6
	Some	556	10%	28	40	21
	None	625	8%	22	41	30
Age of respondent:						
Men:	21-29	244	ı 33%	33	27	7
	30-39	192	21%	26	43	12
	40-49	187	18%	23	39	19
	50-59	123	16%	27	34	22
	60 plus	160	19%	25	34	21
Women:	21-29	338	23%	24	37	16
	30-39	270	10%	29	42	20
	40-49	283	5%	27	42	25
	50-59	218	12%	23	37	29
	60 plus	252	8%	22	42	29
Church attendance						
Men:	None	468	28%	29	34	11
	Most	108	12%	22	33	33
Women:	None	577	14%	27	39	20
	Most	201	5%	24	39	32

Source: Abelson H., Cohen, R., Heaton, E., & Suder, C. Public attitudes toward
and experience with erotic materials. *Technical reports of the Commission
on Obscenity and Pornography*. Vol. 6.

to say that they would "discuss, and not discourage" child
masturbation.

The relationship between use of erotic materials and sex
attitudes is also documented in a national study of Sweden
(Zetterberg, 1970). Among the Swedish, persons who were
more accepting of erotic materials were also more accepting
of contraceptive use, sex education in the schools, and premarital and extramarital sexuality.

These studies suggest that persons who are more experienced
recently with erotic materials are indeed attitudinally different from those with less experience. Experienced persons
tend to be more liberal and more tolerant in their sexual
attitudes. The data in Table 23 show that highly experienced

TABLE 22

Tolerance of Masturbation
and Exposure to Erotica

[Question: "Most children play with themselves sexually while
they are growing up. If a young person does this and has a sexual
climax, this is called masturbation. Suppose a 12 or 13 year old
boy or girl does something like this. Which one of these
statements comes closest to your opinion of what a parent should
do? " (Q 15, SAQ)]

| | Recent exposure to erotica: | | | | | |
| | Men | | | Women | | |
	Most	Some	None	Most	Some	None
Number of people	256	342	313	189	556	625
Punish	1%	4%	8%	5%	2%	6%
Forbid, but not punish	7	10	17	4	9	13
Discourage, not forbid	26	34	24	21	23	17
Discuss, not discourage	50	33	23	48	40	29
Ignore	11	7	8	11	9	7
Don't know, No answer	5	13	20	12	17	28

Note — Adapted from Abelson, H., Cohen, R., Heaton, F., & Suder, C. Public
attitudes toward and experience with erotic materials. *Technical reports
of the Commission on Obscenity and Pornography.* Vol. 6.

persons, as compared with others, are more supportive of
First Amendment rights, less restrictive regarding the availability of erotica, and more active in local and national
politics. They are also more highly educated and more frequently read books and magazines and view motion pictures
(Abelson, et al., 1970).[38]

Taken together, all of these findings suggest that neither
all nor part of this attitudinal constellation is a consequence
of exposure to sexual stimuli. Rather, it appears that a "self-
selection" mechanism operates in such a way that persons
who are more socially and sexually active[39] and tolerant are
also more likely to have encountered sexual stimuli in the
ordinary course of social participation. Although the available
data do not prove such a relationship, at least three national
surveys (Abelson, et al., 1970; Berger, et al., 1970a; Zetterberg, 1970) are supportive of this interpretation.[40]

A series of experimental studies suggest, however, that
exposure to erotic stimuli has little or no effect on already
established attitudinal commitments regarding either sexuality
or sexual morality. A series of four studies (Howard, et al.,

TABLE 23
Selected Correlates of Recent Exposure to Erotica

| | Recent Exposure to Erotica | | | | | |
| | Men | | | Women | | |
	Most (N=267)	Some (N=345)	None (N=372)	Most (N=193)	Some (N=578)	None (N=722)
Mass Media Consumption						
Low	13%	29%	45%	9%	18%	38%
Medium	37	42	41	34	52	46
High	50	29	14	57	31	15
Political Activism						
Least	12	18	27	16	18	38
Somewhat	25	30	36	29	33	30
Moderate	31	33	24	34	31	23
Most	32	19	13	22	18	9
Restrictiveness Index on Availability of Erotica						
Restrictive	10	24	42	8	27	46
Moderate	50	57	44	51	52	42
Tolerant	40	18	10	41	19	7
Supportive of First Amendment Rights						
Least accepting	13	32	41	25	39	53
Somewhat	20	21	28	21	22	26
Moderately	23	21	17	14	17	12
Most	44	26	15	41	21	9

[1] For a description of these indices, see Abelson, et al.

Note — Adapted from Abelson, H., Cohen, R., Heaton, E., & Suder, C. Public attitudes toward and experience with erotic materials. *Technical reports of the Commission on Obscenity and Pornography.* Vol. 6.

1970; Kutschinsky, 1970a; Mann, et al., 1970b; Mosher, 1970a), employing a large array of indicators found practically no significant differences in such attitudes before and after exposure to sexual material. In one study (Howard, et al., 1970) the sex attitudes of 23 males were measured before and after they had the opportunity to view and read erotic materials 90 minutes a day for three weeks. No changes were observed on eight of ten attitude scales comprising 148 items (sex drive and interest, sexual maladjustment and frustration, neurotic conflict associated with sex, expression of sexuality, conservative attitudes toward sexuality, loss of sex controls, admission of homosexual tendencies, denial of homosexuality, and sex role confidence).[41] Small but significant changes were observed on two of the (Thorne Sexual Inventory) scales. Subjects reported changes in attitudes toward both greater "repression" of sexual activity and greater acceptance of "promiscuous" attitudes.[42] The investigators noted the apparent paradox, and indicated that "the changes on both scales are from low to more central values and seem to reflect a tempering or moderating opinion" (Reifler, et al., 1970). The investigators, utilizing data from psychiatric interviews and other questionnaires concluded that "the increase in 'promiscuous' attitudes seems more related to tolerance for such behavior in others, as the subjects' own behavior and attitudes for personal conduct did not change." Subjects' increased "repression" was interpreted as relating to their disapproval of personally engaging in various sexual practices (e.g., group sex and homosexual activities) about which they were not previously conversant.

Analysis of an additional indicator, an attitude inventory, revealed that there were no significant changes in subjects' attitudes toward petting or premarital intercourse or in attitudes toward school, work, politics, and friends.

In an experimental study (Mosher, 1970a) of 194 single males and 183 single females, attitudes about premarital sexual intercourse, extramarital sexual intercourse, standards of sexual behavior, and a rating of subjects' own sex attitudes compared to other persons[43] were assessed before and after viewing two erotic films. This study found, that there were no changes in subjects' somewhat conservative attitudes about extramarital sex. Opinions about premarital intercourse became somewhat more liberal two weeks after viewing films; "more sexually experienced subjects, in particular, became more liberal while less sexually experienced subjects changed little." This change reflected subjects' greater agreement, after film-viewing, that "sexual intercourse is all right with a lesser degree of intimacy or affection" (Mosher, 1970a). One significant change was observed in regard to a measure of subjects' own sex standards, although this change was somewhat complicated. Sexually experienced males became slightly more conservative while less sexually experienced females became more liberal in their attitudes about sex standards. More sexually experienced males, however, became more liberal after than before while the more sexually experienced females became more conservative after than before. One other finding of this study may be noted. Before and two weeks after film-viewing, all subjects rated themselves "in comparison to the average person" on a 5-point liberal-conservative sex attitude scale. It was found that more sexually experienced subjects saw themselves as less liberal in "comparison to the average person" two weeks after film viewing. Less sexually experienced persons saw themselves as somewhat more liberal after than before.[44]

A study of 85 married couples (Mann, et al., 1970) assessed sex attitudes before and after couples viewed erotic films once a week for four weeks. Items comprising "romanticism" and "sexual liberalism" scales (Athanasiou and

Shaver, 1969) were employed. Analysis revealed no significant changes for either males or females on either scale, nor were any changes found among individuals who viewed sadomasochistic and group-sex films as opposed to those who viewed other films. The researchers concluded that exposure to erotic film did not change attitudes in these areas. Two other findings may be noted. An additional before-after inventory, a "marital adjustment survey"[45] revealed no significant changes in scales designed to measure "sexual satisfaction (self)," "sexual satisfaction (spouse)," and other indices of marital interaction. It was also found (as discussed in Section C) that over 20% of these couples reported that their participation in the experiment had "lowered inhibition toward spouses" and 16% of the husbands and 12% of the wives reported "increased satisfaction with marital sex life" as a result of the experiment (Mann, et al., 1970b). Another study (Byrne and Lamberth, 1970) of 42 young married couples found that some subjects reported "increased love," "increased willingness to experiment," and "increased feeling of closeness one week after a one-hour session in which couples viewed and read erotic material.

Another study (Kutschinsky, 1970a), employing predominantly married students, administered inventories designed to measure sex attitudes and attitudes about sex crimes before and after a one-hour session in which subjects viewed and read a variety of erotic materials.[46] It was found that "severe-lenient" attitudes about sex crimes did not change four days after exposure, nor 14 days after exposure. In regard to sex attitudes, it was found that subjects reported significantly less interest in "desire to engage in unusual sex practices" four days after exposure, and even less interest 14 days later.

"SEX-CALLOUSED" ATTITUDES TOWARD WOMEN

It is often asserted that a distinguishing characteristic of sexually explicit materials is the degrading and demeaning portrayal of the role and status of the human female. It has been argued that erotic materials describe the female as a mere sexual object to be exploited and manipulated sexually.

One presumed consequence of such portrayals is that erotica transmits an inaccurate and uninformed conception of sexuality, and that the viewer or user will (a) develop a calloused and manipulative orientation toward women and (b) engage in behavior in which affection and sexuality are not well

239

integrated. A recent survey shows that 41% of American males and 46% of the females believe that "sexual materials lead people to lose respect for women" (Abelson, et al., 1970). Recent experiments (Mosher, 1970a, b; Mosher and Katz, 1970) suggest that such fears are probably unwarranted.

Mosher (1970b) observed that during the socialization of adolescent males in American society, beliefs and attitudes are transmitted and learned which encourage a calloused and exploitive orientation toward females. This kind of orientation, Mosher suggests, is believed by young males to ensure sexual access to and success with women. In this study of 256 college males, Mosher (1970b) found that over half of them had used one or more exploitive techniques in an attempt to gain intercourse. These sex "calloused" males more often professed love, used physical force, alcohol, and sexual materials to increase the probability of sexual intercourse. A second study (Mosher, 1970a) tested the hypothesis that sex "calloused" attitudes in males would increase after exposure to sex stimuli. Results showed that exposure to two erotic films did not increase already established frequencies of exploitive sexual behavior—nor in sexual behavior of any kind. Sex "calloused" attitudes toward women decreased immediately after viewing the erotic film (depicting heterosexual petting, coitus, and oral sexuality) and continued to decrease slightly 24 hours and two weeks later. Sex "calloused" males did, however, report greater sexual arousal during exposure than males holding less "calloused" attitudes, and were slightly more likely to report that they found the film enjoyable (Mosher, 1970a).

The author concluded that exposure to erotic stimuli does not increase sex "calloused" attitudes toward women, nor does it dispose persons with "calloused" attitudes toward subsequent exploitive or manipulative activity. The interpretation offered by the author is that:

Seeing a 'stag' film in the presence of male peers bolsters masculine esteem; it serves the same needs as endorsing calloused attitudes. Following the viewing of the films, the males had less need to endorse calloused attitudes since they had just shared the masculine activity of watching a 'stag' film with male peers. . . . If this interpretation does stand the test of further research, it would add some support to the argument that pornography may serve a function as an outlet or safety valve (Mosher, 1970a).

240

Some psychologists have argued that hypotheses which predict that exposure to sex stimuli results in direct and substantial increases in rape, homosexuality, and other forms of sexual behavior are not plausible because they tend to discount the effects of ordinary socialization and other behavioral influences. It has been argued that if exposure to erotic materials affects an individual at all, it would be a more subtle effect—the development of defective character. A recent study systematically investigated this problem (Davis and Braucht, 1970b).

Psychological inventories were developed to assess four aspects of moral and interpersonal character. Item scales were designed to assess moral "blindness," inclination to act upon a moral basis, level of moral reasoning, and quality of interpersonal character. The questionnaires also assessed respondents' experience with erotic materials and the extent to which family background and peer associations served as conforming or deviant influences. The inventories were administered to over 300 men between the ages of 18 and 30, including imprisoned offenders and university and theology students representing a range of ethnic groups.

Results of this study show that moral character was statistically unrelated to the amount of exposure to erotica (r = -.14), but associated with deviant home backgrounds[47] (r = -.45) and deviant peer influences[48] (r = -.41). Additional analysis revealed that character was unrelated to the age of first exposure to erotic materials, and that deviant homes and peers exerted a much stronger influence on both the amount of exposure and age of first exposure. The authors suggest that "these analyses provide no evidence for a detrimental effect of exposure to pornography on character" (Davis and Braucht, 1970b). The importance of peers in determining the age and amount of exposure to sex stimuli has been observed in several other studies (Report of the Traffic Panel, 1970).

Available research in this area suggests that exposure to erotica has no independent impact upon character.

ATTITUDES ABOUT "PORNOGRAPHY"

Several experimental studies have found that exposure to sexual stimuli tends to change attitudes about such material. In three studies, persons became less fearful of the supposed detrimental effects of exposure after they actually had been exposed (Davis and Braucht, 1970a; Howard, et al., 1970; Mann, et al., 1970b). Several experimental studies suggest that both increased familiarity with erotic materials and certain established sexual preferences determine attitudes about the restriction of "pornography." In a repeated exposure experiment (Howard, et al., 1970), attitude changes toward "pornography" were regarded by the investigators as the most striking result of the project. Subjects' initial attitudes ranged from a desire to maintain current controls to a feeling that all controls should be abolished. After three weeks of exposure to sex stimuli, all except two subjects moved toward a more tolerant attitude regarding restrictions, and all subjects agreed that "pornography" would not harm an adult or a stable adolescent. Of 23 subjects, 17 favored the abolition of all controls on the sale and distribution of "pornography" (Howard, et al., 1970).

A study of 85 married couples showed substantially the same results. Female subjects, whose prior experience with erotica was limited, became significantly more permissive toward legal exhibition of erotic films after exposure, and males, whose prior experience was more extensive, also showed increased permissiveness (Mann, et al., 1970b). It was also found that increased permissiveness was affected by the order in which subjects viewed erotic films. Females who viewed films in increasing order of sexual explicitness (e.g., from "suggestive" films to depictions of heterosexual coitus to depictions of homosexual activity, depictions of group sex and, finally, sadomasochistic activity) became more permissive toward the public availability of each depiction than did females who viewed, for example, sadomasochistic films first. The researchers suggested that this finding supported the expectation that a graded exposure to stimuli in a hierarchical order of "innocuousness" results in more attitude change than initially viewing material generally considered most deviant and aversive.

Two other experiments suggest that in addition to increased familiarity with erotic materials, certain established personality and sexual dispositions affect attitudes about restrictiveness. After viewing three erotic films, 121 males indicated that they were generally less fearful of detrimental consequences of exposure to "pornography" (Davis and Braucht, 1970a). Decreased fear of "pornography's" effects was associated with not having been introduced to heterosexuality early ($r = .18$)

or frequently in high school (r = .38), and greater (reported) sexual tension after film-viewing (r = .34).[49]

Byrne and Lamberth (1970) found that personal reactions to erotic depictions tended to determine positions about restriction. It was found that restrictiveness was associated with authoritarianism, feelings of disgust during exposure, and the absence of arousal from certain sexual themes. Regardless of restrictive attitudes, however, these subjects expressed willingness to return to view additional erotic materials.[50]

EMOTIONAL RESPONSES TO EROTICA

Recent research has demonstrated that even a brief presentation of sexual stimuli elicits strong and divergent affective responses in addition to sexual arousal. While the range of emotional responses studied is narrow and the number of studies small, the data suggest that people's position on whether or not erotica should be restricted depends more upon their emotional reactions to such stimuli than upon their views regarding the behavioral effects of such material (Byrne and Lamberth, 1970).[51]

Many investigators have observed "multiple" responses to erotic stimuli, including reported and observed sexual arousal, disgust, and other reactions suggesting an aversive response. Available studies show that exposure to sexual stimuli may produce (a) diffuse, or general, (nonsexual) activation of moods, tension, and other emotional and vegetative states, and (b) affective responses, such as interest, pleasure, liking and dislike, shock, and repulsion. These emotional responses are transitory and, in general, they vary according to certain personality dimensions of the viewer or user and the sexual theme presented.

DIFFUSE EMOTIONAL ACTIVATIONS[52]

Several experiments in which individuals viewed or used sex stimuli show that both mood and emotional states may be temporarily activated as a result of exposure, and that these nonsexual[53] emotional changes are apparent to the viewer during the 24 hours after exposure. After one session of viewing erotic films, male and female university students described themselves as feeling generally more "innerly agitated," and "irritated." Males reported feeling more "gregarious" and "impulsive," and females described themselves as feeling more "emotional," "wild," "uninhibited," "jumpy," and "dizzy." (Schmidt and Sigusch, in press). Twenty-four hours later, between 4% and 38% of these subjects reported increased "inner uneasiness," diminished "concentration ability," increased "general activity," and females reported feeling "more restless" during sleep (18%) and an increase in "autonomic complaints" (14%) (Schmidt and Sigusch, in press).

In another study utilizing the same film stimuli, males aged 18 to 30 tended to describe themselves as having "difficulty concentrating," feeling "uneasy," "active," and having "difficulty sleeping" during the 24 hours after a single exposure (Davis and Braucht, 1970a). It was found that this general increase in emotional tension (i.e., ability to concentrate, aggression, activity level, uneasiness, quality of sleep) was marginally related to reported sexual arousal during exposure $(r = +.16)$, and more strongly related to increased sexual desire $(r = +.34)$ and having fantasized the erotic stimuli during masturbation or coitus after exposure $(r = +.36)$. Increased emotional tension was also related to greater fear of "pornography's ill effects" $(r = +.26)$.

A third film study, again using the same film stimuli, showed that in the 24 hours after exposure both males and females reported mild increases in "internal unrest," "gastro-intestinal complaints," "sexual tension," and slightly decreased "concentration capacity." Females reported increased "nervousness" and "guilt feelings" (Mosher, 1970a).

A fourth experiment (Howard, et al., 1970), in which college males had the opportunity to view or read erotic materials five times a week for three weeks, asked subjects to describe certain moods and emotions prior to each daily exposure session. This study differed from those cited above both in its longitudinal character and in other methodological aspects. Mood ratings, for example, were performed immediately before each exposure. The study found that in reference to 5 of 6 "moods" measured, subjects indicated that they were no more nor less "dizzy," "sleepy," "clear-thinking," "aggressive," or "friendly" throughout the experiment. For one mood, however, subjects did show significant change: they described themselves as initially less "unhappy" on exposure days than on other days. The study did find that during the first of three weeks of daily exposure, as compared with the previous week, subjects reported substantial changes in general "areas of functioning" including increased "thoughts and daydreams of sex," "sexual feelings," and "arousal and anxiety in anticipation" of the daily sessions. Each of these declined, however, during the second and third weeks of the experiment, and remained relatively low throughout the remainder of the experiment. This study also found that feelings of "boredom" and "indifference" decreased significantly during the first week of daily sessions from the week prior to exposure, but by the third week feelings of "boredom" were not significantly different from the week prior to exposure (Howard, et al., 1970).

In general, these studies suggest that exposure to sex stimuli temporarily activates mild emotional responses in substantial proportions of viewers. The studies also show, however, that there is considerable variation among individuals in the specific emotional responses elicited. For example, in one study (Mosher, 1970a) persons who had feelings of guilt before exposure reported significantly more "nervousness," "internal unrest," and "guilt" in the 24 hours after exposure. Sexually inexperienced individuals reported significantly more "guilt" after exposure. The considerable variability in the specific emotional responses to sex stimuli suggests that established response dispositions of individuals largely determine what emotional state is stimulated. The notion that persons differ in their propensities toward certain emotional responses is consistent with studies which show that individuals also differ in their propensities[54] to specific physiological manifestations of emotion (e.g., in some persons, emotional excitement is associated with increased respiratory rates, and in others with glandular activation) (Hain and Linton, 1969, Zuckerman, 1970).

Research on emotional responses to sex stimuli must, however, be considered incomplete. There are distinct limits to the populations studied, the varieties of stimuli, and the context in which exposure was experienced. In many of the experiments, novelty was a major complicating factor, since in most of the experiments, the subjects had very little and quite remote experience with explicit erotic material. Despite their relative naivete and the wide variety of emotional responses engendered, there is no evidence that any of the exposed subjects were emotionally traumatized. In the one experiment which used such indicators in reference to repeated exposure (Howard, et al., 1970) it was found that, as novelty diminished, so too did both the sexual and nonsexual components of emotional arousal.

Available research indicates that both males and females report a variety of affective responses to erotic stimuli. It has already been noted that sexual arousal is reported by substantial proportions of males and females as a result of exposure to erotic stimuli. Experiments by Amoroso and his colleagues (1970), Byrne and Lamberth (1970), Davis and Braucht (1970a), and Schmidt and Sigusch (in press) indicate that feelings of guilt are sometimes experienced as a response by both sexes.[55] These experimental findings are supported by retrospective reports obtained in several surveys (Abelson, et al., 1970; Berger, et al., 1970a; b; Elias, 1970).

A study in which college freshmen and sophomores viewed two erotic films, notes that moderate changes were reported for nearly all of the affective states measured. The data in Table 24 show that males reported feeling more "excited,"

TABLE 24

Summary of Means, Standard Deviations, and
Significant F Ratios of Affective Reaction
for All Ss as a Function of Gender

Affects	Males M	Females M	F Ratios
Interested	1.19	.69	F = 10.43 b
Peaceful	-.44	.89	F = 10.21 b
Attracted	.93	.12	F = 28.01 c
Repelled	-.55	.30	F = 26.25 c
Excited	1.39	1.06	F = 7.47 b
Shocked	-.31	.57	F = 32.98 c
Irritated	-.45	.33	F = 27.61 c
Pepped-Up	1.14	.53	F = 27.23 c
Impulsive	.69	.32	F = 14.12 c
Driven	.63	.19	F = 16.49 c
Jumpy	.32	.60	F = 7.66 b
Disgusted	-.30	.72	F = 45.30 c
Angered	-.49	.08	F = 23.62 c
Benumbed	-.15	.25	F = 8.41 b
Depressed	-.44	.10	F = 19.50 c
Anxious	.93	.45	F = 18.03 c
Serene	-.41	-.73	F = 6.80 a
Ashamed	-.38	.12	F = 21.58 c
Happy	.46	-.15	F = 10.40 b
Embarrassed	-.32	.45	F = 13.22 c
Guilty	-.40	.02	F = 10.54 b

$^a p < .05$ $^b p < .01$ $^c p < .001$

Note — Adapted from Mosher, D. L. Psychological reactions to pornographic films. *Technical reports of the Commission on Obscenity and Pornography.* Vol. 8.

"interested," "pepped up," and less "angry," less "depressed," and less "ashamed" after exposure. Females were more ambivalent in their reported feelings: they were both "interested" and "attracted" but also "shocked," "irritated," and "repelled." Differences between the sexes tended to be both quantitative and qualitative (Mosher, 1970b).

Another study (Mann, et al., 1970) presented erotic films to married couples weekly, over the course of four weeks. These subjects also reported both sexual arousal and various aversive reactions to the sex stimuli. When subjects rated each film as "favorable-unfavorable," negative (disapproving) responses were more often reported than positive (approving) responses.

These studies also indicate that persons may differ in what sexual themes are defined as either arousing or aversive. In one study (Mann, et al., 1970), males more often reported "arousal" than "aversion" while females commonly reported the opposite. Middle-aged females, for example, found lesbian themes more aversive than did their husbands, and males found male homosexual depictions more aversive than did their wives. Among younger married couples (Byrne and Lamberth, 1970), responses to depictions of masturbation (male and/or female) were found to be significant indicators of affective responses: females were more aroused and less repelled by depictions of male masturbation, while males responded similarly to female masturbation. Unmarried college males and females (Mosher, 1970a) tended to differ in their responses to depictions of oral sexuality, with sexually inexperienced persons reporting more "disgust" and less sexual arousal, especially among females. Certain personality and background characteristics are also associated with specific effective responses to sex stimuli. For instance, "disgust" was found to be associated with authoritarianism, religious participation and religious affiliation (Byrne and Lamberth, 1970), and sex guilt (Mosher, 1970a).

AROUSAL AND BEHAVIOR: SOME UNRESOLVED ISSUES

The studies reviewed in this and the previous section show that sex stimuli elicit both sexual and nonsexual emotional arousal. This research permits the formulation of problems yet to be investigated. One question, for example, concerns the impact of erotic stimuli upon persons who are disposed to find such stimuli aversive. The expectation might be that such reactions would function to diminish interest in exposure

247

to sex stimuli. However, one experiment in this area (Amoroso, et al., 1970) suggests that the opposite may be the case. The data in Figure 7 show that when subjects viewed erotic slides which they previously had judged as "unpleasant, bad, dirty, and harmful" they spent substantially more time looking at them when they were permitted to view them alone than when viewing them in the presence of observers.

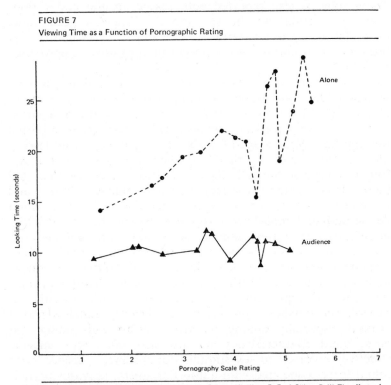

FIGURE 7
Viewing Time as a Function of Pornographic Rating

Note — Adapted from Amoroso, D. M., Brown, M., Pruesse, M., Ware, E. E., & Pilkey, D. W. The effects of arousal and the presence of others on voluntary exposure to erotic stimuli. *Technical reports of the Commission on Obscenity and Pornography.* Vol. 8.

These data suggest that although some erotic materials may be regarded as aversive, they are not found to be less interesting. The study also found that the slides judged to be most "pornographic" were also regarded as the most sexually stimulating (Amoroso, et al., 1970).

Another question of both theoretical and practical importance pertains to the relative contribution of sexual arousal, emotional arousal, stimulus content, and availability

248

of a sexual partner (opportunity) in generating sexual activity following exposure to sex stimuli. The studies reviewed have shown that substantial proportions of persons report both sexual arousal and activated emotional states after exposure to sex stimuli, but that coital and masturbatory responses are considerably less frequent. When they do occur, the selection of one over the other appears to be determined by opportunity. The importance of sexual arousal or emotional activation, or both, as dispositional or motivational factors is not yet clear. Davis and Braucht (1970a) found that higher levels of sexual arousal during exposure were associated with subsequent masturbatory activity ($r = +.33$), but unrelated to petting or coitus, whereas general emotional activation in the 24 hours following exposure was not associated with masturbation, but rather with increased frequencies of coitus ($r = +.25$) and petting ($r = +.26$). This study also found that conversations about sex in the 24 hours after exposure were associated with increased coital and petting frequencies, and hence, emotional activation. These data suggest that sexual and emotional arousal differentially affect subsequent sexual activity. Additional studies are needed to clarify these patterns.

A third unresolved issue in this area involves the relationship between emotional arousal and the likelihood of overt sexual behavior. Mosher (1970b) found that persons with sex-"calloused" attitudes reported more highly activated emotional states than non-"calloused" persons after exposure; they were more often reported feeling "excited," "eager for sexual contact," "interested," "attracted," "impulsive," "wilder," and "driven." It was hypothesized that the greater activation of this group could potentially be discharged through subsequent sexual behavior. The data showed, however, that this group reported no changes in sexual behavior and that, in fact, exposure to the erotic films reduced existing levels of sex-"calloused" attitudes (Mosher, 1970a).

Yet another question is suggested by a series of experiments (Tannenbaum, 1970) which provide preliminary support for the notion that general emotional arousal, nonspecific to any emotional state, leads to higher levels of response, regardless of the particular response called for. When general arousal was measured by heart rate, blood pressure, and skin temperature, it was found that a film containing erotic cues was more generally arousing than a film containing aggressive cues and instigated more intense responses, including both "aggressive" and "altruistic" behaviors. This finding may or may not be compatible with Mosher's and Katz's (1970) finding that sexual arousal induced by viewing erotic films did not lead to increased levels of verbal aggression, except when opportunities to view additional films were contingent upon such responses.

JUDGMENTAL RESPONSES TO EROTICA

One consequence of exposure to sexual stimuli is the formulation of evaluations and judgments. Persons may approve or disapprove of the material viewed or read, and the judgment may be based upon a range of criteria (i.e., aesthetic, intellectual, and/or moral). One of the more interesting questions raised by the objective analysis of erotic stimuli is: under what conditions do persons define sexual stimuli as "obscene" or "pornographic?" The few studies which have explored this question indicate predictably that such judgments tend to be determined by (a) certain characteristics of the stimulus and (b) certain characteristics of the judge.

UNIVERSALISM AND RELATIVISM

It is now well known that specific erotic materials and depictions are judged and valued differently across cultural and subcultural groups, and through time within the same groups. The proposition that obscenity or pornography is "in the eye of the beholder" is trite, but nonetheless true. Anthropological literature suggests that probably all societies have established cultural or legal definitions of what is offensive to the senses or to some principle or ideal (La Barre, 1955). Although virtually all societies have formulated definitions, of "obscene" or "pornographic" representations, words, and acts, there is no universally defined standard with respect to what is obscene.

The cultural relativity of what constitutes obscene or pornographic sexual representations establishes at the outset two fundamentally important considerations. First, informed treatment of these issues will avoid assumptions that parochial values, whether cultural or idiosyncratic, necessarily constitute human absolutes. Second, it will be recognized that when persons are taught and educated to define certain erotic representations as obscene or pornographic, and if that aspect of socialization is successful, such representations will, in fact, be judged obscene or pornographic.

Higgins and Katzman (1969) attempted to isolate the characteristics of erotic photographs which influence judgmental reactions. Ninety photographs, collected from a range of sources, were presented randomly to over 300 adults from various occupations who were asked (for each photograph) "in your opinion, how obscene is this photograph?" and "in your opinion, how sexually stimulating is this photograph?" Results showed that several photograph characteristics were associated with obscenity judgments. Most of the photographs rated obscene were black and white, rather than color, and were aesthetically unappealing. These photos typically portrayed provocative backgrounds, such as bedrooms or bathrooms, and the models, although posed seductively, were regarded by the subjects as unattractive. Total nudity with an exposed pubic area was a characteristic of almost all photos judged obscene. By contrast, photos judged not obscene, or "low" obscene, were judged to have superior technical qualities, to have less seductively posed, but more attractive models, and to portray outdoor or benign backgrounds. Only partial nudity was displayed; breasts, buttocks, and pubis were not shown (Higgins and Katzman, 1969).

A follow-up study (Katzman, 1970a) attempted to determine more specifically the features of those photographs which elicited judgments of obscenity. The study found that characteristics such as clothing, pose, attractiveness, photography, body exposure, and background were all highly related to obscenity ratings. The data in Table 25 show that the factor most highly connected with obscenity judgments was the degree of nudity thought to be acceptable to most other people, not just nudity *per se.*

It was also found that ratings of "sexually stimulating" were associated with "obscenity" ratings (male: $r = +.54$; female: $r = +.33$). The study also showed that persons of varying educational levels differed in the criteria used for judging obscenity.

Other studies have examined stimulus characteristics which determine judgments of *pornography.* Two studies of erotic films (Mosher, 1970a; Byrne and Lamberth, 1970) and a study of photographic slides (Amoroso, et. al., 1970) suggest that depictions of oral sexuality and homosexuality are typically judged to be more pornographic than heterosexual coitus. This generalization is complicated, however, by the concomitant finding that sexually inexperienced persons are

251

TABLE 25

Photograph Characteristics Correlated
with Obscenity Ratings

Scale Titles	r of Scale and Obscenity	Inter-rater r
Propriety of Body Exposed to View	.70	.77
Could be published in common Magazine (excluding Playboy)	-.64	.79
Emphasis in photo on pubic area	.58	.76
Percent of both breasts exposed	.57	.76
Attractiveness of clothing	.56	.70
Artistic merit of photo	-.51	.62
Apparent sexual innocence of model	.51	.61
Sexual suggestiveness of clothing	.50	.53
Body build of model	.47	.68
Propriety of pose or action suggested	.47	.65
Attractiveness of body below waist	.45	.69
Amount of exposure of pubic-genital area	.44	.93
Neatness of general appearance of model	.44	.69
Attractiveness of photo	.44	.66
Age of model	.43	.64
Attractiveness of pose or position	.43	.61
Percent of inside thigh in view	.42	.84
Overall technical quality of photo	-.41	.53
Attractiveness of model (body and face)	.41	.60
Of body in picture, what percent exposed to view	.40	.85

Note — Adapted from Katzman, M. Photograph characteristics influencing the judgment of obscenity. *Technical reports of the Commission on Obscenity and Pornography.* Vol. 9.

generally disposed toward unfavorable judgments of all unfamiliar sexual practices.

Research in this area shows that some sexual themes are judged to be both pornographic *and* sexually arousing, while others are regarded as pornographic and not arousing, and some are defined as arousing but not pornographic. In a rating study employing college males as subjects, Amoroso his colleagues (1970) found that the sexual themes judged as most pornographic were: fellatio, ventral-dorsal coitus, cunnilingus, and ejaculation. This study also found a high positive correlation between pornography ratings and ratings of sexual stimulation (rho = +.73) and a high negative correlation between pornography ratings and "pleasantness" ratings (rho = —.70), although "pleasantness" was unrelated to ratings of sexual stimulation. The authors interpreted these findings to suggest that "material is seen as highly pornographic which is highly stimulating as well as quite unpleasant" (Amoroso, et al., 1970).

252

A study by Byrne and Lamberth (1970) in which young married couples rated visual, textual, and imagined sexual themes found that the most pornographic themes were homosexual anal intercourse, homosexual fellatio, group sex, male sadism toward females, and homosexual cunnilingus. Themes judged to be both pornographic and sexually arousing were: group sex, heterosexual cunnilingus and fellatio, female masturbation, and homosexual cunnilingus. In general, this group, with estabilshed heterosexual commitments, regarded depictions of heterosexual coitus as arousing and not pornographic, and judged homosexual depictions to be pornographic and not arousing. The study suggests that while characteristics of the stimulus determine pornography ratings, individual sexual dispositions seem to determine reactions to stimulus characteristics (Byrne and Lamberth, 1970).

CHARACTERISTICS OF THE JUDGE

Available research indicates that individual sexual preferences, sexual experience, sex attitudes, and educational level are important determinants of judgmental responses to sexual stimuli. Higgins and Katzman (1969) found that occupation and education were significantly associated with judgments of obscenity. The data in Figure 8 show that of six occupational groups, policemen and psychiatrists were significantly less likely than probationary police, physicians, lawyers, and teachers to judge sexual stimuli as obscene or sexually stimulating. It was also found that persons with less than 16 years of formal education rated photos as more obscene and more sexually stimulating than did persons with graduate and professional training.[56] A follow-up study (Katzman, 1970a) suggests that socioeconomic characteristics of the rater are more important than gender differences in rating obscenity; educational level was found to be particularly highly related to rating judgments. It was found that persons with less education were more likely to be concerned with degree of nudity, especially the pubic area, and the sexually stimulating qualities of the photograph. More highly educated persons, on the other hand, tended to judge photographs in terms of aesthetic criteria such as technical quality and attractiveness of the model and background (Katzman, 1970a).

Further analysis of these data (Katzman, 1970b) revealed that, in general, judgments of obscenity tend to be more variable than judgments of sexual stimulation. It was found

FIGURE 8

Occupation Groups' Obscenity Ratings

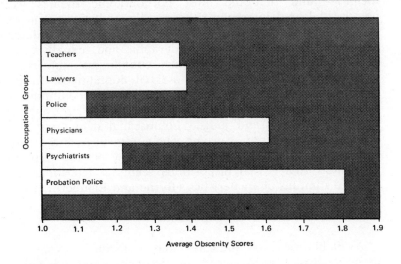

Note — Adapted from Higgins, J. W., & Katzman, M. B. Determinants in the judgment of obscenity. *American Journal of Psychiatry*, June, 1969, *125*(12), 147.

that raters more often agreed on which photographs were sexually arousing than on those which were obscene. It was also found that the relationship between judged obscenity and sexual stimulation varies according to the educational level of the judge. Among less educated judges, photographs which were rated as obscene were also judged to be sexually stimulating. More highly educated judges, however, rated obscenity independently of sexual stimulation (Katzman, 1970b).

Research indicates that persons with comparatively liberal sex attitudes are less likely, and religiously active persons more likely, to judge erotic stimuli as pornographic (Amoroso, et al., 1970; Byrne and Lamberth, 1970). Several studies found that the number of stimuli judged as pornographic was strongly related to authoritarianism (Abse, 1955; Byrne and Lamberth, 1970; Eliasberg and Stuart, 1961).

Sexual inexperience also seems to be related to judgmental responses. In a study of college freshmen and sophomores, Mosher (1970a) found that sexually inexperienced persons judged two erotic films (especially segments depicting oral sex) to be substantially more pornographic, disgusting, offensive, and abnormal than sexually experienced persons. As

254

reported earlier, a study of married couples (Byrne and Lamberth, 1970) showed that homosexual themes were judged to be pornographic. However, it is quite possible that raters with established homosexual commitments would rate homosexual themes as less pornographic. As Byrne and Lamberth (1970) have noted, positive reactions to specific themes may well be in part a function of its familiarity, either behaviorally or symbolically. This interpretation is consistent with the finding that increased frequency of exposure to a stimulus leads to a more positive evaluation of that stimulus (Zajonc, 1968),[57] and suggests that judgments about what is pornographic can be altered by repeated presentations of the same theme.[58]

SUMMARY AND DISCUSSION

Persons who are more experienced with erotica are more liberal or tolerant than those with less experience in reference to other people's behavior. They are, for example, more likely to feel that, "when it comes to sex, there is a great difference between what most people do and what they would like to do" and less likely to agree that "a girl who goes to bed with a boy before marriage will lose his respect." They are also more tolerant of masturbation in their children.

Experimental studies to date indicate that exposure to erotic stimuli have little or no effect on established attitudinal commitments regarding either sexuality or sexual morality. Comparison of attitudes before and after single or repeated exposure reveal almost no significant differences. Such isolated differences as were observed principally involve somewhat increased tolerance for other peoples' activities, and are in some respects contradictory. The overall picture is almost uniformly one of no significant change. A study of 300 young males indicates that exposure to erotica has no direct relationship to "moral character."

Available research indicates that exposure to pornography does tend to liberalize attitudes, regarding whether such material is itself harmful or whether it should be restricted. Such attitudes are also apparently related to feelings of guilt, politicosocial attitudes, and other personality characteristics.

Several attempts have been made to identify the social and psychological variables which determine judgments such as "obscene" and "pornographic" in response to sex stimuli. Available research indicates that characteristics of both the

255

stimulus and the rater influence such evaluations. One factor which has been found to be highly associated with "obscenity" judgments is the degree of nudity thought to be acceptable to most people. Research in this area also shows that individual sexual preferences, sexual experience, tolerant attitudes, and educational backgrounds are important determinants of the judgments made about erotic stimuli. Finally, the data suggest that familiarity with erotica is an important determinant of evaluative reactions.

A set of experimental studies indicates that exposure to erotic material activates a variety of general emotional responses, including agitation and malaise among both males and females. A study of repeated exposure suggests that these effects are transitory (less than 24 hours).

Affective responses are varied, and differ with sociopsychological characteristics of the subjects. Erotic stimuli are variously regarded as both arousing and repelling, arousing but not repelling, and repelling but not arousing.

Section E. Erotica and Antisocial and Criminal Behavior

In its assignment to the Commission "to study the effect of obscenity and pornography upon the public," Congress added for emphasis "and particularly minors, and its relationship to crime and other antisocial behavior" (P.L. 90-100). This emphasis reflects: (a) a long-standing concern that has been voiced by many officials[59] and (b) the state of scientific knowledge at the time the Commission was established.

The paucity of research information regarding the effects of pornography on the antisocial behavior of adults and youth is partly a function of a general sensitivity about the scientific study of private behavior—especially sexual behavior and specifically as it concerns children. The Commission was not immune to social forces restricting research in this area nor to the logistical and methodological difficulties inherent in pioneering efforts. Research that the Commission initiated is, therefore, somewhat more restricted in quantity and in the quality of rigor than that required for unequivocal conclusions. Nevertheless, many more empirical observations

256

were accumulated during the past two years than had been brought to bear on the issue previously. Sufficient information is now available to discuss these issues within the framework of scientific knowledge.

The following discussion is organized around two general research problems: (a) the relationship between availability of erotic material and the incidence of antisocial behavior, and (b) the experience of convicted offenders with sexual materials. Data are first presented for minors and then for adults.

EROTICA AND JUVENILE DELINQUENCY

The causes of juvenile delinquency and its prevention continue to be matters of serious concern to this country. A large literature of scientific research and Congressional testimony of expert witnesses has developed during the past 20 years, and although delinquent behavior is not yet well understood, substantial knowledge about its causes has been accumulated. Perhaps the most important development in scientific thought about the etiology of delinquency has been the discovery of important social and subcultural influences.[60] Traditionally, criminal and delinquent behavior was attributed to conditions such as personal maladjustment and individual pathology, biological, physiological or psychological. During the past decade, however, increasing attention has been devoted to identifying a broader range of cultural and subcultural variables and "the conditions of life that drive people to commit crime and that undermine the restraining rules and institutions erected by society against antisocial conduct" (President's Commission on Law Enforcement and the Administration of Justice, 1967:41).

The history of delinquency research also shows comparatively little concern about literature, film or television as potential causes of delinquent behavior.[61] A review (Kupperstein, 1970) of the scientific research and theoretical literature on delinquency causation showed that "pornography" has never been seriously regarded as a cause of delinquency by criminologists, sociologists, and psychologists. It was concluded that

. . . even the most recent theoretical and empirical investigations of the causes of delinquency—particularly those that are concerned with enumerating significant environmental and cultural variables—fail to mention pornography or to suggest that an investigation be made

257

of the relationship between pornography and juvenile delinquency (Kupperstein, 1970).

In the absence of adequate research, opinions about these relationships have been both numerous and divided. Many people working in law enforcement, for example, believe that exposure to pornography not only is related to the commission of offenses by minors but actually causes such offenses (Hoover, 1965). Other professionals trained in social work, psychology, sociology and similar disciplines having a wide range of experience with youth, generally do not believe that such a causal relationship exists (Lipkin and Carnes, 1970; Wilson and Jacobs, 1970).[62] This difference in expert opinion is due, in part, to different experiences and to different modes of inference used by the two groups. Most testimony by individuals working in law enforcement, for example, cites instances in which offenders are found to have erotic materials on their person, or among their possessions. Based on an accumulation of such instances, a causal relationship is inferred (Senate Subcommittee to Investigate Juvenile Delinquency, 1955: pp. 104, 117; 1959: pp. 68, 164, 212, 314; Kefauver, 1960; House Select Subcommittee on Education, 1967: pp. 85-86).[63] Professional workers, on the other hand, who may have more intensive and extensive contact with minors, tend to base their opinions on knowledge of both delinquent and nondelinquent youth.

It is no longer necessary to rely on expert opinion alone. Several empirical studies are now available to inform discussion regarding the relationship between erotic material and antisocial behavior among minors.

AVAILABILITY OF EROTICA, JUVENILE SEX CRIMES,
AND ILLEGITIMACY

A recent study examined the relationship between increased availability of erotic material in the past decade and the national incidence of juvenile sex offenses during the same period (Kupperstein and Wilson, 1970). Police statistics were drawn from the Federal Bureau of Investigation's Uniform Crime Reports.[64] Analysis showed that the availability of sexual materials increased several fold from 1960 to 1969.[65] During that same period, and as shown in Table 26, the number of juvenile[66] arrests for all offenses, sexual and nonsexual, increased by 105 percent, and the number of such arrests for nonsexual crimes increased by 108 percent.

258

During that same period, however, the number of juvenile arrests for sexual offenses decreased by four percent.

TABLE 26

Number and Percent Change in
Juvenile[1] Arrests: 1960 to 1969

Offense Category	1960	1969	Percent Change
All offenses, sexual and nonsexual	477,262	980,453	+105.4
All sex offenses	10,881	10,395	-4.5
Forcible rape	1,191	2,214	+85.9
Prostitution and commercialized vice	393	860	+118.9
Other sex offenses	9,297	7,321	-21.3
All nonsex offenses	466,381	970,058	+108.0

[1] Under 18 years of age

Note — Compiled from Federal Bureau of Investigation, United States Department of Justice, *Uniform crime reports - 1969*. Washington D. C.: U. S. Government Printing Office, 1970, 110.

The decrease in juvenile arrests for sex offenses is in some part the product of a change in law enforcement policy resulting in the reduction of arrests for certain forms of homosexual behavior. Further, the overall decrease obscures an absolute increase of 86% in juvenile arrests for forcible rape and a 119% increase in such arrests for prostitution and commercialized vice.[67] When population changes are taken into account, however, it becomes clear that the increases in juvenile arrests for these offenses are not so large as the absolute numbers suggest.[68] It is also worthy of note that juveniles accounted for a very small proportion of all arrests for prostitution and commercialized vice (1.5% in 1960 and 2.1% in 1969) and for about one-fifth of all arrests for forcible rape (17.3% in 1960 and 20.6% in 1969) and for other sex offenses (20.5% in 1960 and 19.5% in 1969). Thus, to the extent that arrest data are valid indicators of the changes in the nature and volume of crime, it appears that juveniles did not contribute substantially more to the sex crime rate in 1969 than they did in 1960.

In sum, then, while the availability of sexual materials increased several fold during the period from 1960 to 1969, and while juvenile arrests for all crimes more than doubled, juvenile arrests for sex crimes decreased. Despite the change in arrests for homosexual activity, and the increase in rape,

259

these statistics do not provide support for the belief that increased availability of sexual materials leads to sex crime among juveniles. The data do not, however, disprove a connection between sexual material and forcible rape.

This review (Kupperstein and Wilson, 1970) also examined statistics on illegitimate births[69] between 1940 and 1968. When the first draft of this report was written, rates of illegitimate births had been made available by the Division of Vital Statistics of the United States Public Health Service for the period 1940 to 1965. Those data presented a clear and somewhat surprising picture. In relation to the 1960 to 1965 period, illegitimate birth rates for females 15-19 years rose from 15.7 to 16.7 (a 6.4% increase). Rate increases for all unmarried women 15 to 44, and indeed for almost every age group,[70] were higher, and in some cases vastly higher than the small increase among adolescent females. These 1940 to 1965 and 1960 to 1965 data accordingly cast extreme doubt on the thesis that increased availability of erotica was associated with increased illegitimate births among minors.

In late August, 1970, the Public Health Service released partial data on illegitimate births during the 1965 to 1968 period. These new data tremendously complicate the picture and render it impossible to come to any firm conclusion as to whether there is any relationship between increased availability of erotica and the rate of illegitimate births. In brief, the illegitimate birth rate among females 15-19 increased 18.6%, while illegitimacy rates for every older age group dropped, in some cases to a very marked degree (e.g., by 24.0% among women aged 30-34). Put another way, the years 1965 to 1968 were marked by a virtual reversal of the 1960 to 1965 (or 1940 to 1965) trends for almost all age groups, and the reversals occurred in both directions, i.e., minors went up, while the rate for everyone else went down (See Table 27). What is here manifested is not a simple change in rates but a wholly changed social picture.

The question which is virtually impossible to answer is whether the increased availability of erotica in the 1965 to 1968 period was related to this phenomenon. The picture is simply too complex and is necessarily a product of several causes. It is difficult to conceive, for example, that increased availability of erotica should have had one effect on minor girls and no similar effect—indeed, in a sense, the opposite effect—on all other women. Almost certainly, the increased availability of simple contraceptive methods and of abortion,

260

and differences in such availability for different age groups, must be involved in the picture. The complexity of the phenomenon is further attested by the vast differences in illegitimate birth rates between such population groups as whites and blacks. In brief, the overall picture is simply too complex to lend itself to any simple, let alone single, explanation. In reference to the role of erotica, if any, all that can be said is that it seems unlikely that so complex a change could result from so specific an element. Whether it played

TABLE 27

Estimated Illegitimacy Rates and Percent Change, By Age of Mother: United States, 1940-1968

(Rates are illegitimate births per 1,000 females in specified age group)

Year	15-44 years	Age of Mother						
		10-14	15-19	20-24	25-29	30-34	35-39	40-44
1940	7.1	0.4	7.4	9.5	7.2	5.1	3.4	1.2
1950	14.1	0.6	12.6	21.3	19.9	13.3	7.2	2.0
1960	21.8	0.6	15.7	40.3	42.0	27.5	13.9	3.6
1961	22.6	0.6	16.0	41.2	44.8	28.9	15.1	3.8
1962	21.5	0.6	14.9	41.8	46.4	27.0	13.5	3.8
1963	22.5	0.6	15.3	39.9	49.4	33.7	16.1	4.3
1964	23.4	0.6	16.5	40.0	50.1	41.1	15.0	4.0
1965	23.4	0.7	16.7	38.8	50.4	37.1	17.0	4.4
1968	24.4	-*	19.8	37.3	38.6	28.2	14.9	3.8
Percent Change 1940-1969	+229.6	+75.0	+125.7	+224.2	+600.0	+627.4	+400.0	+266.7
Percent Change 1960-1965	+7.3	+16.7	+6.4	-3.7	+20.0	+34.9	+22.3	+22.2
Percent Change 1965-1968	+4.3	-*	+18.6	-3.9	-23.4	-24.0	-12.3	-13.6

*Figures not available

Note — Adapted from Public Health Service, United States Department of Health, Education and Welfare, *Trends in illegitimacy, United States 1940-1965*. Washington, D. C.: U. S. Government Printing Office, 1968. Figures for 1968 received directly from the Public Health Service, Division of Vital Statistics.

any role at all is a question that simply cannot be answered on the basis of available data.

JUVENILE DELINQUENTS' EXPERIENCE WITH EROTIC MATERIAL

Several recent studies suggest that the experience of delinquent youth with erotic materials is not generally different from that of nondelinquent youth. Both delinquent and nondelinquent youth report: (a) substantial experience with sexual materials at relatively young ages; (b) friends and peer group networks as a principal source of erotic materials; and (c) psychosexual stimulation from such materials.

EXTENT OF EXPERIENCE[71]

Recent research has assessed the extent to which youth are experienced with erotic materials. Studies of high school students (Abelson, et al., 1970; Elias, 1970) and college youth (Berger, et al., 1970a) show that about 80% of American males and 70% of the females have seen visual depictions or read textual descriptions of sexual intercourse by age 18. Adults report that most of their experience with erotic materials, generally, occurs during adolescence and young adulthood, and declines substantially after age 30.[72]

These findings are consistent with studies of delinquent youth. Juvenile offenders also widely report experience with sexual materials. A study of 100 incarcerated male juveniles found that 94% reported experience with "eight-pagers" and "sixteen-pagers" (cartoon booklets) depicting sexual activity (Haines, 1955). A comparison study of 39 delinquents and 39 nondelinquent youth[73] (Berninghausen and Faunce, 1964) found no significant differences between these groups in the number of "sensational" books they had read. Nondelinquent youth were somewhat more likely (75%) than delinquent youth (56%), however, to report having read at least one "possible erotic" book.[74] A similar finding was reported by Schiller (1970) in a study of pregnant high school girls and 91 junior college girls. The unwed pregnant girls reported reading fewer books of any kind than did the college girls. Nearly all the girls in both groups, however, reported experience with "confession" and "romance" magazines and Playboy.

A recent study (Propper, 1970) of 476 incarcerated delinquent[75] males revealed that 95% reported experience with

262

at least one erotic visual depiction, and 83% with at least one textual depiction.[76] In comparison, a national survey (Abelson, et al., 1970) found that of a representative sample of boys between the ages of 15 and 20 years, 87% reported exposure to at least one visual depiction, and 80% to at least one textual depiction. The depictions with which the majority of both nondelinquent and delinquent males were experienced included sex organs, oral sexuality and heterosexual intercourse. Experience with depictions of homosexuality and sadomasochistic activities was considerably less widespread in both groups.

These studies suggest that the proportion of youthful offenders who have had experience with erotic materials is not significantly different from the proportion of other adolescents and young adults in American society, regardless of their age or social background. Table 28 summarizes the relevant data with respect to one often used indicator, viz. exposure to depictions of heterosexual intercourse.

TABLE 28

Extent of Exposure Among Delinquent
and Nondelinquent Youth[1]

Population	Erotic[2] Books	Erotic[2] Pictures
Incarcerated delinquents, 17-20 years (Propper, 1970)	77%	84%
National sample males, 18-20 years, living in parents' home (Abelson, et al., 1970)	68%	63%
National sample males, 21-29 years (Abelson, et al., 1970)	82%	81%
National sample college students 17-24 years (Berger, Simon & Gagnon, 1970a)	88%	95%
Urban working class high school students (juniors and seniors) (Elias, 1970)	95%	81%
Urban working class adolescents, 13-18 years (Berger, Simon & Gagnon, 1970b)	79%	77%
Los Angeles working class white males reporting on their adolescent experience (Goldstein, et al., 1970)	80%	85%
Los Angeles Black "Ghetto" males reporting on their adolescent experience (Goldstein, et al., 1970)	81%	78%

[1] "Extent" refers to the proportion of a given population reporting any experience with erotic material.
[2] Refers to depictions of heterosexual intercourse.

American adults have their first exposure to erotic materials at a relatively young age. A survey (Abelson, et al., 1970) shows that 74% of adult males report experience with erotic material before age 21, over half (54%) before age 18, and nearly one-third (30%) before age 15. Females generally report slightly later ages of first exposure.

The same survey found that about half (53%) of young people 15 to 17 reported first exposure to visual erotica before the age of 15, and 49% reported reading textual erotica before 15. Among males 15 to 17,[77] 63% reported exposure to visual material before age 15 (39% before age 13). Fifty-three percent of these males reported experience with erotic textual material before 15 (21% before age 13). It appears, then, that today's youth have had earlier experience with erotic material than did the preceding generation.[78]

Propper's (1970) study of incarcerated delinquent males also found relatively early ages of first experience with visual and textual erotica. Over half reported first exposure to visual depictions of sex organs (62%), oral-genital contact (51%), and intercourse (52%) prior to age 15. Corresponding figures for first exposure to textual erotica are, in each of these cases, under 30 percent. (See Table 29).

TABLE 29

Percentage of Nondelinquent and Delinquent Males
First Exposed to Erotica Prior to Age Fifteen

	Visual	Textual
Nondelinquents[1]		
All depictions	63%	53%
Delinquents[2]		
Sex organs	62	26
Oral-genital contact	51	26
Intercourse	52	27
Homosexuality	30	16
Sado-masochism	18	12

[1] 15-17 year old males (Abelson, *et al.*, 1970) Question asked of approximately half of young male sample

[2] 17-20 year old incarcerated delinquent males (Propper, 1970)

Recent studies suggest that substantial proportions of American youth have seen or read depictions of sexual activity more than once or twice. A national survey (Abelson, et al., 1970) of American youth 15 to 20 years found that 87% of the boys and 80% of the girls had some experience with visual erotica; 81% of the boys and 73% of the girls had such experiences within the last two years. Of those who had, 32% of the males and 29% of the females reported exposure to erotic visual material on more than five occasions during the past two years.[79] Forty-nine percent of the males and 45% of the females reported having seen five or more types of visual and textual erotic depictions in the course of their lives.

Extensive experience is also reported in several studies of selected populations. A study of 473 working class, white, predominantly Catholic adolescents age 13–18 (Berger, et al., 1970b) found that among males, over half (53%) had seen photographs of human genitalia and about a third (32%) had seen pictures of sexual intercourse more than ten times. A study of 476 incarcerated youthful male offenders age 17 to 20, 67% Black and 21% Puerto Rican, also reported exposure on more than ten occasions to visual depictions of sex organs (49%), or oral sex (36%), of heterosexual intercourse (44%), of homosexual activity (23%), and of sadomasochistic activity (13%) (Propper, 1970).

THE SOCIAL CONTEXT OF EXPERIENCE

Research shows that exposure to erotic photographs, cartoons, snapshots, and erotic stories in books, magazines, and typewritten sheets ordinarily occurs in a social context. Such material circulates among adult male friendship and work groups (Abelson, et al., 1970; Davis and Braucht, 1970b), within university fraternities (Berger, et al., 1970a), and adolescent social networks in neighborhoods and schools (Abelson, et al., 1970; Berger, et al., 1970b; Elias, 1970), and among juveniles incarcerated in reformatories (Propper, 1970). Research also suggests that the circulation of erotic materials among females tends to originate with males; wives obtain erotic materials from their husbands (Abelson, et al., 1970) and college, high school and younger females frequently obtain such materials from male peers (Berger, et al., 1970a, 1970b; Elias, 1970).

265

A small proportion of both delinquent and nondelinquent youth report purchasing or receiving sexual materials through the mail (Abelson, et al., 1970; Berger, et al., 1970a, 1970b; Elias, 1970b; Haines, 1955). Rather, a principal avenue of traffic and distribution of erotica is the social network of age-peers (Berger, et al., 1970a, 1970b; Elias, 1970; Haines, 1955; Propper, 1970; Davis and Braucht, 1970b).

These findings suggest that exposure to erotica is part of the more general exchange of sex information that ordinarily occurs among adolescent peers, and is related to other social and sexual experiences. Davis and Braucht (1970b) found moderate correlations among the three variables; exposure to pornography, peer group pressures for sex, and sexual deviance. The interpretation of these correlations is very difficult. One of the problems is that the sexual deviance scale has very low internal consistency and the incidence of sexual deviancy in the sample is very low. Among the three correlations, those between peer group pressures for sex and, first, exposure to pornography (r = .43), and, second, sexual deviance (r = .40) are larger than the correlation between exposure to pornography and sexual deviance (r = .33). These data would be consistent with the hypothesis that peer group pressures produce both exposure to pornography and sexual deviancy. Unfortunately, the age at which peer group pressures and sexual deviancy occurred was not obtained. The authors correctly note that these data are not sufficient to rule out the hypothesis that early exposure to pornography may play some role in the development of sexually deviant life styles. Berger and his colleagues (1970a), for example, found that socially isolated youth are less likely than the socially active to have had experience with erotic material, and that general participation in high school social activities is associated with exposure to erotica.

PSYCHOSEXUAL STIMULATION

It was reported earlier that substantial proportions of adults report sexual arousal as a response to erotic material, and that arousal tends to vary with sexual theme and medium of presentation.[80] Visual depictions of nudity, heterosexual intercourse and oral sexuality are generally regarded as more arousing than portrayals of homosexual or sadomasochistic activities (Byrne and Lamberth, 1970; Levitt and Hinesley, 1967; Wallace, et al. 1970). An early study (Ramsey, 1943) of 280 male youth found that "sex conversation," "female nudity," and "obscene pictures" were rated as most arousing by boys 11 to 14. For older boys (15–18), "female nudity," "daydreaming" and "obscene pictures" were judged as most arousing.

A comparison of unwed pregnant high school girls with junior college girls (Schiller, 1970) found that romantic themes in television, books, romance magazines, motion pictures and musical recordings were generally considered more arousing than "pornographic" materials among both groups. The two groups of girls differed, however, in that the pregnant girls considered television to be most sexually provocative, while college girls reported that movies were most stimulating.[81]

An early study of 100 incarcerated delinquents 16 to 21 (Haines, 1955) found that 14% of those who had experience with "eight" or "sixteen-pagers" depicting sexual acts reported being sexually aroused by them.[82]

Comparison of 476 incarcerated delinquents, median age 19 years, (Propper, 1970) with a representative sample of 18 to 20 year-old nondelinquent males (Abelson, et al., 1970) suggests that the delinquents were approximately three times as likely to report arousal from visual erotica. When the same delinquents are compared with a sample of 473 working-class adolescents 13 to 18 years of age (Berger, et al., 1970b), however, the differences in reported arousal diminish markedly. Forty-four percent of the delinquents, compared with 36% of the working-class boys, reported arousal from visual depictions of heterosexual intercourse, and 38% of the delinquents, as compared to 31% of the working-class youth, reported arousal from visual depictions of genitalia (Propper, 1970; Berger, et al., 1970b). Part of the residual difference is probably a function of age.

SUMMARY: EROTICA AND DELINQUENCY

Two important findings emerge from the studies reviewed: (a) experience with erotic materials is widespread among American youth; and (b) the experiences of delinquent and nondelinquent youth, though not identical, are generally similar. The small differences which appear to be in the amount of exposure and the reactions to it, seem to be attributable to age and subcultural variables. Taken together, these data provide no particular support for the thesis that experience with sexual materials is a significant factor in the causation of juvenile delinquency.

267

There is some evidence that both juvenile misbehavior and certain dimensions of experience with erotic materials may be explained by the subcultural and social processes operative in the home, neighborhood, and school peer groups. One study, in particular, addressed these relationships. Davis and Braucht (1970b) examined the relationships between moral character and experience with erotic materials among young males. Results indicated that the statistical relationship between moral character and amount of experience with sexual materials ($r = -.142$) was a function of the relationship of each of these variables to the influence of deviant peers. There were strong relationships between associating with deviant peers and moral character ($r = -.453$) and deviant peers and amount of exposure to erotica ($r = -.430$). This study also found that an early age of first exposure to sexual materials was more strongly related to deviance in the home ($r = .302$) and the influence of deviant peers ($r = .423$) than to moral character ($r = .280$). These results were interpreted by the authors to indicate that "it may well be that an early age of exposure has no impact on character over and beyond that of a generally deviant background" (Davis and Braucht, 1970b). Among persons whose first experience with sexual materials occurred in late adolescence, those with low character scores more often pursued such experience, and this pattern was strongly associated ($r = .585$) with having deviant friends and neighbors. This analysis concluded that "at the very least, this argues for a pattern in which exposure to pornography is part of a strongly deviant life style" (Davis and Braucht, 1970b).

Needed Additional Research. Available research concerning the effects of erotic material upon juveniles has not included experimental studies in which the direction of relationships is more systematically assessed. Continuing fears about the consequences of controlled exposure studies have precluded the accumulation of strong evidence. The generally wide experience of adolescents with sexual materials, however, suggests that concerns about detrimental effects of experimentation may well be unwarranted. Additional research is needed and existing studies with slightly older populations suggest its feasibility. Future research might include: (a) retrospective and comparative studies of youth with histories of those antisocial behaviors deemed to be consequences of exposure to sexual materials; (b) longitudinal studies of the consequences of exposure to erotica among youths with similar social and demographic characteristics; (c) experimental studies of the consequences of controlled exposure to erotic materials with a wide range of youth.

Gaps in available knowledge suggest that such studies should expand the experimental circumstances of exposure, the types of consequent variables observed, and the length of observation periods. The observed relationships between exposure and certain sexual behaviors suggest that particular attention be devoted to the social and psychological processes which mediate these relationships.

EROTICA AND SEXUAL DEVIANCE

The belief that reading or viewing explicit sexual materials causes sex crimes is widespread among the American public. A recent survey of a representative sample of adults in the United States (Abelson, et al., 1970) showed that 47% of the men and 51% of the women believed "sexual materials lead people to commit rape." Law enforcement officials, students of criminal behavior and other professionals working with criminals are also divided in their opinions about this relationship. Although some law enforcement officials attest to a causal relationship between exposure to pornography and the commission of sex offenses (Hoover, 1965), few psychiatrists and psychologists report having encountered such cases in their professional experience (Lipkin and Carns, 1970).

AVAILABILITY OF EROTICA AND SEX OFFENSES

Reports of increased availability of erotic materials coupled with reported statistical increases in sex crimes over the past decade may, in part, account for the public's apprehensions in this area. The Commission variously sponsored and performed several studies of the relationship between availability of erotic materials and the incidence of sex offenses in both the United States and Denmark.

The United States: 1960-1969. A recent analysis of national police statistics in the Uniform Crime Reports for the period 1960 to 1969 (Kupperstein and Wilson, 1970) showed that both the availability of erotic materials and the incidence of sex offenses increased over the past decade. Increases in the availability of erotica,[83] however, generally outweighed the overall increase in adult arrests for sex offenses. With respect to sex offenses, there was an absolute increase of 50% in adult arrests for forcible rape and a 60% increase in adult arrests for prostitution and commercialized vice. At the same time, however, there was a decrease in arrests for all other sex offenses which may, at least in part, be attributable to a reduction in arrests of homosexuals (See Table 30).

TABLE 30

Number and Percent Change in Adult[1]
Arrests for Sex Crimes: 1960 to 1969

Offense Category	1960	1969	Percent Change
All offenses, sexual and nonsexual	2,846,479	3,145,763	+10.5
All sex offenses	66,860	79,069	+18.3
Forcible rape	5,671	8,533	+50.5
Prostitution and commercialized vice	25,240	40,405	+60.1
Other sex offenses	35,949	30,131	-16.2
All nonsex offenses	2,779,619	3,066,694	+10.3

[1] 18 years of age and over

Note — Compiled from Federal Bureau of Investigation, United States Department of Justice, *Uniform crime reports - 1969*, Washingtion D. C.: U. S. Government Printing Office, 1970, 110.

Two other points regarding the offenses of forcible rape, prostitution and commercialized vice deserve mention here. First, these offenses, combined, accounted for only 1.1% of all adult arrests in 1960 and 1.6% in 1969. Further, the number of known cases of and arrests for forcible rape increased less than did four out of the other six serious crimes which comprise the F.B.I. Crime Index[84] (See Figure 9) and less than such other serious offenses as narcotic drug law violations (adult arrests up 380.4% from 1960 to 1969) and weapons law violations (adult arrests up 129%). Once again, however, the relatively crude comparisons of the absolute number of arrests or offenses over time may be misleading. The figures in Table 31 show that the differences in known cases and arrests for forcible rape between 1960 and 1969 become smaller as the index is refined. This would, of course, also be true for other crimes.

In sum, available evidence shows that although adult arrests for sex offenses have increased on the whole, the increase has not been as great for these offenses as for such other serious offenses as robbery and narcotic law violations.

FIGURE 9

Percentage Change in Number of Adult Arrests for, and Known Cases of
Index Offenses, 1960-1969

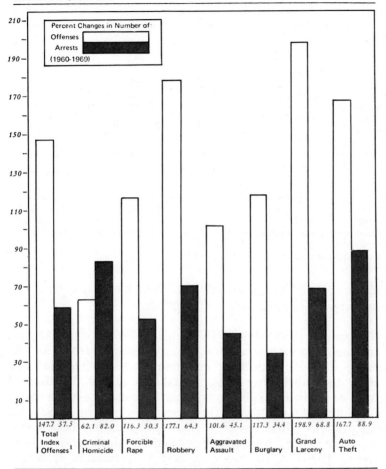

Note — Adapted from Federal Bureau of Investigation, United States Department of Justice. *Uniform crime reports* — 1969. *Washington, D. C.: U. S. Government Printing Office, 1970, pp. 57, 110.*

1. The seven offenses included in the FBI's crime index are: criminal homicide, forcible rape, aggravated assault, robbery, burglary, grand larceny, and auto theft.

Further, arrests for sex offenses constituted no more than 2% of all adult arrests during the period studied. If the heightened availability of erotica were directly related to the incidence of sex offenses, one would have expected an increase of much greater magnitude than the available figures indicate. Thus, the data do not appear to support the thesis of a causal connection between increased availability of erotica

271

TABLE 31

Percentage Change in Known Cases of and
Arrests for Forcible Rape 1960-1969

Unit of Count	1960	1969	Percent change
Number of forcible rapes known to police[1]	16,860	36,470	+116.3
Number per 100,000 inhabitants[1]	9.4	18.1	+92.6
Number per 100,000 male 10-49 years[2]	34.5	64.2	+86.1
Number of arrests for forcible rape[1]	6,862	10,747	+56.6
Number per 100,000 inhabitants[3]	3.8	5.3	+39.5
Number per 100,000 males 10-49 years[2]	14.5	19.0	+31.0

[1] Federal Bureau of Investigation, United States Department of Justice. *Uniform crime reports -1969*. Washington, D. C.: U. S. Government Printing Office, 1970, 57, 110.
[2] Based on figures supplied by the United States Department of Commerce, Bureau of the Census.
[3] Adapted from *Uniform crime reports - 1969*.

and the commission of sex offenses; the data do not, however, conclusively disprove such a connection.

Denmark: 1958-1969 In June, 1967, the Danish Parliament voted to remove erotic literature from its obscenity statute[85] and then, on June 1, 1969, repealed the statute, thus abolishing legal prohibitions against the dissemination of sexually explicit materials to persons sixteen years of age and older. Despite the general prohibition which existed prior to 1967, however, literary erotica has been available since 1965, and graphic material since 1967 (Ben-Veniste, 1970). Estimates furnished by producers of sexual materials indicated that dissemination of erotic literature, particularly paperback novels, began to increase during 1960, and reached a peak around 1967. By that time, an increase in production of explicit graphic materials apparently reduced consumer demand for literary erotica and the market for explicit graphic materials increased.[86]

Ben-Veniste (1970) compiled statistics on sex offenses reported to the police in Copenhagen, Denmark, over a twelve year period, 1958 to 1969. These figures show that the number of reported sex crimes declined during the period, even though pornography became increasingly available to the general public. As shown in Table 32, the sharpest con-

272

tinuous reduction in sex offenses began in 1967, and has continued through 1969. The onset of this decline occurred when prohibitions regarding dissemination of literary sexual materials were relaxed.

TABLE 32

Total Sex Crimes Reported to the Police
in Copenhagen, Denmark: 1958-1969

Year	Total Crimes[1]	Percent increase or decrease over previous year
1958	982	-0-
1959	1,018	+3.66
1960	899	-11.69
1961	1,000	+11.23
1962	749	-25.10
1963	895	-19.49
1964	732	-18.21
1965	762	-4.10
1966	783	-2.75
1967	591	-24.52
1968	515	-12.86
1969	358	-30.48

[1]Total reported sex crimes, 1958-1969 = 9284. These include: rape and attempted rape, coitus with minors, "indecent interference short of rape" with both minor girls and adult women, exhibitionism, peeping (voyeurism), homosexual offenses and verbal indecency. The original investigator omitted from his analysis, and without explanation, the "quasi-sex offenses" of bigamy, incest, livings off the earnings of a prostitute, inducing to prostitiution, propositioning, and obscenity offenses (the latter eliminated by repeal of prohibitions against the dissemination of sexual materials).

Note — Adapted from Ben—Veniste, R. Pornography and sex crime — the Danish experience. *Technical reports of the Commission on Obscenity and Pornography.* Vol. 7.

Further analysis found that all classes of sex crimes decreased, but that some decreased more than others. Rape and attempted rape decreased less than did exhibitionism or "unlawful interference short of rape" with children, and these latter offenses decreased less than voyeurism and homosexual offenses which showed the most dramatic decreases (see Table 33).

Additional studies (Ben-Veniste, 1970; Kutschinsky, 1970c) attempted to determine whether the reported decrease in sex offenses was attributable to changes in legislation, law enforcement procedures or practices, police reporting and data collection procedures or people's definition of sex crimes, their readiness to report offenses to the police, and their ex-

TABLE 33

Number and Percent Change in Sex Crimes Reported
to Copenhagen Police, by Offense Category, 1958-1969

Offense Category	1958	1969	Percent Change
Heterosexual offenses	846	330	-61.0
Rape (including attempts)	52	27	-48.1
Intercourse on threat of violence or by fraud, etc.	11	8	-37.5
Unlawful interference short of rape with adult women	100	52	-48.0
Unlawful interference short of rape with minor girls	249	87	-65.1
Coitus with minors	30	19	-57.9
Exhibitionism	264	104	-60.6
Peeping	87	20	-77.0
Verbal indecency	53	13	-32.5
Homosexual offenses	128	28	-78.1

Note - Adapted from Ben-Veniste, R. Pornography and sex crime - the Danish experience. *Technical reports of the Commission on Obscenity and Pornography*. Vol. 7.

perience with such offenses. It was found that changes in the incidence of sex offenses could not be attributed to legislative change, alteration of law enforcement practices or modified police reporting and data collection procedures[87] (Ben-Veniste, 1970). A survey (Kutschinsky, 1970c) of Copenhagen residents found that neither public attitudes about sex crimes nor willingness to report such crimes had changed sufficiently to account for the substantial decrease in sex offenses between 1959 and 1969.

SEX OFFENDERS' EXPERIENCE WITH EROTIC MATERIAL

Prior to 1960, there were few empirical studies of the relationship between exposure to erotic materials and the commission of sex offenses. They provided, however, a baseline and point of departure for the Commission's studies.

Two early studies investigated the relationship between choice of reading matter and the nature of offenses committed by male prisoners. Von Bracken and Schafers (1935) found that murderers reported preferences for "high-grade information" books and adventure stories, swindlers preferred light novels, thieves chose books on "practical culture," and sex offenders preferred "sex books." A study of more than

3,000 sex offenders (Le Maire, 1946) concluded that literature was not generally a factor in the commission of these offenses.

Between 1961 and 1968, several studies probed beyond overt deviant behavior and found that responses to sexual stimuli were also associated with sexual guilt, conflict, and psychosexual development (Galbraith and Mosher, 1968; Leiman and Epstein, 1961; Thorne and Haupt, 1966).

The most extensive study during this period (Gebhard, et al., 1965) analyzed the sexual histories of 1,356 white male sex offenders, 888 male nonsex offenders and a control group of 477 males (volunteers) from the general population. The study found that: (a) exposure to sexual materials was almost universal among all three groups, and (b) there were no significant differences in exposure between the two groups of offenders and the nonoffender control group. Respondents were asked: "Does it arouse you sexually to see photographs or drawings of people engaged in sexual activity?" Findings revealed no substantial differences in reported arousal between these groups. Table 34 shows that 33% of the control group reported little or no arousal, and 31% reported strong arousal. The corresponding percentages for the imprisoned

TABLE 34

Percentages Reporting Arousal from
Visual Depictions of Sexual Activity

Groups	Degree of Sexual Arousal				Cases		Proportion of total N unknown %
	Little or none %	Moderate %	Strong %	Formerly, none currently %	Known N	Total N	
Control	32.8	24.2	30.7	12.2	475	477	0.4
Prison	37.7	22.0	36.3	4.0	885	888	0.3
Heterosexual offenders vs.							
Children	39.4	19.7	28.3	12.6	198	199	0.5
Minors	53.2	12.7	26.6	7.5	173	174	0.6
Adults	60.8	17.0	18.0	4.1	217	217	0.0
Heterosexual aggressors vs.							
Children	50.0	16.7	25.0	8.3	24	25	4.0
Minors	25.9	22.2	44.4	7.4	27	27	0.0
Adults	41.4	25.7	26.4	6.4	140	140	0.0
Incest offenders vs.							
Children	34.5	23.6	25.4	16.4	55	56	1.8
Minors	53.0	21.2	13.6	12.1	66	66	0.0
Adults	62.5	12.5	16.7	8.3	24	25	4.0
Homosexual offenders vs.							
Children	43.2	21.0	25.3	10.5	95	96	1.0
Minors	37.0	21.5	33.3	8.1	135	136	0.7
Adults	25.5	26.5	42.8	5.1	196	199	1.5
Peepers	37.5	21.4	28.6	12.5	56	56	0.0
Exhibitionists	35.8	21.6	32.8	9.7	134	135	0.7

Source: Gebhard, P. H., Gagnon, J. H., Pomeroy, W. B., & Christenson, C. V. *Sex offenders*: An analysis of types. New York: Harper and Row, 1965.

275

nonsex offenders were 38% and 36% respectively. On the whole, sex offender groups reported least arousal from pornography, with the exceptions of heterosexual aggressors against minors and homosexual offenders against adults, whose rates of reported "strong arousal" are higher but not statistically significantly so. Exhibitionists reported more arousal than nonsex offenders but less than controls.

The study also found that about one-third of the control group and one-half of the prison group reported having owned pornographic materials. Sex offenders fell between these two groups. The researchers concluded that:

> About all that can be said is that strong response to pornography is associated with imaginativeness, ability to project, and sensitivity, all of which generally increase as education increases, and with youthfulness, and that these qualities account for the differences we have found between sex offenders, in general, and nonsex offenders. Since the majority of sex offenders are not well educated nor particularly youthful, their responsiveness to pornography is correspondingly less and cannot be a consequential factor in their sex offenses unless one is prepared to argue that the inability to respond to erotica in general precludes gaining some vicarious stimulation and satisfaction and thereby causes the individual to behave overtly which, in turn, renders him more liable to arrest and conviction.

The results of these studies indicate that sex offenders are somewhat less responsive than other adults to erotic stimuli.

Several recent studies of sex offenders generally support and extend knowledge about the relationship between exposure to erotic material and sexual deviance, and indicate more specifically how sex offenders' experience with erotica is different from that of other adults.

Early Experience with Erotica. Available research indicates that both the extent and frequency of sex offenders' experience with erotic material is substantially less than that of non-sex offenders and nonoffender adults during preadolescence (Cook and Fosen, 1970; Johnson, et al., 1970) and during adolescence[88] (Cook and Fosen, 1970; Goldstein, et al., 1970; Johnson, et al., 1970). One indicator of the extent of adolescent exposure to erotica is the proportion of persons who report ever and never having encountered specified materials during this period.

When sex offenders and sex deviants were compared with

nonoffender adults, Goldstein and his colleagues (1970) found that several specific offender and deviant groups, e.g., male object pedophiles, had significantly less adolescent experience with several specific depictions (e.g., photos of partially and fully nude women, heterosexual intercourse and sadomasochistic activity as well as books describing intercourse and mouth-genital relations). No significant differences in the other direction were observed. The data in Figure 10 show the proportion of sex offenders, sex deviants and nonoffender adults who ever encountered photographs of human coitus during adolescence (Goldstein, et al., 1970).

FIGURE 10

Percent Reporting Adolescent Exposure to Photographic Depictions of Coitus

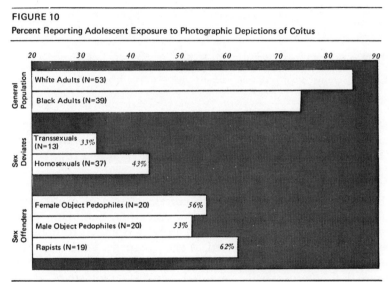

Note — Adapted from Goldstein, M. J., Kant, H. S., Judd, L. L., Rice, C. J., & Green, R. Exposure to pornography and sexual behavior in deviant and normal groups. *Technical reports of the Commission on Obscenity and Pornography.* Vol. 7.

Although the number of subjects in the various categories is small, sharp and statistically significant differences are nonetheless evident. Table 35 shows that substantial proportions of the offender and deviant groups reported no experience with photographic depictions of human coitus during adolescence, and that the percentage for each of the groups was greater than that for nonsex offenders.

These data show that as compared with nonsex offenders, sex offenders and sexual deviants have comparatively little experience with erotica during their adolescence, and also suggest that sex offenders differ from other adults in the kinds

TABLE 35

Frequencies of Exposure Among Sex Offenders, Sexual Deviants and Non-Offender Adults Reporting Adolescent Exposure to Photographic Depictions of Coitus

(Figures in Percentages)

| Population | None | Number of Photographs Seen | |
		1 to 10	11 or more
White non-offenders (N=53)	15%	28%	57%
Black non-offenders (N=39)	26	23	51
Rapists (N=19)	38	38	24
Male object pedophiles (N=20)	47	24	29
Female object pedophiles (N=20)	44	17	39
Homosexuals (N=37)	57	14	29
Transsexuals (N=13)	67	8	25

Note — Adapted from Goldstein, M. J., Kant, H. S., Judd, L. L., Rice, C. J. & Green, R. Exposure to pornography and sexual behavior in deviant and normal groups. *Technical reports of the Commission on Obscenity and Pornography*. Vol. 7.

of material seen or read during adolescence. Sex offenders' experience appears to be limited to less explicit sexual material (Cook and Fosen, 1970; Goldstein, et al., 1970; Walker, 1970).

Among both sex offenders and sexual deviants, it appears that adolescent experience with certain classes of erotic stimuli tend to reflect an established, or emerging, dominant sexual orientation. Homosexuals and pedophiles oriented to male objects, for example, reported more frequent adolescent experience with depictions of male nudity and homosexuality than did heterosexually oriented persons (Goldstein, et al., 1970). Of all the sexual offender and deviant groups studied, the early experience with erotica of transsexuals is most different from that of adults in the general population. The apparent psychosexual maladjustment of transsexuals is reflected in their inexperience with erotic materials, particularly their comparatively infrequent exposure to depictions of female nudity, oral sexuality, and heterosexual intercourse. Transsexuals reported that they found objects associated with the opposite sex, particularly clothing, to be considerably more stimulating during adolescence than commercially produced sexual stimuli (Goldstein, et al., 1970).

The limited extent and amount of sex offenders' adolescent experience with erotica suggests that there may be differences between sex offenders, nonsex offenders and nonoffender

278

adults in the age of first exposures, to these materials. Two studies bear directly on this issue.[89]

A study of 63 incarcerated sex offenders and a matched group of 66 incarcerated nonsex offenders (Cook and Fosen, 1970) found a significant difference in that 50% of the nonsex offenders, as compared with 28% of the sex offenders, reported experience with erotica between six and ten years of age (all subjects reported experience at a later age.)

Another study (Walker, 1970) compared 60 incarcerated rapists[90] with a matched group of 60 nonsex offenders. All subjects were asked at what age they first saw each of fifteen erotic depictions, and mean ages of first exposure were computed for each of the two groups and each of the types of erotica. The data in Table 36 shows that the mean age of first exposure of the rapists was one-half a year or more later than that of the matched nonsex offenders in reference to eight of the fifteen items and one-half a year or more earlier in reference to two. The biggest difference between the groups occurred in relation to depictions of heterosexual intercourse, for which nonsex offenders had a mean age of first exposure of 14.95, and rapists a mean age of first exposure of 18.19. Rapists were also found to have a generally later mean age of first exposure to erotica than a nonmatched sample of college students and a lower age than a nonmatched sample of members of men's clubs.

TABLE 36

Mean Ages at Which Various Categories of Pornography Were First Seen

		Experimentals (N=60)	Controls (N=60)	College (N=60)	Men's Club (N=30)
1.	"... [materials with] 4-letter words"	13.19	13.11	11.88	13.50
2.	"... nude females with breasts exposed"	14.83	15.09	13.51	13.90
3.	"... nude females showing sex organs or hair between leg . . . legs"	17.76	15.87	16.00	16.64
4.	"... nude males [with] sex organs"	16.15	16.25	15.74	16.67
5.	"... nude or partially nude couple kissing" kissing"	17.50	16.12	15.11	16.67
6.	"... male and female having intercourse"	18.19	14.95	16.45	16.78
7.	"... homosexual activities"	17.70	17.85	16.91	20.28
8.	"... humans and animals having sex relations"	16.94	17.50	15.89	19.09
9.	"... sexual activity with whips, belts or ropes"	20.05	18.13	17.67	20.91
10.	"... mouth-sex organ contact"	17.46	17.57	17.54	19.17
11.	"... a sex activity involving a group of people"	19.96	18.09	18.02	21.00
12.	"... a male or female masturbating "	18.67	17.73	16.21	19.50
13.	"... advertisements [of various sexual material] sent [in] the mail"	18.64	20.00	16.18	23.77
14.	"... live burlesque strip-tease, etc."	20.46	18.73	18.51	21.48
15.	"... live show [with] a sex act"	18.00	19.18	19.36	24.33

Source: Walker, C. E. Erotic stimuli and the aggressive sexual offender. *Technical reports of the Commission on Obscenity and Pornography.* Vol. 7.

In summary, recent studies of sex offenders' early experience with erotic materials indicate that these offenders have somewhat later and relatively less experience during adolescence. These findings cast considerable doubt on the theory that sexual deviance can be attributed to early experience with erotica.

Recent Experience with Erotica. Although sex offenders reported relatively less adolescent experience with erotica than nonoffender adults, the amount and frequency of their recent adult experience[91] is not significantly different from that of other adults in the general population, although there is a slight tendency for sex offenders to report somewhat less experience (Cook and Fosen, 1970; Goldstein, et al., 1970; Johnson, et al., 1970; Walker, 1970).

On certain specified depictions, however, substantial differences do remain (see Figure 11).

FIGURE 11

Percent Reporting Recent Exposure to Photographic Depictions of Coitus

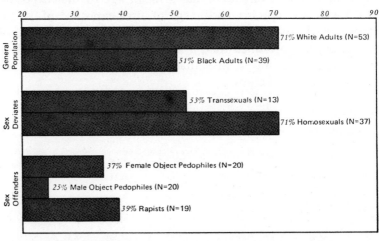

Note — Adapted from Goldstein, M. J., Kant, H. S., Judd, L. L., Rice, C. J., & Green, R. Exposure to pornography and sexual behavior in deviant and normal groups. *Technical reports of the Commission on Obscenity and Pornography.* Vol. 7.

When sex offenders and sex deviants were compared with nonoffender adults, for example, Goldstein and his colleagues (1970) found that in several instances specific offender groups, e.g., female object pedophiles, had significantly less experience with several specific depictions (e.g., photos of partially nude females, fully nude females and partially nude males, and

280

movies involving nude females, nude males and heterosexual intercourse). No significant differences in the other direction were observed.

Walker (1970) asked matched groups of incarcerated sex and nonsex offenders and unmatched samples of college students and men's club volunteers how often, if ever, they had seen any of fifteen erotic depictions. The mean frequencies of exposure on the basis of six depictions[92] (nude females with sex organs showing, nude males with sex organs showing, mouth-genital contact, heterosexual intercourse, homosexuality, and sadomasochistic activities) revealed no significant differences between the sex offenders and either the nonsex offenders, the college students or the men's club members. Such tendency as exists is in the direction of greater experience among the controls and higher status groups. Walker similarly found no significant differences between these groups in relation to the proportions who knew a store or bookshop in their community where erotic materials could be purchased or in the proportions who reported that they had ever collected pornography.[93]

These data raise the question about what factors account for differentials in experience. Research would be required to sort out the constellation of subcultural variables, both social and psychosexual, which determine (a) the availability of sexual material, and (b) other sources of sexual knowledge.

In brief, these studies underline the similarity of sex offenders and other population subgroups[94] in reference to recent exposure to erotic materials and present no basis for the assumption that recent experience with erotica leads to the commission of sex crimes.

Responses to Erotic Material. Research shows that sex offenders and other adults in the general population generally do not differ in their reported immediate responses to reading or viewing erotic materials—substantial proportions of both groups report psychosexual stimulation. As in the case of recent exposure, however, such tendency as does exist is in the direction of less reported arousal on the part of sex offenders (Cook and Fosen, 1970; Gebhard, et al., 1965; Goldstein, et al., 1970; Johnson, et al., 1970; Walker, 1970). For example, in one experimental study (Cook and Fosen, 1970) 63 incarcerated sex offenders and a matched group of 66 incarcerated nonsex offenders were asked to rate their level of arousal to each of 26 erotic slides. Ratings of the two groups did not differ significantly. Upon leaving the experimental situation, only 6% of the sex offenders and 11% of the nonsex offenders reported being "very highly" or "extremely excited." About one-third of the offenders in each group reported "stimulation, enjoyment and arousal" as their primary reasons for reading or viewing erotic materials prior to the experiment.

Another study (Walker, 1970) which involved nonoffender adults as well as sex offenders and nonsex offenders found no significant differences between the two offender groups in the proportions who reported arousal from sex stimuli either during adolescence or adulthood. In reference to the comparison between sex offenders and nonoffender groups, the sex offenders reported significantly less arousal than the college students with respect to two out of fifteen erotic depictions, and significantly more than men's club volunteers with respect to one of the fifteen.

Johnson and his colleagues (1970) compared the responses of 47 probationary male sex offenders with those of 652 adult males in the same age range in the general population (survey by Abelson, et al., 1970). The study found that seven percent of the sex offenders and six percent of the nonoffender adults reported sexual arousal to erotic visual materials. The sex offenders were significantly more likely than the comparison group, however, to report arousal from textual depictions.

Retrospective reports of the sexual behavior of sex offenders and various adult comparison groups indicate that these groups do not differ substantially in the proportions reporting sexual behavior following exposure to erotic stimuli although there appear to be differences in the kinds of sexual behavior reportedly activated by exposure (masturbation vs. coitus). Walker (1970), for example, asked matched groups of sex and nonsex offenders and unmatched groups of college students and men's club members whether they did anything sexually while using "pornography." There were no significant differences between the sex offenders and any of the other groups except in one instance in which college students responded more affirmatively than did the sex offenders. In the same study the investigator asked, "Do you think that your experience with erotic materials has increased or changed your sexual behavior in any way?" Although the majority of both the sex offenders (63%) and the nonsex offenders (83%) said no, more than twice as many sex offenders (37%) as nonsex offenders (17%) responded affirmatively. However, there were no significant differences between the sex offenders and either the college students or the men's club volunteers.

Two studies found differences in the kinds of sexual behavior reportedly activated by exposure to erotic materials prior to incarceration. Sex offenders significantly more often reported increased frequencies of masturbation (Cook and Fosen, 1970; Goldstein, et al., 1970). Nonsex offenders more often reported increased heterosexual intercourse (Cook and Fosen, 1970). Goldstein and his colleagues (1970), however, found no significant differences between sex offenders and nonoffender adults in the proportions reporting that erotic materials "excited them to sexual relations."

A retrospective survey (Goldstein, et al., 1970) involving sex offenders, sexual deviants and nonoffender adults inquired into the degree to which they wished to imitate and the degree to which they did imitate highly salient erotic depictions during adolescence and adulthood. The data in Table 37 show that all groups reported greater interest as teenagers than as adults in imitating the act depicted, and all except homo-

TABLE 37

Reactions to Most Salient Experience with Erotica
(Figures in Percentages)

	Wished to try act seen		Did try shortly after exposure		Wished to try other sex after exposure		Did try other sex shortly after exposure	
	Teen	Adult	Teen	Adult	Teen	Adult	Teen	Adult
Rapists (N=19)	80	35	30	15	75	40	25	20
Male object pedophiles (N=20)	65	35	25	15	70	60	40	40
Female object pedophiles (N=20)	40	25	20	25	55	45	25	15
Homosexuals (N=37)	39	33	14	6	51	61	28	36
Transsexuals (N=13)	29	14	14	7	50	28	21	0
White non-offenders adults (N=53)	48	30	28	13	63	65	22	35

Note — Adapted from Goldstein, M. J., Kant, H. S., Judd, L. L., Rice, C. J. & Green, R. Exposure to pornography and sexual behavior in deviant and normal groups. *Technical reports of the Commission on Obscenity and Pornography.* Vol. 7.

sexuals reported greater interest as teenagers than adults in wishing "to try other sex shortly after exposure." On the critical question of whether they reported imitating the act depicted shortly after exposure, sex deviants replied affirmatively less often than nonoffender adults in reference to both adolescence and adulthood, and the reports of sex offenders did not differ significantly from the reports of the nonoffender controls.[95] With respect to trying sex other than that depicted shortly after exposure, the only conspicuous difference observed was the total absence of such activity on the part of transsexuals during adulthood. In this regard, male object pedophiles were consistently, but not significantly, higher than all other groups in both adolescence and adulthood.

While considerable ingenuity was required to gain these data, this study necessarily involved small numbers of participants and thus the findings, while suggestive, require further test and confirmation to substantiate the pattern of results.

Walker's (1970) retrospecive survey found no significant differences between sex offenders, nonsex offenders, and men's club volunteers in the proportions reporting what kinds of sexual activity they felt like performing during or after exposure to fifteen erotic depictions. For two out of the fifteen erotic depictions, college students were more likely than sex offenders to report a desire to engage in certain types of sex activity.

In summary, the available research indicates that sex offenders do not differ significantly from other adults in their reported arousal or reported likelihood of engaging in sexual behavior during or following exposure to erotica. There is some indication that sex offenders are more likely to respond to stimulation by masturbation as compared with nonsex offenders or nonoffender adults who are more likely to engage in coitus.

In three studies, sex offenders were given the opportunity to say that erotica (or "pornography") has played a part in their criminal behavior. Such a "scapegoat" question is rarely used because it provides persons with an opportunity to blame their difficulties on something outside themselves, and may therefore invite wide, but not necessarily valid, affirmative replies.

The three studies came to different findings, as indicated below, but taken together found that about 10% of sex offenders said that there was some kind of relationship in their own cases.

One study (Johnson, et al., 1970) found that among 47 probationary sex offenders, none of the rapists, and only one other offender, a pedophile, claimed that erotic material had led them to commit rape. A second study (Cook and Fosen, 1970), found no significant differences in the proportion of sex offenders and nonsex offenders who were exposed to pornography within 24 hours prior to their offense or who claimed that pornography "encouraged them to commit their offense."[96] A third study (Walker, 1970) found no significant differences between incarcerated sex offenders, nonsex offenders, and nonoffenders in the proportions reporting preoccupation with erotic books and pictures, or "moral break-down," but found sex offenders significantly more likely than others to say that erotica had led them to commit sex crimes; he reports that "a small but significant minority" of sex offenders said pornography "was partially responsible for their offense." Thus, in relation to the "scapegoat" question, two studies found no statistically significant differences between sex offenders and comparison groups and one did find such a difference.

These data are difficult to interpret, not only because of the scapegoat nature of the question, but also because the question used in all group comparisons referred either to rape or to sex crimes, and does not seem equally applicable to all persons convicted of sex crimes or to persons convicted of nonsex crimes of nonoffenders. In view of the nature of the question, the ambiguity of the findings, and the weight of other available research comparing sex offenders and other persons, these particular data do not seem to constitute significant evidence of erotica leading to sex crime. Further research would be desirable, however, to determine precisely what is meant by the responses of those sex offenders who replied affirmatively.

A growing body of research literature on the etiology of sexual offenses emphasizes the difference between sex offenders and other adults in psychosexual development. Research shows that the early social environments of sex offenders may be characterized as sexually repressive and deprived. Sex offenders frequently report family circumstances in which, for example, there is a low tolerance for nudity, an absence of sexual conversation, and punitive or indifferent parental responses to children's sexual curiosity and interest. Sex offenders' histories reveal a succession of immature and impersonal sociosexual relationships, rigid sexual attitudes, and sexually conservative behavior (Amir, 1965; DeRiver, 1956; Gagnon and Simon, 1967b; Galbraith and Mosher, 1968; Gebhard, et al., 1965; Karpman, 1954; Leiman and Epstein, 1961; Reinhardt, 1957; Thorne and Haupt, 1966).

Such literature, coupled with the studies reported in this chapter, suggest that sex offenders' inexperience with erotic material is a reflection of their more generally deprived sexual environment. The relative absence of such experience probably constitutes another indicator of atypical and inadequate sexual socialization.

Analyses of the United States crime rates do not support the thesis of a causal connection between the availability of erotica and sex crimes among either juveniles or adults. Because of limitations in both the data and inferences which can validly be drawn from them, the data cannot, however, be said absolutely to disprove such a connection. Similar analyses for Denmark show that in that country the increased availability of erotica has been accompanied by a decrease in sex crimes.

Studies of juvenile delinquents indicate that their experience with erotica is generally similar to that of nondelinquents in reference to extent and amount of experience, age of first exposure, and arousal. Such small differences as exist appear to be products of age and subculture variables. Research does suggest that exposure to erotic materials may sometimes be part of a deviant life style and may reflect, rather than affect, the character, attitudes, and conduct of delinquent youth. There is no basis in the available data, however, for supposing that there is any independent relationship between exposure to erotica and delinquency.

Studies show that in comparison with other adults, sex offenders and sexual deviants are significantly less experienced with erotica during adolescence. As adults, sex offenders are not significantly different from other adults in exposure or in reported arousal or reported likelihood of engaging in socio-sexual behavior following exposure to erotica.

Various studies revealed no significant differences between sex offenders and other groups in reference to whether erotica had affected their morals or produced preoccupation with sexual materials. When explicitly given the opportunity to do so, a small minority of sex offenders say that erotica or pornography had some relationship to their committing sex crimes, but for reasons detailed above, these data cannot be regarded as reliable evidence of such a relationship.

Sex offenders generally report sexually repressive family backgrounds, immature and inadequate sexual histories and rigid and conservative attitudes concerning sexuality. Research suggests that childhood experiences which encourage sexual repression and inhibition of sexual curiosity are associated with psychosexual maladjustment and antisocial sexual behavior.

Research to date thus provides no substantial basis for the belief that erotic materials constitute a primary or significant

286

cause of the development of character deficits or that they operate as a significant determinative factor in causing crime and delinquency.

This conclusion is stated with due and perhaps excessive caution, since it is obviously not possible, and never would be possible, to state that never on any occasion, under any conditions, did any erotic material ever contribute in any way to the likelihood of any individual committing a sex crime. Indeed, no such statement could be made about any kind of nonerotic material. On the basis of the available data, however, it is not possible to conclude that erotic material is a significant cause of sex crime.

NOTES

1. The adequacy of legal definitions of "obscenity" is discussed elsewhere (Bender, 1970) and for the purposes here only one observation is necessary: the legal definition, or test, of obscenity is made identical with the assumed effect. The effects in question, *i.e.*, prurient appeal and the violation of "community standards" can be assessed empirically, providing, of course, that some consensus of opinion exists in regard to the referents of *prurience* and *community* standards.

2. *I.e.*, systematic re-analysis of data originally gathered for different purposes.

3. The survey was funded by the Commission and the objectives of the survey were formulated by the members of the Effects Panel. The study was conducted by Response Analysis Corporation, Princeton, New Jersey, and the Institute for Survey Research, Temple University, Philadelphia, Pennsylvania. Hereafter, references to the findings of this survey will cite Abelson, *et al.*, 1970. The full data file is available upon request.

4. Probability sampling methods were used at each stage in the selection of survey respondents, *i.e.*, each dwelling unit in the coterminous United States had a known and equal probability of being selected for the sample. "Quota" sampling criteria, followed by many polling organizations, were not used. For a thorough description of sampling procedures, including estimates of sampling tolerances, see LoSciuto, *et al.*, 1970.

5. These represent the following completion rates for adults: 70% for the general interview and 66% for the accompanying self-administered questionnaire. Ninety percent of the adolescents completed interviews. See LoSciuto, *et al.*, 1970.

6. All participants in these studies were volunteers who agreed to viewing or reading erotic materials, and endorsed their willingness to participate with written consent.

7. A brief description of research problem and methods of each Commission-funded study cited in this Report is provided in the Appendix.

8. Opinion researchers have become increasingly sensitive to the difficulty of probing beyond "social rhetoric" in attitude surveys. It has been found that certain topics, and certain forms of questioning, tend to elicit stereotyped responses. This is a particular danger in questions about morality, especially in the realm of sex. One of the important contributions of the Institute for Sex Research (Kinsey) studies was the finding of differences between private and public reporting of sexual behavior. A recent study of moral issues revealed the ease with which persons respond with "a whole string of old verities of morality" (Harris, 1969).

9. It appears that the diversity characteristic of American public opinion is also characteristic of public opinion in Denmark. A recent probability survey in Copenhagen (Kutschinsky, 1970c) also found varied beliefs about the effects of exposure to erotic materials. About half (53%) of the Danish respondents believed that "pornography might be or might perhaps be considered harmful" (45% disagreed). At the same time, about three-fourths

287

(77%) believed that "pornography might be or might perhaps be considered beneficial" (18% disagreed). Like Americans, Danish adults more frequently mentioned socially neutral or desirable effects. The most commonly mentioned were: "alleviates the sexual urge for some people in some places" (25%), reduces sex crime (18%), and provides information (17%).

10. For variations by sex, see Abelson, et al., 1970.

11. "Recent experience" in the survey is defined as "during the past two years."

12. "Highly experienced" persons are those who reported experience with five or more specified visual and textual depictions in the past two years. See Abelson, et al., 1970, for a discussion of index construction.

13. Seven questionnaire items were combined to form a sex attitude index. The items were: "A girl who goes to bed with a boy before marriage will lose his respect;" "Young people today have healthier attitudes towards sex than do their parents;" "First of all, sex is for fun;" "Homosexuals should be excluded from regular society;" "There is an element of homosexuality in all of us;" "It is important that the government strictly enforce existing sex laws;" and "When it comes to sex, there is a great difference between what most people do and what they would like to do." Assignment of values to response categories and cutting points for the index are discussed in Abelson, et al., 1970.

14. Mail questionnaires were distributed to a national sample of 1725 persons in the cited professions compiled from various professional directories. Usable replies were received from 73.8% of the police chiefs and 74.1% of all others.

15. Mail questionnaires were sent to 7,484 psychiatrists and 3,078 clinical psychologists. Tabulations were based on a 35% response rate.

16. Mail questionnaires were sent to 640 American sex educators and counselors. Tabulations were based on 324 usable questionnaires (response rate of 54%).

17. The methodological problems associated with the measurement of human sexual arousal are discussed in more detail in two Commission-funded reviews: Mann, 1970; Zuckerman, 1970.

18. Masters reports that erotic materials have been used in his laboratories for stimulative purposes only 41 times since 1957. "Opportunity for direct physical observation was present and physiologic recording techniques were established. Although there was adequate recording objectivity we could demonstrate no specific variation in pornographically stimulated response from the study-subjects' previously recorded response patterns during masturbatory or precoital activity. There was no significant variation in either rapidity or intensity or recorded or observed sexual responsivity . . . in our minimal series, the women were essentially as stimulated by pornographic materials, either visual or descriptive, as were the men. We are aware that this return is in direct variance to the Kinsey reports which claim little female response to pornographic materials. It should be emphasized, however, that the materials were presented to a selective group of individuals. Both male and female study-subjects by definition are selected only if they are sexually responsive or orgasm." Personal communication.

19. This "multiple response" phenomenoi was first observed in studies which attempted to use galvanic skin response (GSR) as an indicator of sexual arousal. It was found that the arousal level, as measured by GSR, did not discriminate between sexual arousal and a highly aversive effect. Several studies in which introspective reporting and semantic differential methodology accompanied GSR measurement found that some persons experienced aversive reactions to exposure which produced relatively high GSR levels (Hain and Linton, 1969; Jordan and Butler, 1967; Koegler and Kline, 1965; Loiselle and Mollenauer, 1965).

20. There is some evidence that the assessment of sexual arousal varies according to the reporting or recording method. Retrospective reports, in which respondents are asked to recall an experience which occurred months and years past, yield more conservative estimates than introspective reports during, or immediately after, exposure. Physiological assessment, especially penile plethsymography for males, indicates greater arousal than accompanying verbal reports. These studies also suggest that females are more similar to males when asked to report certain physiological manifestations of arousal such as genital sensations, vaginal lubrication, etc.

21. Differences in questioning may be responsible for this difference. Respondents in the latter study (Abelson, et al., 1970) were specifically asked to recount their predominant response ("Think back to your reaction when you last saw this. Were you mostly aroused sexually, disgusted, pleased or

what?"). The questioning followed by Kinsey was apparently not standardized although it is clear that the interviewers asked about "ever having been aroused," rather than about respondents' predominant response. In the Abelson study, multiple and conflicting responses (recorded by other studies, e.g., Berger, *et al.*, 1970b; Byrne and Lamberth, 1970; Byrne and Sheffield, 1965; Mosher, 1970a; Paris and Goodstein, 1966; Schmidt and Sigusch, in press) were not recorded. Thus, whatever bias may be due to dissimulation and inaccurate recall is multiplied by the "forced single response," and the extent and frequency of sexual arousal is probably underreported in this study.

22. In this study, "visual" referred to erotic photographs, snapshots, cartoons, and motions pictures (but no stag films or "skin flicks"). "Textual" refers to printed materials, including books, magazines, paperback books and typewritten stories. Film (or movies) refers only to "stag films" and "skin flicks."

23. Two of the (Hamburg) Institute of Sex Research 10 minute color films were utilized. One film depicts a "couple undressing one another, kissing and manual genital petting, cunnilingus, and fellatio to ejaculation." The second film depicts "the couple undressing one another, kissing and manual-genital petting, and face-to-face coitus (Mosher, 1970a).

24. Seven films were utilized, and these included 10 to 12 minute depictions of: (a) female homosexual fondling and mutual oral-genital activity; (b) two females and one male engaging in oral sexuality, coitus, fondling, and anal play; (c) three male homosexuals engaging in oral sexuality and mutual masturbation; (d) a male and a female in a whipping and coital activity; (e) a female masturbating to orgasm; (f) a couple fondling, oral-genital activity, and coitus, involving a number of positions; and (g) oral sexuality, penile insertion and other heterosexual activity.

25. For "imaginary media" respondents were simply provided with a card upon which was printed a short descriptive phrase, e.g., "heterosexual intercourse, face to back, female sitting on male."

26. "Arousal," as used by Tannenbaum, refers to physiological arousal as measured by heart rate, systolic and diastolic blood pressure, and skin temperature, and may or may not indicate sexual arousal.

27. "Overall arousal" refers to summated scale values for all 19 ratings.

28. One study found that heterosexual inexperience and a relatively late age of first heterosexual petting and intercourse are associated with reported higher sexual arousal (Davis and Braucht, 1970a).

29. The experimenters, a psychologist and two physicians, reported: "By the end of the experiment our subjects' experience with pornography had been considerably greater than that which most people would have in their entire lifetime. On this basis alone they could be considered experts. It was impressive to the investigators that despite this extensive experience only one subject reported that, transiently, he felt more in favor of legal controls on this type of material. All the other subjects reported either no change or some increased tolerance to the existence of such materials . . . even though they themselves were considerably less interested in it by virtue of their exposure" (Reifler, *et al.*, 1970: 18-19). ". . . not only did subjects become satiated to pornography but there is no evidence that this massive exposure to erotically stimulating material had any major lasting effect upon their attitudes or behavior. What changes did occur seemed to be in a favorable direction and quite minor. Psychological tests given before and after the experience showed that the subjects opinion of themselves had moved in the direction of greater self esteem . . ." (Howard, *et al.*, 1970).

30. Unmarried subjects included both coitally experienced and inexperienced persons.

31. Different questioning procedure not susceptible to reporting in Table 15.

32. The strength of these relationships varied, however, by gender. The relationship between frequency of exposure and high school socio-sexual experimentation was (gamma) .39 (males) and .16 (females) and .38 (males) and .12 (females) during college. See Berger, *et al.*, 1970a.

33. In a study of young married couples, no change in any sexual activity was reported after these couples viewed erotic slides. The method of reporting, however, may have underestimated the effects of exposure upon these couples' sexual behavior. See Byrne and Lamberth, 1970.

34. A third study (Kutschinsky, 1970a) of sexually experienced young couples, both married and unmarried, reported increases for both males and females which appear to be statistically significant, although no significance test was actually employed.

35. Both color films portrayed the same man and woman in the same

physical setting. One film depicted the couple undressing one another, kissing and manual-genital petting, cunnilingus, and fellatio to ejaculation. The second film depicted the couple undressing one another, kissing and manual-genital petting, and face-to-face coitus.

36. Seven films were utilized, and these included depictions of heterosexual intercourse and oral sexuality, male and female homosexuality, group sexual activity, female masturbation, and sadomasochistic activity.

37. "more experienced recently" refers to having seen or read five or more erotic visual and textual depictions in the past two years. See Abelson, *et al.,* 1970.

38. See Report of the Traffic and Distribution Panel to the Commission on Obscenity and Pornography.

39. Regarding sexual activity, see Section C.

40. A national study of American college students (Berger, *et al.,* 1970a) found that this relationship is apparent at a relatively early age. Frequency of exposure to erotic materials is related to frequency of high school dating (gamma: males equals +.51; females equals +.58), number of persons dated during high school (gamma: males equals +.20; females equals .13), and "going steady" during high school (gamma equals +.20), but only for males. For college males, frequency of exposure to erotic film is also associated with fraternity membership (gamma equals +.49).

41. These items were adapted from the sex attitude and experience inventory developed by Thorne and Haupt, 1966.

42. The terms "repression" and "promiscuity" are not the investigators', but these scales are so identified by Thorne, 1965. Actually, both terms seem exaggerated: "liberality" and "rigidity" might be more apt.

43. These scales consisted of 39 items developed by Athanasiou and Shaver, 1969.

44. Mosher (1970a) suggests that this change may be artifactual, i.e., a function of a regression toward the mean.

45. The investigators used an abridged form of the 33-item *Marriage Council of Philadelphia Adjustment Survey.*

46. Couples viewed a 15-minute film depicting "group" sexual activities of two females and one male, looked at five "explicit" magazines, listened to a tape recorded erotic narrative, and viewed a second film of two couples, one heterosexual and one homosexual.

47. Six scales were developed as measures of deviance in the home. The components of the overall index included exposure to deviant models in the home, exposure to sexually deviant models in the family, absence of sanction networks within the family, perceived quality of mother-father relationship, and paternal/maternal warmth and fairness. See Davis and Braucht (1970b).

48. Four scales constituted an index of deviance in the neighborhood and peer group. The components included the extent of delinquency and crime in the neighborhood and peer group, and heterosexual and homosexual deviance in the peer group. See Davis and Braucht (1970b).

49. In this study, even though subjects were less fearful of potential detrimental effects after exposure to ten-minute erotic films, they tended to be somewhat less willing to have "pornography freely available to the public" after exposure. See Davis and Braucht, 1970a.

50. While these studies suggest that exposure to sexual stimuli may change attitudes about erotic materials, it should be noted that persons who participated in these studies were (a) volunteers, (b) generally well educated, and (c) relatively sexually liberal prior to participation. A cautious interpretation of these data would emphasize that already liberally oriented persons became, after exposure, even more liberal. These studies do not demonstrate that such changes occur, or would occur among persons with established restrictive attitudes regarding erotic materials.

51. After analyzing findings of an experiment in which young married couples viewed and read erotic material, Byrne and Lamberth (1970) observed "individuals who respond to the stimuli with positive affect judge them not to be pornographic and would not impose legal restrictions on their dissemination to others. Those who respond to the stimuli with positive affect judge them not to the be pornographic and would not impose legal restrictions. It would seem to be these personal reactions rather than any evidence about the effects of 'pornography' which are the determinants of one's position on this issue."

52. The studies reported in this section generally employed semantic differential or adjective checklist methods. Terms such as "internally agitated," "aggressive," "wild," etc., were presented to participants in these studies

as brief verbal descriptions of the range of possible feelings these persons experienced prior to, during, and after viewing or reading erotic-stimuli. As such, a behavioral interpretation of these data should proceed with caution.

53. Some of the "diffuse emotional activation" reported here, e.g., "inability to concentrate," "impulsiveness," may or may not be related to, or associated with, sexual arousal, i.e., sexual emotions, moods, etc.

54. Zuckerman (1970) notes that "Most subjects seem to have a most likely, or most powerful, channel of response. One subject may be a GSR responder, another subject a heart responder and so on." ʾIn this regard, Masters and Johnson (1966) report that a "sex flush" develops in response to sexual stimulation in about 75% of females but in only 25% of the males observed.

55. In one experiment (Mosher, 1970a), after viewing two erotic films, "high sex-guilt," college males and females reported less intense physiological sexual reactions than "low sex-guilt" persons. Feelings of sex guilt does not, however, preclude sexual arousal from erotic stimuli. Mosher also notes that "high sex-guilt" subjects rated films as more "pornographic," "disgusting," "offensive," and less "enjoyable" than did low guilt subjects. "High sex-guilt" subjects experienced more negative affects such as "repelled," "shocked," "irritated," "disgusted," "embarrassment," "ashamed" and "guilty" after film viewing.

56. These educational data, as reported by Katzman, are difficult to reconcile with the occupational data regarding physicians and full-time police. It would be supposed that the mean education level of physicians would be considerably higher than that of full-time police, but physicians are reported as considerably more likely (not less likely, as would be supposed) than full-time police to rate stimuli as obscene.

57. One implication of this is that repeated exposure to erotica or the increased availability of it, will produce progressively wider acceptance of the material, but not necessarily the sexual practices depicted.

58. Howard, et al. (1970) noted the satiation effect of repeated exposure, as discussed above.

59. National Council of Juvenile Court Judges, 1954; Senate Subcommittee to Investigate Juvenile Delinquency, 1955, 1959; J. Edgar Hoover, 1965; House Select Subcommittee on Education, 1967.

60. The existence of subcultural factors implies that there are values, beliefs, and norms which are learned and shared and that differ from those in other subcultures or from the dominant value system. (See Cloward and Ohlin, 1960; Cohen, 1955; Miller, 1958).

61. There have, however, been studies of the effects of the mass media on behavior, including antisocial behavior. Studies of the effects of literature (Bird, 1940; Jahoda, 1954; Kvaraceus, 1965; Muhlen, 1949; Waples, et al., 1940; Wertham, 1948, 1949, 1968; Wolfe and Fiske, 1949), film (Blumer and Hauser, 1933; Green, 1962) and television (Himmelweit, et al., 1958; Schramn, et al., 1961; Shayon, 1951) on delinquent behavior have produced inconclusive results. A more recent body of research concerning the effects of violence in the mass media (Bandura, 1965; Berkowitz, 1964; Maccoby, 1964; National Commission on the Causes and Prevention of Violence, 1969; Weiss, 1969) suggests highly qualified and conditional findings.

62. The diversity in expert opinion is illustrated by a survey conducted at the University of Minnesota Library School from 1962 to 1965 (Berninghausen and Faunce, 1965).

63. These inferences tend to disregard instances of offenses that are unaccompanied *by association* with obscenity and to ignore the incidence of exposure to erotica by nonoffenders.

64. The *Uniform Crime Reports* present arrest statistics for three categories of sex offenses: (a) forcible rape (rape by force, assault to rape and attempted rape, excluding statutory offenses where no force is used and the victim is under age of consent.) (b) prostitution and commercialized vice ("sex offenses of a commercialized nature and attempts, such as prostitution, keeping a bawdy house, procuring, or transporting women for immoral purposes"); and (c) other sex offenses ("statutory rape, offenses against chastity, common decency, morals and the like," including attempts).

65. See Report of the Traffic and Distribution Panel of the Commission on Obscenity and Pornography (1970).

66. Under 18 years of age.

67. It should be noted, however, that an accurate index of a given social phenomenon should be based on an appropriate age-, and where necessary, sex-specific rate, thus taking into account changes over time in the population

of interest. In the case of illegitimacy (discussed below), the best index is based on the number of unmarried females in the population of childbearing age (15 to 44 years). In the case of forcible rape, the most appropriate base would consist of males in the population, 10 to 49 years of age. By definition, only males can be charged with this offense, and males in this age range accounted for 98% of all arrests for forcible rape during the period under study (1960-1969). For all other sex offenses a reasonably accurate basis for estimating changes in volume and trends of juvenile arrests would be the number of juvenile males and females in the ten to seventeen year age category. The same kind of refinement calculated for all offenses would undoubtedly reduce the magnitude of the percentage increase of decrease over time. Sex offenses and illegitimacy were selected as a focus of refinement here because of the Commission's particular interest in their relationship to the availability of erotica.

68. The rate of juvenile arrests for forcible rape was 9.3 (per 100,000 males, 10 to 17 years) in 1960 and 13.9 in 1969. The rates (per 100,000 juveniles 10 to 17) of juvenile arrests for prostitution and commercialized vice are 1.5 in 1960 and 2.7 in 1969.

69. There are three different statistics variously used to estimate the volume and trends of illegitimate births. These statistics include: (a) the *number* of reported illegitimate birth, (b) the *ratio* of illegitimate to total live births, and (c) the *rate* of illegitimate births per 1,000 unmarried females of childbearing age (15-44 years). The illegitimacy rate, however, is the most reliable indicator and will be used as the basis for discussion here. Differences in calculations of percentage increases in terms of absolute number as opposed to rate may be illustrated as follows:

Age of Childbearing Females	Number of Illegitimate Births			Illegitimacy Rate		
	1960	*1968*	*% change*	*1960*	*1968*	*% Change*
All ages (15-44)	224,300	339,200	+51.2	21.8	24.4	+11.9
Under 15 years	4,600	7,700	+67.4	0.6	0.7*	+16.7*
15-19 years	87,100	158,000	+81.4	15.7	19.8	+26.1

*Rates for age group under 15 years available only for the period 1960-1965.

Note: Adapted from Public Health Service, Division of Vital Statistics, United States Department of Health, Education and Welfare (1967, 1968). 1968 figures (unpublished) made available directly from the Division of Vital Statistics.

70. The rate decreased among women aged 20-24.

71. Two dimensions of experience with erotic material—extent and amount— are discussed in this report. "Extent" of experience refers to the proportion of a given population reporting any experience with erotic material. "Amount" of experience refers to both the number of different erotic depictions ever viewed or used and the number of occasions of exposure to such depictions.

72. These data are reported in the Report of the Traffic Panel to the Commission on Obscenity and Pornography (1970).

73. The two groups were individually matched on the basis of age, grade in school, school attended, reading ability, and father's occupation.

74. It should be noted, however, that nondelinquents read more, in general, than did the delinquents. This finding is consistent with the reports of several other researchers who investigated the reading habits of delinquent and nondelinquent youth (Glueck & Glueck, 1950, Kvaraceus, 1965; Havighurst, 1959; Schiller, 1970).

75. The boys were 17-20 years old (98%), mostly of Negro or Puerto Rican ethnic background (88%), and had lived in the same city since age 10 (92%). They were incarcerated for a variety of crimes against persons and property, including robbery, larceny, possession of drugs, and burglary. Only 3% of the sample had been incarcerated for assault, and only 2% for sex offenses.

76. Propper reports that informal conversation with both reformatory officials and inmates revealed that there was a considerable amount of erotica circulating clandestinely within the reformatory. He points out that responses to the two questions, "Have you ever been exposed?" and "Have you been exposed recently?" produce almost exactly the same percentages of affirmative answers, and thus speculates that the high rates of exposure to erotica may reflect the experience of these delinquents within the reformatory itself.

77. Due to a technical problem, questions generating these specific data in Abelson, *et al.* (1970) were asked of only about half the young males. They should therefore be regarded as indicative, but not wholly precise.

78. It is difficult to assess how much of the youth-adult differential is a function of inaccurate recall.

79. This is probably a low frequency estimate because respondents were asked about different depictions, and some depictions, e.g., sadomasochistic activities, are likely to be seen less frequently than others.

80. Pertinent findings are discussed in detail in Section C.

81. Several other studies have suggested that such themes evoke feelings and fantasies of affection, sentimentality and romance among females generally (Kinsey, *et al.*, 1953; Cairns, *et al.*, 1962; Elias, 1970).

82. The researcher concludes from these data that pornography "plays a distinct role in the creation of antisocial behavior in susceptible teenagers" (Haines, 1955; p. 198). The inference of casuality, however, seems premature in the absence of data for a nondelinquent control group. There is no indication in the study that delinquents' experience with sexual materials was or was not different from that of nondelinquent youth.

83. See Report of the Traffic and Distribution Panel of the Commission on Obscenity and Pornography (1970).

84. The F.B.I. Crime Index is comprised of the following offenses: criminal homicide, forcible rape, robbery, aggravated assault, burglary, larceny of $50 or over, and auto theft.

85. Sec. 234 of the Danish Penal Code.

86. As one researcher has noted, "spirited public discussion in the newspapers, radio and television alerted the populace to its accessibility. The existence of magazine vending machines outside some 'porno shops' and mail order solicitation in the daily newspapers has ensured that even the most inhibited consumer may purchase pornography with a minimum of anxiety" (Ben-Veniste, 1970).

87. With the exception of arrests for homosexual activity, which for several years reflected a change in the legal age of consent for homosexual relations and a short-lived police "crackdown" on homosexuals.

88. Although the percentages reporting adolescent exposure sometimes differed according to the characteristics of the stimulus (medium and content), the differences were all in the same direction—i.e., sex offenders and sex deviants tended to report *less* exposure.

89. Not reported here are survey data which cite ages of first exposure but do not report comparative ages for sex offenders and others. Reported age of first exposure will vary from study to study with the precise wording of the question and with the ages of the respondents (older people tend to report later ages of first exposure). Comparison of offenders and nonoffenders is therefore valid only if exactly the same question is asked of both groups and if the two groups are matched on age.

90. Group includes seven persons convicted for "attempted rape."

91. Because a substantial amount of erotica circulates among prison populations, the offenders in this study were asked about their adult experience with erotica *prior* to incarceration. See Goldstein, *et al.*, 1970.

92. The six depictions were those which correspond most closely to the standardized depictions used in several other studies.

93. See, however, one datum reported by Gebhard, *et al.*, which may possibly be inconsistent with the weight of the new research here reported.

94. Studies of adult bookstore and motion picture patrons consistently report that the clients of these establishment are predominantly White, middle aged, middle class males, most of whom present the physical appearance of economical success and social respectability. (Finkelstein, 1970a; Massey, 1970; Nawy, 1970; Winick, 1970). A recent market analysis (Nawy, 1970) of erotic bookstore and motion picture patrons in San Francisco found that, in proportion to their representation in the population, Blacks were underrepresented and Chinese overrepresented among these patrons. An examination of sex crime statistics in San Francisco, showed that Blacks were overrepresented and Chinese underrepresented. This relationship between ethnicity and sex offenses has been reported elsewhere (Amir, 1965; Guttmacher, 1951).

95. The apparent greater incidence of action on the part of female object pedophiles is based on an N of 20 and does not constitute a statistically significant difference.

96. More specifically, only six of 63 sex offenders and five of 66 nonsex offenders report exposure within 24 hours before committing their crime; four of the six sex offenders said the exposure had encouraged the offense

and none of the five nonsex offenders said this. The numbers involved in the latter comparison are extremely small and the difference is not statistically significant.

REFERENCES

Abelson, H., Cohen, R., Heaton, E., & Suder, C. Public attitudes toward and experience with erotic materials. *Technical reports of the Commission on Obscenity and Pornography.* Vol. 6. Washington, D.C.: U.S. Government Printing Office, 1970.

Abse, D. W. Psychodynamic aspects of the problem of definition of obscenity. *Law and Contemporary Problems,* Autumn, 1955, *20(4),* 572.

Adorno, T. W. *The authoritarian personality.* New York: Harper, 1950.

Amir, M. *Patterns in forcible rape.* Unpublished doctoral dissertation. University of Pennsylvania, 1965.

Amoroso, D. M., Brown, M., Preusse, M., Ware, E. E., & Pilkey, D. W. An investigation of behavioral, psychological, and physiological reactions to pornographic stimuli. *Technical reports of the Commission on Obscenity and Pornography.* Vol. 8. Washington, D.C.: U.S. Government Printing Office, 1970.

Athanasiou, R. & Shaver, P. A research questionnaire on sex. *Psychology today,* July, 1969, 64-69.

Bandura, A. Vicarious processes: A case of no-trial learning. In Berkowitz, L. (Ed.) *Advances in experimental social psychology.* Vol. 2. New York: Academic Press, 1965.

Banning, M. C. Filth on the newsstands. Cited in Report of the Select Committee on Current Pornographic Materials, H.R. 2510. 82nd Congress, 1st Session, 1952, 135.

Baker, R. K., Ball, S. J., & Lange, D. L. *Mass media and Violence.* Task Force reports to the National Commission on the Causes and Prevention of Violence. Vol. 9. Washington, D.C.: U.S. Government Printing Office, 1969.

Bender, P. The definition of "obscene" under existing law. *Technical reports of the Commission on Obscenity and Pornography.* Vol. 2. Washington, D.C.: U.S. Government Printing Office, 1970.

Ben-Veniste, R. Pornography and sex crime—the Danish experience. *Technical reports of the Commission on Obscenity and Pornography.* Vol. 7. Washington, D.C.: U.S. Government Printing Office, 1970.

Berger, A. S., Gagnon, J. H., & Simon, W. Pornography: high school and college years. *Technical reports of the Commission on Obscenity and Pornography.* Vol. 9. Washington, D.C.: U.S. Government Printing Office, 1970. (a)

Berger, A. S., Gagnon, J. H., & Simon, W. Urban working-class adolescents and sexually explicit media. *Technical reports of the Commission on Obscenity and Pornography.* Vol. 9. Washington, D.C.: U.S. Government Printing Office, 1970. (b)

Berkowitz, L. Some aspects of observed aggression. *Journal of Personality and Social Psychology,* 1965, *2,* 359-369.

Bernick, N., Borowitz, G., & Kling, A. Effect of sexual arousal and anxiety on pupil size. Presented at the Rocky Mountain Psychological Association, Denver, 1968.

Berninghausen, D. K., & Faunce, R. W. An exploratory study of juvenile delinquency and the reading of sensational books. *Journal of Experimental Education,* Winter, 1964, *33(2),* 161-168.

Berninghausen, D. K., & Faunce, R. W. Some opinions on the relationship between obscene books and juvenile delinquency. Unpublished manuscript, University of Minnesota Graduate School, 1965.

Bird, C., *Social Psychology,* New York: D. Appleton-Century, 1940.

Blumer, H., & Hauser, P. M. *Movies, delinquency and crime.* New York: MacMillan, 1933.

Brady, J. P., & Levitt, E. E. The relation of sexual preferences to sexual experiences. *The Psychological Record,* 1965, *15,* 377-384. (a)

Brady, J. P., & Levitt, E. E. The scalability of sexual experiences. *The Psychological Record,* 1965, *15,* 275-279. (b)

Brown, P. T. On the differentiation of homo or hetero-erotic interest in the male: An operant technique illustrated in a case of a motorcycle fetishist. *Behavior Research and Therapy,* 1964, *2,* 31-37.

Buchwald, A. M. Personal communication. In R. B. Cairns, J. C. N. Paul,

& J. Wishner. Sex censorship: The assumptions of anti-obscenity laws and the empirical evidence. *Minnesota Law Review,* 1962, *46,* 1009-1041.

Bullock, D. H. Note on "looking at pictures" behavior. *Perceptual and Motor Skills,* 1959, *9,* 333.

Bureau of the Census, United States Department of Commerce, *United States census of population, 1960. United States summary, detailed characteristics, 1960.* Washington, D.C.: U.S. Government Printing Office, 1962.

Burgess, A. What is pornography? In *Perspectives on pornography.* New York: St. Martin's Press, Inc., 1970.

Byrne, D., & Lamberth, J. The effect of erotic stimuli on sex arousal evaluative responses, and subsequent behavior. *Technical reports of the Commission on Obscenity and Pornography.* Vol. 8. Washington, D.C.: U.S. Government Printing Office, 1970.

Byrne, D., & Sheffield, J. Response to sexually arousing stimuli as a function of repressing and sensitizing defenses. *Journal of Abnormal Psychology,* 1965, *70(2),* 114-118.

Cairns, R. B. Psychological assumptions in sex censorship: An evaluative review of recent (1961-68) research. *Technical reports of the Commission on Obscenity and Pornography.* Vol. 1. Washington, D.C.: U.S. Government Printing Office, 1970.

Cairns, R. B., Paul, J. C. N., & Wishner, J. Sex censorship: The assumptions of anti-obscenity laws and the empirical evidence. *Minnesota Law Review,* 1962, *46,* 1009-1041.

Carroll, V. A., Testimony before House of Representatives Subcommittee on Postal Operations, Committee on Post Office and Civil Services, 90th Congress, 1st session. Hearing on H.R. 426 and H.R. 8215, June 9, 1967, 37.

Clark, R. A. The projective measurement of experimentally induced levels of sexual motivation. *Journal of Experimental Psychology,* 1952, *44,* 391-399.

Clor, H. *Obscenity and public morality.* Chicago: University of Chicago Press, 1969.

Cloward, R. A., & Ohlin, L. E. *Delinquency and opportunity.* New York: Free Press, 1960.

Cohen, A. K. *Delinquent boys: the culture of the gang.* Glencoe, Ill.: Free Press, 1955.

Cook, R. F., & Fosen, R. H. Pornography and the sex offender: Patterns of exposure and immediate arousal effects of pornographic stimuli. *Technical reports of the Commission on Obscenity and Pornography.* Vol. 7. Washington, D.C.: U.S. Government Printing Office, 1970.

Corman, C. Physiological response to a sexual stimulus. B. Sc. (Hed.) Thesis. University of Manitoba, 1968.

Davis, K. Prostitution. In R. K. Merton, & R. A. Nisbet (Eds.), Contemporary social problems. New York: Harcourt, Brace & World, Inc., 1961.

Davis, R. C., & Buchwald, A. M. An exploration of somatic response patterns: *Stimulus and sex differences. Journal of Comparative and Physiological Psychology,* 1957, *50,* 44-52.

Davis, K. E., & Braucht, G. N. Reactions to viewing films of erotically realistic heterosexual behavior. *Technical reports of the Commission on Obscenity and Pornography.* Vol. 8. Washington, D.C.: U.S. Government Printing Office, 1970. (a)

Davis, K. E., & Braucht, G. N. Exposure to pornography, character and sexual deviance: A retrospective survey. *Technical reports of the Commission on Obscenity and Pornography.* Vol. 7. Washington, D.C.: U.S. Government Printing Office, 1970. (b)

De River, D. The sexual criminal. Springfield, Illinois: Charles C. Thomas, 1956.

Egan, D. Testimony before Senate Subcommittee to Investigate Juvenile Delinquency, Committee on the Judiciary, 84th Congress, 1st Session, Hearings pursuant to S. Res. 62, May 24, 26, 31, June 9, 18, 1955, 72.

Elias, J. E. Exposure to erotic materials in adolescence. *Technical reports of the Commission on Obscenity and Pornography.* Vol. 9. Washington, D.C.: U.S. Government Printing Office, 1970.

Eliasberg, W. G., & Stuart, I. R. Authoritarian personality and the obscenity threshold. *Journal of Social Psychology,* 1961, *55,* 143-151.

Federal Bureau of Investigation, United States Department of Justice. *Uniform crime reports—1969.* Washington, D.C.: U.S. Government Printing Office, 1970.

Finkelstein, M. M. The traffic in sex-oriented materials, part I: adult bookstores in Boston, Mass. *Technical reports of the Commission on Ob-*

scenity and Pornography. Vol. 4. Washington, D.C.: U.S. Government Printing Office, 1970.

Fitzgerald, Thomas J. Testimony before House of Representatives Select Committee on Current Pornographic Materials, 82nd Congress, 2d. Session. H.R. 2510, 1952, 47.

Freund, K. Homosexualita u muze. Stat. zdrav. nakl., Prague, 1962.

Freund, K. A laboratory method for diagnosing predominance of homo- or hetero-erotic interest in the male. *Behavior Research and Therapy,* 1963, *1,* 85-93.

Freund, K. Diagnosing heterosexual pedophilia by means of a test of sexual interest. *Behavior Research and Therapy,* 1965, *3,* 229-234.

Freund, K. Diagnosing homo- or hetero-sexuality and erotic age preference by means of a psychological test. *Behavior Research and Therapy,* 1967, *5,* 209-228. (a)

Freund, K. Erotic preference in pedophilia. *Behavior Research and Therapy,* 1967, *5,* 339-348. (b)

Freund, K., Diamant, J., & Pinkava, V. On the validity and reliability of the phalloplethysmographic diagnosis of some deviations. *Rev. Czech. Med.,* 1958, *4,* 145-151.

Frignito, N. G. Testimony before House of Representatives Select Sub-committee on Education, Committee on Education and Labor, 90th Congress, 1st Session. Hearings on H.R. 2525, Washington, D.C., April 20 and 24, 1967, 86.

Gagnon, J. H., & Simon, W. Pornography—raging menace or paper tiger? *Trans-action,* 1967, *4,* 41. (a)

Gagnon, J. H., & Simon, W. *Sexual deviance.* New York: Harper & Row, 1967. (b)

Galbreith, G. G., & Mosher, D. L. Associative sexual responses in relation to sexual arousal, guilt, and external approval contingencies. *Journal of Personality and Social Psychology,* 1968, *10,* 142-147.

Gallup, G. Gallup Opinion Index: Political, Social and Economic Trends. Report No. 49. Princeton, N. J.: Gallup International, Inc., July 1969.

Gebhard, P. H., Gagnon, J. H., Pomeroy, W. B., & Christenson, C. V. *Sex offenders: an analysis of types.* New York: Harper & Row, 1965.

Giese, H., & Schmidt, G. Sexuality of students: behavior and attitudes. A Poll at 12 West German Universities, Rowoiilt Publishing Company, 1968.

Glock, C. Y., & Stark, R. *Religion and Society in Tension.* Chicago: Rand McNally & Co., 1965.

Glueck, S., & Glueck, E. *Unraveling juvenile delinquency.* Cambridge, Massachusetts: Harvard University Press, 1950.

Goldstein, M. J., Kant, H. S., Judd, L. L., Rice, C. J., & Green, R. Exposure to pornography and sexual behavior in deviant and normal groups. *Technical reports of the Commission on Obscenity and Pornography.* Vol. 7. Washington, D.C.: U.S. Government Printing Office, 1970.

Green, B. Obscenity: censorship and juvenile delinquency. *University of Toronto Law Journal,* 1962, *14(2),* 229-252.

Guttmacher, M. S. *Sex offenses.* New York: W. W. Norton, 1951.

Hain, J. D., & Linton, P. H. Physiological response to visual sexual stimuli. *Journal of Sex Research,* 1969, *5(4),* 292-302.

Haines, W. H. Juvenile delinquency and television. *Journal of Social Therapy,* Oct. 1955, *1(4),* 192-198.

Harris, Louis. Time Morality Poll. New York: Harris and Associates, May, 1969.

Hartley, R. The impact of viewing aggression. Columbia Broadcasting System, Office of Social Research, multilithed, 1964.

Havighurst, R. J. Poor reading and delinquency may go hand in hand. *Nation's Schools,* 1959, *64,* 55-58.

Hess, E. H., & Polt, J. M. Pupil size as related to interest value of visual stimuli. *Science,* 1960, *132,* 349-350.

Hess, E. H., Seltzer, A. L., & Shlien, J. M. Pupil response of hetero- and homosexual males to pictures of men and women. *Journal of Abnormal Psychology,* 1965, *70(3),* 165-168.

Higgins, J. W., Katzman, M. B. Determinants in the judgment of obscenity. *American Journal of Psychiatry,* June 1969, *125(12),* 147.

Himmelweit, H. T., Oppenheim, A. N., & Vince, P. *Television and the child,* London: Oxford University Press, 1958.

Hoover, J. E. Cited in Interim report of the Committee on the Judiciary made by its subcommittee to investigate juvenile delinquency pursuant to S.

Res. 62 and S. Res. 173. *Obscene and pornographic literature and juvenile delinquency*. 84th Congress, 2d Session. June 28, 1956. 2.

Hoover, J. E. The fight against filth. Personally revised (1965) and distributed reprint of an article originally appearing in *The American Legion magazine*, 1961, *70(16)*, 48-49.

House of Representatives Select Subcommittee on Education, Committee on Education and Labor, 90th Congress, 1st Session. Hearing on H.R. 2525, Washington, D.C., April 20 and 24, 1967.

Howard, J. L., Reifler, C. B., & Liptzin, M. B. Effects of exposure to pornography. *Technical reports of the Commission on Obscenity and Pornography.*. Vol. 8. Washington, D.C.: U.S. Government Printing Office, 1970.

Hughes, D. A. *Perspectives on pornography*. New York: St. Martin's Press, 1970.

Hyman, S. E. In defense of pornography. In Hughes, D. A. *Perspectives on pornography*. New York: St. Martin's Press, 1970.

Jahoda, M. *The Impact of literature: A psychological discussion of some assumptions in the censorship debate*. Prepared for the American Book Publishers Council, March 1, 1954.

Jakobovits, L. A. Evaluational reactions to erotic literature. *Psychological Reports*, 1965, *16*, 985-994.

Johnson, W. T., Kupperstein, L., & Peters, J. Sex offenders experience with erotica. *Technical reports of the Commission on Obscenity and Pornography*. Vol. 7. Washington, D.C.: U.S. Government Printing Office, 1970.

Jordan, B. T., & Butler, J. R. GSR as a measure of the sexual component in hysteria. *Journal of Psychology*, 1967, *67*, 211-219.

Karpman, B. *The sexual offender and his sex offenses*. New York: The Julian Press, 1954.

Katzman, M. Photograph characteristics influencing the judgment of obscenity. *Technical reports of the Commission on Obscenity and Pornography*. Vol. 9. Washington, D.C.: U.S. Government Printing Office, 1970. (a)

Katzman, M. The relationship of socioeconomic background to judgments of sexual stimulation and their correlation with judgments of obscenity. *Technical reports of the Commission on Obscenity and Pornography*. Vol. 9. Washington, D.C.: U.S. Government Printing Office, 1970. (b)

Kefauver, E. Obscene and pornographic literature and juvenile delinquency. *Federal Probation*, Dec. 1960, *24(4)*, 3-12.

Kilpatrick, J. J. Testimony before House of Representatives Select Subcommittee on Education. Committee on Education and Labor. 90th Congress, 1st Session. Hearing on H.R. 2525, April 20 and 24, 1967, 24.

Kinsey, A. C., Pomeroy, W. B., & Martin, C. E. *Sexual behavior in the human male*. Philadelphia: Saunders, 1948.

Kinsey, A. C., Pomeroy, W. B., Martin, C. E., & Gebhard, P. H. *Sexual behavior in the human female*. Philadelphia: W. B. Saunders, 1953.

Koegler, R. R., & Kline, L. Y. Psychotherapy research: An approach utilizing autonomic response measurement. *American Journal of Psychotherapy*, 1965, *19*, 268-279.

Kronhausen, E., & Kronhausen, P. *Pornography and the law*. New York: Ballantine Books, Inc., 1959.

Kubie, L. Testimony before House of Representatives Select Subcommittee on Education, Committee on Education and Labor, 90th Congress, 1st Session. Hearings on H.R. 2525, Washington, D.C., April 20 and 24, 1967, 69.

Kupperstein, L. The role of pornography in the etiology of juvenile delinquency: A review of the literature. *Technical reports of the Commission on Obscenity and Pornography*. Vol. 1. Washington, D.C.: U.S. Government Printing Office, 1970.

Kupperstein, L., & Wilson, W. C. Erotica and anti-social behavior: An analysis of selected social indicator statistics. *Technical reports of the Commission on Obscenity and Pornography*. Vol. 7. Washington, D.C.: U.S. Government Printing Office, 1970.

Kutschinsky, B. The effect of pornography—an experiment on perception, attitudes, and behavior. *Technical reports of the Commission on Obscenity and Pornography*. Vol. 8. Washington, D.C.: U.S. Government Printing Office, 1970. (a)

Kutschinsky, B. Pornography in Denmark: Studies on producers, sellers, and users. *Technical reports of the Commission on Obscenity and Pornography*. Vol. 4. Washington, D.C.: U.S. Government Printing Office, 1970. (b)

Kutschinsky, B. Sex crimes and pornography in Copenhagen: A study of attitudes. *Technical reports of the Commission on Obscenity and Pornography*. Vol. 7. Washington, D.C.: U.S. Government Printing Office, 1970. (c)

297

Kvaraceu, W. C. Can reading affect delinquency? *American Library Association Bulletin*, June 1965. *59(6)*, 516-522.

La Barre, W. Obscenity: an anthropological appraisal. *Law and Contemporary Problems*, 1955, *20*, 533.

Leiman, A. H., & Epstein, S. Thematic sexual responses as related to sexual drive and guilt. *Journal of Abnormal and Social Psychology*, 1961, *63*, 169-175.

Le Maire, L. L'importance de la litterature comme factor criminogene. *Acta Psychiatrica*, 1946, *21*, 585-593.

Levin, M. Stated cited in House of Representatives Subcommittee on Postal Operations, Committee on Post Office and Civil Services. 90th Congress, 1st Session. Hearing on H.R. 426 and H.R. 8215, June 9, 1967, 51.

Levitt, E. E. Pornography: some new perspectives on an old problem. *The Journal of Sex Research*, November 1969, *5(4)*, 247-259.

Levitt, E. E., & Brady, J. P. Sexual preferences in young adult males and some correlates. *Journal of Clinical Psychology*, 1965, *21*, 347-354.

Levitt, E. E., & Hinesley, R. K. Some factors in the valences of erotic visual stimuli. *The Journal of Sex Research*, February 1967, *3(1)*, 63-68.

Lindner, R. Cited in E. Kronhausen & P. Kronhausen, *Pornography and the law*. New York: Ballantine Books, Inc., 1959.

Lipkin, M., & Carns, D. E. Poll of mental health professionals. Cited in the University of Chicago Division of the Biological Sciences and the Pritzker School of Medicine Reports, Chicago, Illinois, Winter 1970, *20(1)*.

Loiselle, R. H., & Mollenauer, S. Galvanic skin responses to sexual stimuli in a female population. *Journal of Genetic Psychology*, 1965, *73*, 273-275.

Lorang, M. C. *Burning ice:* The moral and emotional effects of reading. New York: Charles Scribner's Sons, 1968.

LoSciuto, L., Spector, A., Michels, E., & Jenne, C. Methodological report on a study of public attitudes toward and experience with erotic materials. *Technical reports of the Commission on Obscenity and Pornography*. Vol. 6. Washington, D.C.: U.S. Government Printing Office, 1970.

MacCoby, E. Effects of mass media: in M. L. & L. W. Hoffman (Eds.) *Review of child development research*. New York: Russell Sage Foundation, 1964.

Mann, J. The experimental induction of sexual arousal. *Technical reports of the Commission on Obscenity and Pornography*. Vol. 1. Washington, D.C.: U.S. Government Printing Office, 1970.

Mann, J., Sidman, J., & Starr, S. Effects of erotic films on sexual behaviors of married couples. *Technical reports of the Commission on Obscenity and Pornography*. Vol. 8. Washington, D.C.: U.S. Government Printing Office, 1970.

Marriage Council of Philadelphia, *Marriage adjustment schedule 1B*, Philadelphia, 1950.

Martin, B. Expression and inhibition of sex motive arousal in college males. *Journal of Abnormal and Social Psychology*, 1964, *68(3)*, 307-312.

Massey, M. A marketing analysis of sex-oriented materials in Denver, Colorado, August 1969. *Technical reports of the Commission on Obscenity and Pornography*. Vol. 4. Washington, D.C.: U.S. Government Printing Office, 1970.

Masters, W. H., & Johnson, V. E. *Human sexual response*. Boston: Little Brown, 1966.

McConaghy, N. Penile volume change to moving pictures of male and female nudes in heterosexual and homosexual males. *Behavior Research and Therapy*, 1967, *5*, 43-48.

Mercier, V. Master Percy and/or Lady Chatterly in Hughes, D. A. *Perspectives on pornography*. New York: St. Martin's Press, Inc., 1970.

Miller, J. R. Testimony before House of Representatives Select Subcommittee on Education, Committee on Education and Labor. 90th Congress, 1st Session. Hearing on H.R. 2525, April 20 and 24, 1967, 15.

Miller, W. B. Lower class culture as a generating milieu of gang delinquency. *Journal of Social Issues*, 1958, *14*, 5-19.

Money, J. The positive and constructive approach to pornography in general sex education, in the home, and in sexological counseling. *Technical reports of the Commission on Obscenity and Pornography*. Vol. 10. Washington, D.C.: U.S. Government Printing Office, 1970.

Mosher, D. L., & Katz, H. Pornographic films, male verbal aggression against women and guilt. Unpublished manuscript, Commission files, 1970.

Mosher, D. L. Psychological reactions to pornographic films. *Technical* reports of the Commission on Obscenity and Pornography. Vol. 8. Washington, D.C.: U.S. Government Printing Office, 1970. (a)

Mosher, D. L. Sex callousness toward women. Technical reports of the Commission on Obscenity and Pornography. Vol. 8. Washington, D.C.: U.S. Government Printing Office, 1970. (b)

Mueller, G. O. W., Gage, M., & Kupperstein, L. R. The Legal norms of delinquency—a comparative study. Monograph Series Vol. 1, New York University School of Law, 1969.

Muhlen, N. Comic Books and Other Horrors: Prep School for totalitarian society? Commentary, Jan. 1949, 68(1), 80-87.

Mussen, P. H., & Scodel, A. The effects of sexual stimulation under varying conditions on TAT sexual responsiveness. Journal of Consulting Psychology, 1955, 19, 90.

National Council of Juvenile Court Judges, Resolution (1954). Cited in Clor, H. M. Obscenity and public morality. Chicago: University of Chicago Press, 1969.

Nawy, H. The San Francisco erotic marketplace. Technical reports of the Commission on Obscenity and Pornography. Vol. 4. Washington, D.C.: U.S. Government Printing Office, 1970.

Nix, Hon. R. N. C. Testimony before House of Representatives Subcommittee on Postal Operations, Committee on Post Office and Civil Services, 90th Congress, 1st. Session. Hearings on H.R. 426 and H.R. 8215, June 9, 1967, 35.

Nunnally, J. C., Knott, P. D., Duchnowski, A., Parker, R. Pupillary response as a general measure of activation. Perception and Psychophysics, 1967, 2, 149-155.

Paris, J., & Goodstein, L. D. Responses to death and sex stimulus materials as a function of repression-sensitization. Psychological Reports, 1966, 19, 1283-1291.

Polsky, N. Hustlers, beats and others. Chicago: Aldine, 1967.

President's Commission on Law Enforcement and the Administration of Justice, Task Force Report: Juvenile delinquency and youth crime. Washington, D.C.: U.S. Government Printing Office, 1967.

Propper, M. M. Exposure to sexually oriented materials among young male prison offenders. Technical reports of the Commission on Obscenity and Pornography. Vol. 9. Washington, D.C.: U.S. Government Printing Office, 1970.

Public Health Service, United States Department of Health, Education and Welfare. Trends in illegitimacy, United States—1940-1965. Washington, D.C.: U.S. Government Printing Office, 1968.

Public Health Service. United States Department of Health, Education and Welfare. Vital statistics of the United States. Vol. 1. Washington, D.C.: U.S. Government Printing Office, 1967.

Public Law 90-100, 90th Congress, October 3, 1967.

Orne, M. T. On the social psychology of the psychological experiment: With particular reference to demand characteristics and their implications. American Psychologist, 1962, 17, 776-783.

Ramsey, G. The sexual development of boys. American Journal of Psychology, 1943, 56, 217.

Reifler, C. B., Howard, J., Lipton, M. A., Liptzin, M. B., & Widmann, D. E. Pornography: An experimental study of effects. Presented at the American Psychiatric Association Annual Meeting, 1970.

Reinhardt, J. M. Sex perversion and sex crimes. Springfield, Illinois: Charles C. Thomas, 1957.

Legal considerations relating to erotica: The report of the Legal panel. In The report of the Commission on Obscenity and Pornography. Washington, D.C.: U.S. Government Printing Office, 1970.

Traffic and distribution of sexually oriented materials in the United States: The report of the traffic and distribution panel. In The report of the Commission on Obscenity and Pornography. Washington, D.C.: U.S. Government Printing Office, 1970.

Rosenthal, R. Experimenter effects in behavioral research. New York: Appleton-Century-Crofts, 1966.

Rosenthal, R. On the social psychology of the psychological experiment: The experimenter's hypothesis as unintended determinant of experimental results. American Scientist, 1963, 51, 268-283.

Sampson, J. J. Traffic and distribution of sexually oriented materials in the United States, 1969-1970. Technical reports of the Commission on

Obscenity and Pornography, Vol. 3. Washington, D.C.: U.S. Government Printing Office, 1970.

Schiller, P. The effects of mass media on the sexual behavior of adolescent females. *Technical reports of the Commission on Obscenity and Pornography,* Vol. 1. Washington, D.C.: U.S. Government Printing Office, 1970.

Schmidt, G., & Sigusch, V. Psychosexual stimulation by films and slides: a further report on sex differences, in press.

Schmidt, G., Sigusch, V., & Heyberg, U. Psychosexual stimulation in men: Emotional reactions, changes of sex behavior, and measures of conservative attitudes. *The Journal of Sex Research,* August 1969, *5(3),* 199-217.

Schramm, W. J. Lyle and E. B. Parker. *Television in the lives of our children.* Palo Alto, Cal.: Stanford University Press, 1961.

Senate Subcommittee to investigate Juvenile Delinquency of the Committee on the Judiciary, 84th Congress, 1st Session. *Juvenile delinquency: Obscene and pornographic materials.* Hearings pursuant to S. Res. 62, May 24, 26, 31 and June 9, 18, 1955.

Senate Subcommittee to Investigate Juvenile Delinquency, Committee on the Judiciary, 84th Congress, 2nd Session, on S. Res. 62 and S. Res. 178. *Interim report on obscene and pornographic literature.* Report no. 2381, 1956.

Senate Subcommittee to Investigate Juvenile Delinquency of the Committee on the Judiciary, 86th Congress, 1st and 2nd Sessions. Hearings on S. J. Res. 116, S. J. Res. 133. and S. 2562, August 29, September 9, November 12, 1959, and January 14, 1960.

Senate Subcommittee to Investigate Juvenile Delinquency of the Committee on the Judiciary, 89th Congress, 2nd Session, 90th Congress, 1st Session. Part 17, *Youth, obscene materials, and the United States mails,* Dec. 16, 1966 and Feb. 9, 1967.

Shayon, R. L. *Television and our children.* New York: Longmans, Green, 1951.

Sigusch, V., Schmidt, G., Reinfeld, R., & Weidemann-Sutor, I. Psychosexual stimulation: Sex differences. *The Journal of Sex Research,* February 1970, *6(1),* 10-24.

Slap, J. Testimony before the House of Representatives Subcommittee on Postal Operations, Committee on Post Office and Civil Services, 90th Congress, 1st Session. Hearing on H.R. 426 and H.R. 8215, June 9, 1967, p. 54.

Solyom, L., & Beck, P. R. GSR assessment of aberrant sexual behavior. *International Journal of Neuropsychiatry,* 1967, 3, 52-59.

Sonenschein, D. Pornography: A false issue. *Psychiatric Opinion,* 1969, 6, 11-18.

Steiner, G. Night words in Hughes, D. A. *Perspectives on pornography.* New York: St. Martin's Press, 1970.

Tannenbaum, P. H. Emotional arousal as a mediator of communication effects. *Technical reports of the Commission on Obscenity and Pornography.* Vol. 8. Washington, D.C.: U.S. Government Printing Office, 1970.

Thornberry, T. P., & Silverman, R. A. The relationship between exposure to pornography and juvenile delinquency as indicated by juvenile court records. *Technical reports of the Commission on Obscenity and Pornography.* Vol. 1. Washington, D.C.: U.S. Government Printing Office, 1970.

Thorne, F. C. *The sex inventory.* Brendon, Vermont: Psychological Associates, 1965.

Thorne, F. C., & Haupt, T. D. The objective measurement of sex attitudes and behavior. *Journal of Clinical Psychology,* 1966, *22,* 395-403.

Tynan, K. Dirty books can stay in Hughes, D. A. *Perspectives on pornography.* New York: St. Martin's Press, Inc., 1970.

van den Haag, E. Is pornography a cause of crime? *Encounter,* 1967, *29(6),* 52-56.

Van den Haag, E. Case for pornography/case for censorship in Hughes, D. A. *Perspectives on pornography.* New York: St. Martin's Press, 1970.

Von Bracken, H., & Schafers, F. Ueber die haltung von strafgefangenen zur literatur. *Zeitschrift fur Angelwandte Psychogie,* 1935, *49,* 169-207.

Walker, C. E. Erotic stimuli and the aggressive sexual offender. *Technical reports of the Commission on Obscenity and Pornography.* Vol. 7. Washington, D.C.: U.S. Government Printing Office, 1970.

Wallace, D., Wehmer, G., & Podany, E. Contemporary community standards of visual erotica. *Technical reports of the Commission on Obscenity and Pornography.* Vol. 9. Washington, D.C.: U.S. Government Printing Office, 1970.

Walters, R. H., Bowen, N. V., & Parke, R. D. Influence of looking behavior of a social model on subsequent looking behavior of observers of the model. *Perceptual and Motor Skills,* 1964, *18,* 469-483.

Waples, D., Berelson, B., & Bradshaw, F. *What reading does to people.* Chicago: University of Chicago Press, 1940.

Weiss, W. Effects of the mass media of communication. In Lindsey, G., & Aronson, E. (eds.) *The Handbook of social psychology.* Vol. 5 (2nd ed.). Reading, Mass.: Addison-Wesley, 1969.

Wenger, M. A., Averill, J. A., & Smith, D. D. B. Autonomic activity during sexual arousal. *Psychophysiology,* 1968, *4,* 468-478.

Wertham, F. Are comic books harmful to children? *Friends Intelligencer,* July 10, 1948.

Wertham, F. What are comic books? *National Parent-Teacher,* March, 1949.

Wertham, W. What do we know about mass media effects? *Corrective Psychiatry and Journal of Social Therapy,* Winter 1968, *14(4),* 196-199.

Wheeler, S. Sex offenses: A sociological critique. *Law and Contemporary Problems.* Spring 1960, *25(2),* 258-278.

Wilson, W. C., Horowitz, B., & Friedman, J. The gravity of the pornography situation and the problems of control: A survey of prosecuting attorneys. *Technical reports of the Commission on Obscenity and Pornography.* Vol. 2. Washington, D.C.: U.S. Government Printing Office, 1970.

Wilson, W. C., & Jacobs, S. Survey of sex educators and counselors. *Technical reports of the Commission on Obscenity and Pornography.* Vol. 10. Washington, D.C.: U.S. Government Printing Office, 1970.

Winick, C. A study of consumers of explicitly sexual materials: Some functions of adult movies. *Technical reports of the Commission on Obscenity and Pornography.* Vol. 4. Washington, D.C.: U.S. Government Printing Office, 1970.

Wolfe, K., & Fiske, M. The children tell about comics. In P. Lazarsfeld & F. Stanton (eds.) *Communications research, 1948-1949.* New York: Harper, 1949.

The World Almanac, 1970 Edition. New York: Newspaper Enterprise Association, 1970.

Zajonc, R.B. Attitudinal effects of mere exposure. *Journal of Personality and Social Psychology,* 1968, *8(2),* Part 2, 1-27.

Zamansky, H.S. A technique for assessing homosexual tendencies. *Journal of Personality,* 1956, *24,* 436-446.

Zetterberg, H. L. The consumers of pornography where it is easily available: The Swedish experience. *Technical reports of the Commission on Obscenity and Pornography.* Vol. 9. Washington, D.C.: U.S. Government Printing Office, 1970.

Zillman, D. Emotional arousal as a factor in communication—mediated aggressive behavior. Unpublished doctoral dissertation, University of Pennsylvania, 1969.

Zuckerman, M. Physiological measures of sexual arousal in the human. *Technical reports of the Commission on Obscenity and Pornography.* Vol. 1. Washington, D.C.: U.S. Government Printing Office, 1970.

Zurcher, L. A., & Kirkpatrick, R. G. The natural history of an *ad hoc* anti-pornography organization in Midville, U.S.A. *Technical reports of the Commission on Obscenity and Pornography.* Vol. 5. Washington, D.C.: U.S. Government Printing Office, 1970.

Section G

APPENDIX 1: ANNOTATED REFERENCES*

Abelson, H., Cohen, R., Heaton, E., & Slider, C. Public attitudes toward and experience with erotic materials. *Technical reports of the Commission on Obscenity and Pornography.* Vol. 6. Washintgon, D.C.: U.S. Government Printing Office, 1970.

Problem: To identify the amount, frequency, and circumstances of the public's exposure to erotic materials; to describe community standards

---

*The research *problem* and *method* of 39 Commission-funded studies cited in the Effects Panel Report are described here. For a detailed account of each study, see the *Technical reports of the Commission on Obscenity and Pornography.* Vols. 1-10. Washington, D.C.: U.S. Government Printing Office, 1970.

301

and norms pertaining to distribution, consumption, and control of erotica; to collect other relevant data concerning the correlates of exposure to erotic materials, and to identify the public's perceptions of the effects of exposure to erotic materials.

Method: A probability sample interview survey of 2,486 American adults over 20 and an additional sample of 769 young persons, 15 to 20. Face-to-face interviews were conducted in the 48 contiguous states during February, March, and April of 1970.

Amoroso, D. M., Brown, M., Pruesse, M., Ware, E. E., & Pilkey, D. W. An investigation of behavioral, psychological, and physiological reactions to pornographic stimuli. *Technical reports of the Commission on Obscenity and Pornography.* Vol. 8. Washington, D.C.: U.S. Government Printing Office, 1970.

Problem: To obtain subjective ratings of erotic slides and to assess the effect upon these ratings of social context of viewing, presence of physiological instrumentation, and order of presentation of the erotic stimuli.

Method: Ss were 60 male undergraduate students, 18 to 25, who viewed 27 color erotic slides. Each slide was rated on 11-point scales for "pornographic—not pornographic", "pleasant-unpleasant", and "sexually stimulating—not sexually stimulating". Half the Ss viewed slides alone, half in groups of five. Half of each of these was "wired" in simulation of physiological measurement. Slides were presented in three different orders over the groups. Attitude and behavioral data were obtained before exposure and one week atfer.

Ben-Veniste, R. Pornography and sex crime—the Danish experience. *Technical reports of the Commission on Obscenity and Pornography.* Vol. 7. Washington, D.C.: U.S. Government Printing Office, 1970.

Problem: To examine the statistical relationship between availability of erotic materials and the incidence of sex crimes in Copenhagen, Denmark for the 1958-1969 period.

Method: Refined sex crime data were obtained by reviewing over 9,000 police reports in Copenhagen. Estimates of the dissemination of erotic materials were developed with statistics furnished by producers of these materials through face-to-face interviews or self-administered questionnaires.

Berger, A. S., Gagnon, J. H., & Simon, W. Pornography: high shool and college years. *Technical reports of the Commission on Obscenity and Pornography.* Vol. 9. Washington, D.C.: U.S. Government Printing Office, 1970.

Problem: Through secondary data analysis, to analyze relationships between experience with erotic material and selected social and sexual behaviors among American college students.

Method: Data utilized were obtained in a national probability sample of full-time male and female undergraduates at four-year American colleges and universities during 1967 (sample stratified by year in school). Data based on 1,177 interviews with white students between 17 and 24; 593 males and 584 females.

Berger, A. S., Gagnon, J. H., & Simon, W. Urban working-class adolescents and sexually explicit media. *Technical reports of the Commission on Obscenity and Pornography.* Vol. 9. Washington, D.C.: U.S. Government Printing Office, 1970.

Problem: To describe the type, frequency, and amount of experience with erotic material and to examine the relationship between such experience and certain attitudes and sexual behaviors among working class adolescents.

Method: A self-administered questionnaire was completed in group sessions by a nonprobability sample of 473 working-class youth in Chicago. Youths ranged from 12 to 18, and the sample was obtained on an *ad hoc* basis through a YMCA agency and street corner workers.

Byrne, D., & Lamberth, J. The effect of erotic stimuli on sex arousal, evaluative responses, and subsequent behavior. *Technical reports of the Commission on Obscenity and Pornography.* Vol. 8. Washington, D.C.: U.S. Government Printing Office, 1970.

Problem: To explore the effects of identical erotic depictions presented in three different conditions upon sexual arousal, various evaluative and judgmental responses, and sexual behavior.

Method: Ss were 42 married couples who were assigned randomly to three experimental groups. One group viewed 19 erotic slides, a second group read 19 erotic stories, and a third group was asked to "imagine" each of 19 erotic depictions. Ss rated each depiction in terms of "sexually exciting",

302

"pornographic", and "restrictiveness". Inventories concerning emotional states and opinions about erotic material were administered before and after exposure. A followup questionnaire was completed one week after exposure.

Cairns, R. B. Psychological assumptions in sex censorship: an evaluative review of recent (1961-1968 research. *Technical reports of the Commission on Obscenity and Pornography*. Vol 1. Washington, D.C.: U.S. Government Printing Office, 1970.

An evaluative review of the psychological literature pertaining to the effects of exposure to erotic stimuli. Studies cited in *Psychological Abstracts* (1961-1968) and published in other relevant journals are discussed.

Cook, R. F., & Fosen, R. H. Pornography and the sex offender: patterns of exposure and immediate arousal effects of pornographic stimuli. *Technical reports of the Commission on Obscenity and Pornography*. Vol. 7. Washington, D.C.: U.S. Government Printing Office, 1970.

Problem: To compare patterns of experience with erotic materials and actual responses to such materials after controlled exposure of incarcerated sex offenders and incarcerated non-sex offenders.

Method: Matched samples of 63 sex offenders and 66 non-sex offenders viewed 26 color erotic photographic slides depicting heterosexual petting, coitus, and oral activities. Each slide was rated on a six-point "arousal" scale. Slides were presented either randomly or in a "story-line" sequence. All Ss were interviewed about the type and frequency of experience with erotic material during childhood. A follow-up questionnaire was completed during the 24 hours after exposure.

Davis, K. E., & Braucht, G. N. Reactions to viewing films of erotically realistic heterosexual behavior. *Technical reports of the Commission on Obscenity and Pornography* Vol. 8 Washington, D.C.: U.S. Government Printing Office, 1970.

Problem: To distinguish types of reactions to erotic film, utilizing post-experimental inventories and a pre-experimental survey of sexual history, attitudes and "moral character."

Method: Ss were 121 males, representing a range of socio-sexual background characteristics. Ss viewed three erotic films depicting heterosexual petting, coitus, and oral sexuality. After film-viewing, Ss completed a questionnaire pertaining to immediate emotional and sexual responses. Another questionnaire was completed 24 hours later.

Davis, K. E., & Braucht, G. N. Exposure to pornography, character, and sexual deviance: a retrospective survey. *Technical reports of the Commission on Obscenity and Pornography*. Vol. 7. Washington, D.C.: U.S. Government Printing Office, 1970.

Problem: To evaluate hypotheses about the impact of erotic stimuli upon moral character and deviant behavior by examining behavioral and attitudinal correlates of experience with such materials.

Method: Respondents were 365 males from eleven different natural groups including jail inmates, Mexican-American college students, Black college students, white fraternity members, conservative Protestant students, and Catholic seminarians. Scales were developed to measure amount and age of first exposure to erotic material and various dimensions of family and peer environments associated with deviant behavior.

Elias, J. E. Exposure to erotic materials in adolescence. *Technical reports of the Commission on Obscenity and Pornography*. Vol. 9. Washington, D.C.: U.S. Government Printing Office, 1970.

Problem: To describe the amount, type, and frequency of experience with erotic materials among high school students, and to describe the social and psychological circumstances of such experience.

Method: A probability sample of 405 high school students was drawn from a school district in a large midwestern city. Questions dealt with experience with erotic materials as well as with preferred and actual sources of sex information. A subsample was drawn for face-to-face interviews.

Finkelstein, M. M. The traffic in sex-oriented materials, part I: adult bookstores in Boston, Mass. *Technical Reports of the Commission on Obscenity and Pornography*. Vol. 4. Washington, D.C.: U.S. Government Printing Office, 1970.

Problem: To examine adult bookstore traffic in sex-oriented materials in Boston and to develop preliminary information concerning possible involvement of organized crime in distribution of such materials.

Method: Interviews with law enforcement officers, public officials, participants in bookstore traffic; examination of public business records; periodic onsite inspections of adult bookstores; review of arrest, court and probation records.

Goldstein, M. J., Kant, H. S., Judd, L. L., Rice, C. J. & Green, R. Exposure to pornography and sexual behavior in deviant and normal groups. *Technical reports of the Commission on Obscenity and Pornography.* Vol. 7. Washington, D.C., U.S. Government Printing Office, 1970.

Problem: To determine comparative frequency of adolescent and recent (prior year) exposure to erotic materials and the attitudinal and behavioral correlates among selected adult subpopulations.

Method: Data were gathered from a clinical research instrument administered to samples of institutionalized sex offenders (rapists and two groups of pedophiles), non-institutionalized sex deviates (homosexuals and transsexuals), pornography users (customers of adult book stores, patrons of "skin flick" movie theaters and persons whose names were on mailing lists and identified as having purchased 8 mm erotic movies), Black (a Black ghetto group and a Black middle-class group), and normal white community controls.

Howard, J. L., Reifler, C. B., & Liptzin, M. B., Effects of exposure to pornography. *Technical reports of the Commission on Obscenity and Pornography.* Vol. 8. Washington, D.C.: U.S. Government Printing Office, 1970.

Problem: To assess the effects of repeated exposure to erotic materials upon sexual arousal, interest in erotica, attitudes toward sexuality and erotic materials, and certain emotional responses.

Method: Ss (23 experimental and 9 control) were male college students, 21-23. Ss viewed two erotic films during two exposure sessions occurring five weeks apart. Prior to each exposure session Ss participated in a psychiatric interview and were administered various personality and sex history inventories. Experimental Ss, between the two films, participated in 15 90-minute sessions during which they had the opportunity to view and read additional erotic (or nonerotic) material. Various physiological measurements were obtained during the 15 daily sessions, and additional data were obtained from self-administered questionnaires.

Johnson, W. T., Kupperstein, L. & Peters, J. Sex offenders' experience with erotica. *Technical reports of the Commission on Obscenity and Ponography.* Vol. 7. Washington, D.C.: U.S. Government Printing Office, 1970.

Problem: To compare male sex offenders with an age-matched group of non-offender male adults from the general population with respect to experience with and attitudes toward erotic materials.

Method: Respondents were 47 probationary male sex offenders who were interviewed with a questionnaire identical to that used in a national survey (see Abelson, *et al.,* 1970). The sex offender sample included rapists, pedophiles, homosexuals, and exhibitionists.

Katzman, M. Photograph characteristics influencing the judgment of obscenity. *Technical reports of the Commission on Obscenity and Pornography.* Vol. 9. Washington, D.C.: U.S. Government Printing Office, 1970.

Problem: To determine the specific features of erotic photographs which are correlated with "obscenity" judgments.

Method: 90 photographs were rated on five-point scales for "obscene" and "sexually stimulating". From these ratings, 46 photograph characteristics were identified and a value for each characteristic was allocated to the photographs. These values were correlated with each photograph's overall "obscenity" score.

Katzman, M. The relationship of socioeconomic background to judgments of sexual stimulation and their correlation with judgments of obscenity. *Technical reports of the Commission on Obscenity and Pornography.* Vol. 9. Washington, D.C.: U.S. Government Printing Office, 1970.

Problem: To analyze data collected earlier on judgments of sexual stimulation; to compare sexual stimulation ratings of different educational and occupational groups, and to investigate correlations of judgments of sexual stimulation with obscenity judgments and make comparisons between different educational and occupational groups.

Method: Comparison of different educational and occupational groups on mean "sexual stimulation" scores by analysis of variance technique and comparison of educational groups on rankings of mean photo "obscenity" scores.

Kupperstein, L. The role of pornography in the etiology of juvenile delinquency: a review of the literature. *Technical reports of the Commission on Obscenity and Pornography*. Vol. 1. Washington, D.C.: U.S. Government Printing Office, 1970.

Problem: To answer the question: what do the major empirically-based studies of juvenile delinquency have to say about the relationship between exposure to pornography and juvenile delinquency.

Method: Review of seletced professional theoretical and research studies on delinquency causation.

Kupperstein, L. & Wilson, W. C. Erotica and antisocial behavior: an analysis of selected social indicator statistics. *Technical reports of the Commission on Obscenity and Pornography*. Vol. 7, Washington, D.C.: U.S. Government Printing Office, 1970.

Problem: To examine the statistical relationship between availability of erotic materials and the incidence of sex crimes and illegitimacy in the United States for the 1960-1969 period.

Method: Analysis of the sex crime data reported by the Federal Bureau of Investigation in its *Uniform Crime Reports* for the years 1960-1969, and of the illegitimacy data compiled by the United States Department of Health, Education and Welfare. Estimates of the dissemination of erotic materials were developed by the Commission.

Kutschinsky, B. The effect of pornography—an experiment on perception, attitudes, and behavior. *Technical reports of the Commission on Obscenity and Pornography*. Vol. 8. Washington, D.C.: U.S. Government Printing Office, 1970.

Problem: To assess the effects of exposure to erotic film, magazines and narratives upon sexual behavior and attitudes toward sex crimes.

Method: Ss were 70 sexually experienced Danish university students (42 males and 28 females), assigned randomly to three experimental groups differing in pretest-posttest measurement procedures. All Ss participated in a 90 minute "group" session in which two 15 minute films were viewed, 5 color picture magazines were distributed and examined, and an erotic narrative was read via loudspeaker.

Kutschinsky, B. Pornography in Denmark: studies of producers, sellers, and users. *Technical reports of the Commission on Obscenity and Pornography*. Vol. 4. Washington, D.C.: U.S. Goverment Printing Office, 1970.

Problem: To survey the nature and volume of erotic materials available in Copenhagen, Denmark and to ascertain the social characteristics of the buyers and users of such material.

Method: Face-to-face interviews were conducted with a large number of producers, wholesalers, and retailers of erotic material in the Copenhagen area. In addition, 30 "porn shops" were selected for observation which included the collection of data pertaining to amount and kind of sales as well as social characteristics of buyers.

Kutschinsky, B. Sex crimes and pornography in Copenhagen: a survey of attitudes. *Technical reports of the Commission on Obscenity and Pornography*. Vol. 7. Washington, D.C.: U.S. Government Printing Office, 1970.

Problem: To describe public attitudes about sex crimes and about reporting sex crimes in Copenhagen, Denmark for the purpose of ascertaining changes in these attitudes.

Method: A sample of 398 Copenhagen by two methods (a random sample stratified by marital status and a nonprobability "quota" sample). Face-to-face interviews were conducted by same-sex interviewers.

LoSciuto, L. Methodological report on a study of public attitudes toward and experience with erotic materials. *Technical reports of the Commission on Obscenity and Pornography*. Vol. 6. Washington, D.C.: U.S. Government Printing Office, 1970.

A technical discussion of the methodological procedures and problems involved in the Commission-funded national survey (see Abelson, *et al.*, 1970). Topics discussed include sampling procedures and sampling errors, field procedures, completion rates and an analysis of non-response, coding and editing procedures, and scale and index construction.

Mann, J. The experimental induction of sexual arousal. *Technical reports of the Commission on Obscenity and Pornography*. Vol. 1. Washington, D.C.: U.S. Government Printing Office, 1970.

A review of the psychological and social psychological literature pertaining to the experimental induction of human sexual arousal. Clinical implications of results and possible directions of future research are discussed.

305

Mann, J., Sidman, J. & Starr, S. Effects of erotic films on sexual behaviors of married couples. *Technical reports of the Commission on Obscenity and Pornography*. Vol. 8. Washington, D.C.: U.S. Government Printing Office, 1970.

Problem: To assess the effects of exposure to specific types of erotic films upon sexual and general marital behavior and upon sexual attitudes of married couples throughout a twelve week period.

Method: Ss were 85 couples, 40-50 years of age, married more than ten years. Ss were assigned randomly to four film viewing groups or a control group. All Ss recorded daily sexual activities with a mail-in log book for 84 consecutive days. After four weeks of recording daily activities (baseline phase), Ss were exposed to either erotic or nonerotic films, once a week for four weeks. Control group did not view films. After four weeks of exposure phase, Ss continued to record daily activities for an additional four weeks.

Massey, M. A marketing analysis of sex-oriented materials in Denver, Colorado, August 1969. *Technical reports of the Commission on Obscenity and Pornography*. Vol. 4. Washington, D.C.: U.S. Government Printing Office, 1970.

Problem: To collect and interpret information related to the marketing activities, environment and community climate directly related to sex-oriented materials in Denver, Colorado.

Method: Marketing analysis with emphasis on observation and interview techniques.

Mosher, D. L., & Katz, H. Pornographic films, male verbal aggression against women, and guilt. Unpublished manuscript, Commission files, 1970.

Problem: To explore whether sexual arousal from viewing a pornographic film increases the likelihood of verbal aggression against women and to assess the influence of guilt on verbal aggression against women.

Method: Ss were 120 male college students (volunteers) watched either pornographic or neutral films. Prior to viewing, base level of aggression was established. After viewing, half of the Ss were told that seeing a second film was contingent upon obtaining a high but unspecified level of aggression against a female confederate; the remaining Ss were simply asked to aggress a second time against the female assistant.

Mosher, D. L. Psychological reactions to pornographic films. *Technical reports of the Commission on Obscenity and Pornography*. Vol. 8. Washington, D.C.: U.S. Government Printing Office, 1970.

Problem: To investigate affective responses of college men and women to viewing erotic film as a function of the situation, past sexual histories, psychological maladjustment and sex guilt.

Method: Ss were 194 males and 183 females, freshman and sophomore college students. Various inventories were used to assess sexual experience prior to exposure, "sex guilt," maladjustment and various affective states (sexual arousal, anxiety, shame, guilt, and various sex attitudes). Ss were exposed to erotic films in same-sex groups of 30. Behavioral changes were assessed 24 hours after exposure and again two weeks later.

Mosher, D. L. Sex callousness toward women. *Technical reports of the Commission on Obscenity and Pornography*. Vol. 8. Washington, D.C.: U.S. Government Printing Office, 1970.

Problem: To develop a self-reported measure of sex calloused attitudes toward women and to relate it to reports of sex aggression and exploitation.

Method: 256 single, male college students completed newly constructed measure of sex calloused attitudes toward women as well as measures of guilt and sex experience. All measures were correlated with reported sex aggression and other exploitive tactics.

Nawy, H. The San Francisco marketplace. *Technical reports of the Commission on Obscenity and Pornography*. Vol. 4. Washington, D.C.: U.S. Government Printing Office, 1970.

Problem: To determine the nature and extent of the distribution of sex-oriented materials in San Francisco, and to describe and analyze the sociological and psychological attitudes, experiences and behavior of the consumer population of the San Francisco marketplace for erotic literature and films.

Method: Field observations (100% visual coverage of 6 out of 7 districts where sale of erotic materials is possible); interviews with bookstore owners and distributors, arcade managers and movie theater owners; collection of over 4700 detailed demographic observations of consumer popula-

306

tion in bookstores, arcades, and movie theaters; and in-depth questionnaires to random sample of bookstore and movie patrons.

Propper, M. M. Exposure to sexually oriented materials among young male prison offenders. *Technical reports of the Commission on Obscenity and Pornography*. Vol. 9. Washington, D.C.: U.S. Government Printing Office, 1970.

Problem: To determine experience with and attitudes toward erotic materials among a sample of youthful offenders (16 to 21 years) serving sentences in the reformatory of a large northeastern city.

Method: Ss were 476 incarcerated males. Data collected from a respondent questionnaire inquiring into experience with erotic materials, social and sexual attitudes and demographic background; a peer rating schedule inquiring into offender's character as judged by his peers; and oral interviews using the survey questionnaire developed specifically for the Commission by Abelson, *et al.*, 1970 (*supra.*).

Schiller, P. The effects of mass media on the sexual behavior of adolescent females. *Technical reports of the Commission on Obscenity and Pornography*. Vol. 1. Washington, D.C.: U.S. Government Printing Office, 1970.

Problem: To identify the various popular media which function as catalysts for evoking or reinforcing the "love theme"—and associated erotic feelings—among adolescent females, and to examine the ways and degree to which these stimuli affect their sexual behavior.

Method: The data were gathered from interviews and questionnaires administered to a group of inwed pregnant junior and senior high school age girls and a group of sophomores in a girls' junior college.

Tannenbaum, P. H. Emotional arousal as a mediator of communication effects. *Technical reports of the Commission on Obscenity and Pornography*. Vol. 8. Washington, D.C.: U.S. Government Printing Office, 1970.

Problem: To experimentally test a "theory" which postulates that increased physiological arousal, by whatever means it may be induced, leads to a heightened level of responsiveness—regardless of whatever response the individual is called upon to make.

Method: Several experiments, using college students as Ss were conducted in which different films (aggressive, erotic, humorous, neutral) were used to induce physiological arousal (measured by heart rate, systolic and diastolic blood pressure, skin temperature) and after which, Ss were asked by the E to make various responses ("aggressive," "helping," humorous, etc.).

Thornberry, T. P. & Silverman, R. A. The relationship between exposure to pornography and juvenile delinquency as indicated by juvenile court records. *Technical reports of the Commission on Obscenity and Pornography*. Vol. 1. Washington, D.C.: U.S. Government Printing Office, 1970.

Problem: To determine whether juvenile court records reflect, to any significant degree, the role of pornography in the commission of delinquent acts, particularly sex offenses, or in the personal or social maladjustment of the juvenile offender.

Method: Detailed examination of the juvenile court records of a sample (representative) of 436 delinquents brought to the attention of the Neuropsychiatric Division of a large, urban juvenile court in Eastern United States during the calendar year 1968.

Walker, C. E. Erotic stimuli and the aggressive sexual offender. *Technical reports of the Commission on Obscenity and Pornography*. Vol. 7. Washington. D.C.: U.S. Government Printing Office, 1970.

Problem: To provide information regarding the relationship between experience with erotic materials and sexual offenses.

Method: The basic procedure was to administer a structured interview and three psychological tests to seven groups of 30 respondents, including two groups of incarcerated aggressive sexual offenders, two matched groups of incarcerated nonsexual offenders, and three unmatched groups of college students and men's service club members.

Winick, C. A study of consumers of explicitly sexual materials: some functions of adult movies. *Technical reports of the Commission on Obscenity and Pornography*. Vol. 4. Washington, D. C.: U.S. Government Printing Office, 1970.

Problem: To study the characteristics of consumers of explicitly sexual materials, particularly adult movie theater patrons.

Method: A total of 100 interviews with patrons of heterosexual adult movies was conducted in New York (45), Chicago (15), Atlanta (20),

Kansas City (10), and Los Angeles (10). Respondents were men who had just viewed an adult movie.

Zetterberg, H. L. The consumers of pornography where it is easily available: the Swedish experience. *Technical reports of the Commission on Obscenity and Pornography*. Vol. 9. Washington, D.C.: U.S. Government Printing Office, 1970.

Problem: To describe attitudes toward erotic material and the correlates of these attitudes in Sweden.

Method: Through secondary analysis (of data obtained from a probability sample of 2,001 respondents, 18 to 60), a typology of attitudes about "pornography" was developed. Various other attitudinal constellations and patterns of social and sexual behavior were examined.

Zuckerman, M. Physiological measures of sexual arousal in the human. *Technical reports of the Commission on Obscenity and Pornography*. Vol. 1. Washington, D.C.: U.S. Government Printing Office, 1970.

A technical discussion of contemporary developments in the physiological measurement of human sexual arousal. Areas reviewed include skin potential and skin resistance, cardiovascular changes, respiration, penile erection measures, uterine contractions, temperature, pupillary response, and evoked cortical response.

Zurcher, L. A., & Kirkpatrick, R. G. The natural history of an *ad hoc* anti-pornography organization in Midville, U.S.A. *Technical reports of the Commission on Obscenity and Pornography*. Vol. 5. Washington, D.C.: U.S. Government Printing Office, 1970.

Problem: To document the natural history of an *ad hoc* anti-pornography organization.

Method: Descritpion. and review of anti-pornography activities in Midville from 1950-1969, the origins, growth and accomplishments of the anti-pornography organization, and the role of key participants and community formal organizations and agencies as they relate to the evolution of the *ad hoc* organization.

TABLE A

Approximate Sampling Tolerances
for Survey Percentages — Adults'
(95% Confidence Level)

	Sample Size	10% or 90%	20% or 80%	Percentage Near 30% or 70%	40% or 60%	50%
Total	2500	2%	3%	3%	3%	4%
Female	1500	2	3	3	3	3
	1200	2	3	3	4	5
	900	3	3	4	4	4
	600	3	4	5	5	5
	300	4	6	7	7	7
	100	8	10	12	12	13
Male	1000	3	4	4	4	4
	800	3	4	5	5	5
	600	3	5	5	6	6
	400	4	6	6	7	7
	200	6	8	9	10	10
	100	8	11	13	14	14

Source: LoSciuto, L., *et al.*, Methodological report on a study of public attitudes toward and experience with erotic materials. *Technical reports of the Commission on Obscenity and Pornography*. Vol. 6.

	Sample Size	10% or 90%	20% or 80%	Percentage Near 30% or 70%	40% or 60%	50%
Total	750	3%	4%	5%	5%	6%
Female	400	4	6	7	7	7
	300	5	7	8	8	9
	200	6	8	10	10	11
	100	9	12	14	15	15
	50	13	17	19	21	21
Male	350	¼4	6	7	7	7
	300	5	6	7	8	8
	200	6	8	9	9	9
	100	8	11	12	13	13
	50	11	15	17	18	19

Source: LoSciuto, L., *et al.*, Methodological report on a study of public attitudes toward and experience with erotic materials. *Technical reports of the Commission on Obscenity and Pornography.* Vol. 6.

III. POSITIVE APPOACHES: THE DEVELOPMENT OF HEALTHY ATTITUDES TOWARD SEXUALITY[1]

Report of the Positive Approaches Panel to the Commission on Obscenity and Pornography.

Commission Panel Members

Edward D. Greenwood—
    Chairman
Irving Lehrman
Cathryn A. Spelts
Frederick H. Wagman
William B. Lockhart—
    ex officio

Staff Members

Karen Green
Sylvia Jacobs
Bobbie J. Wallin
W. Cody Wilson—
    Executive Director and
    Director of Research

I. Introduction

Attitudes toward sex have varied from society to society and from era to era. Most societies have noted the presence of explicit sexual materials but reactions to such materials have varied considerably. Contemporary society is experiencing social innovations with extraordinary rapidity and undoubtedly the mass media play a substantial role in this, bombarding individuals with various kinds of stimuli, including the sexual. Perhaps never before has it seemed so important that society address itself to such questions as, "How should human sexuality be viewed?" "What attitudes should be taken toward explicit sexual materials?" and "What approaches are desirable in dealing with explicit sexual materials?"

One of the tasks assigned to the Commission on Obscenity and Pornography by Congress was "To recommend such legislative, administrative, or other advisable and appropriate action as the Commission deems necessary to regulate effectively the flow of such traffic, without in any way interfering with constitutional rights." While exploring alternatives to legislative and administrative action, the Positive Approaches Panel of the Commission on Obscenity and Pornography identified three areas for implementing this congressional mandate.

The first of these is an emphasis on healthy sexual attitudes through appropriate educational channels. Another is self-regulation by the communications industries, and yet another is action by organized groups of citizens.

Although there has been considerable public concern and much public discussion about obscenity and pornography during the past decade, very little consideration has been given to extra-legal approaches to the solution of the problem, and almost no empirical research evidence exists in this area. However, studies conducted for the Commission indicate that the public is supportive of this Positive Approaches position.

A national survey conducted by Abelson and his associates (1970) asked a representative sample of adults about several alternatives to legal control in the regulation of sexual materials. Nearly all (96%) approved of "parents teaching children what is good for them and what is not"; about three-quarters (76%) of the respondents approved of "librarians keeping objectionable materials off the shelves"; 76% approved of "instruction in school that teaches children what is good for them"; 72% approved of industry self-regulation; 72% approved of local boards of citizens from different walks of life keeping objectionable things out of the community; and nearly half (49%) approved of every person being allowed to decide for himself, as compared with 42% who disapproved. Women tended to approve all of these procedures more than did men.

Opinions varied as to whether laws would be more or less effective than these several alternatives: 49% felt that laws would be more effective, and 40% believed that laws would be less effective. Women preferred legal sanctions more than did men. On the whole, however, the positive, nonlegal approaches in dealing with explicit sexual materials received broader support from the sample than did the legal approaches.

II. Sex Education

A. BACKGROUND

Attitudes toward sexuality are developed in a social context. Although American society is experiencing a transition in relation to its attitudes toward sexuality, a great deal of ambivalence remains in these attitudes and there is confusion in the area of sexuality and its treatment. Sanctions still inhibit the open discussion of sex, particularly in the relationships between young people and their parents as well as between young people and other adults. Such communication tends in many cases to be limited, uncomfortable, and anxiety-provoking. In addition, many older persons do not possess adequate information about important aspects of sexuality, and as a consequence communication is further hampered. Embarrassment, uncertainty, and negative emotional responses to sexuality frequently determine the course of such discussions.

The fear of pornography felt by many people is a symptom of this confusion and ambivalence about sexuality. Exposure to pornography is thought to degrade moral values and to affect adversely sexual behavior and social behavior in general. It directly represents to many people the danger and the unpleasantness which is actually associated by them with sexual behavior, and indeed with the very concept of sexuality. It is the opinion of this Panel that only education can truly change the basic concepts which shroud sexuality with so many negative connotations. When a healthy and informed attitude toward sexuality exists, pornography is not a significant source of information about sexual behavior. Sex education, straightforward and adequate, begun in the home, continued in school, and supplemented by community agencies such as religious, medical, and other service institutions, can reduce interest in pornography as a source of information and can assist in developing a healthy attitude toward sexuality.

Sex education is thought to be necessary by young people, their parents, school administrators and teachers, and by the public in general. Yet adequate, reliable channels of sex information are not often available through which this information may be acquired in an open, positive manner. Most adults have had no formal sex education, and those young people who have taken sex education courses in school (less than 40%) find these courses inadequate. Young people also report that their parents have failed to give them adequate sex information; they feel that their parents themselves need instruction in that field. Most young people believe that they should learn about sex in school and that such instruction should begin early and continue through high school. Biological studies indicate that boys and girls enter pubescence earlier than formerly was the case, and, as a result, are aware of their sexual feelings earlier. It is highly desirable at this stage in their development that they receive straightforward information from their parents, from the school, and from qualified community agencies.

Lack of teacher preparation and opposition from conservative groups have hampered the implementation of sex education courses in many schools. Moreover, inadequate preparation of religious and medical personnel has limited their participation in programs of sex education. Finally, lack of information and embarrassment in discussing sexual matters also have prevented parents from communicating adequately with their children in this area. This creates a serious problem, since sex education in the schools should be supplementary to information and values transmitted in the home and in religious and medical contexts.

312

The need for early and adequate sex education was stressed by two groups of young people who discussed these issues with the Positive Approaches Panel. One group which met in Washington, D. C., was comprised of young people of a variety of ethnic and geographical backgrounds who were summer interns from the White House Conference on Children & Youth. The other group, which met in Los Angeles, was comprised of concerned college students, some of whom had been present at the Commission's West Coast hearings. These young people indicated that pornography was of little concern to them, while more "obscene" aspects of contemporary life such as violence, poverty, war, racial discrimination, etc., were the real problems faced by our society. They felt that it was primarily the adults rather than the young people who were concerned about explicit sexual materials. They were concerned, however, that sex education be an integral part of every young person's education, and that it be initiated early enough to help him deal with his various stages of psycho-sexual development.

A study by Offer (1969) defines the levels of sexual development that young people in high school and college experience, and suggests that as interest in the opposite sex begins to crystallize, attitudes are more important initially than overt sexual behavior. These developing attitudes must be based on accurate and complete information regarding sexuality if subsequent behavior is to be responsible and mature.

Sex education, then, must be expanded and more fully developed as an integral element of general health education to insure its adequacy to meet the needs of the whole community. Both parents and young people require adequate sources of reliable information, and the community should provide these sources through its trained personnel and institutions.

SOURCES OF INFORMATION ABOUT HUMAN SEXUALITY

The national survey (Abelson, et al., 1970)[2] asked people what they considered to be the best source of sex education. The data indicate that people are dissatisfied with the sources of information about sex that have been provided in the past. Parents were overwhelmingly preferred by both men and women as a desirable source of sex information for young people. Nearly 90% indicated the mother as a preferred source and 80% indicated the father as a preferred source. Sixty percent of the respondents named the family doctor as a pre-

313

ferred source of sex information and forty percent preferred the school as a source. Twenty-six percent named the church and books as preferred sources; whereas only 10% listed siblings and only five percent indicated friends as the preferred source.

Preferred sources contrast sharply, however, with the actual sources reported by these same people in the national survey. In actuality, friends were the principal source of sex information for 53% of the men and for 35% of the women. Mothers were an actual source of sex information for 46% of the women; but parents served as an actual source for only about a quarter of the men (25% of the men named their fathers and 18% listed their mothers). Only eight percent of the adult men and nine percent of the adult women indicated that the school had been an actual source of sex information.

Among adolescents surveyed regarding the actual sources of their sex information, 67% of the adolescent males and 59% of the adolescent females named friends. Fifty-four percent of the girls named their mothers as an actual source. On the other hand, 38% of adolescent males and 38% of the adolescent females noted that schools were an actual source of sex information for them. Considerably more young people in the survey named schools as a source of sex information than did the adults (38% versus eight and nine percent), thus reflecting changing attitudes and trends in sex education.

Regarding other sources of sex information, one-quarter of the boys and one-third of the girls gave books as a major source of sex information. Two other potential sources, clergy and physicians, were named by less than five percent of the adults and adolescents.

A survey of 342 sex educators and counselors (Wilson & Jacobs, 1970) showed that 72% of these professionals felt that friends about the same age were the principal source of sex information for adolescents. Seventy-two percent of those surveyed also indicated that this information was generally unsatisfactory.

EXPLICIT SEXUAL MATERIALS AS A SOURCE OF SEX INFORMATION

In view of the dissatisfaction with actual sources of sex education, the Panel felt that it would be fruitful to investigate the possibility of a relationship between sex education and exposure to pornography.

In fact, the findings indicate that exposure to explicit sexual material seems to occur in the context of conversation with friends in the general quest for sex information:

In the normal course of an adolescent's development, it would seem that exposure to pornography and learning new things about sex from explicit sexual materials and from one's friends is a common experience. The national survey inquired about people's exposure to ten kinds of explicit sexual depictions and descriptions. These ranged from nudity with sex organs showing through sexual intercourse, oral-genital activity, homosexual activity, to sadomasochistic activity in either pictorial or textual form. Of the adults, 84% of the males and 69% of the females reported having seen at least one of these depictions. More striking is the fact that 49% of the boys and 45% of the girls reported having seen at least five or more of these kinds of depictions. Friends were the principal source of these explicit sexual materials. Berger, Gagnon, and Simon (1970) also noted that exposure to explicit sexual materials or pornography appears to be part of socializing with friends. For example, they found that their adolescent respondents who date most frequently were substantially more likely than those who dated least frequently to have been exposed to a relatively large number of sexually explicit materials.

The data indicate that 1) most people learn about sex from their peers, and 2) exposure to pornography occurs within the context of the peer group.

The national survey investigated the possibility of a relationship between the extent of use of explicit sexual materials and the actual source of sex information. In the case of both sexes, there was, in fact, a relatively high proportion whose source of sex information had been friends or books, or both, and who also had been comparatively heavy users of explicit sexual materials.

The national survey also found the people whose major source of sex information was their parents were less likely to use explicit sexual materials; whereas people for whom friends about the same age were the major source of sex information were more likely to use explicit sexual materials.

The latter finding was also evident in the work done by Elias (1970). He found that the group who had frequent exposure to explicit sexual materials and who reported having learned a great deal about sex from peers of their sex was considerably larger than the group who had frequent exposure to explicit sexual materials but who learned little about sex from peers of their sex. Elias (1970) also found that in

315

the case of both male and female high school students, those who received sex information and education from their parents reported using explicit sexual materials or pornography less frequently than those who were given no information by their parents.

OPINIONS ABOUT PORNOGRAPHY AS A SOURCE OF
SEX INFORMATION

Sixty-two percent of the adult men surveyed in the national survey felt that explicit sexual materials could provide information about sex. And 43% of the adult men reported that explicit sex materials had provided information about sex either for themselves or for someone they had known personally.

Also, 60% of the women surveyed felt that explicit erotic materials could provide information about sex, and 35% of them said this was true for themselves or for someone they had known personally (Abelson, 1970).

Among young people, Berger, Gagnon, and Simon (1970) also investigated the possibility of an informational function of pornography and found that 47% of the 473 urban working class adolescents they interviewed reported that they had learned something new about sexuality from the explicit materials to which they had been exposed.

Winick (1970) also inquired into some of the functions served by adult movies as related by patrons of those movies. He reported that 56 out of 100 adult movie patrons interviewed reported the information function as a significant element in adult films.

In the opinion of most adults, especially most professional people, learning about sexuality; from friends of the same age or from pornographic or explicit sexual materials, may lead to misconceptions, myths and distortions, and is not the preferred or ideal way to learn about sex.

EXTENT OF FORMAL SEX EDUCATION IN THE UNITED STATES

SEX EDUCATION AS PREFERRED SOURCE OF SEX INFORMATION

Of the 342 sex educators and counselors who were asked about the relationship between sex education and pornography, 45% felt that sex education would provide a context that might prevent potential harmful effects of later exposure to pornography. Thirty-five percent felt that sex education would satisfy curiosity and reduce interest in pornography. On the other hand, 16% felt that sex education was not relevant to pornography and only two persons indicated a belief that sex information increased interest in pornography.

A survey of state departments of education conducted by Quality Educational Development, Inc. (1970) also asked about the potential impact of sex education on interest in pornography. Fifty-eight percent of the 35 state departments of education reported their belief that an effective sex education program would reduce interest in pornography; 30% said they did not know; and 12% felt that it would not.

Furthermore, the national survey showed that Americans generally endorse education as a way of regulating the traffic and distribution of pornography or explicit sexual materials. According to this survey 96% of adults approved of "parents teaching children what is good for them and what is not," and 76% approved of "instruction in school that teaches children what is good for them" as ways to regulate the traffic and distribution of explicit sexual materials. Forty percent of the sample thought such educational techniques by parents and schools would be as effective as legal means of regulating the traffic and distribution of explicit sexual materials.

CURRENT ATTITUDES TOWARD SEX EDUCATION
IN PUBLIC SCHOOLS

In practice, sex education courses in school are increasingly becoming prominent as sources of sex information. Whereas 10% of the 2,486 adults surveyed in the national sample (Abelson, 1970) indicated that they had such a course in school, 34% of the adolescent males and 44% of the adolescent females of the total 769 adolescents surveyed, reported having had such a course.

This trend toward delegating to schools some responsibility for sex education is approved by the majority of citizens in our country. Among the national survey sample 58% of the men stated they were for sex education in the public schools, 22% were opposed, and 13% qualified their support. Among the women 54% favored sex education in the public schools, 23% were opposed and 16% qualified their support. Approval of sex education was found to be more common among people in their 20's, among the college educated and among those with liberal sex attitudes. Over three-quarters of these groups

317

favored sex education in the public schools. Opposition was found to exist especially among those who were over 60, who had less than a high school education, and who had conservative sex attitudes. Less than 50% of these groups were in favor of sex education in the public schools.

Educators have also been found to favor the inclusion of sex education in public school curricula. The National Education Association (NEA Journal, 1965) surveyed a representative sample of public school teachers and reported that more than 79% favored sex education in the nation's high schools.[3]

CURRENT STATUS OF SEX EDUCATION PROGRAMS IN THE SCHOOLS

A study to evaluate the current status of sex education programs in the public schools of the United States was conducted by Quality Educational Development, Inc. (1970). When making inquiries at the state and local levels regarding sex education in the schools, several respondents asked whether the inquiries were sponsored by right wing organizations opposed to sex education, particularly the John Birch Society. Harassment from right wing organizations and from a vocal minority of conservative parents has in fact prevented effective implementation of sex education programs in many districts. The National Education Association reports that courses have been cancelled or suspended in 13 states as a result of such harassment. In March, 1970, the NEA published a booklet entitled, "Suggestions for Defense Against Extremist Attack: Sex Education in the Public Schools," as a guideline for districts under pressure to withdraw or not begin sex instruction in the schools. Usually, as the experiences of the Anaheim, California, and Nashville, Tennessee, school districts illustrate (where sex education programs were cancelled after harassment) attacks originate with extreme right wing organizations and take the form of associating sex education and its supporters with communist causes and with moral degeneracy. The resulting publicity causes school administrators great difficulty and embarrassment, and results in an unpleasant climate in which to try to improve sex education in the schools.

Bearing in mind these obstacles to the successful implementation of sex education programs in the public schools in many communities at present, it is not surprising that the study made by Quality Educational Development Inc. (June,

318

1970) revealed that the programs in existence throughout the country presently represent many different stages of development and adequacy. The survey of the current status of sex education in the public schools of the United States, undertaken by Quality Educational Development, Inc. (1970) for the Commission, elicited information from 35 states. The following data are based upon these replies.

The United States Office of Education, beginning in 1966, offers federal grants to schools, communities, and state agencies for the purpose of establishing or improving programs in sex and family life education. Funds available under Title III of the Elementary and Secondary Education Act of 1965 have provided support for program development and research at the state level since that time but state offices of education, frequently in conjunction with other state agencies such as health departments, have taken varying positions on sex education in their school systems. In a few instances, legislation has been introduced to eliminate or limit the teaching of sex education. Most legal attacks aimed at sex education programs, including those directed against specific materials, have been dismissed in the courts, but this situation has resulted in the withdrawal of some programs and has impeded the implementation of others as local administrators are hesitant to proceed in such an atmosphere.

On the other hand, fifteen of the 35 state departments of education responding to this survey reported that they actually provide curriculum guidelines for sex education programs for schools in their districts (12 of these 15 sent copies of their guidelines in response to the survey questionnaire); seven of the 35 reported that they have developed policy or position statements regarding the teaching of sex education in their states, and two reported that they are in the process of developing programs for their schools. Eleven of the 35 state departments of education reported that sex education programs are left completely to the discretion of local schools and communities. In short, 24 of the 35 states have developed guidelines or policy statements or are developing a program for their schools, and 11 have left the matter to local discretion. A variety of policies is also evident regarding student attendance in sex education programs. According to Quality Educational Development, Inc.'s findings, such attendance may be either at local option or by student choice, and in some cases no regulation regarding attendance is stated in the guideline.

Where sex education is given it is done, in every case, in

319

both elementary and high school, but it is almost always integrated into other courses rather than offered as a separate course. Some states report that no topics in the field of sexuality are excluded. Others specifically exclude controversial topics such as contraception, venereal disease, birth control, methods, and erotic techniques, or they limit the grade levels at which reproduction may be discussed.

Both state and local school organizations agree that an appropriate and adequate sex education program must encompass the following aspects: 1) The importance of community sentiment should be recognized and efforts made to tailor programs to community standards. (Seventy-three percent of those offering state programs indicated that parents are involved in the preparation.) 2) The need for adequate in-service teacher preparation in sex education should be stressed. 3) Sex education should be introduced in a family-living framework and should not be presented in an isolated fashion. 4) Provision should be made for a continuing evaluation of the programs.

The need for expanded, in-depth sex education has been recognized by such organizations as the National Congress of Parents and Teachers, The National Council of Churches, The American Medical Association, the National Education Association and the American Psychiatric Association, to name only a few. Commercially prepared educational materials, prepared under the supervision of professionals in medicine, psychology, and psychiatry, are sometimes used in conjunction with teacher-prepared materials to design a program appropriate for each community. National, federal, educational, health, and religious organizations offer assistance to communities and schools in establishing sex education programs.

EVALUATIONS OF PUBLIC SCHOOL SEX
EDUCATION PROGRAMS

Unfortunately, there is little empirical evidence available to evaluate the potential effectiveness of public school sex education programs. Kirkendall and Miles (1968) in a recent review of sex education research say ". . . one finds an amazing paucity of research on structure, content, and results. That which is available is for the most part simplistic and often narrow in scope. The questions are there but data for answering them often are not."

One attempt at such a systematic evaluation of public

320

school sex education programs was made by Nation's Schools, an educational journal, (1966) which surveyed a representative sample of school administrators to obtain information regarding national practices in sex education. Of the 43% of the school administrators who responded, only 37% reported that their schools provided sex education courses and only 53% of the latter felt that their programs were effective.

Regarding the possible influence of sex education on attitudes and behavior, some data are provided in one systematic behavioral study that was reported by Quality Educational Development, Inc. (1970).

The Keokuk, Iowa senior high school has taught a marriage and family course for many years. During the period 1947-1966, it was discovered the illegitimacy rate among girls who had taken the course was significantly lower than among girls who had not. A smilar study of the divorce rate among males from 1952 through 1964 also showed that significantly fewer males who had taken the course were divorced than those who had not.

Some studies have asked young people themselves to evaluate the effectiveness of public school sex education programs. One such study was reported by Byler, et al., (1969) in Teach Us What We Want To Know. This study surveyed 5,000 Connecticut school children from kindergarten through the 12th grade. The authors report that certain major topics of concern were common to all students, regardless of socio-economic and urban-rural differences. They found that young people felt they lacked an adequate vocabulary with which to discuss, directly and openly, their concerns about their bodily functions. Children in the lower grades expressed curiosity about their bodies and about the origin of babies. Beginning at grade five, interest was expressed in such topics as puberty, reproduction, sex relations, conception and birth, marriage and family role problems. From grade seven on, young people stated that they wanted to learn about additional topics such as premarital and extramarital sex relations, birth control and venereal disease, and they were especially concerned with values and standards associated with sexual behavior.

Ninth graders reported that most parents do not talk openly or honestly about sex. They advocated a strong program of sex education, beginning in the primary grades, to help young people understand one another. At the school level, students reported that they felt most parents had failed to give their children an adequate foundation in sex education

321

with which to guide their lives. These high school students felt that the school should supplement their knowledge. They also believed that the school should provide some sex education for parents as well as students. When asked to recommend an appropriate program in sex education for their schools, high school students reported that sex education should be taught in all grades and that parents should participate in the program.

Another evaluative study of public school sex education was reported by Seventeen magazine, July, 1970. Seventeen surveyed a representative sample of its subscribers, 1,500 adolescent girls between the ages of 13 and 19, on the topic of public school sex education. Ninety-eight percent of the girls surveyed were in favor of broader and more thorough sex education in the schools. They also felt that sex education courses in the schools should begin earlier than they presently do, that they should emphasize both the idealistic and the practical aspects of sexuality and that sex education courses should be taught without shame or embarrassment in the schools. More than three-quarters of the girls surveyed indicated that they felt that instruction in sex should not be left to mothers alone. The girls were also asked whether they were learning as much as they wished in their sex education courses about such topics as the physiology of reproduction, pregnancy, abortion, birth control methods and contraception, premarital ethics, loss of virginity, orgasm, impotence, male and female sexual drives, homosexuality, lesbianism, and masturbation. The answers indicated that there is a considerable gap between what the schools are presently teaching and what the students wish they would teach. Less than half of the girls responding in the survey indicated that they had ever been taught anything in school about premarital sexual ethics; only two-fifths had been taught anything about abortion, male homosexuality, or loss of virginity; and only about one-third had been taught anything on birth control, impotence, masturbation, perversions or orgasm. But on every one of these topics, anywhere from 78 to 90 percent of the girls surveyed felt that the object should be covered in sex education courses.

Two-thirds of the girls reported that their sex education courses had been incorporated into or made part of other courses in school, such as physiology, health education, and biology. They indicated a preference for sex education taught as a separate course, thereby eliminating the fragmentary

322

character of sex education when it is merely a part of other courses.

When asked whether they thought sex education would make young people want to experiment sexually, seven out of 10 girls replied that they did not believe that this would be a consequence. The major concern of the girls seemed to be directed toward mature and responsible sexual behavior based on adequate information regarding biological, emotional, and ethical factors.

STATUS OF PROFESSIONAL TRAINING IN SEX EDUCATION

LACK OF TRAINED SCHOOL TEACHERS

A common argument against offering sex education courses in the public schools in the United States today is the contention that few teachers are adequately prepared to teach this subject. Evaluations in this area reveal that this criticism tends to be valid. U. S. educators have widely endorsed sex and family living curricula as appropriate topics in public schools but our teacher training institutions infrequently include specific instruction in this area in their curricula.

Education, U.S.A. (Special Report: Sex Education in Schools, 1969) cites a survey conducted in 1967 by Malfetti and Rubin who found that only eight percent of the 250 teacher training institutions responding to the survey at that time offered specific courses for prospective teachers in the field of sex education. In addition, of the 229 institutions which did not offer sex education courses, only six had plans to offer such courses in the future.

Two other surveys that have been conducted more recently (1970) also revealed similar shortcomings in teacher training. The 342 sex educators and counselors surveyed by Wilson and Jacobs (1970) reported, for the most part, that they had received less than adequate formal training. Of the 342 educators responding 33% reported that they had had less than one course; 30% reported that they had had one or two courses; 19% reported that they had had three to five courses, and 14% reported that they had had more than five courses. Forty-two percent reported more than five weeks of training received in informal workshops and seminars; 16% reported three to five weeks of such training, 21% reported one to two weeks, and 18% reported less than one week of such informal training.

Quality Educational Development, Inc. (1970) surveyed

323

the curricula of a representative sample of 100 teacher training institutions, including private and small state schools as well as large universities, summer workshops and special programs. The results of this survey revealed that only 13% of these 100 teacher training institutions provided any kind of specific training for teachers of sex education at the elementary and high school levels.

They also gathered data on teacher preparation and training from questionnaires sent to 250 local school systems. The data, based upon a 50% return, indicated that most teachers are inadequately prepared to deal with sex education. Only 17% of the total number of local school systems responding reported any specific undergraduate or graduate training in sex and family living as part of their teachers' preparation. Fewer than one-third of the school systems reported their view their teachers were adequately prepared to teach sex education as a result of their having had courses in physical education or biology at teacher training institutions. Sex education courses are still infrequently offered, even in health education curricula, as part of standard undergraduate teacher training programs. In-service training seems to be the norm. Fifty percent of the local systems responding reported that in-service training was the primary source of preparation for their teachers and 61% of the local school systems responding reported that they make provision for in-service training programs for their teachers.

LACK OF TRAINED PHYSICIANS AND CLERGY

As noted in the national survey, the family doctor and clergyman, along with parents and schools, are also considered to be desirable sources of sex information for young people. Unfortunately, most members of both the medical and clerical professions have received little, if any, training in the area of human sexuality.

Regarding those in the medical profession, Vincent (1968) reported that a 1966 study by Sheppe and Hain revealed that first-year medical students, in spite of their premedical background, possessed no more sex information than first-year law students. After completing their medical education, fourth-year students did have more information about sex than senior law students, but they were still found to be lacking in adequate information in a number of significant areas related to human sexuality. Vincent reported that a frequent response to discussions of sexuality on the part of

324

medical students was one of anxiety. Another survey of 29 medical schools, representing about one-third of the medical colleges in the United States and Canada, conducted by Coombs (1968), revealed that only five of the medical schools out of the total 29 surveyed in the 1966-67 school year provided mandatory courses in human sexuality. Eight of the medical schools offered such courses as electives, and only four of the schools reported that they planned to offer such courses in the coming year. In most of the remaining 16 medical schools, approximately five to 20 hours of the entire medical curriculum were devoted to subjects relating to sexuality. However, a report by Lief in 1969 revealed that about half the medical schools in the United States and Canada were planning to introduce such material into the curriculm. The medical profession is obviously attempting to remedy this deficiency in training physicians. In the meantime, however, it remains true that too many practitioners are not adequately prepared to deal with their patients' emotional problems involving sex or to provide them with comprehensive sex information.

Most clergy are also inadequately prepared to provide sex information. Their training at the present time usually consists of instruction in the moral position taken by the church on sexual matters. Only infrequently does it deal with the practical aspects of sexual behavior that are of major concern to those seeking guidance. The climate of opinion, however, appears to be changing. Many religious organizations are becoming involved in serious debate regarding the changing moral standards evident in our society today, and some religious organizations are also becoming actively involved in the preparation and implementation of sex education programs in their communities. The National Council of Churches and the Episcopal, Methodist, and Congregational Churches have made available materials based on programs now being implemented with their help. The General Committee on Family Life of the United Methodist Church has provided its pastors and coordinators of family ministries with resource information regarding the Church's support of sex education in the schools and communities. It has also provided a comprehensive listing of national organizations that offer assistance to sex education programs. In particular, they have suggested ways in which churchmen can support sex education in the home, the church, the schools, and the community.

A recent development in the United States has been the

325

acceptance of a document by the General of the United Presbyterian Church which discusses such controversial areas of sexual behavior as masturbation, premarital and extramarital sexual behavior, homosexuality, and virginity in terms of their meaning for the individual, rather than from the viewpoint of a rigid moral code. It is likely that religious groups will begin to play a larger and more important role in the area of sex education in the future.

Three programs that represent striking departures from the traditional approach to sex education for professionals in medicine and religion are noteworthy, in that the use of erotic materials has been incorporated into the training programs. Two medical schools (Indiana University and Johns Hopkins School of Medicine) and one religiously affiliated training center (Glide Foundation of the Glide Methodist Church, San Francisco) have pioneered in the area of using explicit sexual materials to train professionals to deal with the area of human sexuality. The National Sex Forum of the Glide Foundation is presently conducting training courses for professional persons with specific interest in human sexuality. It has been in operation since October of 1968, and was developed to meet a longstanding need for objective, factual, comprehensive information, education, training and research on human sexuality. The materials used include a wide range of explicit sexual materials including films. These were developed instead of more traditional sex education materials because persons attending the Forum's courses indicated that they were more helpful. In a formal study (Glide Foundation 1970), five groups evaluated the Forum's training program: directors and ministers of Christian education; students in a social ethics class of a seminary; participants in a regularly scheduled Forum course for professional workers; students and faculty at Drake University; and students and advisors at the University of California. These groups were asked to evaluate three basic assumptions upon which the Forum bases its work: 1) the most significant factor in sex education is that sex can be talked about casually and non-judgmentally; 2) individuals should be allowed meaningful exposure to a realistic objectification of the range of behavior into which their own experiences and those of other humans fall; and 3) the person who teaches, counsels or gives advice (regardless of professional qualifications) should have a low burden of sexual guilt feelings in order to be of service to others rather than serving his own needs. Over 90% of the participants agreed with all of these assumptions. Participants were asked to evaluate separate aspects of the program in terms of how helpful they were to them. The multimedia approach used by the Forum in presenting its materials was ranked first, with 93% reporting that it was helpful. Historic and current sex action films, the setting of the room in which the course is conducted, and talking about sex freely and openly were ranked next, with over 80% reporting that these factors were helpful. Responses of persons who had attended the courses at an earlier date and had had time to reflect upon their experiences indicated that the films had helped them most. Ninety-six percent of all responses indicated that the explicit sex films had been helpful. The Forum's introductory course on human sexuality has been given in ten locations other than its headquarters in San Francisco where courses are conducted continuously, and has been sponsored primarily by church-related agencies such as urban training centers. The Forum's sex education materials are, in addition, currently being used independently by a group of American Lutheran Churchmen and by a practicing psychologist in the San Francisco area in training programs of their own.

The Indiana University Medical School also utilizes, in its curriculm, explicit sexual materials prepared by the Institute for Sex Research located at the University. Teachers at the medical school have demonstrated their teaching methods to other concerned groups, including the recent convention of the American Association of Sex Education and Counselors held in Washington, D. C. early in 1970.

The Johns Hopkins Medical School also has introduced the use of explicit sexual materials in an educational context. A detailed discussion regarding the program was prepared for the Commission by Dr. John Money (1970). Dr. Money teaches a course in human sexuality to freshmen medical students at Johns Hopkins, and has utilized explicit sexual materials in other educational contexts as well. He states that children learn not only factual content from their experiences but also the moral context in which that content must be considered. In regard to explicit sexual materials, Money states:

> The moral standard that we teach today's children regarding pornography is that it is dirty and forbidden. By default, we teach them that, if they learn about it, they must do so surreptitiously in secret, and then protect us adults from knowing that they know. The standard we impart is that the visual or narrative portrayal of all

327

eroticism is bad and forbidden—even the portrayal of what they will one day be required to accept as normal. . . . The sex education of minors already includes, behind the scenes, materials that either legal or conventional standards, today, qualify as indecent, obscene or pornographic. . . . Let us, therefore, be honest and bring these materials into the open for serious discussion, as a basis for moral guidance as to their proper place in preteen and teenaged life.

Dr. Money states that if exposure to explicit sexual materials first occurred in the home, parents could educate their children regarding the various aspects of these materials so that they would assume a rational perspective in relation to the children's sexuality, and could be utilized in terms of their educational potential. In connection with Dr. Money's use of explicit sexual materials in teaching medical students, he notes that the impact of explicit sexual materials upon people is considerably lessened after a few hours of exposure. He further states:

The medical school curriculum traditionally has included instruction in fertility, conception and childbirth, and in surgery of the sexual organs, but not in the sexual behavior of human beings. Even in psychiatry, where the physician is trained to listen to anything the patient has to disclose, there has been no direct training in human sexual behavior per se. In consequence, the majority of medical students graduated in the past were intellectually and emotionally unequipped to listen to their patients' talk about problems of sexual function and erotic adjustment. Such problems are more widespread than the layman imagines, and often lurk behind other, more "respectable" presenting symptoms in 25% or more of all complaints presented to the general practitioner. The physician needs to be trained to be emotionally composed and at ease, if he is to be able to be of maximum help to the patient with a sexual problem. The use of pornographic slides and movies proved to be completely successful in enabling medical students to "shake up the molecules of their thought" and to regroup and professionalize them—that is, to examine their preconceived attitudes toward sexual behavior and its aberrations, and to reformulate them professionally. They were then, by universal consent, better prepared to be expert in their approach to their first patients with sexual behavior disorders, and to help them. The use of pornographic

movies for teaching purposes is being pioneered in a
few medical schools across the country. The movies
used in my course at Johns Hopkins have been requested
for use in the teaching program at Harvard and at the
University of New South Wales, Australia . . . .

Pornography can be put to good use in the sex education
and counseling of individuals with birth defects and related disabilities of the genital organs, especially in cases
of doubt or anxiety concerning adequacy of appearance
and of ability to perform. Acquaintance with demonstrations of love-making and coital technique can improve the sexual happiness of many couples, not only
those whose relationship is impaired, sexually and otherwise, and who need special counseling.

Money also notes that explicit portrayals of anatomy and
techniques are not available except as erotica.

Apart from these special programs, which purposely stress
all aspects of human sexuality, the topic of human sexuality
is seldom covered adequately in the formal educational curricula to which most professionals are exposed during their
training. In fact, it appears that the most extensive training
available currently is still in the form of in-service programs
and special summer seminars held at educational institutions
throughout the country. During the summer of 1970, 47
training courses were announced by universities and colleges
in 24 states. This compares with 23 programs offered in
16 states in 1969, indicating the rapidly increasing interest
of professionals in learning more about human sexuality.

III. Industry Self-Regulation

A. BACKGROUND

Industry self-regulation can be effective if it is responsive
to community standards and remains flexible enough to reflect changes in those standards. It can be detrimental to
the artistic endeavor if it impairs creativity and limits the exploration of socially relevant themes. Most mass communication media do function under some kind of voluntary
industry self-regulation practiced by members of the industry
associations. These various self-regulation policies are concerned with the portrayal of sexual as well as other sen-

sitive themes. Self-regulation by industry may have a variety of aims, for example, to protect the specific industry from competition, to protect the consumer, or to protect the industry from threats of external regulation.

Most of the mass communication media attempt some sort of self-regulation, usually voluntary and intended both to protect consumers and to ward off external threats of control or censorship. The usual vehicle for self-regulation in the mass communication media is a voluntary code such as the Comic Magazine Code or the National Broadcasting Code. These usually specify the kinds of content that should be prohibited. In particular, concern is often focused on protecting children and adolescents from possible harmful effects of exposure to themes considered suitable only for adult consumption.

B. Comic Book Industries

The comic book industry has maintained an industry code since 1954 specifying standards that must be met by each issue of each member's publications. All material published by each member must be submitted for review prior to publication. Any material that deals with obscenity, nudity, horror, and excessive violence is not acceptable for publication. One hundred seventy-nine comics publishers (90% of the industry) are members of the Comics Magazine Association and adhere to the industry code. Very few complaints have come to public notice during the past decade concerning the sexual content of children's comic books and the industry has been commended for its vigilance in effective self-regulation by several national organizations, including the National Congress of Parents and Teachers and the Chamber of Commerce of the United States.

During the last year or so several publications have appeared which treat explicit sexual themes in a comic book format. These are somewhat reminiscent of the "eight pagers" of the 1920's and 1930's. They are circulated clandestinely and are not available in the same racks as children's comic magazines. This does illustrate one of the weaknesses of voluntary industry self-regulation, however; it is powerless in the face of noncompliance by nonmembers.

C. Broadcasting Industry

The National Association of Broadcasters has long maintained radio and television codes as guidelines and standards

330

against which all member stations are advised to review their programming and broadcasting practices. Circumspection is advised in dealing with adult themes. Profanity, obscenity, sexual material, and vulgarity are forbidden. Both codes stress that the broadcaster should develop programs which foster and promote the commonly accepted moral, social and ethical standards and ideals characteristic of American life. Both radio and television operate in a commercial system which causes them to be extremely responsive to what they interpret to be community sentiment regarding program content. The size of the audience is the crucial factor in determining sponsorship and whether a program remains on the air. The resulting quality of the programs has often been the focus of critics both within and without the industry who have pointed to the lowest common denominator appeal of the product as another weakness of industry self-regulation.

D. MOTION PICTURE INDUSTRY

The motion picture industry provides the most thoroughly documented case history of mass media industry self-regulation. Since its beginning, the industry has been the target of criticism directed at the sexual content and themes of motion pictures. Randall (1968) states that the first recorded protest against a movie was directed at Dolorita in the Passion Dance which appeared as a peepshow in Atlantic City two weeks after the introduction of Edison's new machine around the turn of the century.

From 1920 to 1950, the motion picture industry was dominated by the large studios, known in the trade as the "majors."[41] As a result of public criticism of the sexual content of many motion pictures, the Motion Picture Producers and Distributors Association (MPDAA, now the Motion Picture Association of America) was founded in the 1920's as a self-regulatory body. By 1934, renewed criticism led to the formation of the Production Code Administration (PCA), a quasi-independent agency. Since the PCA's code approval was required for a picture to be shown at a theater controlled by a "major," the Administration's approval became an economic as well as a moral necessity.

The PCA and the "majors" rigorously controlled the sexual content of motion pictures for about 20 years. However, the end of World War II signalled the beginning of a new era of turmoil and change in motion pictures which has continued to the present day. Great economic and social changes

331

have contributed to a relative decline in the industry. During this same period, there has been a corresponding increase in sexual content in movies. Among the factors that contributed to the change in the industry and in the sexual content of movies was an anti-trust decision in 1948[51] that forced the "majors" to divest themselves of control of theaters, and made it possible for an independent producer to defy the PCA.[61] During the 1950's, also, foreign films (which did not carry the PCA seal) began to attract American audiences in such large numbers that a regular foreign film circuit was established. Many of these films treated sexual topics in a manner not acceptable to the PCA.

A new attempt at self-regulation was instituted in November 1968, when a motion picture rating system under the joint sponsorship of the Motion Picture Association of America, the National Association of Theater Owners, and the International Film Importers and Distributors of America went into operation. This rating system was designed to inform potential consumers regarding the content of films and especially to inform parents as to the suitability of rated films for viewing by children and adolescents. A report evaluating the rating system was issued jointly by the Broadcasting and Film Commission of the National Council of Churches and the National Catholic Office for Motion Pictures after the system had been in operation for approximately 18 months. The report notes several areas of concern, including the validity of the ratings, the extent of public knowledge of the system, advertising practices, and enforcement of the system, especially at the box office. The Commission had already initiated studies into several of these areas of concern (Abelson, et al., 1970; Randall, 1970).

The rating system utilizes four categories: G indicates that the film is suitable for general audiences, including children of all ages; GP indicates that all ages are admitted to the film but parental guidance is suggested; R indicates that patrons under 17 years of age must be accompanied by a parent or guardian; and X indicates that no patron under 17 years of age will be admitted to the film.

A national survey carried out approximately 15 months after the initiation of the movie rating system (Abelson, et al., 1970) found that 75% of all adults over 21 had heard about this system of rating. Among adults under 40, nearly nine in ten claim to have heard of it. About two-thirds of the families who have children at home and who have

332

heard about the system report using the rating system to select movies for their children.

The regulations of the rating system require that all films produced or distributed by the members of the Motion Picture Association of America, including most of the large American production and distribution companies, be submitted to the MPAA Code and Rating Administration. From November 1968 to May 1970, the Code and Rating Administration had reviewed and rated a total of 655 films (Valenti, 1970). These films included 29% with a G rating, 40% with a GP rating, 26% with an R rating, and 6% with an X rating. These figures do not include self-rated X films. X is the only rating which may be applied by film proprietors to films produced by themselves or by nonmember companies which are not submitted to the MPAA for rating. Approximately 60% of the films rated so far have been released by member companies and approximately 40% by nonmember companies who have, nevertheless, submitted their films for rating. Randall (1970) reports that during the first 10 months of the rating system's operation 460 new feature films were listed in the trade press; 79% of these were rated by the MPAA and 21% were not rated. Randall (1970) estimates that approximately 93% of the exhibitions of feature films in the U. S. since the rating system has gone into effect have been rated by MPAA. Most of the unrated films apparently were minor films which had limited distribution and short runs. Sampson (1970) notes that there are two principal types of films which are not a part of the "general release" film industry. There are the so-called exploitation or "skin flick" films and the super-exploitation or sex art films, each of which has a special limited distribution system. The traffic and distribution section of the Commission Report deals with these categories in more detail.

Randall (1970) examined the percentages of rated films accounted for by exhibitions in 20 metropolitan areas and 20 smaller cities throughout the country during four sample periods in 1969. In the metropolitan areas rated films accounted for 93% of all exhibitions. These figures do not include self-rated X films; if these are included the percentages are 96% and 97%, respectively. The percentages of exhibitions in these cities accounted for by each rating category during the sample periods are: G, 38%; GP, 41%; R, 20%; and X, less than 2%.

Code approval is required for all advertising and publicity for rated films and such advertising is required to bear the

333

rating symbol. Randall (1970) also examined newspaper advertisements for theater exhibitions in the same 40 cities in the same sample periods. He found that of 16,831 advertisements 34% (not including self-rated X films) did not carry the rating symbols. Of those ads displaying ratings, two percent were in error, showing the wrong symbol. Randall also found that for ads carrying the rating, defects of size, placement, or readability rendered the symbol useless in 13% of the cases. Combined defects (missing rating, incorrect rating, visually defective rating) were apparent in 44% of all advertisements studied. Randall also gathered information regarding the display of rating symbols at theaters by observing 40 theaters in the metropolitan New York area during the summer of 1969. The rating and usually the age limits of admittance were displayed in the box office in 28 of these theaters. In four of the theaters the box office sign stated the age limit only. A large poster-sized sign explaining all of the ratings and the rating system was in evidence at nearly two-thirds of the theaters. Four theaters displayed the rating on the marquee, and one theater displayed an "adults only" sign on the marquee.

The MPAA maintains a special staff for the purpose of reviewing films for rating. The Code and Rating Administration is reputed to be specially cognizant of public opinion, and the rating system is sufficiently flexible to respond to public opinion. Several films have been recalled for a second consideration by the Code and Rating Administration after public outcry had indicated a lack of acceptance of the rating given the movie.

Randall (1970) conducted two separate inquiries comparing the MPAA ratings with outside opinions concerning the suitability for various audiences. In the first study, Randall obtained evaluations of the MPAA ratings given to 31 feature films from 260 newspaper movie editors in 46 states and the District of Columbia. Responses combined for the 31 films indicate that 70% of the evaluations agreed that the MPAA rating was the most appropriate one, in 17% it was felt that the MPAA rating was too restrictive, and in 12% that the MPAA rating was too permissive. In the second study, Randall compared the ratings given by the MPAA to all films rated during the first nine months of the rating system with those given to the same films by eight other agencies: The Dallas Motion Picture Classification Board; The Milwaukee Motion Picture Commission; The British Board of Film Censors; Film Reports (formerly the Green Sheet, a

publication of the Film Board of National Organizations);
Parents' Magazine; the National Catholic Office for Motion
Pictures; and the Southern California Motion Picture Council.
The classification categories of the several agencies are not
strictly comparable, of course. Nevertheless, Randall found
that the ratings given by these agencies to films already
rated by the MPAA were consistent with the MPAA rating
in 74% of the cases. Of the inconsistent ratings, 24% were
more restrictive than MPAA ratings, and two percent were
more permissive.

The eight agencies whose ratings were compared with
those of the MPAA represent a variety of interests ranging
from religious through organized-parental to public-govern-
mental. The degree of inconsistency between the MPAA
ratings and those of the independent agencies differed from
agency to agency. The greatest number of discrepancies in
ratings was found between the MPAA ratings and the ratings
of the National Catholic Office on Motion Pictures. Nearly
one-third of the ratings by this organization were inconsistent
with those of the MPAA. The greatest degree of consistency was found in comparing the MPAA ratings with those
of two municipal agencies which by nature should be more
representative of the wide range of viewpoints in society.
For example, only 13% of the Dallas Board's ratings were
inconsistent with those of the MPAA and in one-quarter of
the latter inconsistencies the MPAA was the more restrictive.

Randall (1970) felt that enforcement of the age restrictions on admission was the weakest link in the rating procedure. His conclusion is based on both observations of admission practices and interviews with theater personnel. A
trained observer directly observed the admission practices
for R and X films at 40 theaters in the metropolitan New
York area during July and August 1969. Observations were
made on all evenings of the week covering the time range
from 5:15 to 11:20 p.m. and on Sunday afternoons from
2:00 to 3:40 p.m., although most of the observing was done
between 7:00 and 9:00 p.m. Thirty-one of the theaters
were showing R films, two were showing films rated X by
the MPAA Code and Rating Office, and seven were showing
self-rated X films. The observer was stationed outside the
theaters where he could observe both the ticket-selling office and the doorman. He made judgments regarding the
customers' ages and recorded the theater's response to each
prospective customer whose age in his judgment was ques-

tionable. Four categories of questionable age were recorded: clearly under age; probably under age; marginal; and probably over minimum age. Three types of action by the theater were recorded: admitted without questioning; admitted after questioning; and not admitted after questioning.

Two hundred sixty-nine prospective customers were observed about whom the observer felt it was questionable whether they met minimum age requirements. Thirty-six of these were classified as clearly or probably under age, 107 as marginal, and 126 as probably over the minimum age. Of the thirty-six who were clearly or probably under age, half were admitted without questioning, and approximately a quarter were not admitted after questioning. Of the 107 who were judged marginal in age, nearly three-quarters were admitted without questioning, and about half of those who were questioned were admitted. Of the 126 who were judged to be probably over the minimum age, over 90% were admitted without questioning and all but one of the remaining 10% were admitted after questioning.

Enforcement of age limits was more rigorous for the X rated films than for the R rated films. All of the prospective patrons who were clearly under age were not admitted to the X films and one-sixth of those who appeared marginal in age were not admitted. The degree of enforcement of the age restrictions varied greatly, although at several theaters there was evidence of determined enforcement of the ratings.

Ticket sellers, doormen, and some managers were interviewed. Understanding of the rating system and the meaning of individual ratings are generally imperfect and often garbled on the part of ticket sellers and doormen. This is less often the case with respect to theater managers. The ticket sellers and doormen appeared to be uninterested, or inhibited, in the enforcement of age restrictions, and also appeared to be poorly instructed by the management regarding the rating system and enforcement policy. In general, the weakness of the enforcement of age restrictions on admission seems to lie in the motivation of the ticket sellers and doormen.

Drive-in theaters present special problems in enforcement of age restrictions on admittance, since the process of checking ages is so difficult in such theaters. In addition the delays occasioned by the cumbersome checking process causes waiting cars to back up on the highway at times and creates a potential hazard.

Randall (1970) indirectly observed a high level of "self-enforcement" of the age restrictions on admission to R and X rated movies—that is, underage persons did not usually attempt to enter the theaters. Accurate counts of all patrons were kept at 34 theaters; slightly over 3,100 patrons were observed. Only .8% fell into the "clearly under" category, .4% into the "probably under" category, 3.5% were in the "marginal" category, and 4.1% in the "probably over" category. Thus, few underage persons attempted to view these restricted movies.

Other research confirms some of Randall's (1970) observations of the enforcement of age restrictions. These studies have observed the patrons of "adult" movie theaters which show "skinflick" or "sexploitation" movies. These are outside of the MPAA system which deals with "general release" films. These "adult" movie houses apparently enforce their age restrictions very rigorously. There also appears to be a high degree of self-enforcement at these theaters since few underage patrons attempt to enter them. For example, Winick (1970a) observed 5,000 customers of adult movie theaters in nine different cities; only one or two persons who might have been under 18 years old were observed attempting to gain admission. And Nawy (1970) observed 2,791 customers at three 'adult theaters in San Francisco; very few potential customers appeared to be under 18 years old. Similar observations regarding enforcement of age restrictions by proprietors of adult book stores—and self-enforcement by youth—have been made by Massey (1970), Finkelstein (1970a), Nawy (1970), and Winick (1970a). In each case the proportion of possibly underage patrons observed entering the stores was less than one percent.

Randall (1970) reports that much of the motivation within the movie industry for the rating system derives from an interest in fending off possible governmental or other external censorship activities directed at movies. A similar motivation was found among the proprietors of adult bookstores and adult movie theaters (Massey, 1970; Finkelstein, 1970a; and Nawy, 1970).

337

IV. Citizen Action Groups

A. BACKGROUND

Citizen action groups formed to deal with the problem of pornography in their communities exist primarily in large cities rather than in small communities. This probably reflects the fact that explicit sexual materials are more likely to be available in large communities, and also that more opportunity exists in the large community for exposure without censure from a tightly organized peer structure.

Two studies completed for the Commission indicate that citizen action groups tend to attract as members socially and politically conservative individuals, those in the community who are more religiously and traditionally oriented, those who are older, and those who have had less formal education. The members of such groups tend to feel that they represent the sentiment of the entire community, even when they do not. Frequently they engage in activities that are more symbolic than utilitarian. Such groups can be a positive force in the community if they are truly representative of that community and if their goals are positive. Otherwise they can be damaging to the community, if, as sometimes is the case, they harass and intimidate merchants, thereby suppressing the distribution of legitimate materials in the community, or if they try to interfere with the decisions of professionals, such as librarians and school personnel, regarding suitable materials for the community and the schools.

The Commission feels that citizen action groups should always emphasize positive goals, such as promoting good reading materials for young people and cooperating in community efforts to implement sex education programs involving parents, school, religious, and medical personnel. These groups can most effectively achieve the goal of limiting interest in explicit sexual materials by contributing to community efforts to educate individuals about the socially approved, positive, and normal aspects of their sexuality.

B. EMPIRICAL STUDIES

The Commission staff conducted a national survey of prosecuting attorneys in the summer of 1969 (Wilson, Horowitz, & Friedman, 1970). A questionnaire was sent to 426 District Attorneys in a stratified random sample throughout the United States and to 306 Municipal Attorneys in the county seats of those counties with over 20,000 population in the sample. Two-thirds of the prosecuting attorneys returned the questionnaire.

The first question asked these prosecuting attorneys was, "Are the volume of traffic and pattern of distribution in obscene and pornographic materials within your jurisdiction sufficient to constitute a matter of serious concern in your community?" The weighted response to this question indicates that fewer than one-third (27%) of the District Attorneys in the nation would answer affirmatively. The reason for this perhaps surprising result is to be found in another result of the survey: obscenity and pornography are much more likely to be reported as constituting a matter of serious concern in the community by district attorneys from more heavily populated counties than by district attorneys from counties with small populations. The survey indicates that whereas 72% (96 of 132) of the district attorneys from counties with populations over 100,000 would say, "Yes, it is a matter of serious concern," only 23% (40 out of 163) of district attorneys from counties with populations less than 100,000 would so reply.

What it is about the size of the community that makes such a tremendous difference in whether or not the volume of traffic and patterns of distribution of obscene and pornographic materials constitute a matter of serious concern is only speculative. It is probable that a certain density of population is required for a sufficiently large number of customers for erotic materials to exist before the distribution of these materials becomes profitable. It is also probable that informal sanction systems that operate successfully in smaller communities break down in the large urban complex.

The smaller a community is, the more homogeneous and less pluralistic it is likely to be in terms of values, attitudes, and norms for behavior. A much larger proportion of a smaller community, as compared with a larger one, is likely to be linked in a network of personal acquaintance. The value structure of smaller communities is also more likely to reflect the values of traditional Christianity. Thus, it is probable that there is less liklihood of the development in a small community of a pattern either of using or of supplying erotic materials. The pressure of opposition from the total acquain-

339

tance structure keeps both the potential consumer and the potential supplier very much in line. In larger communities the acquaintance structure breaks down because of the sheer weight of numbers. Smaller subcommunities develop which can nourish a variety of different values, attitudes, and behavior norms. A single value structure can no longer be enforced by the threat of exclusion from the single acquaintance structure. A single dominant viewpoint can no longer enforce its values, attitudes, and norms on the community by means of informal sanction systems. The threat of exclusion from a monolithic social structure, based on ties of personal acquaintance, is not valid in a larger community.

It is likely, on the basis of this analysis, that organized citizen action groups to deal with problems of obscenity and pornography would be active primarily in situations where informal sanctions no longer operate successfully in controlling behavior related to these materials—that is, in large cities and in communities where the traffic in these materials is perceived to be on the increase.

The results of the national survey of prosecuting attorneys (Wilson, et al., 1970) support this hypothesis. This survey asked each attorney if a citizens group organized for the purpose of dealing with obscenity and pornography had been active in his community during the past three years. Whereas 80% of the district attorneys from counties with populations larger than 500,000 reported that such a group had been active in their communities, an affirmative reply was received from only 46% of the counties with populations between 100,000 and 500,000, from 20% of the counties with populations of 20,000 to 100,000, and from only four percent of the counties with less than 20,000 population. A similar relationship was found between the presence of a citizens action group and the perception of the traffic in obscenity and pornography as a matter of serious concern in the community.

An intensive analysis (Zurcher & Kirkpatrick, 1970) of two ad hoc citizens action groups is consistent with the idea that these groups organize to exert more overt and formal social influences when informal sanction systems become ineffective. The authors interpret the actions of these groups and the motives of the members as an attempt to reinforce and reinstate value systems and behavioral norms which are perceived to be in danger of eroding away. Because a number of people will no longer voluntarily subscribe to the system and conform to the norms under the pressure

340

of informal sanctions, an attempt is made to arouse the community to a reaffirmation of its values and norms in this area and to formalize them with new external sanction systems, usually in the form of laws or prosecutions.

Zurcher and Kirkpatrick (1970) analyzed the development of two ad hoc anti-pornography organizations, one in the Midwest and the other in the Southwest, as cases of collective behavior. They find confirmation for the idea that the development and functioning of these organizations manifested dynamics, stages and elements that characterize other collective behavior movements. They also collected data on demographic and value variables for a sample of active participants in the two ad hoc anti-pornography organizations and for a sample of the people they felt were opposed to their actions. The opposition was not very well organized in either case and tended to be motivated principally by a civil libertarian viewpoint. Those who were actively engaged in anti-pornography organizations, in comparison with those who tended to oppose the activities of these organizations, were more likely to be reared in rural communities, older, religiously active, family oriented, politically conservative, traditional, and restrictive in their sexual attitudes. They were also more likely to score higher on scales of authoritarianism and dogmatism, and to be intolerant of individuals whose political views differed from their own. Both of the groups were principally middle-class and both tended to be relatively active politically and socially.

These characteristics are likely to hold more generally. The national survey found that persons in favor of restricting the availability of erotic materials, in comparison with persons not favoring restricting their availability, were more likely to be older, less educated, more frequent and regular in church attendance, conservative on other issues, and less tolerant of freedom of expression, generally.

Evaluating the success of an ad hoc anti-pornography organization may be a relatively difficult task because the goals tend to be amorphous and ill-defined. Zurcher and Cushing (1970) report that in one of the citizens groups they observed, the leader of the organization spent a great deal of effort in maintaining a single delimited focus for the organization's effort—the passing of new legislation regarding the attendance of minors at movies with explicit sexual content. In maintaining this narrow and specific focus, he lost a number of potential participants in the organization but he faciliated the accomplishment of the specific goal.

341

Zurcher's observations indicate that the practical effect on the availability of erotica in the community was minimal, however. In the other citizens group that was observed the goals were so nonspecific that it was impossible to make evaluations regarding achievement. The anti-pornography organization created operating difficulties for the principal target, an adult bookstore, but the availability of erotica and the distribution of such materials probably increased during the period when the anti-pornography organization existed. This organization also was instrumental in the passage of local legislation which later was declared unconstitutional.

The national survey of prosecuting attorneys (Wilson, et al., 1970) reveals that district attorneys are quite divided in their opinions regarding the helpfulness of citizen action groups to law enforcement. Sixty percent of the district attorneys felt that such groups are helpful and 40% felt that they are not. The key factor in the district attorneys' opinions regarding helpfulness is not whether there is a problem in the community but whether the citizens action group is representative of the total community. The more representative of the total community, the more likely is the group to be judged helpful. Twenty-three percent of the district attorneys who have experience with citizen action groups report that the group in their community is very representative of the opinion held in the community, 56% report the group to be only fairly representative, and 21% report the group to be not very representative of community opinion. The responses of municipal attorneys are similar to those of the district attorneys except that they report the citizen action groups to be less representative of the community and less helpful in law enforcement. The prosecuting attorneys report that citizen groups can be helpful in locating and reporting violators, influencing merchants in the direction of self-regulation, and alerting the community to the problem. They also report that such groups sometimes hinder law enforcement by not knowing what the law is, by pressing for action that is illegal, and by over-zealousness and attempting to impose their standards on the community.

The issues of representatives and of imposing a minority opinion on the total community are very difficult to deal with because perception tends to be selective. Zurcher and Kirkpatrick (1970) report that the members of ad hoc anti-pornography organizations tend to feel that there is widespread community support for their position and to

342

dismiss people who do not agree with them as not representative of the real community. Abelson and his colleagues (1970) report general misperceptions nationally. Although there is actually a good deal of diversity of opinion regarding erotic materials, individuals who want the most restrictions on availability generally think that others in the community want about the same degree of restriction that they themselves do. The actual national distribution of attitudes toward availability and control of explicit sexual materials is as follows: permissive even if the materials are harmful, seven percent; permissive if the materials are not harmful, 23%; restrictive only if the materials are harmful, 21%; restrictive even if the materials are not harmful, 35% and unclassifiable, 14%.

One further point needs to be made regarding the effectiveness of citizen action groups. Zurcher and Kirpatrick (1970) conclude that many, if not most, of the accomplishments of the two ad hoc anti-pornography organizations that they observed were symbolic rather than utilitarian. The groups' activities did not materially influence the availability of erotic materials in their commmunities and the authors conclude that it appeared to be more important to demonstrate belief in, and support of, a specific set of basic values, to have a large number of others join in that demonstration, and to have the demonstration recognized by prestigious members of the community than to implement restrictions which would effectively eliminate the problem of pornography.

In summary, citizen action groups typically arise in situations where voluntary compliance and informal sanction systems are no longer effective in controlling the flow of explicit sexual materials. They are effective to the extent to which they genuinely reflect the opinion of the larger community and undertake specific, well-defined and delimited goals. They act as community censors to the extent that they bring pressure to bear upon retail outlets. This can result in the suppression of legitimate materials which are thereby denied to the entire community. The desirable strategy for citizen action groups should be persuasion rather than coercion.

The Positive Approaches Panel recommends:
The Continuation of Research in the Area of Human Sexuality. The research sponsored by the Commission is an important beginning but by no means constitutes a defini-

343

tive statement. It is hoped that the Commission has helped to validate this area of study and that others will continue to seek new avenues for obtaining information.

The Development and Improvement of Viable Alternatives to Increased Legal Control. It is felt that current nonlegal approaches, such as sex education, industry self-regulation, and organized citizen groups (which have a positive purpose, such as promoting good sex education or encouraging good reading), can be effective if properly implemented. There is and will be, however, a continuing need for new and constructive positive steps in the future. It is hoped that such proposals will be accepted and acted upon with an open mind.

The Panel feels that the implementation of these recommendations will increase knowledge of human sexuality, resulting in a more informed citizenry. Such positive approaches can reduce ignorance and fear and can increase the possibilities for a healthy society.

NOTES

1. This report is based on detailed data which appear in full in the Commission's Technical Reports.
2. Hereinafter referred to as the national survey.
3. In Sweden, where attitudes toward sexuality are much more liberal and pornography is minimally restricted, sex education programs in the public schools have been offered for quite some time. Zetterberg (1970) reports that since 1956 all Swedish schools have been required to provide sex education, and that the Swedish government is involved in family education through state-supported adult education programs. Sex education in public schools is favored by 86% of the Swedish population, and a 1968 survey revealed that 98% of the students completing the last compulsory grade of their education at age 16 had received sex education.
4. These companies not only produced most of the motion pictures, but also controlled the theaters in which they were shown. Today, the "majors" are Allied Artists, Avco Embassy, Columbia, MGM, Paramount, 20th Century Fox, United Artists, Universal, and Warner Brothers. Five other large companies (American International, Buena Vista, Cinerama, Commonwealth, and National General) operate in the same manner as the "majors."
5. *United States* v. *Paramount Pictures,* 334 U.S. 131 (1948).
6. In 1953, a picture entitled *The Moon is Blue* was denied the PCA seal of approval because of its treatment of adultery. The industry believed the picture was economically doomed because no one would exhibit it. The skeptics were proven wrong, however; the picture grossed over $6 million on a $450,000 investment.

REFERENCES

Abelson, H., Cohen, R., Heaton, E., & Slider, C. Public attitudes toward and experience with erotic materials. *Technical reports of the Commission on Obscenity and Pornography.* Vol. 6. Washington, D.C.: U.S. Government Printing Office, 1970.

Berger, A. S., Gagnon, J. H., & Simon, W. Pornography: high school and college years. *Technical reports of the Commission on Obscenity and Por-*

344

nography. Vol. 9. Washington, D.C.: U.S. Government Printing Office, 1970 (a).

Berger, A. S., Gagnon, J. H., & Simon, W. Urban working-class adolescents and sexually explicit media. *Technical reports of the Commission on Obscenity and Pornography.* Vol. 9. Washington, D.C.: U.S. Government Printing Office, 1970(b).

Byler, R., Lewis, G., & Totman, R. *Teach us what we want to know.* Published for the Connecticut State Board of Education by the Mental Health Materials Center, Inc. New York, 1969.

Coombs, R. H. Sex education in American medical colleges, in C. E. Vincent (ed.) *Human sexuality in medical education and practice,* 1968.

Elias, J. E. Exposure to erotic materials in adolescence. *Technical reports of the Commission on Obscenity and Pornography.* Vol. 9. Washington, D.C.: U.S. Government Printing Office, 1970.

Finkelstein, M. M. The traffic in sex-oriented materials, part I: adult bookstores in Boston, Mass. *Technical reports of the Commission on Obscenity and Pornography.* Vol. 4. Washington, D.C.: U.S. Government Printing Office, 1970.

Glide Foundation, Effects of erotic stimuli used in national sex forum training courses in human sexuality. *Technical reports of the Commission on Obscenity and Pornography.* Vol. 10. Washington, D.C.: U.S. Government Printing Office, 1970.

Kirkendall, L. A., & Miles, G. J. Sex education research. *Review of Educational Research,* Dec., 1968.

Lief, H. I. Sex education of medical students and doctors, in C. E. Vincent (ed.) *Human sexuality in medical education and practice,* 1968.

Massey, M. A marketing analysis of sex-oriented materials in Denver, Colorado, August 1969. *Technical reports of the Commission on Obscenity and Pornography.* Vol. 4. Washington, D.C.: U.S. Government Printing Office, 1970.

Money, J. The positive and constructive approach to pornography in general sex education, in the home, and in sexological counseling. *Technical reports of the Commission on Obscenity and Pornography.* Vol. 10. Washington, D.C.: U.S. Government Printing Office, 1970.

Nawy, H. The San Francisco erotic marketplace. *Technical reports of the Commission on Obscenity and Pornography.* Vol. 4. Washington, D.C.: U.S. Government Printing Office, 1970.

Offer, D. Sex and the normal adolescent. Paper presented at the 46th Annual Meeting of the American Orthopsychiatric Assoc., New York, April 2, 1969.

Quality Educational Development, Inc. Sex education programs in the public schools of the United States. *Technical reports of the Commission on Obscenity and Pornography,* Vol. 10. Washington, D.C.: U.S. Government Printing Office, 1970.

Randall, R. S. Classification by the motion picture industry. *Technical reports of the Commission on Obscenity and Pornography.* Vol. 10. Washington D.C.: U.S. Government Printing Office, 1970.

Sampson, J. J. Traffic and Distribution of sexually oriented materials in the United States, 1969-70. *Technical reports of the Commission on Obscenity and Pornography.* Vol. 3. Washington, D.C.: U.S. Government Printing Office, 1970.

Vincent, C. E. *Human sexuality in medical education and practice.* Charles C Thomas: Springfield, Ill., 1968.

Winick, C. A study of consumers of explicitly sexual materials: some functions served by adult movies. *Technical reports of the Commission on Obscenity and Pornography.* Vol. 4. Washington, D.C.: U.S. Government Printing Office, 1970.

Winick, C. Some observations on characteristics of patrons of adult theaters and bookstores. *Technical Reports of the Commission on Obscenity and Pornography.* Vol. 4. Washington, D.C.: U.S. Government Printing Office, 1970.

Wilson, W. C., Horowitz, B., & Friedman, J. The gravity of the pornography situation and the problems of control. *Technical reports of the Commission on Obscenity and Pornography.* Vol. 2. Washington, D.C.: U.S. Government Printing Office, 1970.

Wilson, W. C., & Jacobs, S. Survey of sex educators and counselors. *Technical reports of the Commission on Obscenity and Pornography.* Vol. 10. Washington, D.C.: U.S. Government Printing Office, 1970.

Zurcher, L. A., & Bowman, C. K. The natural history of an ad hoc anti-

345

pornography organization in Southtown, U.S.A. *Technical Reports of the Commission on Obscenity and Pornography.* Vol. 5. Washington, D.C.: U.S. Government Printing Office, 1970.

Zurcher, L. A., & Cushing, R. G. Some individual characteristics of participants in ad hoc anti-pornography organizations. *Technical reports of the Commission on Obscenity and Pornography.* Vol. 5. Washington, D.C.: U.S. Government Printing Office, 1970.

Zurcher, L. A., & Kirkpatrick, R. G. The natural history of an ad hoc anti-pornography organization in Midville, U.S.A. *Technical Reports of the Commission on Obscenity and Pornography.* Vol. 5. Washington, D.C.: U.S. Government Printing Office, 1970.

Zurcher, L. A., & Kirkpatrick, R. G. Collective dynamics of ad hoc anti-pornography organizations. *Technical reports of the Commission on Obscenity and Pornography.* Vol. 5. Washington, D.C.: U.S. Government Printing Office, 1970.

IV. LEGAL CONSIDERATIONS RELATING TO EROTICA

Report of the Legal Panel to the Commission on Obscenity and Pornography.

Commission Panel Members
Thomas D. Gill - Chairman
Morton A. Hill
Barbara Scott
Kenneth B. Keating - Resigned
   June 1969
William B. Lockhart - ex officio

Staff Members
Paul Bender
Jane Friedman
W. Cody Wilson - Executive
   Director and Director of
   Research

Introduction

Public Law 90-100 directed the Commission, "with the aid of leading constitutional law authorities, to analyze the laws pertaining to the control of obscenity and pornography; and to evaluate and recommend definitions of obscenity and pornography." The Commission was also directed "to recommend such legislative . . . action as the Commission deems necessary to regulate effectively the flow of such traffic [in obscenity and pornography] without in any way interfering with constitutional rights."

The Congressionally assigned tasks of analyzing existing obscenity laws, evaluating and recommending definitions of

346

obscenity and exploring constitutional limitations were assigned by the Commission to its Legal Panel in the first instance. The Panel also decided to study the actual present enforcement of obscenity laws and the problems connected therewith, the history of obscenity legislation, and obscenity legislation in other countries. Finally, the Panel believed it appropriate to set out for the Commission's use a discussion of the legal factors relevant to the Commission's task of recommending appropriate legislative action.

Much of the investigation and research within the Legal Panel's concern was done by the Commission's legal staff, which analyzed existing laws, studied their enforcement, and reported to the Panel on constitutional and definitional considerations. In addition, the Panel drew significantly upon several outside sources. With regard to the definitional and constitutional problems before it, the Panel retained four legal consultants who reported to it, and sent a detailed letter of inquiry to several hundred professors of constitutional law in United States law schools. The consultants' papers and the results of the inquiry among law professors are contained in the Commission's Technical Reports. On problems of law enforcement, the Panel was informed through nationwide surveys of the opinions and experience of both state and municipal prosecutors. Historical and comparative law papers were done for the Commission by retained consultants. The Panel also drew upon the Commission's national survey of public opinion for empirical evidence relevant to the application of present definitions of obscenity and to attitudes within the American population relating to the wisdom and appropriateness of various types of obscenity prohibitions.

Near the beginning of its life, the Commission asked the Legal Panel to begin drafting various types of legislative controls of obscene materials in order to have such statutory drafts available for the Commission's use at a later time. The Panel, with the aid of the Commission's legal staff, engaged in such drafting activity throughout its life. The Panel's drafts were not intended as legislative recommendations of the Panel, but merely as sound statutory formulations which the Commission might utilize if it deemed certain types of legislative regulation appropriate. The Panel's drafts, and explanation of the functioning and coverage of these drafts, were laid before the Commission when it came to consider its final conclusions and recommendations.

Some of the Panel's drafts were, with modifications, adopted by the Commission in formulating its legislative recommendations. These drafts appear in Part Two, Section III of the Commission's Report (Drafts of Proposed Legislation). One Panel draft and commentary, which was considered but not ultimately adopted in whole by the Commission, appeared in the Commission's Progress Report of July, 1969. Other Panel drafts which were considered by the Commission are referred to at various points in the Legislative Recommendations Section of the Commission's Report (Part Two, Section I), with explanations of why they were not deemed appropriate legislation by the Commission.

Section A. Historical Background[1]

The crime of creating or distributing "obscene" sexual materials is of relatively recent origin in Anglo-American law. In England, it was held authoritatively as late as 1708[2] that such materials were not indictable at common law, although "obscene libel" was found punishable in England through judicial decision in 1727.[3] The first legislation in England authorizing the prosecution of obscene materials was enacted in 1824[4], and covered public exposure of obscene books or prints. England did not enact legislation generally prohibiting the distribution of obscenity until Lord Campbell's Act in 1857[5], and a broad definition was not formulated for application through this legislation until the decision of Queen v. Hicklin in 1868.[6]

In the United States, the distribution of obscenity never became firmly established as a common-law offense, although there were one or two common-law prosecutions in the 1800s.[7] Only one colony—Massachusetts—enacted an obscenity statute;[8] the other colonies apparently left the subject unregulated. The first state statute was enacted in Vermont in 1821.[9] The first federal statute, prohibiting the importation of pictorial obscene matter, was enacted in 1842.[10] Obscenity was first prohibited in the mails in 1865.[11]

Nor were the earliest obscenity prohibitions directed toward explicit sexual materials as such. The crime of obscenity started in both England and the United States as a crime in which sexual matter was incorporated in materials which directly attacked religious institutions and beliefs. The earliest prosecutions all pertained to sexual works which were con-

348

demned for their explicit anti-religious content. It was not until after 1850 that a distinct offense of publishing explicit sexual material—unconnected with any expressed anti-religious content—fully evolved in the United States and England. The primary forces behind the ultimate creation of these prohibitions upon sexual materials appear, moreover, to have been religious ones.

The following paragraphs briefly summarize the steps in the legal development of the offense of obscenity which led to the emergence in the late 19th Century of a prohibition upon published sexual explicitness. The development and elaboration of obscenity law after the late 19th Century is described in succeeding Sections of this Report which deal with present legal doctrines.

EARLY BEGINNINGS IN ENGLAND

Censorship for political and religious reasons dates back, at least, to Greek and Roman times. In both cultures, however, sexual licentiousness was tolerated in drama (a principal means of popular entertainment) and was often combined with religious themes. During medieval times, bawdiness was apparently quite acceptable in ballads (again, frequently mixed with religious themes) and even in religious works. The Exeter Book, for example, a largely devotional work which is the earliest example of Anglo-Saxon literature, contains explicit sexual riddles which were collected by a monk.

The printing of books increased greatly in England in the 15th Century. Royal censorship began in England in 1538 through a licensing system established by Henry VIII.[12] Like earlier manifestations of governmental censorship in other cultures, however, English censorship at this time was not directed toward sexual content, but only against seditious and heretical works. Subsequently, the strong influence of Puritanism in England in the first half of the 17th Century led to authorization of proceedings against the use of profanity by actors on stage in 1605 and the total abolition of the play houses by Parliament in 1642. The licensing system may have been used to prohibit sexual explicitness during this time. After the Restoration in 1660, however, licensing was again limited to suppressing sedition and heresy in printed works, and the play houses were revived.

The only prosecution in England prior to the 18th Century which somewhat related to what was later deemed to be "obscenity" was King v. Sedley[13] in 1663. Sir Charles Sedley, an intimate of Charles II, became drunk with two friends at a tavern. They climbed to the balcony of the tavern, which overlooked Covent Garden, and removed their clothes. Sedley thereupon gave a speech which included profanities and poured bottles of urine down upon his audience. A riot followed. Sedley was given a substantial fine and committed to jail for a week for breaking the peace. The case is often referred to as the first reported obscenity case, apparently because it showed that common-law courts would, even in the absence of a statute, penalize conduct which is grossly offensive to the public. Sedley's case, however, did not concern the distribution of sexual materials, but involved both a physical assault upon others and the public broadcasting of profanity and nudity upon unwilling recipients. It has little direct relationship with the offense of distributing sexual works to consenting recipients which was later evolved by the law.

The end of the 17th Century in England brought the beginning of long-term governmental concern with the morals of the public in the sexual area which culminated in the Victorian period. Puritan repression of stage plays was renewed. A Society for the Reformation of Manners, which blacklisted persons guilty of "vice," was formed under Royal patronage and Queen Anne issued a proclamation denouncing vice. On the other hand, the Licensing Act was allowed to lapse by Parliament in 1695 because of practical considerations. This, coupled with the spread of literacy and the increased popularity of reading, led to a new class of "popular" literature which often had sexual content and which caused concern because of its attraction for lower-class readers. Nevertheless, in 1708 a man named Read was acquitted for writing a book called, The Fifteen Plagues of a Maidenhead.[14] The book was held by the court to be "bawdy stuff," but since it libelled no one, did not reflect upon the government and did not attack religion, it was held to be "punishable only in the spiritual court."[15]

THE DEVELOPMENT OF THE ENGLISH
LAW OF OBSCENITY

In the 1720s one, Curl, was prosecuted for "obscene libel" for publishing a book entitled Venus in the Cloister or the Nun in her Smock. The judges were troubled by the Read decision and by the fact that, previously, the common law had not recognized as crimes acts which did not tend to a breach of the peace, as Curl's book did not. However, after several

continuances a conviction was rendered in 1727.[16] As shown
by its title, the work in issue in Curl's case was not offensive
solely because of its sexual content, but because of its anti-
religious content as well. An early report of the case states
that the court found there to be an offense because "religion
was part of the common law; and therefore whatever is an
offense against that is evidently an offense against the common law."[17]

Eighteenth Century legal writers treated the offense of obscene libel created by Curl as an offense against God. Eighteenth Century obscenity cases which followed Curl similarly
limited themselves to sexual material in the context of anti-
religious works.[18] In fact, some very sexually explicit books
and pamphlets of the type often referred to today as hard-
core pornography circulated quite freely in England throughout the 18th Century, apparently because their lack of anti-
religious content kept them outside the law's proscription.

Near the beginning of the 19th Century, the common law
appears to have evolved by degrees in England to where it
began to be applied in some cases to prohibit purely sexual
works which did not attack or libel religious institutions. It
has been estimated[19] that there were about three obscenity
prosecutions per year in England between 1802 and 1857.
Obscenity legislation was first enacted in England as part of
the Vagrancy Act of 1824,[20] which prohibited exposing an
obscene book or print in public places. In 1853, a statute,
apparently aimed at French postcards, was passed to prohibit
the importation of obscene materials[21] and in 1857 the so-
called Lord Campbell's Act, generally prohibiting the dissemination of obscenity, was enacted.[22]

Lord Campbell's Act did not contain a definition of what
was deemed "obscene." In 1868, in Queen v. Hicklin[23] an
authoritative judicial definition was adopted. The Hicklin case
involved an anti-religious pamphlet with sexual content entitled, The Confessional Unmasked, showing the depravity of
the Roman Priesthood, the iniquity of the Confessional and
the questions put to females in confession. The opinion of
the court, however, did not expressly limit itself to material
with anti-religious content. It held instead that the test of obscenity was

> whether the tendency of the matter charged as obscenity
> is to deprave and corrupt those whose minds are open
> to such immoral influences, and into whose hands a pub-
> lication of this sort may fall.

Hicklin thus made it clear in England, for the first time,

351

that publications might be prohibited as "obscene" solely because of their sexual content, and not because of their attack upon the government or upon religious institutions.

THE DEVELOPMENT OF OBSCENITY LAW IN THE UNITED STATES

There appears to have been no common-law development in the American colonies, during the 18th Century, of the offense of anti-religious obscenity which was recognized in England in Curl's case in 1727. Only in the Massachusetts colony were there statutes in the area. The Puritan authorities in Massachusetts early prohibited offenses against religion, such as blasphemy (which was punishable by death until 1697 and by boring through the tongue with a hot iron thereafter), and possession of writings containing Quaker opinions. A strict general censorship system was instituted in 1662, but was not aimed at sexual materials. In 1711, however, apparently because of the appearance in the colony of sexual materials imported from England, a statute was passed[24] which recited that "evil communication, wicked, profane, impure, filthy and obscene songs, composures, writings or prints do corrupt the mind and are incentives to all manner of impieties and debaucheries, more especially when digested, composed or uttered in imitation or in mimicking of preaching, or any other part of divine worship," and which prohibited the "composing, writing, printing or publishing of any filthy, obscene or profane song, pamphlet, libel or mock-sermon, in imitation of preaching, or any other part of divine worship." This statute, although closely related to anti-religious material, was apparently potentially applicable to solely sexual material as well. There are, however, no recorded prosecutions under the Massachusetts statute until the "Fanny Hill" case in 1821, which is described below. All the other colonies appear to have left sexual materials entirely unregulated by the criminal law, although some such materials were in circulation in the colonies.

The first obscenity case in the United States occurred in 1815 in Pennsylvania.[25] There the court found the private showing for profit of a picture of a man and woman in an "indecent posture" to be a common-law offense because it was in violation of the public decency. In 1821, the publisher of Fanny Hill was found guilty in Massachusetts under both the colonial statute and the common law.[26] Subsequent state-law development was statutory. In 1821, Vermont became the first state to pass an obscenity statute.[27] A Connecticut statute followed in 1834[28] and in 1835 Massachusetts amended and broadened its statute, lessened its tie to anti-religious works, and defined the obscene to be works "manifestly tending to the corruption of the morals of youth."[29] Subsequent state statutes also typically emphasized a purpose of protecting youth.[30] The proliferation of state obscenity statutes coincided with an increase in literacy among the American population, the beginnings of free universal education, and a decline in the direct influence of the Church over community life.

The first federal obscenity statute in the United States was part of the Customs Law of 1842[31] and prohibited the importation of "indecent and obscene prints, paintings, lithographs, engravings and transparencies." Like the first English customs statute, this was apparently aimed at the French postcard trade. In 1865, Congress passed the first mail obscenity legislation.[32]

There was very little enforcement in the United States of either state or federal obscenity statutes during the first 70 years of the 19th Century. This situation changed significantly after 1868, largely as the result of the efforts of Anthony Comstock. In 1868, the New York legislature, at the urging of Protestant leaders in New York City and the Young Men's Christian Association, enacted legislation prohibiting the dissemination of obscene literature.[33] Comstock, a grocery-store clerk by profession, began, on his own initiative, to investigate violations of the 1868 Act by local retail dealers and to report them to prosecutors.[34] Comstock then joined efforts with the YMCA to work for national obscenity legislation to reach publishers as well as local dealers. They formed the Committee for the Suppression of Vice, with Comstock as chief Washington lobbyist. In 1873, Congress responded to these efforts by broadening the 1865 federal mail act to essentially its present form.[35] Comstock was made special agent of the Post Office in charge of enforcing the federal law and he vigorously pursued these duties.

States which had not previously had obscenity legislation enacted such statutes following the 1873 federal enactment,[36] and by the end of the 19th Century at least 30 States had some form of general prohibition upon the dissemination of "obscene" materials. The basic definition of "obscene" used in federal and state prohibitions between the middle of the 19th and the middle of the 20th Centuries was the Queen v. Hicklin definition, quoted above, although there was increasing

353

judicial dissatisfaction with, and some significant modification of, this definition as the 20th Century progressed. Present obscenity law is based primarily upon the 1957 decision of the Supreme Court of the United States in Roth v. United States,[37] which narrowly formulated the definition of "obscene" for adults and held prohibitions utilizing this definition to be constitutionally valid, and upon subsequent Supreme Court cases which have sharply distinguished between what may be deemed obscene for adults and what may be prohibited under mere narrowly drawn prohibitions—such as those upon sales to juveniles, public displays, and unsolicited mailings—which do not interfere with what adults may read or see when they so wish.

Section B. The Constitutional Basis for Prohibitions Upon the Dissemination of Explicit Sexual Materials

As noted in the historical review presented above, by the end of the 19th Century the United States government had broadly prohibited the importation and mailing of "obscene" matter and at least 30 States had some form of general prohibition upon the dissemination of "obscene" materials. Through the years, the Supreme Court had appeared to assume the validity of these prohibitions in writing opinions in other areas.[38] It was only in 1957, however, in the case of Roth v. United States[39] that the Court first ruled directly that broad obscenity prohibitions had a constitutional basis. Twelve years after the Roth decision, in its 1969 decision in Stanley v. Georgia,[40] the Court again spoke to the constitutional basis for broad obscenity prohibitions in an opinion which suggested that general obscenity prohibitions may not, in fact, be constitutionally valid in all contexts.

General prohibitions upon the dissemination of explicit sexual materials regulate the books and pictures which individual citizens may read or see. Our constitutional traditions place strict limitations upon the right of government to interfere with these activities. Constitutional limitations are contained primarily in the First Amendment to the Constitution, adopted in 1791, and in the Fourteenth Amendment, adopted in 1868, which has been held to have applied the free-speech guarantees of the First Amendment to state and local prohibitions.[41] These Amendments provide that government "shall make no law . . . abridging the freedom of speech, or of the press . . ." Materials covered by obscenity prohibitions—i.e., books, magazines, pictures and films—are ordinarily all deemed to be speech within the protection of these Amendments.[42] Under well established constitutional doctrine the dissemination of "speech" protected by the Amendments may ordinarily be prohibited only where the contents or subject matter of the material create a "clear and present danger" of significant social harm.[43] Applying the approach, some lower court judges reasoned before 1957 that, in the absence of a finding that certain sexually explicit materials create such a danger, general prohibitions upon the dissemination of "obscene" speech were constitutionally invalid.[44]

In the 1957 Roth case the Supreme Court rejected this analysis and held that general prohibitions upon the dissemination of "obscene" material do not conflict with the First and Fourteenth Amendments to the Constitution, so long as such prohibitions utilize a particular circumscribed standard, laid down by the Court, for determining whether the material constitutes obscenity.[45] The Court did not arrive at this conclusion through an application of the "clear and present danger" test described in the preceding paragraph. It did not, that is, find or assert that the dissemination of obscene material ordinarily either causes or creates danger of actual social harm. The Court held, rather, that the protections of the First and Fourteenth Amendments—including the requirement that harm or an immediate danger of harm be shown in justification of a governmental prohibition—do not apply to the dissemination of "obscene" material because "obscenity is not within the area of constitutionally protected speech or press.[46]

This basic conclusion that the constitutional guarantees which ordinarily protect speech from prohibition in the absence of a clear and present danger of harm do not apply to "obscene" speech, was rested by the Court on three findings. In the first place, the Court said that the existence in almost all of the States, at the time of the adoption of the First Amendment, of statutes prohibiting libel, blasphemy and profanity showed "that the unconditional phrasing of the First Amendment was not intended to protect every utterance." The Court then found that, while "at the time of the First Amendment, obscenity law was not as fully developed as

355

libel law, . . . there is sufficiently contemporaneous evidence to show that obscenity, too, was outside the protection intended for speech and press."[47] Finally, the Court noted a "universal judgment that obscenity should be restrained, reflected in the international agreement of over 50 nations, in the obscenity laws of all of the 48 States, and in the 20 obscenity laws enacted by the Congress from 1842 to 1956."[48]

In the 12 years following the Roth decision there was considerable litigation over the meaning and application of the standard for determining what is "obscene" which the Court in Roth had required to be followed in order for general prohibitions upon the dissemination of obscenity to be regarded as constitutional. This litigation, which is discussed in detail in Section C of this Panel Report, resulted in a very narrow scope of constitutionally permissible application to such broad prohibitions. During this period, however, the Supreme Court appeared to adhere, in principle at least, to its holding in Roth that, should material properly be determined to be "obscene" under the required narrow standard, it would be wholly outside the protection of the First and Fourteenth Amendments, so that its dissemination might be broadly prohibited. Then, in 1969, in Stanley v. Georgia[49] the Court suggested substantial doubt regarding the continuing validity of the fundamental premise of the Roth case that the dissemination of "obscene" materials may be broadly prohibited wholly without reference to First Amendment values.

In the Stanley decision, the Supreme Court held that "the First and Fourteenth Amendments prohibit making mere private possession of obscene material a crime."[50] The Court assumed in Stanley that the material involved in that litigation was "obscene" under the narrow standard which had been laid down in the Roth decision.[51] Its decision that the private possession of such material cannot constitutionally be prohibited was based on the holding that the individual nevertheless has a right, protected by the First and Fourteenth Amendments, "to read or observe what he pleases—the right to satisfy his intellectual and emotional needs in the privacy of his home," even if the material involved is entirely without social value and "obscene."[52]

By thus invoking the constitutional guarantees of speech and press to protect possession of materials which were assumed to be "obscene" under Roth the Supreme Court in Stanley v. Georgia appears to have departed from its holding in Roth that obscene materials are inevitably outside the area of constitutionally protected speech or press. In place of this

356

prior absolute disqualification of obscenity from First Amendment protection, the Court in Stanley utilized an approach which recognized a First Amendment right in adults to possess and peruse obscene materials, at least in the privacy of the home, but which also recognized that government has "a valid . . . interest in dealing with the problem of obscenity"[53] which may potentially limit the unfettered exercise of this right.

The question of the social effect of obscenity, which the Roth opinion had deemed irrelevant, thus assumed critical importance in Stanley in order to determine whether the State there had a valid regulatory interest in adult private possession of obscene materials in order to justify a prohibition of that activity. The Stanley Court rejected two such governmental interests put forward by the State. The Court held, first of all, that government has no legitimate interest whatsoever in "protect[ing] the individual's mind from the effects of obscenity"; rather, governmental "control [of] the moral content of a person's thoughts . . . is wholly inconsistent with the philosophy of the First Amendment."[54] The Court also dealt with the assertion "that exposure to obscene materials may lead to deviant sexual behavior or crimes of sexual violence" and that this danger is, therefore, a basis for governmental regulation. The Court noted that "there appears to be little empirical basis for that assertion" and that, even "more importantly," "the deterrents ordinarily to be applied to prevent crime are education and punishment for violations of the law," rather than prohibitions upon the possession of literature.[55] On the other hand, the Court appeared to recognize that government may, in view of present knowledge, legitimately seek to guard against unrestricted public distributions which may create "the danger that obscene materials might fall into the hands of children" or the danger that such materials "might intrude upon the sensibilities or privacy of the general public." Prohibition of private possession was not, however, sufficiently tied to vindicating these interests to justify governmental action.

The Supreme Court's opinion in Stanley v. Georgia "discerned . . . an important interest in the regulation of commercial distribution of obscene material" and stated that "Roth and the cases following that decision are not impaired by today's holding."[56] Yet broad prohibitions upon the commercial dissemination of obscenity to adults may interfere to a substantial degree with the exercise of the right of adults to read or see what they wish to in their own homes. It may also be impossible to maintain tenable distinctions between the right of adults to read or view sexual materials at home and their right to view them privately elsewhere—as, for example, in a motion picture theater where admission is restricted to adults.[57] Therefore, while it recognizes certain governmental interests in regulating the dissemination of obscenity—such as the protection of youth and the protection of privacy from unwanted intrusion of sexual materials—the Stanley opinion, unlike the Roth decision 12 years earlier, may require that each prohibition be narrowly drawn to serve only such legitimate interests, and not to interfere unnecessarily with the First Amendment right of an adult to "read or observe what he pleases."

The Supreme Court has not, in the short time since its decision in Stanley, yet ruled expressly on the question whether sufficient governmental interests support prohibitions upon dissemination of obscenity in various contexts. The Stanley decision has been considered in this regard by a number of state and lower federal courts. Among these cases, five federal district court decisions have held obscenity prohibitions in areas other than private possession to be unconstitutional on the basis of the Stanley case. Two of these decisions concerned the federal customs statute,[58] and held it unconstitutional insofar as it prohibits individuals from importing "obscene" materials for their own use;[59] one held that the federal mailing statute[60] may not be constitutionally applied to prohibit the commercial mailing of "obscene" matter to adults who request such materials;[61] and two decisions dealt with state obscenity statutes, one holding it unconstitutional to prohibit an "obscene" film from being shown commercially in a theater to which minors were not admitted[62] and one holding that the dissemination of "obscene" material may not be prohibited unless the restriction is limited to "commercial or public" distribution.[63] These cases have, to various degrees, relied upon the Stanley decision's recognition of a right to private possession of obscenity as requiring the recognition of a correlative right in adults to acquire obscene materials when they so wish. In the context of private or unobtrusive distributional activity limited to consenting adults, they have found no greater governmental interest than was present in Stanley to justify the prohibitions involved. Three of these cases are presently before the Supreme Court for decision.[64] At the same time, courts in three States, the federal courts of appeals for the Fourth and Fifth Circuits, and five federal district courts have sustained obscenity prohibitions in the context of commercial dissemination against challenges invoking Stanley v. Georgia. Two of these cases have dealt with the federal prohibition upon interstate transportation of obscene material[65] and the remainder have dealt with state prohibitions upon commercial exhibition or dissemination.[66]

To sum up the present constitutional position of obscenity prohibitions: After many years of assuming, without deciding, that laws barring the dissemination of obscenity were consistent with the First and Fourteenth Amendments, the Supreme Court in 1957, in the case of Roth v. United States directly held that such laws were constitutional, subject to a narrowly restrictive standard of what may be considered "obscene." Under the Roth case, once material was found to be obscene under the required standard, it was deemed not to be "speech" entitled to constitutional protection. The question in each case thus became solely whether or not the material was, in fact, "obscene."

The fundamental premise of Roth—that the protections accorded to speech by the Constitution are wholly inapplicable to "obscene" material—was apparently rejected by the Supreme Court in 1969 in Stanley v. Georgia. There the Court indicated that, even where material is "obscene," the individual citizen nevertheless has, a constitutionally protected right, if he so wishes, to read or view such material at least in his own home. Obscenity prohibitions which interfere with this right appear to require the support of a sufficient governmental interest. The protection of juveniles from exposure to obscene materials and the protection of individual sensibilities against materials involuntarily thrust upon persons who do not wish to see them were recognized in Stanley as legitimate governmental concerns. On the other hand, Stanley appears to have held that government may not rest prohibitions upon what consenting adults may read or view upon a desire to control their morality, or upon a desire to prevent crime or antisocial behavior, at least, in the absence of a solid empirical foundation.

The Supreme Court has not, as yet, expressly applied the principles of the Stanley decision to prohibitions other than those upon private possession of obscenity (which was involved in Stanley itself). Lower federal courts and state courts have arrived at somewhat conflicting conclusions as to the application of Stanley and some cases are presently before the Supreme Court for decision. In the situations which have been litigated which appear closest to private possession, however—federal prohibitions upon importation of obscene material for private use and upon the mailing of obscene material to persons who request it, and state prohibitions applied to films exhibited at theaters to which minors were not admitted—federal courts have relied upon Stanley in holding the prohibitions to be unconstitutional. These courts have held that the right to possess established in Stanley implies a correlative right to acquire material through unobtrusive channels.

Section C.   Constitutionally Permissible Definitions of Prohibited Sexual Materials[67]

THE DISTINCTION BETWEEN "GENERAL" AND "SPECIFIC" OBSCENITY STATUTES

A single factor has, more than any other, been productive of confusion surrounding the meaning and application of the law regarding explicit sexual materials. This is the failure to notice the difference between prohibitions which seek generally to prevent the distribution of certain materials, even to adult persons who wish to obtain them, and prohibitions which restrict themselves to impeding certain types of distributional conduct—such as distributions through unsolicited mail or distribution to minors—without interfering with the right of individuals to obtain materials they wish to see.

Several different legislative objectives may have motivated government in the past to regulate or prohibit such materials: Such materials may have been thought to be harmful to minors; government may have desired to protect persons who do not wish to be confronted with such materials from having them thrust upon them, as in public displays or unsolicited mailings; vigorous commercial exploitation of sexual appetites and curiosities may have been deemed socially harmful; and some materials may have (as in Georgia at the time of the Stanley decision) been deemed to be inappropriate for viewing or reading even by consenting adult persons in a wholly noncommercial context. It is apparent that some of these asserted objectives might be accepted within a jurisdiction, while others were rejected, and it also seems evident that the definition of material to be prohibited where one

360

objective is to be served may well vary significantly from the definition appropriate to serve a different legislative objective. A concern with public displays, for example, would naturally lead to a definition focusing on pictorial rather than verbal material. To take another example, a much more inclusive definition might be deemed appropriate where distributions to children were to be stopped than where unobtrusive distributions to consenting adults were sought to be regulated.

Despite these differences in legislative objective and in the definitions of material appropriate to serving such diverse objectives, until very recent years statutes regulating explicit sexual materials almost invariably tended to set forth a single definition of the "obscene" and to prohibit all or virtually all dissemination of the defined material, without creating distinctions turning on whether the distribution was to a minor or an adult, whether it was public or private, solicited or unsolicited, and even, in many cases, without regard to whether it was commercial or noncommercial. The federal mailing statute, for example, still broadly prohibits mailing "obscene" material, without regard to whether the mailing is to a child or an adult, whether it is for commercial or noncommercial purposes, or whether it is an unsolicited advertisement which is part of a mass indiscriminate mailing or a work specifically requested by the recipient. A single definition of "obscene" is employed in the statute to cover all of these cases. Prohibitions which thus utilize a single concept of the "obscene" to regulate a broad range of distributional conduct, including distributions to consenting adults who wish to see the material deemed obscene, are referred to in this Report as "general" or "adult" prohibitions.

When the Supreme Court determined, in Roth v. United States, that obscenity prohibitions were consistent with the First and Fourteenth Amendments, it had reference to such "general" or "adult" prohibitions. The very limited permissible definition of "obscene" which the Roth case imposed—and which is discussed in detail immediately below—was, similarly, imposed only upon the application of general prohibitions for adults. In a series of cases subsequent to Roth, however, the Court made clear that where attempts were made to prohibit only specific distributional activities connected with sexual materials—and not to prevent consenting adult individuals from obtaining material they wished to see —more inclusive definitional standards than that imposed in Roth would be permitted to be applied.

The first case leading in this direction was Ginzburg v.

361

United States.[68] There the Court "assume[d] without deciding"[69] that the materials involved could not be deemed "obscene" for consenting adults under the standard required by the Roth case. The Court found the question of obscenity under Roth a close one, however, and it permitted the conviction of the defendant to stand because he was found to have "pandered" the materials in an offensive manner rather than merely to have sold them to persons who wished to obtain them. Thus, the Court permitted a conviction which it would not have permitted had the defendant merely been engaged in neutral dissemination to consenting persons. In Redrup v. New York[70] the Court made this definitional division between general and specific prohibitions explicit; in addition, it made a general statement about the kinds of specific prohibitions which would be permitted to employ more inclusive definitions than that required by Roth for adults. In Redrup, as in Ginzburg, the materials were held not to be "obscene" under the Roth standard. The Court, however, stated that prohibitions might have been permissible if "the statute in question [had] reflected a specific and limited state concern for juveniles," if the case had been one where there was "an assault upon individual privacy by publication in a manner so obtrusive as to make it impossible for an unwilling individual to avoid exposure to it," or if there had been "evidence of the sort of 'pandering' which the Court found significant in Ginzburg v. United States."[71] Subsequent to Redrup, in Ginsberg v. New York[72] a statute prohibiting only commercial distribution to juveniles, and containing a definition applying to works which, the Court held, were "not obscene for adults,"[73] was, in fact, upheld by the Court. Recently, in Rowan v. Post Office Department[74] the Supreme Court also sustained legislation protecting postal patrons from unsolicited mail advertisements which could not be deemed "obscene" under Roth. Limited prohibitions like the statutes upheld in Ginzburg and Rowan are referred to in this Report as "specific" obscenity prohibitions.

Considerable confusion is avoided if the distinction between "general" and "specific" prohibitions is borne in mind. A general prohibition, which broadly prohibits distribution of "obscene" materials even to adult persons who wish to obtain them, may only be applied in accordance with the narrow standard set forth in Roth v. United States (and, indeed, in light of Stanley v. Georgia, discussed above, such general prohibitions may be wholly inapplicable in some contexts as impermissible impingements upon individual rights). Proper

362

specific prohibitions, which limit their operation to particular types of distributions which cause special social concern, but do not seek to disturb consensual adult distributional activity generally, may utilize broader definitions shaped to respond to the specific concern of the prohibition.

The Verbal Standard for Defining "Obscene" Under General Statutes

Before the Roth decision, legislation ordinarily did not attempt to define the word "obscene." For about one hundred years before the Roth decision, the basic definition of "obscene" used by courts under such statutes was derived from the decision of the Court of Queens Bench in England in 1868 in Queen v. Hicklin[75] which held that:

the test of obscenity is this, whether the tendency of the matter charged as obscenity is to deprave and corrupt those whose minds are open to such immoral influences, and into whose hands a publication of this sort may fall.

In the decades immediately prior to the Roth decision, there was increasing dissatisfaction, among both judges and reform-minded lawyers, with the Hicklin test and some aspects of its application. Specifically, criticism was directed at, among other things, the fact that the Hicklin test might be applied without regard to the social purpose or value of a work; the related fact that application of Hicklin might permit obscenity to be found by examination, out of context, of particular passages or parts of a work, rather than by examination of a work as a whole; the fact that Hicklin judged a work by its effect upon "those whose minds are open to such immoral influences," which was often taken to mean that obscenity for all adults was to be judged by the supposed effect of material on the most susceptible persons in society, including children; the fact that Hicklin focused upon the effect of a work upon thoughts, rather than upon conduct; and the fact that Hicklin as applied, was often unresponsive both to changing community standards regarding the permissible depiction of sexual matters and to the reputation of a work among respected critics and scholars.[76] Some of these elements of Hicklin were subjected to judicial modification as this Century progressed.[77] Just before the Roth decision of 1957, in response to these and other objections to Hicklin a Tentative Draft of the Model Penal Code of the American

363

Law Institute proposed abandonment of the Hicklin standard and substitution of the following test for "general" statutes:

A thing is obscene if, considered as a whole, its predominant appeal is to prurient interest, i.e., a shameful or morbid interest in nudity, sex or excretion and if it goes substantially beyond customary limits of candor in description or representation of such matters.

The 1957 Roth decision accomplished two principal objectives. As described in Section B of this Panel Report, it directly held that government might impose general prohibitions upon the dissemination of material on the ground of its "obscenity" consistently with the First and Fourteenth Amendments to the Constitution. At the same time, it rejected the Hicklin test for judging whether materials are "obscene," and set out a different standard by which "obscenity" must be determined under general prohibitions, if such prohibitions are to be deemed constitutionally valid. The Roth decision was thus a two-edged sword: While it upheld the validity of general obscenity prohibitions, it also subjected such prohibitions—for the first time—to a uniform federal constitutional standard defining the "obscene." In view of the narrow scope of application subsequently accorded to the Roth standard to defining what is "obscene," the net effect of the Roth decision, even before Stanley v. Georgia was, in fact, to restrict the scope of application of general obscenity prohibitions, even though the case upheld the constitutional validity of such prohibitions.

Before considering the intricate details of the standard constitutionally required by Roth for defining "obscene," it should be noted that the standard required in Roth may be of very limited practical importance today. In the first place, the shift of constitutional doctrine intimated by the Supreme Court in Stanley v. Georgia, if given full effect, would mean that general adult prohibitions are not, as Roth appeared to assume, constitutional in all contexts, but that the adult individual's right to see materials of his own choice may only be overcome where there is a substantial social basis for governmental regulation. As a result, many applications of general prohibitions may no longer be permissible. The Roth constitutional standard for determining the "obscene" retains potential validity only in those areas where adult prohibitions may validly continue to apply. Moreover, as noted above, courts are not bound to utilize the narrow Roth standard if they apply "specific" prohibitions which reflect a legitimate governmental interest in regulating particular distributional conduct. Such specific prohibitions may utilize more inclusive definitions than Roth would permit. Roth's particular constitutional standard for judging obscenity thus remains important only where (1) the area regulated is one where a "general" prohibition may still be constitutionally applied, and (2) the area is not covered by a "specific" prohibition which properly utilizes a more inclusive definition than Roth permits. These significant qualifications should be borne in mind in considering the following material on the meaning of the Roth standard.

The standard for the "obscene," which the Roth decision constitutionally requires to be applied in "general" or "adult" prohibitions, is as follows: Material may constitutionally be deemed "obscene" under such a prohibition only if

> to the average person, applying contemporary communi-
> ty standards, the dominant theme of the material, taken
> as a whole, appeals to prurient interest.[78]

This standard closely follows that suggested in the same year as the Roth decision by a tentative draft of the Model Penal Code of the American Law Institute.

As thus formulated, the Roth test clearly rejected two elements which had been present in applications of the Hicklin rule—the examination of only isolated passages or excerpts in judging the obscenity of an entire work and the focus upon the effect of material on particularly susceptible persons. Roth requires examination of a work "as a whole" to find whether its "dominant theme" is "obscene" and it requires that the "obscene" effect of a work be judged by its effect upon the "average person." These changes alone are largely responsibile for narrowing the application of general obscenity statutes under Roth as compared with many applications of Hicklin.

Roth also somewhat shifts the verbalization of what is "obscene" from that utilized under Hicklin. Under the earlier case, the test of the "obscenity" of material dealing with sex was whether "the tendency of the matter . . . is to deprave and corrupt." Under Roth material dealing with sex may not be deemed "obscene" in a general statute unless it "appeals to prurient interest." This prurient-interest material is defined in the Roth opinion as material "having a tendency to excite lustful thoughts." It would appear that, in this particular respect, the Roth standard may be potentially somewhat more inclusive of material than the earlier Hicklin test, for it would perhaps be easier to find that material excites lust, as Roth requires, than to find that it actually tends to "deprave and corrupt," as Hicklin required.[79] As noted below, however, other elements than appeal to prurient interest have been required in the determination of what is obscene under Roth.

In a number of opinions rendered since the Roth decision the Justices of the Supreme Court have elaborated upon the meaning of the constitutional standard for determining the "obscene" under general prohibitions.[80] Only one of these opinions has obtained the adherence of a majority of the Justices. In 1966, in Mishkin v. New York[81] a majority of the Court modified somewhat the requirement of Roth, that material prohibited by a general statute be obscene to the "average person" by deciding that

Where the material is designed for and primarily disseminated to a clearly defined deviant sexual group, rather than the public at large, the prurient-appeal requirement of the Roth test is satisfied if the dominant theme of the material taken as a whole appeals to the prurient interest in sex of the members of that group.[82]

Other opinions in the Supreme Court since Roth bearing on the constitutional standard for the "obscene" in applications of general prohibitions have not been joined in by a majority of Justices. Some of the Justices have not accepted the Roth decision at all, despite the fact that it was joined in by a majority of the Justices at the time of its announcement. Two of these—Justices Black and Douglas—who dissented from the decision in the Roth case, have adhered since that case to the view that no general obscenity prohibitions are constitutional, on the ground that such prohibitions inevitably conflict with the freedom of speech guaranteed by the Constitution.[83] A third Justice—Justice Stewart—has adopted the view that general obscenity prohibitions are constitutional only if limited in application to "hard-core pornography," a term defined by Justice Stewart through reference to certain very explicit sexual materials,[84] and his now famous remark that, while there are considerable difficulties of accurate verbal definition, "I know it when I see it."[85] A fourth Justice— Justice Harlan—has adopted the "hard-core pornography" test as setting a constitutional limit on federal general prohibitions, but has urged that a more inclusive standard than the Roth standard be applied to state prohibitions:

As to the States, I would make the federal test one of rationality. I would not prohibit them from banning any material which, taken as a whole, has been reasonably found in State judicial proceedings to treat with sex in a fundamentally offensive manner under rationally established criteria for judging such material.[86]

The two newest Justices—Chief Justice Burger and Justice Blackmun—appear to have agreed initially with Justice Harlan's view of the increased latitude to be permitted under state legislation.[87]

Among the Justices who have accepted the majority Roth verbalization of the permissible constitutional reach of general prohibitions, two important differences exist. While no single case has ever so held in a majority opinion, six Justices who have accepted Roth—Justices Brennan, Goldberg, Warren, Fortas, Clark and White—have agreed that Roth requires, not only that "obscene" material appeal to prurient interest, but also that, to be "obscene," material be found to be

> patently offensive because it affronts contemporary community standards relating to the description or representation of sexual matters.[88]

This element was part of the American Law Institute test which the opinion in Roth professed to follow. There has, however, been no agreement regarding the "contemporary community" whose standards are relevant in judging such offensiveness. Two Justices—Justices Brennan and Goldberg—have said the community should be the "national" community under both federal and state law;[89] two Justices—Justices Harlan and Stewart—have urged the national community for federal statutes;[90] two other Justices—Justices Warren and Clark—have urged the permissible use in State prohibitions of local "community standards—not a national standard";[91] and, as noted above, Justice Harlan and initially Justices Berger and Blackmun have stated that they would in general, accord the individual States considerable definitional latitude. The remaining Justices who follow Roth have not spoken directly to the question. The question of the relevant community, therefore, remains unresolved by the Supreme Court.[92] Nor has the Court elaborated upon what is meant by the "community" standard of offensiveness. A "community" standard would appear to require at least that a majority of the relevant community adhere to that standard, and it more likely implies a standard of offensiveness adhered to by a large preponderance of the members of the community, for otherwise it would be difficult to assert that the community had any single standard.

The second important verbal definitional difference among the Justices accepting the Roth decision concerns the role

367

of the "social importance" or "social value" of the material charged as obscene under a general prohibition, and what degree of social value a work must have for that factor to be controlling. The Roth opinion noted that[93]

All ideas having even the slightest redeeming social importance—unorthodox ideas, controversial ideas, even ideas hateful to the prevailing climate of opinion—have the full protection of the guarantees [of the First and Fourteenth Amendments] unless excludable because they encroach upon the limited area of more important interests. But implicit in the history of the First Amendment is the rejection of obscenity as utterly without redeeming social importance.

The Court thus appeared to say that material with any social importance can only be prohibited if the prohibition satisfies First Amendment requirements. All the Justices who accept Roth thus agree that the social value of a work has constitutional relevance in determining its obscenity. One Justice—Justice Clark—used such value as one of three relevant factors, along with prurient appeal and offensiveness,[94] in determining obscenity. Another Justice—Justice White—finds social value relevant "only to determine the predominant prurient interest of the material."[95] In the plurality opinion in the Court's decision of Memoirs v. Massachusetts[96] three Justices—Justices Brennan, Warren and Fortas—stated their somewhat different view that a valid application of a general obscenity prohibition requires independent examination of the question whether the material has "redeeming social value" and that a finding of "obscenity" can be upheld only as to material found to be "utterly without redeeming social value." These Justices thus stated their view that a work must be:

"unqualifiedly worthless before it can be deemed obscene." A book cannot be proscribed unless it is found to be utterly without redeeming social value. This is so even though the book be found to possess the requisite prurient appeal and to be patently offensive. Each of the three federal constitutional criteria is to be applied independently; the social value of the book can neither be weighed against nor cancelled by its prurient appeal or patent offensiveness.[97]

Thus, these three Justices, who also accepted the need to incorporate a test of patent offensiveness in applying general statutes, required what amounts to a three-part test for

368

judging "obscenity" under general statutes. They summarized this test as follows:

> . . .[T]hree elements must coalesce: it must be established that (a) the dominant theme of the material taken as a whole appeals to a prurient interest in sex; (b) the material is patently offensive because it affronts contemporary community standards relating to the description of representation of sexual matters; and (c) the material is utterly without redeeming social value.[98]

Not only have the Justices not agreed on the precise role to be accorded to social value in determining obscenity under general prohibitions, but the Court has also not made clear what values are to be classed as social values and what, if any, significance is to be accorded to the requirement that such value be "redeeming" (where that modifier is used in opinions of one or more Justices). With regard to the meaning of "redeeming," the Justices who use this term as part of a three-part test also insist, as noted above, that social value cannot be outweighed by prurient appeal or offensiveness, so that a balancing of value against other factors appears fairly plainly not to be contemplated by them through their use of this word. As to the values which qualify as social values, presumably political, philosophical, literary, artistic, educational, scientific and other similar values are included. In addition, in Stanley v. Georgia, in a somewhat different context, a majority of the Court noted that it was not relevant that the material there before the Court was "arguably devoid of any ideological content," for "the line between the transmission of ideas and mere entertainment is much too elusive for this Court to draw, if indeed such a line can be drawn at all."[99]

There is, in sum, a considerable and confusing contrariety of views within the Supreme Court regarding the verbalization of the test of "obscenity" required by the Constitution for "general" obscenity prohibitions. The Court, itself, in a 1967 per curiam opinion joined by seven Justices in Redrup v. New York, recognized and stated these verbal differences, although noting that the "hard-core pornography" and three-part tests are "not dissimilar."[100] In this situation, the overwhelming majority of state courts and lower federal courts have utilized the three-part test for obscenity under general prohibitions stated in the plurality opinion in Memoirs v. Massachusetts.[101] This general employment of the three-part test in the lower courts appears warranted, even though no majority opinion of the Court has expressly incorporated that

369

verbalization. This is true because Justices Black and Douglas, who remain on the Court, continue to take the view that no "general" obscenity prohibitions are constitutionally permissible. Thus, so long as at least three other Justices employ the three-part verbalization as the constitutional standard for general prohibitions, no application of a general prohibition which does not employ this test will be upheld by the Court on appeal. State and local legislatures which have formulated general obscenity statutes in recent years have also almost uniformly employed the three-part standard, presumably for the same reasons which have guided lower courts in this direction. These definitional difficulties under general prohibitions are, in all events, of limited practical significance today in view of the significantly wider definitional latitude permitted under specific prohibitions and the possible invalidity of imposing any general prohibition for adults in at least some contexts under Stanley v. Georgia.

APPLICATION OF THE STANDARD FOR DEFINING "OBSCENE" UNDER GENERAL STATUTES

The verbal Roth standard for determining what is "obscene" for adults through the application of general prohibitions does not, by itself, afford a great deal of information regarding the actual materials which, in fact, may properly be determined to be obscene under that standard. The actual application of the Roth standard in particular cases has, however, not been left to lower courts and juries by the Supreme Court. The Court has, on the contrary, reviewed (and almost uniformly reversed) findings of obscenity in a relatively large number of cases arising from application of general prohibitions since the Roth decision. The actual limiting significance of the Roth standard may be judged through examination of these cases.

The Supreme Court has not ordinarily written opinions in the cases in which it has applied the Roth standard to particular materials. There have, indeed, been only four cases decided by the Court since the Roth decision[102] in which members of the Court agreeing with the Court's disposition have written opinions explaining their application of the Roth standard to the materials in issue. All of these cases were decided before 1967 and in three of the four cases judgments of obscenity were reversed. Only one of these opinions represents the views of a majority of the Court and in that case the only issue discussed was whether material might be obscene which appealed to the prurient interests of members of "deviant" sexual groups.[103] In the Roth case itself the Court did not actually apply its standard because it found that the parties had made no issue of the obscenity of the material involved, but had urged only the general proposition that obscenity prohibitions were unconstitutional.[104]

The Court's more usual course in applying the Roth standard to particular works has been to utilize summary per curiam dispositions, rendered without written opinion (and usually without prior oral argument), and merely stating the result of affirmance or reversal. The Court has used this device on about 30 occasions since Roth, and since the Court's 1967 decision in Redrup v. New York, it has utilized the per curiam disposition without opinion as the exclusive means by which it has determined questions of obscenity under Roth. In all but one of these per curiam decisions, judgments of obscenity were reversed by the Supreme Court.[105] Since 1967, per curiam dispositions reversing findings of obscenity have almost invariably cited the Redrup decision.[106] There the Court reversed findings of obscenity under general adult prohibitions. After summarizing the different views among the Justices regarding the precise verbalization of the Roth[107] standard the Court said:

whichever of these constitutional views is brought to bear upon the cases before us, it is clear that the judgments cannot stand. Accordingly, the judgment in each case is reversed.[108]

The Supreme Court's per curiam dispositions do not contain descriptions of the materials involved. A number of lower court decisions in the cases, however, have been reported which do contain such descriptions, and some descriptions are present in the four cases in which opinions have been written, so that the scope of the Roth standard has been elucidated somewhat. The cases involve three kinds of material—books (ordinarily not containing illustrations except for their covers), picture magazines and films (both feature films designed for theater viewing and films primarily designed for individual viewing in so-called "peepshow" format). Where books have been concerned the Court has reversed findings of obscenity as to novels entirely devoted to describing the sexual activities of their characters and which have contained quite detailed descriptions of heterosexual intercourse, oral-genital intercourse, masturbation, sadomasochism and homosexual activity.[109] In the most

371

recent case involving such novels the descriptions of sexual activities reached the greatest possible degree of explicitness, including the frequent use of vernacular terms for sexual organs and actions as part of the descriptions.[110] The Court several years ago also reversed a judgment of obscenity in a case involving a book which contained extremely explicit descriptions of sexual activity in vernacular terms, but in which such descriptions were in the context of a broader literary purpose.[111] In the area of picture magazines, the Court has reversed findings of obscenity with regard to collections of pictures of totally nude women, of totally nude men, of nude men and women together, and of women being subjected to "bondage" practices.[112] These pictures have often clearly displayed and focused upon pubic hair and male sex organs (although not in a state of excitation) and upon occasion they have focused directly upon female genitalia. Among the films which the Court has found not to be "obscene" under the Roth standard have been films showing entirely nude women, films showing nude or partially nude women engaging in gyrations, simulated intercourse and simulated oral intercourse and emphasizing and displaying pubic and rectal areas, films showing two partially nude women simulating lesbian activity, and films showing heterosexual activity between a man and a woman (but not revealing genital areas during such activity).[113]

It is difficult to extrapolate general conclusions from these dispositions, largely rendered without opinions. Moreover, in the case of pictorial material, works entirely devoted to the most explicit type of photographic depiction of sexual intercourse and other activity have not been involved in these cases, so that the status of these works necessarily remains in doubt.[114] However, it appears that the Court believes that the Roth standard does not permit a finding of obscenity to be made under a general prohibition (i.e., a prohibition upon what consenting adults may obtain) with regard to a large class of pictorial material with exclusively sexual content, which is quite graphic in detail and description, and which has a strong capacity both to arouse and offend. It further appears that, where verbal material is involved, not even the most explicit type of material is obscene, at least when presented in the context of a story or novel. Some courts have, indeed, appeared to conclude on the basis of these decisions that no material at all can any longer be found to be "obscene" under a general prohibition.[115] In the absence of authoritative opinions in the Su-

372

preme Court explaining the application of the Roth standard to particular materials, it remains uncertain which aspects of that standard account for these results. It appears most probable, however, that they flow from judicial conclusions regarding changing standards of community acceptance of explicit sexual materials and from the difficulty of concluding that works are entirely or almost entirely without social value for all adults.[116]

"SPECIFIC" PROHIBITIONS

The Supreme Court has enumerated three types of specific prohibitions which may be applied to material whose dissemination to consenting adults could not broadly be prohibited for adults under a "general" prohibition. These are: (1) prohibitions under statutes "reflect[ing] a specific and limited state concern for juveniles"; (2) prohibitions applied to prohibit "an assault upon individual privacy by publication in a manner so obtrusive as to make it impossible for an unwilling individual to avoid exposure to it"; and (3) prohibitions applied to "the sort of 'pandering' which the Court found significant in Ginzburg v. United States."[117] The Court has upheld one application of a federal prohibition to "pandering" conduct, it has upheld one state statute aimed at protecting juveniles (while striking down two such statutes), and it has upheld one federal statute seeking to protect individual privacy from obtruding publications.

PANDERING

In 1966, the Court in Ginzburg v. United States[118] held that where the question of obscenity of material for adults under the Roth standard is in doubt, when the material alone is considered, a dissemination of the material may nevertheless be prohibited if undertaken in a "pandering" manner, because such pandering may "resolve all ambiguity and doubt" as to the question of obscenity.[119] What constitutes "pandering" is not satisfactorily explained in the Ginzburg case. The Court's opinion appears to equate pandering with "the business of purveying textual or graphic matter openly advertised to appeal to the erotic interests of their customers."[120] The Court's opinion appears to rely heavily upon the fact that the Ginzburg defendant utilized massive unsolicited mailing campaigns in attempting to sell his materials. These unsolicited mailings contained material deemed

373

by the Court to be of a potentially offensive nature. "Pandering" may thus be a form of "assault upon privacy" which the Court in Redrup said might be comprehensively regulated through specific prohibitions, although it may be that a defendant who represents his publications as arousing to consenting persons may also be guilty of pandering. The Court has never addressed itself to this latter question. In Rowan v. Post Office Department[121] the Court upheld the federal mail "Anti-Pandering Act," which is designed to safeguard mail recipients from repeated exposure to unwarranted unsolicited mail campaigns such as carried out by the Ginzburg defendant.

CONCERN FOR JUVENILES

The Court has twice struck down legislation reflecting a special concern for juveniles. In 1957, in Butler v. Michigan[122] a state statute was held unconstitutional which generally prohibited dissemination to all persons of material "tending to incite minors to violent or depraved or immoral acts, or manifestly tending to the corruption of the morals of youth." The Court held the due process clause of the Fourteenth Amendment to be violated because "the incidence of this enactment is to reduce the adult population of Michigan to reading only what is fit for children." A specific concern for juveniles, therefore, may not find expression in legislation which prohibits adults from obtaining material deemed harmful to juveniles. In 1968, in Interstate Circuit v. Dallas [123] the Court struck down another juvenile statute—in this instance one, unlike that in Butler, prohibiting dissemination only to juveniles—on the ground that its definition of the prohibited material was excessively vague.

In Ginsburg v. New York,[124] decided in 1968 on the same date as the Interstate Circuit case, the Court held constitutional a state statute prohibiting the commercial distribution of certain defined material to persons under seventeen years of age, although the materials involved were assumed to be "not obscene for adults." As in the earlier Roth opinion, the Court did not rest its finding of constitutionality on a conclusion that certain sexual materials create a clear and present danger of harm for minors. Rather, the Court appears to have based its decision either on the view that, where minors are the purchasers of material, what is "obscene" for them (and, hence, what is not within the protection of the First and Fourteenth Amendments for them) may be assessed in terms of the sexual interest of minors, which may lead to a more inclusive definition of prohibited material than is permissible for adults.[125] On the other hand, the view that minors are not entitled to the same scope of constitutional protection to read or view material of their own choice as are adults and, specifically, that restrictions for minors need only be "rational," and do not need to be supported by the existence of a "clear and present danger" appears to be a basis for this decision. In this latter connection, the Court in Ginsburg noted that a State might rationally seek to protect minors from explicit sexual materials which are not obscene for adults either in order to afford "parents and others, teachers for example, who have primary responsibility for children's well-being" "the support of laws designed to aid discharge of that responsibility," or in pursuance of the State's "independent interest in the well-being of its youth."[126]

The definition used in the statute approved in the Ginsburg case is a complex one.[127] Essentially, to be prohibited for distribution to minors, material must fall within one or more objectively defined categories of explicit sexual material, and must also be "harmful to minors," a term defined through the use of a three-part test similar to that used under the Roth case, but modified to require appeal to the prurient interest of minors, patent offensiveness in light of prevailing standards in the adult community with respect to what is suitable for minors, and utter lack of redeeming social importance for minors. The Ginsburg case, however, does not appear to require that minor statutes conform in their application to this particular definition. Rather, the Court's opinion states that definitions in minors' statutes may be constitutionally applied so long as it is "not irrational for the legislature to find that exposure to material condemned by the statute is harmful to minors.[128] Since the Ginsburg case, a large number of jurisdictions have adopted minors' legislation incorporating the definition (or a very similar version thereof) used in the statute upheld in Ginsburg.[129]

PROTECTION OF SENSIBILITIES FROM
OBTRUDING PUBLICATIONS

In Rowan v. Post Office Department[130] the Supreme Court upheld the constitutionality of federal legislation pursuant to which mail recipients may require that their names be removed from the mailing lists of mailers who have sent them material which the recipient "in his sole discretion believes to be erotically arousing or sexually provocative.[131] The Court held that this unqualified right of an individual to insulate himself from unsolicited mail was consistent with the constitutional guarantees of freedom of expression because "the right of every person 'to be let alone' must be placed in the scales with the right of others to communicate."[132] The Court found the right of privacy predominant in the context of mail deliveries and consequently held that there is no constitutional "right to press even 'good' ideas upon an unwilling recipient." The Court has not, however, directly passed upon the constitutionality of prohibitions designed to protect sensibilities from assault outside the home, as in open displays upon public thoroughfares,[133] nor has it suggested what definitions might be appropriate in such statutes, which obviously cannot leave the determination of what is offensive to the sole discretion of each person who may be confronted with such a display.

The Court, in sum, has permitted a "pandering" manner of dissemination of material to play a relevant role in the determination of questions of application of the Roth standard, and it has also found that the constitutional guarantees of speech and press do not prohibit legislation which reasonably responds in a limited way to a desire to protect children from material rationally deemed harmful to them, nor do they prohibit legislation reasonably protecting individuals against communications of explicit sexual material which are offensive to them. Definitions in legislation serving either of these latter two interests apparently need only be rationally related to preventing the social harms at which the statutes are directed.

Section D. Procedural Limitations

The Requirement of Proving Scienter

Where either a general or specific obscenity prohibition has been violated by a defendant, he may nevertheless not be punished for such a violation unless he is proved to have had some degree of knowledge of his violation. This requirement of scienter was established by the Supreme

Court in 1959 in Smith v. California,[134] where the Court held unconstitutional an ordinance which had been applied to permit the conviction of a defendant for possessing obscene materials for sale, even where the defendant was not proved to have had any knowledge of the contents of these materials. The Court found such a prohibition in conflict with the free expression guarantees of the First and Fourteenth Amendments since, "if the bookseller is criminally liable without knowledge of the contents he will tend to restrict the books he sells to those he has inspected; and thus the State will have imposed a restriction upon the distribution of constitutionally protected as well as obscene literature."[135] Other than determining that some knowledge by the defendant respecting his violation is required by the Constitution, the Court in Smith did not determine precisely what degree of knowledge or understanding need be demonstrated:

> We . . . do not pass today on what sort of mental element is requisite to a constitutionally permissible prosecution of a bookseller for carrying an obscene book in stock; whether honest mistake as to whether its contents in fact constituted obscenity need be an excuse; whether there might be circumstances under which the State constitutionally might require that a bookseller investigate further, or might put on him the burden of explaining why he did not, and what such circumstances might be.[136]

The Supreme Court has not, since its decision in Smith v. California, finally resolved the questions regarding the scienter requirement left open by that case. In Mishkin v. New York[137] the Court upheld a conviction under a statute which was applied to require that the defendant be "in some manner aware of the character of the material" so that only "calculated purveyance of filth" was prohibited.[138]

It thus appears clear that proof of knowledge of contents, combined with a conclusion that the defendant, having knowledge of the contents, would undoubtedly realize that he might well be in violation of the obscenity laws in distributing the material, will meet the constitutional scienter requirements. It is not yet clear, however, to what extent, if any, proof of the existence of a reason to inquire into contents may substitute for actual knowledge of contents[139] nor has the Court since the Smith case, made it clear in what circumstances, if any, a defendant may be convicted without his being found to have been conscious of substantial likelihood that the materials would be deemed legally obscene.[140]

377

Where special prohibitions have been applied only to distributions to minors, these statutes have ordinarily required the prosecution to prove that the defendant either knew the age of the recipient or have had reason to inquire about age and have failed to do so reasonably;[141] and the Court has not, in consequence, been required to determine the constitutional necessity of such provisions.

LIMITATIONS ON SEIZURES AND INJUNCTIONS

One of the most well-established propositions of constitutional law relating to the guarantees given to free expression is that government may not prevent the dissemination of a particular book or work until after a judicial determination is made that the prohibition of that work is consistent with applicable law and with the Constitution. This rule has generally been interpreted to permit the application of criminal statutes to the dissemination of books judicially determined to be obscene only subsequent to their dissemination,[142] but not to permit a specific judicial injunction to be imposed upon the distribution of particular material prior to a judicial determination of the obscenity of that material. In cases involving the constitutionality of systems for licensing films prior to their distribution, the Supreme Court has held that distribution may be required to await the determination of the licensing authority as to obscenity but only where "any restraint imposed in advance of a final judicial determination on the merits . . . is limited to preservation of the status quo for the shortest fixed period compatible with sound judicial resolution."[143] Similarly, in cases involving material prevented by customs officials from being imported into the United States on the ground of its obscenity, lower federal courts have held that officials may delay the importation of material thought by them to be obscene only for the short period of time required to obtain a judicial determination of obscenity.[144]

In recent years, the Supreme Court has applied these principles to seizures of material by law enforcement officials ancillary either to prosecution for violation of obscenity laws or to proceedings leading toward the condemnation and destruction of allegedly obscene material. The seizures involved in these cases have been either seizures in large quantities of all the copies of a book or magazine held by a particular distributor or retailer, or seizures of films for exhibition. In three cases the Court has held that such seizures, at least when they effectively prevent distribution of particular material within the jurisdiction while they are in effect, may be conducted only if preceeded by a sufficient prior judicial determination that the material to be seized is, in fact, obscene.[145]

In Marcus v. Search Warrants[146] a search and seizure warrant was obtained from a judge by a police officer for a large-scale seizure of materials. The Supreme Court held the warrant procedure inadequate because "[T]he warrants issued on the strength of the conclusory assertions of a single police officer, without any scrutiny by the judge of any materials considered by the complainant to be obscene," and because "there was no step in the procedure before seizure designed to focus searchingly on the question of obscenity."[147] In a Quantity of Books v. Kansas[148] the procedures acceptable as a prior judicial determination were somewhat further suggested. There, the judge had "scrutinized" 7 of 59 books identified specifically by title before issuing a warrant for seizure of all 59 titles. While there was no opinion of a majority of the Court, four Justices found the procedure deficient even in respect to the seven books examined by the judge, on the ground that any prior procedure which did not include an adversary hearing on the question of obscenity was inadequate:

> It is our view that since the warrant here authorized the Sheriff to seize all copies of the specified titles, and since P-K (the distributor) was not afforded a hearing on the question of obscenity even of the seven novels before the warrant issued, the procedure was constitutionally deficient.
>
> We therefore conclude that in not first affording P-K an adversary hearing, the procedure leading to the seizure order was constitutionally deficient.[149]

In a per curiam opinion in Lee Art Theater v. Va.[150] the Supreme Court again held a state procedure prior to seizures inadequate on the ground that the judge, in authorizing seizure, had improperly relied upon the conclusory assertion of a police officer as to the question of obscenity.

There has been considerable litigation in lower courts regarding the precise meaning and elaboration of the prior judicial determination requirement established by these three cases. There has also been litigation regarding the circumstances under which it is appropriate for lower federal courts to interfere with state criminal prosecutions prior to final conviction because invalid seizures have occurred. The

379

Supreme Court will very likely speak further on these matters in the near future. It is clear, in all events, that broad injunctive or seizure procedures are ordinarily appropriate only in aid of "general" adult obscenity prohibitions. If prohibitions are restricted to specific distributional conduct—such as sales to children—it would appear inappropriate (except, perhaps, in the case of repeated adjudicated violations) to authorize the seizure or confiscation of materials or a broad injunction against their distribution to adults.

Section E. Existing Federal and State Obscenity Prohibitions—Their Content and Enforcement[151]

Lengthy technical papers prepared for the Commission by its staff describe in detail the content of existing state and federal obscenity statutes. Staff and contract research papers—including a nationwide survey of prosecuting attorneys—explore in detail the methods and problems of enforcement of these statutes. The salient features of present obscenity law in the United States, as revealed by this research, are summarized here. Reference should be made to the underlying research reports for details not presented here and for complete citations to statutes and other authorities.

1. State Statutes

a. "General" Criminal Statutes. Forty-eight of the fifty states have "general" obscenity statutes—that is, laws generally imposing criminal penalties on those who make distribution of obscene materials to any person, including consenting adults.

i. Statutory definitions of obscenity. Eighteen jurisdictions do not define the term "obscene" in their general statutes. The majority of the remaining jurisdictions have adopted the language of the Roth case as their definition. That is, "Obscene means that to the average person, applying contemporary community standards, the dominant theme of the material taken as a whole appeals to the prurient interest."

Several other states incorporate as their statutory definition of obscenity the tripartite Memoirs test, thus requiring the coalescence of appeal to prurient interest, patent offensiveness, and utter lack of redeeming social value before the material can be found obscene.

Only one state has failed to adjust its definition to the Roth or Memoirs standards for determining obscenity. There, a thing is still obscene if it "tend[s] to corrupt the morals of youth, or tend[s] to corrupt the public morals."

ii. Penalties. The typical state statutory maximum penalty for a first-time violator is a $1,000 fine and/or a one-year prison sentence. The actual range runs from $100 and no prison sentence (Minnesota) to $5,000 and/or ten years in prison (Oklahoma).

In addition, 14 states impose a more stringent penalty on those who have already been once convicted of an obscenity violation.

iii. Statutory exemptions. Many state statutes exempt from criminal liability those persons who distribute obscene materials in the course of scientific or artistic pursuits. Another common exemption provision relates to materials which have been "cleared" by a Federal agency, usually Customs or the Post Office. A third type, found in at least three states, is an exemption for noncommercial distributions to adult personal associates. Finally, a few states provide immunity to motion picture projectionists or exemptions for daily and weekly newspapers.

iv. Prohibitions on Tie-In sales. Twenty-three states have statutory provisions prohibiting publishers and distributors from requiring as a condition to a sale of magazines, books, papers, etc. that the purchaser also receive obscene material.

v. Extradition. While the statutes of four states specifically provide for the extradition of persons violating injunctions or other civil decrees relating to obscenity, only one state specifically provides, by statute, for the extradition of persons charged with violating the general criminal obscenity laws of the state.

vi. Pandering. In its recently enacted obscenity statute, the state of Georgia, apparently in an effort to codify the Ginzburg decision, included the following provisions:

Material, not otherwise obscene, may be deemed obscene under this section if the distribution thereof, or the offer to do so, or the possession with the intent to do so is a commercial exploitation of erotica solely for the sake of their prurient appeal.

381

The obscenity statutes of three other states likewise contain pandering provisions. In one of these, however, evidence of "pandering" may be considered only for the purpose of ascertaining whether the material is totally lacking in social value.

vii. Scienter. Although most obscenity statutes require an offense to be committed "knowingly" or "intentionally," very few state obscenity statutes contain provisions relating to the proof required to satisfy this scienter requirement. Those which do contain such statutory references are of two types. The first type is exemplified by an Oregon statute which provides that scienter on the part of the defendant can be proved by evidence of

"the advertising, publicity, promotion, method of handling or labeling of the matter, including any statement on the cover or back of any book or magazine."

The other type of scienter provision is the statutory presumption. For example, in New York,

A person who [disseminates] . . . obscene material, or possesses the same with intent to [disseminate] it, in the course of his business is presumed to do so with the knowledge of its content and character.

viii. Use of tangential statutes. Several state legislatures have expressly authorized the use of nonobscenity statutes as a device for controlling distributions of obscene materials. Among these are an Ohio statute which permits obscenity to be enjoined as a nuisance and a Texas statute permitting theaters showing explicit sexual films to be treated as "disorderly houses." In addition, law enforcement officers in some places may use nonobscenity statutes, such as statutes prohibiting "contributing to the delinquency of a minor," to penalize distribution of obscenity.

b. Statutes Prohibiting Distributions to Young Persons. The statutes of forty-one jurisdictions contain some type of special prohibition regarding the distribution of erotic materials to young persons. Eighteen of these statutes are either identical to or closely patterned after the New York statute upheld in Ginsburg v. New York.

i. "Ginsburg" Statutes. "Ginsburg" statutes prohibit the commercial dissemination of certain explicit sexual materials to minors. In order to be proscribed, the material must meet two tests. It must depict nudity, sexual conduct, or sadomasochistic abuse (or contain a verbal description of sexual excitement, sexual conduct, or sadomasochistic abuse) and it must be "harmful to minors." The terms "nudity,"

382

"sexual conduct," "sexual excitement," and "sadomasochistic abuse" are all defined quite explicitly and objectively. The test of what is "harmful to minors" is essentially the tripartite Memoirs test, adapted for youth as follows: The predominant appeal of the material must be to the prurient interest of minors and the material must be patently offensive to prevailing standards in the adult community with respect to what is suitable material for minors, and it must be utterly without redeeming social importance for minors.

ii. Statute containing either the Roth or Memoirs test as applied to minors. In Massachusetts, material cannot be distributed to minors if it appeals to the prurient interest of minors, is contrary to community standards as to what is suitable for minors and is utterly without redeeming social value for minors. Four other states likewise have minors' laws which embody either the Roth or Memoirs definition as applied to minors.

iii. Statutes containing a "General" obscenity provision and a separate but identical "Minors" provision. The statutes of six states contain "Minors" provisions which are virtually identical to their "General" obscenity provisions.

iv. Statutes which prohibit the dissemination to minors of both erotic and violence-oriented materials. The "Minors" statutes of four states prohibit the disseminating of both erotic and violence-oriented materials to young persons.

v. Statutes which prohibit the dissemination to minors of materials which "Tend to Corrupt [Their] Morals" or "Appeal to [Their] Lust." Three states prohibit the dissemination to youth of materials which have a tendency to corrupt their morals. Two other states prohibit the dissemination to a minor of materials "presented in such a manner as to exploit lust for commercial gain and which would appeal to the lust of persons under the age of 18 years."

vi. Utah's statute forbidding the sale to minors of hard-core pornography. A newly enacted Utah statute makes it illegal to sell or offer for sale hard-core pornography to minors. Hard-core pornography is defined as material "that shows people, or people and animals, in actual genital contact of any kind."

vii. Washington's "Labelling" Statute. In the state of Washington, it is illegal to distribute erotic materials to minors. The definition of erotic material is, in essence, the tripartite Memoirs test as applied to minors. In addition, the statute provides that when it appears that material which

383

might be erotic is being sold or distributed within the state, the prosecuting attorney may apply for a hearing and obtain an adjudication as to whether the material is erotic within the meaning of the statute. If the court rules that the material is erotic, an order is then issued requiring that an "Adults Only" label be placed upon it. Failure to comply with a court order so issued subjects the dealer or distributor to contempt proceedings. Any person who sells or distributes labelled materials to a minor is, for the first offense, guilty of a misdemeanor; for a second offense, guilty of a gross misdemeanor; and for all subsequent offenses, guilty of a felony.

c. Civil Statutes.

i. Declaratory Judgment Actions. In a recently enacted obscenity statute, the Georgia state legislature included a provision to the effect that no prosecution for general distribution of obscenity may be commenced unless the district attorney serves the accused with prior written notice that he (the district attorney) has determined the material to be obscene. Any person receiving such notice is then given thirty days to bring a declaratory judgment action, thereby seeking a judicial determination as to whether or not the material is obscene.

Georgia appears to be the only state in which prior notice to the accused and opportunity for him to bring a declaratory judgment action may be a mandatory prerequisite to a criminal prosecution. However, several other states do empower their law enforcement officials to bring declaratory judgment actions when they deem such action to be advisable. Such an action may be used as a method of establishing scienter on the part of the defendant. One state statute explicitly gives sellers and distributors the opportunity to institute, affirmatively, actions for declaratory judgments.

The notice provision contained in most of the declaratory judgment statutes appears to have been drafted so as to virtually guarantee actual notice of the pending litigation to all persons who are known to have a possible interest therein.

ii. Injunctions In Rem. The obscenity statutes of five states contain provisions for injunctions in rem i.e., injunctions which are directed against a book or material qua book or material, as opposed to injunctions in personam which are directed at particular persons and the conduct of those persons. These provisions appear as corollaries to declaratory judgment provisions and require that the complaint must designate as respondents all persons known to have a commercial interest in the matter. Permanent injunctions against any person distributing or possessing with intent to distribute the obscene matter and seizure and destruction of the material are authorized.

iii. Injunctions in Personam. The legislature of eighteen states have explicitly authorized their courts to restrain prospective violations of their obscenity laws through the issuance of injunctions in personam. These are decrees which are directed at specified persons, enjoining them from specified conduct or activities.

Most injunction statutes empower only the state's attorney or other public official to institute the action. However, in Kentucky, "any citizen" may maintain the action, and in Colorado, private citizens, by use of a mandamus action, can compel the district attorney to do so. In some states, the courts may also grant temporary restraining orders pending the outcome of the litigation.

iv. Seizure Statutes. Most injunction and declaratory judgment statutes contain a provision to the effect that the Government's complaint shall request the "surrender, seizure, and destruction" of the objectionable material after a final adjudication that it is obscene.

Some states have separate seizure statutes in terms such as the following.

"An obscene or indecent writing, paper, book, picture, print or figure found in possession, or under control of a person arrested therefor, shall be delivered to the magistrate before whom the person arrested is required to be taken, and if the magistrate finds it is obscene or indecent he shall deliver one copy to the county attorney of the county in which the accused is liable to prosecution, and at once destroy all other copies. The copy delivered to the county attorney shall be destroyed upon conviction of the accused."

The application of such provisions to permit that material be seized and destroyed prior to an adequate judicial hearing on the issue of its obscenity would appear to be unconstitutional.

Additionally, several seizure statutes contain provisions allowing law enforcement personnel to "seize any equipment used in the photographing, filming, printing, producing, manufacturing or projecting of pornographic, still or motion pictures and . . .[also] any vehicle or other means to transportation . . . used in the distribution of such obscene prints and articles." The materials so seized are then subject to forfeiture proceedings.

v. Motion picture licensing and classification boards. Maryland is the only state which still has a state-wide motion picture licensing board. The issue of the constitutionality of the Maryland licensing procedure is presently pending before the Supreme Court. In addition, the state of Tennessee has empowered its municipalities to establish boards for the classification and regulation of the presentation of motion picture films to minors.

d. Enforcement Procedures and Difficulties. The actual methods for enforcing the foregoing statutes vary widely from jurisdiction to jurisdiction. Where criminal statutes are concerned, the primary enforcement agency is the police. Police Departments in larger cities ordinarily have a special unit or officer who is initially responsible for all enforcement. Police act against allegedly obscene materials in response to citizen complaints and they also conduct either periodic or continuing surveillance of known distributors of explicit materials. If complaints or surveillance reveal material which police deem to be obscene, they frequently issue a warning to the distributor that he will be arrested unless distribution of the objectionable material is stopped. This warning process may often result in withdrawal of material from circulation in a jurisdiction without the institution of a formal proceeding or a determination of whether the material is, in fact, obscene. If not, arrests (and often seizure as well) will take place. In many jurisdictions police do not issue warnings, but conduct arrests and seizures upon concluding that "obscene" material is being distributed.

The most difficult enforcement problem experienced by police is in making the determination whether particular material is or is not "obscene." This has not been a serious problem under juvenile statutes, which, typically, contain relatively objective definitions. For perhaps the same reason, detected violations of juvenile statutes are rare, i.e., most commercial distributors appear to have little incentive to violate such prohibitions and they do not often do so when they can confidently determine to what materials the prohibitions apply. Where general statutes regulating distribution to adults are concerned, however, neither existing statutes nor court decisions give any satisfactory guidelines as to what material is prohibited. Police often consult with the prosecutor before initiating formal action, but prosecutors too are without any firm basis for deciding whether particular materials are or are not obscene for adults under present standards. A nationwide survey of prosecutors conducted by the Commission revealed that their most frequent criticism of present obscenity laws for adults was that the definition of obscenity is too subjective, vague and ambiguous. All parts of the Roth constitutional standard appeared to create some problems in this regard, but the ascertainment and application of "contemporary community standards" of offensiveness appears particularly difficult.[152]

In these circumstances, prosecutors often rely upon self-made practical guidelines which they formulate and revise on the basis of the most recent authoritative judicial decision of which they are aware. Such guidelines may change rapidly and they vary significantly from place to place. It has been particularly difficult to utilize Supreme Court decisions in formulating such guidelines, since these decisions have recently been rendered without opinion or any description of the materials involved. Because of these definitional difficulties, prosecutors and police are rarely confident of obtaining convictions in cases of public distribution of erotic materials. Perhaps as the inevitable result of such uncertainties, and also because of other law enforcement problems requiring police and prosecutorial attention, consistent uniform and vigorous enforcement of obscenity laws for adults is exceedingly rare. More typically, law enforcement "campaigns" are conducted from time to time by police and prosecutors either in response to mounting numbers of complaints or in order to make the public periodically aware of law enforcement "concern" with obscenity; between such campaigns, formal enforcement is infrequent but informal enforcement through police warnings may be substantial.

Definitional difficulties do not ordinarily arise regarding material sold "under the counter" or which is otherwise treated as illegal material by its distributor. Law enforcement in this area is infrequent, however, both because the incidence of this activity may be decreasing and because the location and identification of such underground sources requires a considerable investment of police personnel which is often not deemed warranted in view of other demands upon law enforcement.

A second apprehended difficulty in enforcement of criminal obscenity prohibitions relates to constitutional restrictions upon searches and seizures. Police have been accustomed in many places to instituting prosecution through seizure of allegedly obscene material, and such seizures have frequently been large-scale seizures of all copies of an allegedly obscene work. Judicial decisions in recent years have established that such seizures are unconstitutional, unless preceded by an adequate judicial decision on the question of the obscenity of the seized material. (Evidence which is illegally seized is ordinarily inadmissible in a prosecution). Few jurisdictions have an existing explicit procedural framework for obtaining such a judicial determination. It appears that some police departments have been deterred from instituting action against obscene material because of the difficulty in validly seizing material at the time of arrest.

Ordinarily, the difficulty of seizing material at the time of arrest should not defer law enforcement. Where books, magazines or any other materials sold in individual copies are involved, these materials may be purchased by the police, and the material thus purchased can form the basis for arrest and prosecution. The prosecution of film exhibitions, however, does create significant problems in the absence of authority for some form of seizure or attachment prior to trial which can insure that the allegedly obscene film will be available as evidence.

2. Federal Statutes

a. Postal Statutes. During the last several years, virtually all of the major cases prosecuted by the Justice Department have involved the use of the mails and have, therefore, been brought under the basic mail statute, 18 United States Code Section 1461.

i. 18 United States Code Section 1461. This federal statute provides that whoever knowingly uses the mails for the mailing or delivery of obscene materials shall be fined not more than $5,000 and/or imprisoned not more than five years for the first offense and not more than $10,000 and/or ten years for each subsequent offense.

Suspected violations of this statute are investigated by the United States Postal Inspection Service. This agency locates mail obscenity both through complaints from the public and purchases under pseudonymns.

Venue. At some point in the investigation, the postal inspector will consult with the U.S. attorney who has jurisdiction over the area from which the material was mailed or in which it was delivered. Until 1958, there was only one possible federal venue for each obscenity case involving the use of the mails, i.e., the jurisdiction from which the material was mailed. This made successful prosecution difficult, for many of the dealers operate from the Los Angeles area where community standards presumably were less conducive than some others to obtaining convictions. To remedy this, Congress, in 1958, amended 18 U.S.C. Section 1461 so that a dealer may be prosecuted not only where the material was mailed, but also in any place it was delivered. Of the cases which are currently pending on the federal level, none is pending in the Los Angeles area.

There are currently no exact standards for the selection of a federal venue, decisions being made ad hoc in each case. Two criteria are usually considered: The volume of mailings (as measured by complaints received) into the area under consideration; and the willingness and the ability of the particular United States Attorney in that area to undertake prosecution.

Level of and standards for prosecution. In recent years, the Justice Department has annually initiated several cases (usually between five and ten) pursuant to Section 1461 against major public prominent interstate producers and distributors of nonhard-core erotica. The materials involved in most of the cases are paperback novels, nude photographs concentrating on pubic or genital areas, lesbian magazines, pseudo marriage manuals, nonfiction works on oral-genital activity, etc. These materials, in and of themselves, do not, in the view of the Justice Department, warrant prosecution under present legal standards. Almost every case is grounded instead on the allegation that the defendant has pandered his material within the prohibition of Ginzburg v. United States. "Pandering" as thus used by the Justice Department, appears to have two components: (1) An explicit suggestion in advertising of sexual excitement or illegal sexual activity; and (2) Distribution in an obtrusive manner—usually, but not always, meaning unsolicited mailings. Of those "pandering" cases which have been terminated, the conviction rate is approximately 50 percent.

Administrative procedures. Most of the cases investigated by the Postal Inspection Service pursuant to Section 1461 are never prosecuted but instead are settled administratively through the use of three procedures—"suppressions," denial of second-class mailing privileges, and declarations of nonmailability.

(1) Suppressions. An inspector suppresses mail when he notifies the sender that what he is dispatching is illegal. The sender agrees to refrain from further activity of this type in return for the inspector's promise that no criminal

prosecution will be instituted. The current rate of successful suppressions is approximately 2500 per year.

(2) Denial of second-class mailing privileges. Section 132.2 of the Postal Manual provides: "Only newspapers and other periodical publications, may be mailed at the second-class rates. The copies may not contain obscene . . . material that would cause them to be nonmailable."

The Post Office Department, which promulgated this regulation, construes its power of denial to encompass not only those publications which have been adjudicated obscene but also those which, in the opinion of the Department, do not conform to current obscenity standards.

(3) Declarations of nonmailability. Under this procedure, the Post Office simply halts allegedly obscene mail in transit, usually at the point of entry, thereby denying the use of the mails for the distribution of publications which violate the obscenity standard as construed by the Post Office. Two current members of the Supreme Court have indicated that they do not believe that Section 1461 authorizes the Post Office to declare publications nonmailable and thus to remove them from the mails. The Department, while still occasionally employing this procedure, is rather circumspect about its use.

ii. 18 United States Code Section 1463. This statute imposes a penalty of not more than $5,000 and/or five years imprisonment on any person who knowingly mails any obscene material on postcards, envelopes, or outside wrappers. This statute does not appear to be a useful tool for the regulation of obscenity and has not, in recent history, provided the basis for suit against a major producer of erotica.

iii. 39 United States Code Section 3006—The "Mail Block" statute. This statute authorizes the Postmaster General, upon evidence satisfactory to him that the mails are being used to solicit remittances for obscene matter, to order mail addressed to the violator to be marked "unlawful" and returned to the sender. Two three-judge federal district courts have declared this statute unconstitutional and the matter is presently pending before the Supreme Court.

iv. 39 United States Code Section 3008—The Anti-Pandering Act. This statute empowers the Post Office Department to assist postal patrons who do not wish to receive unsolicited erotic mail. Section (b) of the statute provides as follows:

Upon receipt of a notice from an addressee that he has received [an advertisement for matter which he, in his

390

sole discretion believes to be erotically arousing or sexually provocative] . . . the Postmaster General shall issue an order, if requested by the addressee, to the sender thereof directing the sender and his agents or assigns to refrain from further mailings to the named addressees.

Within 30 days after the receipt of the order (which is called a "prohibitory order"), the sender must delete the name of the designated addressee from all mailing lists which he controls, and must thereafter refrain from making any further mailings to the named addressees.

If the addressee receives a second mailing of any type, from the sender, the Postmaster General must serve a complaint on the sender. An administrative hearing is then held, if the mailer requests one.

If, after the hearing (or without a hearing if one is not requested), the Postmaster General determines that the prohibitory order has been violated, he is authorized to request the Attorney General to make application to the United States District Court encompassing the area where the mail was sent or received for an order directing compliance.

If the Attorney General makes the application and the District Court enters the order, "failure to observe such order may be punished by the Court as contempt thereof."

In addition, upon request of any addressee, the prohibitory order of the Postmaster General must include the names of any of the addressee's minor children who are under the age of nineteen.

Under the Anti-Pandering Act, the postal patron can invoke the aid of the Post Office, and ultimately the courts, in having his name deleted from the lists of all mailers who send out unsolicited mail, for the Act leaves the matter of erotic arousal and sexual provocation entirely to the "sole discretion" of the individual postal patron.

With the exception of two "saturation" mailers, the industry appears to be responsive to the receipt of prohibitory orders. Of 325,000 prohibitory orders issued between April 14, 1968 (the effective date of the Act), and December 31, 1969, there have been only 2,000 cases of noncompliance. The offenders in virtually all 2,000 cases were the two producers mentioned above.

There are two "unsolicited mailing" problems to which the Anti-Pandering Act is not addressed: A postal patron cannot invoke the Act until he has received one mailing from the mailer against whom the prohibitory order is desired, nor does a prohibitory order against one mailer prevent other mailers from sending similar unsolicited mail to the objecting recipient.[153]

The Supreme Court of the United States upheld the constitutionality of this statute in 1970 in Rowan v. Post Office Department.

b. The Customs Statute—19 United States Code Section 1305. Section 1305 of the Tariff Act (Title 19, United States Code), prohibits all persons from importing obscene materials into the United States. The statute, which also gives the Secretary of the Treasury power to permit the importation of "obscene" books of literary or scientific merit, vests final exclusionary authority in the courts rather than in Customs officials.

i. Procedures. Approximately three percent of all packages arriving at a port are set aside, at random, for examination by Customs officials. If the Bureau deems any of the inspected items to be obscene, the United States Attorney is notified. This official then files a "libel" action in federal district court, which will culminate in a judicial determination as to whether or not the material violates current obscenity standards.

Movies are handled in a special way in that, with rare exceptions, all are screened for obscene content by a Customs film reviewer. Those which Customs believes to be obscene are handled in the same way as are packages. That is, the final determination is made at the judicial rather than administrative level.

ii. Sealed Mail. Until very recently the privacy of the seal was felt to be inviolate. Therefore, the Bureau opened and inspected first class mail from abroad only after receiving authorization from the addressee. If the addressee refused to consent to the opening of the envelope or package of suspected mail, it was returned unopened to its sender. However, on February 3, 1970, a notice appeared in the Federal Register to the effect that the Post Office Department and the Customs Bureau intend to amend their regulations so as to permit the opening of sealed mail from abroad without the necessity of requesting the permission of the addressee.

Two federal district courts have recently held that Section 1305 violates the Constitution as an impermissible interference with the right of private possession of obscenity established in Stanley v. Georgia. The matter is on appeal to the Supreme Court.

c. The FCC Statutes. 18 United States Code Section 1464 provides that: "Whoever utters any obscene, indecent, or profane language by means of radio communication shall be fined not more than $10,000 or imprisoned not more than two years, or both."

This statute, violations of which are investigated by the Federal Communications Commission, has been used primarily as a basis for prosecution of persons who utter vulgar expressions over ham radios.

47 United States Code Section 503(B) and 510 permit the FCC to impose a fine of not more than $1,000 on persons who use vulgar language on broadcast radio or citizens bands. If the broadcaster or operator refuses to pay, the Commission must commence an enforcement action in federal district court. This statute, like the FCC's criminal statute, has been used primarily as a basis for penalizing ham radio operators for improper use of their licenses. One proceeding, however, has been brought against an educational FM radio station, resulting in the imposition of a $100 fine on the broadcaster.

The FCC will usually not impose either criminal or civil penalties on broadcasters or operators, except in response to citizens' complaints. It does not independently monitor stations for the purpose of detecting violations of the obscenity statutes.

d. The FBI Statutes—18 United States Code Sections 1462 and 1465. Section 1462 prohibits the use of common carriers for the importation or interstate transportation of obscene materials. Violations are punishable by fines not exceeding $5000 and/or imprisonment not exceeding five years for the first offense and $10,000 and/or ten years for subsequent offenses.

Section 1465 prohibits the interstate transportation of obscene material for sale or distribution. All modes of transportation fall within the purview of the statute, and the transportation of two or more copies of any publication or a combined total of five such publications creates a rebuttable presumption that the materials are intended for sale or distribution. Violations are punishable by fine of not more than $5,000 and/or imprisonment of not more than five years.

Suspected violations of both of these statutes are investigated by the FBI. Despite the fact that most major producers of erotica transport their wares to retail outlets by truck and rail rather than through the mail, virtually all of

393

the major cases prosecuted by the Justice Department during the past several years have been postal cases brought pursuant to Section 1461. In only relatively few of these did the indictment contain a secondary count based on a violation of Section 1462 or 1465.

    e. Overlapping Federal Jurisdiction. Four federal agencies are charged, by statute, with the duty of investigating violations of the obscenity laws. The jurisdiction of three of these agencies—the Post Office Department, the FBI, and the Customs Bureau—are, to some extent, overlapping. That is, large scale producers and distributors of erotica are often the subject of three simultaneous investigations by these three agencies. For example, one Baltimore producer imports large amounts of erotica from Europe and is therefore subject to the jurisdiction of the Customs Bureau. He then ships much of the material by truck and rail to various retail outlets throughout the country, thus subjecting himself to FBI investigation. This same operator also produces a large volume of material, which he advertises via the mails. This latter activity may be separately investigated by the Post Office. The Commission's investigations have revealed no systematic cooperation among these agencies in their law enforcement activities.

Section F. Obscenity Laws in Other Countries

    The Commission retained legal consultants familiar with the criminal laws of other countries to report to it on the state of the law of obscenity in 15 countries with various legal traditions. The detailed reports of these consultants are contained in the Commission's Technical Reports. The consultants and the nations covered in their reports are as follows:

    1. Scandanavian Countries (Denmark, Sweden and Norway): Knud Waaben, Professor of Law, University of Copenhagen, Denmark.

    2. European Countries (West Germany, France, Italy, Yugoslavia, Hungary and the Soviet Union): Mirjan Damaska, Professor of Law, University of Zagreb, Yugoslavia.

    3. Australia and the United Kingdom: Brian Bromberger,

an Australian lawyer engaged in graduate study at the University of Pennsylvania Law School.

4. Israel: Dr. Ernst Livneh, Research Fellow, Institute for Legislative Research and Comparative Law, Faculty of Law, Hebrew University, Jerusalem.

5. Argentina and Mexico: Helen Silving, Professor of Law, University of Puerto Rico.

6. Japan: Peter Hocker, Faculty of Law, Keio University, Japan.

Presented below are brief summaries of the consultants' reports. The summaries are arranged in alphabetical order of country.

ARGENTINA

GENERAL STATUTES

The federal Penal Code prohibits the dissemination of "obscene matter" and imposes a penalty of imprisonment for a period of between two months and two years. The code does not define the term "obscene," but one criminal court has defined it as "all that which by writing or image tends to excite vile instincts and base sexual appetites, offending the public sense of shame." Unless the sole object of the publication is to arouse base sexual instincts, or to provoke licentiousness, the publication does not qualify as obscene. However, even if a book or other material is judicially decreed to be not obscene, the executive power may still intervene and ban the book as "immoral." An executive ban of this type was placed on the book Lolita by Nabakov.

JUVENILE STATUTES

A special provision proscribes the dissemination to any person less than 16 years of age of material which, though not obscene, "may seriously affect his sense of shame or excite or pervert his sexual instincts."

MOTION PICTURES

The National Institute of Cinematography (a governmental agency) screens all motion pictures prior to their exhibition. The Institute can order cuts or age restrictions, but apparently it cannot prohibit the entire exhibition.

Even after the Institute approves a film for exhibition, the film may still be prosecuted under the Penal Code.

AUSTRALIA

CUSTOMS ACT

Since the vast majority of all literature is imported, the most significant prohibitions on the distribution of obscenity are those which are embodied in the Customs Act. The Act prohibits the importation of "obscene" works and provides that the Minister of Customs may refer any imported literature to the National Literary Board of Review for a determination of obscenity. The Board's proceedings are informal and there are no definitional criteria as to what is obscene. Titles of books prohibited by the Board are published. The list currently includes such titles as Mailer's An American Dream, Selby's Last Exit to Brooklyn, and Young's Eros Denied. No imported book may be sold or offered for sale until it has received approval from the Customs Department.

POSTAL AND TELEGRAPH ACT

This statute provides that obscene materials may not be sent through the mails. The Postmaster General has almost complete discretion to refuse service for transmittal of materials which he deems obscene.

STATE OBSCENITY LAWS

In addition to the nationwide restrictions imposed by the Customs and Postal Acts, each state has laws prohibiting the dissemination, within its jurisdiction, of obscene materials. For example, in New South Wales and Victoria, material is obscene and hence may not be published or disseminated if it is likely to deprave or corrupt persons in one class or age group, not withstanding that other classes or age groups might not be similarly affected. Distributors and publishers may not distribute any matter unless it has been duly registered. A list of titles which have been banned includes Erskine Caldwell's God's Little Acre and Mary McCarthy's The Group. In Queensland and Tasmania, it is a crime to distribute any material which has been prohibited by a

Board of Review. If the banned publication consists, in substantial part, of pictures, there is no appeal to the courts.

MOTION PICTURES

A Censorship Board may ban or cut any imported film which, in the opinion of the Board, is blasphemous, indecent or obscene; is likely to be injurious to morality; is likely to be offensive to the people of a friendly nation; or depicts any matter, the exhibition of which is undesirable in the public interest.

Of 475 feature length films imported in 1965-66, one in four was banned or cut. A list of those either banned or so cut as to render them unscreenable includes: Ulysses, Bunuel's Veridiana, Charles Laughton's Night of the Hunter and Goddard's A Married Woman.

Films made within Australia are also subject to prior censorship.

RADIO AND TELEVISION

Television and radio networks are subject to stringent control by the Postmaster General and the Australian Broadcasting Control Board. There is an absolute prohibition against the broadcasting of blasphemous, indecent or obscene material.

DENMARK

REPEAL OF GENERAL OBSCENITY STATUTE

In 1964, the Minister of Justice asked a Criminal Law Committee to consider the issue of pornography. The Committee, which published its report in 1966, proposed that general criminal law provisions on obscene books and other publications be repealed. The Committee's recommendations were based on the following findings:

(1) That the then existing laws had an extremely narrow scope of application, i.e., only a small category of publications were punishable;

(2) That the definition of obscenity was vague and uncertain, and that legal authorities ought not to participate in decisions which might seem arbitrary and lacking legal basis;

(3) That, as a matter of principle, people should be permitted to publish, write and read whatever they wish;

(4) That there was no support for the hypothesis of harm to either children or adults and that, on the contrary, there was support for a hypothesis of no effects or even beneficial effects; and

(5) That morality should not be legislated.

The recommendations of the Committee were subsequently enacted into Danish law in two stages. In 1967, obscene books and other textual materials were removed from the coverage of the Penal Code. In 1969, pictorial matter was decriminalized as well. Danish law now contains no prohibitions on distribution of obscene materials to adults who wish to obtain them.

EXISTING STATUTES

The law does, however, still contain prohibitions on sales of pictures or "objects" to persons under 16 years of age. Fines are imposed for violations. Restrictions applicable to unsolicited mailings of offensive materials are still part of the law and local regulations applicable to offensive public displays also continue to exist.

There is also no censorship for sexual content of motion picture films which are being shown to audiences composed solely of persons 16 years of age and over. If the movie is to be shown to persons under 16, it is subject to prior censorship. The censor may order cuts or he may impose an age limit of 16 years or 12 years.

FRANCE

GENERAL STATUTES

The French Penal Code prohibits the dissemination of material which is "outrageous to good morals." The term "outrageous to good morals" has never been judicially defined. Each case presents an ad hoc issue for the trier of fact, whose finding is not reviewable by the higher courts.

Special rules of procedure apply to prosecutions involving allegedly immoral books which carry the name of their author, publisher and certain other required information. Prior to instituting a prosecution involving such a book, the prosecutor must secure an opinion from a special Commission as to whether the book is contrary to good morals. The Commission's opinion is not binding on law enforcement officials or the courts, but all procedural actions taken prior to securing the opinion are null and void.

398

A separate provision of the Code provides that publications primarily designed for youth may not "present debauchery in a favorable light."

Moreover, if any publication (even those designed primarily for adults) appears to the Minister of Interior to present a danger to juveniles by reason of its "licentious or pornographic character or the place given to crime or violence," he is given the option to impose either a ban on the distribution of the material to juveniles or a ban on the advertisement and public display of the publication.

MASS MEDIA

All motion pictures are screened in advance by a special Commission. The Commission may either ban the movie altogether or may impose an age limitation of 18 years or 13 years. Moreover, movie scripts must be transmitted to the Commission for preliminary review prior to the actual shooting of the movie. Even after the Commission has licensed a film, a movie may still be judicially banned as contrary to good morals.

All radio and television programs are also subject to advance screening by special Commissions.

Live theater performances are not screened in advance but may be prosecuted as a morals offense under the Penal Code.

CONFISCATION AND DESTRUCTION OF OBJECTIONABLE MATTER

After conviction on an obscenity charge, the court is required to decree confiscation and destruction of the objectionable material. There are no provisions for separate in rem proceedings.

WEST GERMANY

GENERAL OBSCENITY STATUTES

The West German Penal Code contains a provision which broadly bars disseminations of "lewd" materials. According to a recent Supreme Court decision, material can be banned as "lewd" only if it severs sexual phenomena from all other aspects of life through "brazen" and "obtrusive" presentation. (This formulation appears to be similar to Justice Stewart's "hard-core pornography" concept.)

A lower court has held the general obscenity statute unconstitutional on the grounds that the statute, in denying the "need" of some adults to consume erotica, has encroached on the Constitutional rights to "free development of personality" and "free access to information." The matter is presently pending before the Constitutional Court.

JUVENILE LEGISLATION

The "Filth and Smut Statute" prohibits the dissemination of "immoral matter" to persons under the age of eighteen. The statutory procedure is as follows. A Federal Board keeps a list of all materials which it deems to be "immoral." New titles are added from time to time. In contrast to "lewd" matter (proscribed by the general statute) which has been limited to hard-core pornography, "immoral matter" is construed much more broadly. Once a title is entered on the list, it cannot be made available to persons under 18 years of age, and restrictions are also placed on its advertisement, display, commercial dissemination, and library lending.

MASS MEDIA

The mass media are subject to rather stringent industry self-regulation. All movies are screened in advance by an examining board which has been set up by an association of movie producers, distributors, and cinema owners. The Board has the power to ban a movie altogether, to order cuts, or to impose age restrictions of 18 years or 16 years (children under 6 are not allowed to attend any movie).

Radio and television networks have adopted guidelines for programming, one of which is the "Safeguard of the Morals Code."

Live stage performances are not subject to prior censorship but may fall within other provisions of the Penal Code such as the prohibition on "causing public annoyance by lewd acts."

CONFISCATION AND DESTRUCTION OF OBJECTIONABLE MATERIAL

Following conviction under the general statute or the "Filth and Smut Statute," all copies of the prohibited material are confiscated and destroyed. Though the use of in rem proceedings, material may also be subject to destruction even in the absence of a criminal prosecution and/or conviction.

HUNGARY

Under the Hungarian Criminal Code, the circulation of "obscene objects" is punishable by deprivation of liberty for a term not exceeding one year. "Obscene" matter has been judicially defined as matter which "seriously offends the general moral sentiment by reason of its orientation to the sexual."

In addition, dissemination of obscene objects to juveniles is punishable by loss of liberty for a period not exceeding three years if the disseminator is "a person charged with the education, care or custody of minors."

The Postal regulations provide that letters or shipments containing obscene materials cannot be forwarded. It is not known what criteria are used by Postal authorities in determining whether the letter or shipment contains "obscene" matter.

ISRAEL

EXISTING LAWS AND THEIR APPLICATION

The Penal Code prohibits the sale, distribution and advertisement of any "obscene printed or written matter or any obscene picture, photograph, drawing or model or any other object tending to corrupt morals." A Post Office Ordinance prohibits the use of the mails for the transmission of obscene matter.

Public displays of obscene pictorial matter are prohibited. There are apparently no special provisions designed to prohibit disseminations of sexual materials to juveniles. However, one rather unique provision prohibits publication of a picture of a nude person of between nine and eighteen years of age.

In 1962, a district court adopted the Roth definition of obscenity, holding that the test was whether to the average person, applying contemporary community standards, the dominant theme of the material, taken as a whole, appeals to the prurient interest.

In practice, the aforementioned penal provisions are largely dead letters. Erotic materials are widely available and there have been very few criminal prosecutions.

401

MOTION PICTURES

All motion pictures are screened in advance for violence, cruelty and sexual content. Of 450 films screened in 1967-68, 15 were banned—12 because of cruelty and only 3 on the basis of erotic content. An additional 150 films were restricted to adult audiences.

MOVEMENT TOWARDS REFORM

A 1968-69 study committee recommended liberalization of the obscenity laws. It found, among other things, that:

(1) Pornography is not a troublesome problem and does not lead to crime; (2) Definitional problems render enforcement exceedingly difficult; (3) Pornography does not corrupt morals; and (4) Pornography may have positive effects such as the release of deviant impulses and the diversion of impulses into "permitted" channels.

The Committee recommended that obscenity be defined as "material which, according to standards accepted at the time and in the society in question, injures the feelings of a considerable sector of the population." The Committee further recommended that two types of cases be exempt from the scope of the law:

(1) Cases involving books and pictures having bona fide redeeming social value and (2) Cases involving a dissemination to an adult who requests it (so long as there is no public exhibition).

The Committee recommended less liberal rules for public performances and films. It also recommended that an existing Committee for the Examination of Literature be given statutory recognition so that it could authoritatively advise those applying to it on the question of whether certain materials are obscene. If the materials were approved by the Committee they could not be subject to criminal prosecution.

ITALY

GENERAL STATUTE

The Italian Code prohibits the dissemination of obscene materials which it defines as those acts and objects "which according to the common sentiment are offensive to shame." Offensiveness to shame has been judicially equated with in-

402

jury to the "usual feelings of reserve which people express with regard to sexual matters."

Sexual materials which are not legally obscene may still be punishable under other provisions of the Code. Three such provisions are those which prohibit general dissemination of materials which offend public decency, are offensive to family morals, or are "capable of disturbing the common moral sentiment."

JUVENILE LEGISLATION

Under the general statute described above, works of art and science are not to be considered obscene unless offered for sale, sold or otherwise procured to a person under 18 for a motive other than that of study.

In addition, a separate statutory provision prohibits public exhibitions or displays of drawings and other pictorial objects "designed for exposure to the public view which . . . [are] offensive to shame or public decency, judged with reference to the particular susceptibility of minors under the age of 18 and assessed with regard to the need for protection of their morals. "Apparently this statute prohibits public exhibitions to all audiences of those pictorial materials considered inappropriate for minors.

An additional statutory provision prohibits the inclusion of obscene matter in "publications designed for children or adolescents."

MASS MEDIA

All motion pictures are screened in advance by a special Commission within the Ministry of Tourism and Public Performances. The Commission may ban the movie altogether or may impose age limitations of 18 years or 14 years.

Live musical comedies and variety shows may not be performed without prior approval. Other live stage performances are not subject to prior censorship, but those not submitted for advance approval are considered to be for audiences of adults only. All live stage performances are subject to potential prosecution under the general obscenity provisions and other related statutes.

Radio and television networks are run by a public corporation which is required to submit its broadcasting program to the Ministry of Mail and Telecommunications every three months. The Ministry forwards the programming schedule to a special Commission which is empowered to order changes. Movies and stage shows which have been banned for minors may not be broadcast on the networks.

JAPAN

The Japanese Penal Code prohibits the sale and display of "obscene" materials. "Obscene" is not defined in the Code, but has been the subject of judicial definition on several occasions. In a decision which held the book Lady Chatterly's Lover obscene, the Supreme Court stated that an object may be considered to be obscene if it does injury to man's sense of shame (bashfulness) or if it excites or stimulates the sexual desires or if it is contrary to proper sexual morality.

There are no separate statutory provisions designed to protect juveniles, nor are there any special display or unsolicited mailing statutes.

Film censorship is carried out on a voluntary basis by a Committee set up by the film industry. Films not passed by that Committee are generally not sold or handled by any of the film distributors or exhibitors.

MEXICO

GENERAL STATUTE

The Mexican Penal Code prohibits the dissemination of "obscene" materials and imposes a penalty thereon of imprisonment for a period of between six months and five years and a fine of up to 10,000 pesos. The term "obscene" has been judicially defined as that which is "contrary to the sense of shame or modesty, or of decorum."

ADMINISTRATIVE SANCTIONS

In addition, an administrative Regulation provides, among other things, that "it is immoral and contrary to education to publish, distribute, circulate, exhibit or sell materials . . . that stimulate excitement or evil passions or sensuality. This Regulation is not prohibition on distributions to juveniles but rather a general ban on dissemination of offensive materials.

The same Regulation creates a federal Qualifying Commission which has the authority to:

(a) Examine any publication which might be in violation of the aforementioned standards; (b) Impose an administrative fine of from 500 to 5,000 pesos upon the offenders; (c) Declare that the publication is illegal and file with the Post Office Department a motion for its withdrawal from the mails; (d) Inform the Federal Prosecutor's Office of the fact that the material has, in the view of the Commission, a criminal character; and (e) Communicate its decision to other appropriate authorities for execution by such authorities.

Material which has been approved by the Qualifying Commission may still be subject to criminal prosecution under the general statute.

MOTION PICTURES

All motion pictures must be approved in advance of showing by the Directorate of Cinematography. The relevant regulation provides that authorization shall be denied when "one attacks morals" or when "one makes apology for any vice."

If the motion picture is approved, it is then placed into one of four classifications. These are:

(1) Permitted for children, adolescents and adults;
(2) Permitted for adolescents and adults;
(3) Permitted solely for adults; and
(4) Permitted for adults in "exhibitions specially authorized."

NORWAY

GENERAL AND JUVENILE STATUTES

The Penal Code prohibits the following acts: (1) Public lectures, exhibitions or performances with obscene content; (2) Sale or distribution or exhibition of obscene writings or similar objects; (3) Delivery of obscene writings, pictures of similar objects to persons under 18; and (4) Obscene conduct which is in public or in the presence of persons who have not consented or in the presence of persons under 16 years of age.

Norwegian law has been applied to a broader range of materials than has its Swedish counterpart. For example, the novels Sexus and Without A Stitch have both been held obscene.

MOTION PICTURES

All motion pictures are screened in advance. Outright bans are placed on those films which are "contrary to law or decency" or which have a "brutalizing or morally deteriorating effect." The censors are also permitted to impose age limitations of 12, 16, or 18 years if they believe that a movie is apt to have a harmful effect on the relevant age group.

RECOMMENDATIONS OF ADVISORY COMMITTEE

In 1955, the Minister of Justice appointed a Criminal Law Committee to study the obscenity provisions. The Committee recommended a broadening of the law so as to proscribe (for all audiences) materials which are "clearly offensive" or which "have a tendency to exert a brutalizing or debasing effect on children or youth." The recommendations were not adopted.

SOVIET UNION

The Soviet Union's Criminal Code prohibits the production and dissemination of "objects of a pornographic character." The term "pornographic" has not been either statutorily or judicially defined. However, in a commentary to the Code, it is stated that an object is pornographic if "it contains indecent descriptions or representations of circumstances connected with sexual relationships whose aim or possible result is the stirring up of sexual passion." Both the production and dissemination of pornographic materials are punishable activities, and can result in a fine of up to 100 rubles or the deprivation of liberty for a term not exceeding three years. (Apparently, the fine and imprisonment are alternative measures.) In addition to the punishment specified in the Code, a violator may also be subject to social censure, dismissal from office, or forfeiture of the right to engage in certain activities or occupy certain offices.

SWEDEN

EXISTING LAW

All disseminations of writings or pictures which "offend morality and decency" are prohibited. Proscriptions are also placed on distributions among youth of any writing or picture "which, due to its content, can coarsen or otherwise involve serious risk for the moral nurture of the young." There are also restrictions on public displays and other public offenses to morality and decency.

The actual application of the law is a very narrow one, especially for verbal or textual materials. Prosecutions of textual materials are limited to works of a sadistic, perverse or brutalizing character.

All motion picture films are screened in advance. Films which have a "brutalizing or harmfully exciting effect" or which "entice crime" are banned. The censors are also authorized to place age limits of 15 years old or 11 years old if the films are apt to impose psychological harm to persons in those age categories.

PROPOSED CHANGES

In 1965, the Minister of Justice appointed a Committee to study existing obscenity legislation. The Committee, which issued its report in 1969, found that there was scarce support for a hypothesis of harmful effects flowing from the reading or viewing of pornographic materials. It recommended narrowing the scope of legislation to "extreme" cases. The Minister of Justice disagreed with the recommendations of the Committee, and recommended instead that the existing general statute be repealed. He further recommended the enactment of prohibitions on advertising, public displays and unsolicited mailings and the retention of juvenile legislation. The recommendations of the Minister of Justice have been once adopted by Parliament. Under Swedish law, they must again be laid before the new Parliament after the general elections in the Fall of 1970. If approved by that body, they will then go into effect.

THE UNITED KINGDOM

GENERAL STATUTES

The Obscene Publications Act of 1959 imposes a prison sentence of up to three years plus a fine (amount unspecified) on those who publish or distribute obscene articles. An article is obscene under the Act if its effect, taken as a whole, has a tendency to deprave and corrupt persons who are likely to read or see it. The words "deprave" and "cor-

407

rupt" have been further defined in judicial decisions. To deprave is "to make morally bad, to pervert, to debase or corrupt morality." "To corrupt" means "to render morally unsound or rotten, to destroy the morality or chastity or, to pervert to ruin a good morality, to debase, to defile."

The Customs Act prohibits the importation of both obscene and indecent works. The courts have held that the words "indecent" and "obscene" are to be dealt with disjunctively and that the importation of either type of work is prohibited under the Act. A work is "indecent" if it offends the ordinary, normal person.

The Post Office Act prohibits the sending of indecent or obscene materials through the mails, and there are three statutes which prohibit the public display of indecent or obscene materials.

Unlike most of the other countries studied, in the United Kingdom, the courts have held that the term "obscenity" encompasses not only sexual materials but also other topics such as drug addiction.

JUVENILE LEGISLATION

The "Children and Young Persons Harmful Publications Act" of 1955 places a general prohibition on the printing or dissemination of any book or magazine which is likely to fall into the hands of young persons and which consists of stories told in pictures portraying the commission of crimes or violent and repulsive or horrible acts or incidents in such a way that the work as a whole would tend to corrupt a child or a young person into whose hands it might fall.

MOTION PICTURES

The British Board of Film Censors is a quasi-legal body established by the Motion Picture Industry. It makes recommendations to local licensing authorities as to the conditions which the latter might attach to the licensing of motion pictures. These recommendations, while not binding, are almost automatically followed by the local licensing bodies. The model condition recommended by the Board is as follows:

No film shall be shown, and no poster or other advertisement of a film . . . shall be displayed which is likely to be injurious to morality or to encourage or to incite to crime, or lead to disorder or to be offensive to the public feeling or which contains any offensive representation of living persons.

The Board of Censors screens each film to ascertain whether the model condition has been met. It is primarily concerned with violence and horror, rather than sex. If a film is approved, it is then given one of four recommended classifications:[153a]

(1) "X"—only for adults; no one under 18 years of age admitted; (2) "AA"—no one under 14 years of age admitted; (3) "A"—suitable for general exhibition, but parents advised that the film contains material which they may not deem suitable for children under 14 years of age to see; (4) "U"— suitable for general exhibition.

A local licensing authority, even though it has adopted the Board's model condition, is free to reject the Board's classification of any given film.

RADIO AND TELEVISION

Radio and television networks are governed by the British Broadcasting Commission and the Independent Television Authority. They have no formal code or regulations but, in general, refuse programs which are offensive to good taste and decency.

MOVEMENTS TOWARD REFORM

The Committee of the Arts Council, a quasi-official body, has recommended repeal of the general laws prohibiting disseminations of obscenity. In its report, it stated that there is no evidence that such a repeal would be injurious to society. It also recognized that it is reasonable to protect individuals who may be affronted by offensive displays or behavior in public places, and therefore recommend retention of the various statutes dealing with these specific offenses. It further recommended the retention of the Children and Young Persons (Harmful Publications Act) and the practice of film classification by the British Board of Film Censors.

YUGOSLAVIA

GENERAL STATUTE

The Penal Code prohibits the dissemination or production (even without intent to disseminate) of matter which is "seriously injurious to morality." Violators are punished by imprisonment for a period of not more than one year.

All material which has been printed must be forwarded (by the printer or publisher) to the public prosecutor for examination. If the latter finds the matter to be "injurious to morality," he may issue a temporary ban on the publication. The ban remains in effect until a final court adjudication of the matter. If the court agrees with the prosecutor's finding, it will make the injunction permanent. If the court disagrees, the injunction will be dissolved.

JUVENILE LEGISLATION

Material which is "damaging to upbringing" may not be disseminated to juveniles. This is a very broad statutory provision which has been used to suppress mere salacious jokes and spicy stories. One court has held, however, that a publication cannot be generally banned under this provision unless it primarily circulates among immature readers.

MASS MEDIA

Each of the constituent republics of Yugoslavia has a special Commission to examine domestic motion pictures. Foreign films are examined by a federal Commission. The Commissions are empowered only to ban or approve a film. They may not impose age classifications.

Sexual expressions on the stage do not fall within the purview of the statutory provisions discussed above. However, objectionable performances could be punished under provisions prohibiting "public conduct which is offensive to moral sentiment."

Radio and television are not subject to prior censorship and, to date, there has been little need for the exercise of legal control of any kind.

Section G. Relevant Empirical Data

PUBLIC OPINION ABOUT OBSCENITY LAWS

Public opinion about the wisdom or necessity of obscenity prohibitions is often considered relevant in determining the propriety of such laws. The Commission sponsored a national survey of American opinion, one of the components of which was a survey of the opinions of the American public regarding laws prohibiting the distribution or availability of explicit sexual materials. This survey utilized a probability sample of American adults; its results closely approximate the actual opinion of the American people.[154]

ADULTS

With regard to the sexual materials which adults may obtain, it is clear that American public opinion does not strongly favor restricting such materials. Indeed, a majority of American adults (almost 60%) believe that adults should be allowed to read or see any explicit sexual materials they want to. This majority is composed of persons who believe that "people should be allowed to read or see anything they want to [in the way of explicit sexual materials]" (32%) and persons who believe that there should be restrictions upon such materials but that such prohibitions should "apply just to children and young people" (27%). The sexual materials to which these questions referred included materials often referred to as "hard-core pornography," that is, pictures mainly for the purpose of showing sex organs, pictures of men and women having (or appearing to have) sexual intercourse, pictures of mouth-sex organ contact between men and women, pictures of homosexual activities and of sex activities including whips, belts or spankings, and textual descriptions of these same themes.

At a different point in the interview, 52% of the adults agreed that it would be "all right" to have these sexual materials available to adults who wished to read or view them privately. The somewhat lower percentage of persons interviewed who agreed with this statement than with the statements referred to in the previous paragraph may be attributable to ordinary fluctuations in responses. It may also flow from the fact that, when asked if consensual private adult exposure to erotica was "all right," some respondents may have answered "no" because they did not deem such exposure to be correct or advisable behavior, although they do not favor legal prohibitions upon such consensual adult exposure.

At yet another point in the interview, respondents were asked to address themselves separately to five different types of explicit sexual depictions, and to answer for whom it is "all right" for these depictions to be made available in

411

movies and in textual material. Responses indicating it is all right for these materials to be available for adults varied from 53% of the respondents, who believed that it is all right for textual materials containing descriptions of the sex organs of a man or a woman to be available for adults, through 45%, who believed it all right to admit adults to movies of a man and a woman having (or appearing to have) sexual intercourse, to 29% who believed it all right to admit adults to movies showing sex activities which include whips, belts, or spankings. Percentages in the 30's and 40's were obtained for the other explicit pictorial and textual depictions (oral-genital sexual activity, homosexual activities and heterosexual intercourse).

It thus appears that, when confronted with a particular explicit sexual depiction in a particular medium, a lower percentage of respondents believe it all right for such a depiction to be available to adults than the percentage who generally believed that adults should be allowed to read or see any sexually explicit materials they want to. This discrepancy may again be caused by the fact that respondents here were asked whether it was "all right" for the materials to be made available—not whether the law should prohibit the availability. It may also be true that persons react more restrictively to very narrowly defined classes of materials which they happen to deem particularly inappropriate than to a general range of sexually explicit materials such as laws would prohibit. In all events, even for the narrow category of sexual materials found not "all right" for adults by the largest group of respondents (i.e., films of sex activities which include whips, belts, or spankings), about 30% of the American public believes it is "all right" for adults to have such materials available to them. There is, therefore, no consensus among the American public that even such explicit sadomasochistic sexual materials should be subject to legal prohibitions for adults.

YOUNG PERSONS

A substantial consensus of American adults believe that young persons should not have access to some sexual materials. American adults were asked their views about to whom (if anyone) it should be "all right" to make available the types of sexual materials described in the preceding paragraph. In reference to none of these types of sexual

412

material did more than 7% feel it would be all right for the materials to be available to persons under 16.

RELEVANCE TO PUBLIC OPINION OF CONCLUSIONS AS TO THE EFFECT OF SEXUAL MATERIALS

The views which Americans hold regarding the advisability of laws restricting sexual materials for adults and young persons are strongly influenced by their views about the harmful effects of such materials. In the national survey, persons who said that they favored no restrictions upon sexual materials were then asked if their views would change "if it were clearly demonstrated that materials dealing with sex had harmful effects." About two-thirds of persons who favor no legal restrictions said that their views would change through such a demonstration. On the other hand, persons favoring restrictions upon either children or adults were asked if these views would change "if it were clearly demonstrated that materials dealing with sex had no harmful effects." About one third of these people stated that such a demonstration would change their view. In all, some two-fifths of American adults indicated that they would change their views in one direction or another on the basis of clear demonstrations that there were or were not harmful effects.

EFFICACY OF LEGAL PROHIBITIONS

Almost half the population believes that laws against sexual materials would be "impossible to enforce." If laws restricting the availability of sexual materials are to be passed, a substantial majority (62%) of the people would rather have "federal laws passed by Congress for the whole country," as opposed to "state laws for each state," or "laws passed by each community who wants them."

CHARACTERISTICS OF PEOPLE FAVORING RESTRICTIONS

Two questions in the national survey were used as a basis for classifying respondents according to the degree to which they favor restrictions. These classifications show that advocacy of restrictions on the availability of explicit sexual materials is related to a general orientation of less acceptance of freedom of expression. People who oppose the availability of explicit sexual materials tend to be more likely to believe that newspapers should not have the right to print

413

articles which criticize the police, that people should not be allowed to publish books which attack our system of government, and that people should not be allowed to make speeches against God. In addition, men are somewhat less likely to be restrictive about sex materials than women; adults under 30 are more likely to be tolerant than older adults; adults with 8 or fewer years of education are more likely to be restrictive than those with more education; and regular church attenders are more likely to be restrictive than those who attend church less frequently or never.

ACCURACY OF AMERICAN PERCEPTION ABOUT
AMERICAN PUBLIC OPINION

The national survey asked respondents not only for their own opinion about the advisability of obscenity laws, but also about their perception of the opinions of others in their community. More respondents (29%) believed that the opinions of most others in their community were more restrictive than their own opinion than believed the opposite (12%). This suggests that, in evaluating the opinions of others in their community, more Americans tend to judge erroneously that others are more restrictive than themselves than tend to judge erroneously that others are less restrictive than themselves. Similar results were obtained in another study of a single community (Massey, 1970).

EMPIRICAL DATA RELEVANT TO THE APPLICATION
OF PRESENT CONSTITUTIONAL STANDARDS
FOR ADULTS

A growing body of empirical evidence is being accumulated regarding the three dimensions referred to in the constitutional standards for obscenity: prurient interest, offensiveness, and social value. The empirical evidence is often only indirectly related to the standards because of definitional problems. For example, prurient interest is perhaps not a unidimensional concept and it must be simplified in order to bring the methods of empirical research to bear on it. Empirical research has tended to focus on sexual arousal or sexual stimulation. While sexual arousal may not be identical to prurient interest it would seem to be a vital ingredient. "Social value" is also not a unidimensional concept. Empirical research has examined several possible social value dimensions such as education or entertainment.

414

The research projects which have investigated these matters have studied a wide variety of kinds of people: adult males of varying socio-economic backgrounds (Katzman, 1969); Canadian male college students age 18-25 (Amoroso et. al. 1970); male and female college students (Mosher, 1970); young married couples (Byrne et. al. 1970); and adult males and females in a variety of natural groups in a large metropolitan area (Wallace et. al. 1970). They have also studied a wide variety of explicit sexual materials: pictures of individual females in various degrees of dress and undress (Katzman, 1969); slide projected pictures covering a range from nude males and females through explicit depictions of a variety of heterosexual activities (Amoroso et. al. 1970; Wallace et. al. 1970); colored motion pictures of heterosexual nude petting and intercourse (Mosher, 1970); and pictures and written descriptions of explicit heterosexual and homosexual activity (Byrne, 1970).

These studies all used a variation on a standard experimental procedure in which the subject is exposed to a stimulus and then asked to rate that stimulus on one or more scales such as the degree of sexual arousal, the degree of offensiveness, or the degree of obscenity made manifest by the stimulus. The results of these several studies are quite consistent even though they used different kinds of subjects, different kinds of stimuli, and different procedures.

Perhaps the principal finding relevant to our interests here is that people do not agree about whether or not a given sexual stimulus is "sexually arousing," "offensive," or "pornographic." Some of the studies asked for judgments of these dimensions on a 6 point scale, others on a 7 point scale, and still others on an 11 point scale. In nearly every case the judgments provided by a group for a given stimulus ranged from one extreme to another. For example (Amoroso, et. al. 1970), 60 male students aged 18 to 25 were asked to judge a colored slide of an attractive couple roughly their own age engaged in sexual intercourse: (1) on the dimension of "pleasantness" using an 11 point scale from "extremely pleasant" to "extremely unpleasant"; (2) on the dimension of "sexually stimulating" using an 11 point scale from "not at all" to "extremely"; and (3) on a "pornographic" dimension from "not at all" to "extremely." These young men so differed among themselves in their judgments of this picture on each of these dimensions that their judgments were distributed on each of the eleven points of the scale. That is, some said that this picture was "not at all sexually stimulating" while others said that it was "extremely sexually stimulating"; some said that it was "extremely pleasant" while others said that it was "extremely unpleasant"; and some said that it was "extremely pornographic" while others judged it to be "not at all pornographic." And, of course, there were judgments that fell on all the intervening points. Similar distributions of judgments on these dimensions were obtained on a variety of depictions ranging from nude female through couple in underwear, nude couple petting, genital intercourse, to oral-genital intercourse.

Similar findings, regarding the lack of consensus among members of groups in their judgments of explicit sexual stimuli along dimensions related to constitutional standards for obscenity, were found by other investigators using a variety of kinds of subjects and stimuli (Katzman, 1969; Mosher, 1970; Byrne et. al. 1970; Wallace, et. al. 1970).

A second important finding of these studies is that groups with different demographic characteristics differ in their judgments of explicit sexual materials. Middle class men differ from working class men (Katzman, 1969); males differ from females (Byrne, et. al. 1970; Mosher, 1970); sexually experienced differ from sexually inexperienced (Mosher, 1970); persons with more feelings of guilt about sex differ from those with less guilt feelings (Mosher, 1970); members of religious organizations, social service organizations, professional organizations, and student groups differ from each other (Wallace et. al. 1970). Such differences are not surprising to social scientists. These differences become important, however, in considering who might be a representative spokesman for a community on issues of obscenity, and the empirical demonstration of the differences is a contribution to the social process.

A third finding is that sexual arousal and offensiveness are independent dimensions. A specific sexual depiction that tends to be sexually arousing may or may not be offensive; and sexual material that tends to be offensive may or may not be sexually arousing. Amoroso and his colleagues (1970) found that for a wide range of sexual depictions the judgments of these depictions on the "stimulating" and "pleasantness" scales were not related, but that each bore an approximately equal relationship to judgments on the "pornographic" scale. That is, to be judged "pornographic" a depiction had to be both highly stimulating sexually and extremely unpleasant, but these two reactions did not occur together most of the time. Results generally consistent with this finding were

416

also obtained by Katzman (1969) and Wallace and his associates (1970).

A fourth finding from empirical research in this area is that "social value" is attributed to explicit sexual materials by substantial portions of the population. In the national survey conducted for the Commission (Abelson, 1970) representative samples of adult men and women, after having been questioned extensively about experience with explicit sexual materials including nudity with sex organs exposed, heterosexual intercourse, mouth-sex organ contact, homosexual activity, and sadomasochistic depictions, were asked about the effects of looking at or reading sexual materials. Of the men, 62% said that these materials provide information about sex, and 43% reported that this had occurred for him or someone he knew personally; 58% said that these materials provide entertainment, and 46% reported that this had occurred for him or someone he knew personally; and 50% said that these materials improve sex relations of some married couples, and 26% reported that this had happened to him or someone he knew personally. Not as many women as men attribute these effects to looking at or reading sexual materials, but 35%, 21%, and 24% of the women report that these materials, respectively, provide information about sex, improve sex relations of some married couples, and provide entertainment for themselves or someone they knew personally.

Another study (Wallace et. al. 1970) found that substantial portions of adults in a large metropolitan area judged a variety of explicit depictions of sexual activity to have some educational and entertainment value.

These findings raise considerable question about the empirical validity of the concepts of "prurient interest of the average person" or "offensive according to contemporary community standards." They also indicate that desirable social value is attributed to explicit sexual materials by a considerable number of people in our society at the present time.

417

Section H. Summary and Analysis of the Legal Considerations Relevant to the Commission's Legislative Recommendations

Four different types of substantive legislative regulation of explicit sexual materials have been suggested to the Commission: (1) Prohibition upon distribution and dissemination generally, including prohibition of commercial distribution to consenting adults; (2) Prohibition upon unconsented distribution, such as public displays and unsolicited mailings, which may offend persons who do not wish to be exposed to explicit sexual material; (3) Prohibition upon direct dissemination of explicit sexual material to young persons; (4) Prohibition upon "pandering." Previous parts of this panel report have described the possible constitutional bases for and constitutional limitations upon these potential types of regulation, as well as the present pattern of legislation and law enforcement in these areas and the relevant empirical data. This part will summarize and briefly analyze the legal considerations bearing upon each of these legislative questions. It will also comment upon three closely related procedural matters—proof of scienter, seizures of material by law enforcement officials, and proposals to withdraw or limit appellate jurisdiction over obscenity determinations.

SHOULD "GENERAL" PROHIBITIONS UPON DISSEMINATION OF "OBSCENE" MATERIAL TO CONSENTING ADULTS BE IMPOSED?

In the past, the Supreme Court has considered the constitutionality of general regulations of explicit sexual materials—which prohibit, among other things, distribution to consenting adults—without overt reliance upon assumptions or conclusions regarding the social effect of such material upon adults who desire to or consent to receive it. In response to Congress' direction in establishing this Commission, the Commission has, for the first time, made a comprehensive effort to study these effects. Set forth below are, first, a summary of the legal considerations bearing upon "general" obscenity regulations in the absence of reliable data as to

418

effects and, second, a discussion of the relevancy of effects data to such regulations.

IN THE ABSENCE OF DATA AS TO EFFECTS

The Roth case (Roth v. United States) held prohibitions upon the distribution of "obscene" material to consenting adults to be constitutional, without reliance upon authoritative findings or conclusions regarding the social effects of such material. The Court's holding was based upon three subsidiary conclusions: (1) that some kinds of printed material, such as blasphemy, profanity, and libel, were not thought by the Framers of the First Amendment to be entitled to the constitutional protection which is ordinarily accorded to speech; (2) that there was evidence that the Framers viewed certain "obscene" explicit sexual materials as within this category of unprotected expression; and (3) that there was a virtually universal judgment that "obscene" explicit sexual materials are entirely without social value and should be prohibited. The Court also undoubtedly relied to an extent upon the fact that, for many years, it had assumed the validity of such prohibitions, although not deciding the question directly.

Developments since the Roth decision have suggested both practical and constitutional doubts about the appropriateness of its conclusion that distribution of "obscene" material to consenting adults may constitutionally be broadly prohibited without reference to considerations of social harm. These developments have been in three areas: (a) The enormous practical difficulties under Roth of meaningfully defining what is "obscene" for consenting adults and of fairly applying such definitions in legal proceedings; (b) Changing public opinion regarding the need for and wisdom of prohibiting distribution of sexual materials to consenting adults; (c) Developing constitutional doctrine holding that free expression guarantees are applicable to "obscene" materials in at least some adult contexts.

PRACTICAL DIFFICULTIES WITH GENERAL PROHIBITIONS

Practical experience with the actual application through the law enforcement process of prohibitions upon the dissemination of "obscene" material to consenting adults under the Roth case has been decidedly unsatisfactory. The difficulties have principally been caused by the unsatisfactory quality of the definition of "obscene" which has been applied in order to comply with the limitations which Roth placed upon what may

419

be deemed "obscene" under a general prohibition. These difficulties exist to a significant degree whichever particular version of the Roth standard is utilized. The discussion here will focus upon the three-part definition adopted in the plurality opinion in the Fanny Hill case, since that version of the Roth standard is the one which is almost universally used in state and lower federal courts.

Perhaps the most obvious problem with the Roth standard is the extreme vagueness and subjectiveness of the test of what constitutes "obscene" material. In most areas of criminal law the law itself makes the judgment regarding what particular conduct is to be penalized and that conduct is described by the law with considerable specificity. The primary question for the trier of fact in each case under such laws is whether the historical facts of the case show that the prohibited conduct has been committed. Where criminal law is less specific as to what conduct is prohibited—as with laws penalizing conduct which is "unreasonable" or "reckless"—the conduct prohibited is ordinarily deemed criminal because it creates an immediate threat of physical danger. In such cases, while the trier of fact in an individual case must do more than ascertain what the defendant did, he may at least judge the criminality of the defendant's act with respect to the actual dangers created by that act, and a judge or juror is aided in making such judgments by a core of common objective experiences in, for example, what kind of automobile driving conduct is reckless because it is unnecessarily productive of a great chance of injury to others.

The Roth standard for defining the "obscene" differs radically from this pattern in that it leaves to the trier of fact in each case a vast judgmental function under a legal standard which does not call upon any common experience with objective phenomena but which relies, instead, upon subjective moral, aesthetic and even psychoanalytic determinations by those charged with application of the law. The test under Roth is not whether materials bear certain specified contents, nor is it even whether they have certain dangerous or harmful effects, for the Roth standard was formulated without reference to such effects. Rather the tri-partite standard calls for a judgment about the "appeal" of the material involved to the average person, about the "social value" of the material, and about the way the material compares with standards of offensiveness prevalent in the community. These judgments are enormously difficult to make with regard to particular materials and it is very easy for different judges and jurors to reach opposite conclusions as to the same works. Expert testimony in these issues may, at times, be helpful, but as often as not there are experts on each side of each issue and the judge or juror is left quite at sea as to which expert view to adopt. It is probably not erroneous therefore to conclude that, in actual practice, application of this test most often comes down to the trier's individual subjective judgment whether the particular work involved ought to be permitted in society, and that this judgment is frequently made primarily with reference to personal belief about the morality of certain sexual practices and the aesthetic appropriateness of publicizing or communicating about those practices. Hence, law is made in each case by the judge or jurors who happen to try it.

Such indefiniteness and subjectiveness makes it impossible in many instances to know in advance whether materials may or may not be legally distributed. Thus, persons may either be unfairly convicted—because they honestly believed they were free to distribute material later held to be obscene—or they may, out of fear of prosecution or upon receipt of police "warnings," forebear from distributing materials which are, in fact, constitutionally protected. In either event, the result is unduly repressive and in some communities constitutionally protected material may simply not be available because of the dangers of attempting to engage in distribution of sexually explicit works. The alternative of non-enforcement of the law because of these uncertainties, which has been adopted by police and prosecutors in some places, is equally unsatisfactory to a portion of the public which justifiably believes that existing laws should be enforced. In addition, the vagueness and subjectiveness of the Roth standard often causes the same book or film to be condemned in one court proceeding, while exonerated in another under exactly the same legal standard.

Thus, the results in individual cases may legitimately be seen by the community and the defendant as the reflection of the personal predilections of particular police, prosecutors, judges and jurors, rather than as the evenhanded result of law. This is not satisfactory criminal law.

The elements of the tri-partite test are unsatisfactory, even aside from their extremely vague and subjective quality.

The "prurient-interest" test is ambiguous in meaning. In addition, to the interest in sex appealed to must be a morbid or shameful one (as the Roth case suggested), the test may be circular. Morbidity or shame may become associated with an

421

interest in material solely or principally because such material is prohibited by law and the social customs which develop under the influence of law. If so, the law's prohibition in this area contributes to or causes the very element which is necessary to satisfy a test of illegality.

The community-standards test unduly favors the established national publisher or distributor of material as compared with his smaller, less established counterpart. An established national distributor can, through widespread exploitation in media, which have become recognized as setting standards of taste, actually change community standards for adults to a great degree by the time a prosecution can be finally decided. It is almost impossible to imagine that material distributed through such an established mass media source could ever be found to offend community standards as required by the test. Thus, to a significant degree, the community-standards test delegates to certain established distributors the setting of the line between the legal and illegal. The same immunity is not given to smaller or less established distributors or to those which do not seek a mass audience.

The social value test either makes the law virtually unenforceable against any material or it creates distinctions which are extremely difficult to justify. The critical question in this regard is whether social value can include entertainment or amusement value as well as value in imparting information or "ideas." If it can, all material which has a market would appear to be excluded from the law by the test. If, on the other hand, entertainment or amusement value is not social value then works of fine art would not have the protection accorded works of historical or philosophical interest—an unhappy result. In practice, works of fine art appear to be recognized as bearing social value. As a result, the test probably is applied to discriminate in an unjustifiable way against "low brow" amusements (as compared with "fine" art) although the functions served by each kind of art may be basically the same. The Supreme Court's recent opinion in Stanley v. Georgia appears to recognize the difficulties here: "The line between transmission of ideas and mere entertainment is much too elusive for this Court to draw, if indeed such a line can be drawn at all."[155]

Apart from its subjectiveness and uncertainties, the tripartite test is also unsatisfactory because it is not coherently formulated to prevent any recognizable evil; it requires a combination of two negative elements—pruriency and offensiveness—the collection together of which as a standard for guilt does not appear designed to achieve any rational social purpose. Specifically, if the arousal of lustful instincts in adults is harmful, it is not clear why a crime is committed only when this element is combined with affront to community standards of decency. Conversely, if excessive candor in the treatment of sexual matters is harmful, it is not clear why a crime is committed only when the material appeals to prurient interest as well. Nor is it clear why, if these elements do not individually call for societal prohibition upon adults, their combination is an occasion for such prohibition. The fundamental problem, again, appears to be that the Roth standard of what may be prohibited for consenting adults was formulated by the Court without reference to any harm caused by the prohibited materials.

Many of the foregoing difficulties would be eliminated if it were possible to formulate an objective definition specifically describing in easily applicable terms what materials were to be prohibited for dissemination. Such a definition, however, is exceedingly difficult to construct. The objective difference, for example, between valuable and even profound works of fiction dealing with sex, and pulp novels which are widely viewed as merely trash, is enormously elusive so as virtually to defy legislative definition. The definitional task is somewhat easier where pictorial materials are concerned, but even there almost every picture, no matter how explicit, can be presented in a context, such as sex instruction manual for married persons, where it would have conceded social importance, and which would thus be constitutionally immune from a general prohibition upon distribution. More basically, in the absence of conclusions as to the harm caused by sexual materials, no basis exists for including some materials within a definition, while excluding others.

Statutory definitions should not seek to define obscenity in the abstract, but should be drafted to describe as clearly as possible in objective terms, the particular kind of erotic material sought to be controlled for the particular purpose. Therefore the definition for a juvenile statute may appropriately differ, and encompass a broader scope than adult prohibitions, and a statute permitting a mail patron to direct that unsolicited mail advertisement of erotic materials not be delivered to him may appropriately be very broad. See the Drafts of Recommended Legislation in Part Two of the Commission's Report.

Since the Commission has decided that a general obscenity statute forbidding sales to adults should not be recommended,

423

the Panel has included no proposed statute of this kind in its Report. The Commission's Legislative Recommendations, however, do include the definition which the Panel deemed most appropriate had the Commission decided to recommend such a statute.

It will be noted that some subjective limitation to protect social value is considered necessary in all of the Commission's recommended definitions. The ideal is to restrict such subjective elements to the minimum consistent with sound policy and constitutional necessity. This we have sought to do.

Finally, it should be recognized that any attempt to use the criminal law to prohibit consensual conduct among adults inevitably creates enormous problems of law enforcement, no matter how clear the statutory definition of what consensual conduct is to be prohibited. Consensual crimes are victimless crimes and they will, in consequence, go undetected in most cases. Because of the substantial interest among adults today in sexual materials, it is probable that an enormously disproportionate investment of law enforcement time, energy and manpower would be required to obtain significant enforcement of the prohibitions of a law regulating dissemination between consenting adults. In view of the many existing problems caused by crimes which do have victims and which cause immense harm to our society today, it is thus difficult to recommend vigorous enforcement of laws against a crime of distributing obscenity to persons who wish to obtain it in the absence of evidence as to any significant harm which such distribution might cause. On the other hand, it would appear unwise to perpetuate laws against consensual distributions on the understanding that they would not often be enforced, for such a situation breeds widespread disregard and disrespect for law and results in unjustifiable inequities in the occasional instances when enforcement does take place.

CHANGING PUBLIC OPINION

In addition to its reliance upon an historical exclusion of obscenity from constitutional protection, the Roth decision appeared to stress what it found to be a virtually universal condemnation of certain explicit sexual materials as having no social value—a condemnation which, at the time of Roth, was expressed in legislation in every State, in federal legislation in this country and in legislation in many other countries. As described in Section G of this Panel Report, however, data obtained in a nationwide study of public opinion sponsored by this Commission indicate that public attitudes today are not as set against even so-called "hard-core" sexual materials as the Court in Roth supposed. Specifically, it appears that well over half of adult Americans believe that these materials have effects which may be deemed socially useful. There certainly is no consensus that such materials are inevitably without such value.

On the question of whether obscene materials should be regulated for consenting adults, the data indicates a similar lack of consensus. On the basis of their present knowledge about effects, more than half of the population believes that prohibitions should not be placed upon what consenting adults may read or view. The only consensus regarding the desirability of prohibitions aimed at consenting adults emerges when persons are asked to assume that harmful effect are in fact caused by obscene material.

DEVELOPING CONSTITUTIONAL DOCTRINE

In the thirteen years since the Roth decision, the Supreme Court has, to at least some extent, modified its position in that case that obscenity may be prohibited for consenting adults without evidence as to the harmful effect of such material. This development has occurred in two ways. First, in applying the Roth standard governing what may be deemed obscene for consenting adults, the Court has held in a number of cases that certain very explicit sexual materials cannot be deemed obscene for consenting adults. These decisions have most often been summary per curiam reversals of determinations of obscenity which have cited the court's decision in Redrup v. New York as authority. In view of these decisions, it is questionable whether any verbal material whatsoever may any longer be deemed obscene for adults under general prohibitions and it appears that only certain highly explicit pictorial material may be so deemed. It would appear to be very difficult, at the least, to defend legal distinctions between material which has thus been held not to be obscene by the Court and the small class of more explicit material.

Secondly, the Supreme Court in Stanley v. Georgia expressly held that concededly "obscene" materials are nevertheless entitled in at least some contexts to the constitutional protection generally accorded to free expression, so that the existence of conclusions regarding social harm is required to justify prohibitions for adults. While this case dealt directly only with adult private possession of obscenity, it rested upon

425

the premise that adults have a constitutionally protected right to read and view what they choose, regardless of the apparent lack of objective "social value" in the material involved. It appears evident that many distributions of sexual material to consenting adults are as much manifestations of the right of such persons to read and view what they wish as was the private possession of materials protected in Stanley—indeed, except where material is self-produced, it appears impossible to exercise the right of possession and perusal of materials of one's own choice without the availability of some sources of distribution. The logic of Stanley may thus require the holding that at least some distributions of obscene material to consenting adults may no longer be constitutionally prohibited unless legislation is supported by reasonably apprehended social harms.

There are, in sum, very serious legal and practical difficulties which counsel against retaining present prohibitions upon dissemination of explicit sexual materials to consenting adults in the absence of authoritative conclusions indicating that such materials have socially harmful effects. Constitutional doubts have been increased by evidence as to changing public opinion which appears to tolerate—and even find value in—the dissemination of "obscene" materials to consenting adults, and by developing legal doctrine within the Supreme Court which has seemed to recognize a constitutional right in adults to obtain obscene materials for private use unless prohibitions are socially justifiable. Perhaps even more importantly, the present state of the law under general prohibitions is decidedly unsatisfactory because of vagueness and subjectivity in the constitutional standard for ascertaining what is obscene for adults, and because of the difficulty of rationally distinguishing between materials which have been held not to be obscene for adults and the small class of materials which may be considered obscene. In the absence of social reasons for imposing prohibitions there could, in all events, appear to be no legal or constitutional basis for recommending the expansion of present controls upon material which may be made available to consenting adults.

THE "EFFECTS" RELEVANT TO GENERAL PROHIBITIONS

Since existing "Supreme Court decisions upholding the validity of general obscenity prohibitions upon distributions to consenting adults do not rest upon conclusions regarding effects, there is no basis for certain prediction as to what effects might be relied upon to justify such prohibitions when they would otherwise be deemed to conflict with the right of the individual to read or view material of his own choice. The small guidance which is available is summarized immediately below.

It seems quite clear that apprehended effects upon "morality," that is, effects upon the thoughts and attitudes of consenting adults, do not afford a basis for regulation. Stanley v. Georgia found the regulation of these matters through the prohibition of reading or viewing matter to be entirely inconsistent with the First and Fourteenth Amendments. The same would appear to be true of effects upon behavior which is not, or which cannot be, deemed to be anti-social behavior. Thus, an increase in the frequency or variety of intercourse between married persons would seem beyond the legitimate concern of government;[156] hence such an effect of exposure to sexual materials, even if established, would not seemingly constitute a basis for regulation.

Any demonstrable effect of sexual materials in inducing clearly anti-social behavior would, on the other hand, appear to afford a potential constitutional basis for regulating the consensual dissemination of such materials. Whether prohibitions would be justified in light of particular evidence as to a causal connection between such materials and certain behavior depends upon a number of factors, and also upon whether the Supreme Court would apply a "clear-and-present-danger" test to such prohibitions, or a less strict test requiring merely a "rational relationship" between regulation and harm. The seriousness of the apprehended harm must in all events be taken into account, as must the strength of the causal link, i.e., the statistical probability that consensual exposure to the material in question will, in fact, precipitate undesirable conduct. The apprehended danger which emerges from consideration of these two factors must, in turn be weighed against any positive or helpful effects which are causally related to dissemination of the materials. If the Supreme Court were to use a clear-and-present-danger standard, that would require that the apprehended danger invoked to justify prohibition be an immediate and significant, rather than a speculative, one and that it clearly outweigh any social benefits to be derived from distribution. Use of a rational relationship test by the Court would permit more speculation and a closer balance between positive and negative effects.[157]

The Stanley opinion, however, contains a somewhat puzzling dictum that general dissemination of explicit sexual material may be justifiably prohibited as a means of avoiding two additional anti-social effects—exposure of children to such materials and the thrusting of such material upon unwilling recipients. As noted in the next two succeeding sections of this report, regulations narrowly drawn to prevent these effects would, indeed, appear to have a firm constitutional basis at the present time. On the other hand, the Supreme Court's 1957 decision in Butler v. Michigan[158] squarely holds that a legitimate desire to safeguard young persons from sexual materials may not be used to forbid such materials to the adult population generally. An identical analysis would seem applicable to efforts to protect persons against unwanted offense by forbidding unobtrusive distribution to persons who wish to receive material offensive to others. The most likely accommodation between these somewhat conflicting precedents would appear to be to conclude that the interests in protecting privacy and juveniles may indeed be invoked against general public dissemination, but only to the extent of requiring that such disseminations make all reasonable efforts to avoid offense to those who do not wish to be exposed and to exclude young persons as recipients. Thus legislation might be designed to restrict the general dissemination of certain explicit materials to places where children are not admitted and from which such material is not unnecessarily displayed to the public at large.

Should Prohibitions upon Public Displays and Unsolicited Mailings Be Imposed?

In two cases—Redrup v. New York and Rowan v. Post Office Department—the Supreme Court has stated that a constitutional basis exists for legislation prohibiting explicit sexual material from being thrust upon persons who do not wish to see it. In the latter case—Rowan—the Court upheld federal legislation prohibiting the mailer from sending mail advertisements to persons who previously notify him that they do not wish to receive advertisements from him. The Court found such legislation consistent with the First Amendment on the ground that the freedom of speech does not extend to communications to unwilling recipients.

The Commission's National Survey and other research shows that, while there is no consensus that particular sexual materials are offensive, a substantial number of persons do, in

428

fact find certain of these materials offensive, while many other persons do not. The number of persons finding some materials offensive, and the fact that the degree of offense to some persons is undoubtedly quite high, appears to provide a basis for a broader utilization of the constitutional theory of the Rowan case. The principal constitutional problem in constructing valid public-offense legislation to vindicate this interest is the necessity to avoid interfering unduly with consensual distributions, while seeking to prohibit offensive unconsented distributions. Supreme Court precedents would not appear to permit prohibiting those persons who want to see material from doing so, in order to safeguard other persons who do not wish to be offended.[159] In the Rowan case, this distinction was observed, for the legislation there prohibited distributions only to persons who signified in advance that they did not wish to receive material.

In order to insure the constitutionality of public-offense legislation, therefore, care must be taken to avoid requiring such substantial financial outlays or other burdens from complying distributors so as to make it unprofitable or impossible for a distributor to engage in consensual distributions. Public display legislation is more dangerous in one of these respects than was the legislation approved in Rowan since a particular public display simultaneously reaches both consenting and unconsenting recipients, while the mailings in Rowan were individually addressed and some could be prohibited while others were permitted. Public display legislation should therefore take care to permit a distributor to advertise his wares in a descriptive but nonoffensive way, so that the patronage of consenting recipients may be solicited, and also to permit political and similar messages to be conveyed through displays on billboards, television, etc., and to permit general public exhibition of works of fine art.[160] The definition of material prohibited for public display should probably, therefore, apply only to pictorial material of the most explicit kind, since the prohibition of such material is least likely to interfere with legitimate advertising or with the substance of political or social messages; an exception to the prohibition for works of artistic value would also appear warranted.

SHOULD JUVENILE PROHIBITIONS BE IMPOSED?

As in the case of public-offense legislation, the Supreme Court has held that properly restricted juvenile legislation is constitutionally valid.[161] Such legislation need not rest upon a clear and present danger of harm to juveniles or others from the distribution of material to juveniles, but need only rest upon a rational legislative conclusion that certain material is harmful to juveniles. Thus, considerably more speculation about possible harm is probably permissible here than in the case of legislation imposing prohibitions upon consenting adults. Legislation for juveniles based upon such a legislative conclusion as to harm to juveniles, however, must be restricted to distributions to juveniles, and may not prohibit adult distribution generally.[162]

If data as to effects show that the danger of harm to juveniles from certain material is somewhat greater than any anticipated benefits or value which that material may have for young persons, a basis for legislation would appear to exist. In the absence of such persuasive effects data, a more doubtful basis for legislation may be provided if opinion that certain material is, indeed, harmful for young persons. The reason for doubt in this regard is that children have been recognized by the Supreme Court to have some constitutional right of free expression.[163] It would seem questionable whether this right should be subject to infringement because of uninformed—albeit widespread—adult public opinion. It also seems relevant here that data as to the source of materials which reach the hands of young persons indicate that commercial channels are not ordinarily utilized, so that juvenile legislation restricting direct commercial distributions to young persons are unlikely to have a very great practical impact. On the other hand, the concern of parents, who wish to protect their children from what they deem to be inappropriate sexual materials, may itself warrant a legislative response which supports the parents and subordinates the child's right during a limited period of early adolescence, so long as the existence of harmful effects remains an open question. In addition, the social value of material for children may be protected to a significant degree if prohibitions do not extend to what parents may wish to have their own children read or see. Legislation which responds to widespread parental concern should fairly plainly apply only to distributions made without the consent of the parent of the juvenile recipient and should permit parents—and perhaps teachers and clergymen as well—to authorize or undertake distributions to children in instances where they deem such action beneficial.

A significant practical problem is present in connection with the formulation of a definition to be incorporated in child legislation. Such a definition should be as objective and specific as possible, so as to reduce the uncertainty over what may be disseminated to young persons and to increase the level of compliance with the legislation. A relatively specific definition can be formulated to cover pictorial material. The problem is much greater, however, where verbal material is concerned, for many works with a considerably explicit sexual content may also contain unquestionable literary, educational and other social values for young persons. In view of the difficulties in formulating a definition of verbal materials which would not prohibit juveniles from obtaining these works, and in view also of the somewhat doubtful empirical basis for juvenile legislation, the Commission has decided to recommend that juvenile statutes cover only pictorial material.

SHOULD "PANDERING" PROHIBITIONS BE IMPOSED?

In Ginzburg v. United States,[164] the Supreme Court held that evidence of "pandering" in the distribution of materials might, in close cases, be deemed relevant in determining the applicability of the Roth standard to distributional conduct. It seems advisable thus to permit the manner of distribution to be taken into account, where relevant, in determining the applicability of legislation restricting such distribution. This is done automatically in specific prohibitions upon displays, unsolicited mailings and distributions to juveniles, where the form and manner of distribution is part of the defined offense. If legislation prohibiting certain distributions to consenting adults were also to be recommended, it would appear advisable to permit the manner, extent and form of distribution to be used, if relevant, to determine issues regarding the applicability of the definition contained in such legislation.

The Supreme Court has never held that "pandering" may be prohibited as a separate offense, and it does not appear advisable to attempt to create such an offense at this time. The meaning of pandering is quite elusive, and any attempts to define the concept in criminal legislation would introduce the same factors of vagueness and subjectivity which have plagued the application of the Roth standard. Moreover, pandering, both in practice, and in its inception in the Ginzburg case, appears to be used to refer to wholly unrestricted public distributions which reach unwilling recipients and children, or to offensive advertisements which are generally disseminated. These matters are best regulated in specific terms in carefully drawn prohibitions. There appears to be no basis

431

for concluding that addition and distinct social harm is caused by nonoffensive advertisements for sexual materials or by the communication to consenting adults of the fact that certain materials have erotic content.

PROCEDURAL RECOMMENDATIONS

Three matters of procedure are closely related to the substantive issues discussed above: The problem of proving scienter, the regulation of law-enforcement seizures of material, and the suggestion that the jurisdiction of appellate courts be limited so as to place the decision whether material is "obscene" entirely in the discretion of the trier of fact.

Scienter   It is well established that some proof of scienter —i.e., knowledge by the defendant of the character of the materials involved—is required in order to obtain conviction under an obscenity type of prohibition. Scienter problems fall into two main areas—the problem of proving the defendant's knowledge of the factual contents of material and the problem of defendants who distribute material, whose contents they know, but which they believe in good faith not to constitute material forbidden by the law. The latter problem can be solved to a considerable extent by the utilization of specific objective definitions of what material is prohibited in certain context. Under such definitions a defendant with knowledge of contents will be very unlikely to be misled as to the legal characterization to be given to those contents. Where less specific definitions are used, so that the definitions alone do not provide guidance as to the legal posture of particular material, it would appear appropriate, in all but the clearest cases of violation, to require the use of a declaratory judgment procedure to establish the applicability of the statute to the materials, and to provide that criminal penalties are not applicable to distributions undertaken before notice of a judicial declaration of obscenity. The problem of establishing a defendant's knowledge of the factual content of material which he distributes is more difficult in view of the vast number of different works which a retail dealer may handle. One possible means for providing knowledge of contents to retail dealers or exhibitors would be a federal requirement that manufacturers or importers of material, who will inevitably be familiar with the contents of their works, affix notice to their materials indicating that they

432

fall within a uniform federal definition of explicit sexual materials which may be prohibited in certain contexts. States might adopt the federal definition in specific prohibitions— such as upon distributions to young persons—and prove scienter through proof that the retail dealer obtained the manufacturer's notification as to the contents of the material. Such a notice requirement would again seem most satisfactory if it incorporated definitions which were as specific and objective as possible. For reasons set forth in the Commission's Legislative Recommendations (Part Two of the Commission's Report) the Commission has determined not to recommend such labelling legislation.

SEIZURES

The Supreme Court has made clear that mass seizures of material by law enforcement officials may not be undertaken without an adequate prior judicial determination that the material to be seized is, indeed, prohibited for distribution. The Court is in the process of elaborating the particular procedural requirements of an adequate hearing. The most persistent present problem in this area is that of permitting law enforcement officers to obtain materials to be used as evidence in criminal proceedings, without permitting them actually to prevent the dissemination of material through its seizure before its obscenity is adjudicated. This problem is not ordinarily of great significance where books or magazines are involved, for evidence may be obtained in such cases through purchase of a copy of the accused material. Where films are involved, however, there is often only one copy of the film within the jurisdiction and it may not be exhibited if it has been seized and impounded by the police. Legislation can, however, be drafted to require an exhibitor or distributor to make a film available for a judicial hearing, while permitting its exhibition pending that hearing. The adoption of such legislation consistent with local practice, would appear warranted in jurisdictions which may continue to seek to prosecute film exhibitions for adults, contrary to the Commission's recommendations.

WITHDRAWAL OF APPELLATE JURISDICTION OVER THE ISSUE OF OBSCENITY

Legislation has in recent years been introduced in Congress which would withdraw the jurisdiction of all federal courts to review findings made by federal juries or by state juries or courts that particular material is obscene.[165] Such legislation appears dangerously unwise from the point of view of the protection of constitutional rights of free expression. Experience has shown that, where obscenity statutes utilize vague and subjective definitions of what material is prohibited, errors in application of the definitional standard are frequently made, the initial results of prosecutions turn frequently upon subjective criteria, and identical materials are often condemned in one trial proceeding and exonerated in another. Not only do these errors and differing results create a great danger of unequal application of the law, but they often result in convictions in lower courts regarding material which, because of its social value or lack of harmful quality, is affirmatively protected by the First and Fourteenth Amendments to the Constitution. The insulation of even the grossest errors in application of obscenity statutes from appellate review thus poses a grave threat to constitutional rights and would constitute a dangerous precedent for the safeguarding of such rights in other areas of intense public concern. On the other hand, there would appear to be legitimate cause for concern over frequent unexplained judicial reversals of obscenity determinations, particularly by the Supreme Court of the United States. This phenomenon appears to flow primarily from the exceedingly subjective quality of the issue put to the trier of fact where the Roth standard is utilized as the definition of "obscene." Restriction of the use of obscenity prohibitions to contexts where specific and objective definitions can be and are utilized should eliminate most or all of these unexplained judicial reversals, and, in consequence, remove any felt need for restrictions upon appellate jurisdiction. The Commission's Legislative Recommendations elaborate somewhat further upon its reasons for recommending against legislation withdrawing appellate jurisdiction over obscenity cases.

NOTES

1. This section of the Legal Panel Report is based upon findings reported to the Commission in a paper by Martha Field Alschuler, Assistant Professor of Law at the University of Pennsylvania. Professor Alschuler's paper will be found in the Commission's *Technical Reports.*
2. *Queen* v. *Read,* 11 Mod. Rep. 142.
3. *King* v. *Curl,* 2 Stra. 788.
4. 5 Geo. 4, c. 83. In 1853, legislation was enacted in England forbidding the importation of obscene materials. 16 & 17 Vict., c. 107.
5. 20 & 21 Vict., c. 83.

6. L.R., 3 Q.B. 360.

7. *Commonwealth* v. *Sharpless,* 2 S. & R. 91 (1815) (Penna.); *Commonwealth* v. *Holmes,* 17 Mass. 336 (1821).

8. The statute was enacted in 1711, was entitled "An Act Against Intemperance, Immorality and Profaneness, and In Reformation of Manners," and can be found in *Ancient Charter, Colony Laws and Province Laws of Massachusetts Bay* (1814).

9. Laws of Vermont, 1824, ch. XXIII, No. 1, Section 23.

10. 5 Stat. 566.

11. 15 Stat. 50.

12. 16 November 1538, S.T.C. 7790.

13. 1 Keble 620 (K.B.), Mich. 15 Car. II B.R. See L. Alpert, *Judicial Censorship of Obscene Literature,* 52 Harv. L. Rev. 40, 41-43 (1938).

14. *Queen* v. *Read,* 11 Mod. Rep. 142.

15. It does not appear that even the power of the ecclesiastic courts to impose spiritual penalties—ultimately excommunication—was often exercised in the case of purely sexual materials on the ground of their explicitness.

16. 2 Stra. 788.

17. *King* v. *Curl,* Barnardiston's Rep. 29 (1744). The Court relied for this proposition upon *King* v. *Taylor,* 1 Ventris 293, in which the defendant was convicted for libelling Christ and calling religion a cheat.

18. See, *e.g., Rex* v. *Wilkes,* 4 Burr. 2527 (1768); *King* v. *Gallard,* W. Kelynge, p. 162 (1733).

19. St. John-Stevas, *Obscenity and the Law,* 66 (1956).

20. 5 Geo. 4, c. 83.

21. 16 & 17 Vic., c. 107.

22. 20 & 21 Vict., c. 83.

23. L.R., 3 Q.B. 360.

24. Province Laws, 1711-12, ch. 6, Section 19.

25. *Commonwealth* v. *Sharpless,* 2 Serg. & R. 91.

26. *Commonwealth* v. *Holmes,* 17 Mass. 336.

27. Laws of Vermont, 1824, ch. XXIII, No. 1, Section 23 (1821). The statute provided: "That if any persons shall hereafter print, publish or vend any lewd or obscene book, picture or print, such person, on conviction . . . shall be sentenced to pay a fine not exceeding two hundred dollars."

28. Stats. of Conn. (1830), p. 182-184 (1834).

29. Mass. Rev. Stat., ch. 130, Section 10.

30. *E.g.,* Mich. Rev. Stat. (1846), title XXX, ch. 158, Section 13.

31. 5 Stat. 566, Section 28.

32. 13 Stat. 50.

33. 7 N.Y. Stats. 309.

34. For accounts of Comstock's career, see Trumbull, *Anthony Comstock, Fighter* (1913); Cushing, *Story of Our Post Office* (1893); Brown & Leech, *Anthony Comstock: Roundsman of the Lord* (1927).

35. 17 Stat. 598.

36. See, *e.g.,* No. Dak. Pen. Code (1877); La. Act. of 1884, No. 111; So. Car. Stats. of 1885 (19) 334.

37. 354 U.S. 476.

38. *E.g.,* Cantwell v. Connecticut, 310 U.S. 296.

39. 354 U.S. 476 (1957).

40. 394 U.S. 557 (1969).

41. Obscenity regulations are also frequently challenged for undue vagueness. *See Interstate Circuit* v. *Dallas,* 390 U.S. 676 (1968). Such a challenge, however, does not ordinarily test the constitutional power to pass the regulation, but only the form in which the regulation is couched.

42. See *Burstyn* v. *Wilson,* 343 U.S. 495 (1952). *In re Giannini,* 69 Cal. 2d 563 (1968). The Supreme Court of California held dance to be within the protection of the First Amendment.

43. *E.g.* Dennis v. *United States,* 341 U.S. 494 (1951). Two Justices—Justice Black and Justice Douglas—have consistently taken the position that material in the form of speech is absolutely protected from governmental prohibition. See their opinions in *Dennis,* 341 U.S. at 579, 581.

44. See Judge Frank concurring in the Court of Appeals in *Roth* v. *United States,* 237 F. 2d 796 and Judge Curtis Bok's opinion in *Commonwealth* v. *Gordon,* 66 D. & C. 101 (Phila. Com. Pleas 1949).

45. The definition of "obscene" required by *Roth* is discussed in Section C. of the Legal Panel Report. The *Roth* opinion was joined in by 5 of the 9 Justices. Chief Justice Warren concurred in the result. Justice Harlan concurred as to state prohibition, but believed that the federal government was

435

more strictly limited in the obscenity area than reflected in the Court's opinion and result. Justices Black and Douglas dissented on the ground that no general obscenity prohibitions are constitutionally valid.

46. 354 U.S. at 485.

47. 354 U.S. at 483.

48. 354 U.S. at 485.

49. 394 U.S. 557.

50. 394 U.S. at 568. The *Stanley* opinion written, by Justice Marshall, was joined in by 6 of the 9 Justices (Justices Warren, Black, Douglas, Harlan, Fortas, and Marshall). The three remaining Justices (Justices Brennan, Stewart, and White) did not disagree, but preferred to decide the case on other grounds.

51. 394 U.S. at 559, n.2.

52. 394 U.S. at 565.

53. 394 U.S. at 563.

54. 394 U.S. at 565-566.

55. The Court in *Stanley* appeared to require more than a chance that "obscene" materials might cause harm in order to justify their prohibition, but to require, instead, a significant probability of such harm. Thus, the Court noted that, "given the present state of knowledge, the State may no more prohibit mere possession of obscenity on the ground that it may lead to anti-social conduct than it may prohibit possession of chemistry books on the ground that they may lead to the manufacture of homemade spirits.

56. 394 U.S. at 563-564, 568.

57. This latter problem was raised in *Karalexis* v. *Byrne*, 306 F. Supp. 1363 (D. Mass. 1969), prob. juris. noted, March 23, 1910, 397 U.S. 985.

58. 19 U.S.C., Section 1305.

59. *United States* v. *37 Photos*, (Luros claimant) C.D. Calif., Jan. 27, 1970, *United States* v. *Various Articles* (Cherry claimant), S.D.N.Y., June 8, 1970. *Contra, United States* v. *Ten Erotic Paintings*, 311 F. Supp. 884 (D. Md. 1970).

60. 18 U.S.C., Section 1461.

61. *United States* v. *Lethe*, E.D. Calif., Apr. 29, 1970.

62. *Karalexis* v. *Byrne*, 306 F. Supp. 1363 (D. Mass. 1969), prob. juris. noted, March 23, 1970, 38 U.S.L.W. 3369.

63. *Stein* v. *Batchelor*, 300 F. Supp. 602 (N.D.Tex. 1969), cert. granted, Dec. 8, 1969, 296 U.S. 954.

64. The *Karalexis* and *Stein* cases were argued at the 1969 term of the Supreme Court, but were not decided and were set over for reargument at the 1970 term. The *Luros* case will be argued before the Supreme Court at the 1970 term. A jurisdictional statement has been filed by the Government in the *Luros* case.

65. *U.S.* v. *Melvin*, 419 F. 2d 136 (4th Cir. 1969); *U.S.* v. *Fragus*, 422 F. 2d. 1244 (4th Cir. 1970).

66. *291 Gable* v. *Jenkins*, 309 F. Supp. 998 (N.D. Ga. 1969), affirmed, 397 U.S. 592; *Grove Press* v. *Evans*, 306 F. Supp. 1084 (E.D. Va. 1969); *Florida* v. *Reese*, 222 So. 2d 732 (Fla. 1969); *Raphael* v. *Hogan*, 305 F. Supp. 749 (S.D.N.Y. 1969); *Copeland* v. *O'Connor*, 306 F. Supp. 375 (C.D. Calif. 1969); *Youngstown* v. *de Loreto*, 251 N.E. 2d 491 (Ohio 1969); *Hewitt* v. *Md. Bd. of Censors*, 254 A. 2d 203 (Md. 1969); *Waggonheim* v. *Md. Bd. of Censors*, 258 A. 2d 240 (Md. 1969); *Overstock Books* v. *Barry*, 305 F. Supp. 842 (E.D. N.Y. 1969).

The affirmance by the Supreme Court of the *Gable* case, without oral argument and without written opinion, would not appear to settle existing questions about the reach of the *Stanley* case. The Supreme Court sometimes utilizes such summary affirmances as the equivalent of a denial of certiorari— *i.e.*, a refusal to exercise jurisdiction to review the case on its merits. In *Gable*, the district court, while preventing plaintiff's prosecution by state authorities, refused to issue a declaratory judgment that the state obscenity statute was overbroad. This contention was based upon a number of grounds, one of which was *Stanley* v. *Georgia*. In refusing to hear the *Gable* case on the merits, the Supreme Court may have been motivated by the fact that complete relief as to pending prosecutions had been obtained below, and only an abstract declaration of unconstitutionality was sought in the Supreme Court. In all events, the Court has presently scheduled for argument two cases (*Karalexis* and *Stein*) involving the meaning of *Stanley* v. *Georgia* in various contexts.

67. This Section is based in part upon a *Commission Technical Paper, The Definition of "Obscene" Under Existing Law*, written for the Commission by

its General Counsel, Paul Bender, Professor of Law at the University of Pennsylvania.

68. 383 U.S. 463 (1966).

69. 383 U.S. at 466.

70. 386 U.S. 767 (1967).

71. 386 U.S. at 769.

72. 390 U.S. 629 (1968).

73. 390 U.S. at 634.

74. 397 U.S. 728 (1970).

75. L.R., 3 Q.B. 360.

76. See, *e.g.*, *United States* v. *Kennerley*, 209 Fed. 119 (S.D. N.Y. 1913) (L. Hand J.) and the cases in the following footnote.

77. See, *e.g.*, *United States* v. *One Book Entitled "Ulysses,"* 72 F. 2d 705 (2nd Cir., 1934); *Commonwealth* v. *Gordon*, 66 D. & C. 101 (Phila., 1949); *Butler* v. *Michigan*, 352 U.S. 380.

78. 354 U.S. at 489. Most courts hold that statutes need not actually verbally incorporate the constitutional *Roth* standards. That standard will be applied through general prohibitions, unless their language precludes such incorporation. *Contra, Stein* v. *Batchelor*, 300 F. Supp. 602 (N.D. Tex., 1969).

79. The *Roth* opinion notes the essential similarity between its definition of "obscene" and that recommended by the American Law Institute Draft Penal Code. The A.L.I. defined a thing as "obscene" "if, considered as a whole, its predominant appeal is to prurient interest, *i.e.*, a shameful or morbid interest in nudity, sex or excretion, and if it goes substantially beyond customary limits of candor in description or representation of such matters." The Court has never explained its rather confusing assertion of equivalency between material tending to "excite lust" and material appealing to "shameful" or "morbid" interests in sex. In practice, a tendency to excite sexual arousal has appeared to be the principal ingredient of "prurient" interest.

80. In addition to the opinion of the Court in the *Roth* case (written by Justice Brennan, and the opinions of Chief Justice Warren and Justice Harlan in that case indicating their view of the constitutional standard, see *Manual Enterprises, Inc.* v. *Day*, 370 U.S. 478 (1962) (opinion of Justice Harlan and Stewart); *Jacobellis* v. *Ohio*, 378 U.S. 184 (1964) (opinions of Justices Brennan and Goldberg, Justice Stewart, Justices Warren and Clark, and Justice Harlan); *Memoirs* v. *Massachusetts*, 383 U.S. 413 (1966) (opinions of Justices Brennan, Warren and Fortas, Justice Harlan, Justice Clark and Justice White); *Mishkin* v. *New York*, 383 U.S. 502 (1966) (opinion of the Court by Justice Brennan); *Ginzburg* v. *United States*, 383 U.S. 463 (1966) (opinion of the Court by Justice Brennan); *Redrup* v. *New York*, 386 U.S. 767 (1967) (per curiam opinion of the Court); *Stanley* v. *Georgia*, 394 U.S. 557 (1963) (opinion of the Court by Justice Marshall); *Cain* v. *Kentucky*, 397 U.S. 319 (1970) (opinion of Chief Justice Burger); *Walker* v. *Ohio*, 398 U.S. 434 (June 15, 1970) (opinion of Chief Justice Burger); *Hoyt* v. *Minnesota*, 399 U.S. 524 (June 29, 1970) (opinion of Justices Blackmun, Burger and Harlan).

81. 383 U.S. 502.

82. 383 U.S. at 508.

83. See, *e.g.*, the opinions of these two Justices in *Ginzburg* v. *United States*, 383 U.S. at 476 and 482.

84. In *Ginzburg* v. *United States*, 383 U.S. at 499 n.3. Justice Stewart "borrowed from the Solicitor General's brief" the following description "of the kind of thing to which I have reference": "Such materials include photographs, both still and motion picture, with no pretense of artistic value, graphically depicting acts of sexual intercourse, including various acts of sodomy and sadism, and sometimes involving several participants in scenes of orgy-like character. They also include strips of drawings in comic-book format grossly depicting similar activities in an exaggerated fashion. There are, in addition, pamphlets and booklets sometimes with photographic illustrations, verbally describing such activities in a bizarre manner with no attempt whatsoever to afford portrayals of character or situation and with no pretense of literary value."

85. *Jacobellis* v. *Ohio*, 378 U.S. at 197.

86. 378 U.S. at 204.

87. See *Cain* v. *Kentucky*, 279 U.S. 319 (1970); *Hoyt* v. *Minnesota*, 399 U.S. 524 (1970). But note Chief Justice Burger's use of the *Roth* test in his opinion in *Walker* v. *Ohio*, 398 U.S. 434 (1970).

88. See *Memoirs* v. *Massachusetts*, 383 U.S. 413, 418, 441, 460; *Jacobellis* v. *Ohio*, 378 U.S. 184. This test is sometimes stated as a requirement that sexual material exceed "customary limits of candor." In addition to the

437

Justices named in the text, the Justices who apply a hard-core pornography test include offensiveness as part of that test. See *Manual Enterprise, Inc.* v. *Day,* 370 U.S. 478 (1962).

89. *Jacobellis* v. *Ohio,* 378 U.S. at 193-196.

90. *Manual Enterprises, Inc.* v. *Day,* 370 U.S. 478.

91. *Jacobellis* v. *Ohio,* 378 U.S. at 200.

92. In *In re Giannini,* 69 Cal. 2d 563, 577 (1968), the Supreme Court of California held that a statewide, rather than local community, standard was applicable in that State.

93. 354 U.S. at 484.

94. *Memoirs* v. *Massachusetts,* 383 U.S. at 441 *et seq.*

95. *Memoirs* v. *Massachusetts,* 383 U.S. at 462.

96. 383 U.S. 413.

97. 383 U.S. at 419.

98. 383 U.S. at 418.

99. 394 U.S. at 566.

100. The Court described the differences as follows (386 U.S. 767 (1967) at 770-771):

The two members of the Court have consistently adhered to the view that a State is utterly without power to suppress, control or punish the distribution of any writings or pictures on the ground of their "obscenity." A third has held to the opinion that a State's power in this area is narrowly limited to a distinct and clearly identifiable class of material. Others have subscribed to a not dissimilar standard, holding that a State may not constitutionally inhibit the distribution of literary material as obscene unless "(a) the dominant theme of the material taken as a whole appeals to a prurient interest in sex; (b) the material is patently offensive because it affronts contemporary community standards relating to the description or representation of sexual matters; and (c) the material is utterly without redeeming social value," emphasizing that the "three elements must coalesce," and that no such material can "be proscribed unless it is found to be utterly without redeeming social value." Another Justice has not viewed the "social value" element as an independent factor in the judgment of obscenity.

101. See, *e.g., Hudson* v. *United States,* 234 A. 2d 903 (Dist. of Col., 1967); *United States* v. *A Motion Picture Entitled "I am Curious (Yellow),"* 404 F. 2d 196 (2d Cir., 1968); *Oregon* v. *Childs,* 447 P. 2d 304 (1968); In *In re Giannini,* 72 (1968); *Stein* v. *Batchelor,* 300 F. Supp. 602 (N.D. Tex., 1969); *Contra, Cain* v. *Kentucky,* 437 S.W. 2d 769 (1969), reversed *per curiam,* 397 U.S. 319 (1970).

In *Ginzburg* v. *United States,* 383 U.S. 463 (1966), the opinion of the Court also seemed to recognize the three-part version of the *Roth* test as the operative law. See, also, the apparently similar recognition by Chief Justice Burger, dissenting in *Walker* v. *Ohio,* 398 U.S. 434 (1970).

102. *Manual Enterprises, Inc.* v. *Day,* 370 U.S. 478; *Jacobellis* v. *Ohio,* 378 U.S. 184; *Memoirs* v. *Massachusetts,* 383 U.S. 413; *Mishkin* v. *New York,* 383 U.S. 502.

103. *Mishkin* v. *New York,* 383 U.S. 502. A finding of obscenity regarding similar materials to those involved in the *Mishkin* case was summarily reversed by the Supreme Court in 1967 in *Central Mag. Sales* v. *United States,* 389 U.S. 50.

104. 354 U.S. at 481 n.8.

105. A list of the Supreme Court's *per curiam* reversals of obscenity determinations since the Roth decision is as folllows:

Prior to *Redrup* v. *New York* (1967): *Times Films* v. *Chicago,* 355 U.S. 35; *One, Inc.* v. *Olesen,* 355 U.S. 371; *Sunshine Book Co.* v. *Summerfield,* 355 U.S. 372; *Tralins* v. *Gerstein,* 378 U.S. 576; *Grove Press* v. *Gerstein,* 378 U.S. 577.

Decided with *Redrup: Austin* v. *Kentucky,* 386 U.S. 767; *Gent* v. *Arkansas,* 386 U.S. 767.

Decided on June 12, 1967 (citing Redrup): *Keney* v. *New York,* 388 U.S. 440; *Friedman* v. *New York,* 388 U.S. 441; *Ratner* v. *California,* 388 U.S. 442; *Cobert* v. *New York,* 388 U.S. 443; *Shepard* v. *New York,* 388 U.S. 444; *Avansino* v. *New York,* 388 U.S. 446; *Aday* v. *United States,* 388 U.S. 447; *Corinth Pub.* v. *Westberry,* 388 U.S. 448; *Books, Inc.* v. *United States,* 388 U.S. 449; *Schackman* v. *California,* 388 U.S. 454; *Quantity of Books* v. *Kansas,* 388 U.S. 452; *Mazes* v. *Ohio,* 388 U.S. 453; *Rosenbloom* v. *Virginia,* 388 U.S. 450 (citing *Sunshine Book Co.* v. *Summerfield, supra,* 355 U.S. 372, rather than *Redrup*).

Decided on October 23, 1967 (citing *Redrup*): *Potomac News* v. *United*

States, 389 U.S. 47; *Connor* v. *City of Hammond*, 389 U.S. 48; *Central Magazine Sales* v. *United States*, 389 U.S. 50; *Chance* v. *California*, 389 U.S. 89.

Decided in 1968 (citing *Redrup*): *I. M. Amusement Corp.* v. *Ohio*, 389 U.S. 573; *Robert-Arthur Management Corp.* v. *Tennessee*, 389 U.S. 578; *Felton* v. *Pensacola*, 390 U.S. 340; *Henry* v. *Louisiana*, 392 U.S. 655.

Decided at the 1969 Term of Court (1969-1970) (citing *Redrup*): *Carlos* v. *New York*, 396 U.S. 119; *Cain* v. *Kentucky*, 397 U.S. 319; *Bloss* v. *Dykemea*, 398 U.S. 278; *Walker* v. *Ohio*, 398 U.S. 434; *Hoyt* v. *Minnesota*, 399 U.S. 524.

In only one case, *Landau* v. *Fording*, 388 U.S. 456 (1967) has the Supreme Court *affirmed* an application of an adult obscenity prohibition through a *per curiam* disposition. That decision may have turned, not on the obscenity of the materials as such, but on a lower court finding that they had been "pandered." The *Landau* case concerned a film which included graphic depictions of male masturbation and which strongly suggested male homosexual (oral-genital) activity.

106. 386 U.S. 767 (1967). One case, *Rosenbloom* v. *Virginia*, relied upon *Sunshine Book Co.* v. *Summerfield*, 355 U.S. 372, apparently because State law did not apply the *Roth* test.

107. See footnote 97, *supra*.

108. 386 U.S. 771.

109. *E.g.*, *Memoirs* v. *Massachusetts*, 383 U.S. 413 ("Fanny Hill"): *Aday* v. *United States*, 388 U.S. 447 ("Sex Life of a Cop") (see 357 F. 2d 855, for description of book); *Corinth Publications* v. *Westberry*, 388 U.S. 448 ("Sin Whisper") (see 146 S.E. 2d 764, for description of book); *Mazes* v. *Ohio*, 388 U.S. 453 ("Orgy Club").

110. *Hoyt* v. *Minnesota*, 399 U.S. 524 (1970) ("The Way of a Man With Maid," "Lady Susan's Cruel Lover" and three other books).

111. *Grove Press* v. *Gerstein*, 378 U.S. 577 ("Tropic of Cancer").

112. *E.g.*, *Central Mag. Sales.* v. *United States*, 389 U.S. 50; *Potomac News* v. *United States*, 389 U.S. 47. See 373 F. 2d 633, 635, for descriptions of the material in these cases.

113. *E.g.*, *Shackman* v. *California*, 388 U.S. 454 (see 258 F. Supp. 983, for descriptions of films); *I. M. Amusement Co.* v. *Ohio*, 389 U.S. 573 (see 226 N.E. 2d 567, for descriptions of films); *Jacobellis* v. *Ohio*, 378 U.S. 184 ("The Lovers"); *Cain* v. *Kentucky*, 397 U.S. 319; ("I, A Woman").

114. Compare the description quoted in Justice Stewart's opinion in *Ginzburg* v. *United States*, footnote 47, *supra*.

115. *E.g.*, *United States* v. *127, 295 Copies of Magazines*, 295 F. Supp. 1186 (D. Md. 1968).

116. The evidence permitted or required to be produced in trials of the issue of obscenity under *Roth* has been subject to considerable litigation. In a concurring opinion in *Smith* v. *California*, 361 U.S. 147 (1959), Justice Frankfurter stated that he would make the right of a defendant to introduce evidence "regarding the prevailing literary and moral community standards and to do so through qualified experts" "a requirement of due process in obscenity prosecutions" 361 U.S. at 165. This view rested upon the understanding that the ascertainment of obscenity under *Roth* is not "a merely subjective reflection of the taste or moral outlook of individual jurors or individual judges," 361 U.S. at 165.

The right to thus enlighten the trier of fact on contemporary community standards has generally been accepted, as has been the right to introduce evidence bearing upon the existence of social value in the work in issue. *E.g.*, *United States* v. *"I am Curious (Yellow),"* 404 F. 2d 196 (2nd Cir. 1968). Such evidence is very frequently presented in obscenity trials under *Roth*. Evidence as to prurient appeal is less often offered, and most courts appear to believe that triers of fact are fully capable in most cases to determine that issue solely by examination of the materials in issue. The most frequent issue which arises over the introduction of evidence on the elements of *Roth* concerns the amount and character of materials, other than the materials in issue in the case itself, which may be introduced by a defendant to demonstrate that works similar to that for which he is accused have been accepted by the community. Ordinarily, some works which have had community acceptance will be admitted for purposes of comparison, but judges may exercise strict control over their volume and may exclude materials not deemed by the judge to be comparable to the work in issue or materials which he does not deem to have been accepted by the community. *E.g.*, *United States* v. *West Coast News*, 228 F. Supp. 171 (W.D.Mich. 1964).

Some cases have held that, not only is evidence as to the elements of the

439

Roth standard relevant, but that, except in the clearest cases of obvious obscenity, the prosecution *must* produce evidence (other than the materials in issue themselves) showing that some or all of the elements of that standard are satisfied in order to obtain a conviction. *E.g., Hudson* v. *United States,* 234 A. 2d 903 (Dist. of Col. 1967). The Court of Appeals for the Second Circuit, notably, has held that, where material is charged as obscene because it appeals to a "deviant" group rather than to the average (under the rule adopted by the Supreme Court in *Mishkin* v. *New York*), the prosecution must present affirmative evidence that the material does, indeed, appeal to the prurient interest of the deviant group, for the trier of the fact is quite unlikely to be able to determine this issue through his own knowledge. *United States* v. *Klaw*, 350 F. 2d 155 (2nd Cir. 1965).

117. See *Redrup* v. *New York*, 386 U.S. 767 (1967).

118. 383 U.S. 463.

119. 383 U.S. at 470.

120. 383 U.S. at 467.

121. 397 U.S. 728.

122. 352 U.S. 380.

123. 390 U.S. 676 (1968).

124. 390 U.S. 629 (1968).

125. This analysis is similar to that used in *Mishkin* v. *New York*, 383 U.S. 502, where the prurient appeal of material designed for a particular group was permitted to be assessed in terms of the interest of that group, rather than of the "average" person.

126. 390 U.S. at 639-640.

127. The definitional and prohibitory sections of the *Ginsberg* statute are as follows:

1. Definitions. As used in this section:

(a) "Minor" means any person under the age of seventeen years.

(b) "Nudity" means the showing of the human male or female genitals, pubic area or buttocks with less than a full opaque covering, or the showing of the female breast with less than a fully opaque covering of any portion thereof below the top of the nipple, or the depiction of covered male genitals in a discernibly turgid state.

(c) "Sexual conduct means acts of masturbation, homosexuality, sexual intercourse, or physical contact with a person's clothed or unclothed genitals, pubic area, buttocks or, if such person be a female, breast.

(d) "Sexual excitement" means the condition of human male or female genitals when in a state of sexual stimulation or arousal.

(e) "Sado-masochistic abuse" means flagellation or torture by or upon a person clad in undergarments, a mask or bizarre costume, or the condition of being fettered, bound or otherwise physically restrained on the part of one so clothed.

(f) "Harmful to minors" means that quality of any description or representation, in whatever form, of nudity, sexual conduct, sexual excitement, or sado-masochistic abuse, when it:

(i) predominantly appeals to the prurient, shameful or morbid interest of minors, and

(ii) is patently offensive to prevailing standards in the adult community as a whole with respect to what is suitable material for minors, and

(iii) is utterly without redeeming social importance for minors.

(g) "Knowingly" means having general knowledge of, or reason to know, or a belief or ground for belief which warrants further inspection or inquiry of both:

(i) the character and content of any material described herein which is reasonably susceptible of examination by the defendant, and

(ii) the age of the minor, provided however, that an honest mistake shall constitute an excuse from liability hereunder if the defendant made a reasonable bona fide attempt to ascertain the true age of such minor.

2. It shall be unlawful for any person knowingly to sell or loan for monetary consideration to a minor:

(a) any picture, photograph, drawing, sculpture, motion picture film, or similar visual representation or image of a person or portion of the human body which depicts nudity, sexual conduct or sado-masochistic abuse and which is harmful to minors, or

(b) any book, pamphlet, magazine, printed matter however reproduced, or sound recording which contains any matter enumerated in paragraph (a) of subdivision two hereof, or explicit and detailed verbal descriptions or narra-

440

tive accounts of sexual excitement, sexual conduct or sado-masochistic abuse and which, taken as a whole, is harmful to minors.

3. It shall be unlawful for any person knowingly to exhibit for a monetary consideration to a minor or knowingly to sell to a minor an admission ticket or pass or knowingly to admit a minor for a monetary consideration to premises whereon there is exhibited, a motion picture, show or other presentation which, in whole or in part, depicts nudity, sexual conduct or sado-masochistic abuse and which is harmful to minors.

128. 390 U.S. at 641.
129. See Section E of this Panel Report, *infra.*
130. 397 U.S. 728 (1970).
131. 397 U.S. at 730.
132. 397 U.S. at 736.
133. The *Rowan* opinion notes that the fact "that we are often 'captives' outside the sanctuary of the home and subject to objectionable speech and other sounds does not mean we must be captives everywhere."
134. 361 U.S. 147.
135. 36 U.S. at 153.
136. 361 U.S. at 154.
137. 383 U.S. 502 (1966).
138. See also, *Ginsberg* v. *New York,* 390 U.S. 629, 643-645.
139. Several state and lower federal courts, however, have ruled that there are circumstances which make it incumbent upon defendant to inquire further, and that proof of the existence of these circumstances may be substituted for proof of actual knowledge of the contents. Among these circumstances are: (1) The "erotic," "lurid" or "vile" titles of the books, *United States* v. *Hochman* 277 F. 2d 631 (7th Cir) (1960); *City of Cincinnati* v. *Coy,* 115 Ohio App. 478, 182 NE 2d 628 (1962); (2) "Obscene," "smutty" or "blatant" pictures on the covers of the books, *ibid.; State* v. *Jungclaus,* 176 Neb. 641, 126 NW 2d 858; (3) advertising and other promotional material, *People* v. *Harris,* 192 Cal. App. 2d 887, 13 Cal. Rptr. 642 (Super Ct. App. Dept. 1961); *People* v. *Sikora* 32 Ill. 2d 260, 204 NE 2d 768 (1965); (4) Receipt by defendant of complaints that the book he was selling was "filthy," *People* v. *Williamson,* 207 Cal App. 2d 839, 24 Cal. Reptr. 734 (Dist. Ct. App. 1962), *cert. denied,* 377 U.S. 994 (1964); (5) the fact that the wholesaler from whom the books were obtained dealt in erotic materials, *State* v. *Cercone,* 2d Conn. Cir. 144, 196 A. 2d 439 (App Div. 1963): *State* v. *Onorato,* 2 Conn. Cir. 428, 199 A. 2d 715 (App. Div. 1963). See, however, the opinion of Justices Harlan and Stewart in *Manual Enterprises, Inc.* v. *Day,* 370 U.S. 478, indicating their view that proof or failure to inquire is not sufficient to establish *scienter* under federal mail regulations withdrawing mail privileges in some circumstances.
140. But see *Rosen* v. *United States,* 161 U.S. 29 (1896), indicating that proof of awareness of contents of material is sufficient and that awareness of the legal characterization of materials as obscene is not required.

See also *United States* v. *Oakley,* 290 F. 2d 517 (6th Cir.), *cert. den.* 368 U.S. 888 (1961) in which the Sixth Circuit sustained a federal conviction for sending photographs of nude women through the mails. The defense of belief in the nonobscenity of the materials was rejected by the Court in the following words: "From his experience with these matters, [defendant] was persuaded, he says, that his enterprise was not illegal, and criminal intent was absent . . . [But it] was for the jury here, under proper instructions, and applying 'contemporary community standards' in the context of defendant's conduct, to determine his guilt."

See also *Yudkin* v. *State,* 229 Md 223, 182 A 2d 798 (1962) where the Supreme Court of Maryland reversed the conviction of a bookdealer on the ground that the trial court had erred in refusing to admit expert testimony on the issue of obscenity. While considering that issue, however, the court noted that booksellers in the same area had been arrested for selling the same book and that defendant had actual knowledge of such arrests. As a result, the court concluded that "the defendant, though he had some doubt as to whether the book could be banned, chose to take the risk that a court would not declare it to be obscene," and that his conviction could not, therefore, be reversed on the ground of belief in the nonobscenity of the material.

The *Redrup* case (and its two companion cases) were originally taken for decision by the Supreme Court to resolve some of these questions regarding the meaning of the requirement of *scienter*. The cases, however, were

441

decided by the Court, without reaching the *scienter* questions, on the ground that the materials involved were not "obscene."

141. See, for example, the definition of "knowingly" contained in the *Ginsberg* statute, quoted in footnote 123, supra.

142. *Contra, Delta Book Distributors, Inc.* v. *Cronvich*, 304 F. Supp. 662, 667 (E.D. La., 1969), holding arrests clearly unconstitutional "for lack of a prior adversary determination of the obscenity of the materials upon which the arrests were based." The Supreme Court has accepted jurisdiction in this case, *sub. nom. Ledesma* v. *Perez* 399 U.S. 924 (1970).

143. *Freedman* v. *Maryland,* 380 U.S. 51 (1965).

144. *United States* v. *A Motion Picture "491,"* 367 F. 2d 889 (2d Cir. 1966); *United States* v. *A Motion Picture "Pattern of Evil,"* 304 F. Supp. 197 (S.D.N.Y. 1969).

145. See *Marcus* v. *Search Warrants,* 367 U.S. 717 (1961); *A Quantity of Books* v. *Kansas,* 378 U.S. 205 (1964); *Lee Art Theater* v. *Va.,* 392 U.S. 636 (1968). These cases have not appeared to involve material seized merely to be preserved as evidence while dissemination is permitted to go forward pending a judicial determination of obscenity.

146. 367 U.S. 717 (1961).

147. 367 U.S. ct 731-2.

148. 378 U.S. 205 (1964).

149. 378 U.S. at 210. Two Justices found the procedures adequate, even without prior adversary hearing.

150. 392 U.S. 636 (1968).

151. This Section of the Panel Report is based, in part, upon Commission *Technical Reports* in the areas of existing laws and law enforcement written for it by Mrs. Jane Friedman, Assistant General Counsel of the Commission.

152. See the *Summary* of the prosecution survey in the Commission's *Technical Reports.*

153. These problems are now addressed by Section 3010-3011 of 39 U.S.C., which were enacted into law as part of the 1970 Postal Reorganization Act. These sections were enacted too late (August 12, 1970) for discussing in this Panel Report. They are discussed in the full Commission's Legislative Recommendations.

153a. The consultant's report describes a three-classification system in effect prior to July 1, 1970. The four-classification system was adopted to be effective on that date.

154. The National Survey sponsored by the Commission (Abelson, *et al.,* 1970) is described in detail in the Report of the Effects Panel of the Commission, *supra.*

155. 394 U.S. at 566.

156. See *Griswold* v. *Connecticut,* 381 U.S. 479 (1965).

157. The Court's opinion in *Stanley* v. *Georgia* suggests the use of the more rigorous standard where adult legislation is concerned. Thus it emphasizes that anti-social conduct must ordinarily be regulated directly, rather than through regulations upon speech or expression, and it invokes an analogy to the impossibility of prohibiting chemistry texts because of their possible use in manufacturing illegal products (although such anti-social use is undoubtedly a reality in some instances).

158. 352 U.S. 380.

159. See *Butler* v. *Michigan,* 352 U.S. 380 (1957).

160. Prohibitions enforced by the Federal Communications Commission upon vulgar language in broadcasts, for example, contain a danger of constricting unwarranted intrusions upon political and other expressions.

161. *Ginsberg* v. *New York,* 390 U.S. 629 (1968).

162. *Butler* v. *Michigan,* 352 U.S. 380 (1957).

163. *Tinker* v. *Des Moines School Dist.,* 393 U.S. 503 (1969).

164. 383 U.S. 463 (1966).

165. *E.g.,* S. 4058, 90th Cong., 2nd Session.

442

Part Four

SEPARATE STATEMENTS
BY COMMISSION MEMBERS

Statement by Irving Lehrman

I feel that inasmuch as the studies were undertaken over too short a period of time and no study of long-range effects is yet available, the findings are not sufficiently conclusive to warrant drastic steps.

I therefore recommend that no action be taken at this time on the removal of all legislative prohibitions but that a new commission be set up to consist of leading representatives of contemporary American culture and religion to undertake a broader, in-depth analysis of the problem for a minimum period of five years.

Statement by Joseph T. Klapper

The personal statement of Commissioner Morris A. Lipton and Commissioner Edward D. Greenwood so closely approximates my own position, and is in my opinion so soundly stated, that I would like to assert my general agreement with it. As a professional researcher in the behavioral sciences, I have long been aware that research answers complex questions only by a series of approximations. The pioneering research which the Commission has been able to accomplish in a two-year period is not and could not be either complete or flawless, nor indeed could it have been so if five years had been available. The strengths and limitations of

443

the research bearing on effects are stated at length in the Report of the Effects Panel. Given these imperfections, the research is nevertheless remarkably consistent, and it does not establish a meaningful causal relationship between exposure to erotica and anti-social behavior.

I subscribe also to Dr. Lipton's and Dr. Greenwood's discussion of the drug analogy. I would add, from my own point of view, that the right of adults to read and see what they please is to me so precious a freedom, that I would wish to protect it from any encroachment not dictated by clear, unambiguous evidence of significant social danger. The available research has certainly provided no such evidence. Its findings have thus been a major factor, but not the only factor, in the determination of my position on the issues on which the Commission has voted.

This position can be stated very briefly. In the interest of personal adult freedom, I have voted with the majority against restrictive legislation for adults. In the interest of the individual's right not to be exposed to material which he finds offensive, I have voted with the majority for restrictions on public display and unsolicited mail. In the belief that little is known about the possible influences of erotica on adolescents, and in the belief that such matters should remain a parental prerogative, I have voted with the majority for restrictions on distribution to young persons.

I believe also that erotica is a part of the total environment and that the most likely way to insure that society and the individual are capable of handling it is by the cultivation of healthy sex attitudes through, as Dr. Lipton and Dr. Greenwood put it "age-appropriate sex education presented accurately and truthfully in an appropriate aesthetic and moral context."

Statement by G. William Jones

Although I was appointed to this Commission by virtue of my educational and artistic concern for broadcasting and motion pictures, I am also an ordained Methodist clergyman. Thus, my service on the Commission has grown out of several personal commitments.

Pornography has been a public concern for at least as

444

long as we have a recorded history of human society. Up until the past two years, however, men have apparently been content to argue about its possible anti-social influence or its innocuousness on the basis of their assumptions and prejudices. I consider the birth and ensuing work of this Commission to have been a milestone in the history of human communications—the first time in history in which men cared about the problem enough to seek the truth about it through the best methods known to science. Although the research studies generated by the Commission and forming one basis for its report have the limitations so ably pointed out by my colleagues, Dr. Klapper and Dr. Lipton, I feel very sure that they have brought us closer to the truth about the relationship between pornography and anti-social behavior than has ever before been possible, and that these contributions will be valuable for many years to come.

As a clergyman, and as one who follows a Leader who said, "I am . . . the Truth," and "They shall know the Truth and the Truth shall set them free," I believe that the search for truth is a liberating, and thus a holy, quest and that science has often proven itself to be God's handmaiden in this quest. Although many religious persons may be distressed by the findings of our research, they must certainly rejoice that misconceptions and prejudices are being replaced by knowledge, and that our concern and efforts may now be redirected toward what appears to be the surer roots of the sexual maladies of our people.

I have long been concerned that the burden of blame and the therapy of re-education be focused on the true sources of the sexual crimes and maladjustments which plague our country and its citizens. If certain kind of books or films had been proven the cause, then I was quite willing to join in the crusade against them. However, it has been very adequately shown through our research that the roots of such behavior lie in the home and in the early years of familial and sibling relationships. It is good, I believe, to stop chasing what may have been our unconscious scapegoats in the media and to concentrate these energies instead upon the kind of re-education of the family which will make for health and sanity.

A Minority Statement by Otto N. Larsen ·and Marvin E. Wolfgang

After reviewing the technical reports of the Commission on Obscenity and Pornography and after careful distillation of research ranging from a national representative sample survey to comparative studies in Denmark and Sweden to laboratory research on varied populations, we have reached a policy decision and now submit that decision in the form of a recommendation as members of the Commission.

We recommend the repeal of all existing federal, state, and local statutes that prohibit the sale, exhibition or other distribution of "obscene" material.

This is phrasing similar to that used by most of the Commissioners who recommend repeal legislation concerning adults, but who would legally restrict distribition to juveniles, and who would provide proscriptions against public display and the unsolicited mailing of "obscene" materials. We, instead, recommend no specific statutory restrictions on obscenity or pornography.

There is no need to review the studies that buttress this recommendation for they are clearly described in the final report and other volumes. The few statements we offer here are, however, based on the best evidence available to us.

Definitional problems about "obscenity" and "pornography" that have rendered previous legislation ambiguous, often unenforceable, and open to excessive subjectivity by the police, prosecutors and judges would continue to exist in any statute aimed to restrict the distribution of erotic materials to juveniles.

There is little reason to believe that persons under any specific age would be prevented from having access to what some persons define as pornography. Even with existing restrictions, we know that high percentages of adolescents now read and see pornography.

There is little reason to believe that restrictive legislation, or its repeal, will significantly affect the proportionate amount of exposure that now exists.

There is no substantial evidence that exposure to juveniles is necessarily harmful. There may even be beneficial effects if for no other reason than the encouragement of open discussion about sex between parents and children relatively early in young lives.

We make special note of the fact that convicted sex offenders have had less exposure and juveniles adjudged delinquent no more exposure to erotica than persons not so convicted or adjudged. Moreover, there is no significant association between what society has declared is criminal or delinquent, in general, and exposure to erotic stimuli.

There is no evidence that adolescents are so feverishly interested in erotic material that they will rush in large numbers to purchase such material if there were no restrictions. Evidence from studies in the United States and Denmark suggests the opposite.

A public display statute specifically aimed at erotic material is unnecessary. Very few jurisdictions have such a statute now. The execution of existing statutes and ordinances concerned with the projection of generally offensive objects, erotic or not, before the public provides all the spatial boundaries on public display of offensive erotica that is needed.

A review of that business concerned with the unsolicited mailing of erotic materials, or other materials deemed offensive to the receiver, indicates that profits are small in most cases and that businesses of this sort often fail. Moreover, a cost analysis of the current practice of processing a citizen's request to prevent the further mailing of offensive material reveals enormous expenditures by the Government. Such monies can surely be better spent in a country with many more important demanding priorities. Moreover, most mailers now place a warning on their envelopes, and the most explicitly erotic material is sold in special bookstores. The assaults on individual privacy are so great in so many other areas of a citizen's life that the reception of unsolicited mail that can readily be thrown away can hardly be viewed as socially significant.

Advocating repeal is not advocating anarchy, for we believe that informal social controls will work better without the confusion of ambiguous and arbitrarily administered laws. With improvements in sex education and better understanding of human sexual behavior, society can more effectively handle, without legislation, the distribution of material deemed by some to be offensive to juveniles or adults.

447

Besides the evidence which leads to these conclusions, we concur with those Justices, scholars, and other citizens who believe that the First Amendment to the Constitution is abrogated by restrictions on textual and visual material that may be deemed by some as "obscene" or "pornographic."

We therefore repeat our recommendation for the repeal of all existing statutes concerned with obscenity or pornography.

Statement by Winfrey C. Link

The final sentence of the non-legislative recommendations says: "Coercion, repression, and censorship in order to promote a given set of views are not tolerable in our society." A segment of this Commission has suffered much coercion, repression, and censorship from the leadership since the very beginning in order that a certain set of views might be promoted.

I feel compelled to dissent from the majority recommendation, "that federal, state, and local legislation prohibiting the sale, exhibition, or distribution of sexual materials to consenting adults should be repealed." My reasons have been very well stated in the dissenting report submitted by Commissioners Keating, Hill and myself. However, I feel it necessary to state my reason for joining a separate, dissenting report.

I hoped from the beginning that ample evidence and information could be assembled to enable the Commission to issue a unanimous report. Short of this I wished to see all dissent expressed within one report signed by all members. I expressed this goal many times and felt it sincerely. In fact, it was not until after the final meeting of the full Commission that I changed my thinking as to this procedure. The action that forced me into this decision took place at the final session.

There had been much discussion about the way dissent would be expressed. It was evident many months before that unanimity was impossible. Reasons varied from biased, slanted and inadequate studies, to the suppression of reports and information that was not in keeping with the preconceived

448

ideas of the Commission leadership, to the exclusion of those of opposing views from certain decision making.

To illustrate each of these I point to the following examples: One of the major sources of information is the "Public Attitudes Toward and Experience With Erotic Materials," conducted by Response Analysis Corporation, Princeton, New Jersey, and Institute for Survey Research, Temple University, Philadelphia, Pennsylvania.

Question #6 of the survey reads, "We are also interested in your opinion on national problems. Would you please tell me what you think are the two or three most serious problems facing the country today?"

It is doubtful that any member of the Commission considers erotic materials to be within the two or three most serious problems facing our country today when we consider pollution, racial issues, the economy, youth rebellion, etc. Yet, because only 2% mention erotic materials as being in the top 3 problems facing our country the formulators of the Commission recommendations attempt to make us feel it is no problem. The many file cabinets in congressional offices filled with correspondence protesting the availability of smut attest to it being a major problem.

Other questions on this survey and other studies show the bias and inadequacy of the information gathered.

I suspected that there was information which gave opposing views coming into the Commission office. Things were just too pat. There was too much objection being heard outside for there to be no supporting information filed with the Commission. It was apparent that opposition was being thwarted when the Chairman refused to allow the Commission to hear any results of the public hearings conducted by Commissioner Hill and myself at our own expense. There was information which would have been helpful if admitted for consideration.

My suspicions were confirmed by a UPI story on September 3, 1970 relating that two psychologists reported to the Commission that they had "found that the relations between exposure to pornography and sexual deviance include a broad spectrum from mildly deviant, high frequencies of heterosexual behavior, to group sex, to sex without love, to homosexuality, rape and male prostitution for those subjects exposed to greater amounts of pornography."

According to the story Dr. Cody Wilson, Executive Director, acknowledged that the Davis-Braucht report had been received. This report was never shared with the Commission members holding opposing views either in verbal or written form. How many more such reports that expressed feelings opposite to the predetermined views were withheld we will probably never know.

A final example illustrates the exclusion of all but a select few in highly important steps taken by the Commission. I was quite astonished to arrive at a meeting one day to find that a young lawyer had been employed some time earlier to work with the Traffic and Distribution Panel of which I was a member. He had made several contacts with all other members of the panel but I had neither been informed of his employment nor contacted by him regarding his work.

A similar event occurred with the employment of a writer to fulfill the request for assistance in the preparation of a minority report. No one contacted those most interested in dissent to inform them of the selection or to get their concurrence. While not a prerequisite to his employment, courtesy would have dictated notice to the dissenters but it was not extended.

Perhaps these examples illustrate why it was obvious early that the Commission was being polarized, instead of being drawn together as a working unit. The leadership saw to it that their preconceived notions and theories were hindered in no way.

The last meetings of the full Commission were held on August 26 and 27, 1970. There was clarification on August 26, 1970 for those issuing a separate report that they could have up to 150 pages, 8½ x 11 inches, typed, doubled spaced. I requested the privilege on August 27, 1970 to include my dissent in the main body of the report. Recognizing that any lengthy statement might interfere with the readability of the report, I proposed that any dissent less than a paragraph be placed in the body of the report. More lengthy dissent could then be footnoted. Some Commissioners such as Elson, Hill, Spelts, and perhaps some others agreed to grant me this privilege. The majority voted against the proposal. They dictated that my dissent must be fully footnoted.

We continued with the discussion. I voted against the proposal to abolish all controls. As you will note in reading the majority report there are lengthy reasons given for the recommendation. I objected to the validity of some statements but was told by the Chairman that I was out of order. The reasons, he said, were for the recommendation and I had

450

already voted against it. My dissent was now removed even from the footnotes.

This action is a typical example of the manner in which the Commission has been directed. If you agreed with the leadership there was ample time for discussion, if not, "we must move on." If you yielded to coercion you could be heard, if not, you were cut off or severely reprimanded.

Because full consideration and study have been thwarted I submit that any recognition of the validity of the majority report will be to the detriment of our nation.

Statement by Drs. Morris A. Lipton and Edward D. Greenwood

The Commission Report, the Panel Reports and the Technical Reports upon which they are based offer the substance and record the conclusions and recommendations of the Commission. Editorial comment is purposely lacking, because the data and evidence will be available to individuals and professional groups who may draw their own conclusions. The Commission is, of course, not only a group which has worked conscientiously at its task, but it is also 18 separate individuals, each of whom made his own decisions. Such decisions are inevitably a result of the personal blend of each Commissioner's background and values, plus the learning experience that came from the information generated by the Commission's research and the discussions and debate which occurred in the many meetings of the panels and the full Commission. It is not likely that every Commissioner reached his decision for the same reasons, but the individual reactions are masked by the consensus. We feel that it would serve a useful purpose to document our experience and the reasons for our decisions.

We would like to think we were chosen because of our sustained activity in clinical, educational, preventive, and research aspects of psychiatry. We approached the problem from a research perspective and with a sense of citizen's responsibility. A neutral position has some utility. Lack of special interest implied a lack of strong bias. A background of research implied a faith that adequate investigation would

451

yield a rational solution. A sense of responsibility implied a feeling of commitment, often to the neglect of personal and professional affairs over the past two and a half years.

As physicians, the need to act on available medical evidence is hardly a new experience, but the need to conclude our efforts in the Commission with a set of recommendations bearing upon broad social and legal questions is a relatively new experience. In general, a researcher focuses on small areas in which, after many years of study, he becomes an expert. Despite this expertise he is seldom offered the opportunity to advise on national policy. He tends to welcome this absence of responsibility because he, more than any other critic, is aware of the shortcomings of his work. In the work with the Commission it has been necessary to become an "expert" quickly in broad areas of behavioral and social science and to follow the mandate of Congress to come to closure at a fixed date. We have done this after considerable reflection and study and have voted with the majority of the Commission on all of the major issues.

This was not done without some sense of uneasiness. All research, and especially research in the behavioral sciences, initially produces imperfect results. Truth is achieved through a series of repeated approximations, and the search for truth around which to establish social policy should ideally be multi-faceted and should involve repeated examination of existing and new evidence with sharper and more precise tools. Because of the limited life of the Commission this has not been entirely possible. Nonetheless, much new information has been obtained and much of value has been achieved.

We would have welcomed evidence relating exposure to erotica to delinquency, crime and antisocial behavior, for if such evidence existed we might have a simple solution to some of our most urgent problems. However, the work of the Commission has failed to uncover such evidence. Although the many and varied studies contracted for by the Commission may have flaws, they are remarkably uniform in the direction to which they point. This direction fails to establish a meaningful causal relationship or even significant correlation between exposure to erotica and immediate or delayed antisocial behavior among adults. To assert the contrary from the available evidence is not only to deny the facts, but also to delude the public by offering a spurious and simplistic answer to highly complex problems.

This is not to condone nor to approve hard core pornography. It is vulgar, distasteful, dull, a waste of money, and rapidly boring. Satiation occurred not only in the subjects of those experiments designed to determine whether it occurred, but also in the Commissioners. We find it to be a nuisance rather than an evil. The American public apparently agrees. Very few citizens consider the problem of the control of pornography to be among the most important social problems of the day. We should prefer to see the industry disappear, but we do not feel that the data gathered as a result of more than two years of investigation warrant restrictive legislation. The development of taste, morality and accurate sexual information is more a matter of education than of legislation. The side effects of highly restrictive legislation may well be more damaging than the problem which it aims to solve.

It has been stated that the recommendations of the Commission are softer on pornography than the Violence Commission was on exposure to violence. It has also been stated that pornography, like new drugs, should be considered dangerous until proven innocent. Neither statement has any basis in fact. The recommended restrictions upon public display and the use of the mails, as well as the statutes designed to offer juvenile protection are much stronger than any existing or proposed federal statutes for the control of the exhibition of violence or for the accessibility of potentially violent hardware like knives and guns. Nor is the analogy with drugs accurate. A drug is investigated by purposely exposing large numbers of people to it under specified conditions. Through such studies efficacy, toxicity, side effects and idiosyncratic adverse reactions are evaluated. The drug is then released with appropriate warnings and safeguards. Acceptance of a drug for use depends almost always upon demonstrated effectiveness and the failure to demonstrate acute toxicity. If chronic toxicity shows up in further studies, the drug may later be withdrawn.

By these standards, erotic materials, to the extent that they have been examined, would get a clean bill of health. In the several experimental situations where erotic materials have been purposely given or made available to subjects who are being tested, there is a transient sexual arousal (which is what the product is supposed to achieve) and no evidence of acute or delayed behavioral toxicity. There is no drug which is absolutely safe and which cannot be misused. This may well be true for erotic materials as well. But drugs are not withheld because occasional annoying side effects are found in a very small population nor should erotic materials. However, all of the experimental studies have been carried out with young or middleaged adults whose sexual attitudes and practices are already established. A significant deficiency in the work of the Commission was the failure to comprehensively study the effects of erotica on children and juveniles whose sexual behavior is not yet fixed. Ethical considerations and social taboos prevented such experiments even though there is much evidence that nearly all children are exposed, largely through peer groups, in their teens. If the drug model analogy is to be followed, experiments should now be performed in which larger numbers of individuals, at different ages and with different backgrounds, are exposed in different social milieus in order to define and refine the full limits of safety.

It appears well-established that sexual interests are instinctually derived and that they are present from infancy through old age with different degrees of intensity. Consequently, it is impossible to fully protect children from exposure to sexual stimuli. From the dirty words of the six year old to the graffiti present in the toilets of schools and public buildings to the "dirty" jokes of the early adolescent and the "dirty" stories and pictures of the teenager, it would appear that exposure is omnipresent. One may, therefore, ask whether such an exposure may not be an inevitable part of growing up in any culture and whether it may even serve a purpose. Gradual and age-appropriate exposure to erotic stimuli may lead to the development of socially appropriate defense mechanisms like sublimation, repression, postponement and self control. Although the analogy may be somewhat far-fetched, it seems possible that graded exposure may immunize in somewhat the same fashion that exposure to bacteria and viruses builds resistance. If this analogy has merit, total lack of exposure would render the child who is totally unexposed as helpless as the animal raised in a totally sterile environment who later encounters the invariably contaminated real world. The finding that sex offenders tend to come from highly restricted families and have had less than the usual exposure to erotica suggests that they may not have had the opportunity to develop appropriate self control.

To continue the analogy, overwhelming exposure might cause illness rather than immunization. An especially vulnerable period is likely following puberty when sexual impulses of increasing intensity emerge. A major problem of adolescence is that of impulse control, and in our troubled and rapidly changing world youngsters are already hyper-stimulated. To add to this stimulation by a completely permissive attitude with respect to the availability of sexual materials appears imprudent. For this reason, we have voted for the juvenile legislation.

We are fully convinced that all of the Commissioners felt about pornography as we did and that all sought the same ends. The specific end was the diminution of interest in pornography by the population at large. The more general end was the development of healthy sexual attitudes based upon accurate information and sound moral values. Some disagreement arose as to the nature of healthy sexual attitudes and about the means for achieving these. Our position is that changing values regarding marriage, divorce, contraception, abortion, and even the right to have unlimited children in the face of a pending population crisis would have much more to do with changing sexual values and attitudes than does exposure to pornography. To the moral absolutist such change is sinful, to the relativist it may not be personally desirable but appears to be an inevitable product of newly emerging social problems. We take the position that highly restrictive legislation for adults, like the Volstead Act, would generate more crime and antisocial behavior than it would prevent. For adults and especially children, age-appropriate sex education presented accurately and truthfully in an appropriate aesthetic and moral context should do far more to reduce interest in pornography than any restrictive legislation which might be initiated. Furthermore, it would do so without raising the many controversies which exist regarding definitions of obscenity and pornography and the kinds of material which may or may not be protected by the First Amendment.

Report of Commissioners

MORTON A. HILL, S. J.
WINFREY C. LINK
concurred in by
CHARLES H. KEATING, JR.*

Overview

The Commission's majority report is a Magna Carta for the pornographer.

It is slanted and biased in favor of protecting the business of obscenity and pornography, which the Commission was mandated by the Congress to regulate.

The Commission leadership and majority recommend that most existing legal barriers between society and pornography be pulled down. In so doing, the Commission goes far beyond its mandate and assumes the role of counsel for the filth merchant—a role not assigned by the Congress of the United States.

The Commission leadership and majority recommend repeal of obscenity law for "consenting adults." It goes on, then, to recommend legislation for minors, public display and thrusting of pornography on persons through the mails.

The American people should be made aware of the fact that this is precisely the situation as it exists in Denmark today. The Commission, in short, is presumptuously recommending that the United States follow Denmark's lead in giving pornography free rein.

We feel impelled to issue this report in vigorous dissent.

The conclusions and recommendations in the majority report will be found deeply offensive to Congress and to tens of millions of Americans. And what the American people do not know is that the scanty and manipulated evidence contained within this report is wholly inadequate to support the conclusions and sustain the recommendations. Thus, both conclusions and recommendations are, in our view, fraudulent.

What the American people have here for the two million dollars voted by Congress, and paid by the taxpayer, is a shoddy piece of scholarship that will be quoted ad nauseam

*Mr. Keating, while concurring in this report is preparing a separate dissent.

456

by cultural polluters and their attorneys within society.

The fundamental "finding" on which the entire report is based is: that "empirical research" has come up with "no reliable evidence to indicate that exposure to explicitly sexual materials plays a significant role in the causation of delinquent or criminal behavior among youth or adults."

The inference from this statement, i.e., pornography is harmless, is not only insupportable on the slanted evidence presented; it is preposterous. How isolate one factor and say it causes or does not cause criminal behavior? How determine that one book or one film caused one man to commit rape or murder? A man's entire life goes into one criminal act. No one factor can be said to have caused that act.

The Commission has deliberately and carefully avoided coming to grips with the basic underlying issue. The government interest in regulating pornography has always related primarily to the prevention of moral corruption and *not* to prevention of overt criminal acts and conduct, or the protection of persons from being shocked and/or offended.

The basic question is whether and to what extent society may establish and maintain certain moral standards. If it is conceded that society has a legitimate concern in maintaining moral standards, it follows logically that government has a legitimate interest in at least attempting to protect such standards against any source which threatens them.

The Commission report simply ignores this issue, and relegates government's interest to little more than a footnote— passing it off with the extremist cliche that it is "unwise" for government to attempt to legislate morality. Obscenity law in no way legislates individual morality, but provides protection for public morality. The Supreme Court itself has never denied society's interest in maintaining moral standards, but has instead ruled for the protection of the "social interest in order and morality."

The Commission report ignores another basic issue: the phrase "utterly without redeeming social value." This language has been propagandized by extremists and profit-seekers, and it is so propagandized in this report as being the law of the land. It is not the law of the land, since no Supreme Court ever voiced such an opinion, yet this erroneous concept has been built into the statutes of the states as a result of extremists asserting that it is a necessary "test" enunciated by the Supreme Court. This erroneous conception has led to a vast upsurge in the traffic in pornography in the past four years. The fact is, it is nothing more than an opinion of three judges, binding on no one, neither court nor legislature.

In sum, the conclusions and recommendations of the Commission majority represent the preconceived views of the Chairman and his appointed counsel that the Commission should arrive at those conclusions most compatible with the viewpoint of the American Civil Liberties Union. Both men singlemindedly steered the Commission to this objective.

In the interest of truth and understanding, it should be noted here that the policy of ACLU has been that obscenity is protected speech. Mr. Lockhart, the Chairman of the Commission, has long been a member of the American Civil Liberties Union. Mr. Bender, his general counsel, is an executive of the Philadelphia Civil Liberties Union.

The two million dollars voted by Congress have gone primarily to "scholars" who would return conclusions amenable to the extreme and minority views of Mr. Lockhart, Mr. Bender and the ACLU.

OUR POSITION

We stand in agreement with the Congress of the United States: the traffic in obscenity and pornography is a matter of national concern.

We believe that pornography has an eroding effect on society, on public morality, on respect for human worth, on attitudes toward family love, on culture.

We believe it is impossible, and totally unnecessary, to attempt to prove or disprove a cause-effect relationship between pornography and criminal behavior.

Sex education, recommended so strongly by the majority, is the panacea for those who advocate license in media. The report suggests sex education, with a plaint for the dearth of instructors and materials. It notes that three schools have used "hard-core pornography" in training potential instructors. The report does not answer the question that comes to mind immediately: Will these instructors not bring the hard-core pornography into the grammar schools? Many other questions are left unanswered: How assure that the instructor's moral or ethical code (or lack of same) will not be communicated to children? Shouldn't parents, not children, be the recipients of sex education courses?

Children cannot grow in love if they are trained with pornography. Pornography is loveless; it degrades the human being, reduces him to the level of animal. And if this Com-

458

mission majority's recommendations are heeded, there will be a glut of pornography for teachers and children.

In contrast to the Commission report's amazing statement that "public opinion in America does not support the imposition of legal prohibitions upon the consensual distribution" of pornography to adults, we find, as a result of public hearings conducted by two of the undersigned in eight cities throughout the country, that the majority of the American people favor tighter controls. Twenty-six out of twenty-seven witnesses at the hearing in New York City expressed concern and asked for remedial measures. Witnesses were a cross section of the community, ranging from members of the judiciary to members of women's clubs. This pattern was repeated in the cities of New Orleans, Indianapolis, Chicago, Salt Lake City, San Francisco, Washington, D.C., and Buffalo. (And yet, one member of the Commission majority bases his entire position for legalization on the astounding "finding" of the Commission survey that "no more than 35% of our people favor adult controls in the field of obscenity in the absence of some demonstrable social evil related to its presence and use.")

Additionally, law enforcement officers testifying at the Hill-Link hearings were unanimous in declaring that the problem of obscenity and pornography is a serious one. They complained that law enforcement is hampered by the "utterly without redeeming social value" language. The Commission's own survey of prosecuting attorneys indicates that 73% of prosecutors polled said that "social value" is the most serious obstacle to prosecution. The decision not to prosecute is usually a manifestation of this obstacle. This figure and information is strangely missing from the report's "Overview of Findings."

We point also to the results of a Gallup poll, published in the summer of 1969. Eighty-five out of every 100 adults interviewed said they favored stricter state and local laws dealing with pornography sent through the mails, and 76 of every 100 wanted stricter laws on the sort of magazines and newspapers available on newsstands.

We believe government must legislate to regulate pornography, in order to protect the "social interest in order and morality."

OUR REPORT

To the end that Congress asked for recommendations to

459

regulate the traffic in obscenity and pornography, we will—
at the close of this report—as much as it is in our power,
carry out the mandate given us by the Congress to analyze
the laws on obscenity (see Appendices), recommend definitions, and recommend such legislative, administrative and
other advisable or appropriate action to regulate effectively and constitutionally the traffic in obscenity and pornography.

In addition, we will point up the astonishing bias of the
Commission majority report by presenting to the President,
the Congress and the American people, a history of the
creation of the Commission, and a brief report on the heretofore secret operation of this Commission.

We shall document Commission bias and slant in the area
of Effects, on which the entire report is based, and in the
Legal area where the American people are asked to accept
a misleading philosophy of law.

I. History of Creation of Commission

For several years prior to 1967 legislation to create a
Commission on Obscenity and Pornography was introduced
into the Congress. It passed the Senate each time, and each
time died in House Committee.

Legislation was vigorously opposed by the American Civil
Liberties Union, which reads the First Amendment in an
absolutist way (cf. Annual Report, American Civil Liberties
Union, July 1, 1965 to January 11, 1967, page 9). Their
position that "obscenity as much as any other form of speech
or press, is entitled to the protection of the First Amendment," can be found in an *amicus* brief in *Jacobellis v. Ohio,*
1964, among others.

In 1967, however, the feeling of the Congress was such
that legislation to create a Commission was certain to pass.
Now, the ACLU strategy changed. In April of that year,
the Director of the Washington Office of the American Civil
Liberties Union testified on such legislation before the House
Subcommittee on Education and Labor.

He called for "scientific studies" into effects on the part
of such a Commission, and maintained that *the public* and
private groups should not be involved in the workings of
the Commission.

A bill to create the Commission was considered by the
Senate in May of 1967. The bill made no mention of effects studies, and drew for membership from both houses

of Congress, from various governmental agencies, education, media, state attorneys general, prosecutors and law enforcement. It provided for public hearings and power of subpoena.

The bill which ultimately passed the Congress called for effects studies, drew heavily from the behavioral sciences for membership, and the power of subpoena had been removed. In other words, it was considerably weakened, and much more in line with the libertarian concept of such a Commission.

A White House press release dated January 2, 1968 reported that William B. Lockhart had been "selected" Chairman of the Commission, although public law 90-100 mandated that a chairman and vice-chairman be elected by the Commission from among its members.

Five months later, the Commission met for the first time. After five months, during which Mr. Lockhart had laid much groundwork, talking "effects" with several universities, the Commission voted to affirm his chairmanship.

Mr. Lockhart had present as an observer, at all sessions of the first Commission meeting, Mr. Paul Bender, who was later retained as general counsel to the Commission.

Mr. Lockhart has long contended that "scientific proof" of harmful effects is needed before an item can be adjudged obscene. (See Lockhart-McClure articles, U. of Minn. Law Rev.) This reasoning, followed to its logical conclusion, would have all obscenity law repealed, for it is virtually impossible to prove that one book or one film caused one person to commit an anti-social act or a crime. No court, nor any legislature, has ever demanded such "scientific proof" as requested by Mr. Lockhart and his civil libertarian confreres.

After the appointment of the Commission and the "selection" of the Chairman, no further word was heard, to our knowledge, from the Civil Liberties Union until October of 1969, when the same director of the Washington office testified before the House Subcommittee on Postal Operations. This time, he urged that no legislation against pornography be enacted *until the issuance of the Commission report.*

The Commission thus had its beginnings in bias and never changed course. Using procedures wholly undemocratic, the Commission Chairman has marched the Commission from a preconceived assumption along a precharted path to a predetermined conclusion.

461

II. Operation of Commission

At the first meeting of the Commission, the Chairman asked for "confidentiality" or secrecy on the part of the members. The Commission concurred.

No by-laws have ever been drawn up to our knowledge. No parliamentary procedure has been observed. There has not been a call for approval or amendment of minutes, distributed by mail. Because of this, one of the undersigned asked that meetings be taped or recorded. This request was refused.

Agenda for Commission meetings and for panel meetings were prepared by a hand-picked staff, and received shortly before meetings, giving Commission members little time for preparation.

Two or three members who were in obvious and open disagreement with the Commission leadership were all but excluded from participation. From the beginning, Commission members heard only one viewpoint; seldom hearing alternatives.

Because of this, and because the Commission under its leadership had consistently refused to go to *the public* and hear other views firsthand, two Commissioners conducted public hearings at their own expense in eight cities throughout the country. At the completion of the hearings of Commissioners Hill and Link, the Commission voted to refuse them reimbursement for expenses incurred, deciding to hold two "official" hearings lest their report not receive public acceptance. (Note above the libertarian specification that *the public* should not be involved in the workings of such a Commission. Note also Commission majority explanation for not having conducted hearings until the end of the Commission's life.)

Commissioners themselves were not put into direct contact with the problem of obscenity in the concrete. A few films were shown at the first meeting; samples were "available," but no Commissioner was asked to become conversant with the problem in the concrete, so that he could be equipped to make judgments.

At the first meeting the Commission was summarily divided into four "working" panels. Panel members were not aware of what was transpiring in other panels, except for oral reports at meetings and brief written reports distributed by mail.

Full Commission meetings were held approximately every

other month in the beginning. However, from October 1969 to March 1970 there was a lapse of five months between full meetings.

III. Critique of Commission Behavioral Research

1. INTRODUCTION

Dr. Victor B. Cline, University of Utah psychologist and specialist in social science research methodology and statistics, has called the Commission's Effects Panel Report—upon which the majority report and its recommendations are based—"seriously flawed, and omitting some critical data on negative effects."

Dr. Cline is the author of over 30 published research papers, principal investigator on a number of research projects funded by the Office of Naval Research, National Institutes of Mental Health, Offices of Education, etc. He teaches courses in clinical, experimental, and child psychology, and is a practising clinical psychologist.

Testifying before the Commission in Los Angeles on May 4, Dr. Cline called for, and has since repeatedly called for, the assemblage of an unbiased panel of scientists to (a) evaluate the original research sponsored by the Commission, and (b) assess what conclusions might legitimately be drawn from the assembled evidence. The Commission leadership and majority have ignored his request. In view of this, the signers of this dissenting report asked Dr. Cline to serve as an unpaid consultant. He agreed to do so, in the interest of scientific honesty and truth.

Following is Dr. Cline's evaluation of the Commission report, Effects Panel report, and "findings."

A careful review and study of the Commission majority report, their conclusions and recommendations, and the empirical research studies on which they were based, reveal a great number of serious flaws, omissions and grave shortcomings which make parts of the report suspect and to some extent lacking in credibility.

Readers of the majority report are at the "mercy" of the writers of that report, and must assume that evidence is being presented fairly and in good faith on both sides of the issue. This is also true for most Commission members themselves. It should be stated that members of the Commission Minority were allowed to look at most of the Commission-sponsored 85 research studies but only after re-

463

peated, dogged requests. And then a number were finally and most reluctantly released to them perilously close to the Commission-set deadline for this dissent.

A number of the research studies upon which the report is based suggest significant statistical relationships between pornography, sexual deviancy and promiscuity. Yet, some vital data suggesting this linkage are omitted or "concealed." Findings from seriously flawed research studies or findings which do not follow from the data are sometimes presented as fact without mentioning their very serious limitations.

2. OVERVIEW OF PROBLEM

There are at least two reasons for the existence of laws regulating and controlling the traffic in obscene and pornographic materials. The *first* has to do with potential harmful or adverse effects such materials may have on the user, child or adult (e.g., corrupt one's morals, deprave, feed a neurosis, awaken and provoke the sex appetite in an unstable individual who might thereby sexually harm or molest another, etc.). The *second* involved an "offense to public morality or taste." Examples might include prostitution, public exposure and nudity, etc., the control of which has its basis in the Judeo-Christian values from which our national culture and heritage is derived.

The majority report of the Commission on Obscenity and Pornography has made recommendations which essentially involve repeal of all laws restricting the distribution, sale or exhibition of any kind of pornography[1] to adults and the same for non-pictorial pornography for children.

However, whenever sweeping changes in social policy, laws, regulations, etc., (such as this) are recommended which might affect the health and welfare of the nation's citizens (which their own and other surveys suggest a significant proportion of the population believe to be the case), the burden of proof for demonstrating "no harm" or "no adverse results" is ordinarily thought to be on the shoulders of the innovators or "changers".

Thus our task here will be to look carefully at the research presented and see if "no harm" has been adequately demonstrated. The issue of pornography being "an offense to public morality and taste" which involves values will not be an issue in this discussion.

---

[1]They would approve control of unsolicited mailed advertisements for pornography and certain open displays of same.

464

TABLE 1
"Exposure to Sexually Oriented Materials
Among Young Male Prison Offenders" (1970)
(By Martin Propper)

Sample: 476 male reformatory inmates, ages 16-21

Activity Engaged In	Subjects Having Lo Exposure to Pornography	Subjects Having Hi Exposure to Pornography	Source
1. Age of first intercourse 11 or under	37%	53%	Table 31
2. Age of first intercourse 14 or under	65%	86%	Table 31
3. Having sex intercourse 3 or more times a week prior to incarceration	28%	45%	Table 29
4. Having intercourse with 7 or more partners	63%	96%	Table 28
5. Intercourse with *more* than 1 person at a time	35%	59%	Page 68
6. Engaged in *passive* mouth sex organ contact (sometimes or frequently)	27%	56%	Table 34
7. Engaged in *active* mouth sex organ contact (sometimes or frequently)	16%	49%	Table 33
8. *No* homosexual experience	53%	37%	Page 66
9. Several times to frequently did anal intercourse	20%	40%	Table 35
10. Belongs to a high sex deviant peer group[1]	44%	78%	Table 36 Page 72
11. Belongs to high anti-social "crime" group[2]	55%	82%	Table 37 Page 73

	Seeing Textual Depictions of Homosexual Activity		
12. Participation in homosexual activity one or more times	Never 12%	10 or more times 40%	

13. Table 32 in the Propper study also reveals among the younger age boys a very high relationship between (a) the *age* at which they saw a picture of sexual intercourse, and (b) the *age* at which they first engaged personally in sexual intercourse. This means that if a boy saw pictures of intercourse at a very early age, he engaged in intercourse at a very early age. If he saw intercourse pictures later, he engaged in intercourse later. While the data do not provide evidence of causal linkage it certainly raises the possibility. It also reminds one of Bandura's work in "imitative learning" where children learn by imitating what they've seen.

[1]The sex behaviors which constituted this measure included: (a) sex intercourse, (b) "gang bangs," (c) going to a whore, (d) getting a girl pregnant, (e) participating in orgies.
[2]The activities which constituted this measure included: (a) friends' suggestions to violate the law, (b) friends in jail or reform school, (c) friends in trouble with the law, (d) purchase of stolen goods by friends, and (e) friends who were members of gangs.

465

3. THE PROPPER STUDY

The Commission in the summary of their Effects Panel Report conclude:

In sum, the empirical research has found no evidence to date that exposure to explicit sexual materials plays a significant role in the causation of delinquent or criminal behavior among youth or adults. The Commission cannot conclude that exposure to erotic materials is a factor in the causation of sex crime or sex delinquency.

Based on the above paragraph, cited again and again in various forms throughout the whole report, we have the basis for recommending the removal of all pornography controls for adults and all controls (except pictoral pornography) for children.[1]

Yet if we review the research of Propper, in his study of 476 reformatory inmates (see Table 1) we noted again and again a relationship between high exposure to pornography and "sexually promiscuous" and deviant behavior at very early ages, as well as affiliation with groups high in criminal activity and sex deviancy. This study was financed and contracted by the Commission, and while they refer to Propper's study often, no mention is made of any of these specific results in the Commission Report. This study was for many months in the hands of the professional committee that assembled and wrote the report as well as available for inspection of any of the Commission members who wished to read it (but no one else). As the reader can scarcely fail to note, there are striking statistical relationships between heavy use of pornography and various kinds of sexual "acting out," deviancy, and affiliation with high crime risk groups.

4. THE DAVIS AND BRAUCHT RESEARCH

Davis and Braucht (1970) in a study of seven different populations of subjects comprising 365 people assessed the relationship between exposure to pornography and moral character, deviance in the home, neighborhood, sex behavior, etc. Samples of city jail inmates, Mexican-American college students, black college students, white fraternity men, conservative protestant students and Catholic seminarians were

---

[1]Control of unsolicited mail order pornography and open public displays are recommended.

studied intensively. In addition each had one female friend fill out a character scale about their behavior.

In their study, which was impressive in its rigorous methodology and statistical treatment, they state, *"One finds exposure to pornography is the strongest predictor of sexual deviance among the early age of exposure subjects* [p. 35]." Later, they again note, *"In general, then, exposure to pornography in the 'early age of exposure' subgroup was related to a variety of precocious heterosexual and deviant sexual behaviors* [p. 36]." They note that since exposure in this subgroup is NOT related to having deviant peers (bad associations and companions) and similar type variables, it would be difficult to blame the sexual promiscuity and deviancy of these subjects on other influences such as being influenced by friends (rather than pornography) into these kinds of anti-social activities.

It should be noted that this research was contracted and financed by the Commission, was in the hands of the Commission staff for many months, is referred to many times in their report—but not a single mention is made of these negative finds. In fact, the September 3 issue of *The New York Daily News* and an earlier edition of the *Washington Post* carried stories on their research linking exposure to pornography with sex deviancy. This is a particularly important finding in that it suggests real dangers in exposing children and young adolescents to heavy quantities of pornography, the strong implication being that pornography can affect and stimulate precocious heterosexual activity and deviant sex behavior (homosexuality). Obviously more research must be done here, but like with the early studies linking smoking with lung cancer, it would seem most irresponsible not to report such findings and especially in the Commission's Effects Panel Report when so few people have access to the original research, and where publication in the scientific literature would be at least one or two years in the future.

5. THE BERGER RESEARCH

Alan Berger and associates in Illinois had contracts with the Commission to do two studies. In one they surveyed 473 adolescents primarily in the age range of 14-18 (from working class backgrounds) with an extensive questionnaire which asked questions about their exposure to pornography, their sexual behavior, etc. In the second study 1177 college students were interviewed about similar issues. In carefully reviewing these findings it is once again distressing to note that those data "not favorable" to the majority point of view are either played down or not mentioned.

The two most significant (highest) relationships (between independent variables) were between having been exposed to large amounts of pornography and engaging in high levels of sexual activity. This was true for both high school students (gamma .394 [males] page 48) and college age subjects (gamma .380, page 62). These relationships are lower (but still significant) for women. An example of this relationship can be seen in Table 2 below.

TABLE 2

	Amount of Pornography Exposed to Student	Percent College Males Engaging in Sex Intercourse, etc.
Hi	5-6	77%
	4	62%
	3	60%
	2	44%
Lo	1	4%

There are also substantial relationships between exposure to pornography (high) and grades (low), especially in high school, but also college for males (gammas of −.256, page 30; and −.216, page 67). The relationship between these two in college declines when one controls out the influence of high school grades, but still remains true for the top college men academically (who have low pornography exposure indices).

In their study of the 473 high school students they found a relationship between frequency of seeing movies depicting sexual intercourse and the adolescent engaging in intercourse (their Table 46, page 101, is duplicated in part below).

TABLE 3

	Frequency of adolescents seeing movies depicting sex intercourse			
	Not at all	1-4 times	5-10 times	11 or more times
Percent of Males engaging in premarital intercourse	53	62	73	88
Percent of Females engaging in premarital intercourse	10	29	44	

468

The above data are in the Commission financed reports, but are not discussed or presented, despite the fact that they have an important bearing on the "effects" question.

And while it is recognized that there are some people in our society with more libertarian views who would not be concerned if pornography did "cause" more young people to engage in premarital intercourse, there are still others, including many parents, who would be concerned and would wish to be so informed. The Commission Report fails in fully informing its readers about such associations or linkages as noted above.

6. THE MOSHER AND KATZ STUDY

In another Commission sponsored study by Mosher and Katz (1970) studying male aggression against women in a laboratory setting, they concluded (page 23) that, "The data clearly support the proposition that aggression against women increases when that aggression is instrumental to securing sexual stimulation (through seeing pornography)." This finding was particularly true for men with severe conscience systems as well as for those feeling guilt about being aggressive. This suggests that the need for sexual stimulation (via pornography) can overrule conscience and guilt in "permitting" aggressive behavior towards women. And while this is only a laboratory demonstration, with many limitations, it still constitutes another "negative effects" type of evidence in which virtually no attention is paid by the writers of the Commission report.

7. THE GOLDSTEIN STUDY

In another Commission financed research project by Goldstein (1970)[1] a study was made of the exposure to pornography and its relationship to sex activities of groups of sex offenders and others. In all, nine separate groups of male subjects were studied and compared. They found that the rapists were the group reporting the highest "excitation to masturbation" rates by pornography both in the adult (80%) as well as teen (90%) years. Considering the crime they were imprisoned for, this suggests that pornography (with accompanying masturbation) did not serve adequately as a catharsis, prevent a sex crime or "keep them off the

---

[1]Table 9-10, pages 48-50.

streets." Fifty-five percent of the rapists report being "excited to sex relations by pornography." When reporting on "peak experiences" in exposure to pornography during their teens, 80% of the rapists report "wishing to try the act" that they had witnessed or seen demonstrated in the pornography exposed to them. This is far higher than with any other group. When asked if in fact *they did follow through* with such sexual activity immediately or shortly thereafter 30% of the rapists replied "yes." An even higher number of blacks (38% replied "yes") which is consistent with many studies showing very high rates of sexual activity early in life for this group. Even among the "normal" controls 28% replied "yes." If we can accept what they say at face value, this would suggest that pornography potentially does affect behavior and possibly adversely. This would also suggest serious concerns about exposing young people, especially to thematic material involving pornographic-violence. Since the writers of the Commission Report base most of their findings on data using "verbal self report" there is little reason not to at least consider as partially valid what these people say about pornography and its influence in their lives. When one asks them about their *adult* years and to what extent they "tried out behaviorally" what pornography had suggested to them, the figures drop somewhat (15% for rapists, 25% for child molesters, etc.) but still suggest an "effect."

8. THE OPINIONS OF PROFESSIONAL WORKERS ABOUT PORNOGRAPHY

In their summary section the Commission states, "Professional workers in the area of human conduct generally believe that sexual materials do not have harmful effects." While this appears to be true these conclusions are based on a mail-back survey in which only a third of their sample responded. They also neglect to state that in this study 254 psychiatrists and psychologists *had* cases where they reported they had seen/found a direct causal linkage between involvement with pornography and a sex crime. While another 324 professionals reported seeing cases where such a relationship was suspected, this totals in actual numbers 578. While these therapists represent a minority group percentagewise, it would seem to this reviewer irresponsible to gloss over them as if they didn't exist. What if 900 of 1000 physicians indicated that they had observed no relationship

470

between cancer of the cervix and use of the coil contraceptive, but the other 100 physicians indicated that in their practice they had come across cases where there was a suspected or definite relationship. Do we discount the experience of the minority because they are outvoted where a possible health hazard is involved?

Additionally they do not report (though they were aware of its existence) of another survey conducted by a religious group, the Archdiocese of New Jersey, in 1967 of professionals seeing a relationship between involvement with pornography and anti-social sex behavior. The majority of therapists here reported noting such a relationship at some time during their practice. This study is also flawed because of a low return of "mail-backs" by the professionals. But such is also true of the Lipkin and Carns study. Such omission of contrary evidence is difficult to understand.

9. SEX OFFENDERS REPORT PORNOGRAPHY CONTRIBUTED TO THEIR CRIME

In another Commission sponsored study by Walker (1970) seven groups of adult males (sex offenders, mental hospital patients, university students, etc.) were tested and interviewed relative to exposure to pornography and a great deal of personal background data. In their analysis of the data they found that the sex offenders significantly, more often than their controls (non sex offenders who they were compared with), increased their sexual activity after viewing pornography. A significant minority (39%) of the sex offenders indicated that "pornography had something to do with their committing the sex offense they were convicted of." The researchers also found that their offenders significantly more often claimed that they had been influenced by pornography to commit a sexual crime.

The writers of the Commission Report note this evidence and rightly raise the possibility that these sex offenders may be "scapegoating" here (blaming something or somebody else for their problem). This possibility is certainly a reasonable one. The alternate possibility, that they might indeed be telling the truth, however, *is* another reasonable alternative. And until this issue is settled it would seem most injudicious and unwise to claim that pornography has "no effects" or that "no effects" can be demonstrated which would constitute the basis for major social change, repeal of laws, etc.

471

10. THREE EXAMPLES OF IMPROPER REPORTING OF RESEARCH DATA

(a) The Berninghausen and Faunce Study
(b) The Kutschinsky Study
(c) The Walker Research

(a) *The Berninghausen and Faunce Study*

In Chapter V of the Effects Panel Report, the Commission states

A comparison study of thirty-nine delinquents and thirty-nine nondelinquent youth (Berninghausen & Faunce, 1964) found no significant differences between these groups in the number of "sensational" (obscene) books they had read. Non-delinquent youth were somewhat more likely (75%) than delinquent youth (56%) however, to report having read at least one "possibly erotic" book.

But what the Commission doesn't tell the reader is that:

(a) a significantly greater number of delinquent boys (than non-delinquent) had read two or more adult books (with erotic content); and a significantly greater number of delinquents had read three or more "erotic books" than the non-delinquents.

(b) the authors of the research concluded that "limitations of the study precluded having any great confidence in the stability of the conclusion" meaning the findings are unreliable and probably shouldn't be cited.

The writers of the Commission Report make three errors:

(a) They cite data to prove a point from a "worthless" study.

(b) They don't tell the reader that the study is flawed.

(c) They present only that evidence which favors their point of view. They again fail to cite contrary findings.

Since most readers will never read the original study they are "at the mercy" of the writers of this report to present complete and honest data. Once again we see an example of where this did not occur.

(b) *The Kutschinsky Study*

In the final "Effects Panel Report" the Commission staff write,

A survey (Kutschinsky, 1970) of Copenhagen residents found that neither public attitudes about sex crimes nor willingness to report such crimes had changed sufficiently to account for the substantial decrease in sex offenses between 1958 and 1969.

472

In the Final Report summary section they put it even more strongly,

Other research showed that the decreases in reported sexual offenses cannot be attributed to concurrent changes in the social and legal definitions of sex crimes or in public attitudes toward reporting such crimes to the police. . . .

The average reader and most social scientists will never get an opportunity to see what this Danish psychologist actually wrote in this report or what he did. He, of course, was studying the issue of why with increasing pornography in Denmark has the rate of sex crimes apparently dropped. Maybe pornography has a "therapeutic effect" on sex criminals. What Kutschinsky did, in fact, was intensively interview a carefully drawn sample of adult men and women throughout Copenhagen surveying (a) whether they had ever been a victim in a sex crime, (b) did they report it, (c) would they report certain types of sex crimes now (or ignore them), (d) have they changed their mind over the past few years about the seriousness of certain sex offenses, and (e) how did they feel about these same things ten years ago. He found that 26% of the men[1] and 61% of the women of Copenhagen had been victims of some category of sex crime (some minor, some serious). However, only 6% of the males interviewed and 19% of the female victims reported it to the police. This is consistent with statements made by the U.S. Department of Justice in their 1970 Unified Crime Reports referring to rape. "This offense is probably one of the most under reported crimes due primarily to fear and/or embarrassment on the part of the victims." This means overall that sex crimes statistics are very "shaky" and have to be viewed with caution simply because most are probably never reported.

Kutschinsky concludes after a careful and extended analysis of his data that, *The decrease in (sexual) exhibitionism registered by the police during the last ten years may be fully explained by a change in people's attitudes toward this crime and towards reporting it to the police.* He concludes in about the same terms with regards to the sex crime of *"indencency towards women"* (which can involve anything short of a direct rape attempt on a female). If the reader will go back and read again what the Commission said about the Kutschinsky findings, we again get an example of critical

---

[1]Involving primarily "homosexual molestation."

473

omissions and misrepresentations of important factual data.[2]

The Commission's presentation of the Denmark sex crimes data omits certain types of sex offenses such as incest (apparently unavailable) which many people would regard as fairly serious. If as Kutschinsky's study suggests, there have been no real declines in sex crimes in certain categories, only a change in people's conception about their seriousness and a lessened inclination to report them, this should be given thoughtful and careful consideration. That the Danish people have liberal sex attitudes has been documented by various surveys including another by Kutschinksy which indicated that only thirty-two percent of Danes regard sex intercourse with a "consenting" fourteen year old as a crime and only twelve percent would regard the rape of a female as a crime where she permitted the rapist to engage in prior petting.

The kind of sex crime most people would be concerned with would involve a personal assault as in rape, or on a child, or the situation involving exhibitionism which might "traumatize" some women and possibly affect their psycho-sexual feelings and attitudes negatively.

If we look at the Copenhagen rape statistics (combining rape, rape with robbery, attempted rape, and intercourse on threat of violence) which all involve a sexual assault on an-other—we get the following picture.

Year	Rape (all categories)
1958	57 cases
1959	55
1960	37
1961	48
1962	53
1963	50
1964	39
1965	42 Pornography freely available
1966	70
1967	44
1968	50
1969	35

[2]With regards to "peeping" a non-violent sex crime which has declined 79.9% in the last decade his data suggest that the availability of all sorts of visual pornography, films and live sex shows probably have reduced the need of the peeper to risk arrest looking through people's windows when he can see more in any porno shop. We would agree with this conclusion. In the only other sex crime which he evaluated, "Indecency toward girls" his data suggested little or no change in public attitudes towards its seriousness or lack of willingness to report it. The decline in the reporting of this offense remains a puzzle, with Kutschinsky suggesting the possibility of pornography being a (poor) substitute for little girls for this type of offender.

474

If one looks at the table and notes that it was about 1965 when pornography became generally available (even though legal recognition of this wasn't to come for several years). It presents a rather puzzling picture in that until 1969 there were no major changes in rape rate other than the normal fluctuations common to preceding years. In any event it would certainly be injudicious to conclude that there has occurred a true change or decline in some sex crimes, at least yet, in the light of the above statistics or in view of Kutschinsky's findings that with certain sorts of sex offenses the "decline" can be partially or fully attributable to changes in people's attitudes about certain sex crimes and their changes in "reporting" practices. Other sorts of data which would be useful to have in studying this whole problem would be divorce rate figures for the past ten years, venereal disease rates, changes in extra-marital sex patterns, and prostitution figures for the decade.

(c) *The Walker Research*

In Chapter V of the Effects Panel Report the Commission reviews the research of Walker (1970) studying sex offenders and non-offenders.

> . . . the mean age of first exposure (to pornography) of the rapists was one half a year or more later than that of the matched non-sex-offenders in reference to eight of the fifteen items (types of pornography) and one half a year or more earlier in reference to two. The biggest difference between the groups occurred in relation to depictions of heterosexual intercourse for which non-sex-offenders had a mean age of first exposure of 14.95 and rapists a mean age of first exposure of 18.19

The Commission blandly reports this as a fact when a quick look at Walker's tables shows that this is undoubtedly in error. The table below is produced directly from their data.

Type of Pornography Seen	Mean age when Sex Offenders **First** Saw Pornography	Type of Pornography Seen	Mean Age when NON Offenders **First** Saw Pornography
Male-Female Sex Intercourse	18.19 years of age	Male-Female Sex Intercourse	14.95 years of age
Humans Having Sex Relations with Animals	16.94	Nude Female with Breasts Exposed	15.09
Mouth-Sex Organ Contact	17.46	Nude Female Showing Sex Organ or Pubic Hair	15.87
Homosexual Activities	17.70	Nude Males with Sex Organs	16.25
		Nude or Partially Nude Couple Kissing	15.10

475

To claim that the non-sex offenders (see above) saw pictures of a male and female having intercourse 1.3 years *before* they first saw a picture of a male sex organ, or nude female with the breasts exposed, etc. demands a great deal of credulity from the reader. It likewise stretches the imagination for one to believe that the Sex Offender group witnessed pictures of animal-human intercourse, oral intercourse, and homosexual relations a year or less *before* ever seeing pictures of male-female intercourse. These data are obviously in error. And while it is not too difficult to imagine a single typographical error, we have two independent errors here both occurring in the same area. Common sense would have dictated a check on this. Both Walker and the Commission staff say nothing.

11. THE PURCHASERS VS. CONSUMERS OF EROTICA

The Commission Report suggests that the primary purchasers of erotica appear to be well educated, middle class, males in their 30's and 40's. It should be noted that this is based on studies nearly all in downtown urban areas where a surveyor "guessed" at the age, socio-economic level, etc., of those he saw in "adult bookstores" and movies. Where interviews were conducted they consisted of approaching men as they emerged from an "adult movie" and having an "informal conversation over coffee" with them (no notes were taken until later). And of 270 people approached in the Winick study, only 100 agreed to "have coffee," creating sampling problems. When they tried to get people to fill out questionnaires (as in the Nawy study of the "San Francisco Marketplace") only 29 out of 150 bookshop customers cooperated, and 190 out of 800 movie patrons so obliged. This makes generalizing about these data extremely risky. Massey (1970) in his analysis of the Denver area concluded that the type of customer is related to the *location of the store* and *time of day*.

Probably the major issue is who *consumes* and *uses* pornography, not so much who buys it. Because for every purchaser of hard core materials there may be 10-100 viewers or users of the merchandise. In the Abelson National Survey of Youth and Adults we find that girls 15 to 20 see most pornography (for females) and young men in the age range of 15 to 29 get the heaviest doses. Abelson found that more boys than adult men have seen visual pornography (87% vs. 80%) and more girls have seen this than adult females

476

(80% vs. 53%). This means in sum that the heavy users and most highly exposed people to pornography are adolescent females (among women) and adolescent and young adult males (among men).

Though his samples are not random, in Nawy's study of the "San Francisco Marketplace" 70% of the patrons of erotica he surveyed attend sex movies once a month or more. He also found that 49% of these people were currently having sex with two or more partners in and out of their households and 25% had been having sex with 6 or more partners in the past year. Frequency of intercourse rates were very high for his sample, suggesting that erotica may have a "booster" or "accelerating" effect on sex activity. In any event, the data outside the laboratory where people are studied in their own environment, suggest that those interested in erotica or pornography consume it regularly and for "sexual" reasons. But this is suggestive only because of flawed sampling.

12. MISUSE OF QUESTIONNAIRE AND VERBAL
SELF REPORT DATA

Nearly all of the studies presented in evidence relied heavily on "verbal self report" without outside verification. Caution must be exercised in interpreting these kind of data. A number of factors can make these data suspect: (a) The subjects may consciously falsify or distort (especially if the questions might "incriminate" or would require revealing damaging evidence against oneself—this might be particularly true for the prison sex offender inmates), (b) Questions in the sexual area in particular could lead to defensiveness, distortion, or "protective dishonesty" of response (such as having married couples, as in the Commission's Mann study (1970), check off in a daily diary (kept home) whether or not they had had an extramarital sexual experience the night before, and "Did you orally stimulate your partner's genitals to climax?" etc.), (c) The fact that it has been repeatedly demonstrated that slight changes in wording of a question can make major differences in the number of people who will respond "yes" or agree. This was demonstrated in this study in a most dramatic fashion when in the commission sponsored national survey (by Abelson) only 23% of the males admitted that pornography sexually aroused them vs. 77% agreeing to this in the Kinsey studies. Similar differences were found for women (8% Abelson, 23% Kinsey). Who can you believe? Similar gross differences were found

477

when asking people if they felt pornography should be controlled by legislation and laws. Not only is this true across several different studies, but also across several questions within a single study.

  Example: (Abelson, 1970) 88% of a national sample would prohibit sex scenes in movies that were put in for entertainment; but only 50% say that no one should be admitted to movies depicting sexual intercourse.

  The problem with the above example has to do with what question preceded the critical one (which may have established a certain "set" in answering it), or what alternatives were there available in answering; or confusion as to what you mean by a movie depicting sexual intercourse? It could mean a scene in which a couple are in bed together covered by blankets in which intercourse is only suggested or it might mean an explicit stag film. The Commission Report writers tend to treat "verbal report" as fact, and when there are discrepancies they consider as significant and present or emphasize that data which favor their point of view.

  Example: Harris Poll (1969): 76% of U.S. wants pornographic literature outlawed.

      Gallup Poll (1969): 85% of the U.S. favor stricter laws on pornography.

      Abelson (1970): 2% of U.S. viewed pornography as a serious national problem. (A Commission Study)

  However, when one looks at the question which Abelson in this Commission financed study asked U.S. citizens, it's not difficult to figure out why they got such a low percent: *"Would you please tell me what you think are the two or three most serious problems facing the country today?"* It is doubtful that even the most concerned citizen would list "pornography" as among the first two or three when the country is faced with the problems of war, racial conflict, youth rebellion, law and order disruption, drugs, pollution, etc. And as might be expected these head the list.

  Thus when in recommending abolition of nearly all laws regulating pornography the Commission report justifies this by saying: *"A majority of the American people presently are of the view that adults should be legally able to read or see explicit sexual materials if they wish to do so."* They are basing this only on *some* of the responses of U.S. citizens to *Abelson's* survey but not other data from the *same* survey (e.g., 88% would prohibit putting sex scenes in movies that

478

were put there for entertainment)[1] and of course are rejecting out-of-the-hand results of the Harris and Gallup polls (see above) who have been in business for several decades. This kind of manipulation of statistics and reporting of data is indefensible especially when most Americans or even social scientists will never have an opportunity to view the original data on which these recommendations are based.

Another example of distortion in the presenting of "results" is in the Legal Panel's Report. For some reason they *also* review the empirical research findings on pornography's effects, public attitudes toward it etc., duplicating part of the Effects Panel Report.

While the writers of the Effects Panel Report have made major changes and modifications in what they say, but only after heavy fire and criticisms by the minority and others about "flawed methodology" etc., which has resulted in some modesty and more care in their presentation of results—the same cannot be said for Legal Panel Report. Any law student or other reader of that report will find data which have been systematically marshalled to favor one point of view. This is particularly true in the "public attitudes" toward pornography section. Key data giving opposing evidence are excluded.

13. THE ISSUE OF WHETHER SEX OFFENDERS COME FROM SEXUALLY DEPRIVED BACKGROUNDS

The Commission in their Effects Panel Report, and elsewhere again and again cite data to show that sex offenders come from conservative, repressed, sexually deprived backgrounds. Quotations from Chapter V, Effects Panel Report, capture well the essence of their conclusions,

Sex offenders generally report sexually repressive family backgrounds, immature and inadequate sexual histories and rigid and conservative attitudes concerning sexuality.

Or another quote,

The early social environment of sex offenders may be characterized as sexually repressive and deprived. Sex offenders frequently report family circumstances in which, for example, there is a low tolerance for nudity, or absence of sexual conversation, punitive or indifferent parental responses to children's sexual curiosity

---

[1]When the question is worded slightly differently we, as might be expected, get slightly different results: "If a sexual scene were essential to plot development" (not just for entertainment) only 69% would wish to prohibit it.

479

and interest. Sex offenders' histories reveal a succession of immature and impersonal sociosexual relationships, rigid sexual attitudes, and severely conservative behavior.

Or still another quote,

. . . suggest that sex offenders' inexperience with erotic material is a reflection of their more generally deprived sexual environment. The relative absence of such experience probably constitutes another indicator of atypical and inadequate sexual socialization.

There are a number of things very wrong about these conclusions. In some of the studies where they compare sex offenders and non-offenders they, inexcusably, lump all different types of offenders together "into one bag" (e.g., Cook & Fosen, and Johnson et al., 1970). The problem here, as the Kinsey Institute studies well demonstrate, is that there are at least 21 categories of sex offenders, who show striking differences in family, sexual and psychosocial backgrounds. To draw general conclusions about such a diverse group is like doing a study on what religious people are like and include in your group Catholics, Unitarians, Buddhists and Black Panthers, treating them as a single "type." For example aggressive rapists are very impulsive, having extremely high levels of sexual activity from an early age with very high degrees of criminality. They are very dangerous. The "peeper" on the other hand tends to have very low rates of sexual experience, tends not to marry and is poorly socialized and is an entirely different "breed of cat."

Another type of problem is the use of inadequate control groups or none at all. To illustrate how this might cause serious problems, consider the following: "Protestants are a more criminally inclined group of citizens than atheists." We study a group of protestants at the state prison and compare them with atheists taken from the general population, and sure enough our conclusion is correct. Or another (again made purposely absurd to illustrate the point), "Men who drink carrot juice will have a high sex drive" and we compare men 20-25 years of age who drink carrot juice with men age 90 and over who don't drink it, on a variable like frequency of intercourse. If we conclude this study shows that drinking carrot juice is related to or causes a "high sex drive," we are in error. It has demonstrated no such thing. If we report this and *also* fail to mention that we didn't have a comparable control or comparison group, or not mention that the controls exceeded 90 years of age, then we've made a second serious error.

One of the studies that the Commission cites as giving evidence that "sex offenders" come from sexually deprived backgrounds is that of Thorne and Haupt (1966). Six percent of their college students report TRUE "I have never had a sexual orgasm" vs. almost 30% for the rapists. While they don't have a matched control group to compare the rapists to, they do have data on murderers and property crimes offenders who one might guess would tend to be more similar in social class background, intelligence and age to the rapists (than the college students). When we look at their responses to this question we find an amazing 40% who indicate never having had a sexual orgasm. Since by the very nature of their offense it would be difficult to believe that 30% of the rapist sample never had orgasm, and in view of the Kinsey findings that very nearly all of rapists (which they studied) engaged in premarital intercourse and nearly 80% engaged in extramarital sex after they married, these findings appear even more difficult to believe. However, if one is aware of the fact that most rapists, murderers, and property crimes felons who are convicted come from lower socioeconomic backgrounds, have lesser education, etc. a very simple explanation offers itself. A significant number of these men didn't understand what the term "sexual orgasm" meant. Again, incorrect inferences are drawn from data.

Thus one can see the extreme importance of having matched control groups. If we use the murderers and property crimes felons as controls for the rapist sample (a risky thing to do) and compare how this typical sex offender group compares on sexual repression, deprivation, etc. we find that (because they are in jail) they *do* tend to feel more guilty about their sex behavior, but there are no real differences overall. However, if one compares the sex offenders or total prison population against the college students on attitudes we do find them a little more prudish in what they say—but not apparently in what they do, compared to the college students. This undoubtedly reflects the differences between current middle and lower class cultures out of which they emerge.

In the study of Goldstein and associates (1970) they attempted to obtain a good control sample to compare their sex offenders against. But unfortunately they were not too successful. Their controls were significantly younger and better educated than the sex offender groups. (Example: nearly 80% of his controls were under 30 vs. only 25% for one of

481

the child molester groups.) This makes it very dangerous to say that sex offenders are different or the same compared to "normals" when your comparison group is different. Remember the carrot juice example and its relation to sexual activity?

The seeming disregard for these very elementary considerations in evaluating research findings by the Commission report writers leaves one very concerned about how they arrived at their other conclusions.

The evidence from many studies would indeed suggest that certain types of sex offenders are sexually immature and regressed, but other types are sexually aggressive and very promiscuous starting at very early ages. Making these kinds of distinctions would be seen as most important in any evaluation of the research literature. The Commission Report fails badly in this regard.

14. DOES PORNOGRAPHY ALTER BEHAVIOR?

The Commission Report states in their conclusions, "When people are exposed to erotic materials some persons increase masturbatory of coital behavior, a smaller proportion decrease it, but the majority of persons report no change in these behaviors. In general, established patterns of sexual behavior were found to be very stable and not altered substantially by exposure to erotica." There are a number of problems in drawing these conclusions: (a) In a number of the 16 studies reviewed (focusing on this problem) behavior was studied ONLY for the 24 hours before and after exposure to the pornography, (b) In some other studies (Amaroso, 1970) the total exposure time to erotica for all subjects was only 50 seconds, in another study (Byrne & Lamberth, 1970) total exposure time was 6½ minutes (hardly sufficient to conclude that exposure to erotica has or has not an effect) but (c) probably the major methodological problem is the fact that 13 of the 16 groups who were deliberately exposed to pornography were limited to young college students, plus one group of middle aged couples almost all college educated, and a final two groups who were "sex offenders." Since a great deal of evidence from the Commission studies indicate that young college educated persons are those already having high exposure to pornography (compared to conservative, older, lower class subjects)— this means *that most or all of their subjects have already been repeatedly exposed to pornography* which means that if it were to have a "corrupting" effect this would probably have *already* started to occur. This also would mean that one wouldn't expect experimentally great changes in sexual behavior before and after exposure even if in fact pornography were indeed to have a "viciously depraving influence." Failure to control for this factor makes the conclusions drawn by the Commission writers very questionable. And (d) it is highly unlikely that any subject in such an experimental study under such close scrutiny would engage in any anti-social sex behavior, and even if he did admit to it in most studies reported *they fail to even ask this type of question.* (e) All samples were restricted to volunteers who chose to be exposed to pornography which would introduce a systematic bias. And (f) finally, as Davis and Braucht point out these samples (young college educated) are not the people of "popular concern" (e.g., the unstable, more vulnerable, from defective environments). For scientists to confidently conclude that there are essentially no significant sex behavior changes or increase in antisocial sex activity on the basis of these kinds of data takes a considerable amount of "faith, ESP, and some admixture of divine revelation."

15. SEX CRIMES IN THE U.S. AND PORNOGRAPHY

The Commission after being criticized for inaccuracies in their early reports on incidence of sex crimes in America have made a number of corrections. However, it still is incomplete and a summary of this data would be in order here. Some have argued that because sex crimes have apparently declined in Denmark while the volume of pornography has increased, we need not be concerned about the potential effect in our country of this kind of material (because, essentially, of Denmark's benign experience). However two considerations must be noted. First we are a different culture with a greater commitment to the Judeo-Christian tradition; and secondly we are actually only a year or so behind Denmark in the distribution and sale of pornography. Hardcore written pornography can be purchased anywhere in the U.S. now. Hardcore still pictures and movies can now be purchased over the counter in some cities. Anything can be purchased through the mails. And in a few cities people can attend hardcore pornographic movies. About the only thing we don't have, which Denmark has, are live sex shows. What is most relevant are sex crime statistics in this country, not Denmark. Since it was in about 1960, at the beginning of

483

the decade, that pornography began to flower in the U.S. relevant statistics should be examined carefully. One cannot impute cause and effect here, though the Commission infers it (in the other direction) with the Denmark sex crime data.

Reported Rapes (verified)
Up 116%   1960-69 (absolute increase)
Up 93%   1960-69 (controlled for Pop. Growth)
Rape Arrests
Up 56.6%   all ages 1960-69
Up 85.9%   males under 18 1960-69
Source: Unified Crime Statistics 1970

"Sex Offenses" (homosexual acts, statutory rape, etc.)
All Ages: 1960-69: Down 17%   This is a spurious not true decline. Is
Under 18:   1960-69: Down 21%   due to change in law enforcement
Source: Unified Crime Report 1970   policy, primarily involving homosexual
                                    acts between consenting adults—which
                                    are now rarely prosecuted though early
                                    in the decade were.—U.S. Justice Dept.
Prostitution and Commercialized Vice
Up 80.1%   1960-69 all ages
Up 120.2%   1960-69 girls under 18 (numbers are small here)
Note: The bulk of prostitutes are 15-24 years, peak age: 22, and only 13%
      of sex offenses (arrests) are women.
Source: Unified Crime Statistics 1970
Illegitimate Births
1. General Note: During decades 1947-67 rate of illegitimacy doubled per 1,000
                 never married females.
                 1960-67 Illegitimacy ratio up 71% (which is the number of
                 illegitimate births per 1,000 live births)
Source: p. 31, 1970 Natality Statistics
2. Illegitimate Birth Rate
          1940   1967
Under 15   2.1   6.9   (350% increase) During this period the population
15-19   40.5 144.4   (350% increase) of the U.S. increased 50%
Source: 1970 New York Times Encyclopediac Almanac
3. "The greatest current rate of increase in illegitimacy is with 15-19 year olds."
   Source: page 31, 1970 Natality Statistics, U. S. Public Health Dept.)
V.D.—Gonorrhea
All ages: 1960-69: Up 76%
Females 15-19: Up 52% 1965-68
Females 20-24: Up 36% 1965-68
Females 25-29: Up 25% 1965-68
Source: V.D. Fact Sheet, 1969, U. S. Public Health Service
Divorce Rate
   1960   1969
393,000   660,000   Up 70%
(2.2 per   (3.3 per
1000 pop.)   1000 pop.)
Source: Monthly Vital Statistics Report, March 12, 1970, U. S. Public Health
        Service

The above data suggest increases in most types of social pathology in the U. S. While this is associated with an increase in pornography, no claims as to a causal relationship can be made from this data.

16. DO PEOPLE GET SATIATED THROUGH OVER EXPOSURE TO PORNOGRAPHY

In the Commission's single study investigating satiation of sexual arousal and interest in pornography after 15 days of

484

heavy exposure to it on the part of 23 college males, they have pretty well demonstrated the obvious (e.g., that people can get weary of it). But as physician John Cavanaugh has commented, "It is generally recognized that the sex appetite and interest is the one most quickly satisfied but also the one quickest to return." Voltaire's Candide also found this to be true. Clinical experience indicates that a man may be stimulated by his partner's nude body for many years, even though there may be temporary periods of satiation as to need for sex and erotic stimulation. The periodicity of the sex drive suggests continued cycles of interest and satiation continuing throughout life. The Commission's conclusion implies that if people get all the pornography they want, they'll soon get tired of it and not want more. This is certainly one popular theory advanced by some students of the issue. But the evidence here suggests only that if college males are given a great glut of pornography in a laboratory setting they will temporarily satiate. But, essentially the same may be said of having sexual intercourse, eating, drinking, etc. Considering the limited time this experiment ran—not much more can be said about this issue. Another limitation of the Commission study was that it did not approximate a real life situation or use of pornography in one's own milieux. It involved a deliberate forced "over feeding" of pornography for pay. It also meant removing all clothing and putting on a loose robe, hooking up one's penis to a condom and electrodes, attaching electrical instruments to both ears, putting a bellows around one's chest, being observed through a one way window and sitting in an "isolation booth" for 1½ hours a day for 15 days.

According to other Commission studies (such as those by Charles Winick) of consumers of explicit sexual materials "out in real life" (e.g., patrons of "adult" movies and bookstores) 52% are regular customers and are "regular or heavy users" of erotica. In other words there is no evidence that people "satiate" in real life. The consumption of pornography is regulated to the tastes of the individual consumer. In Nawy's study of the "San Francisco Marketplace" 70% of the patrons of erotica he surveyed attend sex movies once a month or more. He also found that 49% of these people were currently having sex with two or more partners in and out of their households, and 25% had been having sex with 6 or more partners in the past year. Frequency of intercourse rates were very high for his sample suggesting that erotica may have a "booster or accelerating" effect on sex activity. In any event the data outside the laboratory where people are studied in their own environment and "on the hoof" suggest that those interested in erotica or pornography consume it regularly and for "sexual" reasons.

Berger (1970) in his survey of 473 working class adolescents concludes, "It would appear that even high levels of exposure to sexually explicit materials did not bore the young people who participated in this study." None of this is mentioned in the Commission report; even though all of this data comes from Commission studies.

17. ETHICAL CONSIDERATIONS IN EXPOSING YOUNG
PEOPLE TO PORNOGRAPHY

The Commission provided many of the researchers with a number of slides and movies depicting explicit hardcore pornography. Certain ethical issues might be raised in exposing large numbers of young people (18 and over) to what sometimes involved large quantities of pornography. And while consent was obtained, sometimes the young people (male and female) were brought together at the research room before being told that the experiment would involve being shown hardcore pornography. They were told that they need not participate if they did not wish to. However backing out at this point and conceivably "losing face" with their peers could create a problem for some people. Since the data from a number of studies did indicate that some people were "emotionally upset", sexually aroused, felt guilty, disgusted, etc., the ethical problems and protection of the rights of human subjects would be a matter for discussion and review here.

18. ADDITIONAL SIGNIFICANT LIMITATIONS IN
COMMISSION'S RESEARCH

(a) No Longitudinal Studies. There were no longitudinal studies considered or contracted by the Commission studying the long range effects of exposure to pornography and its effect on sexual activities, sex offenses, changes in moral values, etc. Nearly all studies cited covered only a few days or weeks for the subjects (and in most cases only an hour to two). The longitudinal study properly done would give the most powerful evidence concerning pornography's effects. There were none here.

(b) No Clinical Studies. There were no in-depth clinical

studies of individuals assessing the impact of use of pornography on attitudes, sex offenses, character, anti-social behavior, etc.

(c) Omission of Studies on "Porno-Violence." No attention was paid to the problem of porno-violence where pornography and violence are linked together in fiction and increasingly in motion pictures. This omission is particularly surprising in view of the findings in the Final Report of the National Commission on the Causes and Prevention of Violence (1969) which link visual presentations of violence to aggressive acting out behavior. Their findings would appear to have some implications for situations where violence and pornography are combined (e.g., sexual abuse and physical injury inflicted on the female/male, etc.).

(d) Omission of Studies and Evidence in "Imitative Learning" Area. There is an omission of discussion of studies in the area of imitative and social learning by such investigators as Albert Bandura and his associates at Stanford University. Since this body of research suggests that a significant amount of learning occurs through watching and imitating the behavior of others this would logically appear to have great relevance to any pornography "effects" studies. If Bandura's work (as well as others in this area) have any validity, it would suggest that certain types of pornography involving whole sequences of behaviors probably would effect some individuals if they saw it consistently modeled on the screen or in fiction (e.g., suggest to them anti-social sex behaviors which they might imitate or repeat). This is certainly indicated by the findings of the violence literature. In view of the type of evidence and findings presented by the Bandura "school" it would seem, at the very least, that the Commission staff would indicate some cautions or concerns. There are none.

(e) Absence of Youth Studies. While the Commission in their Final Report state ". . . . . [there] is no evidence that exposure to or use of explicit sexual materials play a significant role in the causation of social or individual harms such as crime, delinquency, sexual or non-sexual deviancy, or severe emotional disturbances . . . or plays a significant role in the causation of delinquent or criminal behavior among *youth* or *adults*," they do not mention that there was *not a single* experimental study, longitudinal study, or clinical case study involving youth. The only information they have is from questionnaires which are subject to the usual problems of willingness to be truthful (especially about sex

487

data), memory, misinterpretation of questions, etc. Their conclusions about youth would appear extremely incautious in view of the limitations of significant data.

(f) Possible Bias in Using Only Volunteers Who'd Submit to Pornography. All studies which probed sexual histories, or exposed individuals to pornography were to some degree biased by using only those people who would submit to such exposure or questioning. This would be especially true for female subjects. Those rejecting of pornography would not be studied.

(h) Varying Definitions, Types and Amounts of Erotic Material Used. While some studies used similar pornographic slides or movies, there still existed great variation in the type of pornography which was used (sometimes pictures, sometimes movies, sometimes written material). These varied greatly in their erotic and "offensive" qualities. In the case of "retrospective reports" where people were interviewed or filled out questionnaires they often had to necessarily rely on their subject's own definition or unique interpretations of what constituted pornography. Thus saying that one witnessed sexual intercourse on the screen could involve something bland or explicitly offensive.

In some studies (Amoroso, 1970) subjects saw 27 slides projected on a screen for two and one half seconds each, and only twenty of which could be regarded as "pornographic" which means a total viewing time of fifty seconds for the erotic material. To conclude that pornography effects or does not effect behavior on the basis of such limited exposure and no control group would seem incautious at most.

SUMMARY AND CONCLUSIONS

1. The Commission on Obscenity and Pornography (majority report) is recommending major changes in laws and social policy in an area of controversy, public concern, and also in an area having health and welfare implications for adults and minors (e.g., remove all controls on pornography for adults and children—except, in the latter case, pictorial materials).

The basis for recommending these changes is that the Commission found no empirical scientific evidence showing a causal relationship between exposure to pornography and any kind of harm to minors or adults.

2. However it should be stated that conclusively proving causal relationships among social science type variables is

488

extremely difficult if not impossible. Among adults whose life histories have included much exposure to pornography it is nearly impossible to disentangle the literally hundreds of causal threads or chains that contributed to their later adjustment or maladjustment. Because of the extreme complexity of the problem and the uniqueness of the human experience it is doubtful that we will ever have absolutely convincing scientific proof that pornography is or isn't harmful. And the issue isn't restricted to, "Does pornography cause or contribute to sex crimes?" The issue has to do with how pornography affects or influences the individual in his total relationship to members of the same as well as opposite sex, children and adults, with all of its ramifications.

The "burden of proof" or demonstration of no harm in a situation such as this, is ordinarily considered to be on the shoulders of he who wishes to introduce change or innovation. It might be noted that in areas where health and welfare are at issue, most government agencies take extremely conservative measures in their efforts to protect the public. In the case of monosodium glutamate which was recently removed from all baby food by government orler, the evidence against it, in animal studies, was quite weak. However, because the remote possibility of harm existed, measures were immediately taken to protect children from consuming it.

3. The evidence the Commission presents does not clearly indicate, "no harm." There are also many areas of "neglect" relative to the Commission's studies of pornography's effects (e.g., no longitudinal studies, no in depth clinical studies, no porno-violence data, no studies in modeling or imitative learning, etc. etc.).

4. In the Commission's presentation of the scientific evidence there are frequent errors and inaccuracies in their reporting of research results as well as in the basic studies themselves. Frequently conclusions which are not warranted are drawn inappropriately from data. There is a frequent failure to distinguish or discriminate between studies which are badly flawed and weak and those of exceptional merit. But, most serious of all, data from a number of studies which show statistical linkages between high exposure to pornography and promiscuity, deviancy, affiliation with high criminality groups, etc. have gone unreported. This suggests a major bias in the reporting of results which raises a major issue of credibility of the entire report. Regardless of why it occurred, it suggests that at the very least, a panel of independent scientists be called in to reevaluate the Commission research

489

and the conclusions which might be validly drawn from it before any major changes occur in laws and social policy regarding pornography's control.

IV. Legal "Findings" of Commission

We vigorously object to the word "findings" with regard to legal issues. Section IV of the majority report is an attempt to foist upon the people and upon the President and the Congress a philosophy of law which is misleading at best.[1]

The section headed letter "C" states that the "prevailing view" in the Supreme Court is that to be classified as obscene an item must meet three—and all three—criteria. These criteria, the report claims, are: (1) the dominant theme of the material, taken as a whole, must appeal to the prurient interest of the average person; (2) the material must be patently offensive according to contemporary community standards; and (3) the material must lack redeeming social value.

This is a misinterpretation of the law, as counsel to the Commission must know, for he originally stated in his Legal Panel Report that NO MAJORITY OF THE U. S. SUPREME COURT has ever accepted the proposition that "utterly without redeeming social value" is a "test" for obscenity. To say that an item may not be adjudged obscene if it does not meet all three of these criteria is false. It is exactly the promotion of this canard which has brought us to the deplorable state we are in today in this nation insofar as obscenity is concerned. NO SUPREME COURT OPINION SO HOLDS. In fact, the *Roth* case says the opposite. This is the only case where the Supreme Court gives us a definition of obscenity. The "utterly without redeeming social value" language is assumed to have been built into the *Roth* test by an opinion in the *Memoirs* (Fanny Hill) case of 1966.

However, this was the opinion only of three Justices: Brennan, Warren and Fortas. It was not the opinion of the Court, and so is not the law of the land. It is a three-Justice out of nine opinion, not binding on anyone. In 29 American Jurisprudence 2nd, at Section 195 of the topic "Courts," we find the following:

---

[1]On September 10, as this dissent was going to press, Mr. Lockhart called Commissioner Gill and instructed him to make certain modifications in these statements so that the legal panel report no longer reads the same as it did when the Commission was influenced by it to vote for the legalization of obscenity at their first meeting of August 11 & 12 and the final meeting of August 26 & 27.

A decision by an equally divided court does not establish a precedent required to be followed under the stare decisis doctrine. And where the members of the court unanimously or by a majority vote reach a decision, but cannot even by a majority agree on the reason therefor, no point of law is established by the decision and it cannot be a precedent covered by the stare decisis rule.

The Supreme Court of the United States has said in 218 U.S. at 213 that unless a majority of the Supreme Court agrees on an opinion the case cannot become "an authority either in this or in inferior courts."

The *Roth* case gives us only the prurient interest test and this test has not been modified by *any* subsequent Supreme Court decision. In *Roth* the Court said, an item is obscene when to the average person, applying contemporary community standards, the dominant theme of the material taken as a whole appeals to the prurient interest.

This brings us to the Legal Panel Report, prepared by general counsel Bender and staff, with the apparent assistance of Mr. Lockhart, from which the "Legal Findings" section is drawn, and upon which legislative recommendations are based.

The Legal Panel Report should reflect the concepts of the Commission, their conclusions, their interpretations and analysis and their recommendations for legislative action. Instead, the Commission is asked to adhere to ideas, concepts, suggestions, analyses and recommendations prepared by staff members appointed by the Chairman and his general counsel, and reflecting their points of view.

This Bender-Lockhart Panel Report is misleading in many fundamental areas of the law, and so misleads the Commission, so as to cause those members, many of whom are unlearned in the law, to come to fundamentally erroneous conclusions of the state of the law. We object specifically to the following misleading statements in the Bender-Lockhart Legal Panel Report:

1. "Unless there is a basis for finding that certain sexually explicit materials create such a danger [clear and present danger of significant social harm], therefore, general prohibitions upon the dissemination of 'obscene' speech would appear constitutionally invalid under ordinary principles." We are told on the next page that this analysis was rejected in *Roth* by the Supreme Court. Why then do they state it as a fact and ask the Commission to accept it?

2. Shortly after this, the Panel Report begins to take after the United States Supreme Court decision in *Roth* and suggests that it is erroneous and should be reversed and in fact has in effect been reversed by the decision in *Stanley v. Georgia* in 1969. They discuss the meaning of *Stanley* vis-a-vis *Roth* as they interpret it and make the following statements:

(a) Obscenity prohibitions were found constitutional in the *Roth* decision . . . without investigation into or conclusions regarding the actual social effect of the dissemination of obscene materials. It is the conclusion—that obscenity prohibitions regulating what even consenting adults may obtain may be upheld without any indication of social harm—that has been brought into question by . . . *Stanley*.

(b) *Redrup* may be read as doubting whether *Roth* was actually still the law.

(c) In *Stanley* . . . the Court threw greatly into doubt the continuing validity of the fundamental premise of the *Roth* case that the dissemination of "obscene" materials may be prohibited without reference to First Amendment values, and suggested, instead, the strong constitutional significance of the question whether such materials are in fact socially harmful.

(d) The question of the social effect of obscenity, which *Roth* had deemed irrelevant has assumed critical importance in *Stanley* "in order to determine whether the state there had a valid regulatory interest sufficient to prohibit private possession of obscene materials." The Court held in *Stanley* that it did not.

(e) Prohibitions upon the commercial dissemination of obscenity to consenting adults may interfere with the right of adults to read or see what they wish in their own homes.

(f) *Stanley* appears to have held that government may not rest prohibitions upon what consenting adults may read or view upon a desire to control their morality.

(g) It further held that adult prohibitions premised upon a desire to prevent crime or anti-social behavior must, at least, rest upon a solid empirical foundation.

A Commission member, reading these statements and the continual "pounding" of *Stanley v. Georgia* at every opportunity throughout the rest of this panel report, would naturally assume that these statements are true and that *Roth* in some way has been overturned in a very fundamental manner by *Stanley v. Georgia.* But as a matter of fact *Roth* has not been overturned. It has been specifically confirmed in *Stanley* at 22 L. Ed. 2d 542, where the Court says:

Roth and the cases following that decision are not impaired by today's holding. As we have said, the states retain broad power to regulate obscenity; that power simply does not extend to mere possession by the individual in the privacy of his own home.

If the Bender-Lockhart Panel Report was intended to give the Commission an unbiased view of the state of the law, why was not the meaning of this phrase expounded? Since *Roth* is still the law of the land, then the following are the true facts (as stated in *Roth*):

(1) It is not necessary to prove that "obscene material will perceptively create a clear and present danger of antisocial conduct or will induce its recipients to such conduct."

(2) That the basis for federal and state proscription for obscenity is "the social interest in order and morality."

It is also to be noted that the Court said its decisions following *Roth* are not impaired.

In *Ginsberg v. New York,* at 20 L. Ed. 2d 195, the Court said:

Our conclusion in *Roth* . . . that the clear and present danger test was irrelevant to the determination of obscenity made it unnecessary . . . to consider the debate among the authorities whether exposure to pornography caused antisocial consequences.

The *Ginsberg* case was subsequent to *Roth.* Why was it not mentioned? Among other United States Supreme Court decisions subsequent to *Roth* that should have been mentioned are the following, all contradicting the Bender-Lockhart thesis that somehow *Stanley* has changed things:

1. *Times Film (1960)*
   (State has right to censor obscene motion pictures.)
2. *Freeman v. Maryland (1965)*
   (State may require prior submission of motion pictures to a Board of Censors.)
3. *Ginzburg v. U.S. (1966)*
   (State has a valid interest in preventing pandering to

493

"the widespread weakness for titillation by pornography" books and magazines.)

4. *Mishkin v. New York (1966)*
(State has interest in protecting homosexuals from obscenity.)

5. *Interstate Circuit v. Dallas (1968)*
(Municipality may enact an ordinance regulating motion pictures for adults as well as children and censoring those obscene.)

Each of the statements made in (a), (b), (c), (e), (f) and (g) above in the Bender-Lockhart Report are incorrect when we look at *Stanley v. Georgia's* reaffirmation of *Roth* and cases thereafter. The statement made in (d) above is misleading that "private possession" is permissible because it fails to complete the quotation "in the privacy of his home."

It would appear that for purposes of the Bender-Lockhart Panel Report, the "wish is father to the thought." They would like *Stanley v. Georgia* to say what they say it says but that desire is not borne out by the facts of that case.

It is quite clear that *Stanley v. Georgia* stands for a very narrow position and that is that a state may not convict a person of a crime "for mere possession of printed or filmed matter in the privacy of a person's *own home.*" 22 L. Ed. 2d 542. And again, at 22 L. Ed. 2d 551, "the right to be free from state inquiry into the contents of *his library.*" The state has no business "telling a man sitting alone *in his own house,* what books he may read or what films he may watch."

It could not be much clearer that this was the narrow proposition decided. The Court said it *four* times while specifically upholding *Roth* and all subsequent decisions.

3. The Bender-Lockhart Panel Report hits us with two phrases. One appears to be the invention of the authors in lieu of the use of the word "obscene" and that is the phrase "explicit sexual material." The other phrase is the catchword "consenting adults" which is a euphemism to express the authors' position that there are no restraints on "explicit sexual material" as long as "consenting adults" patronize it. Translated simply, it means "Legalize Obscenity for Adults" and the authors of this report should have so labeled it since this is the net effect of their suggestions. Nowhere is it explained that neither of these terms is used in any Supreme Court opinion, nor is it explained that this is the phrase used by those who would have the Court legalize the showing of "I Am Curious (Yellow)" in both Massachusetts and Maryland where it has been held obscene. In fact, there is an amazing

parallel between the Bender-Lockhart Panel Report and the language used in the briefs for the distributors of that motion picture. Both sing the same tune. The Panel Report suggests that adults have "a right to obtain [explicit sexual materials] they wish to see." They cite no justification for setting up this false premise. Certainly *Stanley v. Georgia* never said it. They then proceed to state the motivations of the government in regulating "explicit sexual materials" (which we translate to "obscene"). They fail completely, however, to give the real reason which is the "social interest in order and morality." Having set up two false premises, they then proceed to obfuscate the true situation. There is a bald misstatement of the law when the Panel Report says:

> In a series of cases subsequent to *Roth,* the Court made clear that where attempts were made to prohibit only specific distributional activities connected with sexual materials—and not to prevent consenting adults from obtaining material they wished to see—more inclusive definitional standards than that imposed in *Roth* would be permitted to be applied. The first case leading in this direction was *Ginzburg v. United States.* There the Court . . . permitted the conviction of the defendant to stand because he was found to have "pandered" the materials in an offensive manner rather than merely to have sold them to persons who wished to obtain them. Thus the Court permitted a conviction which it would not have permitted had the defendant merely been engaged in neutral dissemination to consenting persons.

You would assume that Mr. Bender and staff, who ought to know, have told the Commission members what the *Ginzburg* case held. Nothing could be further from the truth. As they ought to know, this is *not* what *Ginzburg* held, since:

(a) The term "consenting adults" is nowhere used or implied in that case.

(b) The Court did not say anything about *Ginzburg* not having "merely sold them to persons who wished to obtain them." It didn't mention that at all.

(c) The implication that the case stands for the right to receive "obscenity" by consenting adults is misplaced. The Court said in *Ginzburg* that the materials *were not* "obscene in the abstract".

4. The Bender-Lockhart Panel Report suggests that "some of" the federal mailing statute may be unconstitutional

under *Stanley*. This is another non-sequitur. The mailing statute has nothing to do with invading a man's home.

5. The implication on page 13 that there is something in *Redrup* which proves a theory that "consenting adults" have a right to receive obscenity is also misplaced. *Redrup* found the materials not to be obscene.

6. On page 16, the Bender-Lockhart Panel Report states that:

Stanley v. Georgia, if given full effect, would mean . . . that the individual's right to see materials of his own choice may only be overcome where there is a substantial social basis for government regulation. As a result, many applications of general prohibitions may no longer be permissible. The *Roth* standard for determining the "obscene" retains potential validity only in those areas where *Stanley* permits general prohibitions to apply.

Now, if this problem were not so important to our country, the immediate reaction to such a non-sequitur from *Stanley v. Georgia* would be to shrug it off as ridiculous. There is absolutely nothing in *Stanley* to warrant this misinformation.

"*Roth* is supreme," says Stanley—not the other way around. *Stanley* cannot be exploited or expanded to help the pornographers in this fashion.

7. Eventually, the Legal Panel Report abandons the position that *Fanny Hill* has modified the *Roth* test and engages in the business of counting Justices who have adopted the "patently offensive" test. Four of these six Justices are no longer on the Court so this maneuver fails. The footnote reference to Black and Douglas also fails since they have never enunciated this standard. The reference to Stewart and Harlan refers to federal cases only. The reference to the American Law Institute standard is misleading since that Institute never used the phrase "patently offensive."

8. Again, the Panel Report abandons its original claim that the *Roth* test included an "utterly without redeeming social value" element, and now tries to give new dignity to the opinion of three Justices (two of whom, if we use his technique, we should note are no longer on the Court) by calling it a plurality opinion. As we point out in our discussion of "Fanny Hill," under the decisions of the United States Supreme Court, an opinion of three Justices is no precedent, does not establish the law and does not bind either the United States Supreme Court or "any inferior court."

9. The Legal Panel Report finally admits that *Memoirs* "utterly without redeeming social value" "test" is not a test

496

at all, not having been adopted by a majority, but they suggest that it is nice to incorporate the same in statutes because Black and Douglas are on the bench and this is two strikes against you. They state, "So long as at least three other Justices employ the three-part test," no application of a general prohibition which does not employ this test will be upheld on appeal. What kind of specious reasoning is this? The Bender-Lockhart Legal Panel Report seems so intent on keeping this unnecessary language in our statutes (which contradicts *Roth*—see our comments under *Memoirs* case) that they employ the scare tactics that you only need two more people against you and you lose. Is this what our statutes should be based on in this vital area? Is this what this Commission was formed for, "to estimate percentages"? Fortas and Warren are gone, leaving only Brennan who adheres to this pernicious concept. Presumably then, eight out of nine Justices will adhere to *Roth,* which rejects this so-called test and says that once it is obscene by the *Roth* test (which has no social value language), then it is proscribable. But this is not our function. We are to interpret *Roth* honestly and give the country an honest definition of obscenity. Such a definition does not include the "Brennan" so-called "test". It is to be noted, that the Legal Panel Report does not quote the recent decisions in Maryland, Massachusetts and Arizona that say that there is no "social value" test in *Roth* (see our comments in Appendix under *Fanny Hill*) nor do they say that New York is proposing repeal of this part of their statute (see our remarks under *Fanny Hill*).

10. The Bender-Lockhart Panel Report states that the Supreme Court believes that the *Roth* standard does not permit a finding of obscenity to be made under a prohibition of what consenting adults may obtain with regard to a large class of pictorial material. Again we note that there is no opinion of the Supreme Court that supports this statement that somehow "consenting adults" are a separate class under the *Roth* standard. That phrase is not used in any Supreme Court opinion.

V. Conclusions

We submit: That the Commission majority has not carried out the mandates of Congress.

We submit: That its legislative recommendations should be excluded from consideration by the Congress and States, since they are not re-

497

sponsive to the mandate of Congress to regulate the traffic in pornography. It is irrelevant legislation and deserves condemnation
as inimical to the welfare of the United
States, its citizens and its children.

We submit: That the purpose of the Commission's report is to legalize pornography.

In the pursuit of the mandates of the Congress, and in
compliance therewith, we have made a review of the law
and the decisions of the United States Supreme Court; and
have analyzed the same in detail. This review is attached as
Appendix I. In the light of that review and comment there-
under, and in view of our other mandates, we make the
following recommendations.

VI. RECOMMENDATIONS

1. RECOMMENDED TEST OR DEFINITION OF OBSCENITY

A thing is "obscene" if, by contemporary community
standards, and considered as a whole, its predominant
appeal is to the prurient interest. As a matter of public
policy, anything which is obscene by this definition shall
be conclusively deemed to be utterly without redeeming social importance. Any slight social value in such
obscenity shall be deemed outweighed by the social interest in order and morality.

"Prurient interest" is defined as a shameful or morbid
interest in nudity, sex or excretion which goes substantially beyond customary limits of candor in description
or representation of such matters. If it appears from
the character of the material or the circumstances of
its dissemination that the subject matter is designed for,
or directed to a specially susceptible audience, the subject matter shall be judged with reference to such audience. When the subject matter is distributed or exhibited
to minors who have not attained their 18th birthday,
the subject matter shall be judged with reference to an
average person in the community of the actual age of
the minor to whom such material is distributed or exhibited. In all other cases, the subject matter shall be
judged with reference to the average person in the community.

Comment. This formulation is taken from the *Roth* case
which is the only case in which the Supreme Court defined

obscenity and the *Ginsberg* case, in which the Supreme Court accepts the concept of variable obscenity as it applies to minors. It rejects the suggestion of three of the nine Justices that "utterly without redeeming social value" is a test for obscenity, since the Supreme Court has never adopted this suggestion. In fact, it is this unnecessary "test" that has caused the floor of hard-core pornography in motion pictures, books, magazines and other publications.

A complete review of the lack of constitutional necessity for this so-called "test" is found in Appendix I in our comments under the *Memoirs* (*Fanny Hill*) case.

The *Roth* Test, it is claimed by some is subjective. Upon examination, however, it is plain that the individual juror is not instructed to apply his subjective concept of what is obscene, but to determine something objective *viz.* "the prurient interest of the average person." This is very similar to what juries are called upon to do in negligence cases where the juror is asked to determine if a person used that degree of care that a "reasonably prudent man" would use. This determination has never been thought to be subjective nor too impractical or difficult to apply. We have confidence in the ability of the Anglo-Saxon jury system to determine obscenity if properly instructed. See Judge's charge in *Roth* case Appendix I).

Our recommendations are squarely based on the concept that the State has, as the Supreme Court says, a right to enact obscenity legislation based on the "social interest in morality." There is a distinction that should be made between individual morality and the level of general morality which the state needs to protect.

A person's beliefs and practices depend on what he relies on for an authority as to what is right and best. As children grow up, they come under various authorities' influences: parents, relatives, friends, teachers, writers, actors, celebrities, clergymen and a host of others. They are also influenced in various ways by other forces of good and evil.

At every point in life a person has a certain moral character. It is the sum total of what he then believes and practices in the area of right and wrong. This overall moral character is constantly changing under the interplay of the aforementioned influences. Thus if a person accepts higher standards, his moral character improves; if he accepts lower standards, his moral character deteriorates.

Not only does every individual reflect a certain moral character, but so does every group of individuals, a club, a city, a state, or even a nation—*the essence of which is determined by a general consensus of individual standards.* It is, stated another way, the distillation of all the individual moralities or the *level* of morality generally. It is this level, this distillation, this average, this essence, which the state has an interest in protecting. The state protects this level from falling and creates an atmosphere by which it can rise. The obvious morals protected are chastity, modesty, temperance, and self-sacrificing love. The obvious evils being inhibited are lust, excess, adultery, incest, homosexuality, bestiality, masturbation and fornication.

A discussion of the background of the other aspects of this definition may be found in our comment on the Model State Obscenity Statute in Appendix II.

2. RECOMMENDED FEDERAL LEGISLATION

We recommend: (a) That the United States Codes Sections 1461, 1462, 1463, 1464, 1465 of Title 18, and Section 1305 of Title 19, and Section 4006 of Title 39 be amended to define "obscene" in accordance with our recommended definition of obscenity mentioned above.

(b) That so much of our recommended Model State Statute, found in Appendix II, which is suitable for incorporation in these federal statutes be therein incorporated.

(c) We recommend that Congress note that Section 4009 of Title 39, Prohibiting of Pandering Advertisements in the Mails, was specifically upheld by the U. S. Supreme Court in *Rowan v. U.S.,* decided May 4, 1970. This statute, it should be noted, gave a parent the right to require, also, that the mailer stop sending mail to "any of his minor children who have not attained their nineteenth birthday, and who reside with the addressee."

While the decision did not turn on this specific point, it is nevertheless an indication that the Supreme Court will accept at least an age 18, and possibly 19 or older, as a division line between minor and adult in the obscenity field. Certainly under 16 is too low.

(d) We have reviewed anti-obscenity legislation now before Congress which we believe will help, effectively and constitutionally, to regulate obscenity. This review is attached as Appendix III.

(e) We recommend legislation or a Presidential Directive establishing a Division, in the Office of the Attorney General of the United States, under the direction of a Deputy Attorney General, made up of a team of skilled lawyers ready and able to assist District Attorneys throughout the nation in prosecutions against sex exploiters. We have personal knowledge of the fact that district attorneys generally are desperately in need of this type of assistance. The urgent necessity for the same was enunciated in March of 1965 by the presiding Judge of Franklin County, Pa., Judge Chauncey M. Depuy, when he said:

> Whenever a prosecution for obscenity occurs in a county, the well-heeled purveyors of smut act with lightning alacrity to provide high-priced counsel for the defendant. Legal smut specialists are called into the county from the nationwide staff. These professionals soon place the local district attorney's staff, unacquainted with a highly specialized field of law, at a great disadvantage. The average district attorney or assistant is no match for these well-experienced "pros" who move from county to county and state to state . . . There is no hope for government to serve the interest of the general citizen in managing this flood of pornography unless a massive effort is made at the Department of Justice level. An effective mechanism must be devised, on a permanent basis, as a division of the department, having . . . highly skilled lawyers ready to be loaned at any time . . . to assist the district attorney in connection with any prosecution against the sex exploiters.

It should be noted that if it is believed that such a mechanism could not be set up on the federal level without enabling legislation, such legislation could be based on the Commerce clause, since most obscenity is transported interstate or imported. A model could be found in language used in the Civil Rights Act of 1964.

(f) We recommend the establishment, by Federal legislation, of a National Crime Research and Reference Library on the Law of Obscenity. The Library will be unique, since the Librarian of Congress has indicated that after diligent search, "no reference to any special law library in this area has been found, and . . . such a library would be unique and unduplicated as a single collection."

The purpose of the library will be to service prosecutors nationwide to expedite preparation of cases. It will be available also to the judiciary, behavioral scientists, clergymen, writers and other professionals who can contribute to the effort to stem the flow of obscene material. The district attorneys of New York City are of the unanimous opinion

501

that such a library will prove invaluable to law enforcement agencies. It will contain everything written on the law of obscenity: statutes, ordinances, decided cases, texts, commentaries, etc. It will also contain a section on medical, psychiatric and psychological research relative to obscenity. Law enforcement officials believe that the convenience of finding all precedents, statutes, briefs, etc. in one location will save countless hours in case preparation.

3. RECOMMENDED STATE LEGISLATION

(a) *Model State Obscenity Statute*

Attached to this Report as Appendix II is our recommended Model State Obscenity Statute based on the concept of variable obscenity and taking into consideration all U.S. Supreme Court cases. We believe it is a constitutionally effective statute that will effectively regulate the traffic in obscenity. The suggested statute is explained and annotated in the Appendix.

(b) We also recommend to the States that they establish, by legislation, a Board of Film Review which would require —under carefully prescribed rules based on Supreme Court decisions discussed in Appendix I—the submission of all motion pictures for licensing prior to their exhibition. This proposed statute is taken from Maryland Statutes Article 66A which has been revised to comply with *Freedman v. Maryland,* a Supreme Court decision. In our opinion it will withstand constitutional attack. A copy of this proposed Model Statute on Film review is attached as Appendix IV.

(c) In addition, we suggest that some States might desire to permit local ordinances for the establishment of Film Review Boards, generally, or for the purpose of establishing classification of films as suitable or unsuitable for minors under 18. Such States should enact legislation confirming the existing right of municipalities to adopt such legislation, and permitting them to apply for injunctive relief in the courts; and requiring a prompt judicial determination of the issue. A suggested statute to be used as a model is Section 418A, again of the State of Maryland, found in Appendix V. It should be used as a supplement to any State statute or local ordinance on Film Review or classification. This model should be modified where used in aid of local ordinances to permit the Chief Legal Officer of the municipality, or the Film Review or Classification Board, to apply also for an injunction in the case of motion pictures.

502

(d) We recommend the employment of the injunctive remedy, found in 22a of the New York Statute or 418A of the Maryland Statute, to supplement the Model State Statute generally. This is a most effective weapon sanctioned by the decisions of the U.S. Supreme Court, and will reach all types of obscenity. See Appendix V.

(e) We recommend that the Attorney General's Office be required to review for possible prosecution any type of suspected obscenity distributed or about to be distributed, of which he gains knowledge, and which falls into any of the descriptive categories listed below:

1. The Stag Film
2. The Sexploitation Film
3. The Commercial X-rated Film
4. The Commercial Unrated Film
5. Advertisements for X and Unrated Films
6. Underground Sex Publications
7. Underground Newspapers
8. Mimeographed Underground Newpapers
9. Sensational Tabloids
10. Homosexual Magazines
11. Sex-violence Magazines
12. "Spreader" or "Tunnel" Magazines
13. Teenage Sex Magazines
14. Pseudo-Scientific Sex Publications
15. So-called Nudist Magazines
16. Lyrics on Commercially Distributed Rock Records
17. Sex-action Photographs
18. Sex-action Records
19. Sex-action Slides and Tapes
20. Mail Order Advertisements for the Above
21. Paperbacks with themes of: Homosexuality, Sado-masochism, Incest, Bestiality
22. Hardcover Books Devoted to Homosexuality, Sado-masochism, Incest

(f) We advocate the establishment in the office of the Attorney General of each State, a team of one or more skilled attorneys, under the direction of a Deputy Attorney General, to be used to assist in the local prosecutions where intrastate commerce is involved or where federal assistance from the Department of Justice is not readily available.

(g) We advocate the establishment in State Police headquarters of a similar division, working closely with the legal staff just mentioned. The state police have experts in arson, ballistics and other specialties. The formation of a special unit on pornography is long overdue.

(h) We advocate the establishment of permanent State Commission to examine the laws on obscenity, to make recommendations to the legislature, and recommendations for more effective means of enforcement. A suggested statute is attached in Appendix VI, and is modeled on a statute of the State of Illinois, approved September 6, 1967.

(i) We recommend the establishment of a State Commission to review and classify Motion Pictures and printed materials for minors. A suggested statute in this respect, based on our review of *Bantam Books v. Sullivan* is attached as Appendix VII.

(j) As minimum legislation, we advocate elimination of the phrase "utterly without redeeming social value" in any State statute. A suggested statute is attached as Appendix VIII.

4. RECOMMENDED LOCAL ORDINANCES

(a) We recommend a review of existing ordinances in the light of our review of U.S. Supreme Court decisions in Appendix I, and the modifying or amending of same to comply therewith, including the elimination of the phrase, "utterly without redeeming social value" whenever found.

(b) We recommend the adoption of local ordinances (wherever the State has not adopted a Film Review Statute) to review Motion Pictures—based on Maryland Statute recommended above.

(c) On an optional basis, or as part of a general ordinance on motion picture review, we recommend a Film Review and Classification Ordinance for minors. The suggested ordinance, attached as Appendix IV is liberally designed to meet Supreme Court requirements.

(d) We recommend an ordinance designed to protect minors from being exposed, on the highway or street, to drive-in movie scenes of motion pictures that are unsuitable for children. The suggested Ordinance attached as Appendix X has been approved by the United States Court of Appeals for the Fifth Circuit in the case of *Chemline Ind. v. City of Grand Prairie,* decided August 8, 1966, 364 F 2d. 721.

(e) We recommend a local ordinance to penalize the showing of obscene motion pictures, and to penalize the licensee found guilty. See Appendix XII, based on a second ordinance upheld in *Chemline* case above, containing pure *Roth* test.

5. RECOMMENDED PRIVATE ACTION BY THE PUBLIC

(a) We recommend that private citizens join with or form private, non-sectarian, community organizations that take organized, but constitutional action against obscenity.

(b) We recommend citizens bring official legal complaints whenever evidence of obscenity comes to their attention.

(c) We recommend that citizens continually urge their municipal, State and federal officials, to prosecute obscenity cases. Here, again, this is best accomplished in an organized manner, working through an existing community organization.

APPENDIX I

LEGAL AND LEGISLATIVE ANALYSIS
AND RECOMMENDATIONS

1. *Duties of the Commission in the Legal Area.*
The 90th Congress, in enacting S. 188 into law as Public Law 90-100, gave to the Commission on Obscenity and Pornography four mandates as follows:

"(1) with the aid of leading constitutional law authorities, to analyze the laws pertaining to the control of obscenity and pornography; and to evaluate and recommend definitions of obscenity and pornography;

(2) to ascertain the methods employed in the distribution of obscene and pornographic materials and to explore the nature and volume of traffic in such materials;

(3) to study the effect of obscenity and pornography upon the public, and particularly minors, and its relationship to crime and other antisocial behavior; and

(4) to recommend such legislative, administrative, or other advisable and appropriate action as the Commission deems necessary to regulate effectively the flow of such traffic, without in any way interfering with constitutional rights."

This part of the report shall concern itself with mandates (1) and (4) which, summarized, require the following:

(a) Analysis of existing Federal and State statutes and municipal ordinances;

(b) A recommended definition of obscenity; and

(c) Recommended legislative and other action to regulate effectively and constitutionally the flow of such traffic.

It is clear, at the outset, that Congress did not by the enactment of this law desire that the Commission's recommendations for effective regulation depend on proof of bad effects of obscenity or that obscenity bore a provable cause and effect relationship to crime and other antisocial behavior. Congress enacted this statute with knowledge of the Supreme Court opinion in the *Roth* case wherein it was stated that obscenity was not constitutionally protected free speech and that it was *unnecessary* in order to proscribe it to prove:

"that obscene material will perceptively create a clear and present danger of antisocial conduct, or will probably induce its recipients to such conduct. . . . Certainly no one would contend that obscene speech, for example, may be punished only upon a showing of such circumstances. . . ." (1 L. Ed. 2d 1508)

Public Law 90-100 was enacted on October 3, 1967. Even after that date, the United States Supreme Court reiterated its position that the question of antisocial behavior was irrelevant to the question of whether or not obscenity was proscribable when in the case of *Ginzberg* v. *New York* a majority of the Court at 390 U.S. 629, 641; 20 L. Ed. 2d 195, at page 205, on April 22, 1968, stated:

"Our conclusion in Roth, at 486-487, 1 L. Ed. 2d at 1507, 1508, that the clear and present danger test was *irrelevant* to the determination of obscenity made it unnecessary in that case to consider the debate among the authorities whether exposure to pornography caused antisocial consequences. . . ."

It is quite apparent that the Congressional mandate to

"recommend . . . action . . . necessary to regulate effectively the flow of such traffic"

is susceptible to no other meaning than that this traffic is to be regulated and that Congress is in the bill expressing the Public Policy of the United States in this respect. The study into antisocial effects was a peripheral project to the major concern.

If further proof is necessary that effective regulation was the main function of the Commission, it can also be discerned from the comments of the members of Congress when Public Law 90-100 was enacted.

On August 7, 1967, the Bill (then H.R. 10347) was considered in the House and the following explanation was offered:

Congressman Daniels: "I am confident that from the work of the commission will come exemplary Federal Laws and model state laws, consistent with constitutional standards."

Congressman Boland: "There does exist a problem with respect to this situation all over America."

Congressman Perkins: "The bill proposes that an advisory commission be established whose purpose shall be, after a thorough study, to recommend effective, advisable and appropriate constitutional means to deal effectively with the growing traffic in obscenity and pornography."

Congressman Langen: "This type of commission recognizes the need for a positive effort and effective tools for stopping the flow of the evil and contamination that forms a vexing thorn in the side of society. . . . A commission on Obscenity and Pornography would . . . come up with recommendations that can be used as guides for action by the Federal, State and local levels of government. . . ."

Congressman Berry: "We must act now to see that the flow of obscenity is checked in a way which will not be voided by the Courts."

Congressman Wyatt: "We must stem this tide of moral decay."

Congressman Fascell: "Passage of this measure will reaffirm the interest that the legislative branch has in stemming the tide of offensive, indecent and fraudulent mail."

506

On September 20, 1967, the Senate passed this bill. Among the comments were the following by

Senator Allott: "I think this prevalence of pornography does an injustice to us, and casts a direct challenge at the Congress of the United States."

When the Chairman of this Commission, Doctor Lockhart, later testified before the Senate Appropriations Committee, this same Senator Allott said to him,

"We want to see the legislation that comes out of this as hard-hitting as any legislation can be."

In the 91st Congressional Session the legislators made it quite clear that they meant what they said about the suppression of obscenity. Without waiting for the Commission report and because of the urgency of the situation, separate bills to suppress obscenity were introduced by 136 different Congressmen.

2. *Analysis of Laws Pertaining to Obscenity.*

A. *The Statutes*

1. *The Federal Statutes.* The Federal Statutes prohibit:
(a) *Mailing* Obscene Matter (Title 18 U.S.C. #1461).
(b) *Importation or Transportation of* Obscene Matter in Interstate or Foreign Commerce (Title 18 U.S.C. #1462).
(c) Mailing Obscene Matter in *Wrappers* or *Envelopes* (Title 18 U.S.C. #1463).
(d) *Broadcasting* Obscene Language (Title 18 U.S.C. #1464).
(e) Transportation of Obscene Matters *for Sale* or Distribution (Title 18 U.S.C. #1465).
(f) *Importation of Immoral Articles* (Title 19 U.S.C. #1305).
(g) *Nonmailable* Matter (Title 39 U.S.C. #4001).
(h) *Unlawful* Matter (Title 39 U.S.C. #4006).
(i) *Detention* of Mail for Temporary Periods (Title 39 U.S.C. #4007).
(j) Prohibition of *Pandering Advertisements* in the Mails (Title 39 U.S.C. #4009).
(k) Obscene *Telephone Calls* (Public Law 90-299, 82 Stat. 112).
(l) They establish a *Commission on Obscenity* and Pornography (Public Law 90-100, 81 Stat. 253).
2. *The State Statutes.*
All of the states have some type of statute prohibiting obscenity.
3. *Local Ordinances.*
It is believed that many municipalities have adopted local ordinances relative to obscenity, but no known up-to-date summary is available. Many of these ordinances relate to the exhibition of motion pictures. Commentaries on the validity of various ordinances will be set forth in this report.

B. *The Court Decisions*

1. *Decisions of the United States Supreme Court.* In any consideration of the validity of a statute on the subject of obscenity, we must of necessity refer to the decisions of the U.S. Supreme Court since the *Butler, Roth* and *Kingsley* cases have made the same subject to the Court's postulations as to its outside limits of control under the First and Fourteenth Amendments. This section of this report shall therefore review and analyze in a

chronological fashion the opinions of the U.S. Supreme Court for the period 1957 to 1970.

(a) *Butler* v. *Michigan*
   352 U.S. 380, 1 L. Ed. 2d 412
   (Decided February 25, 1957)

In this case the defendant, Butler, was convicted of violating a statute of the State of Michigan which made it an offense to make available to the general reading public a book that is found to have a potentially deleterious influence on youth. Mr. Frankfurter, speaking for eight of the Justices, held that the Michigan statute violated the due process clause of the Fourteenth Amendment. The Court stated, at 1 L. Ed. 2d 414:

"The State insists that by thus quarantining the general reading public against books not too rugged for grown men and women in order to shield juvenile innocence, it is exercising its power to promote the general welfare. . . . We have before us legislation not reasonably restricted to the evil with which it is said to deal. The incidence of this enactment is to reduce the adult population of Michigan to reading only what is fit for children . . . ."

Comment

The *Butler* case foreshadowed the "average person" test found in the *Roth* case, decided four months later, to be a requirement for a general statute on obscenity. It should be noted that the Court distinguished between the "adult population" and "juveniles" in one place referring to adults as "grown men and women." An "adult" is defined in the dictionary as "a person who has attained the age of maturity or legal majority." It would appear that the Court here is referring to a person who is either 21 years of age or possibly 18 years of age. Thus age distinction becomes important in drafting a statute especially designed to protect those who are not adults which we shall consider later in this report.

(b) *Kingsley Books, Inc.* v. *Brown*
   354 U.S. 436, 1 L. Ed. 2d 1469
   (June 24, 1957)

The State of New York's Code of Criminal Procedure contained a section known as Section 22-a which supplemented the conventional criminal provision dealing with pornography by authorizing the chief executive or legal officer of a municipality to invoke a "limited injunctive remedy" under closely defined procedural safeguards against the sale and distribution of written and printed matter found after due trial to be obscene and to obtain an order for the seizure in default of surrender of the condemned publications. The section further provided that the persons sought to be enjoined "shall be entitled to a trial of the issues within one day after joinder of issue and a decision shall be rendered by the Court within two days of the conclusion of the trial." The novelty of the procedure was the issuance of an injunction preventing further sale or distribution of the material pending the final order of the Court.

Justice Frankfurter, speaking for a majority of the Court, said at 1 L. Ed. 2d 1473:

"Neither in the New York Court of Appeals, nor here, did

appellants assail the legislation insofar as it outlaws obscenity . . . their attack is upon the power of New York to employ the remedial scheme of Section 22-a."

He continues:

"Authorization of an injunction pendente lite as part of this scheme, during the period within which the issue of obscenity must be promptly tried and adjudicated in an adversary proceeding for which adequate notice, judicial hearing and fair determination are assured is a safeguard against frustration of the public interest in effectuating judicial condemnation of obscene matter. It is a brake on the temptation to exploit a filthy business. . . .

"Resort to this injunctive remedy, it is claimed . . . amounts to a prior censorship of literary product and as such is violative of that freedom of thought and speech which has been 'withdrawn by the Fourteenth Amendment from encroachment by the States'. . . . In an unbroken series of cases extending over a long stretch of this Court's history, it has been accepted as a postulate that 'the primary requirements of decency may be enforced against obscene publications.' 283 U.S. at 716. . . .

"It is not for this Court [thus] to limit the State in resorting to various weapons in the armory of the law, whether proscribed conduct is to be visited by a criminal prosecution . . . or by some or all of these remedies in combination, is a matter within the legislature's range of choice. . . .

"The judicial angle of vision in testing the validity of a statute like 22-a is 'the operation and effect of the statute in substance.' The phrase 'prior restraint' is not a self-wielding sword. Nor can it serve as a talismanic test . . . 'what is needed . . . is a pragmatic assessment of its operation in the particular circumstances. The generalization that prior restraint is particularly obnoxious to civil liberties cases must yield to more particular analysis.' "

One of the dissenting Justices, Mr. Brennan, indicated that Section 22-a required a trial by jury to, in his opinion, make it constitutional. He states:

"The jury represents a cross section of the community and has a special aptitude for reflecting the view of the average person. Jury trial of obscenity therefore provides a peculiarly competent application of the standard for judging obscenity . . . . Of course, as with jury questions generally, the trial judge must initially determine that there is a jury question, i.e. that reasonable men may differ whether the material is obscene."

Comment

In a series of Public Hearings held by Commissioners Hill and Link throughout many principal cities of the United States, the greatest problem to effective enforcement of the laws against obscenity, other than the phrase "utterly without redeeming social value," was the belief by some judges that *Marcus v. Search Warrant of Property,* a 1961 decision of the Supreme Court, in some manner requires a prior adversary hearing before a seizure may be had of alleged obscene material. While we intend to discuss this in more detail in the commentary on that case, it perhaps is in order to point out to the legislatures of the states where such

509

rulings have been made that pending the clarification of this issue by the United States Supreme Court, the adoption of a statute similar to Section 22-a will permit an injunction against the sale and distribution of such material throughout the state pending the trial determination and where a trial judge issues a permanent injunction during the pendency of any appeal. This procedure would appear to be clearly permissible under *Kingsley Books v. Brown.*

The *Kingsley Books* case stands squarely for the proposition that limited prior restraints are permissible and in the meantime offending obscene motion pictures and other forms of obscenity are not thrust upon the public during the time it takes to appeal the case to the United States Supreme Court. It perhaps could be amended along the lines suggested by Justice Brennan to provide for jury trials on an optional basis if demanded by either side. This, however, does not seem legally necessary since the defendant is not being charged with a misdemeanor.

    (c) *Roth v. United States*
         and *Alberts v. California*
         354 U.S. 476, 1 L. Ed. 2d 1498
         (Decided June 24, 1957)

These two appeals were heard together. Roth was charged with violating the Federal obscenity statute and Alberts with violating the obscenity law of the State of California. Roth contended that obscenity was protected free speech under the First Amendment and Alberts contended that the California statute violated the Fourteenth Amendment Due Process Clause. Other constitutional issues were that the statutes were too vague, that only the states could pass obscenity statutes and that the Federal statutes preempted the field.

Justice Brennan, speaking for a majority of the Supreme Court, said at 1 L. Ed. 2d 1505:

"The dispositive question is whether obscenity is utterance within the area of protected free speech and the press. Although this is the first time the question has been squarely presented to this Court . . . expressions found in numerous opinions indicate that this Court has always assumed that obscenity is not protected by the freedoms of speech and press (quoting 10 prior Supreme Court cases). . . .

"It is apparent that the unconditional phrasing of the First Amendment was not intended to protect every utterance. . . .

"All ideas having even the slightest social importance—unorthodox ideas, controversial ideas, even ideas hateful to the prevailing climate of opinion—have the full protection of the guaranties, unless excludable because they encroach upon the limited area of more important interests. But implicit in the history of the First Amendment is the rejection of obscenity as utterly without redeeming social importance. This rejection for that reason is mirrored in the universal judgment that obscenity should be restrained, reflected in the international agreement of over 50 nations, in the obscenity laws of all of the 48 states and in the 20 obscenity laws enacted by Congress from 1842 to 1956. This is the same judgment expressed by this Court in Chaplinsky v. New Hampshire . . .

    . . . There are certain well defined and narrowly limited

classes of speech, the prevention and punishment of which have never been thought to raise any constitutional problem. These include the lewd and obscene . . . *It has been well ob-observed that such utterances are no essential part of any exposition of ideas, and are of such slight social value as a step to truth that any benefit that may be derived from them is clearly outweighed by the social interest in order and morality.* (Emphasis supplied by the Court.)

"We hold that obscenity is not within the area of constitutionally protected speech or press. . . .

"Sex and obscenity are not synonymous. Obscene material is material which deals with sex in a manner appealing to prurient interest."

The Court then refers us to a footnote for the definition of "prurient interest":

"i.e. material having a tendency to excite lustful thoughts . . . we perceive no significant difference between the meaning of obscenity developed in the case law and the definition of the American Law Institute Model Penal Code . . . viz. 'a thing is obscene if, considered as a whole, its predominant appeal is to prurient interest, a shameful or morbid interest in nudity, sex, or excretion and if it goes substantially beyond customary limits of candor in description or representation of such matters . . .'

"The early leading standard of obscenity allowed material to be judged merely by the effect of an isolated excerpt upon particularly susceptible persons. Regina v. Hicklin (1868), L.R. 3 QB 360. Some American Courts adopted this standard, but later decisions have rejected it and substituted this test: whether to the average person, applying contemporary community standards, the dominant theme of the material taken as a whole appeals to the prurient interest. The Hicklin test . . . must be rejected as unconstitutionally restrictive of the freedom of speech and press. On the other hand, the substituted standard provides safeguards adequate to withstand the charge of constitutional infirmity. Both trial courts below sufficiently followed the proper standard.

"In Roth, the trial judge instructed the jury as follows:

'. . . the test is not whether it would arouse sexual desires or sexual impure thoughts in those comprising a particular segment of the community, the young, the immature or the highly prudish or would leave another segment, the scientific or highly educated or the so-called worldly-wise and sophisticated indifferent and unmoved . . . the test in each case is the effect of the books, picture or publication considered as a whole, not upon any particular class, but upon all those whom it is likely to reach. In other words, you determine its impact upon the average person in the community. The books, pictures and circulars must be judged as a whole, in their entire context, and you are not to consider detached or separate portions in reaching a conclusion. You judge the circulars, pictures and publications which have been put in evidence by present day standards of the community. You may ask yourselves does it offend the common conscience of the community by present-day standards.

'In this case, ladies and gentlemen, you and you alone are

511

the exclusive judges of what the common conscience of the community is, and in determining that conscience you are to consider the community as a whole, young and old, educated and uneducated, the religious and irreligious—men, women and children.'

"It is argued that the statutes do not provide reasonably ascertainable standards of guilt and therefore violate the constitutional requirements of due process. . . . The federal obscenity statute makes punishable the mailing of material that is 'obscene, lewd, lascivious, or filthy . . . or other publication of an indecent character.' . . . The . . . argument is that these words are not sufficiently precise . . . .

"Many decisions have recognized that these terms of obscenity statutes are not precise. This Court, however, has consistently held that lack of precision is not itself offensive to the requirements of due process. . . . 'The Constitution does not require impossible standards'; all that is required is that the language conveys sufficiently definite warning as to the proscribed conduct when measured by common understanding and practice.

"These words, applied according to the proper standard for judging obscenity, already discussed, give adequate warning of the conduct proscribed and mark boundaries sufficiently distinct for judges and juries fairly to administer the law."

Justice Harlan in his concurring opinion in the *Alberts* case, at 1 L. Ed. 2d 1516, states:

"It seems to me clear that it is not irrational, in our present state of knowledge to consider that pornography can induce a type of sexual conduct which a State may deem obnoxious to the moral fabric of society. . . .

"Furthermore, even assuming that pornography cannot be deemed ever to cause, in an immediate sense, criminal sexual conduct, other interests within the proper cognizance of the States may be protected by the prohibition placed on such materials. The State can reasonably draw the inference that over a long period of time the indiscriminate dissemination of materials, the essential character of which is to degrade sex, will have an eroding effect on moral standards. . . .

"Since the domain of sexual morality is pre-eminently a matter of State concern, the Court should be slow to interfere with State legislation calculated to protect that morality."

Comment

The *Roth-Alberts* decision is of the greatest importance not only because it firmly decided that obscenity is proscribable both under state and federal law, but because it is the *only* decision of the United States Supreme Court which sets forth the test for obscenity.

The Court made the following points: 1. The test for obscenity is

"whether to the average person, applying contemporary community standards, the dominant theme of the material taken as a whole appeals to the prurient interest."

2. Once material is adjudged to be obscene by a jury (or Judge) applying this test or its equivalent then, since it is obscenity, it is conclusively presumed as a matter of law to be "utterly without redeeming social importance." 3. Such lewd and obscene utter-

512

ances may have some "social value" but "any benefit that may be derived from them is clearly outweighed by the social interest in order and morality." 4. Obscenity is not protected free speech. 5. A charge to a jury that includes only the prurient interest test (or its equivalent) is constitutionally valid. 6. A statute proscribing "obscene or lewd" material is sufficiently precise. 7. Since obscenity is not protected free speech, it is unnecessary to prove that obscenity will "create a clear and present danger of antisocial conduct or will probably induce its recipients to such conduct." 8. The legal base for obscenity laws is the "social interest in order and morality," or the prevention of "an eroding effect on moral standards."

It seems clear that since there is no later *Court* decision modifying the definition of obscenity found in the *Roth-Alberts* case, then this case may be used as the basis for the state and federal legislative recommendations mandated by Congress as a task of this Commission. Such suggested legislation will be discussed in a later part of this report.

(d) *Smith v. California*

361 U.S. 147, 4 L. Ed. 2d 205

(Decided December 14, 1959)

Smith, the proprietor of a bookstore, was convicted under a Los Angeles city ordinance which made it unlawful for any person to have in his possession any obscene or indecent writing or book in any place of business where books are sold or kept for sale. The lower courts had defined the offense literally in the words of the statute without requiring any element of scienter, i.e. knowledge by defendant of the contents of the book for the possession of which he was convicted. Justice Brennan, speaking for a majority of the Court, said at 4 L. Ed. 2d 210:

"We have held that obscene speech and writings are not protected by the constitutional guarantees of freedom of speech and the press. Roth v. United States. . . . The ordinance here in question, to be sure, only imposes criminal sanctions on a bookseller if in fact there is to be found in his shop an obscene book. But our holding in Roth does not recognize any state power to restrict the dissemination of books which are not obscene; and we think the ordinance's strict liability feature would tend seriously to have that effect, by penalizing booksellers even though they had not the slightest notice of the character of the books they sold. . . .

"By dispensing with any requirement of knowledge of the contents of the book on the part of the seller, the ordinance tends to impose a severe limitation on the public's access to constitutionally protected matter. For if the bookseller is criminally liable without knowledge of the contents . . . he will tend to restrict the books he sells to those he has inspected; and thus the State will have imposed a restriction upon the distribution of constitutionally protected as well as obscene literature. . . .

"It is argued that unless the scienter requirement is dispensed with, regulation of the distribution of obscene material will be ineffective as booksellers will falsely disclaim knowledge of their books' contents or falsely deny reason to suspect their obscenity. We might observe that it has been some time now since the law viewed itself as impotent to explore the actual state of a man's

513

mind. . . . Eyewitness testimony of a bookseller's perusal of a book hardly need be a necessary element in proving his awareness of its contents. The circumstances may warrant the inference that he was aware of what a book contained despite his denial. . . .

"Doubtless any form of criminal obscenity statute applicable to a bookseller will induce some tendency to self censorship and have some inhibitory effect on the dissemination of material not obscene, but we consider today only one which goes to the extent of eliminating all mental elements from the crime."

Comment

The Court opinion, here reduced to its simplest terms, is to the effect that a law that prohibits the possession in a book shop by a bookdealer of an obscene book is unconstitutional unless the bookseller is somehow aware of the contents of the book. The decision does not require that he "know" the book is obscene. It seems to be sufficient if he is somehow generally aware of the contents of a book which is later found to be obscene.

From the experience of law enforcement officers throughout the country and from our own experience, we believe that this requirement of "scienter" has been one of the greatest inhibitory factors in successful obscenity prosecutions at the retail level. Justice Harlan in his separate opinion chides the Court for suggesting that "proving the state of a man's mind is little more difficult than proving the state of his digestion." This Commission is charged with the duty, nevertheless, of recommending appropriate action to constitutionally and effectively regulate obscenity. It appears to us then, that we must meet the issue of "scienter" head on. This means that we must devise a method of making those who retail books and writings that may or may not be obscene in some manner "aware of the contents" so that they are put on notice that they may be selling or keeping for sale "obscenity." Those retailers who prefer not to sell such material will have the benefit of this information and those who do prefer to vend it will be unable to "insulate themselves against knowledge about an offending book."

On August 7, 1964 the then Mayor of the City of New York, Robert F. Wagner, in view of widespread concern with the problems of obscenity, appointed a 21-member "Mayor's Citizens Anti-Pornography Commission." That Commission, in its report on April 9, 1965, devised an 11-point plan for combatting obscenity. One of those recommendations seems admirably suited to the problem of making those who sell obscenity "aware of the contents." This was the suggestion of the Mayor's Commission to establish "citizens advisory commissions." Their recommendation in this respect is as follows:

"5. *Peer Groups or Citizens Advisory Commissions.*

This Commission advocates that, in addition to the official Commissions on Noxious and Obscene Matters and Materials, that a permanent city-wide Citizen's Anti-Pornography Commission be established, appointed by the Mayor, which would be a self-governing organization supported by contributions from individuals, corporations and foundations, members of said Commission to serve without pay, no member of which to be directly concerned with the enforcement of any criminal statutes.

514

"Said Commission would then prepare a set of by-laws for its own regulation and prepare a program for the establishment of borough-wide Citizen's Advisory Groups to which said Commission would refer material alleged to be salacious or obscene for an advisory opinion after said members had been advised in writing as to the definition of said terms. These local groups of 12 citizens each to be selected by lot, by the Commission, from the voter's registration list and to serve for a three-month term. The findings of these juries are to be reported to the Citizen's Anti-Pornography Commission, which would have the right to add its opinion of the propriety of the findings to the jury verdict. These opinions, then to be released to the press and to be recorded in the Journal of the Commission. Where deemed appropriate, advertising space would be taken in the 'Book Review' columns of local newspapers.

"It is the opinion of this Commission that such a Commission and such Local Citizen's Advisory Groups may be legally established under the decisions of the Courts in *American Mercury Inc.* v. *Chase et al,*[5] *Bantam Books* v. *Sullivan*[6] and *Sunshine Book Company* v. *McCaffrey.*[7] For example, in *American Mercury Inc.* v. *Chase et al,* the Federal District Court in Massachusetts stated, relative to a Citizen's Literature Review Society:

'The defendants have the right of every citizen to come to the courts with complaints of crime. . . . *the distributors have the right to take advice* as to whether publications which they sell violate the law and to act on such advice *if they believe it to be sound. The defendants have the right to express their views as to the propriety or legality of a publication,* but the defendants have not the right to enforce their views by organized threats, either open or covert, to the distributing trade to prosecute persons who disagree with them. . . .' [emphasis supplied]

"See also New York University Law Review, Vol. 33, November 1958.

"We strongly urge the organization of such Peer Groups, or Citizen's Commissions and, in fact, we go further and urge the Legislature of the State of New York and the Legislatures of other states throughout the United States to consider if State inaugurated and supported committees should be established. In the meantime, however, there seems to be no inhibition to the establishment of such an organization by private groups."

We therefore urge the establishment of such local private citizen's groups.

It seems clear that such a local commission and advisory group would be exercising its right of free speech under the Constitution and at the same time preventing pornography vendors and distributors (who might also be notified) from using lack of "scienter" as a sword instead of a shield. See also our comments relating to the *Bantam Books* case discussed later in this report.

Insofar as state criminal obscenity statutes or municipal ordinances are concerned, it seems clear that "scienter" must be in-

---

[5] 13 F. 2d 224 (Dist.Ct.Mass., 1926).
[6] 372 U.S. 65, 9 L. Ed. 2d 590 (1963).
[7] 168 N.Y.S. 2d 268 (1957).

515

corporated therein or if not such law must be deemed to require a showing of the same.

(e) *Kingsley International Pictures*
Corporation v. Regents
360 U.S. 684, 3 L. Ed. 2d 1512
(Decided June 29, 1959)

A New York State statute which in part provided for the prohibition of motion pictures that portrayed acts of sexual immorality as desirable was construed by the New York Court of Appeals as prohibiting a motion picture which presented adultery as being right and desirable for certain people under certain circumstances. Justice Stewart, for a majority of the Court, stated that the statute as so construed was invalid under the First Amendment as made applicable to the states by the Fourteenth. The New York Court in its decision rejected any notion that the film was obscene.

Comment

This case stands for the proposition that absent a claim or showing of obscenity, the mere fact that a motion picture advocates an idea that is not shared by the majority is not in itself sufficient grounds to suppress the same. This, in effect, is not an obscenity case.

(f) *Times Film Corporation*
v. Chicago
365 U.S. 43, 5 L. Ed. 2d 403
(Decided January 23, 1961)

An ordinance of the City of Chicago required submission of all motion pictures for examination prior to their public exhibition. The Times Film Corporation attacked the ordinance as a "prior restraint" within the prohibition of the First and Fourteenth Amendments.

Justice Clark, in delivering the opinion of the Court, stated at 5 L. Ed. 2d at page 405:

"The petitioner complied with the requirements of the ordinance, save for the production of the film for examination. The claim is that this concrete and specific statutory requirement, the production of the film at the office of the Commissioner for examination, is invalid as a previous restraint on freedom of speech. . . . Admittedly, the challenged section of the ordinance imposes a previous restraint, and the broad justifiable issue is therefore present as to whether the ambit of constitutional protection includes complete and absolute freedom to exhibit, at least once, any and every kind of motion picture. It is this question we must decide. We have concluded that Section 155-4 of Chicago's ordinance requiring the submission of films prior to their public exhibition is not, on the grounds set forth, void on its face. . . .

"Obviously, whether a particular statute is 'clearly drawn' or 'vague' or 'indefinite' or whether a clear standard is in fact met by a film are different questions . . . to be tested by considerations not here involved. . . .

"Petitioner would have us hold that the public exhibition of motion pictures must be allowed under any circumstances. The State's sole remedy, it says, is the invocation of criminal process.

516

. . . But this proposition is founded upon the claim of absolute privilege against prior restraint under the First Amendment—a claim without sanction in our cases. . . .

"We recognized in Burstyn . . . that capacity for evil may be relevant in determining the permissible scope of community control . . . and that motion pictures were not necessarily subject to the precise rules governing any other particular method of expression. . . .

"Certainly petitioner's broadside attack does not warrant . . . our saying that . . . the State is stripped of all constitutional power to prevent, in the most effective fashion, the utterance of this class of speech. . . .

"It is not for this Court to limit the State in its selection of the remedy it deems most effective."

Comment

This case stands for the proposition that some prior restraint of the exhibition of motion pictures is constitutional and that one of the constitutional forms of that prior restraint is the requirement that the exhibitor submit it for review to a city official prior to exhibition under an ordinance which included a provision relative to denial of the right to exhibit if found by the city official to be obscene. The court expressed no opinion as to the validity of the ordinance generally.

In response to our mandate from Congress to suggest constitutional methods of controlling obscenity, we believe that *Times Film Corp. v. Chicago* is a firm base from which to devise an ordinance that will, as the Court says, "prevent in the most *effective* fashion this type of speech." One of the gravest problems facing this country is the thrusting of pornography on the population and then keeping it on the market during the period of a trial for the criminal offense up to the final appeal with innumerable delays. When the last appeal is denied and the conviction is affirmed, the damage caused by the offending motion picture or other obscene publication cannot be redressed. The very existence of such a Board to review motion pictures guarantees that the state or city will be on constant alert to proceed swiftly, expeditiously and knowledgeably against obscene motion pictures. It is important to note the caveat of the Court to the effect that such an ordinance, however, should not be otherwise "vague" or "indefinite" or have other constitutional infirmities in application. We shall further discuss the validity of such ordinances and the additional constitutional safeguards needed in our comments under *Tietel Film Corp. v. Cusack*, *Freedman v. Maryland* and *Interstate Circuit v. Dallas*. We shall also propose suggested ordinances and statutes for the general public and ordinances and state statutes designed especially for children in the legislative section of this report. It should be noted that the Court had approved a "limited Prior Restraint" in the *Kingsley Book* case discussed earlier.

(g) *Marcus v. Search Warrant of Property*
367 U.S. 717, 6 L. Ed. 2d 1127
(Decided June 19, 1961)

A Missouri statute authorized the search for and seizure of allegedly obscene publications preliminarily to their destruction if found by a court to be obscene. The statutory procedure was supplemented by a rule of the Supreme Court that permitted the issuance of the warrant on "probable cause" to believe that obscene matter is being held in any place . . . to any peace officer. The owner of the property was not afforded a hearing before the warrant issued, but the judge had to fix a date not more than 20 days after the seizure for a hearing to determine obscenity. No time limit was provided within which the judge must announce his decision.

Justice Brennan delivered the opinion of the Court and stated at 6 L. Ed. 2d 1136:

"We believe that Missouri's procedures as applied in this case lacked the safeguards which due process demands to assure nonobscene material the constitutional protection to which it is entitled. Putting to one side the fact that no opportunity was afforded the appellants to elicit and contest the reasons for the officers belief, or otherwise to argue against the propriety of the seizure to the issuing judge, still the warrants issued on the strength of the conclusionary assertions of a single peace officer without any scrutiny by the judge of any materials considered by the complainant to be obscene. . . .

"It is no reflection on the good faith or judgment of the officers to conclude that the task they were assigned was simply an impossible one to perform with any realistic expectation that the obscene might be accurately separated from the constitutionally protected. They were provided with no guide to the exercize of informed discretion, because there was no step in the procedure before seizure designed to focus searchingly on the question of obscenity. . . . discretion to seize allegedly obscene materials cannot be confided to law enforcement officials without greater safeguards than were here operative."

The Court noted that under the warrants issued 280 different publications were seized of which only 100 were later found to be obscene.

The Court then notes the distinctions between this case and *Kingsley Books v. Brown:*

"The differences in the procedures under the New York statute upheld in that case and the Missouri procedures as applied here is marked. They amount to the distinction between 'a limited injunctive remedy' under closely defined procedural safeguards . . . and a scheme which in operation inhibited the circulation of publications indiscriminately because of the absence of any such safeguards. *First,* the New York injunctive proceeding was initiated by a complaint filed with the court which charged that a particular named obscene publication had been displayed, and to which were annexed copies of the publication alleged to be obscene. The court, in restraining distribution pending final judicial determination of the claim, thus had the allegedly obscene material before it and could exercise an independent check on the judgment of the prosecuting authority at a point before any restraint took place. *Second,* the restraints in Kingsley Book, both temporary and permanent, ran only against the named publication; no catchall restraint against the distribution of all 'obscene' material was imposed on the defendants there, comparable to the warrants here which authorized *a mass seizure*

518

and the removal of a broad range of items from circulation [emphasis supplied]. *Third,* Kingsley Books does not support the proposition that the state may impose the *extensive restraints* [emphasis supplied] imposed here on the distribution of these publications prior to an adversary proceeding on the issue of obscenity, irrespective of whether or not the material is legally obscene."

The Court then proceeded to indicate that the restraint prior to hearing included seizure of all copies of the 280 publications (11,000 copies of 280 publications) and indicated that if the distributor had obtained a new supply, these too would be subject to seizure and thus preventing the distributor from displaying publications he believed might be not obscene solely on the contrary judgment of a police officer.

The Court continues:

"Finally, . . . the New York statute required that a judicial decision on the merits of obscenity be made within two days of trial, which in turn was required to be within one day of the joinder of issue. In contrast, the Missouri statutory scheme . . . has no limitation on the time within which decision must be made, only a provision for rapid trial on the issue of obscenity. And in fact over two months elapsed between seizure and decision. In these circumstances the restraint on the circulation of publications was far more thoroughgoing and drastic than any restraint upheld . . . in Kingsley. . . .

"Mass seizure in the fashion of this case was thus effected without any safeguards to protect legitimate expression."

Comment

Marcus v. Search Warrant appears to stand for the following proposition, as indicated in its headnote 6:

"The safeguards which the due process clause of the Fourteenth Amendment demands to assure nonobscene material the constitutional protection to which it is entitled are fatally absent from a state's procedures authorizing the search for and seizure of allegedly obscene publications . . . where (1) the procedures authorize a court to issue a warrant to search for and seize obscene material on the sworn complaint of a police officer stating facts indicating that obscene material is being kept in any place or building, without scrutiny by the court of any materials considered by the complainant to be obscene and (2) the warrant gives the broadest discretion to police officers executing it, leaving to the individual judgment of each the selection of such materials as are, in his view, obscene, notwithstanding that he has not previously examined any of the material he seizes."

It should be noted that the facts in *Marcus v. Search Warrant* involved a *massive* seizure of publications and an inability to keep *any* copies of the publications on the market, the obscenity or nonobscenity of which were determined on the spot by the use of a list or judgment of the peace officer. This was a type of "prior restraint" found to be unconstitutional. The Court reiterated its support of the procedure in the *Kingsley Book* case, but did not indicate that any "prior restraint" procedure more restrictive than

519

Kingsley Book would be condemned. It did indicate that Missouri had stepped over the line.

It would appear that Section 22-a of the New York Code of Criminal Procedure is a constitutional and effective method that should be considered by the various state legislatures. New York and other states that adopt said procedure might contemplate the addition of motion pictures to the type of material against which a limited injunction may issue. The comments made later in this report under film cases should be consulted.

    (h) *Manual Enterprises v. Day*
        370 U.S. 478, 8 L. Ed. 2d 639
        (Decided June 25, 1962)

The Alexandria Virginia Postmaster withheld delivery of copies of three homosexual magazines which had been deposited for delivery as second class mail on the ground that they were obscene for homosexuals applying an "average homosexual" test instead of the "average person" test. The publishers of the magazines brought suit in the U. S. District Court for the District of Columbia.

The Court reporter says:

"On certiorari, the Supreme Court reversed, *but could not agree upon an* opinion" [emphasis supplied].

Two of the Justices, Harlan and Stewart, said that:

"These magazines cannot be deemed so offensive on their face as to affront current community standards of decency—a quality that we shall hereafter refer to as 'patent offensiveness' or 'indecency.' Lacking that quality, the magazines cannot be deemed legally 'obscene' and we need not consider the proper 'audience' by which their 'prurient interest' appeal should be judged. . . .

"Obscenity under the federal statute thus requires proof of two distinct elements: (1) 'patent offensiveness'; and (2) 'prurient interest' appeal. Both must conjoin before challenged material can be found obscene. . . . In most obscenity cases, to be sure, the two elements tend to coalesce, for that which is patently offensive will also usually carry the requisite prurient interest appeal. . . .

"To consider that the 'obscenity' exception in the area of constitutionally protected free speech or press . . . does not require any determination as to the patent offensiveness vel non of the material itself might well put the American public in jeopardy of being denied access to many worthwhile works in literature, science or art. For one would not have to travel far even among the acknowledged masterpieces in any of these fields to find works whose 'dominant theme' might, not beyond reason, be claimed to appeal to the 'prurient interest' of the reader or observer."

Justices Harlan and Stewart went on to say that in their opinion the relevant community under the *federal* statute is a national standard of decency [emphasis supplied].

Three of the other Justices concurred in the judgment of reversal on the ground that the statute did not authorize the Postmaster General to exclude matter from the mails on his own determination of what is obscene.

Comment

It is quite obvious that this is *not* a Supreme Court opinion. The separate opinions are not precedent binding on any court and under familiar principles do not become the law of the land. They represent only the individual opinions of the authors. It seems clear that this case does not modify the *Roth* test in any way, nor can two out of nine Justices establish a principle that the 'community standard' by which Federal Obscenity Statutes are to be tested is a 'national' one. It is to be noted that these Justices based part of their reasoning on the Hicklin Rule, which the Supreme Court rejected in the *Roth* case.

It should be noted, however, in *Roth* that that Court could perceive no significant difference between its test for obscenity and that developed by the American Law Institute (see discussion of *Roth* case above) to the effect that

"a thing is obscene if, considered as a whole, its predominant appeal is to prurient interest . . . *and if it goes substantially beyond customary limits of candor in description or representation of such matters.*"

In *Roth,* however, the remark was that the Court could see no significant difference between the two delineations. It, however, did not adopt the A.L.I. "test" apparently believing that the "average person" and "contemporary community standards" criteria were sufficient to protect masterpieces from proscription even though they might appeal to the prurient interest of a small segment of the community. At all events, *Manual Enterprises v. Day,* not being a precedent, leaves the *Roth* test unchanged and the *Roth* case unmodified.

(i) *Bantam Books v. Sullivan*
   372 U.S. 58, 9 L. Ed. 2d 584
   (Decided February 18, 1963)
The Rhode Island legislature created a commission for the purpose of combatting juvenile delinquency and conferred on it the power to educate the public concerning literature containing obscene material or manifestly tending to corrupt the youth. The commission's practice was to notify a distributor that certain designated books or magazines distributed by him had been declared by a majority of its members to be objectionable for sale, distribution or display to youths under 18 years of age. These notices phrased virtually as orders, reasonably so understood by the distributor of plaintiff's books, in fact stopped the circulation of the listed publications.

Justice Brennan, speaking for the Court at 9 L. Ed. 2d 591, stated:

"It is true that appellant's books have not been seized or banned by the State and that no one has been prosecuted for their possession or sale. But though the commission is limited to *informal sanctions—the threat of invoking legal sanctions and other means of coercion, persuasion, and intimidation*—the record amply demonstrates that the Commission deliberately set about to achieve the suppression of publications deemed 'objectionable' [emphasis supplied]. . . . We are not the first court to look through forms to their substance and recognize that informal censorship may sufficiently inhibit the circulation of publications to warrant injunctive relief.

"It is not as if this were not regulation by the State of Rhode

521

Island. The acts and practices of the members and Executive Secretary of the commission disclosed on their record were performed under color of state law and so constituted acts of the state within the meaning of the Fourteenth Amendment. . . .

"We hold that the system of informal censorship disclosed by this record violates the Fourteenth Amendment. . . .

"We do not mean to suggest that private consultation between law enforcement officers and distributors prior to the Institution of a judicial proceeding can never be constitutionally permissible. We do not hold that law enforcement officers must renounce all informal contacts with persons suspected of violating valid laws prohibiting obscenity. Where such consultation is genuinely undertaken with the purpose of aiding the distributor to comply with such laws and avoid prosecution, it need not retard the full enjoyment of First Amendment freedoms."

Justice Clark, concurring in the result, stated at page 595:

"As I read the opinion of the Court, it does much fine talking about freedom of expression . . . but as if shearing a hog, comes up with little wool. In short, it creates the proverbial tempest in a teapot over a number of notices sent out by the Commission asking . . . cooperation. . . . The storm was brewed from certain inept phrases in the notices wherein the Commission assumed the prerogative of issuing an 'order' to the police that certain publications which it deemed obscene are not to be sold, distributed or displayed to youths under eighteen years of age and stated that the Attorney General will act for us in case of non-compliance. But after all this expostulation the Court, *being unable to strike down Rhode Island's statute,* see Alberts v. California [emphasis supplied] . . . drops a demolition bomb on 'the Commission's practice' without clearly indicating what might be salvaged from the wreckage. . . .

"In my view the Court should simply direct the Commission to abandon its delusions of grandeur and leave the issuance of 'orders' to enforcement officials and . . . criminal regulation of obscenity to the prosecutors who can substitute prosecution for 'thinly veiled threats'. . . .

"As I read the opinion this is the extent of the limitations contemplated by the Court, leaving the Commission free, as my Brother Harlan indicates, *to publicize its findings as to the obscene character of any publication; to solicit the support of the public in preventing obscene publications from reaching juveniles; to furnish its findings to publishers, distributors and retailers of such publications and to law enforcement officials; and finally, to seek the aid of such officials in prosecuting offenders of its State's obscenity laws.* [Emphasis supplied]

"Certainly in the face of rising juvenile crime and lowering youth morality, the State is empowered consistent with the Constitution to use the above procedures in attempting to dispel the defilement of its youth by obscene publications."

Comment

It appears from the *Bantam Books* case that a state may properly set up a "Commission to Encourage Morality in Youth" appointed by the Governor or otherwise to serve with or without compensation as long as such Commission avoids the excesses

522

related in that case of issuing "orders" to police and threatening criminal prosecutions. Such a statute would be constitutional and we recommend it as an effective method of combatting obscenity, since it will be on a constant alert, devoted exclusively to this one area of concern. Suggested state legislation may be found later in this report for those states which desire to adopt it. (See also Mr. Harlan's comments.)

It is also to be noted that *Bantam Books* puts its stamp of approval on police officers giving advice to distributors as to the possible obscene nature of material to be distributed. This type of cooperation is to be encouraged since it, too, assists the distributor or retailer and prevents the obscenity in an effective manner and also eliminates the possibility of the distributor or retailer claiming lack of scienter.

    (j) *Jacobellis v. Ohio*
        378 U.S. 184, 12 L. Ed. 2d 793
        (Decided June 22, 1964)

The manager of a motion-picture theater in Ohio was convicted of violating an Ohio obscenity statute by possessing and exhibiting "The Lovers," a French film depicting an unhappy marriage and the wife's falling in love with a young archaeologist, and including in the last reel an explicit, but fragmentary and fleeting, love scene.

On appeal, the Supreme Court of the United States reversed, but the six Justices voting for reversal *were unable to agree upon an opinion in support of the decision* [emphasis supplied].

Brennan, J., joined by Goldberg, J., stated that (1) the constitutional test for obscenity is whether to the average person, applying contemporary community standards, the dominant theme of the material taken as a whole appeals to prurient interest; (2) under this test the community standards are a national standard; (3) in applying this test the Supreme Court must make an independent constitutional judgment on the facts of each case, and cannot merely decide whether there is substantial evidence to support a finding that certain material is obscene; and (4) under the constitutional test the film, "The Lovers," was not obscene.

Warren, Ch. J., joined by Clark, J., dissented, stating that (1) the constitutional test of obscenity is that expressed by Brennan, J., in (1) above, but that (2) under this test the community standards are local standards, and (3) in applying this standard the Court should avoid sitting as a "Super Censor" and should limit itself to a consideration only of whether there is sufficient evidence in the record upon which a finding of obscenity can be made under the constitutional test.

Harlan, J., dissented on the ground that the Constitution does not prohibit the states from banning any material which, taken as a whole, has been reasonably found in state judicial proceedings to treat with sex in a fundamentally offensive manner, under rationally established criteria for judging such material.

Comment

It is to be carefully noted that this is not a Supreme Court opinion and the only thing here decided was that the defendant was not to be convicted. The individual opinions of the separate Justices are not binding as precedents. In fact, if they were, certain anomalies would follow since: (1) two Justices said the community standards are national; (2) two Justices said that the community standards are local; (3) two Justices said that the Supreme Court must judge every case and cannot limit itself to a consideration of whether there is substantial evidence to support a finding of obscenity; and (4) two Justices said the Court should not be a super censor and should so restrict itself.

In passing, it should be noted that the Brennan-Goldberg opinions contained the remark that "material dealing with sex . . . that has . . . any . . . social importance may not be branded as obscenity and denied the constitutional protection nor may the constitutional status of the material be made to turn on a 'weighing' of its social importance against its prurient appeal, for a work cannot be proscribed unless it is 'utterly' without redeeming social importance."

It cannot be overemphasized that the opinion of two Judges out of nine does not make law or precedent and these remarks of these Justices are not the law of the land any more than their contention that community standards are national. It is interesting to note, however, that this opinion equates "any social importance" with the phrase "utterly without redeeming social importance," so that if you apply this reasoning a showing of "any social importance" would be enough to prevent proscription. This, of course, flys in the face of the *Roth* case on two counts, one that the *Roth* case states that if you apply the prurient interest test and determine it is obscene, then being obscene it is by nature stamped as "utterly without redeeming social importance." The other important statement in the *Roth* case that Brennan's statement is in conflict with, is the fact that *Roth* admits that obscenity has some slight "social value" but under Brennan doctrine (as he elaborates in *Fanny Hill*) anything with any "social value" cannot be obscene. It seems clear that *Roth* and Brennan on any social value theory are not compatible. We shall discuss this divergence at length under the *Memoirs* (Fanny Hill) case.

(k) *A Quantity of Books v. Kansas*
378 U.S. 205, 12 L. Ed. 2d 809
(Decided June 22, 1964)

Pursuant to a Kansas statute, the state attorney general filed an information with the district judge of Geary County, Kansas, alleging that a news service in the county had a stock of obscene paperback novels. Although not required by the statute, the attorney general identified the novels by title, and the district judge conducted a 45-minute ex parte inquiry in which he examined seven of the books. Concluding that the books appeared to be obscene literature, the district judge issued a warrant directing the county sheriff to seize them. After a subsequent full hearing, the Kansas District Court held that the novels were obscene and ordered the sheriff to stand ready to destroy them. The Supreme Court of Kansas affirmed.

On appeal, the Supreme Court of the United States reversed, but the seven justices voting for reversal *were unable to agree upon an opinion* in support of the decision [emphasis supplied].

Brennan, J., joined by Warren, Ch. J., White, J., and Goldberg, J., stated that the procedure leading to the seizure order was constitutionally deficient in not first allowing the news service an adversary hearing.

524

Harlan, J., joined by Clark, J., dissented on the grounds that Kansas could find the books obscene and that the Constitution does not require an adversary hearing on obscenity before seizure of allegedly obscene matter.

Comment

Again it should be noted that this is not a court opinion and therefore not a precedent that need be followed by anyone. It also involved a mass seizure of 1715 copies of 31 novels being all copies of the same to be found and the four Justices noted that "since the warrant here authorized the sheriff to seize all copies of the specified titles . . . the procedure was . . . deficient."

(1) *Freedman v. Maryland*
    380 U.S. 51
    13 L. Ed. 2d 649
    (Decided March 1, 1965)

A Maryland statute made it unlawful to exhibit a motion picture without having obtained a license. *Freedman* attacks the statute as unconstitutional, not on the requirement for submission, but on the procedure for an initial decision by the censorship board, which without judicial participation effectively barred exhibition unless an appeal is taken by the exhibitor to the court.

Justice Brennan, for a majority of the Court, stated at 13 L. Ed. 2d, page 654:

"Applying the settled rule of our cases, we hold that a non-criminal process which requires the prior submission of a film to a censor avoids constitutional infirmity only if it takes place under procedural safeguards designed to obviate the dangers of a censorship system. First the burden of proving that the film is unprotected expression must rest on the censor. . . . Second, while the state may require advance submission of all films, in order to proceed effectively to bar all showings of unprotected films, the requirement cannot be administered in a manner which would lend an effect of finality to the censor's determination whether a film constitutes protected expression. The teaching of our cases is that, because only a judicial determination in an adversary proceeding ensures the necessary sensitivity to freedom of expression, only a procedure requiring a judicial determination suffices to impose a valid final restraint. . . . To this end the exhibitor must be assured by statute or authoritative judicial construction that the censor will within a specified brief period either issue a license or go to court to restrain showing the film. Any restraint imposed in advance of a final judicial determination on the merits must similarly be limited to preservation of the status quo for the shortest fixed period with sound judicial resolution. . . . It is readily apparent that the Maryland procedural scheme does not satisfy these criteria. . . .

"How or whether Maryland is to incorporate the required procedural safeguards . . . is, of course, for the state to decide. But a model is not lacking. In Kingsley Books . . . we upheld a New York injunctive procedure designed to prevent the sale of obscene books. . . .

"The requirement of prior submission to a censor sustained in *Times Film* is consistent with our recognition that films differ from other forms of expression. Similarly, we think that the nature of the motion picture industry may suggest different time limits for judicial determination. It is common knowledge that films are scheduled well before actual exhibition. . . . One possible scheme would be to allow the exhibitor or distributor to submit his film early enough to ensure an orderly final disposition of his case before the scheduled exhibition date— far enough in advance so that the exhibitor could safely advertise the opening on a normal basis. Failing such a scheme or sufficiently early submission under such a scheme, the statute would have to require adjudication considerably more prompt than has been the case under the Maryland statute."

Comment

The Court has clearly indicated to the State of Maryland and to the various states and municipalities the basis for an effective statute to constitutionally inhibit obscenity without interfering with nonobscene motion pictures. After this case the Maryland statute was amended to comply with its requirements. The revised statute may be found in the Legislative Recommendations section of this report and we recommend its adoption by the states. Any state that prefers not to have a state board of review should adopt legislation in aid of those municipalities within the state which desire to utilize the device of local ordinances. This legislation should be designed primarily to assure the prompt judicial determination required by the *Freedman* case.

(m) *A Book Named . . . Memoirs of a*
Woman of Pleasure
v. Attorney General of Massachusetts
383 U.S. 413, 16 L. Ed. 2d 1
(Decided March 21, 1966)

In a proceeding instituted in a Massachusetts state court by the state attorney general, the book commonly known as "Fanny Hill" was declared obscene. On appeal, the Supreme Court reversed. The Court Reporter, at 16 L. Ed. 2d 1, states:

"The . . . members of the Court . . . *did not agree upon an opinion*" [emphasis supplied].

Justices Brennan, Warren and Fortas stated that the Massachusetts court erred in holding that a book need not be "unqualifiedly worthless before it can be deemed obscene," and they stated their opinion at 16 L. Ed. 2d 5 that:

"Three elements must coalesce: it must be established that (a) the dominant theme of the material taken as a whole appeals to a prurient interest in sex; (b) the material is patently offensive because it affronts contemporary community standards relating to the description or representation of sexual matters and (c) the material is utterly without redeeming social value. . . .

"Even on the view of the court below that Memoirs possessed only a modicum of social value, its judgment must be reversed."

Justice Clark's opinion appears at 16 L. Ed. 2d 18:

"*While there is no majority opinion* in this case, there are three justices who import a *new test* into that laid down in Roth [emphasis supplied], namely that 'a book cannot be proscribed unless it is found to be *utterly* without redeeming social value.' *I agree* with my Brother White *that such a condition rejects the basic holding of Roth* and gives the smut artist free rein to carry on his dirty business. My note in that case—which was the deciding one for the majority opinion—was cast solely because the Court declared the test of obscenity to be: 'whether to the average person, applying contemporary community standards, the dominant theme of the material taken as a whole appeals to prurient interest.' I understood that test to include only two constitutional requirements: (1) the book must be judged as a whole, not by its parts; and (2) it must be judged in terms of its appeal to the prurient interest of the average person, applying contemporary community standards. Indeed, obscenity was denoted in Roth as having *'such slight social value as a step to truth that any benefit that may be derived . . . is clearly outweighed by the social interest in order and morality'* [emphasis supplied by Justice Clark]. Moreover, in no subsequent decision of this *Court* has any 'utterly without redeeming social value' test been suggested much less expounded [emphasis supplied]. The first reference to such a test was made by my Brother Brennan in Jacobellis v. Ohio . . . seven years after Roth in an opinion joined only by Justice Goldberg. . . ."

Justice White, in his opinion at 16 L. Ed. 2d 29, stated:

"In Roth v. United States . . . the Court held a publication to be obscene if its predominant theme appeals to the prurient interest in a manner exceeding customary limits of candor. Material of this kind, the Court said, is 'utterly without redeeming social importance' and is therefore unprotected by the First Amendment.

"To say that material within the Roth definition of obscenity is nevertheless not obscene if it has some redeeming social value is to reject one of the basic propositions of the Roth case—that such material is not protected *because* it is inherently and utterly without social value.

"If 'social importance' is to be used . . . obscene material, however far beyond customary limits of candor, is immune if it has any literary style, if it contains any historical references or language characteristic of a bygone day, or even if it is printed or bound in an interesting way. Well written, especially effective obscenity is protected; the poorly written is vulnerable. And why shouldn't the fact that some people buy and read such material prove its social value?

"A fortiari, if the predominant theme of the book appeals to the prurient interest as stated in Roth, but the book nevertheless contains here and there a passage descriptive of character, geography or architecture, the book would not be 'obscene' under the social importance test. I had thought that Roth counseled the contrary: that the character of the book is fixed by its predominant theme and is not altered by the presence of minor themes of a different nature. The Roth Court's emphatic reliance on the quotation from Chaplinsky . . . means nothing less: . . .

'Such utterances are no essential part of any exposition of ideas, and are of such slight social value as a step to truth that any benefit that may be derived from them is clearly

527

outweighed by the social interest in order and morality.'
[Emphasis supplied by Mr. White]

"In my view 'social importance' is not an independent test of obscenity but is relevant only to determine the predominant prurient interest of the material, a determination which the court or the jury will make based on the material itself and all the evidence of the case, expert or otherwise."

Comment

The promotion of the opinion of Brennan-Warren and Fortas as a Court opinion that modified the *Roth* case has been both deceitful and insidious. Many states were urged to and did modify their obscenity statutes to build in a rule that actually contradicted the Supreme Court's holding in the *Roth* case and the Roth test and today we are paying ten-fold for our lack of vigilance. Justice Clark's prophetic statement in the *Fanny Hill* case we know now is true. He said such a condition "gives the smut artist free rein to carry on his dirty business." It is quite obvious that Justices Clark and White are correct when they say in "Fanny Hill" that there is no such test. We submit that "utterly without redeeming social importance" is not part of the definition of the word "obscene" nor part of the test for obscenity for the following reasons:

(1) There is no Court opinion in "Fanny Hill" and the opinions of three Judges out of nine do not constitute a binding precedent so as to require any court or legislature to follow their suggestions. It is not the law of the land.

(2) *Roth* is a Court opinion and it does not use the phrase as part of its test for obscenity.

(3) Once the *Roth* test is applied to a disputed work and it is decided to be "obscene" then *Roth* conclusively presumes the material to be utterly without redeeming social importance.

(4) *Roth* says obscenity has social value, but that value is outweighed by the interest in morality. Three Justices in "Fanny Hill" say if it has any social value it is not obscene. This contradicts *Roth* in an essential manner and is in error.

(5) The charge to the Jury approved in the *Roth* case did not have a "social value" or "social importance" or "utterly without redeeming social value" test or phrase. Since *Roth* is still the *only Supreme Court opinion* on the definition of obscenity, then no social value "test" need be given to any Jury nor be made part of any statute. If it were a necessary charge, *Roth* would have insisted upon it.

(6) The more recent lower court decisions have recognized that *Roth* is still the test unencumbered by subsequent "no majority" opinions, for example.

Judge Barnes in his concurring opinion in *Wagonheim v. Maryland Board of Censors,* Court of Appeals Maryland, October 22, 1969, No. 212, holding "I Am Curious (Yellow)" obscene in that state, said:

"Some have thought that the third 'test' (utterly without redeeming social value) was finally brought into the law by the decision in Memoirs, supra in 1966. But, alas, again the 'test' did not receive the approval of a majority of the Supreme Court . . . Mr. Justice Clark, indeed, in his dissenting opinion in Memoirs observed that the social value test was 'novel' and that *only three* members of the Supreme Court held to it. He further pointed out that in his opinion, such a test *rejects* the *Roth* test to which, as above indicated a *majority* of the Supreme Court *did agree*. Even in the case of *Redrup v. New York,* 386 U.S. 767, 18 L. Ed. 2d 515 (1967) . . . the *per curiam* opinion of the Supreme Court was careful to state that the necessity of meeting the three pronged test was one held *only* by certain justices in Memoirs."

Judge Barnes goes on to say that the recent case of *Stanley v. State of Georgia,* 394 U.S. 557, 22 L. Ed. 2d 542, decided April 7, 1969, "seems to equate the cases subsequent to the decision in *Roth* as continuing the *Roth* test."

Judge Nelson K. Mintz of the New Jersey Superior Court in the case of *Lordi et al v. Grove Press et al,* decided December 9, 1969, stated in the trial of "I Am Curious (Yellow)" in that state that:

"My conclusion is that the dominant theme of this motion picture taken as a whole appeals to a prurient interest. I also find that the film is patently offensive because it affronts contemporary community standards relating to the description or representation of sexual matters . . . on the basis of all the evidence I reluctantly and with regret conclude that 'I Am Curious (Yellow)' does possess a modicum of redeeming social value." (Note the word modicum was used by Justice Brennan in "Fanny Hill." New Jersey statute has "the Social Value test." Contrast this result with the result obtained on the same motion picture in Arizona which does not have this unnecessary "test".)

Judge Paul W. LaPrade, in the County Superior Court of the State of Arizona on December 8, 1969, case No. 228092, rendered an opinion that "I Am Curious (Yellow)" was obscene. This was the case of *National General Corporation v. Mummert, Sheriff of Maricopa County.* As to the context of this film ruled not obscene in New York and New Jersey, Judge LaPrade says:

"1. A few minutes after being introduced to Borje by her father, Lena takes him into her room where they commenced an all night love scene. Their nude bodies were graphically depicted, head to toe, caressing while standing up, on their knees, kissing her breasts and finally lying on their backs tired and pensive. She tells him he is number 24, but the first 19 were no fun. He lies on top of her in the morning for the obvious purpose of more intercourse. After they leave, father urinates in the wash basin.

2. Later that day Lena and Borje engage in a non-violent protest against the monarchy of Sweden. Standing in front of the Royal Palace in broad day light, she takes off her panties, they straddle the balustrade, she sitting on him. The Swedish national anthem plays as they copulate in an explicit and graphic manner.

3. On retreat, Lena reads a sex manual depicting various positions of sexual intercourse. They were clearly shown on the screen.

4. On the grass at retreat, Borje tosses Lena to the ground and performs oral-genital acts (cunnilingus). They make love in the nude, pubic areas and genitals in full view. She caresses and kisses his penis and simulates fellatio. He caresses her genitals.

529

5. In the crotch of a large and ancient tree they experiment for a good sexual intercourse position. Trousers of each are then removed and he mounts her in the tree. Intercourse is explicit and certain.

6. They struggle in a shallow pond. The scene closes with Borje nude on top of Lena, obviously having carnal knowledge.

7. Back at the ranch house, Lena and Borje again disrobe, struggle in the nude in full view. Pubic areas at close up, and he takes her from the rear as they engage in either violent sexual intercourse or sodomy. They retire to the next room on the bare floor, still nude, flat on her back with loins entangled. Intercourse is clear, open and obvious.

8. The fantasy of her dream depicts her twenty-three experimental lovers tied to a tree as Borje approaches. After gunning him down she calmly takes out her knife, unbuttons his pants, pulls them down and emasculates his genitals.

9. The movie closed with Lena and Borje standing nude in full view facing camera while the hospital attendants delouse them."

Judge LaPrade states:

"The Supreme Court of the United States in 1957 in *Roth vs. United States,* 354 U.S. 476, 77 S. Ct. 1304; held that the legal test of obscenity was twofold. To condemn a motion picture it must be established that (a) the dominant theme of the material taken as a whole appeals to a prurient interest in sex, and (b) the material is patently offensive because it affronts contemporary community standards relating to the description or representation of sexual matters.

"*Fanny Hill,* in an opinion written by Justice Brennan, joined only by Justices Warren and Fortas, injected what has been interpreted as establishing a third, independent test of obscenity as applied to a book. Unless it is found to be 'utterly without redeeming social value' it cannot be suppressed. Further it held that the social value could not be weighed against the prurient interest or patent offensiveness tests.

"This third 'social value' test has given the Courts no little difficulty and of late has been seriously questioned.

"In *Roth* the Court held that obscenity was not protected because 'implicit in the history of the First Amendment is the rejection of obscenity as utterly without redeeming social importance . . .'

"*Jacobellis vs. Ohio,* 378 U.S. 184 (1964), the next significant Supreme Court decision on obscenity, unlike *Roth,* did not contain a majority opinion of the Court. Justice Brennan, joined only by Justice Goldberg, announced the Judgement of the Court and therein expanded upon the concept of social value as contained in *Roth.* Then came *Fanny Hill,* where Justice Brennan, misinterpreted, in my opinion, the teaching of *Roth* and pronounced the 'social value' test.

"Justice White foresaw the flaw of the Brennan doctrine in *Jacobellis* at page 461. In *Fanny Hill,* Justices White and Clark criticized it, as did Justice Harlan. The plurality opinion upon which the 'social value' test was founded was criticized by Justice Frances in *G. P. Putnam's Son vs. Calissi,* a New Jersey decision in 1967 reported in 50 New Jersey 397.

"*Stanley vs. Georgia,* 394 U.S. 557 (1960), the Supreme Court's

most recent decision in the field of obscenity supports the view
that the standards for obscenity set forth in *Roth* have not
been superseded by the plurality opinion of Justice Brennan
in *Fanny Hill.* A majority of the Court joined in the opinion
of Stanley. *Roth* was cited frequently as the applicable law.
Fanny Hill, decided nine years after *Roth,* is cited only casually
in a footnote at page 561. Note 6. The highest Court of Kentucky in *Cain vs. Kentucky,* 437 Southwest 2nd, 269, petition
for certiorari filed, 38 U.S. Law Week 3054, stands upon *Roth*
and rejected the *Brennan* doctrine.
"The 'social value' rule, if literally applied to a motion picture
film means that no matter how extremely offensive it may be,
if any part of the film deals with social ideas of some significance, it cannot be declared obscene.
"The 'social value' test is not part of the Arizona Statute
(Supra).
"TRIAL COURT DUTY
"It is the duty of a trial judge to follow the decisions of the
United States Supreme Court on constitutional rules, whether
he agrees with or likes the rule or not. In all faithfulness to
his oath of office it is his duty to follow it. The fact that
Justices Warren and Fortas are no longer on the Court is immaterial.
"The question is not whether I will follow *Fanny Hill,* but
rather, what is the rule of law in that decision.
"A majority of the Court agreed upon the result, and there
is a Judgement. There are five different rules of law expressed
in *Fanny Hill.* The Supreme Court was not able to muster a
majority for any one of them. If the nine Justices cannot agree
on a rule, how can a Superior Court trial judge in Maricopa
County, Arizona, be expected to second guess or speculate on
what the real significance of the Brennan 'social value' rule is.
"At my request, attorney John P. Frank of the Arizona Bar
filed an Amicus Statement in this case on the single question
of his view of the law of obscenity in the light of Fanny Hill.
His article, *Obscenity: Some Problems of Values in The Use of
Experts,* 41 Wash. L. Rev. 631 (1966), anticipates the prob-
lem. Mr. Frank is widely known as a constitutional lawyer.
His writings on constitutional questions have been published
as authoritative and his analysis of the Fanny Hill-Plurality
Opinion was sorely needed by the Court.
"Mr. Frank has counselled the Court that there is no rule of
law in *Fanny Hill* binding upon it except that the result is,
and in a similar book case the same result must be reached.
Further, that I must look to *Roth* as the true test of obscenity.
"He too points out that the recent case of *Stanley vs. Georgia*
barely mentions *Fanny Hill* and is an exposition of *Roth.*
"I concur with Mr. Frank in that the Brennan 'social value'
doctrine of *Fanny Hill* is not a rule of law binding upon this
Court to the extent that I must consider it as a third independent test of obscenity without weighing it against the doctrine
set forth in *Roth* being the prurient interest and patent offensiveness tests.

CONCLUSION

"The motion picture 'I Am Curious (Yellow)' fails to pass

531

the *Roth* test of obscenity in that its dominant theme is the sexual activity of the heroine-Lena, that activity appeals to a prurient interest in sex, and the film taken as a whole clearly affronts contemporary community standards of candor in the expression of sex. By virtue thereof, the subtle and confusing messages concerning politics and social problems lose whatever minimal social importance they may have had. The suppression of this motion picture will not deprive mankind of anything worthwhile. . . .

"My duty is to apply the Arizona law which prohibits the exhibition of such motion pictures. My judgement and opinion herein is a judicial expression in response to the desires of the great mass of the American people.

". . . Chief Judge Lumbard of the Court of Appeals (Second Circuit) in his dissenting opinion in *United States vs. A Motion Picture* Entitled 'I Am Curious (Yellow)', 404 Fed. 2nd 196 (1968), hits the nail on the head when he said:

'the only interest to the viewer arises from the uncertainty of the method of mutual sexual gratification in which the hero and heroine will next indulge . . .'

"The fate of this particular motion picture is not important but the principle involved is. Clever pornographers will soon bombard this country with films depicting increasingly explicit sexuality unless the trial judges and appellate courts take a stand. This is mine."

Mr. Charles Rembar, who won the *Fanny Hill* case, states in his book *"The End of Obscenity"* at page 203, commenting on the California statute:

"The California anti-obscenity statute had been recently amended, and liberals in the legislature managed to incorporate a *value* test in the statute itself (it is a fair assumption that most of the legislators did not know what they were doing)."

[Parenthetical phrase is Mr. Rembar's]

Query does it apply today to the State legislatures and the U. S. Congress? Have Congressmen studied the necessity for this phrase and the vitiating effect it has on otherwise valid legislation? Will they permit a minor "over 17" or "over 15", as the case may be, to see the scenes depicted by Judge LaPrade in Note 3? Why would this be permitted for anyone?

In the case of *Cain v. Kentucky,* 437 S.W. 2d, 769 (1969), a unanimous court, after quoting the rule of law in the *Roth* case, *supra,* held:

"We have found no case subsequent to the *Roth* opinion which has retracted, modified or overruled the above language."

And the court further held:

"Appellants further contend that the legal test of obscenity was modified in *Memoirs v. Mass.,* 383 U.S. 413, 418, 6 L. Ed. 2d 1, 5, 86 S. Ct. 975 (1966), and as a result of that opinion a third separate independent test is added to the requirements of our present statute and that is that the material must be 'utterly without redeeming social value.' We do not read this requirement in the case for the reason that this again was a no clear majority opinion. The test was joined in by only three justices of the court. Conceding that these three justices interpreted the *Memoirs* case as making the redeeming social

532

value test a new factor for the determination of obscenity, this test was not approved by the other justices of the court and, therefore, in our opinion it has not become the law on this subject. We have examined the *Roth-Alberts* case, supra, and believe it still to be controlling authority upon the test of what is obscenity."

Judge Tauro of the Massachusetts Court (Chief Judge of the Suffolk County Superior Court), in the case of *Commonwealth vs. Karalexis et al,* on November 12, 1969, concluded that the test for obscenity as set down in the *Roth* case, *supra,* is still the law of the land, "unencumbered by subsequent decisions." He observed that the so-called "social value" doctrine has never received the support of the majority of the Supreme Court, and so is not an independent test. Judge Tauro contends that the 1969 *Stanley vs. Georgia, supra,* decision, "confirms that *Roth,* the last judicial definition of obscenity to be endorsed by a MAJORITY of the Supreme Court, has not been superseded by the PLU-RALITY OPINION of Justice Brennan in MEMOIRS." [Emphasis by Judge Tauro] In the appendix of his decision, Judge Tauro scored the "theory of social value" as the most influential factor "contributing to the prevailing confusion over the role and power of the courts in this area." He said that in *Jacobellis* and *Memoirs,* in opinions unsupported by a majority of the Supreme Court, Justice Brennan "attempted to postulate the amorphous and ambiguous concept of 'utter lack of redeeming social value' as the determinant for obscenity and as a substitute for the rule of reason endorsed by a majority of the United States Supreme Court in *Roth*."

The remarks of the Judges in these cases and the contrasting situations where the so-called "utterly without redeeming social value" "test" is applied and where it is not, should impress Congress and the legislators of the various states to realize that this unnecessary test should be eliminated from any statute where it now is incorporated (as unnecessary, obscenity breeding and contrary to *Roth*). In those states where it is not incorporated, it should not be and if a Judge of such state has by error deemed it to be part of the definition of obscenity, that error should be corrected by appropriate legislative action.

If further proof is needed that the *Memoirs (Fanny Hill)* three Justice opinion is not a precedent binding on anyone, it may be found in opinions of the United States Supreme Court itself. In 29 American Jurisprudence Second at Section 195 of the topic "Courts", we find the following:

"A decision by an equally divided court does not establish a precedent required to be followed under the stare decisis doctrine. And where the members of the court unanimously or by a majority vote reach a decision but cannot even by a majority agree on the reason therefor, *no point of law is established by the decision and it cannot be a precedent covered by the stare decisis rule.*" [Emphasis supplied]

As authority for this statement, American Jurisprudence quotes the United States Supreme Court case of *United States v. Pink, Superintendent of Insurance of the State of New York,* 315 U.S. 203, 86 L. Ed. 796 (1941).

Referring to that case, we find the following rule:

"Nor was our affirmance of the judgment in that case by an equally divided court an authoritative precedent. . . . The lack of an agreement by a majority of the court on the principles of law involved prevents it from being an authoritative determinate for other cases. Hertz v. Woodward, 218 U.S. 205, 213-214."

In the *Hertz* case the United States Supreme Court made it crystal clear when it said:

"The principles of law involved *not having been agreed upon by a majority of the court sitting prevents the case from becoming an authority either in this or in* inferior courts." [Emphasis supplied]

Applying this to the *Memoirs* case, it is quite clear that three is not a majority and therefore, in the words of the United States Supreme Court, this prevents that case "from becoming an authority either in this or in inferior courts."

The legislature of the State of New York became aware in its 1969 session of the contradiction of the "utterly without redeeming social value" "test" with the *Roth* test and also of the fact that this "test" in that statute was vitiating effective law enforcement and introduced legislation to excise the social value test from its statute. The bill passed the Assembly 123 to 10 and was referred to the Senate where its 20-member Codes Committee reported the same favorably to the Senate two days before final adjournment. In the rush for adjournment, however, the measure was not reached. It is to be reintroduced in the 1970 Session and its sponsors are confident that it will be adopted.

(n) *Ralph Ginzburg v. United States*
383 U.S. 463, 16 L. Ed. 2d 31
(Decided March 21, 1966)

The defendants, an individual and three corporations controlled by him, used the mail for distributing allegedly obscene literature; namely, the magazine Eros, containing articles and photo essays on love and sex; a biweekly newsletter, dedicated to "keeping sex an art and preventing it from becoming a science"; and "The Housewife's Handbook on Promiscuity." A judge sitting without a jury in the United States District Court for the Eastern District of Pennsylvania convicted defendants on charges of having violated the federal obscenity statute (18 USC §1461). The Court of Appeals for the Third Circuit affirmed. (338 F2d 12.)

On certiorari, the Supreme Court of the United States affirmed. In an opinion by Brennan, J., expressing the view of five members of the Court, it was held that even if the material involved was not obscene in the abstract, the trial judge's conclusion that the mailing of these publications offended the statute was supported by evidence showing that defendants engaged in the sordid business of pandering, that is, the business of purveying textual or graphic matter openly advertised to appeal to the erotic interest of defendants' customers.

At 16 L. Ed. 2d 40, the Court said that it could perceive no threat to First Amendment guarantees in thus holding that is close cases evidence of pandering may be probative with respect to the nature of the material in question and thus satisfy the *Roth* test.

534

Comment

This case stands for the proposition that the mode of distribution may be taken into account in determining the obscenity of the material involved. In other words, as the Court says, where the defendant is engaged in "the sordid business of pandering—the business of purveying textual or graphic matter openly advertised to appeal to the erotic interest of their customers," this may tip the scales in close obscenity cases. The Court recognizes that this pandering is to "the widespread weakness for titillation by pornography."

This case is significant in that it clearly shows the concern of the Court for protecting the public from moral corruption by being influenced by titillating advertisements; in other words, from seduction away from morality. It recognizes that the public can be influenced toward obscenity and that the government has a social interest in protecting the public against such influences.

(o) *Mishkin v. New York*
    383 U.S. 502, 16 L. Ed. 2d 56
    (Decided March 21, 1966)

The New York court found appellant guilty of violating a New York criminal obscenity statute by hiring others to prepare obscene books, publishing such books, and possessing them with intent to sell them.

On appeal, the Supreme Court of the United States affirmed. In an opinion by Brennan, J., expressing the views of five members of the Court it was held that the statute was not invalid either upon its face on the ground of vagueness, nor as applied, since the standard of obscenity laid down by the New York state courts was stricter than required by the federal constitutional standard, the state court's definition of scienter as an element of the offenses met the demands of the Federal Constitution, and the proof of scienter was adequate.

The Court also said at 16 L. Ed. 2d 62:

"Where the material is designed for and primarily disseminated to a clearly defined deviant sexual group, rather than the public at large, the prurient-appeal requirement of the Roth test is satisfied if the dominant theme of the material taken as a whole appeals to the prurient interest in sex of the members of that group."

Comment

It is to be noted that the New York statute as it then existed was interpreted as requiring a stricter standard (viz. hard core pornography) than *Roth*. As a result of the Court's remarks that their standard was unnecessarily strict, New York proceeded to amend its statute, but the legislators were led to believe that a social value test was required, so that instead of adopting the *Roth* test (applied in *Mishkin*) the *Roth* test encumbered by the vitiating and unnecessary *Fanny Hill* "social value" embellishment was passed. New York has since discovered that under its present statute it is doubtful that even hard core pornography can be proscribed since hard core pornography will be saved under its test if a "dash" or, as Brennan puts it, a "modicum" of social value is added. New York is actually worse off now than it was at the time of *Mishkin*.

535

(p) *Redmond v. United States*
      384 U.S. 264, 16 L. Ed. 2d 521
      (Decided May 23, 1966)

Comment

This case stands for the proposition that a conviction of a husband and wife of mailing films of each other posing in the nude will be vacated upon motion of the Justice Department that the initiation of the prosecution violated the Justice Department policy. The Solicitor General pointed out in his opinion such prosecution should be confined to those cases involving repeated offenders or other circumstances characterized as aggravated.

(q) *Redrup v. State of New York*
      386 U.S. 767, 18 L. Ed. 2 515
      (Decided May 8, 1967)

In this case certain girlie and other magazines were declared not to be obscene.

Comment

In reversing the judgment of obscenity the Court noted that only certain members of the Court (a reference to the three Justices) held to the "utterly without redeeming social value" test.

(r) *Rabeck v. New York*
      391 U.S. 462, 20 L. Ed. 2d 741
      (Decided May 27, 1968)

A New York statute that was designed to protect minors under 18 years of age (which had been repealed) was struck down as vague because it prohibited the sale of magazines which would appeal to the lust of persons under 18 years of age.

Comment

This particular statute, if properly amended to comply with the *Rabeck* case in the respect indicated, deserves consideration since it was an attempt to be more precise and explicit in defining what is obscene for minors. An example of such statute, amended in this respect, is attached to this report.

(s) *Interstate Circuit v. City of Dallas*
      390 U.S. 676, 20 L. Ed. 2d 235
      (Decided April 22, 1968)

An ordinance of the City of Dallas had classified a motion picture as "not suitable for young persons" by the city's motion picture classification board.

Justice Marshall for the Court held that the ordinance was unconstitutionally vague in that it failed to state narrowly drawn, reasonable and definite standards for the board to follow.

Comment

This Court reiterated the right of municipalities to enact ordinances but required precision. This case is taken into account in the suggested language for state and municipal ordinances in this field in the proposed legislation attached to this report. It is interesting to note that the Court, at 20 L. Ed. 2d 225, implies that it would uphold a properly drawn ordinance when it says:

"It is not our province to draft legislation. Suffice it to say

536

that we have recognized that some believe motion pictures possess a greater capacity for evil, particularly among the youth of a community, than other modes of expression . . . and we have indicated more generally that because of its strong and abiding interest in youth a state may regulate the dissemination to juveniles of, and their access to, material objectionable as to them, but which a state clearly could not regulate as to adults. *Ginsberg v. New York.* . . . Here we conclude that the absence of narrowly drawn, reasonable and definite standards for the officials to follow is fatal."

(t) *Tietel Film Corporation v. Cusack*
    390 U.S. 139, 19 L. Ed. 2d 966
    (Decided January 29, 1968)

In proceedings under the Chicago Motion Picture Censorship Ordinance, the Illinois Courts enjoined the showing of a motion picture. On appeal the United States Supreme Court reversed relying on *Freedman v. Maryland* on the ground that the ordinace was invalid in that it did not assure that the censor would, within a specified brief period, either issue a license or go into court to restrain showing the film, nor did it assure a prompt final judicial decision.

Comment

In this case the administrative process took 50 to 57 days to complete before a judicial decision was sought. The Court said, "The absence of any provision for a prompt judicial decision of the *trial* court" was fatal. It is again apparent that ordinances regulating the showing of motion pictures to adults or children must be carefully drawn to comply with *Freedman v. Maryland.* In some states it may be necessary for the state to aid municipalities by enacting legislation in aid of the municipal ordinance procedure so as to insure "a prompt judicial decision by the trial court." This promptness requirement was foreshadowed by the *Kingsley* decision *infra* and that case might be used as a model on the promptness requirement. See also our remarks under other motion picture cases and recommendations there made.

(u) *Sam Ginsberg v. New York*
    390 U.S. 629, 20 L. Ed. 2d 195
    (Decided April 22, 1968)

Defendant was convicted in New York of selling magazines to a minor under the age of 17 years in violation of a state statute prohibiting a person from knowingly selling to such a minor material "harmful to minors." That phrase was defined by the statute as meaning that quality of any description or representation of nudity, sexual conduct, when it predominantly appeals to the prurient interest of minors, is patently offensive to prevailing standards in the adult community as a whole with respect to what is suitable material for minors, and is utterly without redeeming social importance for minors.

On appeal the United States Supreme Court affirmed. The Court noted that the challenge was not to whether or not the magazines were obscene but to the question of whether the state could enact such a statute. In this case the United States Supreme Court affirmed the validity of the concept of variable obscenity. At page

537

20, L. Ed. 2d 202, the Court quotes with approval the New York Court of Appeals as follows:

"Material which is protected for distribution to adults is not necessarily constitutionally protected from restriction upon its dissemination to children. In other words, the concept of obscenity or of unprotected matter may vary according to the group to whom the questionable material is directed or from whom it is quarantined. Because of the state's exigent interest in presenting [apparently Court said preventing] distribution to children of objectionable material, it can exercise its power to protect the *health, safety, welfare* and *morals* of its community [emphasis supplied] by barring the distribution to children of books recognized to be suitable for adults."

The Court quotes numerous footnote articles on the propriety of protection for minors in this area.

At page 204, the United States Supreme Court, quoting one of its earlier decisions, says:

"The state has an interest 'to protect the welfare of children' and to see that they are 'safeguarded from abuses' which might prevent their 'growth into free and independent well-developed men and citizens'. The only question remaining therefore, is whether the New York legislature might rationally conclude . . . that exposure to the materials proscribed . . . constitutes such an 'abuse'. Section 484-e of the law states a legislative finding that the material condemned . . . is 'a basic factor in impairing the ethical and moral development of our youth and a clear and present danger to the people of the state'. It is very doubtful that this finding expresses an accepted scientific fact. But obscenity is not protected expression and may be suppressed without a showing of the circumstances which lie behind the phrase 'clear and present danger' in its application to protected speech. Roth v. United States.[9] . . . To sustain state power to exclude material defined as obscenity by 484-h *requires only that we be able to say that it was not irrational for the legislature to find that exposure to material condemned by the statute is harmful to minors* [emphasis supplied]. . . . To be sure, there is no lack of 'studies' which purport to demonstrate that obscenity is or is not 'a basic factor in impairing the ethical and moral development of youth . . . .' *But the growing consensus of commentators is that 'while these studies all agree that a causal link has not been demonstrated, they are equally agreed that a causal link has not been disproved either.* [Emphasis supplied] [Quoting numerous authorities] We do not demand of legislators *'scientifically certain criteria of legislation.'* We therefore cannot say that 484-h . . . has no rational relation to the objective of safeguarding such minors from harm." [Emphasis supplied]

The Court then proceeds to uphold the statute against claims of vagueness and notes that it has the required scienter element.

---

[9]"Our conclusion in Roth at 486-487, 1 L. Ed. 2d 1507, 1508 that the clear and present danger test was irrelevant to the determination of obscenity made it unnecessary in that case to consider the debate among the authorities whether exposure to pornography caused anti-social consequences."

Comment

The following should be noted:

1. Legislation which incorporates a concept of variable obscenity is constitutional.

2. Material may be obscene for children even though the same material may not be obscene for adults.

3. The legal basis for obscenity legislation for children is the state's interest in protecting the health, safety, welfare and morals of children. This is the same as the basis for all obscenity legislation, *viz.* "the state's interest in morality." See comments under *Roth*.

4. Obscenity is not protected expression and may be suppressed without regard to whether or not it creates a "clear and present danger" to the state or whether a causal link can be established between obscenity and anti-social effects.

5. The Court did not decide that the "girlie" magazines were obscene for children since Ginsberg did not base his case on their obscenity or non-obscenity. It is quite possible that they may have been declared not obscene on the basis that they were not "utterly without redeeming social importance" for children. As has been shown in prior discussion under the *Memoirs* case, a "modicum" of social importance is all that is required. This apparently means that such material for children can have 95% smut (even hard core pornography) as long as it has some "modicum" or a pinch of social importance. The danger with *Ginsberg v. New York* is that legislation is being drafted at the federal level and at the state level, building in this "social importance" test because the New York statute was upheld. Based on the *Roth* case it seems quite clear that "social importance" is not a necessary test for adults or minors and blind imitation of the New York statute will "foist" smut on our children. This element should be specifically eliminated in any minors statute. See our comments under the *Memoirs* case. Attached to this report is a variable obscenity statute which incorporates the concept of special legislation for children found in *Sam Ginsberg v. New York* without adding the vitiating "test" of "utterly without redeeming social importance" which is not required. The fact that the Supreme Court indicated that the New York statute was valid does not, in the light of the *Roth* case, indicate that a statute eliminating the social value test would not also be upheld.

(v) *Stanley v. Georgia*
   394 U.S. 557, 22 L. Ed. 2d 542
   (Decided April 7, 1969)

The defendant was tried and convicted in a Georgia court of knowingly having possession of obscene matter in violation of a Georgia statute. The obscene matter in question consisted of films which a state officer seized after federal and state agents had found them in a desk drawer in an upstairs bedroom of the defendant's home as they searched it pursuant to a search warrant relating to the defendant's alleged bookmaking activities. On appeal the Supreme Court of the United States reversed.

Justice Marshall, in delivering the opinion of the Court, stated at 22 L. Ed. 2d, page 549:

". . . Appellant is asserting . . . the right to satisfy his intellec-

539

tual and emotional needs in the privacy of his own home. He is asserting the right to be free from state inquiry into the contents of his library. Georgia contends that appellant does not have these rights, that there are certain types of materials that the individual may not read or even possess. Georgia justifies this assertion by arguing that the films in the present case are obscene. But we think that mere categorization of these films as 'obscene' is insufficient justification for such a drastic invasion of personal liberties guaranteed by the First and Fourteenth Amendments. Whatever may be the justifications for other statutes regulating obscenity, we do not think they reach into the privacy of one's own home. If the First Amendment means anything it means that a state has no business telling a man, sitting alone in his own house, what books he may read or what films he may watch."

At page 551, Justice Marshall states:

"Roth and the cases following that decision are not impaired by today's holding. As we have said, the states retain broad power to regulate obscenity; that power simply does not extend to mere private possession by the individual in the privacy of his own home."

Comment

This case stands for the proposition that mere private possession by an individual of matter that may be obscene in the privacy of his home cannot be considered a crime. It essentially decided a very narrow issue, but the pornographers would have us expand it to include the "right" to receive obscenity through the mails or by interstate carrier and the "right" to view obscene motion pictures in public or private theatres. Of course, these so-called "rights" would create corresponding rights in the pornographers to deliver the obscenity in the same fashion and to book and project the motion picture in a public or private theatre.

It is to be noted that the Court specifically held that *Roth* and the cases decided subsequent to *Roth* were not affected. It is quite clear that the basis of obscenity law both for adults (*Roth*) and minors (*Ginsberg*) remains the same and that is the state's interest in "morality". *Stanley v. Georgia* does not change this.

(w) *Van Cleef v. New Jersey*
23 L. Ed. 2d 728
(Decided June 23, 1969)

In this case the Court held that the seizure without a search warrant of several thousand articles including allegedly obscene books and magazines after a three-hour search of a 16-room house containing at least three floors could not be justified on the grounds that the search was incident to an allegedly lawful arrest.

Comment

The case does contain some indication of circumstances where seizure may be incident to an arrest without a search warrant.

Section 1. DEFINITIONS. As used in this Act:

(a) A thing is "obscene" if, by contemporary community standards, and considered as a whole, its predominant appeal is to prurient interest. As a matter of state public policy, anything which is obscene by this definition shall be conclusively deemed to be utterly without redeeming social importance and constitutes a public nuisance which should be abated. Any slight social value in such obscenity shall be deemed outweighed by the social interest in order and morality.

(b) "Prurient interest" is defined as a shameful or morbid interest in nudity, sex or excretion, which goes substantially beyond customary limits of candor in description or representation of such matters. If it appears from the character of the material or the circumstances of its dissemination that the subject matter is designed for, or directed to a specially susceptible audience, the subject matter shall be judged with reference to such audience. For the purpose of Section 7 of this Act, when the subject matter is distributed or exhibited to minors under 18 years of age, the subject matter shall be judged with reference to an average person in the community of the actual age of the minor to whom such material is distributed, or exhibited. In all other cases, the subject matter shall be judged with reference to the average person in the community.

(c) "Matter" means any book, magazine, newspaper, or other printed or written material or any picture, drawing, photograph, motion picture, play, night club performance, television production, or other pictorial representation, or any statue or other figure, or any recording, transcription or mechanical, chemical or electrical reproduction or any other articles, equipment, machines or materials.

(d) "Person" means any individual, partnership, firm, association, corporation or other legal entity.

(e) "Distribute" means to transfer possession of, whether with or without consideration, by any means.

(f) "Knowingly" means having actual or constructive knowledge of the obscene contents of the subject matter. A person has constructive knowledge of the obscene contents, if he has knowledge of facts which would put a reasonable and prudent man on notice as to the suspect nature of the material, and the failure to inspect the contents is either for the purpose of avoiding such disclosure or is due to reckless conduct.

(1) "Reckless conduct" is conduct which consciously disregards a substantial and unjustifiable risk that matter may be obscene. The risk must be of such a nature and degree that, considering the nature and purpose of the actor's conduct and the circumstances known to him, its disregard involves a gross deviation from the standard of conduct that an average law-

abiding person would observe in the actor's situation under like circumstances.

Section 2. AFFIRMATIVE DEFENSE. This Act shall not apply to persons who may possess or distribute obscene matter or participate in conduct otherwise proscribed by this Act when such possession, distribution or conduct occurs in the course of law enforcement activities, or in the course of bona fide scientific, educational, or comparable research or study, or like circumstances of justification. If this issue is not presented by the prosecution's evidence, the defendant may raise the same as an affirmative defense by presenting some evidence thereon. Where raised, the prosecution must sustain the burden of proving the defendant guilty beyond a reasonable doubt as to that issue.

Section 3. JURY TRIAL. Criminal prosecutions and other proceedings involving the ultimate issue of obscenity (as distinguished from the issue of "probable cause") shall be tried by jury, unless both parties to the action waive a jury trial in writing or by statement in open court, entered in the minutes, with the approval of the court.

Section 4. FUNCTION OF JURY AND COURT IN OBSCENITY TRIAL.

(a) The jury represents a cross section of the community and has a special aptitude for expressing the view of the average person. As the trier of fact, it is the exclusive judge of the common conscience of the community and the embodiment of community standards.

(b) Where a jury question is presented, i.e., that reasonable men may differ whether the subject matter or conduct is obscene, the trial court shall have no power either before, during, or after trial to dismiss an obscenity proceeding on the ground that the subject matter, or conduct, is not obscene as a matter of law; nor may an appellate court after trial set aside an obscenity verdict on the same grounds if an examination of the evidence indicates the verdict is supported by sufficient evidence.

(c) Any dismissal by the trial court on such grounds is appealable by the people.

Section 5. PRESUMPTION. Every person is presumed to have knowledge of the standards that exist in the community and what the jury or trier of fact may declare to be obscene.

Section 6. GENERAL SALE OR DISTRIBUTION, ETC., OF OBSCENE MATTER; PENALTY. Every person who knowingly: sends or causes to be sent, or brings or causes to be brought, into this State for sale or distribution or exhibition; or in this State either (1) prepares, publishes, prints, exhibits, distributes, or offers to distribute; or (2) has in his possession with intent to distribute or to exhibit or offer to distribute; any obscene matter is guilty of a misdemeanor.

Section 7. DISTRIBUTION OF OBSCENE MATTER TO MINOR; PENALTY. Every person, who with knowledge that a person is a minor under 18 years of age, or who, while in possession of such facts that he should reasonably know that such person is a minor under 18 years of age, knowingly sends or causes to be sent, exhibits, distributes, or offers to distribute any obscene matter to a minor under 18 years of age, is guilty of a misdemeanor.

542

Section 8. HIRING, EMPLOYING, ETC., MINOR TO ENGAGE IN ACTS DESCRIBED IN SECTION 4; PENALTY. Every person who, with knowledge that a person is a minor under 18 years of age, or who, while in possession of such facts that he should reasonably know that such person is a minor under 18 years of age, hires, employs, or uses such minor to do or assist in doing any of the acts described in Sections 6 or 7, is guilty of a misdemeanor.

Section 9. ADVERTISEMENT, PROMOTION OF SALE, ETC., OF MATTER REPRESENTED TO BE OBSCENE; PENALTY. Every person who writes, creates, or solicits the publication or distribution of advertising or other promotional material for, or who otherwise advertises or promotes the sale, distribution, or exhibition of matter represented or held out by him to be obscene, whether or not such matter exists in fact, or is obscene, is guilty of a misdemeanor.

Section 10. PARTICIPATION IN LEWD EXPOSURE OR SIMULATED ACTS OF SEXUAL INTERCOURSE OR PERVERSION AS A PART OF A PLAY, ETC.

(a) Every person who, during the course of a play, night club act, motion picture, television production, or other exhibition, or mechanical reproduction of human conduct, engages in any lewd exposure or simulated act of sexual intercourse or perversion, which if engaged in offstage or offscreen and in public, would be subject to prosecution under Section _____ of the Penal Code as the misdemeanor crime of lewd exposure or exhibition, or under Section _____ of the Penal Code as the felonious crime against nature, or under Section _____ of the Penal Code as the felonious crime of sexual perversion, is guilty of a misdemeanor.

(b) Every person who procures, counsels, or assists any person to engage in such conduct, or who knowingly exhibits, or procures, counsels or assists in the exhibition of a motion picture, television production or other mechanical reproduction containing such conduct is guilty of a misdemeanor.

Section 11. SINGING OBSCENE SONG, BALLAD, ETC.; PENALTY.

(a) Every person who sings or speaks any obscene song, ballad, or other words in any play, night club act, motion picture, television production, or other exhibition or medium reproducing human conduct, or in any public place, is guilty of a misdemeanor.

(b) Every person who procures, counsels, or assists any person to engage in such conduct, or who knowingly exhibits, or procures, counsels, or assists in the exhibition of a motion picture, television production, or other mechanical reproduction containing such conduct, is guilty of a misdemeanor.

Section 12. REQUIRING PURCHASER OR CONSIGNEE TO RECEIVE OBSCENE MATTER AS CONDITION TO SALE, ETC.; PENALTY. Every person, who, knowingly, as a condition to a sale, allocation, consignment, or delivery for resale of any paper, magazine, book, periodical, publication or other merchandise, requires that the purchaser or consignee receive any matter reasonably believed by the purchaser or consignee to be obscene, or who denies or threatens to deny a franchise, revokes or threatens to revoke, or imposes any penalty, financial or otherwise, by reason of the failure of any person to accept such matter, or by reason of the return of such matter, is guilty of a misdemeanor.

Section 13. CONSPIRACY. A conspiracy of two or more persons to commit any of the crimes proscribed by this Act is punishable as a felony. Any court having jurisdiction of the conspiracy crime has concurrent jurisdiction to try all misdemeanor crimes committed in furtherance of the conspiracy.

Section 14. SPECIAL VERDICT. At the trial of any action arising hereunder, the jury shall render a special verdict, or, if jury trial be waived, the court shall enter special findings, on the issue of obscenity, in addition to a general verdict or general findings. The special verdict or findings on the issue of obscenity shall be: "We find (the court finds) the _____ (title or description of matter) to be obscene," or, "We find (the court finds) the _____ (title or description of matter) not to be obscene," as each item is or is not found obscene. A special verdict shall not be admissible as evidence in any other proceeding, nor shall it be res judicata of any question in any other proceeding.

Section 15. PUNISHMENT.

(a) Every person who violates Sections 6 or 9 is punishable by a fine of not more than one thousand dollars ($1,000) plus five dollars ($5) for each additional unit of material coming within the provisions of this Act, which is involved in the offense, not to exceed ten thousand dollars ($10,000), or by imprisonment in the county jail for not more than six months plus one day for each additional unit of material coming within the provisions of this chapter, and which is involved in the offense, such basic maximum and additional days not to exceed 360 days in the county jail, or by both such fine and imprisonment. If such person has previously been convicted of a violation of this Act, a violation of Section 6 or Section 9 is punishable as a felony and by a fine of not more than two thousand dollars ($2,000) plus five dollars ($5) for each additional unit of material coming within the provisions of this Act, which is involved in the offense, not to exceed twenty-five thousand dollars ($25,000), or by imprisonment in the State prison for not exceeding five years or by both such fine and such imprisonment.

(b) Every person who violates Sections 7, 8, 10, 11, or 12, is punishable by a fine of not more than two thousand dollars ($2,000) or by imprisonment in the county jail for not more than one year, or by both such fine and such imprisonment. If such person has been previously convicted of a violation of this Act, a violation of Sections 7, 8, 10, 11, or 12, is punishable as a felony and by a fine of not more than five thousand dollars ($5,000), or by imprisonment in the State prison not exceeding five years, or by both such fine and imprisonment.

(c) Every person who violates Section 13 is punishable by a fine of not more than five thousand dollars ($5,000), or by imprisonment in the State prison not exceeding five years, or by both such fine and imprisonment.

Section 16. SEIZURE OF OBSCENE MATTER AUTHORIZED. Every person who is authorized to arrest any person for a violation of this Act is equally authorized to seize any obscene matter found in the possession or under the control of the person so arrested and to deliver the same to the court before whom the person so arrested is required to be taken.

Section 17. PROBABLE CAUSE FOR SEIZURE TO BE SUMMARILY DETERMINED.

(a) If the seizure be controverted by any interested person, the court to whom any obscene matter is delivered pursuant to the foregoing section or to the return of a search warrant must within one day after service upon the prosecuting attorney of a motion to suppress the evidence and/or restore the matter, proceed to take testimony in relation thereto. A decision as to whether there is probable cause to believe the seized material to be obscene shall be rendered by the court within two days of the conclusion of the restoration proceedings.

(b) If the motion to suppress the evidence is granted on the grounds of an unlawful seizure, the property shall be restored unless it is subject to confiscation as contraband, as provided for in Section 18, in which case it shall not be returned.

Section 18. CONTRABAND. DESTRUCTION OF OBSCENE MATTER OR ADVERTISEMENT OF MATTER REPRESENTED TO BE OBSCENE.

(a) Obscene matter and advertisements for matter represented to be obscene are contraband and shall be destroyed.

(b) Upon the conviction of the accused or rendition of a court order declaring such matter to be contraband and subject to confiscation, the court shall, when such judgments become final, order, upon five days' notice to the defendant, any matter or advertisement, in respect whereof the accused stands convicted, and which remains in the possession or under the control of the District Attorney or any law enforcement agency, to be destroyed, and the court shall cause to be destroyed any such material in its possession or under its control, retaining only such copies as are necessary for law enforcement purposes.

Section 19. PREPARING, ETC., OBSCENE MATTER OR ADVERTISING ELSEWHERE FOR SALE OR DISTRIBUTION IN THIS STATE. EXTRADITION. Every person, whether or not he is a citizen of or present in this State, who knowingly prepares, publishes, or prints obscene matter for sale or distribution in this State, or who knowingly sends or causes to be sent, or brings or causes to be brought by any means, into this State for sale or distribution herein, any obscene matter, or any advertising promoting the sale or distribution of matter represented or held out to be obscene, whether or not such matter exists in fact or is obscene, shall be subject to the penalties of this Act, and the executive authority of this State shall demand extradition of such person from the executive authority of the State in which such person is found.

Section 20. POLICY. The several sheriffs, constables, state's attorneys, county solicitors, and county prosecuting attorneys (or sheriffs, police chiefs, district attorneys, city attorneys, city prosecutors, and all law enforcement officials) shall vigorously enforce these sections within their respective jurisdictions.

Section 21. POLICY (LOCAL CONTROL). It is not the intent of this Act to occupy the field in the regulation of obscenity, and counties, cities and other political subdivisions of this State are hereby specifically given the right to further regulate obscene materials and conduct.

Section 22. SEVERABILITY. If any provision hereof or the application thereof to any person or circumstance is held invalid such invalidity shall not affect other provisions or applications of the Act which can be given effect without the invalid provision or application, and to this end the provisions of this Act are declared to be severable.

COMMENTS ON THE MODEL OBSCENITY STATUTE

The model statute is patterned after the American Law Institute Model Penal Code drafts. Both employ the "variable" approach to obscenity. Several state legislatures have already adopted this "variable" approach to obscenity. See South Dakota Session Laws of 1968, Chapter 29, Sections 1-16, approved February 15, 1968; New York Penal Laws, Article 235.00-235.22, effective September 1, 1967; Illinois Annotated Statutes, Smith-Hurd, Vol. 28, Sections 11-20; General Statutes of North Carolina, Volume 1-B, Section 14-189.1, and an Act of the South Carolina General Assembly, approved May 12, 1965. Other states have partially adopted its tenets by judicial interpretation: *Conn. v. Sul,* 146 Conn. 78, 147 Atl. 2d 686, 691 (1958); *State v. Jackson,* 224 Or. 337, 356 P2d 495, 507 (1960). The United States Supreme Court has, in its majority opinions, repeatedly cited the Model Penal Code provisions with approval. See also *Sam Ginsberg v. N.Y.,* 20 L.Ed.2d 195 at fn. 4 (April 22, 1968).

Public Nuisance—Section 1(a)

Section 1(a) incorporates into statutory language the Common Law concept that obscenity is a public nuisance. The merit to this approach lies in the resultant focusing on the public welfare issue and muting of the defense cry of "censorship".

In December of 1968, the District Attorney of Allegheny County (Pittsburgh, Pa.) utilized this concept in a successful Common Law action in equity to abate the motion picture film, "Theresa and Isabella" as a public nuisance. *Comm. of Penn. v. Guild Theatre.* Similar actions have also been successful elsewhere, notably in 1970 in Ohio involving the motion picture "Vixen".

"Utterly without redeeming social importance"—Section 1(a)

The majority opinion in Roth-Alberts is clear that "utterly without redeeming social importance" is *not* a required test for factual obscenity. If it were, the judge in *Roth v. U.S.* would have been required to instruct the jury in that case to make a finding on that issue.

At page 484 of the Roth-Alberts opinion, Justice Brennan said, "Implicit in the history of the First Amendment is the rejection of obscenity as utterly without redeeming social importance." Section 1(a) of the Model Obscenity Statute incorporates this understanding. See also extended discussion of the lack of necessity of incorporating this so-called "test" in our comment under the "Memoirs" case in Appendix I and how the incorporation of such a vitiating test is a license for obscenity. As pointed out therein, no opinion of the Supreme Court requires such a "test" which really is a repudiation of the *Roth* standard.

At least two State Supreme Courts have recently refused to

engraph "utterly without redeeming social importance" onto the *Roth* test as a third and separate test. *Cain v. Comm. of Ky.,* ___ Ky. ___ (Feb. 14, 1969), *City of Blue Island, Ill. v. DeVilbiss,* 242 N.E.2d 761 (Nov. 22, 1968). To the same effect are recent decisions in Maryland, Massachusetts and Arizona, cited in Appendix I in comments under "Memoirs."

Variable Obscenity: The Development
of Its Acceptance in the
United States Supreme Court

The philosophy behind the model legislation first appeared in the language of the modern Court's opinions in 1957 in the concurring opinion of Chief Justice Warren in *Roth v. U.S.,* where he said:

> "It is not the book that is on trial; it is a person. The conduct of the defendant is the central issue, not the obscenity of a book or picture. The nature of the materials is, of course, relevant as an attribute of the defendant's conduct, but the materials are thus placed in context from which they draw color and character. A wholly different result might be reached in a different setting." *Roth v. U.S.,* 354 U.S. 476, at 494. See also Justice Warren's opinion in *Kingsley Books, Inc. v. Brown,* 354 U.S. 436, and *Jacobellis v. Ohio,* 378 U.S. 184 (1964).

An examination of the variable treatment afforded the subject matter emphasizes that it is the "act," not the subject matter which is important.

Nine years later, a majority of five justices adopted Warren's rationale in the *Roth* case and, in upholding variable obscenity as consistent with constitutional standards, applied its rationale in interpreting the federal postal obscenity statute. *Ginzburg v. U.S.,* 383 U.S. 463, 475 (Mar. 21, 1966). Justice Harlan would have made it a majority of six, had the *Ginzburg* case not been a federal prosecution.

The "special audience" concept—that portion reading, "If it appears from the character of the material or the circumstances of its dissemination that the subject matter is designed for, or directed to a specially susceptible audience, the subject matter shall be judged with reference to such audience"—was given the approval of six justices in *Mishkin v. U.S.,* 383 U.S. 502, dealing with bondage and flagellation materials and decided on the same day as *Ginzburg v. U.S.,* supra.

The minor's concept—that portion reading, "When the subject matter is distributed or exhibited to minors under 18 years of age, the subject matter shall be judged with reference to an average person in the community of the actual age of the minor to whom such material is distributed or exhibited," as construed by the New York Court of Appeals in *Bookcase v. Broderick,* 18 N.Y.2d 71 (July 7, 1966), and *People v. Tannenbaum,* 18 N.Y.2d 268— was upheld by a majority of five members in *Sam Ginsberg v. U.S.,* ___ U.S. ___, 20 L.Ed.2d 195 (April 22, 1968).

Variable Obscenity: How It Functions

Under the "variable" obscenity approach, the term "obscene" as defined in *Roth-Alberts* functions in accordance with two variable factors: (1) the nature of the materials, and (2) the use of the materials, i.e., the manner in which they are employed.

Under "variable" obscenity, the most objectionable material

547

imaginable (Variable Factor 1) would not be obscene when used by a proper audience (Variable Factor 2). See *U.S. v. 31 Photographs,* 156 F.Supp. 350 (DCSD NY 1957), cited for comparison in *Ginzburg* at page 40, fn. 15, involving the use by Kinsey scientists for research of what was conceded to be blatant pornography. Conversely, material of a less objectionable nature (Variable Factor 1) may be obscene when used improperly, e.g., for the sole purpose of pandering to the prurient interest (Variable Factor 2). See *U.S. v. Rebhuhn,* 109 F.2d 512 (2d Circuit 1940), cited with approval in *Ginzburg* at page 39 and page 40, fn. 15, where a book, "Sex Life In England," having a limited legitimate audience of anthropologists and psychotherapists, was indiscriminately advertised and disseminated in the mail.

Variable Obscenity: Proof

Such evidence may come from either the prosecution or the defense, depending upon who has the burden of going forward with the evidence, and bearing in mind that it is always the prosecutor's burden to establish the violation beyond a reasonable doubt. See Section 2 of the Model Obscenity Statute entitled, "Affirmative Defense". This was graphically illustrated in the majority opinions in the *Mishkin* and *Ginzburg* cases.

In the "Housewife's Handbook on Selective Promiscuity" counts in *Ginzburg,* the United States Government, during its case in chief, presented evidence tending to establish indiscriminate mailings and Ginzburg's intent to pander. Such was sufficient to support the trial court judgment. Had Ginzburg wished to rely on the book's nonprurient appeal in the hands of a special audience of doctors, etc., it was his burden to introduce some evidence in order to overcome the people's prima facie case. Cf. *U.S. v. 31 Photographers, etc.,* 156 F.Supp. 350, cited with approval in *Ginzburg* at fn. 15.

In *Mishkin v. N.Y.,* the people introduced proof of the appeal of the material to a special audience during their case in chief, which supported the judgment on appeal.

Variable Obscenity: Sales to Minors
(a) Historical Background of the
Term "Obscene to Minors"

Under the American Law Institute Model Penal Code Statute and Section 7 of the Model Obscenity Statute, when a person makes a sale to a minor, knowing the purchaser to be a minor, or while in possession of such facts that he should reasonably know that such a person is a minor, then the obscenity is judged by the response of such minor to that material. The Reporter's Comments to American Law Institute Model Penal Code Section 207.10, at pages 36-38, provide:

9. Obscenity Judged by Ordinary Adults. Unless Addressed to Special Audience. A fundamental question in current obscenity law is whether obscenity is to be measured by the response of average or normal individuals or by that of any child or perverted adult to whose notice the material may come . . .

Subsection (a) of proposed Section 207.10 requires obscenity to be judged with reference to ordinary adults *unless the material* is designed for or *directed to* children or other specially susceptible audience . . . (Our emphasis.)

Support authority for this proposition is *U.S. v. Levine,* 83 F.2d

548

156 (1936), and the opinion of the Circuit Court of Appeals, Second Circuit, written by Judge Learned Hand. Judge Learned Hand was one of the drafters of the Model Penal Code sections on Obscenity. That case dealt with a federal prosecution for sending an obscene circular through the mails. At page 157, Judge Hand said:

"What counts is its effect, not upon any particular class, but upon all those whom it is likely to reach. Thus, 'obscenity' is a *function of many variables.*

"The case was not tried on this theory; on the contrary the judge supposed that a book or picture was obscene or innocent by an absolute standard independent of its readers. . . . He was in error. . . ." (Our emphasis.)

And at page 158:

"It may appear that the prospective buyer in the eighth count was a youth and that the accused had reason to suppose that he was. The evil against which the statute is directed would then be the possible injury to such a youthful reader."

U.S. v. Levine was cited in the *Roth* case with approval at fn. 16 as an example of the modern test. See also its citation in *Sam Ginsberg v. N.Y.,* 20 L.Ed.2d 195 at page 202, fn. 5.

Variable Obscenity: Sales to Minors
(b) *"Harmful to Minors", as Used*
in Sam Ginsberg, Means
"Obscene to Minors"

When *Sam Ginsberg v. New York* was handed down April 22, 1968, a blind legislative stampede was started in other states to incorporate into law the provisions of the Special New York Minor's Statute at issue in the *Sam Ginsberg* appeal. In our opinion, a blind application of the language of that statute without more is unwise. If *Sam Ginsberg* is to be properly understood, one must consider the history of the New York statute and the results reached in the New York cases which tested the constitutionality of that provision.

The New York statute is *not* really a "Special Minor's Statute". It is a specific application of the variable obscenity concept as applied to distributions or exhibitions to minors. In reacting to the hard-core pornography rule (constant obscenity) which had evolved in the New York courts, the New York State Legislature in 1965 adopted two minor's statutes, Penal Law Sections 484(h) and 484(i). Although the drafters of those statutes employed the special language "harmful to minors", the New York Court of Appeals, in upholding the constitutionality of such provision, construed the term to mean "obscene to minors". See *People v. Charles Tannenbaum,* 18 N.Y.2d 268, 274 N.Y.S.2d 131, wherein the New York Court of Appeals said:

"In response to the deeply felt needs of the community, our State Legislature enacted . . . statutes . . . proscribing disseminations to infants under 17 . . . of materials *obscene as to such infants.* (Our emphasis.)

"In *Bookcase v. Broderick,* 18 N.Y.2d 71, decided July 7, 1966, we upheld the Legislature's power to *employ variable concepts of obscenity."* (Our emphasis.)

It was this statute and this interpretation which was upheld by

549

the United States Supreme Court in *Sam Ginsberg v. N.Y.*, 20 L.Ed. 2d 195 at 206.

If the law of obscenity is to remain coherent and intelligible, the language employed in the statute must remain rooted to establish historical concept. To illustrate, we need but cite two proposed adaptations of the "harmful to minors" statute. One proposed in Ohio created three crimes: "Obscene to adults," "harmful to minors," and "obscene to minors." To further complicate matters, in the case of the latter two crimes, different penalties were established for each crime. Another proposal in California defined "harmful matter to minors" to mean "that to the average person, applying contemporary standards, the predominant appeal of the matter, taken as a whole, is to prurient interest, i.e., a shameful or morbid interest in nudity, sex, or excretion, which goes substantially beyond customary limits of candor in description or representation of such matters, *and is matter the redeeming social importance of which is substantially less than its prurient appeal.*" (Our emphasis.) The unsoundness of the latter language stems from the fact that as originally employed in *Roth,* it was held that a prurient interest was "utterly without redeeming social importance." The latter definition of "prurient interest" would contradict the *Roth* holding.

The Model Obscenity Statute adopts the "obscene to minors" approach used in the American Law Institute Model Penal Code, which represents the distillation of the best of this nation's obscenity laws, which laws were arrived at by such experienced jurists as Justices Learned Hand, Jerome, Frank, and Curtis Bok, etc.

The proscription of Section 7 only applies to distributions and exhibitions and not to "possession for sale", since possession of such material (i.e., obscene to minors under 18 but not to persons over 18) would be legal for sale to those over 18.

Under Section 7, knowledge of the minor's age is an element of the Minor's Statute. See *Sam Ginsburg v. N.Y.*, 20 L.Ed.2d 195, 206. It is doubtful that an absolute liability standard will succeed. See *Commonwealth of Mass. v. Corey,* 221 N.E.2d 222 (Nov. 3, 1966) involving the sale of the paperback book "Candy" to minors aged 15 and 17, and cf. New York Penal Law 484(i), which required knowledge of the character of the material, but unlike Section 7 of the Model Obscenity Statute and unlike Section 484(h), did not require knowledge of the minor's age. New York Penal Code Law 484(i) was involved in *N.Y. v. Tannenbaum,* 18 N.Y.2d 268, 274 N.Y.S. 2d 131, held to be moot in 18 L.Ed.2d 1300, and was held to be unconstitutionally vague in *Rabeck v. N.Y.,* __ U.S. __, 20 L.Ed.2d 741, 88 Sup. Ct. __ (May 27, 1968).

Variable Obscenity: Special Audience—
Bondage, Flagellation, and Homosexual
Material

The "special audience" proviso in the definition of obscenity is designed to take care of the bondage, flagellation, and homosexual problem.

In this case, prosecution would be brought under the general obscenity proscription. See Section 6. The people in their case in chief can show by expert testimony that the material had a prurient effect on the special audience, and by testimony of vice

550

officers and other experts that it was aimed at a special audience. See American Law Institute Model Penal Code (1957 draft), Section 207.10(2) and the Reporter's Comments thereon at pages 36-38; Proposed Official Draft, Model Penal Code (1962), and *U.S. v. Levine,* 83 F.2d 156. See also *Harold Zucker v. N.Y.,* 15 A.D.2d 883, 225 N.Y.S.2d 154 (Mar. 6, 1962), cert. denied 371 U.S. 863, 83 S.Ct.116, 9 L.Ed.2d 100 (Oct. 15, 1962); *Louis Finkelstein v. N.Y.,* 11 N.Y.2d 300, 229 N.Y.S.2d 367, 183 N.E.2d 661 (May 17, 1962), cert. denied 371 U.S. 863, 83 S.Ct.116, 9 L.Ed.2d 100 (Oct. 15, 1962); *Edward Mishkin v. N.Y.,* 383 U.S. 502, 16 L.Ed.2d 56, 86 S.Ct.958 (Mar. 21, 1966).

Scientier—Sections 1(f) and (2)

The scienter requirement came into the law through Justice Brennan's opinion in *Smith v. Calif.,* 361 U.S. 147 (1959). That case held a strict liability penal ordinance to impose too severe a limitation on the public's access to constitutionally protected matter. The dictum in the *Smith* case seemed to establish, and most state courts so interpreted, the mens rea constitutional requirement as "an awareness of the nature of the contents". See also *Sam Ginsberg v. N.Y.,* 20 L.Ed.2d 195 at 206, and our discussion of *Smith v. California* in Appendix I.

In *Mishkin v. N.Y.* (supra), an argument was made that the state had the burden of proving that the defendant had "subjective" knowledge that the subject matter was obscene. A majority of six rejected this argument, holding that the New York statutory requirement, as interpreted by New York's highest court, was equivalent to the "reckless" standard of the Model Penal Code Test, which satisfied the constitutional standard. Approval of the "reckless" test—an objective standard—put to rest the argument that "subjective" knowledge was a constitutional requirement.

The definition of "knowingly" under Section 1(f) of the Model Obscenity Statute is aimed at keeping the prosecutor's burden of proof for a prima facie case at "knowledge of the contents".

The use of the affirmative defense will permit a defendant latitude in establishing, in his defense, that he was trading in the materials legitimately, once the prosecution has established that he knew or should have known of the contents.

Presumption—Section 5

The presumption in aid of the people's case, established by Section 5, is merely a restatement of the language of the United States Supreme Court in *Roth-Alberts* at fn. 28.

Jury Trial—Sections 3 and 4

Historically, the test for obscenity has been defined in terms of a jury question. See Judge Learned Hand's opinion in *U.S. v. Levine,* 83 F.2d 156, 157:

"As so often happens, the problem is to find a passable compromise between opposing interests, whose relative importance, like that of all social or personal values is incommensurable. *We impose such a duty upon a jury* . . . because the standard they fix is likely to be an acceptable mesne, and because in such matters a mesne most nearly satisfies the moral demands of the community . . . Thus, 'obscenity' is a function of many variables, and the verdict of the jury is not the conclusion of a syllogism of which they are to find only the minor premise, but really *a*

551

small bit of legislation ad hoc, like the standard of care."
(Our emphasis.)

Some states guarantee the right of jury trial to *both* the people and the defendant. See Wisc. Statutes, Vol. 42, Section 957.01; Calif. Const. Art. 1, Sec. 7. In such a situation, the people are not deprived of a jury trial on the issue of "obscenity" where the defendant waives jury trial, unless the people join in the waiver. See 79 A.L.R. 563.

In other states, because of special statutes, the people do not have such a right in situations where the defendant waives jury. See *State of Ohio v. Winters,* 410 App. 146, 12 O.L.Abs. 164, 180 N.E. 559, where the court held it to be error to grant the state's request for a jury trial where the defendant had waived his right to jury trial.

Section 3, in requiring a jury trial unless waived by both parties, focuses attention on the special interest of the people in the value being determined—the common conscience of the community. Section 4 codifies the Common Law concept that the jury is the embodiment of community standards.

Recent cases which faithfully apply this principle are *Nissinoff v. Harper,* 212 So.2d 666 (July 11, 1968), and *Cain v. Comm. of Ky.,* ___ Ky. ___ (Feb. 14, 1969), where the Kentucky Court of Appeals said:

"As we view this matter, it is not the function of this court or any other appellate court to determine whether the material shown is obscene. This is a factual determination to be made by a jury. The film was shown to the jury and they found it obscene. Our function as an appellate court is limited to determining whether the evidence in the record supports the findings of the jury. If so, the verdict must stand. This law is so basic and ancient to the principles of English and American jurisprudence as so elementary in its application as a principle of appellate procedure that we do not feel called upon to cite authorities for its support . . ."

Appeal on Matters of Law—Section 4(c)

Section 4(c) authorizes an appeal by the prosecution in cases where a lower court holds that the subject matter, which is the subject of the charge, is constitutionally protected. This follows the recommendations contained in Section 207.10(3) of the 1957 draft of the Model Penal Code. While in many jurisdictions this right of appeal exists at the present time, in at least one major jurisdiction, the district attorney has refused to appeal, under the claim that, procedurally, the avenue is not open to him.

Advertising Material To Be Obscene—Section 9

Section 9 makes it a misdemeanor to represent or hold out matter to be obscene, whether or not such matter is in fact obscene. This follows the recommendation of Section 207.10(6) of the 1957 Model Penal Code draft and Section 251.4(2)(e) of the Model Penal Code (1962).

The roots for the Model Penal Code proposal are found in principles expressed in several old federal cases which gained acceptance in the 3rd Circuit in the so-called Hornick rule. *U.S. v. Hornick,* 229 F.2d 120 (3rd Cir. 1956). An excellent discussion of this development appears in James Jack Kilpatrick's book, "The Smut Peddlers", at pp. 71-77.

552

A similar provision appearing in California Penal Code Section 311.5 was tested and upheld as constitutional in *Kirby v. Municipal Court of Newhall Judicial District,* 46 Cal. Rptr. 844 (Sept. 30, 1965).

Lewd Exposures, Etc., As A Part Of A Play, Etc.—Sections 10 and 11

The communications media is plagued at the present time with an avalanche of lewd displays and language which, if engaged in off-stage or off-screen and in public, would be subject to criminal penalties as improper public conduct. Sections 10 and 11 codify the rationale applied by the majority of the New York Court of Appeals in *Trans Lux Distributing Corp. v. Board of Regents,* 248 N.Y.S.2d 857 (Mar. 26, 1964), reversed on other grounds in *Trans Lux Distributing Corp. v. Board of Regents,* 380 U.S. 259 (Mar. 15, 1965). See also Justice Clark concurring in *Kingsley International Pictures Corp. v. Regent,* 360 U.S. 684 at 702.

It beggars logic to say that acts of sodomy or actual perversion are punishable as felonies and at the same time hold that a vivid full screen four-minute pictorial display of a simulated act of oral intercourse (sodomy) performed by one teenage girl on another teenage girl ("Theresa and Isabella") or a full-screened five-minute pictorial display of a like lesbianic act ("The Killing of Sister George"), or similar screened conduct or play performance, may not be reached by the law. As was voiced by Justice Burke in the *Trans Lux* case at page 861:

"To all argument predicated on artistic merit as decisive of the constitutional question, it is sufficient answer to say that artists are not such favorites of the law that they may ply their craft in the teeth of a declared overriding public policy against pornographic displays."

These recent developments should even give Justices Douglas and Black second thoughts. See Justice Douglas dissenting in *Roth* at page 512:

"I assume there is nothing in the Constitution which permits Congress from using its power over the mails to proscribe *conduct* on the ground of good morals. No one would suggest that the First Amendment permits nudity in public places, adultery, and other phases of sexual misconduct. . . ." (Our emphasis.)

Felony vs. Misdemeanor—Sections 14 and 15

Section 13 makes a conspiracy to violate the obscenity laws a felony.

While the initial violation of Sections 6, 7, 8, 9, 10, 11 or 12 is a misdemeanor, under the provisions of Section 15, a second violation is treated as a felony.

Special Verdict in Criminal Trial on Issue of Obscenity—Section 14

The procedure should be such as to permit the "obscenity" of all subject matter involved in the case to be decisively decided. This may not be done in three situations:

1. Where there are multiple items involved in one count, e.g., one count charging possession of five publications, and the jury returns a general "guilty" verdict. Under such a verdict, the jury may have considered only one, or all five, obscene.
2. Where the jury returns a general verdict of "not guilty"

553

solely because they could not find the defendant had the requisite guilty mind—"scienter".

3. Where a search and seizure ruling makes prosecution of the criminal case impossible.

At the present time, it is essential that law enforcement be able to point with certainty to that specific material which was found to be obscene as a level of reference and guide for future action. If it is a girlie magazine, the name and number of the edition should be identifiable as the item which was declared to be obscene, so that the community evaluation may be known and understood by law enforcement officials in the same and other jurisdictions, and considered by them as a guide in their future actions.

There are many situations where a jury may be convinced that the material is obscene but will not convict, because of the other considerations involved in a criminal trial—the guilty mind (scienter) requirement. Examples are: The vendor who agrees to remove the material *after* arrest, but who is prosecuted anyway; the situation where a vendor is prosecuted for material which is similar to equally obnoxious material sold elsewhere; prosecution of the "little old lady" who is able to convince the jury she had not been adequately warned, etc.

The above defects may be corrected by the addition of a provision which requires the return of a special verdict on the issue of "obscenity" in addition to the return of the general verdict.

In praise of special verdicts, Sunderland says in 29 Yale L. J. 253, 259:

"The special verdict compels detailed consideration, but above all it enables the public, the parties and the court to see what the jury has done. . . . The general verdict is either all wrong or all right, because it is an inseparable and inscrutable unit. A single error completely destroys it. But the special verdict enables errors to be localized so that the sound portions of the verdict may be saved . . . ."

The special verdict of Section 14 has been made inadmissible as evidence in other proceedings, in recognition of the fact that "use" is a variable factor under variable obscenity concepts (supra). The "conduct" is not always the same in every case, hence the findings shall be restricted to the conduct involved in the case which was tried.

Penalty—Section 15

The graduated penalty of Section 15 is specifically aimed at the manufacturer and distributor. The small retailer does not suffer as much as the area distributor. Any large scale distributor will distribute as many as 2,000 copies of a salacious paperback book. Under intelligent use of this penalty provision, a penalty of major proportions (up to $10,000) can be imposed upon the really culpable operator. This section is modeled after Section 311.9 of the California Penal Code.

Seizure and Summary Determination— Sections 16 and 17

Section 16 specifically authorizes the arresting officer, at the time of an arrest, to seize material reasonably thought by him to be obscene. Section 17 establishes procedures which provide the due process safeguards required in such cases by *Kingsley Books, Inc. v. Brown*, 354 U.S. 436, 77 S.T. 1325, 1 L.Ed.2d

1469 (June 24, 1957), and *Freedman v. Maryland,* 380 U.S. 51, 85 S.Ct. 734, 13 L.Ed.2d 649 (Mar. 1, 1965).

Both provisions are necessary to counter the claim being made by defense attorneys that arresting officers have no right to seize without a prior judicial determination. See *Flack v. Municipal Court of Anaheim-Fullerton Judicial District,* 56 Cal. Reptr. 162, 165 (Jan. 20, 1967), where the California Court of Appeal, Fourth District, rejected such claim, saying:

"No citation of authority seems necessary for the proposition that probable cause need not be previously determined in each instance by a judicial officer before a police officer can make a lawful arrest accompanied by seizure for that which would appear to 'the reasonable man' to be a crime involving contraband. Police officers cannot be relegated to a classification wherein their judgment would not meet the test enunciated in Roth v. United States."

A majority of the ultra-liberal California Supreme Court had a different view, however. See *Flack v. Municipal Court,* 59 Cal. Rptr. 872 (July 3, 1967), reversing the Court of Appeal.

Nor did Philadelphia County law enforcement officers fare any better in the Pennsylvania courts, in a case involving an arrest and the seizure of the motion picture film, "Olga's House of Shame". *Smith v. Crumlish,* 218 Atl.2d 596 (April 14, 1966). In returning the film, Common Pleas Judge Chudoff said that Sections 528 and 529 of the Pennsylvania laws "do not provide any special procedure for the search and seizure of the films." He said he was leaving the solution of the problem to the State Legislature.

Recently the federal courts have intruded upon the scene with startling results. In *Cambist Films, Inc. v. Illinois,* 292 F.Supp. 185 (Oct. 21, 1968), not only did 7th Circuit Federal District Judge Hubert L. Will hold the seizure of the sex exploitation film "Aroused" to be illegal, but he also took it upon himself to hold the film not to be obscene. His opinion cited *Metzger v. Illinois* (June 19, 1968), wherein another Federal District Judge of that Circuit came by a like result as to the motion picture film "I A Woman"—a film which a Louisville jury held obscene and whose verdict the Kentucky Court of Appeals ruled to be supported by overwhelming evidence. *Cain v. Comm. of Ky.,* ___ Ky. ___ (Feb. 14, 1969). A different result was reached by another Federal District Judge in the same circuit in *Metzger v. Pearcy,* 393 F.2d 202 (April 29, 1968), which ordered the film "I A Woman" returned to its owner, but also ordered its return for use at the criminal trial in Indianapolis. A 3-judge constitutional court in the Eastern District of Kentucky also ordered the motion picture film "The Female" returned, but refused to enjoin prosecution, holding the film to be obscene. *Cambist Films, Inc. v. Tribell,* 293 F.Supp. 407 (Nov. 26, 1968). As to this new federal policy of narrowly limiting the policy of abstention, cf. *Dale Book Co. v. Leary,* 233 F.Supp. 754, aff'd in 389 F.2d 40 (Jan. 2, 1968).

Sections 16 and 17 provide the solution to the above problems. By specifically authorizing a seizure incident to an arrest or in execution of a search warrant (obtained from a magistrate in an ex parte proceeding) and, at the same time establishing a procedure which makes possible an immediate adversary hearing *after* the seizure, the same meets the due process requirement of

Kingsley Books, Inc. v. Brown, supra. See *Holden v. Arnebergh,*
71 Cal. Rptr. 401 (August 21, 1968), wherein the California
courts afforded such remedies. Motion to dismiss on the part of
the city granted on March 3, 1969, the United States Supreme
Court opinion reading:
"Per Curiam. The motion to dismiss is granted and the appeal
is dismissed, it appearing that the judgment below rests upon an
adequate state ground."
In the case of the use of search warrants, however, be sure to
avoid the pitfalls described in *Lee Arts Theater v. Va.,* 20 L.Ed.2d
1313 (June 19, 1968).

Contraband—Sections 17(b) and 18

Section 18 adopts the legislative device employed in the Wisconsin jurisdiction and recently upheld by the Wisconsin Supreme
Court in *Wisc. v. Voshart,* 159 N.W.2d 1 (June 7, 1968).

Extradition—Section 19

Section 19 adopts the legislative policy mandated by the Indiana
legislature. It is the public policy of that state to use the extradition laws to bring to justice the prime movers in the industry who
operate abroad under the protection of more tolerant law enforcement attorneys.

Local Control—Section 21

Section 21 contains a grant of local control to the political
subdivisions to further regulate in the area of obscenity control.

APPENDIX III

REVIEW OF LEGISLATION INTRODUCED IN 91ST CONGRESS

We favor:

Bill Number	Description	Remarks
H.R. 9373	Registration of mailing list brokers	
S. 2074	Prohibition of advertisements designed to appeal to prurient interest	Co-sponsored by 34 senators. Many identical Bills in House. Uses pure Roth test.
S. Res. 61	Creates senatorial committee to study film classifications and to suggest legislation	
S. 1077	Jury to be sole judge of what is obscene	Many identical Bills in House.
H.R. 9796	Revocation of mailing permits of pornographers	
H.R. 10941	Non-mailable material	Many identical Bills
H.R. 10108	Withdrawal of mailing permits	
H.R. 12850	Prohibits mailing of specifically defined obscene materials	
S. 2057	Prohibits unsolicited sexually provocative material in mails	
H.R. 11815	Descriptive definitions of word obscene	
H.R. 9878	Strengthens present federal criminal penalties for obscenity	
H.R. 8751	Prohibits mailing erotically arousing material to a person under 19	
H.R. 13459	Sexually provocative mail regulation	

556

There was other legislation introduced in the 91st Congress on this subject having beneficial purposes but containing the "utterly without redeeming social value" phrase. This is unnecessary under *Roth* and permits a pornographer to build in 95 per cent smut and 5 per cent social value. It may be that Congress has been deceived by the compilation entitled "Statutory Regulation of Pornography and Obscenity, a Compilation of Federal and State Statutes," published February 19, 1969 by the Library of Congress, Legislative Reference Service. This book in its first three pages contains blatant misstatements of the law when it says that the Supreme Court has required that matter be "utterly without redeeming social value" and that the community standards to be used are *national* ones. This is serious error since no Supreme Court ever so held. These are simply individual views of some of the justices then on the Court and is not a Court opinion. Not being a Court opinion, it is not binding. See our comments in Appendix I under the *Memoirs* case.

APPENDIX IV

MODEL STATE STATUTE ESTABLISHING FILM REVIEW BOARD

ARTICLE

MOVING PICTURES

§ 1. DEFINITIONS.

The word "film" as used in this article shall be construed to mean what is usually known as a motion picture film and shall include any film shown with or by new devices of any kind whatsoever, such as slot or coin machines, showing motion pictures. The word "view" in this article shall be construed to mean what is usually known as a stereopticon view or slide. The word "person" shall be construed to include an association, copartnership or a corporation.

§ 2. UNLAWFUL TO SHOW ANY BUT APPROVED AND LICENSED FILM.

It shall be unlawful to sell, lease, lend, exhibit or use any motion picture film or view in the State of _____ unless the said film or view has been submitted by the exchange, owner or lessee of the film or view and duly approved and licensed by the _____ State Film Review Board, hereinafter in this article called the Board.

Note Annotation to Maryland Statute

(But present plan is constitutional on its face.—The present Maryland statutory plan for preshowing motion picture censorship is constitutional on its face. Trans-Lux Distrib. Corp. v. Maryland State Bd of Censors, 240 Md. 98, 213 A.2d 235 (1965), decided after the 1965 amendment to §19 of this article.)

557

§ 3. CREATION OF FILM REVIEW BOARD.

The Board shall consist of three residents and citizens of the State of _____ well qualified by education and experience to act as reviewers under this article. One member of the Board shall be chairman, one member shall be vice-chairman and one member shall be secretary. They shall be appointed by the Governor, by and with the advice and consent of the Senate, for terms of three years. Those first appointed under this article shall be appointed for three years, two years and one year, respectively; the respective terms to be designated by the Governor.

§ 4. VACANCY IN BOARD.

A vacancy in the membership of the Board shall be filled for the unexpired term by the Governor. A vacancy shall not impair the right and duty of the remaining members to perform all the functions of the Board.

§ 5. SEAL.

The Board shall procure and use an official seal, which shall contain the words "_____ State Film Review Board" together with such design engraved thereon as the Board may prescribe.

§ 6. BOARD TO EXAMINE, APPROVE OR DISAPPROVE FILMS: WHAT FILMS TO BE DISAPPROVED.

(a) *Board to examine, approve or disapprove films.* The Board shall examine or supervise the examination of all films or views to be exhibited or used in the State of _____ and shall approve and license such films or views which are moral and proper, and shall disapprove such as are obscene, or such as tend, in the judgment of the Board, to debase or corrupt morals or incite to crimes. All films exclusively portraying current events or pictorial news of the day, commonly called news reels, may be exhibited without examination and no license or fees shall be required therefor.

(b) *What films considered obscene.*—For the purposes of this article, a motion picture film or view shall be considered to be obscene if, when considered as a whole, its calculated purpose or dominant effect is substantially to arouse sexual desires, and if the probability of this effect is so great as to outweigh whatever other merits the film may possess.

(c) *What films tend to debase or corrupt morals.*—For the purposes of this article, a motion picture film or view shall be considered to be of such a character that its exhibition would tend to debase or corrupt morals if its dominant purpose or effect is erotic or pornographic: or if it portrays a simulated act of sexual intercourse, perversion or lewd exposure, which if engaged in off stage or off scene and in public, would be subject to prosecution under Section _____ of the Penal Code as the misdemeanor crime of lewd exposure or exhibition, or under Section _____ of the Penal Code as the felonious crime against nature, or under Section _____ of the Penal Code as the felonious crime of sexual perversion.

(d) *What films tend to incite to crime.*—For the purposes of this article, a motion picture film or view shall be considered of such a character that its exhibition would tend to incite to crime if the theme or the manner of its presentation presents the commission of criminal acts or contempt for law as constituting profitable, desirable, acceptable, respectable or commonly accepted behavior, or if it advocates or teaches the use of, or the methods of use of, narcotics or habit-forming drugs.

§ 7. CERTIFICATE OF APPROVAL OR LICENSE.

Upon each film which has been approved by the Board, there shall be furnished by the Board, the following certificate or statement: "Approved by the _____ State Film Review Board No. . . . ." and the Board shall also furnish a certificate or license in writing to the same effect, which certificate shall be the license for such film unless and until the same shall be revoked by the said Board, and said certificate of license shall be exhibited by the holder thereof to any member of the Board or employee thereof upon demand. In the case of motion pictures, such statement shall be shown on the screen to the extent of approximately four (4) feet of film. Upon each film examined and approved by the Board, and upon each duplicate or print thereof, the Board shall stamp, by perforation or otherwise, the serial number and such other initials, words or designs as it may prescribe, the serial number to correspond to the number on the certificate of approval issued by the Board to be shown upon the screen. In the case of slides or views, the Board shall furnish in writing a similar certificate or license and each set of views shall have at least two slides or views shown with a similar statement. Upon satisfactory proof being submitted to the Board that the certificate of approval attached to any film that has been examined and approved by the Board, has been lost, mutilated or destroyed, the Board shall have power in its discretion, and upon payment in advance of the fee prescribed by §11 of this article, to issue a duplicate certificate of approval. Any certificate or license issued as herein provided may be revoked by the Board for any reason which would have justified the Board in refusing to issue such license, or for any violation of law by such applicant in securing such license, or in advertising or using the film or view so licensed. Thereafter any such film may again be submitted to the Board for approval and license.

§ 8. RECORD OF EXAMINATIONS.

The Board shall keep a record of all examinations made by it of films or views; noting on the record all films or views which have been approved, and those which have not been approved, with the reason for such disapproval.

§ 9. REPORT TO GOVERNOR.

The Board shall report, in writing, annually, to the Governor, on or before the first day of September of each year. The report shall show:

(1) A record of its meetings, and a summary of its proceedings during the year immediately preceding the date of the report.

(2) The results of all examinations of films or views.

(3) A detailed statement of all prosecutions for violations of this article.

(4) A detailed and itemized statement of all the income and expenditures made by or in behalf of the Board.

(5) Such other information as the Board may deem necessary or useful in explanation of the operations of the Board.

(6) Such other information as shall be requested by the Governor.

§ 10. OATH AND BOND OF OFFICERS OF BOARD.

The chairman, vice-chairman and secretary shall, before asuming the duties of their respective offices, take and subscribe the oath prescribed by the Constitution of the State of _____ and each shall annually give corporate surety bond to the State of _____ in such sum as the State Comptroller may prescribe, with condition that he faithfully perform the duties of his office and account for all funds received under color of his office.

§ 11. FEES.

For the examination of each and every one thousand feet (1,000) of original motion picture film, or fractional part thereof, the Board shall receive in advance a fee of three dollars ($3.00), where the film averages sixteen (16) frames or less to the foot, and a fee of four dollars ($4.00) where the film averages more than sixteen (16) frames to the foot. For the examination of each original set of views, the Board shall receive in advance a fee of two dollars ($2.00) for each one hundred (100) views or fractional part thereof. The Board shall receive in advance a fee of one dollar ($1.00) for replacing any certificate or stamp of approval in account for and pay all fees received by it into the State treasury.

§ 12. OFFICES, EXPENSES AND COMPENSATION OF BOARD.

The Board shall provide adequate offices and rooms in which properly to conduct the work and affairs of the Board in the City of _____ and the State of _____, and the expenses thereof, as well as any other expenses incurred by said Board in the necessary discharge of its duties and also the salaries of the members of the Board, each of whom shall receive such compensation as shall be provided in the State budget, and each member of the Board shall be reimbursed for actual and necessary expenses incurred in furtherance of the Board's business within the State of _____, such as mileage, at the rate established by the Board of Public Works, hotel bills, the costs of meals and any other incidental expenses incurred in attending meetings or carrying out the other provisions of this article, such reimbursements not to exceed three thousand ($3,000.00) dollars per annum for any member of the Board.

§ 13. DISPOSITION OF FINES.

All fines imposed for the violation of this article shall be paid into the State treasury.

§ 14. RIGHT OF ENTRY.

Any member or employee of the Board may enter any place where films or views are exhibited; and such member or employee is hereby empowered and authorized to prevent the display or exhibition of any film or view which has not been duly approved by the Board.

§ 15. OBSCENE, INDECENT, ETC., ADVERTISEMENTS.

No person or corporation shall exhibit or offer to another for exhibition purposes any poster, banner or other similar advertising matter in connection with any motion picture film, which poster, banner or matter is obscene, indecent, inhuman, sacrilegious or of such character that its exhibition would tend to corrupt morals or incite to crime. If any such poster, banner or similar advertising matter is so exhibited or offered to another for exhibition it shall be sufficient ground for the revocation of the certificate or license for said film issued by the Board.

§ 16. ENFORCEMENT; RULES.

This article shall be enforced by the Board. In carrying out and enforcing the purpose of this article, it may adopt such reasonable rules as it may deem necessary. Such rules shall not be inconsistent with the laws of _____.

§ 17. FILM SUBMITTED FOR APPROVAL: FALSE STATEMENTS.

Every person intending to sell, lease, exhibit or use any film or view in the State of _____, shall furnish the Board, when the application for approval is made, a description of the film or view to be exhibited, sold or leased, and the purposes thereof; and shall submit the film or view to the Board for examination; and shall furnish a written statement or affidavit that the duplicate film or view is an exact copy of the original film or view as submitted for examination to the Board, and that all eliminations, changes or rejections made or required by the Board in the original film or view have been or will be made in the duplicate. Any person who shall make any false statement in any such written statement or affidavit to the Board shall, upon conviction thereof summarily before a justice of the peace, be deemed guilty of a misdemeanor and shall be punished by a fine of not less than fifty dollars nor more than one hundred dollars, and any certificate or license issued upon a false or misleading affidavit or application shall be void ab initio; and any change or alteration in a film after license, except the elimination of a part or except upon writing ten direction of the Board, shall be a violation of this article and shall also make immediately void the license therefor.

§ 18. INTERFERENCE WITH BOARD.

It shall be unlawful for any person to hinder or interfere in any manner with any member or employee of the Board while performing any duties in carrying out the intent or provisions of this article.

§ 19. REVIEW AND APPROVAL OR DISAPPROVAL OF FILM BY BOARD: JUDICIAL DETERMINATION: APPEAL: SALE, EXHIBITION, ETC., OF FILM WITHOUT APPROVAL AND LICENSE.

(a) Any film duly submitted to the Board for examination and licensing shall be reviewed and approved within five (5) days, unless the Board shall disapprove such film under the provisions of §6 hereof, in which event the Board shall, within not later than three (3) days thereafter, apply to the Circuit Court for _____ for a judicial determination as to whether such film is obscene, or tends to debase or corrupt morals, or incite to crime, within the meaning of §6 hereof. Notice of such application shall be forthwith sent by first-class mail, postage prepaid, to the address of the person presenting such film for licensing. The Circuit Court for _____ shall, within five (5) days after the filing of said application conduct a hearing, and shall in connection therewith view such film; within two (2) days after such hearing said court shall enter its decree and order requiring that said film be approved and licensed or be disapproved if in violation of the provisions of said §6 hereof. If the decree and order disapproved said film as being in violation of the provisions of §6 hereof, then the person presenting such film for licensing may appeal such determination to the Court of Appeals of _____, in accordance with the _____ Rules of Procedure, and said Court shall advance such case on its hearing calendar to the earliest practicable date; and in reviewing the order appealed from, said Court shall view the subject film. The burden of proving that the film should not be approved and licensed shall rest on the Board.

(b) Any person who shall sell, lease, lend, exhibit or use any film in this State without having first secured approval thereof and a license therefor in accordance with the procedures set forth in subsection (a) above, shall be guilty of a misdemeanor and upon conviction summarily before a magistrate or the Municipal Court of _____, shall be sentenced to pay a fine of not less than fifty ($50.00) dollars, nor more than one hundred ($100.00) dollars, or to imprisonment for not more than thirty (30) days, or to be both fined and imprisoned in the discretion of the magistrate or judge.

Note Annotation to Maryland Statute

Purpose of 1965 amendment.—By the 1965 amendment, the General Assembly repealed and reenacted this section with the obvious intention of fully meeting the three objections set forth in Freedman v. Maryland, 380 U.S. 51, 85 Sup. Ct. 634, 13L.Ed. 2d. 649 (1965). The legislature succeeded in accomplishing this result. Trans-Lux Distrib. Corp. v. Maryland State Bd. of Censors, 240 Md. 98, 213 A.2d. 235 (1965).

An adversary proceeding is intended.—The use of the language "the burden of proving that the film should not be approved and licensed shall rest on the Board" shows that an adversary proceeding was intended in which the Board would have the burden of going forward with the evidence as well as the burden of proof. Hewitt v. Maryland State Bd. of Censors, 241 Md. 283, 216 A.2d. 557 (1966).

In which the Board should offer testimony.—Save in the rare case where there could be no doubt that the film is obscene, the Board will not meet the burden of persuasion imposed on it by the Constitution and the statute without offering testimony that the picture is obscene in addition to offering the film. Dunn v. Maryland State Bd. of Censors, 240 Md. 249, 213 A.2d. 751 (1965).

§ 20. PENALTIES IN GENERAL.

Any person who violates any of the provisions of this article for which a specific penalty is not provided and is convicted thereof summarily before any magistrate or justice of the peace, shall be sentenced to pay a fine of not less than twenty-five ($25.00) dollars, nor more than fifty ($50.00) dollars, for the first offense. For any subsequent offense the fine shall not be less than fifty ($50.00) dollars, nor more than one hundred ($100.00) dollars. In default of payment of a fine and costs, the defendant shall be sentenced to imprisonment in the prison of the county, or in _____, where such offense was committed, for not less than ten days, and not more than thirty days. All fines shall be paid by the magistrate or justice of the peace to the Board, and by it paid into the State treasury.

§ 21. PARTICULAR PENALTIES: APPEAL.

Any person who shall exhibit in public any misbranded film or film carrying official approval of the Board which approval was not put there by the action of the Board or any person who shall attach to or use in connection with any film or view which has not been approved and licensed by the _____ State Film Review Board, any certificate or statement in the form provided by §7 hereof or any similar certificate, statement or writing, or any person who shall exhibit any folder, poster, picture or other advertising matter, which folder, poster, picture or other advertising matter is obscene, indecent, sacrilegious or inhuman or which tends to unduly excite or deceive the public, or containing any matter not therein contained when the approval was granted by the Board, shall be guilty of a misdemeanor, and upon conviction summarily before a justice of the peace, shall be fined not less than fifty dollars ($50) nor more than one hundred dollars ($100), or imprisonment for not over thirty days, or be both fined and imprisoned in the discretion of the said justice of the peace. In addition to the above penalties, the Board may also seize and confiscate any misbranded film.

In all cases arising under this section there may be an appeal from the decision of the magistrate or justice of the peace where the fine imposed is in excess of fifty dollars ($50.00), or where the penalty imposed includes any term of imprisonment whatever.

§ 22. FAILURE TO DISPLAY APPROVED SEAL.

If any person shall fail to display or exhibit on the screen the approval seal, as issued by the Board, of a film or view, which has been approved, and is convicted summarily before any magistrate, or justice of the peace, he shall be sentenced to pay a fine of not less than five dollars and not more than ten dollars; in default of payment of a fine and costs, the defendant shall be sentenced to imprisonment, in the prison of the county, or in _____ where such offense was committed, for not less than two days and not more than five days.

§ 23. EXEMPTIONS: PERMIT.

This article shall not apply to any noncommercial exhibition of, or noncommercial use of films or views, for purely educational, charitable, fraternal or religious purposes, by any religious association, fraternal society, library, museum, public school, private school or institution of learning. The Board may, in its discretion, without examination thereof, issue a permit for any motion picture film, intended solely for educational, fraternal, charitable or religious purposes, or by any employer for the instruction or welfare of his employees, provided that the owner thereof shall file the prescribed application, which shall include a sworn description of the film. No fee shall be charged for any such permit.

§ 24. SEVERABILITY.

The several sections and provisions of this article are hereby declared to be independent of each other; and it is the legislative intent that, if any of said sections or provisions are declared to be unconstitutional, such section or provision shall not affect any other portion of this article.

§ 25. MONEY DEPOSITED FOR FUTURE RENTAL OF FILM—IN GENERAL.

Whenever money shall be deposited or advanced on a contract

for the future use or rental of motion picture films as security for the performance of the contract or to be applied to payments upon such contract when due, such money, with interest accruing thereon, if any, until repaid or so applied shall continue to be the money of the person making such deposit or advance and shall be considered a trust fund in possession of the person with whom such deposit or advance shall be made, and shall be deposited in a bank or trust company by the person receiving the same, and shall not be commingled with said person's other funds or become asset of such person or trustee, and the person so paying the same shall be notified by the bank or trust company in which said funds are deposited.

§ 26. SAME—WAIVER.

No waiver of the provisions of §25 shall be made so as to evade the provisions of said §25 and any such waiver if so made, shall be considered null and void.

APPENDIX V

MODEL STATE STATUTE
PROVIDING FOR LIMITED INJUNCTIVE RELIEF
ON PUBLICATION OR EXHIBITION
PENDING JUDICIAL DETERMINATION

Injunctive remedy

The circuit courts of the counties and the equity courts of the Supreme Bench of _____ City have jurisdiction to enjoin the sale or distribution of any book, magazine, or any other publication or article (including a motion picture film or showing) which is prohibited from sale or distribution, as hereinafter specified.

1. The State's attorneys of the counties and _____ City in which a person, firm or corporation sells or distributes or is about to sell or distribute or has in his possession with intent to sell or distribute or is about to acquire possession with intent to sell or distribute any book, magazine, pamphlet, newspaper, story paper, writing paper, picture, card, drawing or photograph (including a motion picture film or showing) or any article or instrument of use which is obscene, within the meaning of §___ of this article may maintain an action for an injunction against such person, firm or corporation in the circuit court of the counties or the equity courts of the Supreme Bench of _____ City to prevent the sale of further sale or the distribution or further distribution or the acquisition, publication or possession within this State of any book, magazine, pamphlet, newspaper, story paper, writing paper, picture, card, drawing or photograph (including a motion picture film or showing), or any article or instrument of use which is obscene.

2. The person, firm, or corporation sought to be enjoined is entitled to a trial of the issues within one day after joinder of issue and a decision shall be rendered by the court within two days after the conclusion of the trial.

3. In the event that an order or judgment be entered in favor

of the State's attorney and against the person, firm or corporation sought to be enjoined, such final order or judgment shall contain a provision directing the person, firm or corporation to surrender to such peace officer as the court may direct or to the sheriff of the county in which the action was brought any of the matter described in this section and such sheriff or officer shall be directed to seize and destroy the same.

4. In any action brought pursuant to the provisions of this section, the State's attorney is not required to file any bond before the issuance of an injunction order provided for by this section, is not liable for costs and is not liable for damages sustained by reason of the injunction order in cases where judgment is rendered in favor of the person, firm or corporation sought to be enjoined.

5. Every person, firm or corporation who sells, distributes or acquires possession with intent to sell or distribute any of the matter described in this section, after the service upon him of a summons and complaint in an action brought by the State's attorney of the counties or _____ City pursuant to this section is chargeable with knowledge of the contents thereof.

Note to Maryland State
Effect of amendment (The 1968 amendment, effective July 1, 1968, added the words in parentheses in the first and second paragraphs.)

APPENDIX VI

AN ACT to create an Obscenity Laws Commission, to define its powers and duties and to make an appropriation therefor.

BE IT ENACTED by the People of the State of _____ represented in the General Assembly:

Section 1. There is created an Obscenity Laws Commission, hereinafter called the Commission, consisting of three members of the Senate appointed by the President pro tempore, three members of the House of Representatives appointed by the Speaker thereof, and three persons appointed by the Governor. No more than two members appointed by each appointing authority may be of the same political party.

No vacancy occurs on the Commission because a legislative member is not reelected to serve in the house from which he was appointed. Vacancies occurring because of death or resignation shall be filled by the appointing authority for the group in which the vacancy occurs.

Appointments shall be made within 30 days after the effective date of this Act. As soon as possible after the appointment of all members, the Commission shall meet and select a chairman and such other officers from its membership as it deems necessary. The Commission shall also provide rules for the transaction of its business, and may employ, without regard to the "Personnel Code," such expert legal advisers, employees and assistants as it deems necessary. The members of the Commission shall serve without compensation, but shall be reimbursed for necessary expenses incurred in the performance of their duties under the Act.

Section 2. It is the duty of the Commission to:

(1) Explore methods of combating the influx and distribution, rent, sale or exhibition of obscene matters and materials in their state.

(2) To determine methods of informing the public of the origin, scope and effect of obscene matters and materials through the active cooperation of the leaders of the State, County and local governments and leaders of the mass media throughout the State.

(3) To provide plans for improved coordination between federal, state and local governmental officials in the suppression of the distribution, rent, sale or exhibition of obscene material.

(4) To study laws and ordinances in relation to the distribution, rent, sale or exhibition of obscene matter and materials and make any recommendations which it deems necessary in order to improve or revise such laws and to recommend such other action as it deems necessary.

Section 3. The Commission may conduct hearings, examine witnesses under oath and may compel the attendance and testimony of witnesses and the production of books, records and documents. Oaths may be administered by any member of the Commission. Subpoenas and subpoenas duces tecum may be issued over the signature of the chairman or any other officer of the Commission, and may be served by any adult person designated by the issuing officer.

Any _____ court of this State, or any judge thereof, upon application of the Commission, may, in his discretion, compel the attendance of witnesses, the production of books, records or documents and the giving of testimony before the Commission by an attachment for contempt or otherwise in the same manner as production of evidence may be compelled by the court.

Section 4. The Commission shall make a report of its findings, recommendations and activities on the _____ day of _____ of each year to the General Assembly.

Section 5. This Commission shall remain in effect on a permanent basis unless this Act is repealed.

Section 6. The sum of $_____, or so much thereof as may be necessary, is appropriated to the Commission to carry out the provisions of this Act for the fiscal year ending _____. Future appropriations shall be made in the same manner as are appropriations for other departments of the State Government. This act shall take effect _____.

APPENDIX VII

An Act to Create a Commission to Encourage Morality in Youth and to Prevent its Defilement by Obscene Publications

Be it enacted by the People of the State of _____ represented in the General Assembly:

Section 1. There is hereby created a Commission to Encourage

566

Morality in Youth, consisting of nine members appointed by the Governor. Vacancies occurring because of death or resignation shall be filled by the Governor.

Appointments shall be made within 30 days after the effective date of this Act. As soon as possible after the appointment of all members the Commission shall meet and select a Chairman and such other officers from its membership as it deems necessary. The Commission shall also provide rules for the transaction of its business, and may employ such employees and assistants as it deems necessary. The members of the Commission shall serve without compensation but shall be reimbursed for necessary expenses incurred in the performance of their duties under this Act.

Section 2. It is the duty of the Commission:

(1) to study the source and the extent of the sale or exhibition of obscene matter and materials in this state to children under the age of nineteen;

(2) to publicize its findings as to the obscene character of any publication, motion picture or other obscene matter available to such children;

(3) to solicit the support of the public in preventing obscene publications from reaching such children;

(4) to furnish its findings to publishers, distributors and retailers of such publications and to law enforcement officials;

(5) to seek the aid of such officials in prosecuting offenders of the State obscenity laws.

Section 3. The Commission may conduct hearings, examine witnesses under oath and may compel the attendance and testimony of witnesses, and the production of books, records and documents. Oaths may be administered by any member of the Commission. Subpoenas and subpoenas duces tecum may be issued over the signature of the chairman or any other officer of the Commission and may be served by any adult person designated by the issuing office.

Any _____ court of this State or any judge thereof, upon application of the Commission, may in his discretion, compel the attendance of witnesses, the production of books, records or documents and the giving of testimony before the Commission by an attachment for contempt or otherwise in the same manner as production of evidence may be compelled before the Court.

Section 4. The Commission shall make an annual report to the Governor of its activities no later than the _____ day of _____ of each year.

Section 5. The sum of $_____ or so much as may be necessary, is appropriated for to the Commission to carry out the provisions of this Act for the fiscal year ending _____. Thereafter, appropriations for this Commission shall be included in the General Appropriations Bill in which is included appropriations for other instrumentalities of the State government.

This Act is effective _____.

567

APPENDIX VIII

AN ACT

To amend the penal law, in relation to definition of the word "obscene"

The People of the State of New York, represented in Senate and Assembly, do enact as follows:

Section 1. Subdivision one of section 235.00 of the penal law, as amended by chapter seven hundred ninety-one of the laws of nineteen hundred sixty-seven, is hereby amended to read as follows:

1. "Obscene." Any material or performance is "obscene" if (a) considered as a whole, its predominant appeal is to prurient, shameful or morbid interest in nudity, sex, excretion, sadism or masochism, and (b) it goes substantially beyond customary limits of candor in describing or representing such matters [, and (c) it is utterly without redeeming social value]. Predominant appeal shall be judged with reference to ordinary adults unless it appears from the character of the material or the circumstances of dissemination to be designed for children or other specially susceptible audience.

§ 2. This act shall take effect on the _____ next succeeding the date on which it shall have become a law.

Explanation—Matter in brackets [ ] is old law to be omitted.

APPENDIX IX

AN ORDINANCE REGULATING FILMS NOT SUITABLE FOR YOUNG PERSONS

THE MUNICIPAL COUNCIL OF THE CITY OF _____ does ordain:

SECTION 1. Definition of terms.

(a) "Film" means any motion picture film or series of films, whether full length or short subject, but does not include newsreels portraying actual current events or pictorial news of the day.

(b) "Exhibit" means to project a film at any motion picture theatre or other public place within the city to which tickets are sold for admission.

(c) "Exhibitor" means any person, firm or corporation which exhibits a film.

(d) "Young person" means any person who has not attained his eighteenth birthday.

(e) "Board" means the Motion Picture Board established by Section 2 of this Ordinance.

(f) "Nudity" means the showing of a human male or female genitals, pubic area or buttocks with less than a full opaque covering or the showing of the female breast with less than a fully opaque covering of any portion thereof below the top of the nipple, or the depiction of covered male genitals in a discernibly turgid state.

(g) "Sexual conduct" means acts of masturbation, homosexuality, sexual intercourse, or physical contact with a person's clothed or unclothed genitals, pubic area, buttocks or, if such person be a female, breast.

(h) "Sexual excitement" means the condition of human male or female genitals when in a state of sexual stimulation or arousal.

(i) "Sado-masochistic abuse" means flagellation or torture by or upon a person clad in undergarments, bizarre costume, or the condition of being fettered, bound or otherwise physically restrained on the part of one so clothed.

(j) "Not suitable for young persons" means that quality of any description or representation, in whatever form, of nudity, sexual conduct, sexual excitement, or sado-masochistic abuse, when it:

(1) predominantly appeals to the prurient, shameful or morbid interest of young persons and,

(a) is patently offensive to prevailing standards in the adult community as a whole with respect to what is suitable material for young persons.

(k) "Classify" means to determine whether a film is:

(1) Suitable for young persons; or

(2) Not suitable for young persons.

(l) "Advertisement" means any promotional material initiated by an exhibitor designed to bring a film to public attention or to increase the sale of tickets to exhibitions of same, whether by newspaper, billboard, motion picture, television, radio, or other media within or originating within the City.

(m) "Initial exhibition" means the first exhibition of any film within the City.

(n) "Subsequent exhibition" means any exhibition subsequent to the initial exhibition, whether by the same or a different exhibitor.

(o) "File" means to deliver to the Municipal Clerk for safekeeping as a public record of the City.

(p) "Classification order" means a written determination by a majority of the Board classifying a film, or granting or refusing an application for change of classification.

(q) The term "Board" as used herein shall include the City when attempting to enforce this Ordinance and the Corporation Counsel of the City when representing the Board or the City.

(r) "City" shall mean the City of _____.

(s) "Person" shall mean person, firm, corporation or partnership.

SECTION 2. Establishment of Board:

There is hereby created a Board to be known as the Motion Picture Classification Board which shall be composed of a Chairman and Eight Members to be appointed by the Mayor. Such members shall serve without pay and shall adopt such rules and regulations as they deem best governing their action, proceeding and deliberations and time and place of meeting. If a vacancy occurs upon the Board by death, resignation or otherwise, the

Mayor shall appoint a member to fill such vacancy for the unexpired term.

The Chairman and all Members of the Board shall be good, moral, law-abiding citizens of the City and shall be chosen, so far as reasonably practicable, in such a manner that they will represent a cross section of the community. The Board shall appoint as Secretary of the Board one of its members.

SECTION 3. Classification Procedure:

(a) Before any initial exhibition, the exhibitor shall file a proposed classification of the film to be exhibited, stating the title of the film and the name of the producer, and giving a summary of the plot and such other information as the Board may by rule require, together with the classification proposed by the exhibitor. The Board shall examine such proposed classification, and if it approved same, shall mark it "approved" and file it as its own classification order. If the Board fails to act, that is, either file a classification order or hold a hearing within five (5) days after such proposed classification is filed, the proposed classification shall be considered approved.

(b) If upon examination of the proposed classification a majority of the Board is not satisfied that it is proper, the Chairman shall direct the exhibitor to project the film before any five (5) or more members of the Board at a suitably equipped place and at a specified time, which shall be the earliest time practicable with due regard to the availability of the film. The exhibitor, or his designated representative, may at such time make such statement to the Board in support of his proposed classification and present such testimony as he may desire. Within two (2) days, the Board shall make and file its classification of the film in question.

(c) Any initial or subsequent exhibitor may file an application for a change in the classification of any film previously classified. No exhibitor shall be allowed to file more than one (1) application for change of classification of the same film. Such application shall contain sworn statement of the grounds upon which the application is based. Upon filing of such application, the Municipal Clerk shall bring it immediately to the attention of the Chairman of the Board, who upon application by the exhibitor shall set a time and place for a hearing and shall notify the applicants and all interested parties, including all exhibitors who may be exhibiting or preparing to exhibit the film. The Board shall view the film and at such hearing hear the statements of all interested parties, and any proper testimony that may be offered, and shall within two (2) days thereafter make and file its order approving or changing such classification. If the classification of a film is changed as a result of such hearing to the classification "not suitable for young persons," the exhibitors showing the film shall have seven (7) days in which to alter their advertising and audience policy to comply with such classification.

(d) Upon filing by the Board of any classification order, the Municipal Clerk shall immediately issue and mail a notice of classification to the exhibitor involved and to any other exhibitor who shall request such notice.

(e) A classification shall be binding on any subsequent exhibitor

570

unless and until he obtains a change of classification in the manner above provided.

SECTION 4. Offenses:

(a) It shall be unlawful for any exhibitor or his employee:

(1) To exhibit any film which has not been classified as provided in this Ordinance.

(2) To exhibit any film classified "not suitable for young persons" if any current advertisement of such film by such exhibitors fails to state clearly the classification of such film.

(3) To exhibit any film classified "not suitable for young persons" without keeping such classification posted prominently in front of the theatre in which such film is being exhibited.

(4) Knowingly to sell or give to any young person a ticket to any film classified "not suitable for young persons."

(5) Knowingly to permit any young person to view the exhibition of any film classified "not suitable for young persons."

(6) To exhibit any film classified "not suitable for young persons" or any scene or scenes from such a film or from an unclassified film, whether moving or still, in the same theatre and on the same program with a film classified "suitable for young persons"; provided that any advertising preview or trailer containing a scene or scenes from an unclassified film or film classified "not suitable for young persons" may be shown at any time if same has been separately classified as "suitable for young persons" under the provisions of Section 3 of this Ordinance.

(7) To make any false or wilfully misleading statement in any proposed classification, application for change of classification, or any other proceeding before the Board.

(8) To exhibit any film classified "not suitable for young persons" without having in force the license hereinafter provided.

(b) It shall be unlawful for any young person:

(1) To give his age falsely as eighteen (18) years of age or over, for the purpose of gaining admittance to an exhibition of a film classified "not suitable for young persons."

(2) To enter or remain in the viewing room of any theatre where a film classified "not suitable for young persons" is being exhibited.

(3) To state falsely that he or she is married for the purpose of gaining admittance to an exhibition of a film classified as "not suitable for young persons."

(c) It shall be unlawful for any person:

(1) To sell or give any person a ticket to an exhibition of a film classified "not suitable for young persons."

(2) To make any false or wilfully misleading statement in an application for change of classification or in any proceeding before the Board.

(3) To make any false statements for the purpose of enabling any young person to gain admittance to the exhibition of a film classified as "not suitable for young persons."

(d) To the extent that any prosecution or other proceeding under this Ordinance involves the entering, purchasing of a ticket, or viewing by a young person of a film classified "not suitable for young persons," it shall be a valid defense that such young person

571

was accompanied by his parent or legally appointed guardian, husband or wife, throughout the viewing of such film.

SECTION 5. License:

Every exhibitor holding a motion picture theatre or motion picture show license issued pursuant to Ordinances of the said City shall be entitled to issuance of a license by the Municipal Clerk to exhibit films classified "not suitable for young persons."

SECTION 6. Suspension of License:

Whenever the City Attorney or any person acting under his direction, or any ten (10) citizens of the said City shall file a sworn complaint with the Municipal Clerk stating that any exhibitor has repeatedly violated the provisions of this Ordinance, or that any exhibitor has persistently failed to use reasonable diligence to determine whether those seeking admittance to the exhibition of a film classified "not suitable for young persons" are below the age of eighteen (18), the Municipal Clerk shall immediately bring such complaint to the attention of the Board, who shall set a time and place for hearing such complaint and cause notice of such hearing to be given to the complainants and to the exhibitor involved. The Board shall have authority to require witnesses to appear and testify at such hearing, and any party to such hearing shall be entitled to such process. If, after hearing the evidence, the Board shall find the charges in such complaint to be true, it shall issue and file an order revoking or suspending the license above provided insofar as it grants the privilege of showing such classified pictures for a specific period not to exceed one (1) year, or may issue a reprimand if it is satisfied that such violation will not continue.

The Board likewise, after notice and hearing, may revoke or suspend the license of any exhibitor who has refused or unreasonably failed to produce or delayed the submission of a film for review, when requested by the Board.

SECTION 7. Judicial Review:

(a) Within two (2) days after the filing of any classification by the Board, other than an order approving the classification proposed by an exhibitor, any exhibitor may file a notice of non-acceptance of the Board's classification, stating his intention to exhibit the film in question under a different classification. Thereupon, it shall be the duty of the Board to do the following:

(1) Within three (3) days thereafter to make application to the Superior Court of _____, for a temporary and a permanent injunction to enjoin such defendant-exhibitor, being the exhibitor who contests the classification, from exhibiting the film in question contrary to the provisions of this ordinance.

(2) To have said application for temporary injunction set for hearing within five (5) days after the filing thereof. In the event the defendant-exhibitor appears at or before the time of the hearing of such temporary injunction, waives the notice otherwise provided by the _____ Rules of Civil Procedure, and requests that at the time set for such hearing the Court proceed to hear the case under the _____ Rules of Civil Procedure for permanent injunction on its merits, the Board shall be required to waive its application for temporary injunction and shall join

572

in such request. In the event the defendant-exhibitor does not waive notice and/or does not request an early hearing on the Board's application for permanent injunction, it shall nevertheless be the duty of the Board to obtain the earliest possible setting for such hearing under the provisions of State Law and the _____ Rules of Civil Procedure.

(3) If the injunction is granted by the trial court and the defendant-exhibitor appeals to the _____ Court of Appeals, the Board shall waive any and all statutory notices and times as provided for in the _____ State statutes and _____ Rules of Civil Procedure, and shall within five (5) days after receiving a copy of appealing exhibitor's brief, file its reply brief, if required, and be prepared to submit the case upon oral submission or take any other reasonable action requested by the appealing exhibitor to expedite the submission of the case to the _____ Court of Appeals, and shall upon request of the appealing exhibitor, jointly with such exhibitor, request the _____ Court of Appeals to advance the cause upon the docket and to give it a preferential setting the same as is afforded an appeal from a temporary injunction or other preferential matters.

(4) If the _____ Court of Appeals should by its judgment affirm the judgment of the trial court granting the injunction and the appealing exhibitor should file an application for writ of error to the _____ Supreme Court, the Board shall be required to waive any and all notices and times as provided for in the _____ State Statutes and the _____ Rules of Civil Procedure, and shall within five (5) days after receiving a copy of the applications for writ of error, file its reply brief, if required, and be prepared to submit the case upon oral submission or take any other reasonable action requested by the appealing exhibitor to expedite the submission of the case to the Supreme Court and shall upon request of the appealing exhibitor, jointly with such exhibitor, request the Supreme Court to advance the cause upon the docket and to give it a preferential setting the same as is afforded an appeal from a temporary injunction or other preferential matters.

(5) If the Superior Court denies the Board's application for injunction and the Board elects to appeal, the Board shall be required to waive all periods of time allowed it by the _____ Rules of Civil Procedure and if a motion for a new trial is required, shall file said motion within two (2) days after the signing of the judgment (or on the following Monday if said period ends on a Saturday or Sunday, or on the day following if the period ends on a Legal Holiday), shall not amend said motion and shall obtain a hearing on such motion within five (5) days time. If no motion for new trial is required as a prerequisite to an appeal under the _____ Rules of Civil Procedure, the Board shall not file such a motion. Within ten (10) days after the judgment is signed by the District Court denying such injunction or within ten (10) days after

the order overruling the Board's motion for new trial is signed, if such motion is required, the Board shall complete all steps necessary for the perfection of its appeal of the _____ Court of Appeals, including the filing of the Transcript, Statement of Facts and Appellant's Brief. Failure to do so shall constitute an abandonment of the appeal. On filing the record with the _____ Court of Appeals, the Board shall file a motion to advance requesting the Court to give a preferential setting the same as is afforded an appeal from a temporary injunction or other preferential matters.

(6) If the _____ Court of Appeals reverses the trial court after the trial court has granted an injunction, or if the _____ Court of Appeals refuses to reverse the trial court after that court has failed to grant an injunction, then if the Board desires to appeal from the decision of the _____ Court of Appeals by writ of error to the Supreme Court of the State of _____ it must file its motion for rehearing within two (2) days of rendition of the decision of the Court of Appeals (or on the following Monday if said period ends on a Saturday or Sunday, or on the day following if the period ends on a Legal Holiday), and shall file its application for writ of error within ten (10) days after the _____ Court of Appeals' order overruling such motion for rehearing, and failure to do so shall waive all rights to appeal from the decision of the _____ Court of Appeals. At the time of filing the application for writ of error, the Board shall also request the Supreme Court to give the case a preferential setting and advance the same on the docket.

(b) The filing of such notice of non-acceptance shall not suspend or set aside the Board's order, but such order shall be suspended at the end of ten (10) days after the filing of such notice unless an injunction is issued within such period.

(c) Failure of any exhibitor to file the notice of non-acceptance within two (2) days as required in subdivision (1) of such classification order and such exhibitor shall be bound by such order in all subsequent proceedings except such proceedings as may be had in connection with any application for change of classification under Subsection (c) of Section 3 above.

SECTION 8. Public Nuisances:

The following acts are declared to be public nuisances:

(a) Any violation of subdivisions (1), (2), (3) or (6) of subdivision (a) of Section 4 of this Ordinance.

(b) Any exhibition of a film classified as "not suitable for young persons" at which more than three (3) young persons are admitted.

(c) Any exhibition of a film classified as "not suitable for young persons" by an exhibitor who fails to use reasonable diligence to determine whether persons admitted to such exhibitions are persons eighteen (18) years.

(d) Any exhibition of a film classified as "not suitable for young persons" by an exhibitor who has been convicted of as many as three (3) violations of subdivisions (4) or (5) of subdivision (a) of Section 4 of this Ordinance in connection with the exhibition of the same film.

574

(e) To pander by advertisement for the purpose of inducing by such advertisement "young persons" to view films classified as "not suitable for young persons." Provided such advertisement or advertisements appear on three (3) separate occasions or in three (3) separate media on the (1) occasion.

SECTION 9. Injunctions:

Whenever the Board has probable cause to believe that any exhibitor has committed any of the acts declared in Section 8 above to be a public nuisance, the Board shall have the duty to make application to a court of competent jurisdiction for an injunction restraining the commission of such acts.

SECTION 10. Exemption to State Law:

Nothing in this Ordinance shall be construed to regulate public exhibitions preempted by the Statutes of the State of _____.

SECTION 11.

That any person who shall violate any provisions of this Ordinance shall be subject to a fine not to exceed Two Hundred Dollars ($200.00) and each offense shall be deemed to be a separate violation and punishable as a separate offense, and each day that a film is exhibited which has not been classified according to this Ordinance shall be a separate offense.

SECTION 12. Severability Clause:

Should any section, subsection, sentence, provision, clause, or phrase be held to be invalid for any reason, such holding shall not render invalid any other section, subsection, sentence, provision, clause or phrase of this Ordinance, and the same are deemed severable for this purpose. The Corporation Counsel shall be hereby empowered to prosecute violations in Municipal Court and/or the other courts of the State.

SECTION 13.

This Ordinance shall take effect upon final passage and publication, according to law.

APPENDIX X

MODEL AMENDMENT TO LICENSING ORDINANCE TO PROTECT CHILDREN IN PUBLIC STREETS AND HIGHWAYS FROM VIEWING MOTION PICTURES, SLIDES AND OTHER EXHIBITS NOT SUITABLE FOR VIEWING BY CHILDREN AND TO PREVENT TRAFFIC HAZARDS

Unlawful to Exhibit Nude or Semi-Nude Pictures on Theater Screens within view of Public Street or Highway.

It shall be unlawful for any licensee, ticket seller, ticket taker, usher, motion picture machine operator and any other person connected with or employed by any licensee to show or exhibit at a theater in the city or to aid or assist in such exhibition any motion picture, slide, or other exhibit which is visible from any public street or highway in which the bare buttocks or the bare female breasts of the human body are shown or in which striptease, burlesque or nudist-type scenes constitute the main or primary material of such movie, slide or exhibit.

APPENDIX XI

SPECIFIC DESCRIPTIVE MINORS STATUTE AMENDED
TO COMPLY WITH RABECK V. NEW YORK

A person shall be guilty of a misdemeanor who knowingly sells to a person under 18 years of age any material herewith defined by the phrase "obscene for minors."

Definitions

The following material is "obscene for minors":

1. any picture or other representation which depicts one or more "specified anatomical areas" or "specified sexual activities" and which, by means of posing, composition or format, concentrates prurient interest on the area(s) or activity(ies);

2. any publication or sound recording which contains descriptions or narrative accounts of one or more "specified sexual activities" and which, by means of animated sensual details, concentrates prurient interest on the activity(ies).

"Specified anatomical areas" means:

1. less than completely and opaquely covered; (a) human genitals, pubic region, (c) buttock, and (d) female breast below a point immediately above the top of the areola; and

2. human male genitals in a discernibly turgid state, even if completely and opaquely covered.

"Specified sexual activities" means:

1. human genitals in a state of sexual stimulation or arousal;

2. acts of human masturbation, sexual intercourse or sodomy;

3. fondling or other erotic touching of human genitals, pubic region, buttock or female breast.

"Knowingly" means:

having knowledge of the character and content of any material described herein, or having failed to exercise reasonable inspection which would disclose its character and content.

Presumptions

The sale to a person under 18 years of age of any material proscribed herein shall constitute presumptive evidence:

1. that the defendant made the sale knowingly, and

2. that the defendant knew that the person was under 18 years of age.

Defense

The establishment by a defendant of all of the following facts shall constitute a complete defense to a prosecution hereunder:

1. that the person under the age of 18 years falsely represented in or by writing that he or she was 18 years of age or over, and

2. that the person's appearance was such that an ordinary prudent individual would believe him or her to be 18 years of age or over and

3. that the sale to the person was made in good faith relying upon such written representation and appearance, and in the

576

reasonable belief that the person was actually 18 years of age or over.

Intent of This Act

The Legislature herewith establishes a separate definition of obscenity for persons under 18 years of age in order to adjust the existing definition to social realities, by assessing the appeal of the material defined in terms of the sexual interests of persons under 18. The material intended to be covered by this definition is that appealing to prurient interest, and principally that which emphasizes its sexually provocative aspects and is aimed at a primary audience of mature adults. The Legislature considers that persons under 18 years of age lack the maturity to cope with this material, and that it is harmful to their mental and moral health; this act is intended as a means of insulating them from it.

The Legislature deems the material defined herein as patently offensive to the minimum contemporary standards of the community of the people of relating to the description of representation of sexual matters to persons under 18 years of age, and considers that any social importance the material may have is outweighed by its harmful effect on persons under 18. Accordingly, the definition is intended to exclude further consideration of patent offensiveness or social importance.

Note

Specific minor statutes give the community a false sense of security. However, we include this minor statute because we do not want to give the impression that the Supreme Court in Rabeck had ruled out this type of objective statute. We consider this an improvement on most existing minor statutes. It is not a substitute for general obscenity statutes.

APPENDIX XII

AN ORDINANCE PROHIBITING THE SHOWING OF OBSCENE MOVIES IN THE CITY OF
DEFINING THE TERM "OBSCENE" PROVIDING FOR A PENALTY FOR VIOLATION HEREOF; PROVIDING A SEVERABILITY CLAUSE AND EFFECTIVE DATE HEREOF.

I. DEFINITION.

For purposes of this ordinance, the word 'obscene' is defined as whether to the average person, applying contemporary community standards, the dominant theme of the material taken as a whole appeals to prurient interests.

II. UNLAWFUL TO EXHIBIT OBSCENE MOVIE.

It shall be unlawful for any person operating a motion picture theater in the City of   and for any employee, ticket seller, ticket taker, usher, motion picture machine operator and any other person connected with or employed by any such person to exhibit, or to show or exhibit or to aid or assist in the exhibition of any obscene motion picture, slide or exhibit in the City of

III. PENALTY.

Any person violating any of the terms of this ordinance or

577

failing or refusing to comply with the provisions hereof, shall be deemed guilty of a misdemeanor and upon conviction thereof shall be fined in an amount of not less than $50.00 nor more than $200.00, and the license of such person to operate a movie theater in the City of   shall be suspended for a period of not less than three nor more than sixty days.

IV. SEVERABILITY.

Each word, phrase, paragraph and section of this ordinance is hereby declared to be an individual section or provision, and the holding of any word, phrase, paragraph or section to be void, ineffective or unconstitutional for any cause whatsoever, shall not be deemed to affect any other word, phrase, paragraph or section hereof or the application of any word, phrase, section or paragraph to circumstances or facts not connected with such holding.

V. REPEAL OF CONFLICTING ORDINANCES.

All ordinances or parts of ordinances in conflict herewith shall be and they hereby are, repealed to the extent of such conflict.

VI. EFFECTIVE DATE.

This ordinance shall become in full force and effect from and after five days after its passage and publication as required by law and the Charter of the City of

Report of Commissioner Charles H. Keating, Jr.

INTRODUCTION

"The Congress finds that the traffic in obscenity and pornography is a matter of national concern."

This opening statement of Public Law 90-100 creating the Commission on Obscenity and Pornography is ample evidence that our nation is imperiled by a poison which is all-pervasive. Pornography is not new. But for centuries its invidious effects upon individuals and upon nations has been held in reasonable control by law.

There is good reason for such law, as Reo M. Christenson in an article "Censorship of Pornography? Yes" (*The Progressive,* September, 1970)* writes:

. . . *Sex and Culture* by former Oxford Professor J. D. Unwin, whose massive studies in eighty primitive and civilized societies reveal a distinct correlation between increasing sexual freedom and social decline. The more sexually permissive a society becomes, Unwin says, the

---

*Because of the excellence of this article, I have appended it in full as Exhibit "A" to my Report.

less creative energy it exhibits and the slower its movement toward rationality, philosophical speculation, and advanced civilization.

Harvard sociologist Pitirim Sorokin agrees with Unwin that sexual restraints promote cultural progress; in *The American Sexual Revolution* he contends that immoral and anti-social behavior increased with cultural permissiveness toward the erotic sub-arts. In an article in *The New York Times* magazine entitled "Why I Dislike Western Civilization," May 10, 1964, Arnold Toynbee argued that a culture which postpones rather than stimulates sexual experience in young adults is a culture most prone to progress.

In another article in *The New York Times* magazine, Bruno Bettelheim, the noted psychoanalyst, recently observed: "If a society does not taboo sex, children will grow up in relative sex freedom. But so far, history has shown that such a society cannot create culture or civilization; it remains primitive." Sorokin asserts ". . . there is no example of a community which has retained its high position on the cultural scale after less rigorous sexual customs have replaced more restricting ones."

In slightly less than two centuries of existence, the United States has developed from a frontier nation to a position of predominance in the world in commerce and industry, as well as in the arts and sciences. It is no mere coincidence that this period of unparalleled progress was one in which the rule of law prevailed. The fact that we enjoyed a "Government of Laws and not of Men" provided the intellectual and cultural climate in which the American could develop his talents and the resources of his country to their respective peaks. Throughout our history, we have been successful in adapting and shaping our laws to meet the changing circumstances of the times. Our law has been a living thing, a constant companion which has served us well as our nation came into its maturity. Our tradition and, in fact, our genius has been the adaptation of our laws to meet the challenges of the times. To renounce law as a solution is to abandon our heritage.

Against the general background of the history of nations and against the specific background of the history of the United States, it is apparent the laws prohibiting obscenity and pornography have played an important role in the creativity and excellence of our system and our society—these

579

laws have played an important part in our people coming so far and achieving so much.

Accordingly, it seems incredible to this writer that the majority of the Presidential Commission appointed under Public Law 90-100 opts for a "Danish" solution to the problem of pornography; namely, to remove the controls—to repeal the law.

The shocking and anarchistic recommendation of the majority is difficult to comprehend. It may help to enumerate the Federal laws and State statutes which the majority of this Commission—in spite of the lessons of history, in spite of the will of the overwhelming majority of the people of this nation, and in spite of the circumstances of our times—specifically recommend to be repealed; namely:

18 United States Code, Sections 1461, 1462, 1464, 1465;

19 United States Code, Section 1305;

39 United States Code, Section 4006.s;

Ala. Code, Ch. 64A, Section 374 (4);

Alaska Stats., Title 11, Section 11. 40. 160;

Ariz. Rev. Stats., Title 13, Section 13-532;

Ark. Stats., Vol. 4, Ch. 27, Sections 41-2702, 2703, 2704;

Calif. West's Ann. Code, Ch. 75, Section 311. 2;

Colo. Rev. Stats., Vol. 3, Sections 40-9-16, -17, -18;

Conn. Gen. Stats. Ann., Vol. 28, Title 53, Section 53-243;

Del. Code Ann., Vol. 7, Title 11, Section 711;

Fla. Stats. Ann., Vol. 22A, Section 847.011;

Ga. Code Ann., Title 26, Section 26-2101;

Hawaii Rev. Laws, Ch. 267, Section 267-8;

Ida. Gen. Laws, Vol. 4, Ch. 15, Section 18-1507 and 18-4101 (3), (4), and (5);

Ill. Hurd Ann. Stats., Ch. 38, Section 11-20;

Ind. Stats. Ann., Vol. 4, Ch. 6, Section 9-601 (2085) Fifth, and Section 9-604 (2088) (b); Ch. 28, Section 10-2803;

Iowa Code Ann., Vol. 55, Section 725.3, .5, .6;

Kans. Stats. Ann., Art. 11, Section 21-1102, 1115, 1118;

Ky. Rev. Stats., Ch. 436, Section 436.100, .101 (2);

La. West's Stats. Ann., Vol. 9, Section 106;

Me. Rev. Stats. Ann. 1964, Vol. 9, Title 17, Ch. 93, Section 2901, 2904, 2905;

Md. Ann. Code, Vol. 3, Art. 27, Section 418;

Mass. Gen. Laws, Vol. 44, Ch. 272, Section 28A; B, Section 31, Section 32;

Mich. Compiled Laws Ann., Vol. 39, Section 750.343a through d;

Minn. Stats. Ann., Vol. 40A, Section 617.241, 617.26;
Miss. Code, Vol. 2A, Sections 2280, 2286, 2288, 2674-03;
Mo. Vernon's Ann. Stats., Vol. 41, Section 563.270, .280, .290;
Mont. Rev. Code, Vol. 8, Section 94-3601, 3602;
Neb. Rev. Stats., Ch. 28, Section 28-921, 922;
Nev. Rev. Stats., Vol. 2, Section 201.250;
N. H. Rev. Stats. Ann., Vol. 5, Section 571A;
N. J. Stats. Ann., Title 2A, Section 2A:115-2, -3;
N. Y. McKinney's Consol. Laws, Book 39, Art. 235, Section 235.00, .05, .10, .15;
N. C. Gen. Stats., Vol. 1B, Section 14-189.1, .2; Section 14-190;
N. D. Century Code, Vol. 2, Section 12-21-08;
Ohio Rev. Code Ann., Title 29, Section 2905.34, .342(A), .36, .40, .41;
Okla. Stats. Ann., Title 21, Sections 1021(3) and (4), 1040.8, 1040.13;
Ore. Rev. Stats. Vol. 1, Section 167.151;
Penn. Purdon's Stats. Ann., Title 18, Section 4524, 4528, 4530;
R. I. Gen. Laws, Vol. 3, Section 11-31-1; 11-31-3; 11-31-4;
S. C. Code, Vol. 4, Section 16-414.1, .2;
S. D. Laws of 1968, Ch. 29, Section 1;
Tenn. Code Ann., Vol. 7, Section 39-3003;
Tex. Vernon's Ann. Penal Code, Vols. 1 and 1A, Art. 527-509, Section 1;
Utah Code Ann., Vol. 8, Section 76-39-5 (1) through (5);
Va. Code, Vol. 4, Section 18.1-228, -229, -230;
Wash. Rev. Code, Ch. 9.68, Section 9.68.010, .020;
W. Va. Code Ann., Section 61-8-11;
Wisc. Stats. Ann., Vol. 41, Section 944.21, .22, .23;
Wyo. Stats. Ann., Vol. 3, Ch. 6, Section 6-103, -104;
D. C. Code, Section 22-2001, as amended by Public Law 90-226, Sec. 872(a).s.

Such presumption! Such an advocacy of moral anarchy! Such a defiance of the mandate of the Congress which created the Commission! Such a bold advocacy of a libertine philosophy! Truly, it is difficult to believe that to which the majority of this Commission has given birth.

My Report will go into such detail as is possible on the specifics of the problem, but I cannot undertake consideration of the subject of pornography without commenting on its underlying philosophical and moral basis.

For those who believe in God, in His absolute supremacy as the Creator and Lawgiver of life, in the dignity and destiny which He has conferred upon the human person, in the moral code that governs sexual activity—for those who believe in these "things," no argument against pornography should be necessary.

Though the meaning of pornography is generally understood, reference is seldom made to the root meaning of the term itself. This seems important to me. The Greeks had a word for it, for many "its." And the Greek word for pornography is highly significant. It comes from two Greek words in fact: "prostitute" and "write." So, the dictionary defines pornography as "originally a description of prostitutes and their trade."

Pornography is not merely associated in this historical sense with prostitution, but it is actually a form of prostitution because it advertises and advocates "sex for sale," pleasure for a price.

The use of sexual powers is intimately bound up with both love and life, not merely with the momentary satisfaction of desire. Only a person is capable of love, but any of the lower forms of animal life can experience pleasure as a mere sense reaction. A person is much more than a body, and any form of sexual activity which is impersonal, which uses the body alone for pleasure, violates the integrity of the person and thereby reduces him to the level of an irrational and irresponsible animal.

The traditional Judeo-Christian ethic does not condemn pleasure as an evil in itself; it does condemn the pursuit of pleasure for its own sake, as an end rather than a means, deliberately excluding the higher purposes and values to which pleasure is attached. Everybody knows that the appetite for food makes the necessity of eating more palatable, more pleasurable. To eat to live is rational, sound procedure; to live to eat is an abuse of a basically good thing. The same is true of the sex drive. It serves the individual and the common good of the human race, only when it is creative, productive, when it ministers to love and life. When, however, it serves only itself, it becomes a perversion, actually an anti-social force disruptive and eventually destructive of all love and life. Every word by which the organs of sex are designated bears out this statement: genital, generative, reproductive, procreative. Love is always fruitful of lasting good; mere pleasure is of its nature transitory, barren, the only residue likely to be unhappy, remorseful memories.

582

This thought could be amplified and graphically illustrated.

Those who speak in defense of sexual morality are accused of making sex "dirty." It's the other way around. The defenders of pornography are guilty of degrading sex. Marcel Proust, French novelist *(Sodom and Gomorrah)*, described the effect of his early reading of erotica upon himself: "Oh stream of hell that undermined my adolescence." Literature is a better reflection of life than is scientific opinion; and I am certain that the testimony of men like Proust could be multiplied if someone took the time to assemble the sources.

No, the state cannot legislate virtue, cannot make moral goodness by merely enacting law; but the state can and does legislate against vices which publicly jeopardize the virtue of people who might prefer to remain virtuous. If it is not the proper function of law to offer citizens such protection, then what is it?

The Commission on Obscenity and Pornography —A Runaway Commission

So-called Presidential Commissions do not work. They never will. Such Commissions, in my opinion, are not a valid part of the American political system. The structure of the Commission on Obscenity and Pornography was similar to that of other Commissions. This Commission was not responsible to anyone, either to the President who appointed it, the Congress which created it, or to the people whom the Congress represented.

The selection of the Commission members themselves more often than not is delegated by the President. In the case of the Commission on Obscenity and Pornography, with men such as Jack Valenti and Abe Fortas in key advisory roles in the Johnson Administration, it was more likely than not that the orientation of the Commission for permissiveness would be exactly opposite the orientation intended by Congress; namely, for moral discipline and responsibility. The truth of the matter is that even the Commission members are not those who gather the facts, do the thinking, render the opinions, etc. The bulk of the work is performed by a Staff basically hired by the Commission Chairman, and in the case of the Commission on Obscenity and Pornography, generally consisting of persons of mediocre talent, hangers-on in government, or individuals not yet settled on a course in life who accept interim work on a Commission staff as a

583

place to light and learn during the generally short life of a Commission.

The dispersal of authority and responsibility goes even beyond the Staff. The Commission on Obscenity and Pornography spent by far the greater part of its budget on "contracts" which, as far as I can observe, were principally awarded to persons apparently having predispositions in favor of the Staff's or the Chairman's attitude and philosophy on the subject. These "contractors" are, generally speaking, academicians with ivory-tower views, who have little or no responsibility to anyone or anything, excepting their own thought processes which go unhoned by the checks and balances of a competitive, active, real world. And even beyond the contracting academicians, we find a bulk of work done by their assistants, green graduates, and college students.

To establish the validity of my contentions, I recommend the Commission on Obscenity and Pornography be investigated by the Congress in the following particulars:

(1) The illegality of the appointment of the Chairman.

(2) The influence of the Chairman on the selection of other Commission members.

(3) The expenditure of Commission funds. (See September 12, 1970, letter of Rev. Morton A. Hill, S.J., Exhibit "B.")

(4) The flaunting of the mandate of Public Law 90-100 by the Commission.

(5) The bias of various Commission members in favor of the industries to be affected by the Commission Report.

(6) The failure of the Commission to provide its members with:

(a) Budget information.

(b) Participation in the entire work of the Commission.

(c) A voice in the hiring and retention of Staff.

(d) Approval of contract awards.

(e) Information and reports of the work of Staff or contractors.

(f) Final Technical Reports or final Panel Reports prior to the expiration of the life of the Commission.

(g) Manner in which and by whom the Commission Report, Panel Reports, and Technical Reports will be completed and sent to the Government Printing Office.

Such an investigation, objectively conducted, would settle, for once and for all, the futility of "Presidential" Commissions as an effective arm of government.

584

The Congress, through Public Law 90-100, established the Commission on October 3, 1967, and in January, 1968, President Lyndon B. Johnson appointed William B. Lockhart, Dean of the Law School of the University of Minnesota, Chairman—contrary to Section 2 (d), which states: "The Commission shall elect a chairman . . . from among its members . . ." The Chairman, from the date of his appointment by President Johnson until the first meeting of the Commission in July, 1968, dealt with the Congress, lined up Staff, discussed various studies he proposed for the Commission to take, and otherwise began to mold the direction of the Commission. Actually, it was a full year after the creation of the Commission in October, 1967, that a Director had been procured for the Commission's Staff, i.e., appointed August, 1968, and the nucleus of a Staff assembled, i.e., September, 1968. From the creation of the Commission in October, 1967, until April, 1969, the Commission, including its sub-Panels, had only held twelve meetings. Nevertheless, testifying before a Congressional Committee in April, 1969, Professor Lockhart stated the Commission budget for fiscal 1969 was $643,000 and requested approval of an additional $1,100,000 for the Commission for fiscal 1970.

It should be noted that in his April, 1969, testimony before the Congressional Subcommittee of the Committee on Appropriations, Chairman Lockhart stated that the Director "W. Cody Wilson . . . is a social psychologist who has done a lot of research in the development of adolescent attitudes, although not in the obscenity area. *We wanted someone who was not already involved in the area of obscenity . . .*" Contrast this position with Professor Lockhart's recommendation for the Staff position of Chief Legal Counsel, Mr. Paul Bender. Professor Lockhart recommended Mr. Bender on the *basis of his expertise in the field of law related to obscenity* (italics mine) and, in fact, give the Commission no alternative to the appointment of Mr. Bender, stating at least to Commissioner Link that unless Bender were the Chief Legal Counsel he (Lockhart) would not serve. These references to Professor Lockhart are important because, although Professor Lockhart did not pay his current dues to avoid the telltale association, he is and has been, for all practical purposes, a member of the American Civil Liberties Union.

In June, 1969, when Commissioner Kenneth B. Keating resigned to become Ambassador to India, President Nixon appointed me (no relation to Kenneth B. Keating) as his lone representative to the Commission.

585

As I have said, Public Law 90-100 begins with the following sentence: "The Congress finds that the traffic in obscenity and pornography is a matter of national concern." The history of Public Law 90-100, as it made its way through Congress towards passage, leaves no question whatsoever that both the House of Representatives and the Senate unanimously considered obscenity and pornography to be a serious threat to the United States and to its people, and they wanted something done about it. As a matter of fact, they sought "an appropriate, effective, and constitutional means to deal effectively with such traffic in obscenity and pornography." The only vigorous voice in opposition to the passage of Public Law 90-100 was the American Civil Liberties Union.

It is, therefore, an astounding fact that the man whom the President, in January, 1968, named as Chairman of the Commission on Obscenity and Pornography was not only a member of the American Civil Liberties Union but also as early as 1954, writing with an associate McClure in "Literature, The Law of Obscenity and The Constitution," criticized in systematic form what he regarded as the four basic rationales for obscenity regulation. The criticism analyzed each rationale in terms of "clear and present danger." The authors found that "the evils which are often supposed to result from obscenity are either not really evils or they do not pose such a clear and present danger to substantial social interests . . ." (See Exhibit "A.")

In 1960, the same authors arrived at their concept of variable obscenity. Therein they argued that since there is no such thing as inherently obscene literature, material must be judged by its appeal to and effect upon the audience to which it is directed. However, it appeared in that work that Lockhart and McClure would confine their test to material which was hard-core pornography.

Again in 1962, Lockhart and McClure wrote an article called "Why Obscene" which carried their thesis a step further. ("The First Amendment and the Free Society.")

In March, 1963, the American Civil Liberties Union issued a statement called "Obscenity and Censorship." Based upon a public statement issued on May 28, 1962, which in turn was based on an ACLU Board of Directors' action as of April 16, 1962, which purported to end a three-year review by the ACLU on the issue of censorship of allegedly obscene materials wherein the Union, in effect, concluded that anything goes, that there must be no control of any kind of any expression, no matter what, unless it can be proved that a given expression creates a clear and present danger. That same March, 1963, publication included the text of a press release of February 14, 1963, summarizing "friend of the court" briefs filed with the United States Supreme Court on the defendant's account by the American Civil Liberties Union and the Ohio Civil Liberties Union ("The Lovers," Cleveland Heights, Ohio). I refer to the constant position of the ACLU that no curbs of any kind should be placed upon the obscene, even to the filing of multitudinous briefs in multitudinous cases over the years and across the country as a shield for defense for the pornographers.

In May, 1963, the ACLU distributed widely, as I personally was handed copies in Ohio and in Hawaii, a booklet by Paul Jennison called "Freedom To Read." This booklet underscored and advocated the position of the ACLU of non-control of obscenity and pornography.

In the legislative halls, in the public forum, and particularly in the courtroom, the ACLU has unceasingly sought freedom for the pornographers. The Chairman of the Commission on Obscenity and Pornography is a member of the American Civil Liberties Union; and from the first meeting of the Commission which this writer attended in July, 1969, it was evident that the philosophical orientation and ideology of Professor Lockhart and the majority of the Commission were entirely compatible with the earlier writings of the Chairman as well as with that of the ACLU, and the results of the activities of any Commission under such direction and control were predictable. Contrary to the directives and will of the Congress established in Public Law 90-100, those results are now being imposed upon the American public; namely, that there is no "clear and present danger" from obscenity; that no scientifically valid proof exists that the consumption of pornography produces criminal behavior; and, therefore, obscenity laws should be repealed. (See Effects Panel Report, Legal Panel Report, Overview Report of the Majority, and Complaint for Declaratory Judgment, Injunction, Temporary Restraining Order, and Other Relief, filed September 9, 1970, in the United States District Court for the District of Columbia, Charles H Keating, Jr., Commissioner, Plaintiff, v. William B. Lockhart, Commissioner, et al., Defendants.)

Time and space limitations imposed upon me by the Commission Chairman prohibit a detailed elaboration of the peculiar composition of the Commission and its Staff which have permitted the "runaway" nature of this body, but one additional point must be underscored. Paul Bender, Chief of the Legal Staff of the Commission, is also a member of the American Civil Liberties Union. Prior to his appointment as Chief of the Legal Staff and without my knowing that he was being considered for such appointment, I appeared on a panel for a Cleveland Amory television show wherein Mr. Bender also participated. It was crystal-clear from the position taken by Mr. Bender on that show[1] that he was dedicated to the position on obscenity enunciated by the American Civil Liberties Union—a position, as I have stated, diametrically opposed to the purpose and intent of Public Law 90-100.

When I attended my first meeting of the Commission in July, 1969, the direction and propensities of the Commission toward a "Danish" solution to the problem became immediately obvious. It was also obvious that the Commission was meeting infrequently and the work was being done by a Staff which, with a couple of exceptions, had no background or familiarity with the problem of obscenity and pornography. At this point, I promptly requested the Commission to meet frequently and regularly, suggesting meetings every two weeks or certainly no less often than once a month. My purpose was to have the Commission itself engage in the task at hand and not delegate it to others. This request was denied.

I next asked that I be permitted to serve on each of the four Panels which the Commission had created; namely, Traffic and Distribution, Legal, Effects, and Positive Approaches. (This latter Panel, as constituted and directed, has no basis in Public Law 90-100.) This request was also denied to me; and, further, while I was told that I could attend any Panel session, it was to be strictly a non-participating attendance. The Chairman then arbitrarily assigned me to the Legal Panel, whereon I refused to serve inasmuch as the Panel itself did not do the work but rather delegated it to Mr. Bender whose biased predispositions were obviously opposed to the purport and intent of Public Law 90-100.

I then argued for public hearings to investigate the nature and extent of pornography, the persons who comprised the industry, and other relevant facts, suggesting these public hearings be held in key areas throughout the United States. This request was also denied, although later, after Commissioners Hill and Link (with whom I found myself in almost constant agreement), knowing the importance of public hearings, went ahead on their own and held quite a few such hearings across the country. The majority of the Commission were thus forced into holding public hearings which they did at the end of the life of the Commission in Los Angeles and in Washington, but in a manner so as to effectively exclude meaningful dissent or contradiction to their direction.

I have been accused of non-attendance at the Commission meetings. From the foregoing conduct of the Commission, it became obvious to me that the best service I could render would be to utilize the time I had available for my own investigation, fact-finding, and opinions. This being the case, I repeatedly requested the Commission for copies of any and all Staff or contractors or Panel Reports, studies, memoranda, etc.; for minutes of the Commission's meetings; for budget information; and for information regarding the biographical background of the Staff, etc. These requests were never complied with.

STRUCTURE OF THE COMMISSION REPORT

The method arrived at by the Commission to evolve its Final Report was this: The contracts, along with certain Staff work, would result in a series of "'Technical Reports." These Reports of so-called experts were to be the basis for Panel information and deliberation and subsequently the four Panel Reports. In turn, the four Panel Reports would be the basis for the Commission Overview Report.

As a matter of fact, the Final Draft of the Overview Report was completed prior to the final drafts of the four Panel Reports upon which it was supposed to rest, and the four Panel Reports, which were supposed to rest upon the Technical Reports, were completed before the completion of the Technical Reports. Even today, September 30, 1970, the termination date of the life of the Commission, the Technical Reports are not completed. Improbable as it seems, the Technical Reports continued to be edited by the Staff, after the last full meeting of the Commission on August 25 and 26, 1970, and even today, they continue to be edited and, as a matter of fact, will be assembled and "put together" by an administrative officer of the Commission who will, at that point, have no responsibility to anyone excepting herself, on her own time, as it is possible for her to work into a schedule under the circumstances of a new and different job, and then give them to the Government Printing Office. Similarly, the four Panel Reports, the Commission Overview Report, and the dissenting Reports, even though presented on September 30, 1970, to the President and to the Congress,

589

have not yet been submitted to the Government Printing Office; and this processing will also be accomplished after the life of the Commission terminates under the control and direction of a person responsible to no one.

Obtaining Information from the Commission as a Minority Member

Several facts must be noted; namely, not only were the studies, reports, etc. denied to me, but I understand from the beginning of the Commission's life and certainly while I was a member of the Commission, the awarding of contracts, the hiring of experts, etc., were never submitted for the consideration or the approval of the full Commission. Additionally, those Commissioners whose views did not concur with those of the Chairman were given no right, no authority, nor any funds for studies they considered advisable, and no personnel to in any way assist them to formulate and evaluate their point of view. Considering the fact that I was the lone appointee of the Nixon Administration, it is interesting to compare the total budget of the Commission—approximately $1,750,000—with the total amount expended by the Commission on my behalf of no more than $500, excluding the printing of my dissent. This could hardly be considered a sufficient expenditure to permit presentation of a viewpoint clearly representative of a significant number of persons. I realize I served only one year of the two-year life of the Commission, but it was during the year that I served that the bulk of the $1,750,000 budget of the Commission was expended.

On July 7, 1970, I received First Draft Reports of the Legal, Effects, and Traffic Panels. My point-by-point Reply to the Legal Panel Report was delivered to each Commissioner on August 16, 1970, the result of many painstaking hours of research and writing. At that time, I was given an August 25 deadline for the submission of my total Dissenting Report, the parameters of which had not yet been defined, and, as subsequent events proved, were not to be defined until a full Commission meeting on August 25, 1970. The deadline for my Reply was later extended until August 31, 1970, and then subsequently, after much pressure, the Chairman of the Commission again extended the deadline for my full Reply until September 10, 1970. At 2:30 p.m. on September 8, 1970, two days prior to the deadline to submit my Final Report to the Commission, I received a revision of the Report of the Legal Panel so substantially changed and dramatically different in its content as to be a totally different document and to preclude an effective response. This condition was also true with respect to the Effects Panel Report. Similarly, the Traffic Panel Report. Thus, my Dissenting Report is not able to cover the scope or content of the majority of the Commission, as the only materials available to me to dissent from could give me no more than a general "sense" of what the majority had to say.

Further, the Commission advised dissenting Commissioners Hill, Link, and Keating that the Commission was "so short of funds that their minority reports must be restricted to 150 pages each, or in the event of their agreement, to a composite of 450 pages." Nevertheless, the "Technical Reports" prepared by the "hired hands" of the Commission would be bound in ten books (after "editing by the Staff, which editing is still going on") with a planned publication of 1,000 copies of each book at an estimated cost to the Commission of $100,000. On the other hand, the four Panel Reports, the Report of the Majority of the Commission, and all Minority Reports would be bound into one book, of which 5,000 copies would be printed, at a total expenditure of $12,500.

[For copies of the Report which I submitted to the Commission on September 10, 1970; copies of the original Panel Reports which are quite revealing; or a copy of my initial Reply to the First Draft of the Legal Panel Report, write Citizens for Decent Literature, Inc. 5670 Wilshire Boulevard, Los Angeles, California 90036.]

I only wish that I had some way of summarizing the absurdities collected by the Commission in the Technical Reports which they contracted. Neither time nor space permits me this, nor does time or space permit me to include critiques of those Technical Reports so readily available from the scholarly and practical communities of this country who are experienced in the field of obscenity and pornography—or common sense and logic. I do, however, think that a listing given me by the Commission of those studies is, in itself, revealing. Accordingly, the same follows:

Herbert Abelson, Reuben Cohen, Eugene Heaton, Charlotte Suder. Public Attitudes Toward and Experience with Erotic Materials.

Donald M. Amoroso, Marvin Brown, Manfred Pruesse, Edward E. Ware, Dennis W. Pilkey. An Investigation of

Behavioral, Psychological, and Physiological Reactions to Pornographic Stimuli.

Paul Bender. The Definition of "Obscene" Under Existing Law.

Richard Ben-Veniste. Pornography and Sex Crime—The Danish Experience.

Alan S. Berger, John H. Gagnon, William Simon. Pornography: High School and College Years.

Alan S. Berger, John H. Gagnon, William Simon. Urban Working-Class Adolescents and Sexually Explicit Media.

Donn Byrne, John Lamberth. The Effect of Erotic Stimuli on Sex Arousal, Evaluative Responses, and Subsequent Behavior.

Robert B. Cairns. Psychological Assumptions in Sex Censorship: An Evaluative Review of Recent (1961-68) Research.

Harry M. Clor. Commentary on Constitutional Issues.

Royer F. Cook, Robert H. Fosen. Pornography and the Sex Offender: Patterns of Exposure and Immediate Arousal Effects of Pornographic Stimuli.

Mirjam Damaska. Obscenity Laws in West Germany. Obscenity Laws in France. Obscenity Laws in Italy. Obscenity Laws in Yugoslavia. Remarks on Obscenity Laws in Hungary and the Soviet Union.

Keith E. Davis, George N. Braucht. Exposure to Pornography, Character, and Sexual Deviance: A Retrospective Survey.

Keith E. Davis, George N. Braucht. Reactions to Viewing Films of Erotically Realistic Heterosexual Behavior.

James E. Elias. Exposure to Erotic Materials in Adolescence II.

Marvin Finkelstein. The Traffic in Sex-Oriented Materials, Part I: Adult Bookstores in Boston, Massachusetts.

Marvin Finkelstein. The Traffic in Sex-Oriented Materials, Part II: Criminality and Organized Crime.

Jane Friedman.

Carol Gilligan, Lawrence Kohlberg, Joan Lerner, Mary Belensky. Moral Reasoning About Sexual Dilemmas: The Development of an Interview and Scoring System.

James L. Howard, Clifford B. Reifler, Myron B. Liptzin. Effects of Exposure to Pornography.

Harold S. Kant, Michael J. Goldstein. Exposure to Pornography and Sexual Behavior in Deviant and Normal Groups.

Paul G. Kauper. Commentary on Constitutional Issues Involved in the Legal Control of Obscenity.

592

Marshall Katzman. Photograph Characteristics Influencing the Judgment of Obscenity.

Marshall Katzman. The Relationship of Socio-Economic Background to Judgments of Sexual Stimulation and Their Correlation with Judgments of Obscenity.

Lenore Kupperstein, W. Cody Wilson. Erotica and Anti-Social Behavior: An Analysis of Selected Social Indicator Statistics.

Berl Kutschinsky. The Effect of Pornography—An Experiment on Perception, Attitudes, and Behavior.

Berl Kutschinsky. Pornography in Denmark: Studies on Producers, Sellers, and Users.

Berl Kutschinsky. Sex Crimes and Pornography in Copenhagen: A Survey of Attitudes.

Jack Levin. A Content Analysis of Sex-Related Themes in Underground Press Syndicate Newspapers.

Jay Mann. The Experimental Induction of Sexual Arousal.

Jay Mann, Jack Sidman, Sheldon Starr. Effects of Erotic Films on Sexual Behaviors of Married Couples.

Morris Massey. A Marketing Analysis of Sex-Oriented Materials in Denver, Colorado, August, 1969.

Donald L. Mosher. Psychological Reactions to Pornographic Films.

Donald L. Mosher. Sex Callousness Toward Women.

Donald L. Mosher, Harvey Katz. Pornographic Films, Male Verbal Aggression Against Women, and Guilt.

Harold Nawy. The San Francisco Erotic Marketplace.

Martin L. Propper.

Richard S. Randall.

William J. Roach, Louisa Kreisberg. Westchester College Students' Views on Pornography.

Patricia Schiller. The Effects of Mass Media on the Sexual Behavior of Adolescent Females.

Godfrey P. Schmidt. Comments On and Evaluation of the Definition of "Obscene" Presented by Professor Paul Bender.

Helen Silving. Report on "Obscenity," "Pornography," and "Immorality" in the Laws of Argentina and Mexico.

Alexander B. Smith, Bernard Locke. Response of Police and Prosecutors to Problems in Arrests and Prosecutions for Obscenity and Pornography.

David Sonnenschein, Mark J. M. Ross, Richard Bauman, Linda Swartz, Morgan MacLachlan. A Study of Mass-Media Erotica: The Romance or Confession Magazine.

William N. Stephens. A Cross-Cultural Study of Modesty and Obscenity.

Percy H. Tannenbaum. Emotional Arousal as a Mediator of Communication Effects.

H. Richard Uviller. Analysis and Commentary.

Knud Waaben. The Law on Obscenity in Denmark, Sweden and Norway.

C. Eugene Walker. Erotic Stimuli and the Aggressive Sexual Offender.

Douglas Wallace, Gerald Wehmer. Contemporary Standards of Visual Erotica.

David M. White.

W. Cody Wilson, Jane Friedman, Bernard Horowitz.

Charles Winick. A Study of Consumers of Explicitly Sexual Materials: Some Functions of Adult Movies.

Charles Winick. Some Observations of Patrons of Adult Theaters and Bookstores.

Hans L. Zetterberg. The Consumers of Pornography Where It Is Easily Available: The Swedish Experience.

Marvin Zuckerman. Physiological Measures of Sexual Arousal in the Human.

Louis A. Zurcher, Charles K. Bowman. The Natural History of an *Ad Hoc* Anti-Pornography Organization in Southtown, USA.

Louis A. Zurcher, R. George Kirkpatrick. Collective Dynamics of *Ad Hoc* Anti-Pornography Organizations.

Louis A. Zurcher, R. George Kirkpatrick. The Natural History of an *Ad Hoc* Anti-Pornography Organization in Midville, USA.

Paul Bender. An Analysis of Constitutional Requirements as Manifested in Case Law.

Timothy C. Brock. Erotic Materials: A Commodity Theory Analysis of Availability and Desirability.

Glide Foundation.

Peter Hocker. Report on the Law Relating to Obscenity and Pornography in Japan.

Norman N. Holland. Pornography and the Mechanisms of Defense.

Lenore Kupperstein. The Role of Pornography in the Etiology of Juvenile Delinquency: A Review of the Literature.

Ernst Linveh. The Law of Obscenity and Pornography in Israel.

John Money. The Positive and Constructive Approach to

Pornography in General Sex Education, in the Home, and in Sexological Counseling.

Quality Educational Development, Inc. An In-Depth Review of Research and Educational Programs in Sex Education for Elementary and Secondary Schools in the United States: 1900-1969.

John J. Sampson. Traffic and Distribution of Sexually Oriented Materials in the United States, 1969-70.

Terence P. Thornberry, Robert A. Silverman. The Relationship Between Exposure to Pornography and Juvenile Delinquency As Indicated by Juvenile Court Records.

Louis A. Zurcher, Robert G. Cushing. Some Individual Characteristics of Participants in *Ad Hoc* Anti-Pornography Organizations.

Remember, the cost to the Commission of the above was in the neighborhood of $1,000,000.

More information regarding the majority of the Commission, the tyranny of the Commission Chairman, and the runaway Staff is contained in the Dissenting Report of Commissioners Hill and Link and in the additional Dissenting Report of Commissioner Link, in both of which I concur.

One final fact—one final ironical fact. This Commission, the majority of which have opted for absolute freedom for the pornographers, is the very same Commission which at its very first meeting imposed upon all its members a cloak of secrecy—a vow of silence. No Commissioner was permitted, outside of the hallowed halls of the Commission meetings, to discuss, give interviews, make public statements, etc., regarding the work of the Commission, the opinions of the Commissioners, etc. My request for admission of the press to the meetings of either the Commission or its Panels was refused. Amazing! Incredible! Beyond belief! The "confidentiality rule" of the Commission is understandable when viewed in light of the fact that every effort was made by the majority of the Commission to elimate dissent. As a matter of fact, it was necessary for me to go to Court in order to obtain the right to speak up, the right to dissent.[2]

The record in this regard is clear from a perusal of the Complaint for Declaratory Judgment, Injunction, Temporary Restraining Order, and Other Relief which I filed in the United States District Court, District of Columbia [Civil Action No. 2671-70], on September 9, 1970, and the Order of the Court resulting therefrom, as well as the Stipulation of Dismissal on September 14, 1970.

I hesitated to include so much detail regarding the opera-

595

tion of the Commission. However, upon reflection, it seemed important to me for two reasons:

(1) The fact that the public, particularly law enforcement and the courts, might be misled into thinking that the recommendations of the majority of the Commission were based on worthwhile information and had validity which, indeed, would be a tragedy; and,

(2) The recommendation I have made to abandon the use of Presidential Commissions as an instrument of government required some explanatory detail as an example of the operation of one Commission.

THE QUESTION OF INVOLVEMENT OF THE STATES

Staying with the mandate of Congress in Public Law 90-100 which the majority of the Commission was supposed to do but did not, we find emphasized by placement in Section 1 of that Act the following statement:

The State and local governments have an equal responsibility in the exercise of their regulatory powers and any attempts to control this transmission [i.e., of obscenity and pornography] should be a coordinated effort at the various governmental levels.

and in Section 6 (b):

In carrying out its duties under the Act, the Commission shall consult with other Federal agencies, Governors, attorneys general, and other representatives of State and local government. . . .

In my opinion, the compliance of the majority of the Commission or of its Staff with the foregoing was, for all practical purposes, nonexistent. Even the most liberal interpretation of what was done in this area would have to be classified as an abortive attempt. As a matter of fact, the Chairman of the New Jersey State Commission To Study Obscenity and Depravity in Public Media, (which Commission co-existed in the same time frame as this Commission) made several overtures to the Commission's Staff, specifically W. Cody Wilson, the Executive Director. The attempt of the New Jersey Commission to cooperate, exchange information, and otherwise be of value was formally acknowledged but never accepted.

The States are, indeed, concerned. Witness the Honorary Committee membership of Citizens for Decent Literature, Inc., a nationwide community organization formed (a) to make the public aware of the nature and extent of obscenity

596

and pornography in the United States, and (b) to aid and abet law enforcement, i.e., arrest, prosecution; and conviction of the pornographers.

Citizens for Decent Literature, Inc.
Honorary Committee Members

UNITED STATES SENATORS:
Hon. Carl T. Curtis, Nebraska
Hon. Thomas J. Dodd, Connecticut
Hon. Paul J. Fannin, Arizona
Hon. Barry Goldwater, Arizona
Hon. Jack Miller, Iowa
Hon. Frank E. Moss, Utah
Hon. Karl E. Mundt, So. Dakota
Hon. Jennings Randolph, W. Va.
Hon. John Sparkman, Alabama
Hon. Strom Thurmond, So. Carolina
Hon. Milton R. Young, N. Dakota

U. S. HOUSE OF REPRESENTATIVES:
Hon. Thos. G. Abernethy, Miss.
Hon. E. Ross Adair, Ind.
Hon. Joseph P. Addabbo, N. Y.
Hon. Frank Annunzio, Illinois
Hon. L. C. Arends, Illinois
Hon. John M. Ashbrook, Ohio
Hon. Thomas L. Ashley, Ohio
Hon. Walter S. Baring, Nevada
Hon. E. Y. Berry, South Dakota
Hon. Jackson E. Betts, Ohio
Hon. Ben B. Blackburn, Ga.
Hon. Hale Boggs, Louisiana
Hon. Frank T. Bow, Ohio
Hon. Jack Brinkley, Georgia
Hon. William E. Brock, III, Tenn.
Hon. John H. Buchanan, Jr., Ala.
Hon. J. Herbert Burke, Florida
Hon. Laurence J. Burton, Utah
Hon. Daniel E. Button, New York
Hon. John N. Happy Camp, Okla.
Hon. Bob Casey, Texas
Hon. Chas. E. Chamberlain, Mich.
Hon. Donald D. Clancy, Ohio
Hon. James C. Cleveland, N. H.
Hon. Harold R. Collier, Illinois
Hon. Wm. M. Colmer, Miss.
Hon. Robert J. Corbett, Pa.
Hon. William O. Cowger, Kentucky
Hon. William C. Cramer, Fla.
Hon. Philip M. Crane, Illinois
Hon. W. C. Daniel, Virginia
Hon. Dominick V. Daniels, N. J.
Hon. Robert V. Denney, Nebraska

597

U. S. HOUSE OF REPRESENTATIVES: (Continued)

Hon. John H. Dent, Pa.
Hon. Edward J. Derwinski, Illinois
Hon. Samuel L. Devine, Ohio
Hon. William L. Dickinson, Ala.
Hon. William J. B. Dorn, S. C.
Hon. John Dowdy, Texas
Hon. Thaddeus J. Dulski, N. Y.
Hon. John J. Duncan, Tenn.
Hon. George H. Fallon, Md.
Hon. Michael A. Feighan, Ohio
Hon. Walter W. Flowers, Ala.
Hon. Gerald R. Ford, Michigan
Hon. Samuel N. Freidel, Md.
Hon. Edward A. Garmatz, Md.
Hon. Charles H. Griffin, Mississippi
Hon. James R. Grover, Jr., N. Y.
Hon. G. Elliott Hagan, Georgia
Hon. James A. Haley, Florida
Hon. J. P. Hammerschmidt, Ark.
Hon. James M. Hanley, N. Y.
Hon. Julia B. Hansen, Washington
Hon. William H. Harsha, Ohio
Hon. James F. Hastings, N. Y.
Hon. Wayne L. Hays, Ohio
Hon. Ken Hechler, West Virginia
Hon. David N. Henderson, N. C.
Hon. Lawrence J. Hogan, Md.
Hon. Craig Hosmer, Calif.
Hon. James J. Howard, N. Jersey
Hon. W. R. Hull, Jr., Missouri
Hon. Charles R. Jonas, N. C.
Hon. Carleton J. King, N. C.
Hon. Thomas Kleppe, N. D.
Hon. Earl F. Landgrebe, Indiana
Hon. Odin Langen, Minn.
Hon. Donald E. Lukens, Ohio
Hon. James R. Mann, S. Carolina
Hon. Catherine May, Wash.
Hon. Wm. M. McCulloch, Ohio
Hon. Robert McClory, Illinois
Hon. Jack McDonald, Mich.
Hon. Thomas J. Meskill, Conn.
Hon. Robert H. Michel, Illinois
Hon. Clarence E. Miller, Ohio
Hon. William E. Minshall, Ohio
Hon. Robert H. Mollohan, W. Va.
Hon. John M. Murphy, New York
Hon. Ancher Nelson, Minnesota
Hon. Bill Nichols, Alabama
Hon. Thomas P. O'Neill, Mass.
Hon. Thomas M. Pelly, Washington
Hon. Jerry L. Pettis, California
Hon. Howard W. Pollock, Alaska
Hon. Bob Price, Texas

U. S. HOUSE OF REPRESENTATIVES: (Continued)

Hon. Roman C. Pucinski, Illinois
Hon. Graham Purcell, Texas
Hon. Albert H. Quie, Minnesota
Hon. John R. Rarick, La.
Hon. Charlotte T. Reid, Illinois
Hon. L. Mendel Rivers, S. C.
Hon. H. W. Robison, N. Y.
Hon. Peter W. Rodino, Jr., N. J.
Hon. Richard L. Roudebush, Ind.
Hon. Fernand J. St. Germain, R. I.
Hon. Charles W. Sandman, Jr., N. J.
Hon. John P. Saylor, Pennsylvania
Hon. Henry C. Schadeberg, Wisc.
Hon. Herman T. Schneebeli, Pa.
Hon. Keith G. Sebelius, Kansas
Hon. Robert L. F. Sikes, Florida
Hon. M. G. Snyder, Kentucky
Hon. W. S. Stuckey, Jr., Ga.
Hon. Robert Taft, Jr., Ohio
Hon. Burt L. Talcott, California
Hon. Charles M. Teague, Calif.
Hon. Olin E. Teague, Texas
Hon. Robert O. Tieman, R. I.
Hon. Guy Vander Jagt, Michigan
Hon. Joe D. Waggoner, Jr., La.
Hon. William C. Wampler, Va.
Hon. A. W. Watson, S. C.
Hon. Lowell P. Weicker, Jr., Conn.
Hon. G. Wm. Whitehurst, Va.
Hon. Larry Winn, Jr., Kansas
Hon. Bob Wilson, California
Hon. Jim Wright, Texas
Hon. Chalmers P. Wylie, Ohio
Hon. Gus Yatron, Pennsylvania
Hon. Clement Zablocki, Wisconsin
Hon. Roger H. Zion, Indiana
Hon. John M. Zwach, Minnesota

GOVERNORS:

Hon. Albert P. Brewer, Alabama
Hon. John Dempsey, Connecticut
Hon. Claude R. Kirk, Jr., Florida
Hon. Richard B. Ogilvie, Illinois

■ ■ ■

Paul R. Anderson, President
  Temple University, Philadelphia
Hon. E. Richard Barnes
  Assemblyman, Sacramento, Calif.
Rt. Rev. Francis E. Bloy, Bishop
  Episcopal Diocese of Los Angeles
His Eminence
  John J. Cardinal Carberry
  Archbishop of St. Louis

HONORARY COMMITTEE
MEMBERS: (Continued)

John E. Corbally, Jr.
  President, Syracuse University
Bernard E. Donovan, Ed. D.
  Superintendent of Schools, New York City
Rt. Rev. John H. Esquirol, S. T. D.
  Episcopal Bishop, Connecticut
Rabbi Jacob J. Hecht
  National Com. for Furtherance of
  Jewish Education, New York
Hon. Edward P. Hill, Chief Justice
  Supreme Court of Kentucky
Most Rev. Joseph L. Hogan
  Bishop of Rochester, New York
Jenkin Lloyd Jones, Editor
  and Publisher, Tulsa Tribune
Rabbi Robert I. Kahn
  Houston, Texas
Most Rev. Paul F. Leibold
  Archbishop of Cincinnati
Carl H. Lindner, President
  American Financial Corporation
Robert D. Lindner, V. Pres.
  American Financial Corporation
Mrs. Walter Varney Magee, Pres.
  Gen. Fed. of Women's Clubs
Most Rev. Timothy Manning
  Archbishop of Los Angeles
Rev. Donald F. Miller
  Methodist Minister of Education
  Jefferson City, Missouri
Rev. Kurt P. Nemitz, General
  Church of the New Jerusalem
  Stockholm, Sweden
John W. McDevitt, Supreme Knight
  Knights of Columbus
His Eminence
  Patrick Cardinal O'Boyle
  Archbishop of Washington
Very Rev. Paul L. O'Connor, S. J.
  Pres., Xavier Univ., Cincinnati
Hon. Earl T. Osborne,
  Associate Justice
  Supreme Court of Kentucky
Most Rev. Leo A. Pursley
  Bishop of Fort Wayne-South Bend
Hon. Max Rafferty
  Director of Education, California
Mrs. Belle S. Spafford, President
  National Council of Women,
  Church of Jesus Christ of Latter
  Day Saints, Salt Lake City

600

It has long been apparent that not only are the States concerned but they have been responsible "in the exercise of their regulatory powers and attempts to control the transmission of obscenity and pornography." The police officer, the prosecutor, District Attorney, and Attorney General has not been remiss in vigorous enforcement of the law against the criminal pornographers, excepting only where he is rebuffed and made ridiculous by the courts' subsurvience to the "no-clear-majority" decisions of the Douglas-Black dominated (i.e., in the oscenity field) United States Supreme Court. In May and June, 1967, the United States Supreme Court reversed the obscenity determinations in twenty-two of twenty-six cases. The community standards of eleven states were upset, eight findings of fact by juries and the findings of various tribunals of the judiciary were reversed. The Commission could have, and should have, intimately acquainted and concerned itself with the state authorities in these and other cases—the persons who are on the firing line of the obscenity problem.

Since 1967, the flaunting of morality in the states, i.e., the forcing of immorality on the states by the United States Supreme Court, has gone on unabated insofar as obscenity cases are concerned. The recent appointment of Justices Burger and Blackmun, however, give hopeful indications that this disgusting erosion of morality may be checked— which brings me to the sole legislative recommendation which I now make to the Administration and to the Congress of the United States. In my opinion, this legislation is a positive response to the Congressional mandate of Public Law 90-100 under discussion in this section of my Dissent.

A cursory examination of the State appellate decisions reveals that the High Courts of the fifty States are disenchanted with the performance of the United States Supreme Courts in obscenity matters. A number of the State Supreme Courts have, in strong language, voiced their disapproval of the differing views entertained by certain quarrelsome Justices on the Supreme Court of the United States and the compromising results being reached in that Court's review of State obscenity cases. Most of the State High Courts have

601

refused to acquiesce. See *Henry v. Louisiana,* (magazines), reversed, 20 L. Ed. 2d 1343; *Childs v. Oregon,* (paperback), petition for cert. denied, 22 L. Ed. 2d 460; *Cain v. Commonwealth of Kentucky,* (movie), reversed, 24 L. Ed. 2d 160; *Johnson v. Massachusetts,* (magazines), petition for cert. denied, 24 L. Ed. 2d 452; *Carlos v. New York,* (magazines), reversed, 24 L. Ed. 2d 240; *Spicer v. New York,* (magazines), petition for cert. denied, 25 L. Ed. 2d 653; *Bloss v. Dykema,* (magazines), reversed, 26 L. Ed. 2d 230; *Walker v. Ohio,* (paperback and magazines), reversed, 26 L. Ed. 2d 385; *Hoyt v. Minnesota,* (paperback), reversed, 26 L. Ed. 2d. In each of the above eight states, the State High Court was aware of the nature of the materials considered by the High Court during the 1966 October Term and the results there reached. Yet those Courts refused to reverse the lower State Court decision on their own. Their refusal to so act is an obvious indication that they are reluctant to acknowledge the United States Supreme Court results as controlling—a fact which indicates the State Courts are not confused and recognize wherein the real difficulty lies.

Representative of such disapproval is the language of a unanimous Kentucky Court of Appeals in *Cain, et al. v. Commonwealth of Kentucky,* 437 S. W. 2d 769, at 773: [Note: The Court of Appeals viewed the "Fortas" film[3] approximately two weeks before it handed down its opinion.]

The opinions of Mr. Justice Douglas, when they are only for himself, do not constitute law upon this matter. Mr. Justice Douglas has never purported to follow the law established by his Court or any other Court where matters of obscenity are involved. This fact was noted by Mr. Justice Harlan recently in *Interstate Circuit, Inc. v. Dallas,* 390 U. S. 676, at 705, 88 S. Ct. 1298, at 1314, 20 L. Ed 2d 225, at 244 (April 2, 1968), when he remarked: 'Two members of the Court steadfastly maintain that the First and Fourteenth Amendments render society powerless to protect itself against the dissemination of even the filthiest materials. No other member of the Court, past or present, has ever stated his acceptance of that point of view. . . .'

And at page 774:

Appellants' fifth and final contention is they were entitled to a directed verdict of acquittal because the film shown was not proved to be obscene. As we view this matter, it is not the function of this Court or any other Appellate Court to determine whether the material shown is obscene. This is a factual determination to be made by a jury. The film was shown to the jury, and they found it obscene. Our function as an Appellate Court is limited to determine whether the evidence in the record supports the findings of the jury. If so, the verdict must stand. This law is so basic and ancient to the principles of English and American jurisprudence and so elementary in its application as a principle of appellate procedure that we do not feel called upon to cite authorities for its support. . . .

And at page 775:

. . . The Supreme Court of the United States held in the *Roth* case that obscenity is not protected by the First and Fourteenth Amendments to the Constitution of the United States. As far as we have been able to determine, this holding has never been reversed or modified. The Court has occupied itself since that ruling in a somewhat futile attempt to determine what is obscene and what is not obscene. This problem has given the judiciary of this country the greatest challenge of its history, and as of the date of this opinion, the judicial record reflects nothing more than indecision and failure. While the Courts have vacillated and overexplained, divided and fought, the sentiments of the people of this country have been clear and unassailable, all fifty states of this nation have obscenity laws. From the year of 1800 to 1956, the Congress of the United States passed twenty acts dealing with obscenity. It seems to be universally believed everywhere, except in the whole of the judiciary, that obscenity as such is not entitled to the constitutional protection awarded free speech.

Many times the right to pose a question is tantamount to the right to answer or at least partially so. Down through the years, we have been asking ourselves when dealing with pornography and obscenity, 'Is it harmful?' Of course, this answer cannot come without a certain amount of reservation because the proof is hard to come by and often inconclusive. Therefore, we keep asking the same question and giving the same answers with reservations. If we were to change the form of the question and ask, 'Is is beneficial?' the answer would come loud and clear. Certainly no benefit can come to any individual or any society by the use or dissemination of

603

pornographic and obscene materials. This being so, why should we longer expend the time and energies of the greatest minds of this country in preserving its presence upon the newsstands and in the theaters. . . .

In *State of Florida v. Reese,* 222 So. 2d 732, Justice Spector, speaking in a concurring opinion for three Justices of the Florida Supreme Court, voiced the reaction of the Florida Judiciary at page 737:

However, I doubt the necessity of going through the judicial labor of distinguishing this case from those decided by the United States Supreme Court subsequent to *Roth v. U. S.,* 354 U. S. 476, 77 S. Ct. 1304, 1 L. Ed. 2d 1498, which are cited in the majority opinion. Post-*Roth* cases fail to provide a clear and precise basis upon which the lower court's ruling of invalidity can rest. An examination of those opinions reflect that no single majority of the Court since the Roth case was decided has agreed upon an articulated standard or test satisfactory to a majority of the Justices by which an obscenity statute may be measured against the Constitution.

As I read the cited cases, they are in hopeless conflict, not only as between my views and those expressed in the Federal opinions, but also between the views of the Justices participating in those decisions.

No useful purpose would be served to here list the cast of participants in each of the cases and the views alternately espoused from case to case, it being sufficient for the purpose of my point to observe that there seems to be no perceptible common denominator for the Justices' appearance first on one side of a case and then on another, viz., *A Book Named 'John Cleland's Memoirs of a Woman of Pleasure' v. Attorney General of the Commonwealth of Massachusetts,* 383 U. S. 413, 86 S. Ct. 975 16 L. Ed. 2d 1, (1966), in which six of the Justices agreed upon a reversal but no more than three could agree upon any one *ratio decidendi* to base it on. . . .

In my view, as supported by the foregoing authority, until such time as a readily identifiable standard has been expressly articulated and concurred in by a majority of the United States Supreme Court in a given case, the jurisprudence of obscenity should rest upon the principles of the *Roth* case which, of course, did articulate a constitutional standard susceptible of judical application to obscenity cases. More importantly, the

604

Roth principles were concurred in by a majority of the Court. However, the cases which were later decided by that Court contain opinions of the Justices which are so fractionalized that they are woefully lacking that constancy which is necessary under the doctrine of *stare decisis* before it can be stated with clarion clarity that a given act or circumstance falls within or without the ambit of constitutionality. Thus, when viewed in light of the Roth case, the meaning of the words of the statute, Section 847.011, such as obscene, lewd, lascivious, etc. do fall within the understanding of the meaning.

If courts are to merit the confidence of our citizens, it can no longer be pretended that four-letter-word substitutes for fecal matter and copulation are not obscene merely by veiling them with such hocus-pocus phrasing as 'redeeming social value' and the like.

Even the few Courts which have indicated a willingness to follow the compromising results being reached in the United States Supreme Court have done so with reluctance. Typical is the reproval of a unanimous Supreme Judicial Court of Massachusetts, speaking in *Commonwealth of Massachusetts v. Palladino,* 260 N. E. 2d 653, 656 (June 25, 1970):

We might add that we are entirely in accord with the views stated by Mr. Justice Harlan in his dissent in the *Bloss* case, supra, in which he was of the opinion that proscribing material of the sort there involved was 'the permissible exercise of state power.'

All of the State High Courts, including those which have acquiesced in the United States Supreme Court decisions (supra) are unanimous in their agreement that the constitutional view espoused by Mr. Justice Harlan in the *Roth* case, and concurred in by Chief Justice Burger and Associate Justice Blackmun of the present Court, is the rule of law which should govern in obscenity cases. It is the codification of this rule of law which I now propose:

91st CONGRESS
FIRST SESSION

S.

IN THE SENATE OF THE UNITED STATES
OCTOBER 1970

Mr. _____ introduced the following Bill: which was read twice and referred to the Committee on the Judiciary.

A BILL

TO amend Title 18 and Title 28 of the United States Code with respect to the trial and review of actions involved obscenity, and for other purposes.

Be it enacted by the Senate and House of Representatives of the United States of America in Congress Assembled,

THAT (a) Chapter 71, Title 18, United States Code, is amended by adding at the end thereof the following new section:

Section 1466. Determinations of Fact.

"In any criminal action arising under this chapter or under any other statute of the United States, except those in which trial by jury has been waived by both the people and the defendant, determination of the question whether any article, matter, thing, device, or substance is in fact obscene, lewd, lascivious, indecent, vile, or filthy shall be made by the jury, without comment by the Court upon the weight of the evidence relevant to that question."

(b) The section analysis of that chapter is amended by inserting at the end thereof the following new item:

"1466. Determinations of Fact."

Section 2 (a) Title 28, United States Code, is amended by adding at the end thereof the following new chapter:

"Chapter 176—STATE ACTIONS INVOLVING OBSCENITY

"Sec.

"3001. Judicial Review

"§ 3001. Judicial Review

"In any action, either civil or criminal, arising under any statute of any State or under any law of any political subdivision of any State involving (1) the sale, or distribution, or exhibition, or (2) the preparation, possession, or use for commercial purposes, of any obscene, lewd, lascivious, indecent, vile, or filthy article, matter, thing, device, or substance; or the property rights in any obscene, lewd, lascivious, indecent, vile or filthy article, matter, thing, device, or substance, or in profits arising out of the use of such materials, no court of the United States shall have jurisdiction:

(a) To stay such proceedings in the State Court, or

(b) To review, reverse, or set aside a determination made by a court of such State on the question whether such article, matter, thing, device, or substance, or the use thereof, is in fact obscene, lewd, lascivious, indecent, vile, or filthy, and in vio-

606

lation of the public policy of such State regarding public morality, if such material or its use, when taken as a whole, has been reasonably found in such State judicial proceedings to treat with sex in a fundamentally offensive manner under rationally established criteria for judging such material, such as in any one of the four tests approved by the United States Supreme Court in the 1957 Roth-Alberts case or their equivalents."

(b) The analysis of Title 28, United States Code, preceding Part I thereof is amended by adding at the end thereof the following new item:

"176. State Actions Involving Obscenity . . . . 3001"

(c) The chapter analysis of Part VI, Title 28, United States Code, is amended by adding at the end thereof the following new item:

"176. State Actions Involving Obscenity . . . . 3001"

A Matter of National Concern

Curiously enough, the majority of the Commission on Obscenity and Pornography found that the traffic in obscenity and pornography was not a matter of national concern. As a matter of fact, they went further in their Report, making several patently erroneous, gratuitously insulting remarks:

Discussions of obscenity and pornography in the past have often been devoid of fact. Popular rhetoric has often contained a variety of estimates of the size of the smut industry and assertions regarding the consequences of the existence of these materials and exposure to them. Many of these statements, however, have had little anchoring in objective evidence.

And again:

When the Commission undertook its work, it could find no satisfactory estimates of the volume of traffic in obscene and pornographic materials. Documented evidence *describing the content of materials* included therein were not available. (Italics mine.)

Contradicting the Commission is the language of Public Law 90-100 itself.

Also, for at least the last five sessions, practically all legislatures of the fifty states have considered and in most cases acted upon some form of legislation aimed at tightening their obscenity laws.

There are some 200 bills currently pending before the Congress of the United States to deal more strictly and more effectively with the pornographers.

The Congress of the United States has established a long record documented in the Congressional Record, various Government Printing Office publications, and the Library of

607

Congress the national concern with obscenity and pornography. The first serious investigation brought before a Congressional Committee were the 1952 hearings instituted by Congressman Ezekiel Gathings. Gathings' investigations have been followed to the present time in almost unbroken succession by various Committees and Subcommittees of both the House of Representatives and the Senate. Included among others were the efforts of Kathyrn Granahan, Senators Kefauver, Dodd, and Mundt, and Congressman Dominick Daniels. The most cursory reading of these readily available studies and hearings belies the Commission statements. Literally thousands upon thousands of pages of testimony of well-qualified experts estimate the size of the smut industry and detail the consequences of the existence of the materials and exposure to them. Well-laden with facts and firmly anchored in objective evidence as well as being copiously documented with descriptions of the content of the materials involved, these Congressional hearings provide an absolute gold mine of information for anyone even remotely acquainted with the problem, with the national concern, and looking for an objective evaluation of the situation.

I testified before several of these Committees over a period of years; I have heard many others testify, including men of outstanding reputation and impeccable qualifications. The general theme developed from all the foregoing studies and investigations is that freedom for obscenity is death for morality and that such a condition would result in the enslavement of our society. Such a theme is diametrically opposed to the preconceived conclusions of the Commission majority who are dedicated to a position of complete moral anarchy and is obviously the reason the studies were so completely ignored.

It is said that the Congress of the United States, almost more than any governmental body in history, reflects the will of the people of the United States. Does the conclusion of "non concern" by the Commission majority square with the following fact: Even though the United States Senate knew that the Commission Report was to be made public September 30, 1970, and that the Report would recommend a "soft-line" approach to commercial obscenity, the Senate on September 25, 1970, nevertheless, approved by a unanimous vote of 79-to-0 a bill that would sharply curtail the amount of obscene advertising that pours into American homes through the United States mail.

On August 22, 1970, the Attorney General, John N.

Mitchell, spoke out strongly against the pornographers, reiterating the pledge of the Nixon Administration to "open a new front against filth peddlers . . ." and promised prompt and persistent action to stop the pornographers.

On September 25, 1970, the Vice President of the United States, Spiro T. Agnew, stated the national "need to restrain bad taste and outrageous vulgarity."

Publications over the past several years and today, whether they etc., or in the more technical field, such as the "Newsletter of Research Institute Recommendations", or trade publications of various industrial associations or in magazines of communities, such as "The Cincinnati Magazine" or "Phoenix", all have concerned and do concern themselves with the glut of smut in America as a timely subject.

Most of all, the national concern with obscenity is reflected in the increasing concern of some of the finest people in our nation. I refer specifically to men like Ray Gauer and Jim Clancy of Los Angeles, Bill Pfender of Philadelphia, Dick Bertsch of Cleveland, and Al Johnston of Biloxi. These gentlemen take of their time and their fortunes to participate daily in the battle against the pornographers. They are representative of countless Americans who, awakening to the most serious threat to public decency in history are increasingly becoming aware and active. I suggest the majority members of the Commission ought to communicate more with their fellow Americans. As I inferred earlier in this Report, it is too bad the majority of the Commission are not responsible to the voters. If they were, they would soon feel the brunt of national concern for decency.

The Panel Reports

I will devote the remaining portion of my dissent to comments on the four Panel Reports. It is again necessary to remind the reader that, for all practical purposes, the Panel Reports in their final form were not available for the preparation of this dissent and, therefore, my discussion is not able to be the specific rebuttal which I would have preferred; however, there is ample material to discuss.

Traffic and Distribution of Obscene and Pornographic Material

The Eden Theatre is located in East Greenwich Village. This is a sleazy, disreputable part of New York. The Theatre is old and dilapidated. "Oh! Calcutta!" plays at the Eden Theatre. "Oh! Calcutta!" is pure pornography—a two-hour orgy, principally enacted in the nude. It is not possible to verbally depict the depravity, deviation, eroticism or the utter filth of the play. Male and female players fondle each other, commit or simulate intercouse, sodomy, cunnilingus, masturbation, sadism, *ad nauseam*. This abomination, at the time I write this Report, is proposed to be televised live or by video-tape across the nation via lines of American Telephone and Telegraph and various telephonic communications systems. Never in Rome, Greece, or the most debauched nation in history has such utter filth been projected to all parts of a nation. If there is or ever was any such thing as public decency, these actions offend it. If there is or ever was a constitutional prerogative of the American people to have the exercise of police power in the interests of the public health and welfare, this is it.

On September 17, 1970, a fur farmer in upper New York wrote me regarding migrant Puerto Rican and American Indian workers whom he has employed over the past twenty years. The gentleman advised: "There has been a big change in our workers in the last year or two." He stated that they have changed from rather manly, decent people to rapists being obsessed with sex, including many deviations. "I believe," he said, "this is mostly due to obscene literature and obscene pictures such as I am sending to you". The mail-order obscenity he forwarded included the following:

Source	Description
FSI 7638 Deering, Suite 3 Canoga Park, California 91304	Homosexual magazines, pocket-books and movies. Explicit photos of homosexuals, especially young boys, of their sex organs, their oral and anal engagement of each other's organs, etc.
Barbara Martine Post Office Box 46367 Los Angeles, California 90046	Paperbacks and illustrations. Sexual activity between males and females, female and female, females with instruments such as phallic vibrators, and multi-person perverse activity with close up camera detail of all private parts.
Universal Sales Company Post Office Box 10244	Artificial, battery-driven penises and other "sex apparatus". (The

Source	Description
Denver, Colorado 80210	type of instrument described by columnist Alice Widener, 9/17/69, causing a young surgeon to break down in tears when relating to her: "Lately, I've been on gynecology and obstetrics. It's absolutely frightening to see what's going on—the wards and private rooms are filled with young girls—from as young as 13 to 16 and 17. Their insides are torn to pieces. It's impossible to describe the repair jobs we have to try to do. These girls suffer from the results of every kind of sexual abuse. It used to be that doctors treated prostitutes in such condition. But now we have to treat young girls from the best families for every kind of harm inflicted on them. Every day, we see girls in their teens with diseases and infections and torn-to-pieces insides due to over-indulgence, or sex abuses . . ."
Biofax Productions Post Office Box 34853 Los Angeles, California 90034	Instruments, etc., as above.
Gander Sales Box 569 Union City, New Jersey	Photos, films, slides, instruments, records, as the brochure describes them, in part: "Two Lesbians, Colored and White Girl"; "Mixed Group, Black and White"; "Lesbians, Three Young Girls"; "Group—Mixed"
Private Collectors Post Office Box 46608 Los Angeles, California 90046	Films, photos, etc. Explicit photos of deviated sexual activity, including torture, spanking, group intercourse, etc.
D.G. Sales 1256 S. LaCieniga Blvd. Los Angeles, California 90035	Records: "Incest!" "Lesbianism!" "Wife Swapping!" "Orgies!" Also films with titles such as "The Cream Eaters"; "Fingered for Lust"; "A Real Dog Lover".

The above listing covers less than 10 per cent of the mail I received from this one source. Advertising for this type of

611

material floods the United States Mails and invades the privacy and sanctity of our homes every minute of every hour of every day. For range of perversiveness and volume, it is certain that no nation has ever groaned under such a burden.

Motion picture theaters are to be found in every nook and cranny of the United States. These theaters today present explicit sexual conduct, more often abnormal than normal, as the principal bill of fare. Thanks to Jack Valenti, we have a condition in the motion picture industry today that literally constitutes a course of instruction in decadence, perversion and immorality. Honored companies as Twentieth Century Fox retain pornographers such as Russ Meyer, and produce obscenities such as "Beyond the Valley of the Dolls". It is a sad and dangerous day in America when an industry with as much influence as the motion picture industry turns its back on responsibility and moral code and permits a man such as Russ Meyer access to their most hallowed circles.

To compete with major studio releases in main-line theaters, sexploitation theaters now deal in hardcore pornography disguised as "documentaries" on Danish "sex fairs" or as marriage manuals depicting various positions of intercourse. The showing of explicit sexual activity on the screen under the "Documentary" guise led to the opening of "mini-theaters" in vacant storefronts in New York, San Francisco, Los Angeles, and other cities, which screen unadulterated, undisguised hardcore stag films depicting every imaginable sexual deviation. At the time of this report, there are over 80 such "mini-theaters" in Los Angeles County alone and new ones are opening at the rate of three per week!

An even more alarming, but nonetheless predictable, progression of this deluge of obscenity is the staging of live sex shows which are now taking place in jurisdictions such as Los Angeles, San Francisco, and New York. These "exhibitions" feature live "actors" in actual acts of "normal" sex, as well as perversions such as homosexuality, bestiality, sadism, masochism, etc. One such "show," written up boldly in the Los Angeles "underground" papers, included audience participation to the extent that patrons are invited to the "stage" where oral sex acts and/or intercourse are performed for the voyeuristic pleasure of the other deviates in attendance.

In obvious anticipation of the "soft-line" recommendations of the Commission majority, hard-core pictorial newsstand obscenity that goes beyond anything available in Copenhagen is being displayed openly in innumerable porno shops throughout the country. Many of the shops have display cases containing artificial sexual devices—penises, vaginas, french ticklers, vibrators, etc., as well as penis-shaped candy and inflatable rubber dolls with built-in vagina, etc. Certainly, ancient Sodom and Gomorrah couldn't have been as obsessed with sex as America is today. What is rotten in Denmark is already positively putrid in this country—and all this only in anticipation of the release of the soft-line Majority Report!

Another fact "overlooked" by the majority is that the adoption of their recommendations would open a new "legal" market for the pornographers wares—the *children* of America. They recommend legislation against the sale of *pictorial* obscenity to children—but specifically exempt printed-word or "textual" materials. Thus, while Danish pornographers suffered a drop-off in sales of "textual" material when pictorial obscenity was legalized, their American counterparts will be able to redirect "textual" obscenity to the juvenile market. Ingenious American pornographers will no doubt be quick to devise new techniques to exploit this juvenile market, including mobile porno shops to visit campuses on a monthly basis.

Another most disturbing aspect of legalized pornography as recommended by the Commission majority, is their utter disregard for the moral degradation of the men, women, and children who are forced by economic necessity, or by use of drugs, or simply by seduction, to pose for pornographic pictures. The sexual aberrations and deviations in pornography go far beyond conventional prostitution, and the Commission majority would allow the pornographer who degrades the participants to be raised to the respectability of a legitimate and legal business. Incredible!

In preparing to write this Report, I requested some 50 persons across the United States to send me the entertainment section of their local newspapers. I had intended to elicit from such pages a representative sample of the filth being fed by the entertainment industry into each and every community of this nation. It became obvious through perusal of these newspaper advertisements that a comprehensive presentation of the moral degradation being presented by "show business" today is not only appalling but virtually indescribable. I can only comment that if the majority of the Commission on Obscenity and Pornography has its way and the laws against the pornographers are repealed, we will witness complete moral anarchy in this country that will soon spread to the entire free world.

EFFECTS OF PORNOGRAPHY

We should begin by saying the law is clear. The law founded in reason and common sense recognizes obscenity as intrinsically evil and does not demand the "clear and present danger" test so ardently advocated by Chairman Lockhart and the American Civil Liberties Union. The law rather, proscribes pornography on the basis of the public good—protecting public health and welfare, public decency, and morality, a condition absolutely essential to the well-being of the nation.

Almost immediately after my appointment to the Commission, I wrote Chairman Lockhart a letter memorandum regarding statistical study of the relationship of obscenity to crime and other antisocial behavior, which is attached hereto as Exhibit "C". I urge you to carefully read Exhibit "C". [which was ignored by Chairman Lockhart and the Effects Panel of the Commission]

When my right to dissent was obtained in Court, included was the right theretofore denied me to file certain "Technical Reports" in the Commission's "books of Technical Reports which are to be prepared and printed later". Accordingly, I will submit for such printing certain items bearing upon effects of pornography, including pertinent excerpts from a report prepared for California Senator John L. Harmer, dated May, 1970, and entitled "Obscenity and Pornography in Los Angeles County".

Additionally, in the "technical" reporting, I will incorporate some excellent information and data by Melvin Anchell, M. D., Max Levin, M. D., Victor Cline, Ph.D., and others.

An excellent article was recently forwarded to me by Bernard L. Bonniwell, Ph.D., Department of Psychology, Villanova University, Villanova, Pennsylvania, entitled "The Pornographic Environment and Human Behavior". Same is attached hereto as Exhibit "D".

In the Effects Panel stampede for a "Danish Solution", I noticed in one of their studies a quotation from a young girl interviewed at the "Porno-Fair" in Denmark (regarding the Fair):

There is a complete lack of every kind of affection and solicitude for the other part. They avoid everything human and pleasant.

614

A natural objective for the true scientist, it seems to me, would be to investigate what pornography does to woman, what pornography really is—a despicable thing, a devilish thing, so poignantly brought home to the human heart in the above quotation.

Who, for example, has referred to, investigated, or even discussed in passing the fact that Denmark today is, for all practical purposes, devoid of religion or religious influence. God is gone from the hearts, the minds, and the souls of the people of Denmark. Does this fact not play a significant role in the willingness of the government officials and citizens of that country to accept the legalized degradation for which they are now internationally notorious.

Denmark has a total population of 4,700,000. The "Danish experiment" has only been going on for an extremely short period of time in the history of Man. Shouldn't there at least be some discussion or consideration of whether or not such facts should be the "Pied Piper" for Americans to the extent that this Commission recommends abolition of all obscenity laws in the United States?

And there are many misconceptions regarding Denmark. While I hesitate to refer to a salacious and lewd magazine such as "Playboy" [which is the precursor of immorality and decadence in the United States.] Nevertheless, in a recent article entitled "Pornography and the Unmelancholy Danes", they made the following observations regarding Denmark:

"At ordinary newsstands on perfectly normal street corners, you can buy pictures of laughing girls with semen all over their faces."

". . . the Christian church . . . came very late to Denmark and never achieved rigid political or social control."

". . . two widely and wistfully believed *untruths*.—They are that after the first surge of curiosity it becomes very difficult to sell (Pornography). The second is that porno is sold only—or mostly—to tourists. These notions seemed almost plausible before the celebrated Copenhagen Pornography Fair."

"It is considered normal that teenagers get into bed with each other."

"(A) widely used sex manual both boys and girls had studied in school begins with a statement, 'This book has a moral; namely, that it should be every human being's right to satisfy his sexual needs, regardless of

615

age or sex . . . , he can choose any way of expressing this need.' "

"So it isn't true that the porno business is dying . . . Business has never been better. People who think it is dying are misled because they see the amateurs dropping out. There are between 200 and 300 firms of various sizes making porno in Copenhagen alone."

As Marcellus said in *Hamlet,* "Something is rotten in the State of Denmark".

One can consult all the experts he chooses, can write reports, make studies, etc., but the fact that obscenity corrupts lies within the common sense, the reason, and the logic of every man.

St. Paul, looking upon a society in his time such as ours is becoming today wrote:

They had exchanged God's truth for lie, reverencing and worshipping the creature in preference to the Creator . . . and, in return, God abandoned them to passions which brought dishonour to themselves. Their women exchanged natural for unnatural intercourse; and the men, on their side, giving up natural intercourse with women, were burnt up with desire for each other; men practicing vileness with their fellowmen. Thus they have received a fitting retribution for their false belief.

And as they scorned to keep God in view, so God has abandoned them to a frame of mind worthy of all scorn, that prompts them to disgraceful acts. They are versed in every kind of injustice, knavery, impurity, avarice, and ill-will; spiteful, murderous, contentious, deceitful, depraved, backbiters, slanderers, God's enemies; insolent, haughty, vainglorious; inventive in wickedness, disobedient to their parents; without prudence, without honour, without love, without loyalty, without pity.

If man is affected by his environment, by circumstances of his life, by reading, by instruction, by anything, he is then certainly affected by pornography. The mere nature of pornography makes it impossible for pornography to effect good. Therefore, it must necessarily effect evil. Sexual immorality, more than any other causitive factor, historically speaking, is the root cause of the demise of all great nations and all great peoples. (Ref. Toynbee: Moral decay from within destroyed most of the world's great civilizations.)

Pertinent commentaries rebutting the Effects Panel Report are attached hereto as Exhibits "E" and "F", i.e. "Pornography Report" by Dr. Natalie Shainess and the September 6, 1970, letter of Walter S. Nosal, Ed.D.

The Commission majority bases their recommended repeal of all federal and state laws that "prohibit consensual distribution of sexual material to adults" on the statement that "extensive empirical investigation both by the Commission and by others, provides no evidence that exposure to or use of explicit sexual materials play a significant role in the causation of social or individual harms such as crime, delinquency, sexual or nonsex deviancy or severe emotional disturbances".

While it is a fact that a significant percentage of nationally recognized psychiatric authorities and many law enforcement officials at all levels of jurisdiction would disagree with that statement, the important point I want to make here is that the reasons for obscenity laws are *not* contained in the statement. Obscenity laws have existed historically in recognition of the need to protect the *public morality*.

I submit that never in the history of modern civilization have we seen more obvious evidence of a decline in public morality than we see today. Venereal disease is at epidemic proportions and literally out of control in many large urban centers—despite medicine. Illegitimacy statistics are skyrocketing—despite the pill and other contraceptive devices—and despite the relatively easy access to abortion. Both of these social statistics reflect a promiscuous attitude toward sex which is no doubt contributed to by many factors—but certainly one factor has to be the deluge of pornography which is screaming at young people from records, motion picture screens, newsstands, the United States mail and their peer groups.

To say that pornography has no effect is patently ridiculous. I submit that if pornography does *not* affect a person—that person has a problem. Pornography is intended to arouse the sexual appetite—one of the most volatile appetites of human nature. Once that appetite is aroused, it will seek satisfaction—and the satisfaction sought—without proper moral restraints—is often reflected in the social statistics discussed above.

Proponents of legalized pornography claim that pornography is actually good because it protects society from the sex deviate who might otherwise commit anti-social conduct. He can now read dirty books and get his kicks that way. They point to a 31 percent decrease in sex crimes in Copenhagen to support this thesis.

617

The fact is that in a society such as modern Copenhagen where pre-marital sex and illegitimacy bear no social stigma; where hardcore pornography is sold at every corner kiosk and at the "porno" or "sex shops" that dot the city, where live sex shows are legally conducted and exploited in the daily newspapers; where prostitutes block the sidewalks and wave from apartment windows; in such a society I am amazed that *any* sex crimes are reported. Yet the Chief of Police of Copenhagen, Closter Christionsen, in an interview in January, 1970, with Ray Gauer, National Director of Citizens for Decent Literature, pointed out that violent sex crimes of forcible rape and assault had *not* decreased in that city since legalization of obscenity. The only reason for a 31 percent *statistical* decrease in sex crimes is the fact that what was previously considered a crime is either now ignored or legal.

Denmark is currently experiencing the worst epidemic of venereal disease among young people of any nation in the world.

In addition to the social problems of venereal disease and illegitimacy, it is also of the very nature of obscenity to degrade sex and distort the role that sex plays in a normal life. There is no way to measure the terrible effects that pornography has had and is having on marital infidelity that is reflected in divorce statistics, abortions, suicide, and other social problems that further reflect the decline in public morality.

The effects of obscenity on society can best be summed up by repeating here a quotation written in 1705 by Alexander Pope:

> Vice is a monster of so frightful mein,
> As to be hated, only needed to be seen.
> Yet seen too oft, familiar with her face,
> We first endure, then pity, then embrace.

The majority report of the Presidential Commission on Obscenity and Pornography would have America embrace the monster vice.

POSITIVE APPROACHES

Whittaker Chambers (*Witness,* Henry Regnery Company, Chicago) wrote:

It is idle to talk about preventing the wreck of Western civilization. It is already a wreck from within. That is why we can hope to do little more now than snatch a

618

fingernail of a saint from the rack or a handful of ashes from the fagotts, and bury them secretly in a flowerpot against the day, ages hence, when a few men begin again to dare to believe that there was once something else, that something else is thinkable, and need some evidence of what it was, and the fortifying knowledge that there were those who, at the great nightfall, took loving thought to preserve the tokens of hope and truth.

Chambers was negative; and as he looked upon our society, it was, indeed, difficult for him to be positive. As I look upon the Report of the Positive Approaches Panel and find them concerned with sex education ("how to do it"), I have difficulty breaking away from the pessimism of Chambers.

Nevertheless, without indulging in the temptation to make a detailed but obvious reply to the Positive Approaches Panel Report which advocates sex education without reference to morality, God, or religion, I find there are some positive considerations which should be mentioned.

First of all, the United States gives to each and every one of us a constitutional prerogative heretofore denied to citizens in the history of nations; namely, the undeniable right of free speech and free press guaranteed under the First and Fourteenth Amendments to our Constitution. Throughout history, nations have declined and disappeared coincidental with the rise of the libertines and the moral anarchists in their midst. Here one sees a corresponding denial of freedom and liberty to the dissenting and right-minded people in those societies. It is historically accurate to say that those who would free the creatures of vice would enslave the proponents of decency. Thus, contrary to those nations wherein free speech was denied as libertines obtained power, in the United States we are guaranteed—and our courts will protect—our right to speak. Accordingly, it is possible for me, as a member of this Commission, to obtain per force my right to dissent. It is possible for me and every reader of this opinion to bespeak decency, morality, God—indeed, sanctity and purity throughout this land. This, to me, is a positive approach which I encourage everyone to take. In short, be an articulate, outspoken champion of your principles. That is guaranteed to you; and given your time and attention, the common sense and the logic of your position will prevail.

St. Paul, in a letter to the Ephesians, points out a very positive approach. He said:

Be imitators of God as very dear children, and follow

619

the way of love, as Christ also loved you and gave himself for us, an offering to God, a sacrifice of pleasing fragrance. As for fornication or any kind of uncleanness or lust, let it not be mentioned among you; such is the rule for the saints. Nor should there be any obscenity, or silly and suggestive talk; all that is out of place. Instead, give thanks. And make no mistake about this: no fornicator, no unclean or lustful person, who is really an idolator, has any inheritance in the kingdom of Christ and of God. Do not let anyone deceive you by worthless arguments; these are the sins that bring down God's wrath upon the disobedient; so have nothing to do with them. It is true that you were once darkness; but now you are light in the Lord. Live, then, as children of light; for light produces every kind of goodness and justice and truth.

Alexis Carrel makes an excellent point when he says:

Let us send our sons and daughters, but first let us obtain from them a mode of life which imposes on them a constant effort, a psychological and moral discipline and privation, then we will create an ascetic and mystical minority which will rapidly acquire an irresistible power over this self-indulgent and spineless majority. Without this moral self-denial, intelligence itself becomes anemic. The problem then is not what to do with our own sons and daughters, it is who will train them in the Ten Commandments and morality before they are 16 and 17.

Instead of sex education, i.e., teaching "how to do it," we ought to try Carrel's solution.

As far as sex education is concerned, I am not qualified to comment. Perhaps it is a "give-away" that it is included in a report on pornography. I have seen sex education text books based on Drs. Masters and Johnson. Such references to the works of those "Kooks" for impressionable children are difficult to comprehend.

In any event, on a recent trip to London, I heard a speech on the subject by Robert Clegg, Headmaster, Barden Primary School, Burnley, Lancaster, England, which seemed appropriate to include here, which I have done as Exhibit "G."

LEGAL

I have reviewed the state of the law on the subject of obscenity. My review is attached hereto as Exhibit "H." In view of the all-important role of law in stopping the pornographers, I intend to submit a comprehensive brief as a Technical Report. I, therefore, urge a careful reading of Exhibit "H" hereto; and, further, anyone interested in obtaining a copy of my brief, etc. in the Technical Reports may obtain same by inquiring of Citizens for Decent Literature, Inc., 5670 Wilshire Boulevard, Los Angeles, California 90036.

The real problem in stopping the pornographers obviously lies with the Federal Courts, and especially the United States Supreme Court. The judges of these Courts simply have not looked at the facts in a realistic fashion; by their commissions and omissions they have dictated a level of public morality which relegates us to an animalistic, pagan society.

The actions of the Courts bring to mind the words of G. K. Chesterton, who, referring to Blatchford's remarks that "no English judge would accept the evidence for the Resurrection," answered:

Possibly Christians do not have such an extravagant reverence for English judges as is felt by Mr. Blatchford himself. The experiences of the founder of Christianity have perhaps left us in a vague doubt of the infallibility of courts of law.

Another good indication of the problem was given on September 28, 1970, when a defense attorney, arguing a Petition for Removal in the Federal Court (Southern District of Ohio, Western Division), stated in open court:

I have never won an obscenity case in the Common Pleas Courts of Hamilton County, Ohio, and I have never lost an obscenity case in the Federal Courts.

As I completed my Legal Report, a national closed-circuit video production of the two-hour sex show which I previously referred to in this Report, called "Oh! Calcutta!" was being telecast into numerous cities in the United States. It will, according to Rodney Erickson, President of Color Media Communications Corporation, gross approximately four million dollars as a result of its one-night showing (*Variety*, September 23, 1970). These figures are very significant when one considers that "Airport," a top-grossing movie for the year 1970, has only reached twelve million dollars gross after showing for a ten-month period.

The pornographers thus have found a new market to exploit in their perpetual quest of disseminating filth for profit.

Despite thousands upon thousands of complaints by the

621

American people who cry out daily to their governmental representatives for protection from the pornographers, the Federal Communications Commission and other governmental agencies in the United States have refused and, in fact, took no action to stop this telecast, stating they were powerless under the existing laws to prevent such a showing. If this is true, we are entering a new era of mass dissemination of pornography. What is next? How far are we away from "Oh! Calcutta!" being beamed into our living rooms? Obviously, this is an area which merits serious consideration by the Congress of the United States, and I specifically recommend, in the national interest, that Congress investigate and enact legislation to prevent the pollution of our airwaves.

Closing

At a time when the spread of pornography has reached epidemic proportions in our country and when the moral fiber of our nation seems to be rapidly unravelling, the desperate need is for enlightened and intelligent control of the poisons which threaten us—not the declaration of moral bankruptcy inherent in the repeal of the laws which have been the defense of decent people against the pornographer for profit.

To deny the need for control is literally to deny one's senses, unless such denial is based upon a conclusion that there is nothing evil or dangerous about pornographic material. For a Presidential Commission to have labored for two years at the expense to the taxpayers of almost two million dollars and arrive at the conclusion that pornography is harmless must strike the average American as the epitome of government-gone-berserk.

Credit the American public with enough common sense to know that one who wallows in filth is going to get dirty. This is intuitive knowledge. Those who will spend millions of dollars to tell us otherwise must be malicious or misguided, or both.

The Congress of the United States created a Presidential Commission on Obscenity and Pornography for the purpose of determining legal and constitutional means to protect the country from what the Congress recognized as a threat. Unfortunately, what was intended to provide to our legislators a blueprint for coping with a problem has been turned one-hundred-eighty degrees into a blank check for the pornographers to flood our country with every variety of filth and perversion.

The Commission majority report can only be described as a travesty, preordained by the bias and prejudice of its Chairman, closely followed by his Staff, who has long advocated relaxation of restraints for the dealers in pornography. The Report of the majority of the Commission does not reflect the will of Congress, the opinion of law enforcement officials throughout our country, and, worst of all, flaunts the underlying opinions and desires of the great mass of the American people. Were we not concerned with the morals and life of a nation, the situation represented by the majority Report would be ludicrous.

Far from needing repeal of legislation controlling pornography, what is called for is a return to law enforcement which permits the American to determine for himself the standards of acceptable morality and decency in his community. Our law enforcement in the area of obscenity has been emasculated by courts, seemingly divorced from the realities of our communities, determining from afar the standards of those communities. The law is capable of coping with the problem of pornography and obscenity, but it must be law, coupled with the logic that an American is innately capable of determining for himself his standards of public decency and, beyond that, he has a right to make that determination.

The words of Alexis de Toqueville (during his American visit, 1835-1840) seem appropriate:

I sought for the greatness and genius of America in her commodius harbors and ample rivers—and it was not there; in her fertile lands and boundless prairies—and it was not there. Not until I went to the churches of America and heard her pulpits aflame with righteousness did I understand the secret of her genius and power. America is great because she is good—and if America ceases to be good, America will cease to be great.

Respectfully submitted,

/S/ CHARLES H KEATING, JR.
Commissioner
Commission on Obscenity and Pornography

September 30, 1970

1. I am in possession of a taped copy of the show, which is incorporated herein by reference.

2. Nevertheless, September 7, 1970, found W. Cody Wilson, Executive Director, in Miami Beach, Florida, at Commission expense, attending the American Psychological Association Convention, freely discussing and divulging to the Convention and to the press the reports and findings of the Commission, along with his own opinions thereon. At this same time, the writer had been unable to receive final Panel Reports or the final Commission Report upon which to base his dissent. Further, at this same time, the Commission had advised the writer that there were not sufficient funds to permit a full Minority Report or documentation thereof.

3. The "Fortas" film was a "Report on the United States Supreme Court and Its Recent Decisions in Obscenity Cases," prepared by Citizens for Decent Literature, Inc. and narrated by James J. Clancy, Attorney. The film was a 16 mm., sound documentary, approximately one hour in length, prepared for the use of the United States Senate in connection with its consideration of Abe Fortas for the position of Chief Justice of the United States Supreme Court. Reference: Citizens for Decent Literature, 5670 Wilshire Boulevard, Los Angeles, California 90036.

EXHIBIT "A"

THE PROGRESSIVE September, 1970

Censorship of Pornography?

YES

by REO M. CHRISTENSON

The participants in this debate on the issue of censorship of pornography are long-time friends and colleagues in the Department of Political Science of Miami University, Oxford, Ohio. Their debate on the subject has been conducted in private for the past ten years.

Mr. Christenson specializes in public policy and public opinion. He is the author of Challenge and Decision: Political Issues of Our Time *(Harper and Row), which has gone through three editions, and is the co-editor of two editions of* Voice of the People: Readings in Public Opinion and Propaganda *(McGraw-Hill).*

Mr. Engel specializes in constitutional law and civil rights and liberties. He is the co-author of the forthcoming book, Ideas in Action: Modern Political Ideologies *(Dodd-Mead).*

—THE EDITORS

Tougher censorship laws for America? Speaking as a liberal and long-time member of the American Civil Liberties Union (ACLU), I believe stronger pornography legislation is clearly needed.

To most intellectuals these days, censorship in sexual matters is firmly identified with prim little old ladies, country bumpkins, Bob Jones College, backwater conservatism, cultural yahoos—and

Puritans in general. (A Puritan is someone whose views on sex are less permissive than yours.) Historian Barbara Tuchman (*The Guns of August*) has observed that prominent writers who favor some censorship where sex is concerned are afraid to speak out openly. Attorney Richard Kuh documents the point in a book which has received far too little attention—*Foolish Figleaves.* (Kenyon political scientist Harry Clor's *Obscenity and Public Morality* deserves a bow, also.)

The case for stricter censorship of pornography runs as follows. More than three-fourths of the American people want it, according to a Gallup Poll in June, 1969. They are affronted by books, magazines, movies, plays, erotic displays, pictures, and records which vulgarize, desecrate, and cheapen sex, or which encourage or glamorize deviant sexual behavior. The Middle Americans—and many others—have a deep-rooted suspicion that all of this will undermine certain moral restraints believed to be essential to the public weal.

There is no way of proving whether this suspicion is or is not well-founded. But the public's fears about excessive sexual permissiveness are supported more than they are challenged by such inadequate empirical evidence that we have. In *The Sexual Wilderness,* Vance Packard summarizes the findings of those academicians who have given the most attention to the relation between sexual permissiveness and the progress of society as a whole. He cites *Sex and Culture* by Former Oxford Professor J. D. Unwin, whose massive studies of eighty primitive and civilized societies reveal a distinct correlation between increasing sexual freedom and social decline. The more sexually permissive a society becomes, Unwin says, the less creative energy it exhibits and the slower its movement toward rationality, philosophical speculation, and advanced civilization.

Harvard sociologist Pitirim Sorokin agrees with Unwin that sexual restraints promote cultural progress; in *The American Sexual Revolution* he contends that immoral and anti-social behavior increases with cultural permissiveness toward the erotic sub-arts. In an article in *The New York Times* magazine entitled "Why I Dislike Western Civilization," May 10, 1964, Arnold Toynbee argued that a culture which postpones rather than stimulates sexual experience in young adults is a culture most prone to progress.

In another article in *The New York Times* magazine, Bruno Bettelheim, the noted psychoanalyst, recently observed: "If a society does not taboo sex, children will grow up in relative sex freedom. But so far, history has shown that such a society cannot create culture or civilization; it remains primitive." Sorokin asserts ". . . there is no example of a community which has retained its high position on the cultural scale after less rigorous sexual customs have replaced more restricting ones."

Many social scientists doubt that contemporary research skills are capable of either affirming or denying these charges. The Middle American, then, can hardly be blamed for concluding that, in the absence of scientific proof one way or the other, majority views should prevail. In *The Common Law,* the late Oliver Wendell Holmes, celebrated Justice of the United States

625

Supreme Court, declared that "the first requirement of a sound body of law is that it should correspond with the actual feelings and demands of the community, whether right or wrong." And Justice John M. Harlan, in *Alberts* v. *California,* declared, "the state can reasonably draw the inference that over a long period of time the indiscriminate dissemination of materials, the essential character of which is to degrade sex, will have an eroding effect on moral standards." Harlan has thus established the crucial link between dubious practices and reasonable law.

But should majorities deprive minorities of free expression, whatever their fears may be? When the First Amendment says, "Congress shall make no law . . . abridging freedom of speech or press," should it not mean what it says—*no law?*

The First Amendment does not really mean "no law" and never has. We have had a score of respectable laws abridging freedom of speech and press, some dating back to the earliest days of our republic. A few of these forbid libel, perjury, contempt of court, incitement to violence, disrespect toward command officers, and copyright violation. The First Amendment itself limits free expression; by implication, the "establishment of religion" clause forbids the advocacy of religious doctrines in public schools. The true meaning of the First Amendment is that Congress may place no *unreasonable* restraints on freedom of speech and press. Our entire history attests to this view.

The drafters of the Constitution probably and properly intended an absolute ban on efforts by the Government to forbid the dissemination of any political, economic, religious, or social ideas. John Stuart Mill and others have made an overwhelming cogent case for such freedom; no equally persuasive case has been made for the unlimited freedom of commercial entertainment. There is a right, therefore, to advocate the most disgusting forms of sexual perversion—so long as the proponent is clearly attempting to persuade rather than to entertain commercially. But commercial

---

"It is a mistake . . . to believe that the commercial exploitation of sex frees us from crippling inhibitions . . ."

---

entertainment cannot logically claim the same constitutional protection as normal political discourse.

To the extent that entertainment and persuasion are combined, the case for constitutional protection is proportionately enhanced. But no one has yet demonstrated that the effective dissemination of ideas demands the use of pornographic techniques. The latter are conceivably of peripheral persuasive value but surely no more than that. The marginal loss of free speech involved in sensible pornography legislation, as with other reasonable restrictions on free speech, is more than counterbalanced by the protection of children and the creation of an environment, especially for children, which is more conducive to responsible sex behavior.

The ACLU takes no absolutist position on the First Amendment, but it does oppose limitations on speech and press unless it can be proved that a given expression creates a clear and present danger that it will trigger an act which society has a right to forbid. The ACLU is also convinced that no scientifically valid proof exists that the consumption of pornography produces criminal behavior.

Obviously, the ACLU wants society to consider only short-term effects since it regards long-term effects unknowable. The truth is that short-term effects are also unknowable. The difficulties of delving into the depths of human motivations and sorting out from the richly tangled psychic undergrowth those strands which "cause" a criminal act are so formidable that root causes or even the relative importance of contributory factors may never be satisfactorily established.

Unhappily, all of the major premises on which our society rests derive from the realm of intuition—the viscera. Can anyone *prove* that the family is a desirable institution? That higher education promotes human welfare? That technology makes men happier? That love is better than hate? That democracy is superior to dictatorship? None of these is provable. But this does not stop us from acting on our best judgment, knowing that all human judgment is fallible. If, then, the regulation of pornography comes down to a matter of visceral hunches, why should not the majority of viscera prevail?

Is "pornography" such an imprecise term that it lacks sufficient clarity to meet the "due process" test?

Current state laws could be updated and made more explicit if they were refined to forbid actual or simulated exhibitions of sexual intercourse or sexual perversion on stage or screen—or pictorial representations thereof in other media—when such exhibitions or pictorial representations are primarily intended for commercial entertainment rather than for education.

If the emerging vogue for making a fast buck by portraying such scenes on stage and screen is not an example of moral degradation, that term must be bereft of all meaning. There *are* limits of human decency, and these limits are being transgressed more blatantly year after year in the shameless commercial exploitation of man's baser instincts. Admittedly a few playwrights or motion picture directors may be able to handle these scenes in a sensitive and illuminating manner, but for every artist who can do so, a hundred entrepreneurs will use such themes in a fashion which can only cheapen and coarsen sex. The interests of the general American public are considerably more important than gratifying the erotic-esthetic yearnings of the avant-garde.

Next, the U.S. Supreme Court should modify the interpretation which holds that censorable material must be "utterly without social importance" (*Jacobellis v. U.S.*, 1964). "Utterly" should be stricken, since it invites dealers in pornographic literature to "redeem" their noxious wares by introducing just enough literary "quality" or moral substance to pass judicial muster. The Court should substitute a test of the "predominant" character of challenged material.

Even with these clarifications, the statutory-judicial definition of pornography remains rather vague. But the same applies to numerous other laws. The Sherman anti-trust law forbids monopolies.

627

What is a monopoly? When one firm—or an oligopoly—controls thirty per cent of the output in a field? Fifty per cent? Seventy-five per cent? Ninety per cent? No one knows, and the Supreme Court has never been able to tell us.

What is an "unfair trade practice"? What is a merger which "substantially" reduces competition? What is "negligent" manslaughter? When is guilt proved beyond a "reasonable" doubt?

In terms of imprecision, then, pornography statutes are no more defective than many other well-accepted and adjudicable laws. At one end of their administered continuum, it is clear that a publisher or dealer has not broken the law and no one will take him to court. At the other end, he has so clearly broken the law that he will not bother to appeal the case. But movement toward the center leads to more difficult decisions, until a middle zone is reached in which it is anyone's guess whether the courts will find the defendant guilty. Decisions in this zone inevitably entail a certain amount of arbitrariness and raw subjectivity. Yet those indignant over the lack of specificity in obscenity laws are quite complacent about vagueness in laws they approve.

It is often argued that judges have no special expertise on sexual proprieties. True enough, but if they can bring no special wisdom to bear, they are likely to bring moderation to bear. And that is no mean asset. Furthermore, citizens will accept decisions by judges which they would not so readily accept from others. In brief, entrusting these decisions to the judiciary is a good practical solution to the problem.

Since negative judicial decisions on pornography are sure to be subjected to scathing attacks by civil libertarians—as judges well known—there is much more likelihood of judicial lenience than of excessive restraint. Perhaps it is best to err on the side of leniency, while imposing sufficiently severe penalties where guilt is found to discourage those who specialize in exploring and exploiting the margins of decency.

It is easy to produce a long list of worthwhile books which have been banned and to make censors look ridiculous in the light of modern opinion. But each generation has a right to set its own standards, and if pornography criteria change from time to time, the same is true of legal criteria in other fields. A thousand examples could be cited, including such notable constitutional clauses as "equal protection of the laws" and "the establishment of religion."

Of course, critics are inclined to evaluate censorship solely by its "failures," the banning of works of genuine merit. But it is unfair to exhibit the "failures" of censorship without considering the other side of the coin. If all of the loathsome materials which officials have confiscated and the law has discouraged were balanced against the mistakes, the over-all results would look much less damning of censorship than many English professors would have us believe.

Opponents of pornography censorship sometimes contend that the state should not try to be the moral custodian of the people. Nor should a majority seek to impose its moral standards on a minority, it is said.

Yet *every* criminal law represents a moral judgment. And laws

628

typically constitute a coercion of the minority by the majority. Presumably bigamists resent laws against bigamy, polygamists oppose laws against polygamy, and sexual exhibitionists dislike laws against indecent exposure. Their objections are not decisive once society regards these restrictions as reasonable. The same is true of pornography laws.

If the home, the church, and the school provided adequate sex education and moral training, there would be less need for pornography laws. But the law must deal with social realities, not Utopian visions. Since millions of children receive virtually no moral training, or sex education, the nation is obliged to rely partly upon law for their protection.

Those who say, "Don't tell *me* what *I* can see or read," are consulting their impulses rather than the larger interests of society. A socially responsible person will forego the indulgence of a desire if the policy permitting that indulgence jeopardizes the well-being of others.

Most of us, it should be emphasized, welcome today's freedom to discuss sexual questions and seek greater sexual satisfactions through increased education and scientific knowledge. Nor will the censorship envisaged herein interfere with this salubrious development. It is a mistake, however, to believe that the commercial exploitation of sex frees us from crippling inhibitions and promotes a healthy attitude toward sex. Pornography is more likely to deposit ugly images in the consciousness or subconsciousness of the young than it is to contribute toward the formation of a wholesome attitude toward sex.

The New York Academy of Medicine declared in 1963 that reading salacious literature "encourages a morbid preoccupation with sex and interferes with the development of a healthy attitude and respect for the opposite sex." Certainly if young people are stimulated to experiment with forms of perversion before they understand their implications, traumatic experiences may occur which leave them psychologically scarred for life. Parents who strongly oppose the introduction of unsolicited pornography into their homes display an eminently sensible attitude toward the protection of their children. This outrage, reported to affect more than a million children a year, obviously must be halted.

Sexually abnormal persons who "need" pornography probably need psychiatric care even more. However, since they are unlikely to get the latter, it would probably be unwise to try to eliminate all pornography. If dealers do not solicit or sell to children, do not advertise their wares, and limit their sales to adults who seek them out, perhaps it is best to leave such traffic alone. Sometimes it is prudent to temper the administration of law with a realistic regard for human weakness. The Greek rule applies—"nothing too much."

Are pornography laws unenforceable? Do they tend to make pornography more attractive, since it becomes forbidden fruit?

Enforcement is admittedly difficult. We have not been able to prevent drunken driving, either, or supermarket theft, or income tax evasion, but we do not proceed to make them legal. Instead, we seek more effective enforcement measures.

Laws may make pornography somewhat more attractive to

629

certain persons; so do laws against vandalism and speeding and heaven knows how many other misdeeds. In any case, the repeal of pornography laws would not eliminate the social disapproval associated with the behavior involved. This social disapproval would continue the "forbidden fruit" effect, even in the absence of law.

As for oft-cited Denmark, which has repealed all prohibitions against written pornography (and against pictures sold to persons over sixteen years old), the trial period is far too short to enable us to draw any firm conclusions. Certain kinds of pornography have experienced declining sales; other kinds are flourishing even more. *Newsweek* has called Copenhagen "a veritable showcase of pornography," bristling with shops specializing in every conceivable

---

"Sexually abnormal persons who 'need' pornography probably need psychiatric care even more."

---

form of erotic lingerie, sadomasochistic devices, sexual stimulators, and pornographic jewelry. This may be an appealing demonstration of the delights of a free and liberated society, but a dissenting view is also conceivable.

Paradoxically, the existence of censorship probably assures greater freedom in America than its absence. Morris Ernst, the noted civil liberties lawyer, in *Censorship: The Search for the Obscene,* agrees that the decline of governmental censorship has led to an increase in private vigilantism. If, somehow, the tiny minority (Gallup estimates about six per cent) which wants no censorship were to have their way, it would be an open invitation for vigilante groups to take over. Outraged at the irresponsibles, the Middle American would employ extra-legal pressures as a substitute for law. And a sorry substitute they would be. Controlling pornography by legal means and orderly institutions gives us the best assurance that society's concern will be dealt with in a civilized manner.

To those in the entertainment world, freedom is the supreme value. Whatever makes men more free is believed *ipso facto* good. But freedom is not, standing alone, the *summum bonum* of human society. If it were, we would need no government. Men once saw *laissez-faire* as the culmination of economic progress, only to discover that commercial greed was not quite an adequate guide for achieving human welfare. When freedom is not accompanied by a reasonable amount of self-restraint and social responsibility, it can become a destructive force. I see neither this self-restraint nor this sense of social responsibility being manifested in much of the entertainment world. The most profound (although often subliminal) message which much of modern music, movies, and literature convey to the young is, "Let 'er rip."

A society can tolerate only so much emotional turmoil, so much disruption, so many assaults upon its sensibilities and its mores. At some point, the public's patience becomes exhausted; it cries, "Enough." This denouement may not be far off in America. When it comes, the entertainment industry should be assigned its full share of responsibility in the area of pornographic presentations for the general repression which follows. (Those who condone

630

gross social injustices and those who employ violence for political ends admittedly deserve a larger share of blame.)

For the record, I find much to applaud in our revolutionary age: the refusal to support a senseless war; the challenge to the military budget and to certain military assumptions; the so-called "equality revolution," the demand for justice to the blacks and the poor; the call for sweeping educational reforms; the insistence on higher standards of public morality. But the stresses and strains involved in these movements are hard enough for the body politic to bear. Add to these a dubious sexual revolution powerfully stimulated by the entertainment industry, and society may be bearing an overload of tension.

A final word. Maybe all the "dumb people" are not so dumb after all. Maybe they are right in sensing that sex needs to be treated with some caution, that sexual privacy needs to be preserved from commercial contamination, that sexual relations must not be divested of all sanctity, all mystery, and reduced to the level of leer and titter.

It is a disturbingly democratic idea that the common man just might be smarter, now and then, than many of our avant-garde intellectuals.

EXHIBIT "B"

REV. MORTON A. HILL, S.J.

Member, Presidential Commission on Obscenity and Pornography

980 Park Avenue
New York, N.Y. 10028
(212) 879-6789

September 12, 1970

Mr. William B. Lockhart
Commission on Obscenity and Pornography
1016—16 Street N.W.
Washington, D. C.

Dear Mr. Chairman:
The work of the Commission on Obscenity is now drawing to a close. The American taxpayers are anxious to know if their money has been spent wisely.

I want to voice grave objections as to the way Commission money is being spent. For example, who authorized the spending of a hundred thousand dollars for the printing of the technical reports and only twelve thousand five hundred dollars for the printing of the Commission report? Who authorized Cody Wilson, Executive Director of the Commission, to go to Florida on commission salary and expense—while Commissioners Link, Keating and

631

myself had no financial assistance from this Commission for our minority report, no legal help and no help of professional psychologists to evaluate Commission research. All the people who have helped us have worked after hours on their own time.

Further, Commissioner Link and I spent thousands of dollars to hold public hearings to aid us in our work as Commissioners, so that we could hear the community viewpoint. You never reimbursed us one cent.

Since I do not feel that Commission money has been authorized in a fair and equitable manner, I suggest a special meeting of the Commission to discuss this point. Before the meeting, however, I want to see all the books of the Commission; every cent that has ever been spent; every check that has ever been issued; every voucher that has ever been authorized. In short, I want a complete account of all money expended. This viewing should be done in the presence of a Certified Public Accountant of my choosing, paid by the Commission.

I would also like to see the amount of money that has been paid to you and to all other Commissioners.

Sincerely yours,

/s/ Morton A. Hill

md/
cc: To all Commissioners

EXHIBIT "C"

August 11, 1969

Mr. William B. Lockhart
Office of the President
University of Minnesota Law School
Minneapolis, Minnesota 55455

Memorandum Re Statistical Study of Relationship of
Obscenity to Crime and Other Antisocial Behavior.

Dear Mr. Lockhart:
When the legislation creating the Presidential Commission on Obscenity and Pornography came back to the Senate on September 20, 1967 (Senate Bill 188), after the House amendments of August 7, 1967, Senator Mundt moved for Senate concurrence with 5 additional Senate amendments. All 5 were later to be accepted by the House and became a part of Public Law 90-100.
Addressing himself to the Senate changes, Senator Mundt said (Congressional Record—Senate of Sept. 20, 1967, at page S13320):
"The first two amendments appear in the Finding of Fact and Declaration of Policy in Section 1. *Both of them redirect the*

emphasis toward a coordinated effort by all levels of government rather than leaving it with the Federal Government alone. The original Senate version had this recognition of State concern and responsibility but the House amendment deleted all mention of State and local government with the exception of Section 6, the Powers of the Commission. Section 6, however, is somewhat stronger than the original Senate version in that it declares that the Commission *shall* consult with other representatives, including State and local governments, while the original Senate version read *may* consult. *Between this change made by the House and these two amendments, we have substantially strengthened the legislative mandate to include State and local governments in the investigative stages and in the regulatory stage should stronger laws be deemed advisable.* (My emphasis.)

"The third amendment is in Section 2(a), the establishment of the Commission on Obscenity and Pornography. While it recognizes the necessity of having members who possess expert knowledge in the fields of obscenity and antisocial behavior, it allows for appointment of individuals having special and practical competence or experience with respect to obscenity laws and their application to juveniles. The effect of this amendment is to nullify any possible application of the doctrine of ejusdem generis, the general rule with which you are all familiar which as used in law to limit the application to a specific class of things, *and hence we provide the President with the opportunity to appoint members who have a practical, as opposed to theoretical, knowledge or experience as to the problems surrounding obscenity laws and the relationship between obscene literature and materials and juveniles . . . .*" (My emphasis.)

Sections 1, 2 and 6 of Public Law 90-100, of which Senator Mundt was speaking, is set forth below. The Senate additions of September 20, 1967, to the August 7th House version are underlined as is the use of the mandatory word "shall", referred to by Senator Mundt.

"Finding of Fact and Declaration of Policy.

"Section 1. The Congress finds that the traffic in obscenity and pornography is a matter of national concern. *The problem, however, is not one which can be solved at any one level of government.* The Federal Government has a responsibility to investigate the gravity of this situation and to determine whether such materials are harmful to the public, and particularly to minors, and whether more effective methods should be devised to control the transmission of such materials. *The State and local governments have an equal responsibility in the exercise of their regulatory powers and any attempts to control this transmission should be a coordinated effort at the various governmental levels.* It is the purpose of this Act to establish an advisory Commission whose purpose shall be, after a thorough study which shall include a study of the causal relationship of such materials to antisocial behavior, to recommend advisable, appropriate, effective, and constitutional means to deal effectively with such traffic in obscenity and pornography.

"Commission on Obscenity and Pornography

"Section 2(a) Establishment—For the purpose of carrying out the provisions of this Act, there is hereby created a Commission to be known as the Commission on Obscenity and Pornography (hereinafter referred to as the 'Commission'), whose members shall include persons having expert knowledge in the fields of obscenity and antisocial behavior, including but not limited to psychiatrists, sociologists, psychologists, criminologists, jurists, lawyers, and others *from organizations and professions* who have special *and practical* competence *or experience* with respect to obscenity laws and their application to juveniles . . . .

"Powers of the Commission

"Section 6. . . . (b) Consultation—In carrying out its duties under the Act, the Commission *shall* consult with other Federal agencies, Governors, attorneys general, and other representatives of State and local government and private organizations to the extent feasible.

"(c) Obtaining Official Data—The Commission is authorized to secure directly from any executive department, bureau, agency, board, commission, office, independent establishment, or instrumentality, information, suggestions, estimates, and statistics for the purpose of this Act, and each such department, bureau, agency, board, commission, office, establishment or instrumentality is authorized and directed, to the extent permitted by law, to furnish such information, suggestions, estimates, and statistics directly to the Commission, upon request made by the Chairman or Vice-Chairman.

"(b) Obtaining Scientific Data—For the purpose of securing the necessary scientific data and information the Commission may make contracts with universities, research institutes, foundations, laboratories, hospitals, and other competent public or private agencies to conduct research on the causal relationship of obscene material and antisocial behavior. For such purpose, the Commission is authorized to obtain the services of experts and consultants in accordance with Section 3109 of Title 5, U.S. Code . . . ."

In reading the above Senate amendments, as elaborated upon by Senator Mundt's remarks, it seems to me that it was the clear intent of Congress that (1) practical experience was to play a substantial role in this entire investigation, and (2) the State and local governments were to be active participants in all of the investigative stages.

In reading the Commission report on the work accomplished and in the planning stage, I note that, in the area of antisocial behavior, there is an abundance of projected studies by social scientists into the theoretical aspects of antisocial behavior, but little, if any, time, money or study is being devoted to the practical aspect of what has actually been happening—that is, what the statistics demonstrate regarding police cases, in which a relationship has been found to exist between antisocial sex conduct and obscenity. For example, when one reads a news account

634

of 7 male youths gang-raping a 15-year-old girl and admitting to being incited by reading obscene magazines, it is quite natural for Congress and other legislators to want to know how many more of these and others like them are occurring in that jurisdiction—in that state—in the Nation. All of such "happenings" bear on the "rationality" of obscenity legislation, which is the foundation for its constitutional support. A statistical study of such matters in cooperation with State and local government appears to be in order, utilizing the practical experience of the police profession.

As an attorney who shares the concern of Congress and the Nation in the mushrooming traffic in obscenity, the academic question of direct causation consumes very little of my interest. In my view, that question will not be settled by scientific proof to anyone's satisfaction and, when weighed in the light of other problems that need exposure, its importance seems minimal. At this late date, it appears well settled that that issue is irrelevant insofar as the constitutional question is concerned. As recent as Sam Ginsberg v. N.Y., 390 U.S. 629 at 641 (footnote 9) (Dec. 22, 1968), a majority of the U.S. Supreme Court reaffirmed its holding to that effect in Roth-Alberts in 1957:

> "Our conclusion in Roth, at 486-487, 1 L. Ed. 2d at 1507, 1508, that the clear and present danger test was irrelevant to the determination of obscenity made it unnecessary in that case to consider the debate among the authorities whether exposure to pornography cause antisocial consequence. See also Mishkin v. N.Y., supra; Ginzberg v. U.S., supra; Memoirs v. Mass., supra."

The court went on to say in Ginsberg v. N.Y., supra, at page 641:

> "To sustain state power to exclude materials defined as obscenity by Section 484-h requires only that we be able to say that it was not irrational for the legislature to find that exposure to material condemned by the statute is harmful to minors . . . . We do not demand of legislatures 'scientifically certain criteria of legislation.' "

I therefore seriously question the monetary emphasis placed by this Commission on the "effects" aspect. The law being what it is, it would appear that by emphasizing theory and the paid professional, while neglecting the availability of a fact finding inquiry in support of the rationality of such legislation (available from the experiences of the practiced law enforcement officers through state and local government cooperation), does not put first things first.

The mandate of Congress was not simply to study the "effect" of obscenity upon the public and minors, but more completely:

> ". . . to study the effect of obscenity and pornography upon the public, and particularly minors, *and its relationship to crime and other antisocial behavior* . . . ." (My emphasis.)

I read the "relationship" study (underlined above) as being at least co-equal with the "effect" study. Further, I do not read this duty to study "the relationship (of obscenity) to crime and other antisocial behavior" to be construed so narrow as to require a "direct" cause-effect relationship. For example, in one case of a rape of a 12-year-old girl by a 20-year-old boy, a girlie magazine belonging to the suspect was left at the scene of the attack and

635

was identified by the victim as being in the youth's presence at the time of the attack. The presence of the girlie magazine in the possession of the rapist at the time of the attack is sufficient to warrant notice as a statistic giving evidence of the "relationship" of obscenity to antisocial behavior and bearing on the "rationality" of such legislation.

I have been visibly disturbed by the efforts of the industry, its attorneys and their constant companions, the A.C.L.U. (as amicus in their support) to upset the Roth-Alberts rule noted above. In the 12 years since Roth-Alberts, there have been relatively few briefs from those parties which have not been pushing for the overthrow of this aspect of the Roth-Alberts holding. When it became apparent that this frontal attack on Roth would not disappear, CDL, the organization which I founded 12 years ago, decided that it was going to be necessary to collate the facts in those cases which have constantly been coming to our attention in recent years in which criminal conduct bore a relationship to the use or possession of obscene materials. Toward that end, CDL undertook a pilot project to ascertain whether or not we could reacquire and document the information and experiences of law enforcement personnel during the past 12 years (since Roth-Alberts) by debriefing at this remote point of time the police personnel who were there involved. Our experiences in the two cities of study we undertook were entirely fruitful. See infra. In one of these cities of 100,000 population, we were able to document 25 cases in which obscene material was related to an act of antisocial conduct. The gravity of the relationship ran from vehicles for excitation for a voyeuer to vehicles of inducement to sexual perversion and accidental suicide. In the second city, with the population of 67,000, 9 similar cases were uncovered.

I do not have the professional interest of social scientists in the academic aspect of whether or not obscenity is the direct cause of every antisocial act committed by a person "addicted to" or the "reader" of such materials. It is enough for me that *a* relationship has been found. On this matter, my contacts with law enforcement officers over the past 13 years have confirmed what my own intelligence tells me is so. Time and again, these law enforcement officials have gone on record with statements to that effect, based upon their own personal experiences:

"The circulation of periodicals containing salacious material, and highly suggestive and offensive motion pictures and television, play an important part in the development of crime among our youth."

J. Edgar Hoover, Director,
Federal Bureau of Investigation

"The character of juvenile delinquency has changed as a consequence of the stimulation of salacious publications, being no longer the mischievous acts of children, but acts of violence, armed robbery, rape, torture and even homicide, for which the vicious publications condition the minds of our children."

A Resolution of the National
Council of Juvenile Court Judges.

"The fact that millions of innocent children are exposed in their formative years to reading matter and art depicting shocking sexual travesties is reason enough for serious dismay. Much more important, however, is the growing conviction among law officers that the flood of pornography that has been circulating among our young people for the past ten years is a major factor in today's rapidly rising rate of sex crime. . . .

"What we do know is that in an overwhelmingly large number of cases sex crime is associated with pornography. We know that sex criminals read it, are clearly influenced by it . . . . "A 42-year-old scientist, arrested in the Midwest on charges of taking indecent liberties with a 9-year-old girl, was found to have an impressive collection of pornography in his home . . . .

"I believe pornography is a major cause of sex violence. I believe that if we can eliminate the distribution of such items among impressionable school-age children we shall greatly reduce our frightening sex crime rate."

> J. Edgar Hoover, Director
> Federal Bureau of Investigation,
> writing in This Week Magazine.

"There has not been a sex murder in the history of our department in which the killer was not an avid reader of lewd magazines."

> Herbert W. Case, former
> Detroit Police Inspector

"Our city has experienced many crimes of sexual deviation, such as child molestation and indecent exposure. We find that most of these deviates read obscene materials, and often exhibit them to children in an effort to arouse sexual excitement among their victims."

> Police Chief Paul E. Blubaum,
> Phoenix, Arizona

"Obscene literature is a primary problem in the United States today. Sexual arousals from obscene literature have been responsible for criminal behavior from vicious assaults to homicide."

> O. W. Wilson, Superintendent,
> Chicago Police Department

"The increasing number of sex crimes is due precisely to sex literature madly presented in certain magazines. Filthy literature is the great moron maker. It is creating criminals faster than jails can be built."

> J. Edgar Hoover, Director,
> Federal Bureau of Investigation

"I have never picked up a juvenile sex offender who didn't have this stuff with him, in his car, or in his house."

> Detective Lieutenant Austin B. Duke,
> St. Louis County Police

637

"San Diego County District Attorney Don Keller, on June 21, 1966, reported an increase in child molestation cases in the county, compared with a similar period the previous year.

"Keller said he believed that pornographic material has played a part in the increase of child molesters in the area. He added that stronger laws against pornography and obscenity would be of considerable help in combating the offenses."

Reported in the San Diego
Union, June 22, 1966.

In my opinion, their practical experiences make them experts which warrant special attention beyond that accorded the theorician.

As mentioned above, the Commission report recites an abundance of projected studies by social scientists into the theoretical aspects of antisocial behavior, but little, if any, effort, being devoted to a statistical analysis of crimes on the police blotter. I therefore request this Commission to open the latter area for fuller investigation and examination and in that regard move that adequate moneys be allocated for the project hereinafter described.

Such a project appears to be required by the Senate amendments of September 20, 1967, wherein Senator Mundt made it clear that Congress (1) is desirous of having those with special and practical competence in these areas participate, and (2) has placed an emphasis upon a coordinated effort by all levels of State government. One would be hard put to find personnel with more practical knowledge and experience in this area than the police, sheriffs, vice and juvenile officers in the local communities.

Accordingly, I propose that the attorney generals of each state, the sheriffs of each county, and the police in each city, hamlet, etc., be asked to participate and to examine retroactively the law enforcement files in each jurisdiction for the 12 years since Roth-Alberts for cases such as those mentioned in the hereinafter described statistical study.

Because I am convinced that such a study can be made and will be fruitful, I offer my services as coordinator and request that funds be allocated for personnel to complete the same under the plan as proposed, which is based upon the aforementioned pilot study.

Proposed Statistical Study

Purpose of Statistical Study
The effort here is to demonstrate the validity of the indirect causal rationale by reference to concrete examples which are a part of the ever increasing statistics on crimes in the vice area. This project is *not* an attempt to prove direct causation. Recently a number of rape and attempted rape cases have arisen in which the responsible parties themselves have admitted to having been stimulated to the act by obscene material read before the crime was committed. When informed of the facts of these several cases, one "Douglas view" educator with a Freudian orientation was asked whether 5000 documented histories of a like nature would affect his position. His answer was "No"—he would still want to

638

inquire into the early personal history of the actor. The Douglas requirement of direct causation, which will accept only objectively verified evidence, it is submitted, is impossible of attainment.

Strategy

Jimmie Walker's oft-quoted cliche, "Did you ever know a woman who was ruined by a book" has continued to offer the same tricky argument. It has been as effective in the decade that followed 1957 as it was in 1923, when first used in the New York Legislature to defeat the passage of an obscenity control bill. This issue which was thought to have been defeated so decisively in 1957, has, through constant repetition become one of the principal factors affecting the administration of obscenity controls.

Documentary evidence is needed to point up the connection between the subject matter and our social problems. Under the present regime, to pose the Jimmie Walker question is to raise a negative inference that there is no causal relationship, *direct or indirect*. Statistical information demonstrating *a* relationship between obscenity and social crimes is, at the very least, probative evidence of the latter relationship.

Our concerned, alerted communities need not quibble over how the influence is exerted. This proposition is clearly stated by Justice Harlan in California v. Alberts at page 1516:

"It is well known, of course, that the validity of this assumption is a matter of dispute among critics, sociologists, psychiatrists, and penologists. There is a large school of thought, particularly in the scientific community, which denies any causal connection between the reading of pornography and immorality, crime, or delinquency. Others disagree. *Clearly it is not our function to decide this question. That function belongs to the state legislature.* Nothing in the Constitution requires California to accept as truth the most advanced and sophisticated psychiatric opinion. It seems to me clear that it is not irrational, in our present state of knowledge, to consider that pornography can induce a type of sexual conduct which a State may deem obnoxious to the moral fabric of society. In fact, the very division of opinion on the subject counsels us to respect the choice made by the State.

"Furthermore, even assuming that pornography cannot be deemed ever to cause, in an immediate sense, criminal sexual conduct, *other interests within the proper cognizance of the State may be protected by the prohibition placed on such materials.* The State can reasonably draw the inference that over a long period of time the indiscriminate dissemination of materials, the essential character of which is to degrade sex, will have an eroding effect on moral standards." (My emphasis.)

A society should be concerned over the indiscriminate dissemination of girlie magazines and the like, when such materials are shown to have been a link in the chain of events leading to the forcible rape of a 12-year-old child, or to have been used as an inducement to minors and their moral corruption, etc., where such occurrences are shown to be substantial in number.

Period Under Study

The plan is to concentrate on case histories which have arisen since Roth-Alberts was decided in 1957. The time interval from

639

1957 through 1969 is appropriate, that period spanning the greatest growth in obscenity in any nation's history.

Key to Necessary Data

The case histories which are sought after are not indexed in the police files, so as to be immediately attainable. They are discoverable, however, through a determined investigation. It is simply a matter of searching the mental files of the appropriate law enforcement personnel to provide the key which will locate the paperwork files.

The case histories we are searching for are best described by reference to "type" situations, using actual examples acquired from various sources over the past few years. Some of these are listed below:

1. *Murder—Sexual Perversion.* Male, aged 27, and female, aged 23, murder a girl, aged 10, and boys, ages 12 and 17. Prior to their death murderers employed torture and sexual perversion and tape recorded the events. Lewd photographs of young girls in pornographic poses and a library of pornographic and sadistic literature (DeSade) were found in the male's possession. See Ian Brady/Myra Hingley Moors case, December 9, 1965, and Lady Snow's book, "On Iniquity" by Scribner, discussing this famous Moors case.

2. *Rape.* Male youth, age 20, forcibly attacks minor female, age 12, on her way home from school. The victim reports (and the police find) a girlie magazine belonging to suspect left at the scene of the attack. See James case, Burbank, California, April 3, 1963.

3. *Rape—Murder Case.* Two male youths spend the morning and early afternoon drinking alcoholic beverage and watching lewd motion picture films. At about 3:30 P.M. one youth forcibly enters a car driven by a 19-year-old girl, when it was stopped for a traffic light, forcing her to drive him to a secluded area where he killed her after trying to rape her. See Doss case, Freehold, N. J., November 1, 1966.

4. *Rape Case.* Seven Oklahoma teenage male youths gang attack a 15-year-old female from Texas, raping her and forcing her to commit unnatural acts with them. Four of the youths, two the sons of attorneys, admit being incited to commit the act by reading obscene magazines and looking at lewd photographs. See Fellers case, Oklahoma City, Feb. 1, 1966.

5. *Rape—Murder Case.* Male negro, aged 16, is identified by a 59-year-old female victim as the person who criminally attacked her in her home. Youth admits to having read an account of a criminal assault in a magazine in a neighborhood store after which he walked around the neighborhood, passed the victim's house and decided to break in. The victim told detectives that she pleaded with the man, "I'm an old woman and I don't have any money." She said he replied that he did not want money. The intruder then dragged her into the bedroom and ripped off her clothes. See McGowan case, Akron, Ohio, Nov. 19, 1966.

6. *Assault.* Male youth, aged 13, admits attack on a young girl in a downtown office was stimulated by sexual arousal from a stag magazine article he had previously read in a public drug-

640

store, which showed naked women and an article on "How to Strip a Woman". See affidavit of youth, dated June 30, 1965.

7. *Rape—Juvenile Delinquency.* Investigating the case of a 16-year-old youth who raped a 10-year-old girl, police found in his possession three homosexual playing cards. A number of these cards were found in possession of other boys of that neighborhood, ranging in age from 13 to 16. See Report of Capt. G. E. Matheny, Juv. Off., San Antonio, Texas, Police.

8. *Attempted Rape—Juvenile Delinquency.* A 15-year-old boy grabbed a 9-year-old girl, dragged her into the brush and was ripping off her clothes. The girl screamed and the youth fled. The next day he was picked up by police. He admitted that he had done the same thing in Houston, Galveston, and now in San Antonio. He said that his father kept pornographic pictures in his top dresser drawer and that each time he pored over them the urge would come over him. See Report of Capt. G. E. Matheny, Juv. Off., San Antonio, Texas, Police.

9. *Rape Case.* Woman is raped on the way to church one morning. Just prior to the attack the man was reading obscenity in his panel truck. Cleveland, Ohio. See County Prosecutor Corrigan's story in Universe Bulletin, April 14, 1967.

10. *Rape Case.* Santa Clara County District Attorney Louis Bergna reports, as printed in San Jose, Calif., Mercury, Nov. 23, 1966:

"Santa Clara County Crime File documents cases where teen-age boys have attacked, and killed, women after their sex drives were ignited by lewd photos from readily available men's magazines. One youth after seeing a beautiful young girl kidnapped and held prisoner in the British movie, The Collector, carted off a girl and held her for 18 hours while he forced her to commit every act you can possibly imagine. In his home we found nothing but this type of magazine . . . . The adult bookstores are loaded with books on sadism and masochism—sexual satisfaction through the infliction or receiving of pain." Showing the thin book, he said it contained photos of women tied up or being beaten up by other women and it sells for $5.20. "In Santa Clara County we used to think these things were academic," Bergna said, "but a year or so ago police discovered in Sunnyvale a torture chamber where a young professional man beat other men and committed unnatural sex acts. We just completed another case in the Gilroy area in which a young sailor was bound and beaten by another man bent on fulfilling his sexual hunger. *It just might be we have more of this type of thing in this country than we suspect."*

11. *Murder Case.* Male youth, aged 14, admits slaying of 9-year-old girl. Body was found in a junk-filled shed, which was used as a neighborhood playhouse. Among the articles removed from the shed were some magazines of a pornographic nature. See Lang case, Denver, Colo., June 30, 1966.

12. *Murder Case.* A sackful of pornographic magazines were found near a waterfilled ditch where the bodies of two strangled girls, aged 5 and 6, were discovered. See Tift/Reynolds (victims) case, Cannock Chase, England, Jan. 15, 1966.

13. *Kidnap Case.* Seven-year-old female kidnapped by a 22-

year-old parolee with two previous molesting convictions. Victim was photographed in the nude and was squirted in the eyes with tear gas to prevent identification. Nudist magazines were found in the car and at his home. See Adkins case (victim), Cleveland, Ohio, January 1965.

14. *Juvenile Delinquency—Sex Gang.* A juvenile sex gang involving boys 7 to 15, plus one 3-year-old, was discovered in Oklahoma. An attorney representing one of the 15-year-old boys revealed the boy told him they, themselves, and sub-teenage youngsters had bought magazines at various grocers and drugstore newsstands and were incited by pictures of men committing unnatural acts and men and women in lewd photos. See Wilson case, Valley Blook, Oklahoma, Jan. 27, 1966.

15. *Juvenile Delinquency—Sex Perversion.* Male, aged 42, uses lewd photographs of males and money to entice other male youths to pose for photographs and participate in lewd acts. See Haymaker case, Burbank, Calif., Jan. 11, 1966; San Leandro, Calif. case, July 21, 1967; Welty case, Portage, Mich., Mar. 21, 1965, and Gardiner case, Parkland, Md., Mar. 31, 1965.

16. *Juvenile Delinquency—Sex Perversion.* Police officer making rounds in city park discovers minor boy committing act of sodomy on another minor boy. Center spread of Playboy was being used as means of excitation. See Juvenile Police Officer Frank Meehan, West Covina, Calif., 1964.

17. *Juvenile Delinquency—Sex Perversion.* An interested person discloses conversation with teenage member of gang who revealed that teenage gangs indulging in acts of perversion were using Playboy to get them excited. See letter of Sept. 8, 1965. See also People v. Wrigley, 70 Cal. Rptr. 116 (Aug. 9, 1968).

18. *Juvenile Delinquency—Child Molestation.* Two girls, aged 9 and 12, told police that the male owner of a bookshop, aged 58, located next to a high school, had shown them photographs of naked men and women and had abused one of them. Police indicated that the bookstore owner had previously spent 2 years in jail for molesting a girl 10 years old. When arrested police found thousands of obscene magazines and books in the shop. See Cohn case, New York, N.Y., 1965.

19. *Juvenile Delinquency—Child Molestation.* A male individual brings 2 girls, aged 13 and 15, into his home which is filled with obscene literature and has relations with them. Cleveland, Ohio. See County Prosecutor Corrigan's story in Universe Bulletin, Apr. 14, 1967.

20. *Juvenile Delinquency—Child Molestation.* The Journal of Atlanta, Ga., of Jan. 6, 1966, reports "A psychiatrist examining a man charged with molesting a 10-year-old girl in Fulton County last year reports: 'He states he would often buy . . . books which were illustrated by pictures of women wearing varying amounts of clothing assuming suggestive positions . . . .' "

21. *Juvenile Delinquency—Child Molestation.* First Ass't States Attorney Edward M. Booth, Jacksonville, Fla., writes in his letter of May 27, 1966, ". . . we have four felony charges pending in our criminal courts at this time wherein adults are charged with various sexual offenses involving minor children. In each of these four cases, we have found that obscene literature and

other pornographic materials were used to entice minor children ranging in age from 8 to 16 years, including both boys and girls, into indulging in various lewd and lascivious sexual acts with the adults involved . . . . I have found that most cases involving sexual activities with minor children have obscene and pornographic literature and materials involved, and, *perhaps, this is true throughout the country . . . ."*

22. *Sex Perversion—Juvenile Delinquency.* Defendant male, 28, invited boys, 13 and 15, to a house in Brentwood where they swam, watched TV, were served Vodka and 7-Up, and shown "Playboy" magazines. Defendant engaged in an act of oral copulation. See People v. Cramer, 60 Cal. Rptr. 230, 231, where the California Supreme Court held evidence of one such act was admissible in prosecution for a second offense as evidence of a "common design, plan, or modus operandi", reversing a lower appellate court holding to the contrary in 55 Cal. Rptr. 701.

23. *Juvenile Delinquency—Sex Perversion.* A 5-year-old boy was the victim of sodomy by a 15-year-old boy. The youth arrested said he had seen a number of these homosexual playing cards and had heard men and older boys talk about such acts. He admitted committing these acts on several small boys.

24. *Juvenile Delinquency.* A 17-year-old youth was picked up for writing a most obscene and suggestive letter to a 14-year-old girl. The youth took the officer to the neighborhood drugstore and showed him the books he had been reading—"Vengeful Virgin", "Sex Appeal", "How to Make Love", all available at 35¢ to a dollar on numerous newsstands. See Report of Capt. G. E. Mathony, Juv. Off., San Antonio, Texas, Police.

25. *Juvenile Delinquency.* A 14-year-old boy on the north side was arrested for making obscene telephone calls. He admitted that he had called over 200 women and girls. He had in his home a huge manila envelope stuffed with filthy pictures. These he had traced from pictures in such magazines as "Sun Bathing", "Nudist", etc., because he had looked them over many times but did not have the money to buy them. He further admitted that while talking to the women he had the urge to hurt them. See Report of Capt. G. E. Mathony, Juv. Off., San Antonio, Texas, Police.

26. *Juvenile Delinquency.* Police picked up a 15-year-old boy, who had written an extremely obscene and suggestive letter to a 13-year-old girl, asking her to meet him near a northside elementary school. When arrested he had in his possession a deck of playing cards adorned with pictures of nude women. He had purchased them on Houston Street with no questions asked. See Report of Capt. G. E. Mathony, Juv. Off., San Antonio, Texas, Police.

An examination of the crimes against morality described above indicates that the "key" law enforcement officers for such crimes in any given jurisdiction would be: (1) Juvenile officers, (2) detectives involved in the investigation of sex offenses, and (3) vice officers. Police personnel do not as a general rule leave their profession, nor are they accustomed to wander from job to job within their profession. Those who have occupied the above billets during the period 1957 through 1969 constitute a relatively small number of persons who are still members of the existing police organization.

Re: Attitude of Police Department to Survey

The police in their practice regularly witness that which the legislators in enacting obscenity legislation have acknowledged to be a fact, i.e., that obscenity does bear a substantial relationship to antisocial conduct. They welcome a responsible effort to record their experiences. When approached on the subject, the comment of the Burbank Chief of Police was, "I'm interested in the basic idea." In discussions with other police personnel, the same reaction has been received.

General Outline of Investigative Procedure

The Survey Within The Individual Law Enforcement Agency

The "on the scene" procedure recommended hereafter is based upon a study undertaken in Burbank, California, an incorporated city of about 95,000 inhabitants with its own police force of over 140 men. The approach employed in other cities in California should be the same, or similar, because of the similarity of law enforcement methods within any given state. It should not be too difficult to adapt this procedure to law enforcement agencies in other states, making slight allowances for such differences in organizational structures as may be necessary.

Step I. Ascertain what specific branches of police personnel will be involved in the survey in the jurisdictions being studied. In California, this will be: (1) Juvenile Division, (2) Detectives Division (Sex Crimes), and (3) Vice Division (Prostitution, Homosexuality, Commercial Obscenity).

Step II. Determine from the Personnel Division the names of the persons who headed those divisions during the period 1957-1969.

Step III. After outlining the objectives, conduct a short interview (30 to 45 minutes) with each of the persons identified in Step II above, utilizing the officer's "Activity Record" file to refresh his recollection as to appropriate cases within his knowledge. See Statement of Detective Lane (infra). Make a brief note of the facts of each case recalled and the D.R. number (Desk Report). A small portable tape recorder should be used in these interviews.

Step IV. Examine the M.O. card file (modus operandi), subject Sex Offenses, in the jurisdiction (where available) for case histories in which suspect used smut as a part of his M.O. (for example, shows dirty pictures, movies, books, etc.). Record D.R. number.

Step V. Submit list of D.R.'s to law enforcement agency. D.R. records are pulled from file for study by appropriate officer. Reinterview officers as to specific facts in each case, based upon his present recollection after having refreshed his memory from the police report.

Step VI. Prepare a memorandum for the law enforcement officer recapping the data which has been compiled, requesting the dissemination of such information to each police officer in the command and notification of additional case histories which might be within the immediate knowledge of such officers.

Experience Using The Survey Technique

644

The survey conducted within the Burbank Police Department produced the following information and case histories for the report:

Detective Carl Lane, Vice, Sex Crimes (1957-1964)

Re: Use of Assignment Sheets (Activity Records). "I could go back over my assignment sheets—when I read that, the charge and the defendant—it would come back to me, like the James case. My file contains every case that was assigned to me. It comes to me as a D.R. and the type of case. When the case is solved, the defendant's name goes here. I would have to do what I am doing now."

Re: Use of M.O. File (Modus Operandi). "How much time have you got? If you can get permission, I can tell you how you can do it. They have a M.O. file downstairs. Under Lewd Phone Calls they have words spoken. She will type in the exact words spoken. If you have the time and permission, you can go into the records. The Sheriff's Department has a terrific M.O. file . . . . The C.I.I. (State of California) has a tremendous M.O. file."

1. J---- Case—D.R. 63-2447 (supra).

2. Newspaper Route (1963—no arrest) (Possibly G---- Case— D.R. 63-2703). "We had a newspaper delivery route man. He had a whole boxful of lewd photos. He would show these to the little newspaper boys and then make a pass at them. There wasn't enough evidence to go on him. His M.O. was to show these pictures to get the kids excited and then make a play for them. As I recall, we had two complaints on him but we couldn't make him. He admitted to having the pictures but there wasn't the evidence to prove he showed or fondled them. Even though the boys said he showed them—their ages were such that they wouldn't go on him."

3. Girlie Cutouts (1962—no arrest). "One case comes to my mind and believe it or not, he was never caught. He was shook down on a couple of occasions and he had these girlie magazines in his possession in the car. He had pieces of string tied around the wrist and cut them out and things like that. He had them cut in several places and he had a penis inserted in one. He was in one of the market parking lots at the time. I brought him in and talked to him. He admitted that this was his doings. For a long time I had his name available. I always thought that he was involved or was going to be involved."

The magazines are in the Burbank files. They are all of 1962 manufacture: Figure Annual 1962, Cuddle Bug, Vol. 300, No. 1, Black Lace 1962, Orbit L. N. Flirt, Vol. 1, No. 2. In each of the photographs the individual had cut slits into the vaginal and anal area and inserted human hair. It is interesting to note that this occurred just before the nudist magazines, showing pubic hair, came into being.

4. Sex Perversion. L---- Case—D.R. 58-2928. "We had one child molestation over on Tujunga. The fellow was a projectionist. He would show lewd film and at the same time he was playing with these 5 and 6-year-old girls. He copped out to the whole thing but I lost it in court. The officer who was with me didn't turn on the tape recorder. The defendant got up in court and denied the

645

whole thing. About 5 years later his wife came in. in tears. She found out that he was doing the same thing to his little nieces. He had told the whole thing to her but she had gotten up in court and lied."

5. Re: Lewd Telephone Calls: "A guy will call up and say, 'I'm looking at some pictures and I'm sure you look like this.'" "They have a M.O. file downstairs. Under Lewd Phone Calls, they have words spoken. The typist will type in the exact words spoken."

6. Re: Indecent Exposure and Peeping Toms: "I do know that there have been occasions when we have had prowlers—peepers—they would have magazines in their cars and would frankly admit they were looking for excitment." "The biggest thing we would have would be indecent exposure—then you would have your prowlers which could be broken down into two classes. I found the same thing with them. They had nude pictures and the magazines. It wasn't an uncommon thing and still it didn't happen each time. You thought not too much of it if they were there or they weren't there. There were numerous occasions you would find when you talked to them they had girlie magazines or photographs in their car."

Detective Al Madrid, Vice, Sex Crimes (1964 to present)

7. Indecent Exposure—R---- Case—D.R. 67-4005. "Two girls walked down a sidewalk near the suspect's place of business (commercial). He whistled at them. They looked up to see him standing inside the door. His fly was open and his privates were out with one hand on his privates and one beckoning to the girls. Defendant had pictures cut out of a nudist magazine, showing nude women in various poses, pinned up on a bulletin board. One of the victims saw the defendant remove the photos as they were leaving. The children notified their parents who called the police. When the police arrived (20 minutes later) the pictures were no longer visible but were found by the police among some newspapers."

8. Exhibiting Girlie Magazine Cutouts. (1966—no arrest). "Two or three young girls, 12 and 13, were walking from school on the sidewalk. They observed a vehicle pull up into the driveway a short distance from them and in their path. A male exited from the vehicle and placed something on the sidewalk. He pulled out of the driveway and went down the street a short way. Upon reaching the spot the girls observed the subject matter to be nude pictures. They took them up to their mother who destroyed the pictures before reporting the case."

Lt. Warren King, Vice (1958-1961, 1967)

9. Child Molestation—W---- Case—D.R. 63-8313. "He had these lewd pictures at Olive Recreation Center. Some kid walked by and he conned him into coming into the bushes and forced him to masturbate. It was reported by the victim. This was the earlier case. At that time the suspect was about 13. Victim was also a young boy. In the more recent case (see No. 14, infra), it was a kidnap and oral copulation."

10. Sex Perversion—Glendale case. "A 50-year-old man and

an 8 and 11-year-old girl were involved. The girls reported to the parents who reported to the police. The defendant came over with some lewd pictures and showed them to the girls. He worked for the family. He showed the pictures, had them pull down their pants and then they played games—ball in the pants, etc. He eventually committed 288 (oral copulation) on the children at their home.

11. Exhibition Obscene Photos—M---- Case—D.R. 59-162. "A woman with a Youth Employment Agency had a daughter doing amateur modeling at a restaurant. The daughter passed by the suspect who stopped her and displayed a nude photograph and asked the daughter if this wasn't a picture of her. Another person was offered a drink and shown the same nude photograph."

12. Sexual Perversion—D---- Case—D.R. 67-5847. "A homosexual reported being assaulted with a deadly weapon. The event occurred on graduation night in June. Two boys were involved. One had worked in a restaurant where the suspect worked. The boys came over to his residence. The suspect had promised to take them to Disneyland to the graduation party but reneged. He gave them alcohol and showed them films. The boys had quite a bit to drink, got sleepy and went into the bedroom and he engaged in oral copulation. The boys cut off his hair and took the film. It was submitted but no complaint was filed. There was conflicting evidence—one of the boys might have been a homosexual."

13. Exhibiting Obscene Photos. "In the homosexual bars they show movies on the wall—male nudist type."

Lt. Ernest J. Vandergrift

14. Sex Perversion. W---- Case—D.R. 67-8108. "A 17-year-old boy had access to a vehicle. He picked up a 5-year and 7-year-old boy and, after showing them a cutout from a nudist magazine behind a building, took them to a park in Glendale. He copulated the 5-year-old boy and forced the 5-year-old boy to copulate him. He took them near their home. His record shows he has used a knife. In Burbank he had a prior—he was excluded from Hawaii on the same activity."

15. Sex Perversion—G---- Case. "It was more than 10 years ago. Suspect lived alone. He got himself made Scout Master of the Sea Scouts and took young boys to his hotel. He would talk to them, then give them something to read. In the book it would say, 'Is this making you excited, are you getting a ____ ____? Do you want me to ____ ____?' He had all kinds of pictures of lewd acts, homosexual acts, etc. He was given psychiatric treatment."

16. Sex Perversion—Suicide—H---- Case—D.R. 64-5456. "The body was discovered by the wife of the suspect, who is 24 years old, when she came home from work as a social worker. He attended law school. She found him lying on the bed in a supine position, face down and naked. On top one end of a rope was tied to his ankles, the other end was around his throat. A pair of white sox kept the rope from connection with his skin as did a towel around his throat. She screamed and the neighbor came in and cut the ropes. The Fire Department tried resuscitation and

647

called the police. When the police arrived, his ankles were still trussed but rigor mortis had set in. Just above him on the bed were 5 or 6 nudist magazines (2 were Sun and Sport), all open to female forms. When he was moved, it was found he had a contraceptive on and had an emission on the bed. All windows, doors were locked. The neighbors had seen him enter and he had no visitors until his wife came home. In the investigation with the Coroner's office and Los Angeles County Sheriff disclosed a type of masochism—in which sexual excitement is reached upon tying oneself up and hanging to almost a point of blackout —substantiated by psychiatry and case histories. Interrogation of suspect's wife revealed that ever since their marriage he was unable to obtain satisfactory intercourse without the use of ropes, being tied up and subjected to this before he could perform satisfactorily. He had received psychiatric help for 8 years. The death was accidental—he did not intend to do it. In Los Angeles County, cases of this type occur about 6 times a year in which the defendant goes too far. He had sox on and a towel on his throat to prevent rope marks."

Lt. Don Tutich, Juvenile Division, 1966

17. Sex Perversion—Juvenile Delinquency. H---- Case—D.R. 66-234. "The defendant showed the victims pictures—nudist magazines and nude girls until he got them involved and participating in homosexual activity. He started with pictures of nude women and men and then afterwards just nude males. The story of the use of nudist magazines came from the two boys and other victims. The boys were in the 11, 12 and 14 age group. I came up with 14 victims myself and know there were many others. These were just those who admitted relationships with him and the ones I could identify. In each case the parents were surprised. He was active in the church choir. The boys called him Uncle Harry. The kids used his place as a hangout. They had young girls come over but defendant had nothing to do with them."

18. Voyeurism (1958—No D.R.) "One time we got a call from the pickwick swim park. A man was seated in a car looking at the girls with binoculars. It was suspicious to the ticket woman who called the police. When we drove up he was driving away. He admitted to the M.O. but we let him go since nobody had seen him expose himself. He had a great big jar of vaseline and would masturbate while watching the girls. He had several female type hard backs, pornographic books. Some fly-by-night was producing the material. They were the hardback novel that you could buy in your magazine stores downtown.

19. Sex Perversion (No D.R.) "On one investigation we found a dress dummy in a garage with a hole cut in it. Evidently they would dress the dummy and use it for intercourse. We found a whole mess of girlie magazines at the same time in the garage."

Re: M. O. Card File. The City of Burbank maintains a M.O. Card file that goes back 5 years. The following M.O.'s were found under the general title "Sex Crimes":

20. D.R. 63-4817. Suspect told the young boy, "Come on up to my room and look at some of the magazines." The juvenile re-

648

ported the matter to the police who searched the room and found one book and two magazines.

21. D.R. 63-9691. The suspect "shows pictures of nudes".

22. D.R. 64-7331. A 21-year-old female reported receiving lewd photographs in the mail. She believed that a 24-year-old male whom she had stopped seeing had sent the materials out of spite.

23. D.R. 64-8970. An automobile drove up to the driveway of a home and left photographs of a penis on the driveway. The victims are believed to be two minors, ages 10 and 12, living in the residence.

24. D.R. 66-2942. A man in a car left nude pictures on the sidewalk.

25. D.R. 66-6218. A male approached a 9-year-old juvenile in the public restroom saying, "See this" and "Have you ever seen your mother in the nude?" and shows black and white photographs of nudes.

State Survey

To expand the individual law enforcement agency survey into a statewide survey requires only that the same process be repeated as to each of the other police agencies. This requires an analysis of the state law enforcement structure. By way of illustration, the State of California is selected as the general area under investigation.

California, with a population of over 18 million, is divided into 58 counties, covering an area of over 158,000 miles. The largest of these counties is Los Angeles County with a population of over 6 million, followed by San Diego County with a population of over 1 million, San Francisco County with a population of over 750,000, Orange County with a population of over 700,000, and Sacramento and San Bernardino Counties with populations of over 500,000. Thus one-third of the California population is located in Los Angeles County.

Each one of these counties has its own law enforcement police agency, known as the Sheriff's Department, which provides law enforcement for (1) the unincorporated territory within each county, and (2) the incorporated cities in the county which contract for law enforcement services. Most incorporated cities, however, have their own police department which enforces the law within the jurisdictional boundaries of the city.

In California there are 396 incorporated cities, 54 of which contract for police services with other law enforcement agencies, such as the Sheriff's Department. To cover the police activity in the entire state therefore requires that an examination be made of 400 law enforcement agencies; the 342 cities with independent police departments, and the Sheriff's Department in each of the 58 counties.

A greater portion of the state activity can be covered, with fewer law enforcement agencies involved, by concentrating on the counties with the largest population. Thus, as shown hereafter, Los Angeles County with one-third of the state's population, can be covered by examining only 12% (48) of the total number of law enforcement agencies which exist in the state.

Within Los Angeles County there are 76 incorporated cities.

649

The Los Angeles County Sheriff's Office provides law enforcement for all the unincorporated territory and, under contract, for 29 of these incorporated cities, who have no police force. The 29 cities are:

City	Population	City	Population
Artesia	9,993	Lawndale	21,740
Avalon	1,536	Lomita	19,000
Bellflower	54,000	Norwalk	94,500
Bell Gardens	28,779	Palmdale	7,200
Bradbury	618	Paramount	27,249
Commerce	?	Pico Riviera	51,500
Cudahy	?	Rolling Hills	?
Cerritos	3,508	Rolling Hills Estates	3,941
Duarte	13,962	Rosemead	15,476
Hawaiian Gardens	?	San Dimas	11,520
Hidden Hills	?	Santa Fe Springs	16,342
Industry	?	South El Monte	?
Lakewood	84,000	Temple City	29,000
LaMirada	22,444	Walnut	934
LaPuente	24,723		

The remaining 47 incorporated cities have their own, independent police departments which enforce the law within their cities. Arranged chronologically by population they are:

City	Population	City	Population
Los Angeles	2,695,000	South Gate	57,800
Long Beach	368,000	Redondo Beach	55,000
Glendale	133,000	Monterey Park	48,200
Torrance	129,000	Arcadia	47,200
Pasadena	123,500	El Monte	45,000
Burbank	96,500	Gardena	45,000
Downey	93,500	Hawthorn	45,000
Santa Monica	88,500	Baldwin Park	43,500
Inglewood	86,000	Montebello	40,000
Pomona	83,000	Manhattan Beach	36,000
Compton	77,000	Lynwood	35,500
Whittier	69,500	Beverly Hills	34,500
Alhambra	63,500	Culver City	32,163
West Covina	62,500	Huntington Park	29,920

City	Population	City	Population
Glendora	28,200	Maywood	14,588
Covina	27,600	El Segundo	14,219
Monrovia	27,079	San Marino	13,658
San Gabriel	22,561	Sierra Madre	9,732
Azusa	20,497	Palos Verdes Estates	9,564
South Pasadena	19,706	La Verne	6,516
Claremont	19,400	Signal Hill	4,627
Bell	19,450	Irwindale	1,518
San Fernando	16,093	Vernon	229
Hermosa Beach	16,115		

Therefore, to cover police activity in Los Angeles County completely by personal interview (⅓ of the state population) requires that an examination be made of the police departments for the 47 incorporated cities listed above and the Sheriff's Department (for the unincorporated county territory and the 27 "contract" cities). These 48 agencies, however, represent only 12% of the total number in the state.

Survey by Mail

The administrative burden of interviewing law enforcement agencies can be further reduced if a part of the survey is conducted by mail. If cities in California with a population under 30,000 are surveyed by mail, the number of personal surveys required can be reduced by 40%. A sample form letter to be sent to the respective police chiefs to accomplish this objective is attached as Enclosure A.

Cooperation From Other Sources

Other means of easing the administrative burden present themselves. For example, the attorney general's office in the various States might themselves be moved to sponsor the statewide survey, if given the proper directive.

Assistance may also be forthcoming from sympathetic County Boards of Supervisors and city councils, who have the power to direct their law enforcement agencies to conduct a survey within the county and city. All that would be required would be a formal request, together with a plan of procedure to be followed and examples of successful operation elsewhere.

Collateral Inquiries

The police agency survey has a broad field of inquiry, encompassing not only crimes which have reached the accusatory stage, but also those which are unsolved, as well as matters of routine which turn up in police administration and which never appear on the police blotter. At least two other areas are worth canvassing, both of which encompass a lesser field of inquiry, namely, the judiciary and the probation office.

A personal letter of inquiry to each member of the judiciary and probation department would be an adequate coverage of these professions.

It is very likely that the inquiry of the probation office would be more productive. Whereas responses from the judiciary would turn up cases which were either duplications of matter discovered in the police inquiry or cases which had escaped the recollection of the police agency, responses from the probation department would, in addition, report those matters which were within the personal knowledge of the probationary officer incident to his post-conviction examination of the defendant's case.

Time Element

Very few manhours may be involved in the individual surveys. It may merely require making the personal contact. West Covina (population 67,000—65 police officers) is such a case. There, Juvenile Officer Frank Meehan (presently Chief of Police at Chino, California) explained the procedure in that jurisdiction as follows:

"For the last 6 years, every time any case involving obscenity, any obscenity was picked up, or newspaper obscenity was picked up in the hands of juveniles, who were arrested for

651

anything, a copy of that report automatically went to me and the material itself went to me."

This police force showed a serious concern over the problem. Chief Meehan's words of encouragement were:

"Your best bet is a personal contact with the heads of Juvenile Bureaus of fairly sizeable departments and say, 'This is what I've got—this is what I need—can you help me—I have received cooperation from various other chiefs of police' and you can name them—Chief Sills in West Covina backed your program 100%. He directed me to go through this and forward this information to you. You're going to get some of these guys who have been working these details for such a length of time that they know them and are aware of them and remember specific cases."

The cases uncovered in West Covina were as follows:

1. Sex Perversion—D.R. 69-978. Officer in investigating Walnut Creek at about 5:40 P.M., came upon two youths 15 and 16 years of age, engaged in an act of sodomy. The officer stated, "At the time I came upon these kids, there was a Playboy magazine opened to a double-page spread of nude female photos. The boy that was acting as the passive partner had his head propped up, with his hands resting on his elbows with the magazine spread out before him. The active partner, while on top, was looking at the same magazine over his friend's shoulder. One of the youths had taken the magazine from the drawer of his older brother's dresser, and both had been reading it prior to the act."

2. Indecent Exposure—D.R. 61-2432. Informant, parked at the Alpha Beta parking lot, was waiting for his wife and noticed the suspect in a vehicle, who was looking at the women as they passed and appeared to be masturbating. He called a police officer. "As the officer approached suspect he was observed holding and apparently reading a pocket book 'All About Annette' (Sex Stories Pocket Book). As the suspect turned toward the officer a black suit coat was observed lying on the suspect's legs, the fly to suspect's trousers was unzipped, partially exposing the suspect's penis. The suspect had another sex pocket book lying on the front seat, 'As Bad As They Come', which he grabbed and attempted to put underneath the front seat of the described vehicle . . . . Suspect admitted he was masturbating while he was watching the women that were wearing shorts walking through the parking lot and into the Alpha Beta Market at that location. He also stated that he had been reading the sex pocket books as this occurred and that this would 'excite him'."

3. Indecent Exposure—D.R. 64-4019. A male 36 exposed himself on 7 different occasions in a 2-day period to girls 8 to 12 in the vicinity of a school and a playground area. On one occasion the following occurred: "Females, ages 6 and 13, remained playing in the park at location for approximately 15 minutes when the suspect called them over to his vehicle which was parked in the west parking lot. Upon approaching the vehicle the victims stated that suspect was outside his vehicle in a stooped position with his trouser fly open and his penis protruding. Suspect then gave the victims a book, which is held in evidence, asking if the victims would read it for him. While the victims looked at the book,

the suspect began masturbating. Victims stated they looked at the first page of the comic book and at the suspect and then ran away from the suspect, throwing the book down as they fled. At that time the police unit arrived at the location."

4. Exhibits Obscene Cards—D.R. 64-4425. A juvenile aged 15 exhibited 5 playing cards, all with indecent photographs, to a 12-year-old. Upon investigation, it was revealed that he had received them from a 16-year-old and that many of his friends had similar playing cards in their possession, but that he did not know where they got them.

5. Indecent Exposure—D.R. 65-1611. A male 28 was observed sitting in a car in a shopping area reading a book and masturbating. An officer was called and upon arrival observed suspect to be reading a paperback sex book entitled, "Unfaithful" while masturbating. A paperback book "Punish Lesson" was lying on the seat beside him. Suspect admitted to the offense and to the officer that the passages in the paperbacks he had just bought aroused his sexual desires. Suspect admitted he had a prior record for the same offense in a public place 4 years ago in El Monte.

Officer Meehan also related the following cases:

6. "There was a Los Angeles County Sheriff's Office case that occurred just north of West Covina city limits a couple of years ago. A man was cohabitating with a woman who had a 10-year-old daughter. The woman worked during the day while the man stayed home with the daughter. The man had in his possession numerous catalogs from a firm named 'Nutrix' that was located in New Jersey. The catalogs were labeled, 'Special Bondage Issue' and showed samples of photographs that could be purchased in sets illustrating females in various flagellistic as well as other algolagnic poses. Apparently the pictures excited him to the point that he began to act them out with the young daughter. He began by making her strip and do housework in the nude. While the girl was working around the house, he would strap her bare bottom as the tendency struck him. Later, he suspended the nude girl by her ankles from the rafters in the garage and committed an act of cunnilingus upon her."

7. "Another case that occurred in West Covina a few years ago concerned a barber. He used girlie magazines on his youthful teenage customers and when they were inflamed he would commit an act of fellatio upon them. He was never prosecuted for this due to the fact that we were unable to convince a victim's parents to allow the kids to testify. The barber was arrested for a violation of plain drunk and while he was in custody, I questioned him about the alleged acts and he stated that they were in fact true."

8. "There were other cases there too involving the use of hardcore pornography—one case (a breach of peace) where this guy was mad at his neighbor, so he dropped dirty pictures on the sidewalk and his lawn so that his kids could see them."

9. "There was that knucklehead who was taking the pictures for Fizeek and Trim. The guy lived in the Ventura area. We pinched him on a check warrant. In his possession he had a whole bunch of homosexual stuff—hardcore—some Mickey Mouse movies and also some Trim, View, and Fizeek magazines. Supposedly he was a photographer. He was taking pictures of kids to submit them

653

to these magazines. He had form letters which he would send to his models to get the kids to pose with questions such as, 'What grade are you in?' 'Do you pose in the nude?' etc. He had a kid from San Jose College who wrote him that there was a great market for that stuff in the area—that the kids would go nuts about it."

Yours very truly,
Charles H. Keating, Jr.

CHK:1f
Enclosure A

Enclosure A (Exhibit C)

Dear Chief:

I am writing you on behalf of the Presidential Commission on Obscenity and Pornography. At the present time, we are conducting a nationwide survey aimed at uncovering and documenting case histories of criminal cases in which smut materials are known to have exhibited some relationship in the antisocial conduct involved. We earnestly solicit your cooperation and assistance in this effort.

The cliche most often used by those who oppose obscenity controls is Jimmy Walker's "Did you ever know a woman who was ruined by a book?" The inference flowing from such an argument is that no relationship whatsoever exists. Law enforcement officials can, from experience, attest to the opposite. Our effort here is to collect and document those cases which tend to support the law enforcement's point of view. Examples of the type of case histories we refer to, collected by CDL over the past few years from newspaper clippings, correspondence, etc., are set forth herein: (List material).

Our survey covers the years 1957-1969 (from the Roth-Alberts decisions to date) which period we have found to encompass the greatest growth in the obscenity problem. It has been our experience in the conversations and interviews we have conducted thus far on this subject that police officers can readily recall from their experiences during this 12-year period the type of case we refer to. As an example, in one jurisdiction of 95,000 population, law enforcement officers were able to recall from memory and documents the following case histories: (Set forth case histories).

In another jurisdiction of 65,000 the following case histories were reported by the Juvenile Police Officer, who had himself conducted a special study of such cases: (Briefly list case histories).

The importance of this survey at the present time is beyond question. Congress has recently charged this Commission on Obscenity and Pornography with the duty of studying the effect of obscenity upon the public, and its relationship to crime and other antisocial behavior. It is essential, therefore, *that practical proof of the relationship* be collected for study.

These case histories will be tabulated in a report, a copy of which will be forwarded each law enforcement agency participating in this project. Identity of all parties involved in the police reports will be kept confidential.

Can you help us in this effort? It would be a tremendous assist to the nationwide program if you would conduct a similar survey

654

in your command for inclusion in this report. Administratively, we have found the following procedure to be most effective in this regard and submit it as a possible guide for your approach to this survey: (Set forth Guide Steps noted in Plan for Statistical Study).

I will contact you personally by telephone within the week to discuss this matter more fully. I hope that at that time you will be able to give us the name of someone within your command, who will be able to act as your representative in this effort.

Sincerely

EXHIBIT "D"

THE PORNOGRAPHIC ENVIRONMENT AND HUMAN BEHAVIOR REPORT

BY

Bernard L. Bonniwell Ph D
Department of Psychology
Villanova University
Villanova, Pennsylvania 19085

Pornography is a form of education. As such, it modifies human behavior. The culture which remains indifferent to this principle fails to anticipate the rigid lessons of history.

All education has as its purpose the control and modification of behavior in certain of its aspects. Thus, the selection and manipulation of particular elements in the environment consistently characterizes the accepted types of education undertakings commonly noted in the school system. The nursery school, the elementary school, the junior and senior high schools, the college and the university all selectively attend to the appropriate educational techniques which lead to selected behavior. Among these behavioral goals may be noted the attainment of emotional and intellectual maturation, social sensitivity, and the recognition of mental health as desirable educational ends. In every instance, the manipulation of the environment is co-related with expected behavioral response. Even in the diverse realms of professional education, ranging from civilian occupations to military training, the principle remains the same: selected learning tends to produce behavioral response of a given type. Pornography is not free of this basic trend. It informs, educates and influences in precisely the same manner as does any other behavioral technique. Peculiarly enough, it is an especial form of education applicable only to man, for only man is an ethical animal.

Pornography, then, is an especial form of education for it appeals essentially to man's emotions. Reducing the problem even further, the kind of learning that takes place in a pornographic environment, concentrates a highly specialized excitation at the physiological level of the sex drive. Behaviorally speaking, this is man's most vulnerable area of response, frequently subjecting him to non-rational, anti-social and destructive motivations. Pornography cannot be considered lightly. It is related to

655

a qualitatively powerful human emotion, subject to control under conditions of discipline, yet capable of violently brutal frenzy when unleashed completely. The education of the emotions is as directly subject to the data of pornography as human emotions are subject to the data of the arts, science and literature. It is irrational to hold that pornography is educationally indifferent. It is the environment in a critically compulsive form: at a certain point, it is completely insensitive to rejection by the individual.

The social control of the pornographic environment is a prerequisite for human stability. In every form of human relationship there are rules and regulations which, although modifiable, flow from the nature of man's concept of self, of his needs, and of his desires. One of his prime desires is order. And interestingly enough the expression of order—both personal and cultural—has always been bound by either a wide ranging theo-philosophical concern or by the more precise, but less informative, order of science. In any case, the ordered environment has become his most prized possession, especially in the 20th century. In this sense, then, the pornographic environment—as a part of the whole life experience—is subject to control. It is not a free agent. It is, more precisely, man's socio-legal product and, as such, is subject to control by whatever means are deemed reasonable and necessary. It follows that the recognized pornographic techniques—broadly involving outlets through the modern novel, magazine, motion picture, theatre, and television—are subject to legal supervision and control in precisely the same sense that all education is subject to the principal of law. It is reasonably suggested that pornography is no longer untouchable. It is commonplace, educationally marketable, and like all other wisely distributed commodities subject to the rules and regulations of the marketplace. As an integral part of society, it is subject to social responsibility of a high order, especially as it impacts upon the youth and the adolescent.

It might be hoped that science would materially assist in determining the necessary classifications and reasonable restraints to be placed upon the pornographic environment, just as science assists in the control of medical practice and the appropriate use of drugs. However, the hope is a forlorn one, indeed. Probably no group of conglomerate sciences—the behavioral sciences—has ever tilted so vigorously with complex social issues and arrived at so few demonstrably valid conclusions. In general, for the total society the value of social research is seriously limited: for the malcontent, the disturbed and the abnormal, it has provided an extraordinary and questionable life-stage for the dissident and the alienated, but for the grave issues of society—those involving significant values and goals—the results are depressingly negative. For example, there are no fundamental new insights or answers to the problems of today's society, or even specific 'psychological cures' for today's demoralized youth, forthcoming from the social sciences. It is incredible that such effort, good will and research persistency should have produced so little of profound value to man. The glamorous hardware, the experimental laboratories, the plethora of national grants, would all seem to suggest the processing of extremely worthy research on human behavior.

Apparently contemporary science is simply unable to attack successfully the problem defined as human behavior. Where man is primarily *subjective*—living in the confined inner space of his own being—the behavioral sciences are *objectively* oriented to the external world. Where man lives in a world of distinctive *quality,* science exists in a world of *quantity.* Where pornography is a highly personal, conscience laden dilemma for man, for science it is simply response to the environment. Where man is self punished by moral transgressions, science is non-morally concerned with the problem in the simplistic terms of behavioral neuroses. Thus, for man there is right and wrong, good and bad, while for science there is only modified behavior. Some years ago, at the turn of the century, Monsignor Edward A. Pace of Catholic University, commented: "Either get hold of this instrument (experimental psychology) and use it for proper purposes, or leave it to materialists, and after they have heaped up facts, established laws, and forced their conclusions upon psychology, go about tardily to unravel with clumsy fingers, this tangle of error. Either share the development of the science, or prepare to wrestle with it when it has grown strong in hostile service." Now, in 1970, it is evident that the gross-mouthed purveyor of pornography has succeeded, beyond all expectations, in selling you and your child this 'tangle of error' under the unfortunate guise of social science. Science is not deliberate in its misleading of man in the behavioral sciences: the tragic error—to which even the dedicated Catholic Scholar has succumbed—is a refusal to accept the fact that the methods of research *are inadequate* at the present time. We are given only partial facts of a multi-faceted problem, and we are led to believe we have all the important facts. Our child is behaviorally damned by his love and respect for science—his innocence and gullibility forcing him into self alienation and disbelief of the sacredness of the human venture. Strident parents, ill informed, add to the disorder. The behavioral scientists teach that man is fully determined, not free, a product of his environment, subject to the dark world of the unconscious, a statistical entity, totally conditioned by an uncompromising past, and so ultimately rejected by the society that nourished him to manhood. The destruction of man is so perfect it is to be admired. The behavioral scientists have produced the contemporary negation of man although not fully aware of the extent of the behavioral victory. In plain terms the scientist teaches that science is their God, man their subject, and they will continue to mold him through the control of the educational environment. In contrast to the 20th Century enlightenment, Louis Rene de la Chalotais, writing in 1763, in regard to his plan of studies for the young, observed: "If he is not taught the good, he will necessarily accommodate himself to evil. The mind and the heart cannot remain empty." Thus the distinguishing concern of humanism—a concern *with* humanity—contrasts vividly with the scientific lack of interest in man as a moral being. With the contemporary behavioral sciences faltering badly in the essential areas of human understanding, attention is directed towards the more realistic and pragmatic cultural weight-of-evidence accumulated over the

657

years. The weight-of-evidence indicates a deep and troubled concern with this all too human problem:

Historically—The decline of a culture is consistently linked, in addition to other factors, with the casual acceptance and indulgence in pornography, lewdness and widespread prostitution. It is in the nature of man to resist his own destruction until that critical point is passed beyond which the moral deterioration accelerates with shocking and profound intensity. At this point, the disease is no longer social but personal. The end is historically predictable.

Biblically—The admonition is clear and persuasive. The classic example, starkly outlined in the decline of Sodom and Gomorrah, remains unchallenged as an illustration of man's responsibility towards his own behavior. The treasures of the Bible, looked upon with such intellectual bleakness and disdain by the social scientist, yet remain monuments of insight which reflect the intrinsic motivations of man. Thou shalt not—remains a tremendous psychological directive for all men, regardless of the nature of behavior.

Legally—The problem of pornography insistently haunts the law even into the present hour. The Supreme Court, indecisive, vacillating and affording ill conceived definitions, permits the pornographic *education* of youth to proceed with impunity. A recent comment by the columnist James J. Kilpatrick, May 1970, is socially enlightening in this respect: "Let me be more specific. The rottenness has manifested itself, here on the West Coast, in pornography that startles even the most sophisticated visitors from the East. Here the Chronicle reports routinely upon the 'city's 30 dirty movie theatres' ". In a relatively recent comment by Dr. Benjamin Spock, March 1970, he refers to a contemporary court decision in these terms: "Yet, in a recent federal court decision concerning a film about delinquency that depicted "scenes of brutality, prostitution, homosexuality and sodomy", two of the three judges agreed that, though they were "revolted", the film was not obscene according to the stipulations of the Supreme Court because (1) it was not "designed to appeal to the prurience of the Average American", and (2) was not "utterly without redeeming social significance". Dr. Spock concludes: "I'd suggest that, for public presentations, there should be levels of tolerance or tabu". Apparently the Supreme Court recognizes the problem but cannot realistically resolve it. But, then, the Court does rule on matters of educational significance, such as segregation, in rather precise and clear terms. To a Nation, pornography is also of educational significance, and should be subject to the same responsibility and clarity of ruling.

Psychology—The concept of the pornographic environment has been obscured by a research appeal to the argument of relative behavior. The argument implies a lack of an absolute norm. Who is to be the judge?—and upon what grounds shall a judgment be made? So far, so good. Life is, indeed, a series of prickly value judgments which seem to hang on the insubstantial turn of circumstances. However, the judgments—however they may evolve—do relate eventually to reason and

658

order which constitute, between themselves, a common source of evaluation. Thus, the foundation of our societal process—the life process—is absolute while the *use* of that process is relative. If pornography is defined as relative behavior, no objection: if, however, it is defined as being independent of the total life process, strong objections will be registered. Pornography, like any behavior which offends or threatens the welfare of a society, is immediately suspect and logically subject to restraint or modification.

Education—The traditional instrument of society under which the care and training of its members is a primary goal. In principle, education is the creative enhancement of the total individual in a benign environment. And the protection of the individual from that which is destructive. In a rather exceptional research, Dr. David Rosenhan, Psychologist, has recently re-assessed the traditional principles of human behavior in a laboratory setting, sensitively noting: "The altruistic effect of an adult example appears to be lasting . . . We want to come up with a series of recipes for breeding character into kids." Perhaps the myopic science of psychology is now beginning to perceive its essential possibilities, that is, the study of man as an ethical human being. Pornography will then be re-evalued.

Television—The educational Cyclops of the 20th Century and distributor par excellance of the pornographic environment. Whatever the causes for the present condition, the pornographic trend should be educationally modified. There is at least one active individual with the wit and courage to react to this stupid, violent, lawless giant—Mrs. Mary Whitehouse, general secretary to the National Viewers and Listeners Association (NVLA), England. It is reported, April 1970: "Before it the men of the media tread warily. Whatever changes the NVLA has brought about in television programs might be very subtle indeed—but it's no longer popular to ridicule the rumblings against drugs, homosexuals, bare bosoms, adultery, sadism, long hair, atheism, and anti-British attitudes". The pornography of learning—in America—ceaselessly funnels itself into the homes of every age bracket, despoiling the potential development of human character in endless viewing hours frequently dedicated to the basest instincts of man. Summed up in the words of S. I. Hayakawa, President, San Francisco State College, the behavioral problem unfolds in thought provoking intensity: "Those under 25 (years of age) are the first generation in history to have been brought up as much by the television set as by their parents and teachers. How has this affected them?" Perhaps the full answer lies partly hidden in the depth of the world's unrest. What integral part television has played may never be fully known although the international scope of TV brings to the question a new dimension. TV is the *uncontrolled* educational giant of the day.

Theatre—David Merrick speaks with clarity and firmness and assesses the problem in these terms: "Hard core pornography is nothing new, but rarely in modern history has this kind of material paraded in legitimate theater. . . . Since the days when

659

Romans were entertained by hired actors performing scenes of sodomy, rape and incest, the theater has labored to shed the ancient stigma of immorality. . . . I am concerned about this because live theater, while compared to some of the other arts, is wide in influence. It is a seedbed of our culture. The theater translates many important novels into the spoken word; we pass on to the movies our visions, the fruits of our talent. What we do in the theater affects the texture of our society, influences the moral and, yes, political attitudes of our nation. . . . It is to preserve the theater's right to speak out on all subjects that I would cleanse the stage. To allow license can only result, sooner or later, in public outrage that could lead to a demand for censorship".

Whatever the media, pornography educates. As such, it is clearly subject to legal restrictions.

EXHIBIT "E"

THE EVENING STAR   Washington, D.C., Wednesday, Sept. 2, 1970

PORNOGRAPHY REPORT

Psychiatrist Disputes It

Leaked to the press in recent weeks, the draft report by the President's Commission on Pornography and Obscenity seems to indicate that pornography has no ill effects on society. Dr. Natalie Shainess, a psychoanalyst in private practice who lectures in psychiatry at Columbia College of Physicians and Surgeons and is on the faculty of New York's William Alanson White Institute of Psychiatry, spells out what she feels to be the true danger of pornography in the following copyrighted article.

By DR. NATALIE SHAINESS

Special to The Star

NEW YORK—In advertisements, films and books, pornography washes over us all like a great wave of sewage.

It corrupts the body, and numbs the mind and senses.

So overwhelming is this tide that nobody—not myself, a practicing psychoanalyst—can remain untouched by it.

From my own professional practice, I know that the more we are exposed to things that are degrading, the more we are degraded.

Despite the "research" of the President's Commission on Pornography and Obscenity, this observation should not come as a shock to anybody, especially social scientists.

Repeated Violence

There has been considerable agreement, for example, that repeated acts of violence on television can condition viewers, particularly young viewers, to real-life violence.

660

Dr. Frederic Wertham, the pioneer in this field, graphically demonstrated this in such classic works as "The Show of Violence" and "Seduction of the Innocents."

Businessmen have always known that advertising does sell products. Put a picture of your product in the paper and show attractive, intelligent-looking people wanting it, and the reader will want it, too.

Repeat the ad often enough—in newspapers, magazines, billboards, television—and a national craze for the product can be created.

By what logic, then, can the commission conclude that pornography does not lure its audience into "buying" its wares?

First, let me define what pornography means to me. Then I'll give some examples of the pornography that intrudes on our daily lives, even without our knowledge or approval.

Pornography concentrates on the genitals and accessory sex organs.

It emphasizes and distorts them, and is preoccupied by the ways they can be manipulated to titillate, stimulate, or be stimulated.

One might say that the rest of one's person—body and mind—becomes a mere appendage to the sex organ, rather than the other way around.

The purpose of pornography is to sexually arouse the viewer or reader in a degrading way, rather than to suggest sex in a meaningful interpersonal relationship.

And if the beholder is aroused and unable to achieve mature sexual gratification, then the end result is that pornography leaves him unsatisfied.

You don't have to visit a dirty book store or go to a sex movie house to be raped by pornography. In fact, no matter how you try, you cannot escape it.

Instead of having achieved a sexual liberation, we have become enslaved by sex.

Today, no product seems marketable without a sugar-coating of sex.

Automobile ads show bikini-clad girls sprawling over the new-model cars as if they were the bodies of their lovers. A shaving commercial has a wet-lipped voluptuary urging her man to "take it all off," supercharging an everyday washroom function with the sexuality of a striptease.

But the cigarette ads go furthest.

"It's not how long you make it; it's how you make it long."

"It's what's up front that counts."

(Or, for that matter, the beer with the "ten-minute head.")

Indeed, advertising bombards us with sexual allusions to the exhausting extent that we start finding sexual associations even where none were intended.

This suffusion of sex has reached the point where a New York off-Broadway show tries to top "Oh, Calcutta!" by naming itself "The Dirtiest Show in Town."

On 42nd Street and Times Square the movie houses show films that would make a gynecologist blush.

Children browse in dirty book store windows that flaunt hard-

661

core pornography, with magazines featuring lesbianism, sadism, and male homosexuality dominating the displays. (What must these children wonder about the "adult world" that lies ahead of them?)

Underground newspapers—but there is nothing "underground" about where they are sold, at major newsstands, candy stores and book shops—offer a whole supermarket of perverted sex in their classified ad columns.

Where did it all begin? How did we lose our sexual bearings, to be set loose in this strange and murky sea?

Masters and Johnson

Although there has been a gradual lessening of sexual restraints in our society, it was six years ago, in 1964, that the floodgates were unlocked.

That was the year that Dr. William H. Masters, director of the Reproductive Biology Research Foundation, began reporting his "experiments" on human sexual performance.

Dr. Masters and his partner, Virginia Johnson, are now household names and their two books have been phenomenal best sellers ("Human Sexual Response" and "Human Sexual Inadequacy"). But their fame didn't just "happen."

It was during that same year, 1964, that the Sex Information and Education Council of the U.S., called SIECUS, was organized, with Dr. Harold J. Lief as president and Dr. Mary Calderone as executive director.

Dr. Lief and Dr. Calderone, who have been crusading to teach sex in school as if it were mathematics, were shopping for some scientific backing that would prop up their approach to sex with the appropriate research.

Dr. Masters was their man. In 1964 Dr. Lief, who is the director of Family Studies at the University of Pennsylvania, arranged for Dr. Masters' debut at the American Psychiatric Association, and then at the American Institute of Psychoanalysis.

Lectures to university audiences and reports to scientific journals followed, and the groundwork was laid for the publishing bombshell.

Strangely, nobody to date has verified the Masters and Johnson research, nor has anybody duplicated his experiments. This is unusual in a normally skeptical scientific community.

'Got Off Easy'

In brief, Masters and Johnson "got off easy." Some of their research short-cuts and ill-conceived experiments would be discarded as absurd by the accepted rules of scientific methodology.

For some reason, many psychologists and psychiatrists have winked at the Masters and Johnson infractions.

But even if their methodology were correct, the Masters and Johnson reports would still deserve our reproach. For these two "researchers" regard sex as an object.

Like two auto mechanics working over a car, their sole purpose is to keep the sex organs operating at peak efficiency. Orgasms are sought with religious zeal.

What better demonstration of this trend than the fact that, at

662

a recent rock festival, a young man got up to the microphone and announced, "I need an orgasm."

This change of language, from "I want to love" to "I need an orgasm," lessens the need for interpersonal relationships and vastly diminishes the importance of the particular sex partner—if any sex partner is needed at all!

Although it is exceedingly difficult to get specific information on the Masters and Johnson patients, I do know authoritatively about one man who was sent back to New York by Dr. Masters with a list of sexual partners in Greenwich Village.

"Practice all you can," Dr. Masters told him, giving him the list of names. I also know of another case, of a man who narrowly averted a psychotic breakdown after his "treatment" at the Masters institute.

A constant barrage of pornography encourages marriage partners to indulge their own sexual needs, even if at the expense of the other. For orgasm has become a "right."

With this lowering of self-control, in and out of marriage, the weaker or anti-social individual who cannot get sex when and where he needs it, will take it when and where he pleases—by any means. In this sense, pornography is likely to lead to increased sex crimes.

Despite all this, the President's Commission on Pornography, according to a preliminary draft, will state: "Research indicates that erotic materials do not contribute to the development of character deficits, nor operate as a significant factor in anti-social behavior or in crime and delinquency causation. In sum, there is no evidence in either youths or adults."

The Commission relied primarily on two studies to reach this epochal conclusion.

First, a survey of sex offenders in New York and a Midwestern prison indicated that their maladjustment stemmed from sexually repressive family backgrounds, not from pornography.

This may well be, but it ignores the fact that man is the sum of the input into him and his responses to that input.

It may be quite true that a sex criminal often has a bad family background, but to deny the effect of a later influence, such as pornography, is unscientific.

Next, the Commission subjected 23 University of North Carolina male students to daily pornography viewings—90-minute sessions each day, five days a week, for three weeks running—apparently measuring their response, by their degree of penal erection.

The young men also were asked prior to each session if they had had intercourse or masturbated during the intervening 24 hours.

Too Much Wrong

At the end of the three weeks, the report concluded, there was no heightened interest in pornography among the test cases, thereby "proving" that the materials had no effect on them.

There are so many things wrong with this experiment that one hardly knows where to begin.

But first, nowhere is there an attempt to measure the long-range effects of repeated exposure to pornography.

Surely the experimenters didn't expect the youths to commit gang rape at the end of each test period.

Then there is the fallacy that 23 college-educated boys are representative of the country.

What, for instance, is the effect of pornography on sixth-grade drop-outs?

What, too, was the attitude of the students to the fact that their viewing pornography had the support of the President of the United States, and that they were being paid $100 to boot?

Particularly disturbing is the fact that the three theologians on the Commission were not informed of the nature of this distasteful, indeed obscene, experiment.

The Commission reports that the great increase of explicit sex in films, books and magazines since 1960 has not brought about a corresponding increase in sex crime.

The fact is that forcible rape has increased 57 percent during the last 10 years, and the figure is 86 percent for males under 18.

Nor should it be overlooked that there has been an increase in covert sex misbehavior, by which I mean any kind of sex behavior which entails the use of force and is not mutually agreeable to both partners, whether in or out of marriage.

The Commission's major legislative recommendation is expected to be that all federal, state and local laws against pornography should be repealed for adults, but laws should be enacted to protect children.

To think that we can saturate adults with pornography and effectively isolate their children from it is a fool's dream.

The Commission spent three years and $2 million on its study.

I think one week of work by a few profound thinkers would have been of greater value.

© 1970

EXHIBIT "F"

JOHN CARROLL UNIVERSITY
COUNSELING CENTER

University Heights, Cleveland, Ohio 44118
Area Code 216 -932-3800

September 6, 1970

Mr. Richard M. Bertsch
Bertsch, Edelman, Fludine and Naylor
440 Leader Building
Cleveland, Ohio 44114

Dear Dick,

I have studied the Commission Report on the *Effects* of Pornography and have recorded a number of observations and reactions to that document. Time will not permit a minute analysis of the many assertions and affirmations that punctuate the report as established truths or conclusions. I will comment on the larger dimensions in the sections to follow.

As a rigorous scientific endeavor:

This document would be tossed into a wastebasket by many professional students of behavior. The problem that is admittedly *mercurial* is scarcely examined or analyzed by the methodology (research techniques) that is invoked. Preoccupation with what appears to be a foregone conclusion makes the script appear to be the work of an advertising firm or a propaganda mill.

The poorly devised studies do not give unequivocal conclusions. Yet, the conclusions come through "like a broken record". The statistical analyses of equivocal data leads me to wonder whether the investigators have learned to distinguish causation from correlation in attempts to serve the purpose of explaining human behavior. The recourse to rhetoric rather than research is the chief instrument in trying to convince the reader. It appears that as scientists these investigators have not heard of Morgan's canon or Occam's Razor.

As a model or blueprint for providing constructive learning experiences about life:

Even the apprentice in the field of human behavior is convinced that behavior is the result of many genetic, physical, and *learning experiences* in the life of the person. Moreover, it is recognized that every effort to *partial out* a single thread or aspect of development is virtually impossible. At the present stage of scientific development in human analysis we are forced to deal with events and conditions that candor and honesty would have us state *we think* rather than that *we know*.

Therefore, any major attempt to treat the phenomenon of response effects to erotica in terms of physical reactions rather than in a larger personality-character sense is myopic. To say that the sex response is natural is one fact, but to elicit it deliberately without thought or concern for the consequences or implications is mechanistic and simplistic.

Some Implications

In the United States much time, money, and reflection are devoted to programs in education. It appears that there is overwhelming agreement that the young should be protected, schooled, developed, guided, and eventually join the ranks of responsible adults.

How to achieve such an outcome produces a great variety of programs that range from complete freedom for the child to virtually little freedom for the child to decide what he will do in moving from infancy to adulthood.

Every educational venture is derived from a model or concept of the individual that arranges and gives priorities to guide the participants. Every philosophy of education includes references to the desirability of personality and character development. Every society, even a pluralistic one, develops a system by which the purposes of the people can be pursued. These purposes and goals are translated into value systems and "road maps" by which to order the lives of people. Very often these value systems are the distillations of experiences that have helped form the traditions and values of a group, a family, or a nation. In an analogous sense, this tradition is to a group what memory is to an individual, and

665

no man argues or doubts the dangerous and upsetting consequences of amnesia to an individual. Without guides, norms, models or priorities a person and a group become disoriented, confused, insecure, and eventually disruptive. I am amused at some learned individuals who seem to have devoted large portions of their lives to the purpose of "proving that life is purposeless".

We seem to be so preoccupied with the pollution of the physical environment while at the same time relaxing on the urgency of maintaining some vigilance in what is circulating in terms of psychological stimulation. Many proponents of this "cult of the individual" which espouses "doing your thing whenever you wish" are among the most vehement opponents to the same philosophy when it comes to the economic scene or to some major social issues. The apparent contradiction in their thinking does not deter them from vigorous action.

No civilized nation would risk the spread of infectious agents without imposing some controls to minimize the ill effects to the young. There is a medical axiom that it is better to postpone assaults on the nervous system until the child is reasonably well developed. He will be better able to cope with such disturbances when he is older. In a similar sense too much stimulation in an emotional and psychological sense can be disruptive for one's mental health. Blaine and many other authorities have reported that postponing sheer impulsivity is not detrimental but conducive to mental health. A rough analogy might be found in the observation that "what is needed in the new cars is not more horse power but more braking power". In fact, we might be able to reduce the alarming auto fatalities by putting governors on cars that are driven by the young learners instead of constantly increasing insurance premiums as an antidote that doesn't work to save lives and limbs.

I see the Report as having glaring omissions as a scientific departure as well as indulging in syncretistic intellectualizing. It does not suffice to produce the conclusions rendered.

I have labored in the counseling profession for more than 25 years, and during that period I have counseled with more than 15,000 people. Those experiences have been distilled into a series of writings that I am enclosing as appendices. They provide a more systematic and comprehensive explanation of my convictions than I can produce in this note.

Best wishes,
/s/ Walter S. Nosal, Ed.D, Director

Encls. 3

EXHIBIT "G"

SPEECH BY
ROBERT CLEGG
HEADMASTER, BARDEN PRIMARY SCHOOL
BURNLEY, LANCASTER, ENGLAND

My brief, ladies and gentlemen, is to speak to you for a few minutes about the sex education programmes; and when I asked

666

Mrs. Whitehouse if there was any particular line she would like me to take, she suggested that I might speak from the point of view of a primary school headmaster—which, for my sins, is what I am.

Well, I'll do my best, but I must say that to me, this is not a question to be treated in isolation, just from a school teacher's point of view. I am fairly sure myself that it's something more than just another educational innovation; that it is, in fact, simply a new manifestation of that quite revolting modern concept, the permissive society.

And I, for one, am sick almost to death of the permissive society. Sick of this morbid, compulsive preoccupation with sex, sex, and more sex. I feel sick when I receive literature through the post urging me for the good of my soul to buy books full of beautiful glossy photographs—real models, of course—illustrating the fifty-seven varieties of sex recommended for married couples in this civilised age.

Sick when I read descriptions of pictures painted by Mr. John Lennon, O.B.E., and exhibited, with the sanction of the law, in some gallery in London; picture some of which, if I am to believe what I read, show himself and his wife—clad, of course, in the regulation permissive uniform of nothing at all—actually copulating in some quite ingenious ways.

I am utterly sick of Mr. Lennon's private parts, and of the divine mission he appears to believe he has to display them to the teeming millions of the world. I'm sick of him and of all the other seedy, unwashed apostles of the new morality, whose gospel appears to be that in order to achieve salvation we must all fling off our clothes and copulate feverishly with everyone in sight.

But still—I am myself, in my own way, a fairly permissive character. I am a firm believer in that sadly overworked cliche, the freedom of the individual. And if Mr. Lennon and others of his kind choose to indulge in practices which I find nauseating, they are, as far as I am concerned, welcome to do so. To put it shortly, they are quite at liberty to go to hell in their own way, provided only that they don't interfere with me, or with anyone else.

But that, I would say, is just what the people who have initiated these sex education programmes are trying to do. They amount to a deliberate attempt to interfere with—to change, in fact—the beliefs, standards, and practices of what I would call normal people.

Under the holy name of education, they bring all the apparatus of the new moral thinking into the schools, and use it for the benefit of little children.

Call it education, you know, and you can get away with anything. Full-length pictures—in glorious technicolour naturally—of naked adults of both sexes, carefully disposed so as to bring the sexual parts, particularly the hair surrounding or covering them—what a dreadful immature obsession we seem to have with hair—into the greatest possible prominence. I'm fairly sure that in the ordinary way neither *Playboy* nor any other of the current erotic magazines would care to print them. They would probably be considered too direct for the jaded businessmen who read those publications; but put them under the heading of education, and they can be shown quite freely to eight-year-old boys and girls.

We hear a hymn of praise from those who approve of the programmes about the "tenderness" and the "lyrical beauty" of the pictures. Whether they are beautiful or not, I wouldn't care to say, but the point seems to me quite irrelevant anyway. As I said to someone who praised the pictures for this reason at a private showing which I attended, if Leonardo da Vinci had painted a picture of a woman having relations with a donkey, without any doubt, it would have been a remarkably beautiful picture. But that would scarcely be an argument for showing it to eight-year-old children.

In the television programmes there are moving films of naked people at every stage of development—babies, ten- or eleven-year-olds, adolescents and adults—with the camera zooming in every time to give us a close-up picture of the sex organs. I am not easily shocked myself, but I will remember for a long time the unwholesome-looking female model in the art class, and that broadly-smiling young man exposing himself so proudly and so completely.

And all this is to be a normal subject of study for little boys and girls in junior schools. It is even to be "integrated" into the curriculum as a whole. They are to learn all there is to know—far more, in my opinion, than anyone outside the medical profession needs to know—about their sexual characteristics, how they are developing, how they will develop in the future, and exactly what each new physical manifestation means in terms of their growing sexual powers.

They are to be spared nothing. The little boys are even going to see, along with the little girls, a picture of a female naked except for her sanitary arrangements. What benefit the boys are supposed to get out of this, I can't imagine. I myself had never, in the course of a not-particularly-sheltered life, seen anything like that before, and having seen it now, about all I can say is that I heartily wish I hadn't.

The sexual act itself, and the resulting biological processes, are described baldly and clinically. There is no mention of affection, love, respect, marriage, nothing about discipline, no hint that behaviour in this field is, or should be, governed by any moral code. Pretty well everything that is said, in fact, could apply to the beasts of the field just as well as to human beings.

And what good are the children supposed to derive from all this?

It will prevent unhealthy curiosity, we are told. The facts having been given them in the *right* way, there will be no more furtive street-corner whisperings, no more lurid jokes, no sniggering. The children will accept the information calmly and responsibly, in the way that they accept the fact that two two's make four, and then promptly put the whole thing out of their minds.

What unmitigated nonsense! In the first place, apart from the substitution of a couple of latinised words for Anglo-Saxon ones, I can't see any essential difference between what they will be told in the future in school and what they used to hear on the street-corner.

And as if knowing the facts ever made anyone—child or adult—less interested in sex, or less curious about it! All teaching is aimed at awakening curiosity, not destroying it. Far from stopping the street-corner talk, it will merely provide a license for it, along with a lot of extra material. They will continue to talk, but with much greater knowingness, about themselves, their friends, their parents, their teachers. Just what they will say, I don't know, but I can imagine some of it. I would certainly expect some very animated discussions about just what questions they are going to ask at the next cosy little class discussion on sex.

If I allowed these programmes to be shown at school, and followed them up in the recommended ways, and I subsequently found some of the children examining one another, or trying to achieve a sexual connection, what could I say to them? I can't teach them a subject, openly and comprehensively, especially one which concerns them so vitally as human beings, and then scold them for taking an interest in it. And they would scarcely be human if, after all this indoctrination, they didn't take a very keen interest in it—practical as well as theoretical.

And I am pretty sure that before very long, if these programmes are widely shown, there will be a big increase in sexual practices amongst children at the upper junior and early secondary stages. Instead of worrying about girls of fifteen, we could well be worrying about having to abort girls of twelve and treat them for V. D. What is probably worse, many—if not most—of these children will grow up with an entirely physical, entirely mechanised view of sex, which will give them small chance of ever knowing the real beauty which can, and should, exist in the right kind of relationship between a man and a woman.

I think that they will be the true and logical children of the permissive, or what one eminent politician is pleased to call the "civilised," society. Because I think that it is agencies of the permissive society which are promoting this kind of so-called "education."

I could be wrong. But if I am, I'm not going to say I'm sorry. I've tried to find out exactly who started the whole thing, and exactly whose were the ideas which governed the manner in which the programmes are presented. What I am told is that the ideas came from the School Broadcasting Council, which apparently consists of a positive swarm of delegates from teachers' associations, local authority education officials, former head teachers, college lecturers and inspectors—in addition to a number of people appointed directly by the BBC.

Now, I would be very surprised, indeed, to learn that any teachers' association, or any local authority representative, had originated the scheme, and I can, therefore, only make an educated guess that it probably came in the first place from somewhere amongst the nominees of the BBC. And certainly the BBC does not appear to be without interest. A few weeks ago, at the time when the previewers of the sex programmes were being broadcast, we had on the same evening a "Panorama" programme dealing with sex education, and also a "Horizon" programme which concerned itself with the new science of "sexology." Amongst the so-called experts appearing on the "Horizon" programme were two from America, William Masters and Virginia Johnson, who are the joint authors of a best-selling book called *Human Sexual*

Response. I know nothing about the book, apart from a description by Mr. Masters which I have read of a perfectly incredible mechanical device with which, for the purpose of his researches, some of his female subjects actually had sexual relations.

Besides writing books, Mr. Masters, I understand, is very much concerned with sex education in America. He is, in fact, one of the directors of an organization known as SIECUS, which is the greatest influence in the propagation of this subject in American schools. And it is rather striking that he and his associate should come over here, presumably at the invitation of the BBC, to peddle their disgusting wares on British television, just when the BBC is setting up its own programme of sex education.

I think it was in the same week, too, that I saw a documentary programme for women, in which two self-confessed revolutionary women were preaching the true revolutionary fervour that the institution of marriage had served its purpose, that it should now be abandoned and alternatives found.

All of which seems to me to add up to some kind of campaign by the BBC in favour of what we've got into the habit of calling "permissiveness," and of which sex education is very much a part. It has to be surmised, of course, but if the true authors of these programmes are so shy about coming forward to take the credit, they ought not to blame me if I form my own conclusions based on the evidence available.

Whoever they are, they are doing something which has been regarded for countless generations as one of the most revolting of crimes. They are setting out, with their benevolent voices, their paternal manner, their beautiful arty pictures, even with musical accompaniment, to destroy the innocence of a whole generation of young children.

And however much they talk of the need to transform society, the "changing patterns of sexual behavior"—whatever slick phrases they use, it is still a crime. It is for me, for my acquaintances, for most of the teachers I know, and, I am inclined to believe, for the majority of the people of this country. And I am quite certain that for you, too, ladies and gentlemen, it is a black crime.

And although we may not be able to prevent its commission, at least we can clear our own consciences by continuing to denounce it.

EXHIBIT "H"

THE LAW ON OBSCENITY—WHAT HAS HAPPENED IN THE COURTS—HOW TO CONTROL THE PROBLEM

I. *Obscenity: Its Historical Background.*

At the focal point of this issue is the obscenity crime, which in turn, has its roots in our Judeo-Christian culture, and the Common Law of our Anglo-Saxon heritage.

The first obscene exhibition conviction came about in 1688, when an English community brought Sir Charles Sedley before the Common Law courts for exposing himself in the nude on the balcony of a tavern in Convent Garden, England.

The English society in 1688, referred to in history as the "Gay Restoration Period of Charles the Second," was not unlike society today. Hedonism was rampant. Sir Charles Sedley himself was a rebel playwright, interested in bringing about a change in the social mores. Today, we have "rebels" in the same and other professions, who entertain the same ideas. In place of the lewd exhibition on the balcony, we have such things as lewd movies, pornographic literature, and topless performances in bars throughout communities. In 1688, the English Common Law courts declared Sedley's conduct to be a Common Law crime.

Less than 40 years later, the English novel came into being and immediately thereafter, printed obscenity became a problem. To meet that new social problem, the House of Lords in 1727, in a case involving the distribution of an obscene publication by a printer named Curl, drew an analogy to the law laid down in Sedley's case and held this type of conduct also to be a Common Law crime—the so-called "obscene libel".

In its opinion, the House of Lords, England's Court of Last Resort, reflected upon the "reason" for establishing the offense. A comparison was made with the maintenance of a bawdy house which everyone, at that time, recognized as an offense against the morals of the community. To permit a house of prostitution to exist in public would destroy public morality, which, in turn, would destroy government, for government was nothing more than public order and public order was dependent upon public morality. For the same reason, the dissemination of obscene materials was held to be a Common Law crime.

When the founding fathers settled in America, they brought with them the Common Law of England, including the laws against lewd exhibitions and obscene publications. These principles were immediately absorbed into our laws. Based upon Judeo-Christian norms, and designed for the protection of the family structure, these laws have governed and been the guiding beacon for this Nation for close to 200 years.

A modern attack on these Judeo-Christian principles was made in 1957, when two convicted pornographers, Samuel Roth and David Alberts, urged that the principles expressed in these two English Common Law cases had been overruled by our founding fathers at the time the First Amendment to our Federal Constitution was adopted. The 1957 Supreme Court rejected these arguments by a 7-2 majority in the landmark Roth-Alberts decision, ruling that obscenity was without redeeming social importance and was not constitutionally protected.

The High Court defined obscenity by adopting a test appearing in prior case law, that is, that material is obscene "which to the average person, applying contemporary community standards, the dominant theme of the material, taken as a whole, appeals to prurient interest." Prurient interest was defined as a "shameful or morbid interest in nudity, sex or excretion which goes substantially beyond customary limits of candor in description or representation."

A closer look at the Roth decision is necessary because of an

671

important principle which was involved—important because it relates to the manner in which the United States Supreme Court handled the 26 obscenity cases which were being reviewed in 1966. Who is to make the obscenity determination? Is that issue to be decided by a judge? Or is it to be decided by the people, acting through the jury system?

The question which is posed, frames a conflict which has an ancient origin in our government—the conflict between the powers of the judiciary and the powers of the people.

The most famous of such controversies occurred 50 years before this Nation's founding. There, the early American judges sought to reserve to themselves control of the determination of what in fact constitutes a libel. The matter came to a head in the trial of John Peter Zenger for criminal libel in New York in 1735. Trial Judge DeLancey instructed the jury that they were not to decide the libel issue since that was a matter of law for the judges to decide. Defense attorney Andrew Hamilton argued to the contrary to the Jury—that the matter was for them to decide. In freeing Zenger the jury accepted Hamilton's arguments and rejected Judge DeLancey's view of the law, establishing the supremacy of the jury system on the American Scene as a check and balance against an arbitrary judiciary.

The right of the jury to determine questions of fact has, since this Nation's inception, held a favored position in the hearts of its people. Indeed, its deprivation was one of the causes for the American Revolution. The jury concept was to become one of the foundations of our Federal Constitution. Article 3, Section 2 reads: "The trial of all crimes . . . shall be by the jury; and such trial shall be held in the state where the said crimes shall have been committed." The supremacy of the jury as a fact finder is memorialized in the Sixth, and Seventh Amendments to the Federal Constitution. The Sixth Amendment reads: "In all criminal prosecutions, the accused shall enjoy the right to a speedy and public trial by an impartial jury of the state . . . wherein the crime shall have been committed." The Seventh Amendment reads: "The right of trial by jury shall be preserved, and no fact tried by a jury shall otherwise be re-examined *in any court of the United States,* than according to the rules of the Common Law." (My emphasis.)

In this country, what is obscene has always been regarded as a question of fact for the jury. Judge Learned Hand, one of this country's greatest jurists, pointed out in one landmark case that:

In this country the jury must determine under instructions whether the book is obscene. The court's only power is to decide whether the book is so clearly innocent that the jury should not pass upon it at all.

The rationale behind this rule of law is clear, for the jury has always been regarded as synonymous with the conscience of the community. Maitland, in his History of English Law, says of the jury function: "The verdict of the jurors is not the verdict of twelve men; it is the verdict of the community . . . ."

In *Roth,* the matter was tried to a jury which acted as the fact finder, following the trial judge's instructions on the law covering obscenity. The jury instruction is significant because: (1) it declared that the jury is the sole and exclusive determiner of what was obscene, and (2) it was approved by the United States Supreme Court as a correct statement of the law. It read as follows:

In this case, ladies and gentlemen of the jury, you and you alone are the *exclusive* judges of what the common conscience of the community is . . . You judge the publications which have been put in evidence by present-day standards of the community. You may ask yourselves, does it offend the common conscience of the community by present-day standards.

The 10 Years After Roth-Alberts

The pornographers, however, did not give up with their defeat in 1957 in the *Roth* case. They increased their operations by geometric proportions and more than matched those efforts with their financial expenditures in the courtroom. Their efforts in the courtroom did not fall upon deaf ears.

Justices Black and Douglas, the two dissenters in *Roth-Alberts,* continued their attack against the obscenity laws, refusing to follow or apply the law of the land laid down by the majority decision in 1957. Their unorthodoxy ran contrary to the prevailing rule in Constitutional Law, that, dissenting justices, having participated in a landmark constitutional consideration, are thereafter bound to abide by the majority opinion as are the rest of the jurists throughout the Nation.

In an interview in 1967, Justice Hugo Black was to remark that while he had never won the battle, he had about won the war. The accuracy of Black's statement is demonstrated by the High Court's action in a Florida case where, after jury trial, the book "Tropic of Cancer" was held obscene by the state judiciary. In 1964 the United States Supreme Court reversed that finding in a 5-4 decision. Justices Black and Douglas cast their votes, as members of the 5-man majority, on the ground that there was no such thing as an obscenity law. Had their votes been disqualified as not in consonance with the law, the result would have been 4-3 to sustain the Florida judgment.

To add to this difficulty, the Court's membership was subjected to rapid change. With a change in membership came a change in philosophy. Frankfurter was replaced by Goldberg, who, in turn, was replaced by Fortas, whose law firm had several times represented a publisher whose books were to appear before the Court in 1966—books like "Sin Whisper". Whittaker and Burton were replaced by White and Stewart, neither of whom shares the view of his predecessor in the area of public morals. Justice Stewart ascended to the High Court in October of 1958 from a seat on an intermediate Appellate Court, from which he had one year earlier ruled in the *Volanski* case that, under our Federal Constitution, it was a question for the jury and not for the Court whether the photographs of nude females in provocative poses were obscene. Having attained the High Court, he changed his mind, and in reviewing obscenity determination, adopted a more personal view—that he knew obscenity when he saw it, and "this was not that".

Justice Brennan applied what he called "national standards" to hold the film, "The Lovers", not obscene—a motion picture which

673

for the first time was allowed to depict scenes of sexual inter-course—in this instance, in a bed and bath between the wife and a casual male house guest. A jury and the State of Ohio, speaking through three of its courts and 12 of its Ohio justices, however, had held otherwise.

Chief Justice Warren habitually voted to reverse state obscenity determinations on procedural grounds. While the Chief Justice spoke out forcefully in favor of local standards, in 1967, he was to forget he had ever advocated this view of the law.

In the cases following *Roth,* the Court refused to listen to the communities' protests regarding the people's right to a jury trial and the finality of a jury determination on questions of fact. As new justices mounted the bench, their views grew wider apart.

As a consequence, the High Court's opinions during the period 1958 through 1965, read like masterpieces of confusion. In order for a ruling precedent to be established, a majority of five justices are required to be in agreement on the principle involved. In almost all of these decisions, no such majority was to be found.

Just when it appeared as though the Court was hopelessly dead-locked in its internal struggle, a group of decisions was handed down which gave hopes of a rational solution to the problem. In March 1966, a majority of six justices managed to get together to uphold the conviction of Edward Mishkin in New York for the printing and distribution of sadomasochistic material like "Arduous Figure Training at Bondhaven", "Female Sultan", "Woman Im-pelled", "Screaming Flesh", "Bound in Rubber", "Swish Bottom", "So Firm, So Fully Packed", and "Fearful Ordeal in Restraint-land".

On the same date a majority of five managed to agree that publisher Ginzburg was in violation of the Federal Postal Laws for his mailing of the periodical "Eros", a book named "House-wife's Handbook on Selective Promiscuity" and a newsletter named "Liaison".

In both of these cases, the majority appeared to be in complete agreement that the conduct of the defendant was of primary im-portance and determinative of whether the materials were ob-scene in the constitutional sense.

When the *Ginzburg* and *Mishkin* decisions became final in May of 1966, the stage was being set for the next term of Court. Three retailer cases were ordered to be briefed and set for argument in October, 1966: *Redrup v. New York, Kentucky v. Austin, Gent v. Arkansas.*

The unwholesome results reached in the *Redrup, Austin* and *Gent* cases are now a matter of history. (See in the Technical Reports: Continuity on "A Report on the United States Supreme Court and Its Recent Decisions in Obscenity Cases"). Those who are privy to the facts surrounding the obscenity controversy which centered on Justice Abe Fortas' nomination as Chief Justice to the United States Supreme Court, recognize that there is good cause for concluding that the results reached in the *Redrup-Austin-Gent* and other 1966 Term decisions kept Associate Justice Abe Fortas from becoming Chief Justice of the United States.

The High Court had voted 6-3 to limit the arguments in *Redrup-Austin-Gent* to the scienter issue. When, seven months after oral

674

argument on that issue, the Court found itself unable to arrive at a clear majority decision on that issue, the Court as a whole took that unfortunate and fateful step into the quicksand which was to mark their Waterloo—and the millstone which prevented each individual state government from solving its growing obscenity problems.

As the members continue their random, helter-skelter inquiry into the degrees of obscenity, their methodology draws them deeper and deeper into what appears to be a bottomless pit. In my view, the court has but one chance for rescue—either through acceptance of the Blackmun-Burger-Harlan view voiced in *Hoyt v. Minnesota* (supra) or through adoption by Congress of the legislation I propose, which codifies the Blackmun-Burger-Harlan constitutional view as a legislative limit on the High Courts' appellate review.

II. *Obscenity controls do not attempt to reach private morality. The proscription of obscenity is grounded upon the legitimate governmental aim of controlling and regulating "public morality" i.e., public conduct, which affects the people as a whole.*

Obscenity controls do not attempt to reach *private morality*—such as what a person may read or see. The proscription of obscenity is grounded upon the legitimate governmental aim of controlling and regulating *"public morality"*—public conduct, which affects the people as a whole.

Although it is true that the governmental restraints imposed by such obscenity laws must, of necessity, *indirectly* restrict the availability of such materials for some persons who might wish to see or read such materials, the same result is obtained whenever any "vice" laws are enforced, such as those proscribing prostitution. It is, however, a gross distortion of the law to suggest, as does the legal panel, that this indirect effect on private morals is the *basis* for such criminal sanctions and thus an unconstitutional infringement on the rights of an individual.

Law and morality are not identical. Although interrelated, they are necessarily distinct. Not every moral evil is proscribed by manmade law. *Public* morality is to be distinguished from *private* morality, as to which it is often said, the law does not concern itself. On the other hand, our law has always recognized the importance of maintaining a high *public* morality.

Nowhere was the function of such "vice" laws more clearly stated than in the arguments of the prosecutor two and one-half centuries ago in the first obscenity conviction in *Rex v. Curl,* 2 Strange 789 (1727):

3. As to Morality. Destroying that is destroying the peace of the government for government is no more than public order, which is morality. My Lord Chief Justice Hale used to say Christianity is part of the law, and why not morality too? I do not insist that every immoral act is indictable, such as telling a lie, or the like; *but if it is destructive of morality in general, if it does, or may affect all the King's subjects, it then is an offense of a public nature. And upon this distinction it is that particular acts of fornication are not punishable in the Temporal Courts*

675

(Common Law courts) *and bawdy houses are.* In Sir Charles Sedley's case it was said, that this Court is the custosmorum of the King's subjects. 1 Sid. 168. (My emphasis.)

Louis B. Schwartz, co-reporter of the Model Penal Code, explains the governmental function of the obscenity crime in society in 63 Columbia Law Review, Morals Offenses, and the Model Penal Code (cited by the United States Supreme Court with approval in *Ginzburg v. United States,* 16 L. Ed. 2d page 38, fn. 12; page 39, fn. 14; page 41, fn. 19; *Mishkin v. New York,* 16 L. Ed. 2d page 53, fn. 9; and *Stanley,* 394 U.S. 557, fn. 10) at page 671:

But the great majority of people believe that the morals of 'bad' people do, at least in the long run, threaten the security of the 'good' people . . . . It is hard to deny people the right to legislate on the basis of their beliefs not demonstrably erroneous, especially if these beliefs are strongly held by a very large majority. The majority cannot be expected to abandon a credo, and its associated sensitivities, however irrational, in deference to a minority's skepticism.

And at page 672:

If unanimity of strongly held moral views is approached in a community, the rebel puts himself, as it were, outside the society when he arranges himself against those views . . . the community cannot be expected to make (his) first protests respectable or even tolerated by the law . . . .

Mr. Schwartz continues, at page 681:

But equally, it is not merely sin-control of the sort that evoked Professor Henkin's constitutional doubts. Instead, the community is merely saying, 'Sin, if you must, in private. Do not flaunt your immoralities where they will grieve and shock others. If we do not impose our morals upon you, neither must you impose yours upon us, undermining the restraint we seek to cultivate through family, church, and school.' *The interest being protected is not* directly or exclusively, the souls of those who might be depraved or corrupted by the obscenity, *but the right of parents to shape the moral notions of their children, and the right of the general public not to be subjected to violent psychological affront.* (My emphasis.)

Concerning the power of government to regulate matters relating to *public morals* and power to say what is offensive to *public morality,* the United States Supreme Court said in *Mugler v. Kansas* 123 U.S. 623 (1887):

The power to determine such questions (what is offensive to public morality) so as to bind all, must exist somewhere; else society will be at the mercy of the few, who, regarding their own appetites or passions, may be willing to imperil the peace and security of many, provided only they are permitted to do as they please. *Under our system, that power is lodged in the legislative branch of the government.* It belongs to that department to exert what are known as police powers of the state, *and to determine primarily, what measures are appropriate or needful for the protection of the public morals,* the public health, or the public safety . . . (My emphasis.)

In 1705, Alexander Pope wrote in simple verse in his quatrain

676

"The Monster Vice," why vice must be proscribed if good morality is to be maintained:

Vice is a monster of so frightful mien,
As, to be hated, needs but to be seen;
Yet seen too oft, familiar with her face,
We first endure, then pity, then embrace.

See also Federal District Judge Peirson Hall speaking on "The Monster Vice" in *U.S. v. Four (4) Books,* 289 F. Supp. 972 at 973 (Sept. 10, 1968).

The existence of the vice of obscenity is the symptom of a disorder which probability tells us, will lead to ruin. Arnold Toynbee, the historian, tells us that 19 out of the 21 great civilizations which flourished in world history, crumbled into ruin . . . not because of armed aggression from without but because of moral decay from within. In 1874 Justice Swayne, speaking for an unanimous United States Supreme Court in *Trist v. Child* 21 Wallace 441, 450 (1874) had the following to say about the nature of the underpinnings of this Nation:

The foundation of a republic is the virtue of its citizens. They are at once sovereigns and subjects. As the foundation is undermined, the structure is weakened. When it is destroyed the fabric must fall. Such is the voice of history . . . .

In sum, the case for the governmental action against obscenity was stated by the United States Supreme Court Justice Harlan in his concurring opinion in *Roth-Alberts,* supra, at page 502:

The state can reasonably draw the inference that over a long period of time the indiscriminate dissemination of materials, the essential character of which is to degrade sex, will have an eroding effect on moral standards . . . .

Further, it is my opinion that the awareness by youth that obscene materials are tolerated in the community and presented for entertainment to adults is detrimental to their moral development. This opinion finds support in the reasoning employed by Justice Harlan in *Calif. v. Alberts* (supra) wherein he justified the state obscenity laws on the basis of "indirect" effects on public morals. On this "indirect effects" rationale, it is important to note that the majority opinion in *Ginzberg v. New York,* 390 U.S. 629, 20 L. Ed. 2d 195, 205, fn. 10 thought it of sufficient importance to note and record the observations of Dr. Gaylin thereon. The Court there said:

. . . but despite the vigor of the ongoing controversy whether obscene material will perceptively create a danger of anti-social conduct, or will probably induct its recipient to such conduct, a medical practitioner recently suggested that the possibility of harmful effect to youth cannot be dismissed as frivolous. Dr. Gaylin of the Columbia University Psychoanalytic Clinic, reporting on the views of some psychiatrists in 77 Yale Law at 592-593 said:

'It is the period of growth (of youth) when these patterns of behavior are laid down, when environmental stimuli of all sorts must be integrated into a workable sense of self, when sensuality is being defined and fears elaborated, when pleasure confronts security and impulse encounters control—it is in

677

this period, undramatically and with time, that legalized pornography may conceivably be damaging.'

Dr. Gaylin emphasizes that a child might not be as well prepared as an adult to make an intelligent choice as to the material he chooses to read:

'Psychiatrists . . . made a distinction between the reading of pornography, as unlikely to be per se harmful, *and the permitting of the reading of pornography, which was conceived as potentially destructive.* The child is protected in the reading of pornography by the knowledge that it is pornographic, i.e., disapproved. It is outside of parental standards and not a part of his identification processes. *To openly permit implies parental approval and even suggests seductive encouragement.* If this is so of parental approval, it is equally so of societal approval—another potent influence on the developing ego.'

It seems obvious to plaintiff herein that, in the context employed, the United States Supreme Court recognized that the "indirect" effects merited special attention—that societal approval of obscenity had an indirect effect on public morals in the nature of a scandal-giving seduction.

A nation whose public morals are preoccupied with sex is thought to be sick. The ultimate evil would be a society in which sex pictures, novels and magazines are available at every store, sex pictures on every marquee, sex movies in every theater, sex pictures in every art gallery, and sex language in every dialogue. To the extent that we approach this status by degrees, we recognize we are losing control of public order and are closing the gap on the public morality of the community of "Sodom and Gomorrah." The anti-social conduct of today's society becomes the socially acceptable conduct of the new community. Recognizing that the evolution of man in civilized society is a slow-moving process, I respectfully suggest that the Court should examine and consider the suggestion that in the biblical days of Sodom and Gomorrah there must have been justices like Black and Douglas whose liberal views on public morality led to the destruction of those two cities.

III. *There is a trend developing which treats obscenity as nothing more than an ancient common law scourge whose remedy lies in "abatement" as a common law nuisance.*

Obscenity of indecent exhibitions of a nature to shock the public sense of decency were a public nuisance and indictable at the Common Law. Crain v. State, 3 Ind. 193 (1851). See also Parkins on Criminal Law, Foundation Press, 1954, at page 336:

Obscene or indecent exhibitions of a nature to shock the public sense of decency are also public nuisances and indictable at Common Law. This label includes not only obscene and indecent theatrical performances or side shows, but other disgusting practices such as letting a stallion to mares in the streets or some other public place . . . .

See also, Bloss v. Paris Township, 157 N. W. 2d 260 (Apr. 1, 1968) holding the operation of an outdoor drive-in theater showing motion pictures which "dwell on the subject of sex and the human anatomy" to constitute a public nuisance, the Michigan Supreme Court saying, at page 261, as to the nature of a public nuisance:

What is a public nuisance? Joyce, Law of Nuisances, Section 7, page 15, defines a public nuisance, inter alia, as an act which offends public decency. Cited to Section 66, page 13, is the case of *Hayden v. Tucker,* 37 Mo. 214, in which it was held that the keeping and standing of jacks and stallions within the immediate view of a private dwelling and a public highway is a nuisance which equity will enjoin as a 'disgusting annoyance perpetually bringing the blush of shame to modesty and innocence.' The factual difference between the Hayden and the instant case, is that there involved was a display of equine and here pictures of the human frame, is not a distinction calling for a different conclusion as to the nuisance question.

See also in this regard, *Judson v. Zurhorst,* 30 Ohio Cir. 9, at page 14, where the court said:

There remains one contention for the granting of this injunction on the facts alleged in the petition. That is on the alleged indecency of the pamphlet. The law does not favor obscenity or indecency.

In a proper case instituted by one legally authorized to represent the public, the public exhibition of lewd pictures immodest statuary, or immoral plays would unquestionably be enjoined, or otherwise suppressed; and for the same reason an obscene book or pamphlet is prohibited transit through the United States mail . . . .

On the issue of whether indecency in the form of public lewdness in theatrical performances can be stopped in a civil action to abate a public nuisance in California, see *Weis v. Superior Court of San Diego County,* 30 Cal. App. 730, 159 p. 464 (June 14, 1916). In *Weis,* that issue was before the District Court of Appeals, 2nd District, on a writ of prohibition. The District Attorney had commenced a civil action under Code of Civil Procedure, Section 731, to abate a theatrical performance on the ground that it was a public nuisance. The complaint alleged that under a concession granted by the Panama-California International Exhibition, the defendant was conducting upon the exposition grounds a public resort and place of amusement and entertainment, known as the "Sultan's Harem", in which certain women did make in the presence of the general public a public exhibition and exposure of their naked person and private parts, which performance was alleged to be indecent and offensive to the senses and a public nuisance. The California court dismissed the defendant's application for a preemptory writ holding the action was properly brought. At page 465, the court said:

While the acts here complained of clearly constitute a crime, they also constitute a nuisance within the meaning of Section 3479 of the Civil Code, which defines a nuisance as 'anything which is . . . indecent or offensive to the senses . . . so as to interfere with the comfortable enjoyment of life or property' . . . (Emphasis mine.)

And Section 3480 of the same Code defines a public nuisance as: 'One which affects at the same time an entire community

679

or neighborhood, or any considerable number of persons, although the extent of the annoyance or danger inflicted upon individuals may be unequal.'

Mr. Joyce in his work on Nuisances, Section 409, says:

'A disorderly and disreputable theater may be enjoined, although a common nuisance.'

To the same effect is Wood on Nuisances, Section 68, where it is said: 'A public exhibition of any kind that tends to the corruption of morals, to a disturbance of the peace, or of the general good order and welfare of society, is a public nuisance. Under this head are included . . . obscene pictures and any and all exhibitions, the natural tendency of which is to pander to vicious . . . and disorderly members of society.'

The *Weis* decision and rationale was cited with approval by the California Supreme Court in *People v. Lim,* 18 Cal. 2d 872, 118 P. 2d 472 (Nov. 27, 1941). In the *Lim* case, the California Supreme Court noted, at page 476:

Similarly in *Weis v. Superior Court,* 30 Cal. App. 730, 159 P. 464, it was held that the District Attorney of San Diego County was authorized under Code of Civil Procedure, Section 731, to enjoin the performance of a public exhibition which was shown to have been indecent, and thus within the statutory definition of public nuisances in Civil Code Section 3749 . . . . The courts have thus refused to grant injunctions on behalf of the state *except* where the objectionable activity can be brought within the terms of the statutory definition of public nuisance . . . . (My emphasis.)

As recent as Thursday, September 3, 1970, the City Attorney of Los Angeles used the civil action public nuisance concept in an attempt to halt the lewdness epidemic in Los Angeles. (A newspaper clipping of that action appears below.)

LOS ANGELES TIMES   Fri., Sept. 4, 1970

City Suing Four 'Nude' Bars to Shut Them as Public Nuisances

By DOUG SHUIT
Times Staff Writer

City Atty. Roger Arnebergh said Thursday the city was filing civil suits against four nude entertainment bars in an attempt to close them down as "public nuisances."

Arnebergh said past attempts to win criminal prosecutions against nude bars had been "frustrated by the slow process of the criminal courts and the various legal maneuvers of the defendants."

It is the first time the city has initiated civil suits against bar owners, Arnebergh said.

"Although there have been more than 200 arrests (citywide) during the last six months for lewd conduct, indecent exposure, exhibition of obscene films—and criminal complaints have been issued by this office—these places continue to operate," Arnebergh said at a City Hall press conference. He added that his action was prompted by complaints by "thousands of citizens."

The four bars named in the complaints are the 007 Bar, 10301 West Washington Blvd.; the Frisco Theater, 3607 W. Pico Blvd.; the Honey Bunny, 5667 Lankershim Blvd., North Hollywood, and the Doll House, 8250 White Oak Ave., Northridge.

An attempt by Arnebergh's deputies to get a temporary restraining order to close the bars immediately failed Thursday.

Superior Judge Richard Schauer continued until today a hearing for the restraining order on the grounds the petition was not complete.

Arnebergh called the bars "the worst in the city" and said that confiscated films show "every type of sexual activity you can imagine."

Evidence to support the complaints includes film strips, still photographs taken by police officers and affidavits and petitions from private individuals.

Bar owners maintain they are protected under constitutional provisions for freedom of speech and have in the past charged the city with trying to force them out of business.

"If these (suits) are successful we think others will take the hint and stop this type of entertainment," Arnebergh said.

The laws of most states allow private citizens to initiate such action, either with or without allegations of special damages. In California, where such action is authorized by Sections 11225 and 11226 of the Penal Code, Section 11225 reads, in part as follows:

Every building or place used for the purpose of . . . lewdness . . . and every building or place in or upon which acts of . . . lewdness . . . are held or occur, is a nuisance which shall be enjoined, abated and prevented, whether it is a public or private nuisance.

Section 11226 authorizes a private citizen to bring such action in his own name without the necessity of alleging special damages, as is required with other "public nuisances". See *People v. Casa Company,* 35 Cal. App. 194. Penal Code Section 11226 provides, in part:

Whenever there is reason to believe that a nuisance as defined in this article is kept, maintained, or is in existence in any county . . . *any citizen of the State resident within said county, in his own name may, maintain an action in equity to abate and prevent the nuisance and to perpetually enjoin the person conducting or maintaining it . . . .* (My emphasis.)

In *People v. Bayside Land Co.,* 48 Cal. App. 257, 191 P. 994, the word "lewdness" as employed in Penal Code Section 11225, was given broad significance so as to include all other immoral or degenerate conduct or conversation between persons of opposite sexes and was held not limited to "assignation" and "prostitution".

In *John Harmer v. A Stage Play Entitled "Oh! Calcutta!" Elkins Productions International Corporation, a New York Corporation, et al.* In the Superior Court of the State of California, for the County of Los Angeles, Case No. 967069, a private citizen, John Harmer (also a State Senator) brought a civil action under Penal Code Section 11226 to abate the Los Angeles showing of the stage play "Oh! Calcutta!". That case is presently pending.

In the case of *Bertrand De Blanc, District Attorney of Lafayette Parish, La. v. Jules J. Courille and Gordon Austin, Jr.* (unreported) an action was brought under the provisions of Louisiana Revised Statute 13:4711 et seq. having to do with the abatement of public nuisances. That law generally applies to buildings, structures, land, water craft or movables where assignation, prostitution or "*obscenity* as now defined or as may hereafter be defined by the criminal laws of this state" is carried on. On June 4, 1970, the Honorable Jerome E. Domengeaux, Judge presiding in the Circuit Court of the 15th Judicial District Court upheld the constitutionality of the statute and its application to the exhibition of the motion picture film, "The Minx" at the Center Cinema Theater.

There is a psychological advantage to be gained in framing the relief sought as an action to abate a public nuisance. In an "ob-

681

scenity" action, one cannot escape the false claim that, in truth, the plaintiff was really acting as a censor as to what any one person might read or see. In the public nuisance action, the emphasis is shifted to a different area—the public "good" and social "detriment". Then, too, the abatement action is an action filed in the equity courts, which have traditional powers to mold the relief to the situation. In the latter situations the courts have the potential power to require forfeiture of profits which in and of itself would be a potent force in the development of counter moves against the industry.

At the present time, a number of successful abatement proceedings are on appeal. More often than not, because of the atrocious condition of the motion picture film fare, such cases involve motion picture films. Thus far the status of the cases on appeal is good—the statutes have withstood constitutional attack and the materials have been held to be obscene.

In one of these cases, *State of Ohio ex rel Keating v. A Motion Picture Film Entitled, "Vixen" et al.*, No. A242722, In the Court of Common Pleas, Hamilton County, Ohio, Charles H Keating, Jr., an action was brought by me against the exhibition of the motion picture "Vixen" in Cincinnati, Ohio (Hamilton County). In that trial action, the statute was upheld as against a claim of constitutional invalidity and the exhibition of the film at an indoor movie was held to be a public nuisance under the statute in Hamilton County. On appeal to the Court of Appeals, First Appellate District of Ohio, a similar attack was made against the statute on constitutional grounds, and as applied to the film itself. In *State of Ohio ex rel Keating v. A Motion Picture Film Entitled "Vixen" et al.*, —— Ohio App. ——, decided July 20, 1970, the Court of Appeals, First Appellate District of Ohio (Shannon, Hildebrant, and Hess) after trial de novo, upheld the constitutionality of the statute and declared the exhibition of the film to be a nuisance in the counties of Ohio in which it had jurisdiction.

In *State of Ohio ex rel Clark Ewing v. A Motion Picture Film Entitled, "Without A Stitch" et al.*, In the Court of Common Pleas, Lucas County, Ohio No. 70-1217 Clark Ewing brought an action in Toledo, Ohio under the same statutory grant of authority. In that trial action, the statute was upheld by Lucas Common Pleas Judge Nicholas Nalinski on September 16, 1970 against a claim of constitutional invalidity and the exhibition of the film at an outdoor movie was held to be a public nuisance in the State of Ohio.

Section 3767.01 et seq. of the Ohio Revised Code was recently before a three-judge federal district court, covered under 28 USC Sections 2281-2284 upon a claim of the unconstitutionality of such statute. In that case, *Grove Press, Inc. et al. v. Anthony B. Flask*, Civ No. C69-735, the court, in an unanimous decision (Celebreezze, Battisti and Green), upheld the constitutionality of the statute and its application to the motion picture entitled, "I am Curious (Yellow)".

IV. *The Commercial distribution or exhibition of obscenity is still, and will continue to be a crime.*

The suggestion of the Legal Panel that obscenity might be commercially distributed or exhibited to consenting adults without liability is rash and ill-conceived, being grounded upon an erroneous interpretation of the recent decision of the United States Supreme Court in *Stanley v. Georgia,* 22 L. Ed. 2d 542 (Apr. 7, 1969). An analysis of that decision, and the Court's recent decision in *Gable v. Jenkins,* 25 L. Ed. 2d 595 (Apr. 20, 1970), reveals no justification for such broad conclusions.

In the first place, the majority decision in *Stanley* specifically stated that the *Roth* case and its holding were not affected by the *Stanley* decision. At page 551, the Court said:

Roth and the cases following that decision are not impaired by today's holding. As we have said, the states retain broad power to regulate obscenity; that power simply does not extend to mere possession by the individual in the privacy of his own home. . . . (My emphasis)

To support contrary arguments (i.e., that the *Roth* rule has now been altered to suggest that commercial exhibition to consenting adults has been elevated to a constitutional right) the Legal Panel suggests that the 6-to-3 vote in the *Stanley* case will lead to that result. Nothing could be further from the truth, for the simplest of legal analysis demonstrates the contrary proposition. It is well understood and documented that Justices Harlan and Warren, who were numbered among the majority of six in that opinion, have repeatedly disavowed anything which resembles that philosophy. Justice Fortas, also of the majority, is no longer on the bench.

Further, of the remaining three, the author of the opinion, Associate Justice Thurgood Marshall, gave indications during oral arguments before the United States Supreme Court in *Byrne v. Karelexis* on April 30, 1970, that he also entertains no such intentions. During those arguments, the following colloquy took place between the author of the *Stanley* opinion and Attorney General Quinn of Massachusetts on this issue. Transcript of hearing at page 3, line 17, to page 4, line 18, reading (see Exhibit "3"):

Attorney General Quinn: That is correct, your Honor, In our view this appeal presents two equally important issues which ought to be finally resolved by this Court. The first is whether the court below abused its discretion in enjoining the District Attorney from prosecuting in the future on account of the showing of the film, "I Am Curious Yellow", which the court below assumed to be obscene. The second is whether under this Court's holding in *Stanley vs. Georgia,* any state can constitutionally prohibit public, commercial dissemination of pornographic matter, absent distribution to minors, to nonconsenting adults or by pandering . . .

Justice Marshall: What is there in *Stanley* that protects commercial distribution?

Attorney General Quinn: That is not the way we read it, your Honor, and *I do not think that is the way the author of the opinion wrote it.* (My emphasis)

Justice Marshall: Thank you.

Three attorneys, who were in attendance during the above colloquy, noted that when Attorney General Quinn answered

683

Justice Thurgood Marshall in such a forthright fashion, Justice Marshall was visibly shaken and evidenced the same in the manner in which he said: "Thank you", which was said with sarcasm. One minute later he left the bench.

Such an interpretation of *Stanley v. Georgia,* fails to take into consideration the significance of *Gable v. Jenkins,* 25 L. Ed. 2d 595, affirmed by the Court during the current term (April 20, 1970). Attorney General Quinn in his arguments in *Byrne v. Karalexis* saw otherwise. See Transcript, pages 15-16, where he said (See Exhibit "3"):

Attorney General Quinn: That success depends on the answer to the question, "Can public commercial dissemination of pornography be proscribed by any state?" *Before Stanley v. Georgia,* we submit there was no doubt at all about this principle. *Roth v. U.S.,* the leading case on this subject, based that answer on the fact that obscenity is not protected speech within the First Amendment. We agreed with Mr. Justice Marshall that the holding in *Stanley* in no way impairs the principle so well enunciated in *Roth.* In fact, only last week this Court summarily affirmed in *Gable v. Jenkins,* No. 1049, on the docket of the Court, a case involving action under a distinguishable statute in the same jurisdiction as *Stanley,* distinguishable from the statute in the *Stanley* case, but a statute very much like that upheld in the Roth case and very much like the statute under consideration in the case at bar. The statute upheld *Roth* prohibited commercial distribution of pornography. The Massachusetts statute, Chapter 272, Section 28A, is of like tenure. It strikes at public dissemination. This, we submit, does not affect the situation like that present in *Stanley v. Georgia.*

Associate Justice: Was that case you referred to last week a denial of "cert" or an affirmance?

Attorney General Quinn: It was a summary affirmance, your Honor.

Associate Justice: What is the name of the case?

Attorney General Quinn: *Gable v. Jenkins,* No. 1049. As I recall, I think there were two justices either abstaining or dissenting, your Honor.

Further, such an analysis of *Stanley* completely misses the significance of the Wisconsin Supreme Court decision in *Wisconsin v. Voshart,* 159 N. W. 2d 1 (June 7, 1968). In overlooking *Voshart,* such an analysis fails to observe that the *Stanley* facts actually posed two major questions of law and that but one of these questions was at issue and resolved by the Court's action in *Stanley.* Stated as issues, the two questions were: (1) May a state, within the limits set by the Federal Constitution, *punish as a criminal act* the simple possession of obscene materials (My emphasis), (*Stanley v. Georgia* issue), and (2) *Independent of the former consideration,* may a state, within federal constitutional limitations, declare such materials to be contraband and *subject to forfeiture as against an individuals' claim to a right of property therein* (my emphasis) (*Wisconsin v. Voshart* issue). Only the first issue was answered by the *Stanley* decision.

The distinction between these two issues is the difference between (1) a criminal law motion to suppress such materials as evidence in the criminal trial, and (2) a motion made at the same time or later, based upon property rights, to restore the ownership of such property as against a claim of forfeiture by the state as contraband. See *Wisconsin v. Voshart* (infra).

The right of government to destroy obscene motion picture films as contraband as against the claims of an individual to possession thereof was recently before the Wisconsin Supreme Court in *State v. Voshart,* 159 N. W. 2d 1 (June 7, 1968), on almost identical facts. There, certain motion picture films had been seized under a search warrant and their possessor charged with two counts of obscenity: (1) intentionally having in his possession obscene motion picture film (simple possession), and (2) intentionally having in his possession such film for sale or exhibition (commercial possession). In *Voshart,* however, the trial court granted a motion to suppress the evidence based upon the invalidity of the search warrant and the criminal complaint against him was dismissed as to both counts. Following dismissal of the criminal charge, the defendant filed a motion for return of the obscene motion picture films and the State moved for destruction of the film as contraband. As in *Stanley,* it was conceded that the film was obscene. The Wisconsin Supreme Court, in ruling upon the petitioner's claim to right of possession, adopted the reasoning of the Wisconsin trial court, at page 10:

It seems very clear to us that when contraband articles . . . to which no one can have a property right, are found in an illegal search, they should not be returned to the persons from whom they were taken . . . .

The Wisconsin Supreme Court, in this context, did not recognize any superior right in an individual "to read", "to possess", or to satisfy one's "emotional needs" with obscene motion picture films. Instead, the Court adhered to the Judeo-Christian Anglo-Saxon tradition, namely, at page 9:

Under its police powers, as a matter of public policy, the Legislature may declare to be contraband property that menaces public health, safety and morals. The right to destroy contraband property includes property such as counterfeit money, diseased cattle, contaminated food, and gambling devices. We would sustain the right of the Legislature to place obscene materials in the same category. This is not a case of an innocent article put to an illegal use. It is as impossible to separate the conceded obscenity from the films as it would be to separate the contamination from the food or the gambling from the device . . . .

The *Stanley* decision does not controvert the right of the State of Georgia to destroy obscene motion picture films as contraband and to regard the same as not subject to lawful ownership, as did the State of Wisconsin in *Voshart*. Nor is there anything flowing from any case law interpreting the Federal Constitution which accords to an individual a property right superior to that of the community relative to the possession of obscene motion picture films. Since *Stanley* holds that the rationalization of *Roth-Alberts* is not impaired, the films should be subject to forfeiture as contraband, for that opinion was premised on one fundamental fact— the films were, under prevailing constitutional standards, incontrovertibly obscene as a matter of law. The Atlanta District

685

Attorney refers to them as stag films (Appellee Brief on the merits, at pages 18, 19) and describes their contents as:

These films . . . are not literature in any sense of the word. They contain no plot, no dialogue, no moral lesson, no insight into contemporary social customs or mores, or any other redeeming social value. They are . . . only for lustful private showings. . . . They consist of nothing except close-up scenes of seduction, display of male and female genitalia, and pubic regions, oral sodomy and sexual intercourse in a variety of positions. Thus, we feel the films are pure obscenity . . . .

All litigants were in agreement that the District Attorney's evaluation was correct. At footnote 2, the majority opinion underpins its rationale upon an acknowledgment that the films were obscene as a matter of law:

Appellant does not argue that the films are not obscene. *For the purpose of this opinion, we assume that they are obscene under any of the tests* . . . . (My emphasis)

Having adopted this premise, there is much more concerning the nature of the motion picture films which, under *Roth-Alberts* is not open to question. It must follow that such motion picture films (1) are utterly without redeeming social importance, and (2) are without First Amendment protection because they are utterly without redeeming social importance. In 1957, the majority in *Roth-Alberts* viewed this as being in the order of a "universal judgment". The paramount interest *then* was the Government's interest in "order and morality". See 354 U.S. 576 at 585, where the *Roth* Court said:

But implicit in the history of the First Amendment is the rejection of obscenity as utterly without redeeming social importance. This rejection for that reason is mirrored in the universal judgment that obscenity should be restrained, reflected in the international agreement of over 50 nations, in the obscenity laws of all of the 48 states, and in the 20 obscenity laws enacted by the Congress from 1842 to 1956. This is the same judgment expressed by this Court in *Chaplinsky v. New Hampshire,* 315 U.S. 568, 86 L. Ed. 1031, 1035, 62 S. Ct. 766:

There are certain well-defined and narrowly limited classes of speech, the prevention and punishment of which have never been thought to raise any constitutional problem. *These include the lewd and obscene* . . . . *It has been well observed that such utterances are no essential part of any exposition of ideas, and are of such slight social value as a step to truth that any benefit that may be derived from them is clearly outweighed by the social interest in order and morality* . . . . (Emphasis added.)

We hold that obscenity is not within the area of constitutionally protected speech nor press.

Since the *Stanley* case specifically stated that the *Roth* holding was not impaired, it can hardly be said that a state under the powers reserved to it by the Ninth and Tenth Amendments may not, within constitutional limits, declare such matters to be incapable of ownership and contraband, as against an individual's mere personal claim to a right of ownership. It should be noted that the "chemistry book" reference made by Justice Marshall:

686

The State may no more prohibit mere possession of obscenity on the ground that it may lead to anti-social conduct than it may prohibit possession of chemistry books on the ground that they may lead to the manufacture of homemade spirits . . . .

is inapplicable in such a proceeding, because it is not in the same category of subject matter. Similarly, other language, used in a different context, is similarly distinguishable, for it is a basic rule of constitutional law that the language in an opinion will not be treated as having been written in a vacuum. See *U.S. v. Raines,* 362 U.S. 17, 21 (1960) where the Court said:

This Court, as in the case of all Federal Courts, 'has no jurisdiction to pronounce any statute, either of a state or the United States void, because irreconcilable with the Constitution, except as it is called upon to adjudicate the legal rights of litigants in actual controversies. In the exercise of that jurisdiction, it is bound by two rules, to which it has rigidly adhered, one, never to anticipate a question of constitutional law in advance of the necessity of deciding it; the other, never to formulate a rule of constitutional law broader *than is required by the precise facts to which it is applied.*' *Liverpool, New York and Philadelphia S. S. Co. v. Commissioners of Imigration,* 113 U.S. 33, 39. Kindred to these rules is the rule that one to whom application of a statute is constitutional will not be heard to attack the statute on the ground that impliedly it might also be taken as applying to other persons or other situations in which its application might be unconstitutional.

U.S. v. Wurzbach, 280 U.S. 396.

The *Stanley* opinion is poorly written and should be abandoned by the Court. It would appear that the concurring opinion of Justices Stewart, Brennan and White correctly labels the constitutional principle involved. If simple possession, (without more) of motion picture films which are obscene as a matter of law may not be made a crime, it should turn on the Fourth Amendment to privacy which is a right to one's solitude and is the antithesis of the First Amendment right, which is a right to communicate with others. (Free Speech and Press.) At least under this analysis, the Court does not find itself in the unconscionable position of reconstructing the positive values espoused in the 13 years' region of the *Roth-Alberts* opinion.

V. *There is no requirement that the three elements of the Brennan-Warren-Fortas obscenity test be applied independent of the context in which such materials are used. The only requirement is that they must coalesce.*

That some lower state and federal courts may, in some instances, be backing into a new three-part general test, which means something different from Roth, is indeed unfortunate. Such test, however, cannot analytically be squared away with the *Roth* test and rationale. No legal scholar should be willing to permit Justice Brennan, et al., to change the rules in the middle of the stream without facing up to the responsibility of acknowledging that this is what is being done.

An accurate analysis of the *Mishkin, Ginzburg* and *Fanny Hill* decisions prepared shortly after those decisions were handed down

687

and appearing in the June, 1967, edition of the N. D. R. is attached hereto a part of the Technical Papers. It is therein pointed out at Point E, Page 17:

It should be noted that, in reviewing the book, "Housewife's Handbook on Selective Promiscuity", the majority in *Ginzburg* did *not* apply the social value test independently, but rather considered only the predominant appeal of the material in the light of the precise facts being reviewed.

Both the criminal case, *Ginzburg v. U.S.,* 383 U.S. 463, 16 L. Ed. 2d 31, 86 S. Ct. 942, and the civil case, *A Book Named Memoirs of a Woman of Pleasure v. Attorney General of the Commonwealth of Mass.,* 383 U.S. 413, 16 L. Ed. 2d 1, 86 S. Ct. 975, were decided on the same date. Justices Brennan, Warren and Fortas did not apply the social value test independently in *Ginzburg,* the criminal case. The only way in which the two cases can be reconciled is by the distinction noted in the analysis contained therein.

It should not be overlooked that the reasoning behind some of the lower state and federal court judges in their strained application of the three-part test is not because they are satisfied with the situation, but rather because they want to be sure the state obscenity convictions under review will be upheld *in any event.* See Judge Barnes' concurring opinion in *Wagonheim v. Maryland State Board of Censors,* 258 Atl. 2d 240 at 247, 252 (Oct. 22, 1969):

. . . I have concluded that this Court is not required to follow the "three point test" in motion picture cases so far as any *authoritative and binding holding* of the Supreme Court of the United States is concerned, but that we are required to apply and follow the original *Roth* test. . . .

I reiterate, however, that I think this Court was wise in both the recent *Hewitt* case, supra, and in the majority opinion to apply the "three point test" in view of the unsettled state of the decisions of the Supreme Court in the obscenity field. If a majority of the Supreme Court finally adheres to the three point test (unfortunately from my viewpoint), we will have applied the correct rule; if a majority finally adheres to the *Roth* test, the appellants cannot complain if we have applied a stricter test than the law, as ultimately determined, requires us to do. . . .

See also Justice Spector concurring in *State of Florida v. Reese,* 222 S. 2d 732, 737 (May 21, 1969), the opinion of the Kentucky Court of Appeals in *Cain v. Commonwealth of Kentucky,* 427 S. W. 2d 769, 771 (Feb. 14, 1969) and the opinion of the Illinois Supreme Court in *City of Blue Island v. De Vilbiss,* 242 N. E. 2d 761, 762 (Nov. 22, 1968) for a sensible approach to the Brennan-Warren-Fortas test.

VI. *Similar materials in commerce and trade are not probative on the issue of community standards.*

A. The overwhelming weight of authority excludes such materials as irrelevant and immaterial.

At footnote 75(a) of the First Draft of the Legal Panel Report appears a statement which caused me to reply in part as follows:

688

(See Reply of Commissioner Keating to First Draft of the Legal Panel Report):

I interpret footnote 75(a) to be a subliminal message with advice to defense attorneys, reading as follows: 'Since you can't win in the trial court or in the jury room on the merits of your subject matter, the citation of this footnote and the prestigious position of this Staff Report will support your right to force into the record the rawest content reaching the Supreme Court. Given that misdirection, the jury (being the fair body that it is) will be forced to go against its own instinctive and inherent sense of outrage. . .'

The subject matter appearing hereinafter is in reply to that line of reasoning. There is no question but the United States Supreme Court has overstepped the bounds of appellate review accorded it by the federal constitution. The 1967 Fortas film and magazine cleared by four justices in *Dykema v. Bloss* (1970) are irrefutable evidence in support of that statement. *Those errors must not be perpetuated by the state courts.* This can be accomplished if the State High Courts will accept as a rule of law the views put forth hereinafter.

The overwhelming weight of authority supports the proposition that similar materials appearing in trade are not admissible in evidence on community standards. *State v. Ulsemer,* 24 Wash. 657 (1901); *Burton v. U. S.,* 142 F. 2d 57 (1906); *U. S. v. Levine,* 83 F. 2d 156, 158 (Apr. 6, 1963); *U. S. v. Rebhuhn,* 109 F. 2d 512, 515 (Feb. 13, 1940), cert. den. 310 U. S. 629, 84 L. Ed. 1399, 60 S. Ct. 976; *Schindler v. U. S.* 208 F. 2d 289, 290 (Nov. 30, 1953); *U. S. v. Hochman,* 175 F. Supp. 881, 882 (Sept. 9, 1959); *Womack v. U. S.,* 111 U. S. App. DC 8, 294 F. 2d 204, 206 (Jan. 12, 1961), cert. den. 365 U. S. 859 5 L. Ed. 2d 822, 81 S. Ct. 826 (Mar. 27, 1961), *U. S. v. Oakley,* 290 F. 2d 517, 519 (May 24, 1961); cert. den. 368 U. S. 888, 7 L. Ed 2d 87, 82 S. Ct. 139 (Oct. 23, 1961); *N. Y. v. Finkelstein, et al.,* 11 N. Y. 2d 300, 229 NYS 2d 367, 371, 183 NE 2d 661 (May 17, 1962), cert. den. 371 U. S. 863, 9 L. Ed. 2d 100, 83 S. Ct. 116 (Oct. 15, 1962); *U. S. v. Ginzburg,* 224 F. Supp. 129, 136: aff'd in *Ginzburg v. U. S.,* 383 U.S. 463, 16 L. Ed 2d 31, 86 S. Ct. 969 (Mar. 21, 1966); *U. S. v. West Coast News Co., et al.,* 228 F. Supp. 171, 200 (Mar. 25, 1964), aff'd in *U. S. v. West Coast News Co., et al.,* 357 F. 2d 855, 860 (Mar. 22, 1966); *Books, Inc. v. U. S.*—F. 2d—(Apr. 12, 1966); *Kentucky v. Austin* (unreported) cert, den. on this issue, 16 L. Ed. 2d 438 (Apr. 25, 1966). Compare the opinion of Justice Harlan in *Smith v. California,* 361 U. S. 147, 4 L. Ed. 2d 205, 80 S. Ct. 215, where that justice would hold that it would be a denial of due process to "turn aside *every* attempt by appellant to introduce evidence bearing on community standards, "without passing on the question as to whether" other allegedly similar publications which were openly published, sold, and purchased and which received wide general acceptance" was constitutionally compelled, followed by the California Supreme Court in *In Re Harris,* 56 Cal. 2d 879, 16 Cal. Rptr. 889. Compare *Yudkin v. Maryland,* 229 Md. 223, 182 Atl. 2d 798 (1962), requiring the same to be admitted and read to the jury in full.

One of the leading cases in this area is *Womack v. U. S.*

689

(supra) certiorari denied by the United States Supreme Court, 365 U. S. 859 (Mar. 27, 1961). Womack was convicted by a jury in a federal district court on 26 counts of mailing information as to where obscene material could be obtained and three counts of mailing obscene material. The people's evidence showed that the defendant carried on a mail order business in nude male photographs. At the trial the judge denied Womack's attempt to get into evidence dozens of books and magazines which contained nudes and which were regularly sold in ordinary commerce. On appeal the Court of Appeals for the District of Columbia affirmed, holding at page 206:

> The proffered evidence was immaterial, i.e., of no probative weight in reaching a decision upon the issue at trial. The fact that nudes by Manet, Titian, Raphael, Rembrandt, Picasso, and many others are accepted commercial items is of no possible probative value in deciding whether these particular photographs, which alone are in issue here, are obscene and filthy. If a piece of cloth is bright red, and the cloth itself is in evidence, no testimony, lay or expert, would be admissible to show the cloth is blue. Such testimony would be immaterial, of no probative value, upon the issue of the color. Its admission would be a waste of the court's time, confusing, prolonging, and tending to make a mockery of the processes of justice. Mr. Wigmore treats of this topic in his discussion of relevancy, positing that one of the elements of relevancy is that the proffered evidence have something more than a minimum of probative value. Whether academically we call the principle materiality or relevancy, it is settled that to be admissible a bit of evidence must have some potential probative weight upon the issues of fact under trial. In the case at bar the photographs were filthy, self-evidently and indisputably. We think that photographs can be so obscene—it is conceivably possible that they be so obscene—that the fact is incontrovertible. These photographs are such.
>
> Apart from the foregoing, dispositive of the point, is the fact that Womack made no attempt to show as a foundation for his proffer, any resemblance between the proffered works of art and the photographs he was putting in the mail. The predicate for a conclusion that a disputed piece of mailable matter is acceptable under contemporary community standards, as shown by proffered other material already in unquestioned circulation, must be that the two types of matter are similar. And as another part of his foundation he must show a reasonable degree of community acceptance of works like his own. The impossibility of such showing was fatal to the substance of Womack's case, and his failure to attempt it was a procedural defect. . . .

In short, what Judge Prettyman was saying was that circumstantial evidence of this nature (other material appearing on the market) has little or no probative weight on the issue of fact being tried, but beyond this—before such evidence could be considered, it would have to be shown not only (1) that such material was available, but also (2) that it was reasonably acceptable to the community and (3) that the materials were similar. The court noted that not only did Womack not attempt the proof as to (2) and (3) but also that such a showing was impossible of proof.

As Judge Prettyman points out in his opinion at page 205, all evidential sources are divided into three classes, namely, autoptical, testimonial (direct) and circumstantial. Autoptical evidence proves a principal fact through direct perception by the senses of the tribunal without dependence upon any conscious inference from some other testimonial or circumstantial proof. The subject matter under investigation is itself autoptical evidence. Testimonial (direct) evidence is that which is applied to the principal fact to be proved *directly* and without the aid of any intervening fact or process; as where, on trial for murder, a witness. positively testifies he saw the accused inflict the mortal wound. Circumstantial evidence, on the other hand, is that which is applied to the principal fact *indirectly,* or through the medium of other facts, from which the principal fact is inferred.

Were other material being offered for sale and trade to be admissible as judicial evidence, it could qualify only as circumstantial evidence. Before it could qualify as such it would have to satisfy the legal requirements for materiality and relevancy.

The characteristics of circumstantial evidence as distinguished from that which is direct, are: *First, the existence and presentation of one or more evidentiary facts;* and, *second, a process of inference,* by which these facts are so connected with the principal fact to be proved, as to tend to produce a persuasion of its truth. What is attempted here is an offer of proof as to three collateral evidentiary facts: (1) other films such as B, C, and D are available on the market, (2) B, C and D are acceptable to contemporary standards, and (3) B, C and D are similar to film A in an attempt to establish an inference that principal, film A is acceptable to contemporary community standards. In other words the rationale offered is that film A is acceptable to community standards *if* films B, C and D are available on the market *and if* films B, C and D are acceptable to contemporary community standards.

The ridiculous aspects of this mode of proof can be seen by observing that before such proof was offered, a single issue was before the court, namely, was film A acceptable to contemporary community standards. Were such offer of proof allowed, the Court would oblige itself to hear evidentiary proof on the same identical issue in relation to other films B, C and D *plus* an additional inquiry as to whether the films involved were similar. Having opened the issue thus far, it should then be proper for the people to meet such evidence with additional rebuttal evidence that films B, C and D were not similar and were not acceptable and with evidence on films, E, F and G to establish that such materials were similar to films B, C and D and were unacceptable. Judge Prettyman expressed the overwhelming weight of authority when he said at page 206: "Its admission would be a waste of the court's time, confusing, prolonging, and tending to make a mockery of the processes of justice."

Application of this principal to the case at hand can be seen by reference to the direct testimony of defense witness Frank Huffman in the trial of "Without a Stitch" and the direct testimony of defense witness Louis Pesce in the same trial. Such witnesses were allowed to make comparisons with other motion picture films

691

which were not before the court in support of their opinion that the film under consideration, "Without a Stitch" did not affront the contemporary community standards in relation to sexual matters. The reasoning of both witnesses was the films such as "Sexual Freedom in Denmark" showed scenes which were more explicit than those in "Without a Stitch" and that since those films were being exhibited, they did not affront contemporary community standards, and therefore, it must follow that the film "Without a Stitch" taken as a whole did not affront contemporary community standards. Yet both witnesses refused to render opinions on the separate scenes of "Without a Stitch" in isolation.

That the above line of testimony and mode of proof is improper and should be disregarded by the Court in its deliberations can be seen from the fact that before such proof was offered, a single issue was before the Court, namely was the film "Without A Stitch" obscene. Having opened the offer of proof to comparing films such as "Sexual Freedom in Denmark", which was not before the Court, the Court would be obliged to hear testimony as to what "Sexual Freedom in Denmark" was about, whether the same were acceptable to contemporary community standards, etc., plus the additional inquiry as to whether the film "Sexual Freedom in Denmark" were similar to the film "Without A Stitch". Having opened the issue this far, it should then be proper for the plaintiff to meet this new burden, either by way of cross-examination on those matters or by rebuttal evidence that such proposed "comparable" films were not acceptable, or that such films were not comparable in fact. To allow such testimony would, in the words of Justice Prettyman speaking in *Womack,* be a waste of the court's time, confusing, prolonging and tending to make a mockery of the processes of justice.

The reason for the *Womack* rule is self-evident. If such evidence is permitted, the course of the trial is allowed to take on an excursion into collateral issues. In such a situation, we find ourselves in the position where we must prove the toleration of film B, offered for comparison, so that it in turn; may be used to show the toleration of film A, the challenged film, which, of course, is the main issue—but before that is probative, we must also show that film B is similar to film A, and to do this we must view the same in its entirety to show that the works "as a whole" are similar. How much simpler and more logical, to require *direct* proof on the toleration of the challenged film which is the main issue, than to require the film to make "toleration" judgments and comparisons of 5 or more other films.

Even assuming that the works are *identical* and that film B the comparison work is acceptable, still such evidence would not be material or relevant unless "the circumstances of presentation and dissemination of the material in the market place" were also similar. *Attorney General v. Fanny Hill,* 383, U. S. 413, 16 L. Ed 2d 1, 86 S. Ct. 975; *Ginzburg v. U. S.,* 383 U. S. 462, 16 L.Ed. 2d 31, 86 S. Ct. 969; *U. S. v. Rebhuhn,* supra, cited with approval in *Ginzburg v. U. S.,* supra.

In the *Rebhuhn* case the trial judge refused to allow in evidence a copy of Havelock Ellis' "Psychology of Sex" in which the author had spoken with commendation of the works of several of the

692

authors of the books in question. The Court said at page 515:

But the evidence was neither . . . necessary, nor even important. As we have already said, the books were not obscene per se; they had a proper use, but the defendants willfully misused them, and it was that misuse which constituted the gravamen of the crime. Thus, it meant little to prove the standing of their authors, and the error ought not to be ground for reversal.

(1) Re relevancy and materiality of the proof offered.

The theory on which proof of such collateral facts is being offered in evidence is that an inference is raised that film A is acceptable to community standards *if* films B, C and D are available on the market *and if* films B, C and D are acceptable to community standards and *if* films B, C and D are similar to film A.

It should be observed that if there is a question as to the acceptability of the offered work, then the evidential proposition presented is: The challenged work is *acceptable* because it is similar to an offered work which *might* be acceptable. The logical connection between the evidence offered and the conclusion sought is thus too tenuous for the evidence to be relevant.

On the other hand, if the offered work bears *some* similarities to the challenged work, but is not actually similar as a whole, as in the case of comparing a so-called "comedy" "Without A Stitch" with a so-called "documentary" "Sexual Freedom in Denmark", the logical connection again, is too tenuous for relevancy.

It is doubtful if the acceptability of any work can ever really be proved with sufficient conclusiveness so that the work, even if it were similar to a challenged work, would be relevant proof of the acceptability of the challenged work. All that could be shown are various evidentiary facts, some of which might have relevance if they pertained to the challenged material, but none of which would be conclusive, since, as noted, "in the end it is the jury who must declare what the standard shall be." *U. S. v. Levine,* supra. 83 F. 2d at 158.

Mere proof of availability of the comparison material would obviously not be sufficiently demonstrative of the acceptability of the same, since the mere fact that a book is available for purchase cannot serve to place on it the imprimatur of community acceptance. *U. S. v. Ginzburg,* 224 F. Supp. 129, 136 (Eastern Dist. Pa. 1963) aff'd 338 F. 2d 12, aff'd 383 U. S. 463. See also *Books, Inc. v. U. S.,* Circuit Court of Appeals, First Circuit (F. 2d) (Apr. 12, 1966), and *U. S. v. West Coast News Co., et al.,* 357 F. 2d 855, 860 (Mar. 22, 1966). If mere readership were proof of non-obscenity, then only those materials which failed to sell would be subject to indictment. Nor would evidence that a few persons of "reputable" position buy and read the comparison materials be sufficient. *U. S. v. Hochman,* 175 F. Supp. 881, 882 (Eastern Dist. Wisc. 1959), aff'd 227 F. 2d 1961, cert. den. 364 U.S. 837. As Judge Hand said in *U. S. v. Levine,* supra, 83 F. 2d at 158, in upholding the rejection by the trial court of a proffered list of purchasers of the books there at issue which included a number of well-known persons:

Such a list taken alone told nothing of the standing of the works in the minds of the community; even respectable persons may

693

have a taste for salacity. Obviously it would be impossible without hopelessly confusing the issue to undertake any analysis of such a list by finding out why each buyer bought.

At the least, it would have to be shown that those who read the comparison materials approved of them and that they had the normal tastes in such matters of the average person. Addiction after all, does not necessarily indicate approval. It would appear that such is impossible of proof.

Nor could acceptability of the comparison materials be predicated upon the fact that no legal action had been instituted against the offered film or its purveyor. Those in authority may have been unaware of the film's existence, or content, or, if aware, could have refrained from bringing action for any one of the number of reasons unrelated to community approval. Their decision, moreover, is always subject to revision.

Similarly, acceptability cannot be predicated upon the fact that the subject matter was at issue in a prior trial where the defendant was acquitted. The prior acquittal may have been based upon an issue other than community standards, such as scienter, prior restraint, etc.

Even if the acquittal did, in fact, turn upon the obscenity of the subject matter, an erroneous instruction might have been given the jury by the court or improper and misleading evidence or testimony might erroneously have been admitted or there may have been an improper application of law. The presence of any of these factors would render the verdict nugatory as evidence on the acceptability of the film involved, on the matter of improper application of law, defense, etc.

An example of such an improper application of law appears in the early trial of "Without A Stitch" to the jury in the federal custom's case in Southern California. At that time, the Los Angeles City Attorney and the Los Angeles District Attorney had taken no legal action against the films "I Am Curious (Yellow)" and the lesbian film "The Stewardesses" which had been allowed to play in the area for months. Federal District Judge Hauk allowed both films to be shown to the jury for comparison purposes. That such evidence was erroneously admitted can be seen from the fact that subsequent to the trial of "Without A Stitch", both the City Attorney of Los Angeles and the District Attorney of Los Angeles County commenced police actions against "I Am Curious (Yellow)" which are presently pending. Where a comparison film such as "I Am Curious (Yellow)" is introduced and the opposing party is unable to offer rebuttal evidence as to successful police actions against such alleged comparable film due to a lack of knowledge of the existence of such actions, the trier of fact is totally misled as to the probativeness of such evidence.

Further, when an erroneous result such as that which was reached in the Federal District Court Customs case in Long Beach is admitted into evidence in a subsequent action such as this, without further evidence of other successful actions on the same film, the original error is further compounded.

Furthermore, it is clear that under the *Ginzburg* and *Fanny Hill* cases and the U. S. Supreme Court's approval of the "variable obscenity approach", the use of the alleged comparable materials

694

held not obscene in a different trial is a substantial factor in some cases. Certainly it could not be urged that because the court had found no violation of the obscenity statute in *U. S. v. 31 PHOTO-GRAPHS,* 156 F. Supp. 350, the 31 photographs therein, conceded to be hardcore pornography, were evidence of material which was "acceptable" to the community.

The only way, in fact, to establish for the purposes of a trial that an offered work is sufficiently acceptable to be probative is to submit it to the *same* jury to which is submitted the challenged work. But this would mean no more than that the jury would judge both works by the same *Roth* standards, a useless duplication of efforts which would prove nothing. For if the jury found that the challenged material is obscene and the offered material is not, it would find that the two are not comparable. If it found that they were comparable and the challenged material is obscene, it would find that the offered material is also obscene. And if it found that the challenged material is not obscene, it could arrive at that verdict without the necessity of undertaking a like judgment on the offered material.

In short, all that the admission into evidence of comparison materials would achieve would be to commit to the jury for judgment materials which are not committed to it by the indictment. Such an admission would do no more than to "clutter and confuse the record." *Schindler v. U. S.,* 208 F. 2d 289, 290 (C.A. 9, 1953), cert. den., 347 U. S. 938, and "would be a waste of the court's time, confusing, prolonging, and tending to make a mockery of the processes of justice. *Womack v. U. S.,* supra. 294 F. 2d 206 cert. den., 365 U. S. 859.

In a recent case considering this issue in depth, *U. S. v. West Coast News Co.,* 228 F. Supp. 171, 200 (Mar. 25, 1965), aff'd in *U. S. v. West Coast News Co., et al.,* 357 F. 2d 855, 860, Circuit Court of Appeals Sixth Circuit (Mar. 22, 1966), involving eight paperback books with titles like "Sex Life of a Cop", Federal District Judge Noel Fox said in this respect at page 200:

Under the *Roth* test, a book must be judged by its dominant theme, taken as a whole. Similar books, in order to be probative as to customary limits of candor, must then be judged also by their dominant theme. The book as a whole must be comparable to the challenged book, not just isolated passages. To hold otherwise, as the defendant sought in qualifying the proffered books in this case, would be to apply the Hicklin isolated passages test to the proffered books, while asking the jury to apply the *Roth* test as a whole to the challenged books. Defendant's position is clearly untenable.

A very scholarly discussion on comparable evidence appears in *West Coast News Co.* case at page 191-201. There the defendant sought the admission of eight books, "Fanny Hill", "Tropic of Cancer", "Lady Chatterley's Lover", "Naked Lunch", "Carpetbagger", "Cold Wind in August", "Clip Joint Cutie", and "Sin Binge" on the issue of contemporary community standards. The court ruled that it would admit such evidence if a proper foundation were laid, i.e., three requirements were met, namely: (1) the books enjoyed substantial acceptability in the community, (2) the party testifying is qualified to compare the books introduced to

695

those challenged, and (3) the witnesses' testimony convinced the court first, as a matter of law, that the books are substantially similar to the challenged books. After a hearing outside the presence of the jury, the trial court ruled, as Judge Prettyman had previously in the *Womack* case, excluding all books offered as comparable, holding that all but "Clip Joint Cutie" and "Sin Binge" were not similar as a matter of law, and that as to those two there was no showing that they were "tolerated" by the community, (i.e., substantial acceptability).

The overwhelming majority of the appellate courts have recognized the utter futility of what defense counsel in the *West Coast News Co.* case attempted. In *State v. Ulsemer,* 24 Wash. 657, 1901, the Supreme Court of the State of Washington held as follows in an obscenity case:

> The testimony tendered by appellant as to use of similar pictures in commerce and trade was incompetent. Any use of such pictures by anybody else would not palliate the offense of the appellant. The statute provides . . . 'the jury in all prosecutions under the next preceding section (which defines the crime) shall be the sole and exclusive judges as to whether or not the matter circulated is obscene or indecent.'

In a similar situation, the New York Court of Appeals in *New York v. Finkelstein,* 229 NYS 2, 367 (May 17, 1962), followed the same principle. The court there said at page 371:

> In our opinion, the proffered evidence was properly excluded, as it was irrelevant to the issue of whether or not the two books sold by defendants in this case were obscene. The fact that certain other and different publications were *seen* in bookstores and on magazine stands in New York City is no indication that they were *sold,* or *read,* or that to the average person applying contemporary community standards (*Roth v. U. S.,* supra) they were not obscene.

In *Ginzburg v. U. S.,* 224 F. Supp. 129 (1963) the court said at page 136:

> Defendants place great weight on the requirement of the definition of obscenity, as they see it, which protects works which do not exceed contemporary community standards of candor and expression. There is no question that all three of the indicted materials exceed this standard. Certain materials sold openly on local newsstands were submitted to show what the acceptable limits of candor are today. Without so deciding, it may well be that these materials exceed the contemporary standards themselves. At any rate, supplying this court with such materials does not provide conclusive evidence of the standard set by the community as a whole. Doubtless but a sliver of the community reads such things and there is no doubt the community as a whole does not necessarily tolerate them. For all the court knows, local action before this and in the future will result in the removal of this type of material from the newsstands.

It is submitted that the fact that 20,987 persons saw the film "Without A Stitch" in the Toledo Area does not set the standard for a community of approximately 500,000 persons. In *Books, Inc. v. U. S.* —F. 2d — (Apr. 12, 1966), the U. S. Court of Appeals for the First Circuit said:

696

The other point deserving of our comment is the refusal of the trial judge to permit defendant to introduce in evidence a large number of publications currently available in Rhode Island so that from them the jury could better form its opinion of community standards. It is, of course, true that what is sold in the market reflects to some extent community standards. But it is not true that every item sold is necessarily not obscene. The admission of a number of different publications alleged to be comparable to the publication in issue might make the trial unmanageably complex and lengthy. The trial judge must be allowed wide discretion as to whether to permit the introduction of such allegedly comparable publications, and as to whether to allow the witnesses to be examined in detail on publications other than the one directly at issue. Here the trial judge did not abuse his discretion.

In *U. S. v. 392 Copies of Magazine Exclusive,* 253 F. Supp. 485 (Apr. 4, 1966), the court said at page 496:

Claimant offered the testimony of a former city policeman, now a private detective, and the magazines he had purchased at a dozen stores or newsstands in the city during the trial and before the decision in *Mishkin.* He had started in 'the block' area and had proceeded to particular stores and newsstands which he and many other Baltimorians know deal in pornographic material. His testimony indicates that such material is not available at respectable bookstores, drugstores, newsstands or other outlets for magazines. It is noteworthy that on the very day this case was argued the proprietor of one of the stores where the detective purchased a magazine was convicted and sentenced to prison in the Criminal Court of Baltimore for selling obscene photographs of nude males. Four of the outlets where the detective purchased magazines were located on 'the block' or adjacent thereto. The standards of 'the block' are not the standards to be applied in this case, any more than the standards of the most strait-laced persons. Material purchased in such specialized outlets has little or no value in determining contemporary community standards. *Ginzburg v. U. S.,* 86 S. Ct. 969 (1966).

VII. *A film can be so grossly obscene that it is "obscene, as a matter of law"*

Recently, the Court, in *Morris v. U. S.,* 259 A. 2d 337, (Dec. 2, 1969) had occasion to touch upon a legal concept which is not often mentioned these days—"obscene, as a matter of law." To illustrate this point of law, I incorporate hereinafter that portion of the brief in *Ohio, ex rel. Ewing v. A Motion Picture Entitled "Without A Stitch,"* appearing under the heading "The Film 'Without A Stitch' is Obscene As a Matter of Law."

I urge that each prosecutor of an obscene film study and analyze the arguments herein, for they present what, in my opinion, is the correct rule of law in regard to community standards; that is, the state statutes and city ordinances which prohibit specific immoral conduct define what the moral standards of the State are.

In *Morris,* the Court made the following comment as to material which was "obscene per se," i.e., obscene as a matter of law:

Although the definition and elements of obscenity have been

697

authoritatively stated in *Roth* and *Memoirs,* definition of the oft-used terms 'hard-core obscenity' and 'obscenity per se' has been neglected by the Supreme Court. The Court of Special Appeals of Maryland has faced this problem before and has defined these terms in the following language: hard-core pornography or obscenity per se is obscenity which 'focuses predominantly upon what is sexually morbid, grossly perverse and bizarre without any artistic or scientific purpose or justification.' There is no desire to portray (it) in pseudo-scientific or 'arty' terms. It can be recognized by the insult it offers, invariably, to sex and to the human spirit. It goes substantially beyond customary limits of candor and deviates from society's standards of decency in the representation of the matters in which it deals. It has a patent absence of any redeeming social value; it speaks for itself and screams for all to hear that it is obscene. It is not designed to be a truthful description of the basic realities of life as the individual experiences them but its main purpose (is) to stimulate erotic response. . . . No proof, other than the viewing of it, is required to determine if it is, in fact, obscene.

It is clear to this court that where obscenity per se is involved, the prosecution is not required to offer any evidence (beyond the material or performance itself) that it is pornographic or obscene or that it is below the national community standards. *Womack,* supra; *Hudson,* supra. *In other words, if reasonable men could not differ and they could come to but one conclusion, i.e., that the material or performance is sexually morbid, grossly perverse, and bizarre, without any artistic or scientific purpose or justification,* then the Government on its case-in-chief need not offer any evidence of national community standards. (My emphasis.)

The motion picture "Without A Stitch" is of that genre.

Acts and conduct against the good morals and public decency which result in injury to the people are a public nuisance. Such injury to the public is manifest from defendants' conduct in depicting the following visual and audio presentations, as set forth in Plaintiff's Exhibit "3" (Continuity for "Without A Stitch"):

(1) Scene depicting Dr. Petersen's sexual stimulation of the 17-1/2-year-old girl, Lilian, using physical contact (hands). (Scene 5).

(2) Scene depicting sexual activity between Lilian and Henry in the home of Henry's parents. (Scene 6)

(3) Dialogue of Dr. Petersen instructing Lilian that sexual perversion and promiscuity are acceptable conduct. (Scene 9)

(4) Scene depicting sexual perversion (lesbianic relations) beween Lilian and Brita. (Scene 11)

(5) Scene depicting sexual perversion (oral sodomy) by Dr. Petersen on Lilian in Dr. Petersen's office. (Scene 12)

(6) Scene depicting sexual activity between Lilian and Henry in the home of Henry's parents. (Scene 14)

(7) Scene depicting sexual intercourse between Lilian and Dr. Petersen in Dr. Petersen's office. (Scene 17)

(8) Scene depicting sexual intercourse in a truck between Lilian and Goran, a cameraman. (Scene 20)

698

(9) Scenes depicting Lilian's participation in a stag film. (Scenes 22 and 23)

(10) Scenes depicting sexual perversion (lesbianic relations) between Lilian and Lise in Lise's apartment, including the use of a dildo. (Scenes 29, 30, 31)

(11) Scene depicting sexual perversion (sex orgy) between Lilian, Lise, and a male in Lise's apartment. (Scene 33)

(12) Scene depicting sexual perversion (sadism and masochism) between Lilian and Kurt. (Scene 41)

(13) Scene depicting sexual perversion (sodomy) between Lilian and Freddy. (Scene 45)

(14) Scene depicting sexual perversion (simultaneous sodomy and intercourse) between Lilian, Freddy, and Freddy's friend. (Scene 46)

(15) Dialogue of Dr. Petersen and Lilian approving the above-mentioned sexual conduct as acceptable. (Scene 52)

The visual depiction in public of the above sexual acts, admitted by the defense, if performed off-stage in three-dimensional form, would be indictable. When performed in two-dimensional form, either realistically or simulated, the same are incontrovertibly contrary to the good morals, common custom, public policy, and common conscience of the community of the Nation as a whole.

By way of illustration, plaintiff submits that if sodomy or sexual perversion is a violation of the laws prohibiting "lewdness," then the public display of such acts, real or simulated, by way of motion pictures is also contrary to the public policy and in violation of the obscenity laws as a *matter of law*. In answer, defense counsel responds that if this were so, then the motion picture presentation of simulated murder would be illegal. That, of course, is a non sequitur, for there is no law which prohibits the pictorial portrayal of simulated murder, whereas, there is an almost universally recognized law which prohibits the pictorial portrayal of indecent public conduct and that is the law against "lewdness" in public displays.

The common standards of right and wrong embodied in the statutory law of Ohio should be applied as the rule of law in this case in finding that this film, "Without A Stitch" is UNLAWFUL AS A MATTER OF LAW. This was the view of the unanimous Ohio Court in *City of Youngstown v. DeLoreto*, 251 N.E. 2d 491, (Sept. 10, 1969). The court there said at page 500:

"Ohio Laws Indicating Sex Moral Standards. Laws of Ohio and the City of Youngstown relating to sex, *which indicate the moral standards of the people of Ohio*, prohibit the following: . . . ." (My emphasis.)

Thereafter, the court enumerated the state statutes and city ordinances which prohibited specific immoral conduct. From that the court deduced what the Moral Standard of Ohio People on Sex were: See *DeLoreto* at pages 500 and 501.

It is the prerogative of this Court to take judicial notice of the laws of the State of Ohio relating to sexual morality and apply them in determining the issue of obscenity in this case.

The vast history of the Common Law and the statutes of the State of Ohio make clear those particular areas of public conduct which are so immoral, so contrary to the immemorial custom of propriety of the people, so opposite to the natural sense of con-

699

science and justice of the people, so pervasively at odds with the community notions of right and wrong, so consistently maintained as illegal and contrary to Anglo-American public policy that their display and exhibition to the public either live or recorded is UN-LAWFUL AS A MATTER OF LAW. Fornication, prostitution, adultery, incest, indecent exposure of a human body, public nudism, immoral pictures, lewd pictures, immoral exhibitions, sexual perversion, and sodomy (proscribed by the following respective sections of the Ohio Penal Code: 2905.08, 2905.10, 2905.12, 2905.13, 2905.07, 2905.16-17, 2905.26, 2905:27, 2905.30, 2905.31, 2905.39, 2905.41, 2905.40, 2905.44) all are enumerated acts, the public portrayal of which a judge should recognize as being part of the Common Law specification of "obscenity" and "lewdness."

The courts have always been willing to take judicial notice of those facts and policies that are of general and incontrovertible knowledge. Such matters include those facts of a common or general knowledge that are well and authoritatively settled, not doubtful or uncertain, and known to be within the limits of the jurisdiction of the court. (29 Am. Jur 2d Sec. 22). Such matters have always included the judicial notice of the existence and TENOR of the public laws of the state. (29 Am. Jur. 2d Sec. 34). They also have included a recognition of the ordinary instincts, passions, emotions, and motives which universally, in a greater or less degree, influence the actions and conduct of mankind. (29 Am. Jur. 2d Sec. 114). In addition, judicial notice has been extended to matters of public and social welfare (29 Am. Jur. 2d Sec. 143) and the customs and usages of man which are generally known or accepted to an extent sufficient to make them matters of common knowledge. (29 Am. Jur. 2d Sec. 121).

Lucas County Common Pleas Judge Nicholas J. Walinski's Finding of Fact in the above case, holding the film to be obscene and a nuisance under Ohio law read as follows:

10. That acceptibility by a movie audience is not the true criteria of the measurement of community standards relating to the representation of sexual matters or acceptance of a movie by the community because the attending audience, as in this case, is a very small segment of the community. The proper criteria for a valuation of contemporary standards of the community relating to the representation of sexual matters must necessarily be the enacting and enforcement of laws by that community governing the conduct of citizenry; that simple reference to the Ohio Revised Code sets forth the legal moral standards of the people of Ohio, including Lucas County, on sex matters and that there is generally attempted enforcement in this community. These Sections include, but are not limited to the following:

Sec. 2905.08 O.R.C., Adultery or Fornication
Sec. 2905.10 O.R.C., Prostitution
Sec. 2905.30 O.R.C., Indecent Exposure
Sec. 2905.30 O.R.C., Solicitation of Unnatural Sex Act
Sec. 2905.31 O.R.C., Nudism
Sec. 2905.44 O.R.C., Sodomy

There are existing similar statutes in the majority of states, giving an inference of national community standards.

700